Social Work Practice and People of Color

A PROCESS-STAGE APPROACH

Fourth Edition

DOMAN LUM

California State University,

Sacramento

 **Brooks/Cole**
Thomson Learning

Australia • Canada • Denmark • Japan • Mexico • New Zealand • Philippines
Puerto Rico • Singapore • South Africa • Spain • United Kingdom • United States

Senior Acquisitions Editor: *Lisa Gebo*
Assistant Editor: *Susan Wilson*
Marketing Manager: *Jennie Burger*
Project Editor: *Matt Stevens*
Print Buyer: *Karen Hunt*
Permissions Editor: *Robert M. Kauser*
Text and Cover Designer: *Ellen Pettengell*

Copy Editor: *Laura E. Larson*
Proofreader: *Patterson Lamb*
Compositor/Illustrator: *Summerlight Creative*
Cover Image: *Stephen Daigle/The Stock Illustration Source*
Cover Printer: *Webcom Ltd.*
Printer/Binder: *Webcom Ltd.*

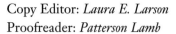

Printed in Canada

2 3 4 5 6 7 03 02 01 00

For permission to use material from this text, contact us by

Web: www.thomsonrights.com
Fax: 1-800-730-2215
Phone: 1-800-730-2214

Wadsworth/Thomson Learning
10 Davis Drive
Belmont, CA 94002-3098
USA
www.wadsworth.com

International Headquarters
Thomson Learning
290 Harbor Drive, 2nd Floor
Stamford, CT 06902-7477
USA

UK/Europe/Middle East
Thomson Learning
Berkshire House
168-173 High Holborn
London WC1V 7AA
United Kingdom

Asia
Thomson Learning
60 Albert Street #15-01
Albert Complex
Singapore 189969

Canada
Nelson/Thomson Learning
1120 Birchmount Road
Scarborough, Ontario M1K 5G4
Canada

Library of Congress Cataloging-in-Publication Data
Lum, Doman, 1938–
Social work practice and people of color : a process-stage approach / Doman Lum. — 4th ed.
    p.   cm.
Includes bibliographical references and index.
ISBN 0-534-35639-7
1. Social work with minorities. 2. Social work with minorities--United States. I. Title.
HV3176.L9 1999
362.84'00973—dc21
99-28881
CIP

Contents

CHAPTER 4

Social Work Knowledge Theory
81

CHAPTER 5

A Framework for Social Work Practice with People of Color
114

CHAPTER 6

Contact
142

CHAPTER 7

Problem Identification 180

CHAPTER 8

Assessment 210

WITHDRAWN

Cultural Studies

Foreword

This book has evolved and been crafted from a career devoted to culturally competent practice. Professor Lum has steadily built this model of culturally competent practice, beginning with the first edition of this book and now through to this fourth edition. In fact, as a sister faculty at California State University, Sacramento, School of Social Work in the 1970s, I witnessed this evolution as I worked closely with him at that school, and throughout the years as we have served together in other settings.

Doman Lum wears a conceptualization and experiential cap that is always enlisting new ideas and perspectives for advancing the art of culturally competent practice. His leadership on the board of directors of the Council on Social Work Education was part of the impetus for the Culturally Competent Social Work Education in the 21st Century Conference at the University of Michigan, Ann Arbor. This effort will seed new theory and practice perspectives for multicultural populations in the new millenium, building on foundations girded by the contributions of pioneers in multicultural practice such as Doman Lum.

This latest edition is one of the most current and substantive works on practice with people of color, designed to address the competency needs of social work practitioners, from those newest in the field to the most seasoned. Doman Lum has again methodically laid out a relevant set of theoretical frameworks to elucidate the multifaceted themes that undergird culturally competent practice. Yet, all this knowledge theory is presented in a writing style that ensures comprehension.

This latest effort exemplifies the incorporation of his most recent formulations, for example, through the addition of multicultural social histories on women of color, gender knowledge theory, and implications for practice, features that duly strengthen what was already a tightly woven framework of practice. An ongoing strength of his accumulating work is his commitment to search out the most recent innovations in this area of practice, inserting vital new research and practice forums such as Young In Song's Woman-Centered Perspective.

The overview of the history of the black women's movement presents critical historical events that highlight the divergence between the needs and politics of the black and white suffrage movements.

Unlike the historical documentation that is made on the black woman's movement, it is more difficult to document the Mexican American and Latina woman's movements at the turn of the century to the present. The common perception in much of the literature is that Mexican American women in the Southwest and western United States were predominantly poor people who immigrated from Mexico in search of a better life, especially after the Mexican Revolution of 1910. In reality, the revolution also pushed into the United States women from the more educated classes in Mexico who, with their families, crossed the border to prevent political repercussions, especially toward husbands and fathers (Meier & Rivera, 1972). The author uses the work of feminist Chicana historians such as Dr. Rosalinda Gonzalez (1981), who has researched how Mexican American women broke traditional gender roles to function as organizers in such diverse arenas as politics, education, mining, shell picking, the garment industry, and the farm workers' struggles.

Thus, the concerns of Latina women, although often very similar to those of other minority and Anglo-American women, display organizing and community endeavors that are broadly focused. Dolores Huerta's life work with the United Farmworkers Union is a present-day example of feminism that is sparked by the priority given to the extensive needs of the Latino population.

The differences in focus, the concern for inclusion of the needs of men of color for many women of color, shades their feminist endeavors with commitments that are often distinct from those of majority group women. The collective stance that Dr. Lum identifies as critical to comprehending diverse populations is very relevant for minority women. To place their needs as women as a priority over the collective or community needs is not a traditional format for many of them.

Thus, their allegiance to the collective and to aspects of their traditional cultures that are imbued with significance often makes their efforts to bring about feminist changes more complex and more challenging than for their nonminority sisters. If and when women of color reach through the glass ceiling, their trajectory there, while similar to that of other women, traverses cultural crossroads that often include painful choices. Although women of color can benefit greatly from the support and understanding of their Anglo-American sisters, it too often is not present in a substantive manner, because of misunderstanding and mistrust.

Similarly, the more rigid sex-role expectations that may exist for women in such tradition-bound groups as Asian and Latino populations may confront women of color with greater risk for rejection, ridicule, or family conflict. Women of color often confront the reality of giving up important cultural supports that have protected them from painful racist realities when they strike out on pioneering moves to break with traditional female roles. The implications for sorting out these similarities and differences for women of color is part of the practice formula and competency mandate that is laid out in this book. The author uses Davis's (1989) work to delineate avenues that all women must traverse if the racism and division that has characterized the women's movements until now will have any hope of changing.

One of the many highlights in this book is the diverse populations that are addressed: minority elderly, gay and lesbian persons of color, multiracial children, immigrants, racial and ethnic families. The uniqueness of each of these diverse groups is captured, identifying the implications for practice in specific and yet meaningful ways.

Similarly, many topics are addressed in a lucid style, such as empowerment, liberation, stratification, power, and powerlessness, all of which are central to viable cultural practice. The organization of the content is threaded carefully so it does not overwhelm the reader.

The tone of the book is an important ingredient, because it uses historical and policy practices to display the institutional racism that has oppressed people of color over time. Yet, the exemplars are well researched and presented without the shards of anger that sometimes accompany this kind of content.

All of this important content sits on the major theoretical framework of a generalist model of practice for social workers. Professor Lum ensures that a sound generalist framework underpins the book, offering key theory insights and practice exemplars for each stage of practice: contact, problem identification, assessment, intervention, and termination. In each of these stages, an array of client-system practice issues are presented that delineate such important aspects to the helping relationship such as addressing client resistance. He notes, for example, how the disparagement many people of color have experienced in other service settings can contribute a unique texture to this classical practice theme. The sections on worker-system practice issues offer a selection of perspectives that divulge family, agency, and community issues of pertinence for culturally competent practice, again using examples that enable the practitioner to recognize both the obvious as well as subtle practice themes for client systems of color.

Dr. Lum has further strengthened this present edition by adding more to the assortment of cultural studies that elucidate his theory perspectives as well as the even more diverse vignettes that delineate culturally competent practice. Through these formats the author integrates the "how to's" for each theory construct he presents so the reader can readily experience the critical application or practice component. There is an evenness to how the variety of cultural/racial groups share the practice forum, to substantiate a critical concept or framework. One of the important similarities among these groups that he highlights is the collective stance that underpins many cultural values and must be entertained for viable practice.

Given the breadth of content that is offered, the book does not suffer from lack of depth. For example, when examining knowledge theory related to gender, current feminist themes are perused yet presented in a manner that focuses on the pivotal and meaty issues. There is genuine sensitivity to the difference in realities that confront women of color as opposed to Euro-American women, a content area that tends to cause political ripples. Issues are presented in an efficient manner that does not belabor the point but quickly takes the reader to the culturally competent practice arena. The author balances the micro-, meso-, and macrolevels of practice in a fashion that ensures that the generalist model is laid out in a theoretically and practice-appropriate manner but one that consistently and methodically pulls in culturally competent practice knowledge and skills. Certainly the focus on a strengths perspective rather than a deficiency or pathological model frames how the practitioner needs to assess culturally distinct clients and research cultures, especially those different from one's own. The inserts throughout the book that encourage the practitioner to self-assess via varied formats reinforce the thread that permeates this book: that culturally competent practice by definition includes ongoing self-assessment so as to effectively serve the varied cultural groups and contexts in which social workers practice.

The paradox that is evident at this time when the population in the United States is becoming so diverse and is projected to only increase in diversity for the new millennium is the conservatism and social climate that is trying to dismantle long-fought resource development efforts that address diversity such as affirmative action policies and bilingual education. The recent racial killing of an African American man who was dragged to death by three white men is another illustration of seemingly regressive trends that are inhumane and frightening. Yet, this book supplies a sense of optimism. It reflects the commitment, the hard work, and the *corazon*, or heart, of social workers and educators such as Doman Lum who continue to address racism and who firmly value and believe in the richness and strengths of a diverse society. This book is evidence that major changes have evolved and will continue to evolve to ensure that all people receive services in a respectful and meaningful manner.

Maria Zuniga, Ph.D.
Professor of Social Work
San Diego State University

REFERENCES

Davis, A. Y. (1989). *Women, culture, and politics.* New York: Random House.

Gonzalez, R. (1981). Chicanas in Mexican immigrant families: 1920–1940. In J. Jensen & L. Scharf (Eds.), *Decades of discontent: The woman's movement 1920–1940.* Westport, CT: Greenwood.

Meier, M. S., & Rivera, F. (1972). *The Chicanos: A history of Mexican Americans.* New York: Hill & Wang.

Preface

Culturally diverse social work practice and social work education are on the brink of beginning a new century and a new millenium. As I reflect on this time change and as I talk with social work colleagues in many universities and around the country at group meetings, I have sensed that there is an anticipation that social work texts and curriculum in the twenty-first century are headed toward outcome measurement results. This is one of the primary reasons for writing a companion volume to the *People of Color* text that appeared in July 1998 entitled *Culturally Competent Practice: A Framework for Growth and Action.* In a real sense the fourth edition of *Social Work Practice and People of Color: A Process-Stage Approach* complements and expands on the knowledge and skills portion of the competency text.

In the midst of the publications of these two texts in 1998 and 1999, the Culturally Competent Social Work Education in the 21st Century Conference at the University of Michigan, Ann Arbor, was an effort to bring together eighty-five of the finest multicultural social work educators and practitioners across the country who have made, are making, and will make major contributions in culturally diverse social work practice. In a real way this network of persons will be developing curriculum design, research studies, and publications in this field in the years ahead. They will carry on the work which many of us in social work education started in the 1970s and 1980s.

The fourth edition of *Social Work Practice and People of Color: A Process-Stage Approach* adds to the current and emerging body of quality culturally diverse social work practice texts and articles.

ABOUT THE BOOK

The structural design of *Social Work Practice and People of Color: A Process-Stage Approach* is still intact: a generalist social work practice-process framework that delineates culture-common and culture-specific social work principles for African, Latino, Asian, and Native Americans. The present literature overwhelmingly makes a case for such unique characteristics of people of color as a collective family hierarchy, interdependence between the individual and family and/or extended family, spirituality, and ethnic identity. The extent that a person of color has acculturated and assimilated into American society determines the influence of these factors in his or her life. However, I have found that residual elements remain even in the most Americanized. Cultural factors are a powerful influence in a person's life.

Among the themes of the book that have remained important for social work practice with people of color are multicultural service delivery, relationship protocols, professional self-disclosure, reframing the problem as an unsatisfied want or an unfulfilled need, socioenvironmental impacts and psychoindividual reactions, and multiple intervention strategies that are appropriate for ethnically diverse clients. I have found these to be valuable teaching themes that strike a responsive chord with students.

About the Changes

The fourth edition has added new changes that reflect recent trends in social work practice and social science materials regarding culture and ethnicity. There are a number of new features:

• Definitions of refugee, asylee, parolee, immigrant, temporary resident, and undocumented person in "Changing Demographics" of Chapter 1
• A new Chapter 2 on "People of Color" that highlights the American multicultural social history of women of color (white feminism and African American women; exclusion from early

women's rights; racism in women's suffrage; black women club movement; Mexican American, Asian American, and Native American women at the turn of the century; women of color feminism) and practice overviews with new arrivals, women of color, gays and lesbians of color, children of color, the racially/ethnically mixed, and older persons of color

• The effects of welfare reform, the 1996 Personal Responsibility and Work Opportunity Reconciliation Act, affecting single women heads of households and their dependent children and restrictions on noncitizens

• Separate chapters on "Culturally Diverse Values" (Chapter 3), featuring the 1997 National Association of Social Workers Code of Ethics and a new Cultural Values Clarification exercise, and "Social Work Knowledge Theory" (Chapter 4), with a new section on gender knowledge theory (including the subsections "The Need for a Multicultural Gender Perspective," "Current Multicultural Feminist Issues," and "Gender Implications for Practice")

• Addition of a framework for black experience-based social work practice, which totals nine framework examples in Chapter 5, "A Framework for Social Work Practice with People of Color"

• A new section on gender assessment that focuses on individual, family group, and community system relationships in Chapter 8 on "Assessment"

• New sections in Chapter 9 on "Intervention" featuring Young In Song's woman-centered perspective, group work, and a mesolevel intervention lay caregiving training program in the local church

• New sections in Chapter 10 on "Termination" covering outcome evaluation and transitions in termination, evaluating destination points, and formulating follow-up strategies

• New sections in Chapter 11, "Epilogue," on culturally competency practice trends and "New Horizons and Challenges for Culturally Diverse Social Work Practice," highlighting themes from McGoldrick's *Re-visioning Family Therapy: Race, Culture, and Gender in Clinical Practice*

• Fourteen new Cultural Studies, for a total of sixty-five in the book

About the Political Climate

Social reform movements have occurred every thirty years in American political, economic, and social life. Franklin Delano Roosevelt and the New Deal of the 1930s and Lyndon Baines Johnson and the Great Society of the 1960s are prototypes for William Jefferson Clinton and his social reform agenda for the 1990s. However, the political and private scandals of the Clinton administration have caused us to close the twentieth century on a different note, other than major social and political change reform.

It will be an interesting process to inaugurate the first president of the United States at the beginning of the new millennium and to witness how this leader will shape and change the country as it enters the new century. Will there be more political and social inclusion of Latino, Asian, and Native American persons in political and administrative positions on the state and federal levels? Will there be new human and civil rights legislation in the twenty-first century that will protect and ensure access for people of color, women, children, the elderly, and gays and lesbians? Will we enter a prolonged period of peace, tranquillity, and readiness so that major global war and killing will be significantly reduced? Will we leave a better America and more global understanding and coexistence to our children?

ACKNOWLEDGMENTS

I wish to particularly thank the staff at Brooks/Cole and Wadsworth, who have maintained a positive, thoughtful relationship with me during the fourth edition of this book: to Lisa Gebo, social work editor, who invited me to work on and improve this book and who has been a constant source of support and assistance; Matt Stevens, production editor; Ellen Pettengell, interior and cover designer; Stephen Rapley, art editor; Bob Kauser, permissions editor; and Laura E. Larson, copy editor.

My social work colleagues at California State University, Sacramento, at the Council on Social Work Education, and in numerous undergraduate and graduate social work programs throughout the country have been valuable sources of feedback for this edition. I particularly want to thank Dr. Yuhwa Eva Lu of New York University, Ehrenkranz School of Social Work, and members of the Cultural Diversity Committee of the Council on Social Work Education Board of Directors (class of 1995–1998) with whom I have had many interesting discussions of concepts addressed in this book. I was fortunate to write material on women of color social work issues that was intended for a book on multicultural feminist social work practice. However, it did not materialize, and instead I integrate women of color content in a number of chapters in this text. Above all, students in my social work graduate course, Multicultural Theory and Practice, cause me to search out new material and to keep up with the growing literature in preparing my classes.

I am most grateful to the manuscript reviewers, who helped shape and refine this edition: Jean W. Granger, California State University, Long Beach; Rebecca A. Lopez, California State University, Long Beach; Norma D. Thomas, Widener University; Barbara W. Shank, University of St. Thomas; and Ellen Whipple, Michigan State University.

I also want to thank Dr. Maria Zuniga of San Diego State University, School of Social Work, for her gracious foreword to this fourth edition; and my family (my wife, Joyce, and my children, Lori, Jonathan, Amy, and Matthew), who have given me the freedom and support necessary to carry out the revisions for this book.

Above all, I want to acknowledge the many professors who contributed to my learning and knowledge over the years at the following institutions of higher education: the University of Hawaii (Departments of English and Philosophy), Fuller Theological Seminary (the Graduate School of Theology), the School of Theology at Claremont (Department of Pastoral Counseling and Psychology), and Case Western Reserve University (the Mandel School of Applied Social Sciences). I want to thank the teachers who have influenced my academic and professional development: Merril F. Heiser, who developed and encouraged my love of English literature and writing; Howard J. Clinebell, Jr., who served as a role model of a classroom teacher par excellence, a friend to students, and a diligent and insightful scholar/writer; Norman L. Farberow, who guided me as a clinical intern and assisted me with difficult cases and was instrumental in my development of crisis intervention theory; Arthur Blum, who impressed me as a teacher who commanded a vast knowledge of social welfare planning and policy analysis, articulated with humor and insight; and Gregory M. St. L. O'Brien, who gave me a model for aspiration to administration in higher education with a driving, hardworking, and highly personal lifestyle. This book is for multicultural social work educators and practitioners, with the hope that they will contribute to the field of culturally diverse social work practice.

Doman Lum, Ph.D, Th.D.
Professor of Social Work
California State University,
Sacramento

About the Author

Doman Lum is professor of social work at California State University, Sacramento. His previous books include *Culturally Competent Practice: A Framework for Growth and Action*, *Social Work and Health Care Policy*, and *Responding to Suicidal Crisis*. He has written articles on Asian Americans, health care delivery and health maintenance organizations, culturally diverse social work practice, suicide prevention, and pastoral counseling. He is a consulting editor for *The Journal of Multicultural Social Work* and *Arete* and has been on the board of directors and the Commission on Accreditation for the Council on Social Work Education. He is an ordained minister of the United Church of Christ, Northern California Conference.

CHAPTER 1

Culturally Diverse Social Work Practice

The last two decades have witnessed the dramatic growth of culturally diverse groups within the population of the United States. Large metropolitan centers (New York, Los Angeles, Chicago, Boston, Houston, San Francisco, Washington, D.C.) have been transformed by new refugee and immigrant clusters. Only the nation's heartland remains relatively homogeneous.

In the 1960s, 1970s, and early 1980s, people of color were generally referred to as *ethnic minorities* in academic texts and in the media. Ethnicity focused on the national-heritage divisions of the population. It underscored the importance of race, which had been at the core of the civil rights movement; that movement's protests culminated in legal safeguards against discrimination and the institution of affirmative action policies. Ethnic affiliation was seen as an important factor in individual and group identity. The term *ethnocentrism* characterized the emotional attitude that a person's own ethnic group and national identity are central to individual and collective belonging. Equally significant was the term *minority*, which highlighted the limited political, economic, and social opportunities of African Americans, Latino Americans, Asian Americans, and Native Americans. Minority status denoted a numerically smaller or politically powerless group in relation to a larger, controlling, and dominant majority. Whites were cast as the majority, whereas nonwhites were the minorities. For many, a minority/majority distinction implied an inferiority/superiority distinction.

In the late 1980s and early 1990s new terms emerged, *multiculturalism* and *diversity*, that may more accurately reflect what has happened in this country. They acknowledge the coexistence of many groups with different cultural practices and traditions in the United States today.

Multiculturalism has both political and academic aspects. The Rainbow Coalition supporting Jesse Jackson's 1988 presidential campaign was an effort to bring people of color together as a political force. On college campuses, multicultural efforts embrace ethnic studies curricula, affirmative action for faculty and students, and organizing activities by people of color.

While seeking unity under the multicultural banner, cultural groups endeavor to preserve their own distinctive identities—their languages, beliefs, and customs. In the multicultural perspective, these distinctive practices represent enormous cultural wealth and are a source of enrichment for the whole society.

Diversity emphasizes the dissimilarity among cultural groups. Ethnic, gender, sexual orientation, and age groups comprise the diversity of the United States. In speaking of diversity, we recognize and respect the differences among cultures.

Culturally diverse social work is concerned with those groups who have historically been oppressed because of differences in ethnicity, color, and customs. There is a growing realization that celebrating cultural variety nourishes the well-being and pride of those in historically oppressed groups. At the same time, we must face the legacy of prejudice and hostility across color lines.

PEOPLE OF COLOR

The population of the United States is composed of ethnic groups. Generation on generation of families from other cultures have assimilated into American society. Yet, to varying degrees, a residue remains of distinctive language, beliefs, and customs. In large cities and rural areas of this country, ethnic neighborhoods and communities have continued to flourish after hundreds of years.

Silva (1983) views people as having a common humanity but also unique differences based on inherited endowment, learned values and culture, developmental histories, specified patterns of problems, and personalized styles of coping. People are products of their cultures and geographic environments, family groups, local settings, regional identities, national identities and experiences, and social situations. In addition, people are influenced by cultural territoriality, discrimination, institutional oppression, and normative behavior. Finally, people are members of ethnic groups and have both individual and group-related identities, experiences, and social realities.

However, the *color factor* has been a barrier to African Americans, Latino Americans, Asian Americans, and Native Americans, in contrast to other ethnic groups who are able to blend into the white-dominated society. Anglo-Saxon and European groups have successfully integrated with each other and become assimilated into the mainstream of American society and power. But, by and large, people of color have not had equal access to the mainstream. The history of racism, discrimination, and segregation binds people of color together and contrasts with the experiences of white Americans.

Social work deals with clients of many socioeconomic and cultural backgrounds. Social work practitioners are responsible for services that range from mental health, corrections, and medical care to grassroots organizations and political change movements that affect the lives and problems of people and their environment. Social workers serve diverse populations and use several theories of practice; these theories must include the knowledge and skills of multicultural practice. It is particularly important that this knowledge and these skills be an integral part of the helping repertoire because people of color have reached a critical turning point. A conservative political and social mood currently prevails in this country. Budget cutbacks have affected poor people of color. At the same time, the resurgence of the conservative right, the dismantling of affirmative action, and racial killings serve to reinforce a racist climate.

Those who stand apart from the dominant society because of color are vulnerable to the difficulties caused by such economic, political, and social conditions. Many of those affected are Latino and Asian immigrants who have fled political oppression in their native countries and who encounter language and employment problems in the United States. These immigrants are vulnerable to social assistance cutbacks and rely on ethnic community survival mechanisms for existence. During the past twenty years, there have been significant changes in the racial composition and cultural diversity of the U.S. population. With the clustering of people of color in major communities and regions, it is important for human services professionals to respond to their psychosocial needs. Culturally diverse knowledge theory, ethnic-sensitive helping skills, and knowledge of cultural factors are essential ingredients in forming appropriate service delivery structures, training ethnic-sensitive workers, and implementing community outreach programs.

The primary aim of this book is to advance the development of culturally diverse social work practice by setting forth a generalist approach to working with people of color. This model consists of four elements: practice process stages, client-system practice issues, worker-system practice issues, and worker-client tasks. These elements are infused with cultural dimensions of meaning; culture acts as a vital bridge between the ethnic community and the dominant society. It includes ethnic customs and beliefs, interdependent family networks, behavioral survival skills, and other distinguishing features. It is my hope that social workers will increase their knowledge of people of color and enhance their culturally diverse practice skills as a result of exploring the themes of this book.

In distinction to the people of color theme, the term *minority* has been set aside and used in the historical context of the sixties. Whereas some feel that *minority* accurately reflects the oppressive nature of American society, in which a dominant majority practices racism, sexism, and homophobia, others strongly object to the continued use of this term in the literature. For example, De La Cancela, Jenkins, and Chin (1993) make the following argument:

> "Minority," used as a label to refer to populations of color, ignores the reality that it is the Caucasian race which is in a numerical minority globally. It also acknowledges what group is in a political majority (i.e., power elite) in the United States and generalizes this to the entire world. We see in this term oppressive connotations of disempoweredness and poverty that are inappropriate and offensive in the context of African, Latino, indigenous, and Asian ethnic groups who are becoming increasingly numerous, economically strong, and sociopolitically organized. (p. 7)

Accordingly, to respect the convictions of many who are writing and actively involved in the field, I refer to people of color in this book not as ethnic minorities but as culturally diverse groups.

HUMAN DIVERSITY

Social work education and practice have focused on human diversity as a curriculum content area and a practice perspective for every social work undergraduate and graduate student in the United States. Human diversity is an inclusive term that encompasses groups distinguished by race, ethnicity, culture, class, gender, sexual orientation, religion, physical or mental ability, age, and national origin. In its broadest sense, human diversity covers the various people who comprise a society. Diversity includes all of us, because each individual is unique and one of a kind,

The 1994 Curriculum Policy Statement of the Council on Social Work Education (CSWE) uses the term *diversity* to denote curriculum content about differences and similarities in the experiences, needs, and beliefs of people. It acknowledges that practitioners who serve diverse populations must use differential assessment and intervention skills.

Components of Diversity

According to Dixon and Taylor (1994), diversity is distinguished by primary and secondary characteristics. The primary characteristics are often visible and may be different for specific groups. However, the differences are not choice driven; the primary characteristics are given traits of particular groups. Among the primary characteristics are race and/or ethnicity, gender, age, physical/mental abilities, sexual orientation, and size. The secondary characteristics, by contrast, are often invisible and may change by individual choice and particular circumstances. They include political ideology, geography, marital/family status, socioeconomic status, religion, occupation/skills, experiences, and education.

These two sets of characteristics help us put primary and secondary trait boundaries around a particular group. For example, we may be focusing on middle-aged Vietnamese males, between the ages of thirty-five and fifty-nine, who are able to read and write in Vietnamese and English and are between five feet and five feet, eight inches tall. These are the visible primary characteristics of the group. However, we may also delineate a number of secondary characteristics. We may want to select middle-aged Vietnamese men who are anticommunist, live in California, are married to a Vietnamese woman, have one to five children, have a single or combined income of $30,000 to $100,000 per year, are active church members in Protestant congregations, have worked in a white-collar occupation in the United States for at least five years, fought in the South Vietnamese armed forces during the Vietnam War between 1961 and 1975, and are college graduates from a university in Vietnam, France, or the United States. Thus, the definition of diversity from Dixon and Taylor (1994) allows us to define a particular group for study in terms of primary and secondary characteristics.

Hoffman and Sallee (1994) present a helpful discussion of human diversity and populations at risk. These two divisions are mutually compatible and must be understood together.

Hoffman and Sallee identify several components of human diversity: dual perspective (our family life nurturing environment and the larger society of the outside world); contextual diversity (the environment as the context for human living and the interaction of individuals and their problems and concerns with the environment); rural-suburban-urban (population size and economic base, which are determining factors in resource allocation); social stratification (differences in income level, education level, and occupation); the life chances of those who are most at risk, regional economies and diversities (differences in occupations, stability, versatility, population heterogeneity, and economic forecasts among various areas of the country); and basic resources (housing, transportation, education, child care).

Hoffman and Sallee cite five major populations that are at risk: women (poor women and children, sexism, the social problems of women, and gender relationships); ethnic minorities of color (institutional racism, individual racism, respectable racism, the last category dealing with subtle forms that support harmful implicit policies or blame individual failure); gay men and lesbian women (AIDS crisis, homophobia, particular forms of prejudice and discrimination); the elderly (ageism, policies adverse to the elderly, care of the elderly); and the physically and mentally challenged (discrimination and adverse policies suffered by the physically disabled, the mentally retarded, and persons with learning disabilities).

Meaning of Diversity

De La Cancela, Jenkins, and Chin (1993) explain the meaning of diversity in the following terms:

> Diversity is the valorization of alternate lifestyles, biculturality, human differences, and uniqueness in individual and group life. Diversity promotes an informed connectedness to one's reference group, self-knowledge, empowering contact with those different from oneself, and an appreciation for the commonalities of our human condition. Diversity also requires an authentic exploration of the client's and practitioner's personal and reference group history. This exploration empowers the therapeutic dyad by providing a meaningful context for understanding present realities, problems of daily living, and available solutions. (p. 6)

At no other time in U.S. history have we witnessed such a rich and varied mixture of people, not only in geographic, social, and ethnic enclaves but also distributed throughout the community. Diversity ought to be a positive element in our country; differences ought to be viewed as assets rather than liabilities.

The development of diversity is the task ahead of us as we move to the end of this century. According to Jenkins (1993), diversity is nurtured through self-knowledge, multicultural education, and empathy.

By *self-knowledge*, Jenkins means an awareness of one's own perceptions of difference on the basis of race, ethnicity, gender, and other factors; positive identification with one's own racial or ethnocultural group helps to develop an appreciation of diversity in others.

Multicultural education has moved from exposure to ethnocultural intricacies (for example, celebration of holidays, native foods, dress, and customs) to the goals of fairness and tolerance, critical thinking and prejudice reduction, resolution of conflict associated with difference, and support for the actualization of basic human rights. It includes professional training programs on stereotypes and prejudice in one's own life, race relations and diversity workshops, and culturally competent supervision.

Empathy is vital for the empowerment of the client; the helper not only connects with the basic human condition of the client but also embraces social and psychological aspects of identity.

Cross-Cultural Diversity

Cross-cultural diversity may be viewed in terms of intra- and interdimensions. Sasao (1996, pp. 185, 186) explains ethnic-cultural diversity as a double-tiered social phenomenon: (l) the within-group diversity consisting of heterogeneity due to changing or diversifying patterns of social relations in family, neighborhood, and communities within ethnic-cultural groups; sexual orientation, gender; political or religious organizations; intergroup marriages and (2) across- or between-group diversity or complexity and intergroup tensions between social groups in work, school, or everyday situations, which is compounded by major urban area diversity due to demographic and social changes.

Cross-cultural studies reveal differences in attitudes toward contrasting Western and Asian helping themes. For example, Chin (1993) identifies differences in Western and Asian attitudes to psychotherapy. She qualifies her remarks by noting that they do not imply uniformity within cultures or among individuals but rather illustrate relative degrees of emphasis between cultures. Also, the attitudes she describes in Asian families are stronger in immigrants and refugees; the American-born tend to be bicultural and able to switch behavior as a coping mechanism.

With these qualifications, Chin reports that Asians who seek assistance expect a generalist helper or advice giver, an authority figure who takes a directive approach and provides concrete social services. Asians are oriented toward a holistic view of health and regard healing as the restoration of balance. Thus, in psychotherapy, somatic concerns must be addressed, and the client requires immediate symptom relief. Restoring an imbalance in the body or family system is an effective approach. Therapists should be aware of the hierarchy of interpersonal relationships, based on obedience to the parents and concern for parental needs and wishes.

Among Asians, the regulation of emotion (self-control, private display, self-expression) is more important to ego development than catharsis or the public display of emotion. To preserve interpersonal harmony, Asians employ polite indirect communication. Silence is used to communicate disagreement; confrontation and overt disagreement are considered aggressive and inappropriate and violate harmony. Asian languages value brevity, with the use of metaphor and implicit meaning. The cultural emphasis is on interdependence (caring for one's family and integration into the extended family); people want to belong.

In short, Chin's understanding of Asian culture provides a framework in which to modify the helping process so as to conform to the client's worldview.

Social Work and Diversity

To sound a note of warning, we must make sure that the diversity debate does not focus on abnormality and innate differences. Espin and Gawelek (1992) believe that the discipline of psychology has distorted diversity.

> Basically, psychology has understood human diversity from diametrically opposed perspectives: Either diversity is a reflection of abnormalities or deficiencies, in which case efforts should be made to change the individuals and make them healthy. Or, these differences are dictated by nature rather than a result of the sociocultural context, so there is no need for any intervention. (p. 89)

In contrast, social work has emphasized the positive worth and reality of human diversity in its curriculum standards and professional practice. Social work can assume the leadership in human diversity research, writing, and practice.

CHANGING DEMOGRAPHICS

During the past twenty years a major influx of refugees, asylees, parolees, immigrants, temporary residents, and undocumented persons has entered the United States, mostly from Asia and Central America. Drachman (1995) explains the following immigration status categories for our understanding:

• *Refugee*—A refugee is a person who is outside and unable or unwilling to avail him- or herself of the protection of the home country because of persecution or fear of persecution on account of race, religion, nationality, membership in a particular social group, or political opinion; the individual who requests refugee status makes an application from abroad, often from a country of asylum, that the Immigration and Naturalization Service accepts or rejects.

• *Asylee*—The asylee applies for asylee status from United States territory, whereas the refugee applies for asylum in the United States from another country; this individual waits a long time for status determination and during the wait remains ineligible for many services.

• *Parolee*—An individual is admitted into the United States under emergency conditions or if the person's entry is considered in the public interest; this person enters the country under the U.S. attorney general's parole authority and is not entitled to federal benefits.

• *Immigrant*—An individual is lawfully granted permission to reside permanently in the United States; a sponsor is required who is a person or organization guaranteeing economic support of the immigrant for the first three years of the immigrant's residence in the United States.

• *Temporary resident*—A person has legal permission to live and work temporarily in the United States and is eligible to become a permanent resident after a set period and must do so or lose legal status; many are undocumented people who legalize their status through the amnesty program.

• *Undocumented person*—An individual with no current authorization to be in the United States who has entered either illegally or legally under a nonimmigrant status for a temporary period (for example, a student or a tourist) and who remains

in the United States after the visa expires; this person is subject to deportation.

Between 1970 and 1980, the U.S. Census recorded marked increases of ethnic groups. The number of African Americans in the United States increased by 17 percent, from 22.6 million to 26.5 million. The Latino American population grew from 9.1 million to 14.6 million, for a 61 percent growth rate.

Asian Americans more than doubled their population, increasing from 1.5 million to 3.5 million (a 126 percent growth rate). The number of Native Americans/Alaskan Natives rose from 800,000 to 1.4 million, for a growth rate of 71 percent.

In 1986, of 601,700 legal immigrants entering the United States, the largest groups came from Mexico (66,500), the Philippines (52,600), and Korea (35,800) (U.S. Bureau of the Census, 1987). By 1987, it was reported that one in every five Americans (Suinn, 1987) and 40 percent of public school students (Vobejda, 1987) were people of color, as were the majority of the population in several states: Hawaii, New Mexico, Alaska, and soon California.

The 1990 U.S. Census reported a surge of immigration to the United States that reflected 30 percent of the nation's population growth during the previous decade. At no other time since the 1920 census has so much growth resulted from migration from other countries.

Between 1975 and 1993, 1,803,527 refugees were admitted to the United States, from East Asia (1,136,957, 63 percent), the Soviet Union (311,165, 17 percent), Eastern Europe (174,985, 10 percent), the Near East and South Asia (84,828, 5 percent), Latin America (46,433, 3 percent), Africa (40,945, 2 percent), and elsewhere. By 1994, the annual ceiling on refugee admissions was 121,000, with the following regional breakdown: Eastern Europe and Soviet Union 55,000; East Asia 45,000; Africa 7,000; the Near East and South Asia 6,000; and Latin America 4,000.

Refugees initially settled in populous metropolitan areas and coastal states. The top five states attracting refugees between 1975 and 1992 were California (532,004), New York (141,653), Texas

(94,192), Washington (62,661), and Illinois (56,066). The pattern of primary refugee arrivals in California between 1985 and 1992 reveals that the leading countries of origin were Vietnam (69,278, 35 percent), the Soviet Union (45,796, 23 percent), Laos (36,106, 18 percent), Iran (18,875, 10 percent), and Cambodia (5,834, 3 percent).

The 1995 projection of resident population, according to the U.S. Bureau of the Census (1993) was 217.5 million white, 33.1 million blacks, 26.5 million Hispanics, 9.8 million Asians and Pacific Islanders, and 2.2 million American Indians and Alaskan Natives. Between 1991 and 1995, the growth rate was expected to be 48.2 per 1,000 among Asian and Pacific Islanders, 30.3 per 1,000 among Hispanics, 14.6 per 1,000 among blacks, 14.2 per 1,000 among American Indians and Alaskan Natives, and 7.1 per 1,000 among whites.

California illustrates the growth of people of color in the population. By 1990, one in every nine Americans lived in California, which had a population equal to those of New York and Pennsylvania combined (Barringer, 1990). According to the 1990 census, people of color accounted for 43 percent of the state's population, as compared with 33 percent in 1980. The number of Latino Americans increased by 70 percent between 1980 and 1990, while the Asian American population doubled during the same period. Twenty-nine of the thirty most ethnically diverse communities in the United States are in California (McLeod & Schreiner, 1991). Between 1990 and 2000, four out of five new Bay Area residents will be persons of color (Schreiner, 1990), and by the beginning of the twenty-first century half of the children in California will be either Latinos or Asian Americans (Policy Analysis for California Education, 1989). In the United States it is estimated that one in every four Americans has African, Latino, Asian, or Native American ancestry (Fiske, 1991).

In the year 2000, the ethnic population is projected to consist of 225.5 million whites, 35.5 million blacks, 31.4 million of Hispanic origin, 11.2 million Asian and Pacific Islanders, and 2.4 million American Indian, Eskimo, and Aleutian Islanders. By the year 2010 there will be significant increases of whites (239.6 million), people of

Hispanic origin (41.1 million), and Asian and Pacific Islanders (15.3 million), whereas there will be moderate increases among blacks (40.1 million) and American Indian, Eskimo, and Aleutian Islanders (2.8 million) (U.S. Bureau of the Census, 1997).

In light of these population shifts, training social work students and practitioners in culturally diverse practice theory and skills is crucial. In the social work tradition, Jane Addams of Hull House and other settlement house workers learned to appreciate and defend the uniqueness of immigrants' cultural heritage (Colburn & Pozzeta, 1979). The essence of the settlement house approach to immigrants was to understand the customs and traditions of each group and then to seek as much opportunity for these groups as possible (Davis, 1967). The settlement houses worked for new policies to protect immigrants, workers, ethnic groups, women, and children. They were instrumental in the organization in 1908 of the Hull House–sponsored immigrant Protective League, which sought to ease the adjustment of newcomers to strange cities by helping them find housing and employment (Magill, 1985). In the 1990s and into the twenty-first century, with the recent influx of immigrants and refugees, we must set up practice strategies, policies, and programs to meet similar needs.

GENERALIST PRACTICE

Beginning with the 1984 Curriculum Policy Statement in the *Handbook of Accreditation Standards and Procedures*, prepared by CSWE's Commission on Accreditation, the term *generalist practice* has been used to describe the professional foundation of social work practice. The 1994 Curriculum Policy Statement reiterates a generalist practice that does the following:

- Emphasizes professional relationships characterized by mutuality, collaboration, and respect for the client system
- Focuses practice assessment on the examination of client strengths and problems in the interac-

tions among individuals and between people and their environments

- Includes knowledge, values, and skills to enhance the well-being of people and to help ameliorate the environmental conditions that affect people adversely
- Includes the following skills: defining issues, collecting and assessing data, planning and contracting, identifying alternative interventions, selecting and implementing appropriate courses of action, using appropriate research-based knowledge and technological advances, and termination
- Includes approaches and skills for practice with clients from different social, cultural, racial, religious, spiritual, and class background and with systems of all sizes

Hoffman and Sallee (1994) propose a bridge model of generalist social work practice, with the following characteristics:

- Establishing a primary goal of facing life's challenges and coping with the environment through the problem-solving method
- Building bridges between people in human relationships or stressful life transitions, so as to bring people together and to use their own strengths
- Connecting people to resources (people, funding, program services)
- Building bridges to create resources through inventive approaches, public policy, and new resources
- Building bridges to empower people through increasing options, using a new perspective on the problem, and enhancing life skills
- Believing in changes at the institutional and societal levels that facilitate changes in people's lives

Kirst-Ashman and Hull (1993) conceptualize the generalist intervention model, with the following basic features:

- A foundation of knowledge, skills, and values that include fields of practice (for example, family and children services, health, mental health, occupational social work, aging, education, and cor-

rections); curriculum content areas (for example, social work practice, human behavior and the social environment, research, social policy); generalist practice micro-, meso-, and macroskills; and professional values and ethics

- A problem-solving orientation that involves individuals, groups, organizations, and social policies and consists of assessment, planning, intervention, evaluation, termination, and follow-up
- Problem analysis that addresses a wide range of perspectives, such as understanding and working with families, making ethical decisions, ethnically and racially sensitive social work practice, gender-sensitive social work practice, advocacy, brokering and case management, and recording
- The flexible application of the problem-solving method in various helping situations

The primary thrust of this book is to formulate a generalist social work practice model for people of color. It articulates generalist practice principles that address people of color and are applicable to all clients. In a sense, good culturally diverse generalist practice is good social work practice for all people.

Culturally Diverse Social Work Practice

Rounds, Weil, and Bishop (1994) offer five principles of culturally competent practice that address diversity areas:

1. Acknowledge and value diversity in terms of understanding how race, culture, and ethnicity contribute to the uniqueness of the individual, family, and community and recognize the differences among and within ethnic, cultural, and racial groups.

2. Conduct a cultural self-assessment in terms of an awareness of your own culture and how it shapes your personal and professional beliefs and behaviors.

3. Recognize and understand the dynamics of difference in terms of the client's and practitioner's behavioral expectations, their interactions, their

degrees of self-disclosure, the client's collective orientation (extended family and community), and issues of racism, rapport, and trust levels.

4. Acquire cultural knowledge in terms of client background (socioeconomic status, education, family history, ethnic group identification, and immigration) and cultural knowledge of the community (informal social network, help-seeking and helping norms, and perception of agency accessibility and roles).

5. Adapt social work skills to the needs and styles of the client's culture (assessment of problems and delayed intervention).

Chapter 2 discusses racial, cultural, and ethnic diversity in terms of African Americans, Latino Americans, Asian Americans, and Native Americans, the four major groups who have historically been oppressed in this country on the basis of color distinctions. However, with the concept of human diversity as a rallying cry, a dialogue is under way between social work theorists and practitioners who have written about those four groups and those who have been formulating similar perspectives regarding women, gays and lesbians, and other oppressed groups. By sharing their theoretical frameworks and practice principles, these writers hope to find transferable knowledge and paradigms and, by that means, to enrich both the discussion of human diversity and social work practice.

Nevertheless, it cannot be forgotten that as long as African Americans, Latino Americans, Asian Americans, and Native Americans are a part of this country, they will be a numerical and political minority on account of their ethnic, racial, and color status. Despite legal and political freedoms guaranteed by the U.S. Constitution, and despite decades of civil rights struggle, these groups still face barriers of social assimilation, class stratification, and political powerlessness.

It may make the majority population uncomfortable to know that racism, along with sexism and homophobia, are still alive and well in the mentality and behavior of many individuals. However, those who read this text and other similar books must confront the reality of the present racial situation in the United States of America.

CRITICAL PERSPECTIVE

Longres (1990) has introduced the notion of a critical perspective on society that analytically identifies problems and solves them. From his vantage point, the critical theory for social service practice is derived from the interaction between individual and social change. He rejects both the "blame the victim" (the individual) and "blame society" (environmental stresses, effects of social forces victimizing the client) approaches. Rather, Longres encourages social workers to develop critical theory that focuses on current strategies linking individual and social change.

A number of thematic linkages focus on the individual and social change, forming a critical perspective for people of color.

Race, Ethnicity, and Power

Pinderhughes (1989) examines the themes of race, ethnicity, and power from a perspective of cross-cultural awareness. She focuses on the effect of psychological and social interaction dynamics on diverse individuals. Starting from the key role of culture in service delivery, Pinderhughes develops a strong case for cultural sensitivity and cross-cultural awareness—that is, for an understanding of difference, ethnicity, race, and power. These concepts form the basis for linking individual and social change because they have micro- (individual) and macro- (societal) implications.

At the same time, Pinderhughes presents culture as a critical factor in problem formulation and resolution and in the clinical process of assessment, relationship development, intervention, and outcome. She strongly emphasizes the need for the social worker to highlight cultural strengths that enable people of color to cope with social conditions. This entails empowering the client, so that he or she has a higher level of self-differentiation and a stronger sense of self, as well as change in the social context of the problem situation.

Ethnic Family Structure, Culturally Sensitive Family Theories, and Culturally Relevant Therapy Phases

Ho (1987) has presented the similarities and differences of family therapy between and among Asian/Pacific Americans, Native Americans and Alaskan Natives, Latinos, and African Americans. Ethnic family structure is based on such cultural values as the relationship of humanity to nature and the environment, harmony, pastime orientation, collective relations with people, being-in-becoming, and a positive view of the nature of humanity. Traditional family structure and extended family ties are reflected in the care of children, distinctive parental and child roles, and hierarchical sibling relationships. Transitional family crisis occurs when the family must cope with immigration, migration, and political and cultural adjustments. Accompanying family role and membership changes also have a disruptive effect. Families turn for help to family and extended family support, to religious healers and leaders, and then to the mainstream care system. The family must be viewed as acting with and reacting to social, economic, and political forces.

Culturally sensitive family theories acknowledge the reality of anxiety and silence, psychophysiological symptomatology, indirect communication, use of the native language when dealing with a crisis or problem solving, dominant-husband and submissive-wife role relations, hierarchical family role structure, and emphasis on humanism and harmonious living. These behavioral responses are embedded in the cultural environment and behavior patterns of the family.

The family therapist is seen as a physician, medicine man or woman, or folk healer. It is important for the therapist to inquire about the family's cultural background, involve extended family members, understand kinship bonds, form a support system from the extended family network, and emphasize the positive aspects of behavior. Ho has blended individual, family, and social environmental factors crucial to ethnic family therapy. They form a critical perspective on the institution of the ethnic family.

Race, Gender, and Class

Davis and Proctor (1989) have stated another set of individual and social themes, concerning race, gender, and class, with practice implications for clients, families, and groups. Acknowledging the phenomenon of difference, Davis and Proctor are concerned about working through differences between client and helper—based on race, gender, and socioeconomic status—that might hinder the relationship. Each theme—race, gender, and class—has parallel sections devoted to individual, family, and group treatment. Thus, there is an infusion between wider social issues (race, gender, and class) and narrower clinical target groups (individual, family, and group). It is simple to compare sections on social issues and treatment foci across the board. Careful attention is also given to similar subsections related to these issues and practice stages.

Race and class are salient issues when there are social class and ethnic differences between the client and the helper. Before working with ethnic clients, workers must gain adequate knowledge of multicultural populations, a self-examination of racial attitudes and values, and a wide repertoire of ethnically effective helping responses. The desired result is managing the early treatment interaction: developing rapport, recognizing the reality of racial and social differences, establishing client trust and confidentiality, and structuring the helping process.

The genders of the worker and client also influence the process and outcome of helping. Practitioners must be aware of sex roles, human physiology and the relationship between biological and emotional functioning, and sexist assumptions in behavior change. It is important to establish trust based on respect at the beginning of a relationship. Workers should take women clients seriously, rather than dismissing their problems as emotional and unreasonable. Practitioners should express appropriate attending skills without sexual connotation and should explore gender difference issues throughout the helping process. In many cases, preference for a worker of the same sex is the basis for a referral.

Practitioners should engage in gender-appropriate treatment on such themes as sex roles, client strengths, personal independence and autonomy, and decision-making abilities. Workers must also be sensitive to sex-role and gender-status issues.

An understanding of socioeconomic status and ethnic-sensitive practice focuses on the needs of low-income persons. Practitioners must set aside notions of the causes of poverty and recognize that poor people hold aspirations and values similar to those of the middle class; the difference is that the poor have limited resources and opportunities. The worker-client relationship must be based on rapport, common ground, trust, and goodwill; understanding of the client's social reality; and mutual respect. The roles and responsibilities of the helping relationship must be clarified. Assessment should explore inadequate economic resources and their impact on the client's problems. Economic constraints and environmental limitations must be addressed with realistic goals and active intervention. It is important for practitioners to be exposed to clients of different economic classes.

Davis and Proctor (1989) have achieved a systematic integration of micropractice principles—individual, family, and group—and macroissues—race, gender, and socioeconomic status. Their approach serves as a uniform model for a critical perspective of social work practice as it relates to people of color.

DEFINITION OF CULTURALLY DIVERSE PRACTICE

Culturally diverse social work practice recognizes and respects the importance of difference and variety in people and the crucial role of culture in the helping relationship. Its primary group focus is on people of color—particularly African Americans, Latino Americans, Asian Americans, and Native Americans—who have suffered historical oppression and continue to endure subtle forms of racism, prejudice, and discrimination. In working with an individual, family, group, and/or community, practitioners draw on the positive strengths of diverse cultural beliefs and practices and are concerned about discriminatory experiences that require approaches sensitive to ethnic and cultural environments.

Social work practice relies on a person-to-person human relationship based on warmth, genuineness, and empathy. At the same time, it draws on relevant theory from those social sciences applicable to social work. Workers target individuals, families, groups, and communities and help them with social problems. But rather than treating people of color as separate and different groups, social workers need to see them as individuals in collective associations: entities in family and community cohorts. Each population has color, language, and behavioral characteristics that distinguish it as a unique group in a multiracial society. Racism, prejudice, and discrimination are often part of the complex of problems that affect the client. As a result, practice approaches must address the interaction of problems that arise from these ethnic social themes.

GOALS OF CULTURALLY DIVERSE SOCIAL WORK

Culturally diverse social work practice addresses individuals, families, and communities who have historically been oppressed on account of ethnic identity and socioeconomic status. Its primary focus is to improve the quality of psychosocial functioning as the person interacts with the social situation. The term *biopsychosocial* refers to the physical, cognitive-affective-behavioral, and environmental forces affecting the person. In social work practice, workers strive to treat the client as a biopsychosocial-gender-cultural-spiritual being. The purpose of a culturally diverse social work curriculum is to educate social work students and practitioners in specific theory and practice skills and to facilitate social change and improvement in the lives of people of color.

Social workers should enhance and upgrade their knowledge and practice approaches to the culturally diverse. Most social workers have completed a required multicultural course in their university education, but fewer have done fieldwork where they could gain practice expertise with multicultural clients or be supervised by instructors with such expertise. This text presents an integrated, direct, practice process model for the culturally diverse, with the worker as social-change initiator.

The Client in Cultural Perspective

Cultural belief systems and behavioral outlook influence people's ideas, customs, and skills. For people of color, the cultural element reinforces positive functioning through family support systems, self-identity and self-esteem, and the ethnic philosophy of living. These cultural resources are coping mechanisms during stress and crisis. On the other hand, a person's ethnic cultural past could be a source of conflict, stigma, and embarrassment. Caught in an acculturation trap, individuals move away from cultural maintenance and toward identification with the majority society. Reacting against their ethnic cultural past, they dissociate from the language, behavior, and values of their cultural roots. Between the extremes of the ethnic traditionalist and the acculturated individual are those who have integrated the best of both worlds, through a sorting-out process. Such people appreciate those cultural elements that express rich customs and traditions, family and ethnic community, and positive values. However, they realize that they must function in, and interact with, the dominant society. Drawing on their upbringing, these individuals achieve a resolution that weaves the cultural element into daily living patterns.

The social worker should be aware of the client's state of cultural development. Northen (1982) points to a particularly important social work principle: "The values, norms, language, customs, and traditions of a culture or subculture influence a person's opportunities for effective functioning or they become obstacles to achieving desired goals" (p. 52). Culturally diverse social work starts by determining whether ethnic and cultural elements are useful functioning forces or barriers to meaningful living. To make such a determination, social workers should find out about family beliefs and practices, community support systems, and other important ethnic information areas. They should ask their clients to share cultural information or viewpoints that relate to the way they see the problem. What particular cultural strengths are appropriate for client coping? Workers should have a resource person who provides background on various cultures and the psychosocial situations, such as a minister, mental health worker, or community leader familiar with the client's community. With professional exploration and consultation, social workers and clients should move toward an integration of cultural resources and the psychosocial situation.

THE RISE OF CULTURALLY DIVERSE PRACTICE

Culturally diverse social work knowledge and practice theory has lagged behind the national focus on people of color. For example, it was not until 1970 that the CSWE stated that its number one priority was, in the terminology then current, ethnic minority group concerns. The CSWE inaugurated a program to recruit people of color as students and faculty and made available scholarships and grant monies (Pins, 1970). It mandated the integration of multicultural content into social work school curricula (Dumpson, 1970). Social work educators of color wrote a series of CSWE publications on the principal nonwhite groups. Many articles and several books appeared on ethnicity, racism, policy and program needs, and the characteristics of selected groups. The number of people of color seeking a master's degree in social work increased by 2.5 percent between 1969 and 1973, but then declined between 1973 and 1977. There was a slight increase nationally in the proportion of people of color among full-time social work faculty (Ishisaka & Takagi, 1981). Multicultural issues were addressed in scattered articles published in social work practice anthologies (Compton & Galaway,

1989; Cox, Erlich, Rothman, & Tropman, 1979; Munson, 1980). In the 1980s, however, professional social work commitment to cultural diversity waned as national attention shifted to women's and gay rights, nuclear disarmament, and other social issues.

Was the emerging interest in multicultural issues during the 1970s reflected in social work texts? If so, undergraduate and graduate students in social work would be exposed to such issues in their reading. A study of thirty-two social work practice texts published between 1970 and 1998 was undertaken to determine how they reflect cultural diversity (Table 1-1). The number of chapters relating to multicultural issues was compared with the total number of chapters, and the number of pages relating to ethnicity, culture, and multicultural concerns, according to the subject index, was compared with the total number of pages in each book. The following observations were made:

• In twenty-five social work practice texts, no chapters were devoted to multicultural issues.

• Seven practice texts contained no chapters on multicultural concerns and no index entries on ethnicity, culture, or multicultural issues.

• Seven practice texts contained between one and six articles or chapters on multicultural issues.

• Nine practice texts contained pages relating to ethnicity, culture, or multicultural issues, according to the index.

• In the thirty-two practice texts, 3 percent (16 of 423) of the chapters focused on multicultural issues.

• Of the total pages, 1 percent (159 of 14,681) were devoted to ethnicity.

• Of the total pages, 3 percent (435 of 14,681) were devoted to culture.

• Of the total pages, 0.0002 percent (35 of 14,681) were devoted to multicultural issues.

• Of the total pages, 3 percent (629 of 14,681) altogether were devoted to ethnicity, culture, or multicultural issues.

The investigation revealed that leading social work practice theorists and texts have only minimally mentioned cultural diversity and related areas. It is beyond the scope of this study to speculate on the reasons for such marginal treatment. However, social work students exposed to these texts have not received adequate information on culturally diverse practice principles.

Minimal Coverage in Journals

If social work practice texts mention cultural diversity only minimally, how well do leading social work journals cover this material? Is their coverage sufficient to make good the deficiencies of the practice texts? In an examination of *Families in Society*, *Social Service Review*, and *Social Work* from 1970 to 1997, the number of articles related to multicultural issues in general and to African Americans, Latino Americans, Asian Americans, and Native Americans in particular was compared with the total number of articles published (Table 1-2, page 16). The study revealed the following trends:

• In the journals, 3 percent (112 of 4,148) of the articles related to general multicultural issues, 2 percent (100) to African Americans, 1 percent (57) to Latinos, 1 percent (42) to Asian Americans, and 1 percent (27) to Native Americans.

• Altogether, 8 percent (349 of 4,148) of the articles in the journals related to general multicultural issues and particular groups.

• In *Families in Society*, 10 percent (167 of 1,635) of the articles related to multicultural issues.

• In *Social Work*, 8 percent (144 of 1,646) of the articles related to multicultural issues.

• In *Social Service Review*, 4 percent (38 of 867) of the articles related to multicultural issues.

• There were nine years (1975, 1976, 1979, 1981, 1983, 1984, 1987, 1993, and 1994) in which *Social Service Review* published no articles on multicultural issues.

• There were two years (1971 and 1991) in which *Social Work* published no articles on multicultural issues.

TABLE 1-1 *Content in Culturally Diverse Social Work Practice Texts, 1970–1998*

Author	Title of Book	Publi-cation Year	Chapters on Multi-cultural Issues	Total Chapters	Pages on Ethnicity	Pages on Culture	Pages on Multi-cultural Issues	Total Pages
Roberts and Nee	Theories of Social Casework	1970	0	9	0	4	0	408
Pincus and Minahan	Social Work Practice: Model and Method	1973	0	13	0	0	0	355
Goldstein	Social Work Practice: A Unitary Approach	1973	0	9	0	0	0	288
Fischer	Interpersonal Helping: Emerging Approaches for Social Work Practice	1973	0	41	No index	No index	No index	668
Klenk and Ryan	The Practice of Social Work	1974	1 article	6 (29 articles)	No index	No index	No index	448
Siporin	Introduction to Social Work Practice	1975	0	12	0	0	0	468
Meyer	Social Work Practice: The Changing Landscape	1976	0	6	0	0	0	268
Fischer	Effective Casework Practice: An Eclectic Approach	1978	0	10	0	0	0	393
Jayaratne and Levy	Empirical Clinical Practice	1979	0	11	0	0	0	340
Gilbert, Miller, and Specht	An Introduction to Social Work Practice	1980	0	12	1	0	0	336
Hollis and Woods	Casework: A Psychosocial Therapy	1981	0	20	14	11	0	534
Northen	Clinical Social Work	1982	0	10	13	20	0	369
Gambrill	Casework: A Competency-Based Approach	1983	0	18	4	4	0	448
Lowenberg	Fundamentals of Social Intervention	1983	0	12	12	12	0	373
Johnson	Social Work Practice	1983	0	15	0	17	0	388
Morales and Sheafor	Social Work: A Profession of Many Faces	1983	5	20	6	5	14	480
Turner	Social Work Treatment	1986	0	24	0	2	0	658
Sheafor, Horejsi, and Horejsi	Techniques and Guidelines for Social Work Practice	1988	0	15	0	7	1	497

TABLE 1-1 *(continued)*

Author	Title of Book	Publication Year	Chapters on Multicultural Issues	Total Chapters	Pages on Ethnicity	Pages on Culture	Pages on Multicultural Issues	Total Pages
McMahon	*The General Method of Social Work Practice*	1990	1	10	1	16	2	348
Schulman	*Interactional Social Work Practice*	1991	0	12	0	4	0	287
Schulman	*The Skills of Helping*	1992	0	18	31	0	0	653
Hepworth and Larsen	*Direct Social Work Practice*	1992	0	21	38	38	0	674
Kirst-Ashman and Hull	*Understanding Generalist Practice*	1993	1	16	2	19	2	568
Compton and Galaway	*Social Work Processes*	1994	6 articles	33 articles	4	30	0	585
Hoffman and Sallee	*Social Work Practice*	1994	0	13	4	11	4	356
McMahon	*Advanced Generalist Practice*	1994	0	10	1	4	9	239
Miley, O'Melia, and DuBois	*Generalist Social Work Practice*	1995	0	16	0	24	0	473
Zastrow	*The Practice of Social Work*	1995	1	24	0	22	0	668
Sheafor, Horejsi, and Horejsi	*Techniques and Guidelines for Social Work Practice*	1997	0	15	8	0	0	635
Hepworth, Rooney, and Larsen	*Direct Social Work Practice*	1997	1	20	9	65	0	615
Locke, Garrison, and Winship	*Generalist Social Work Practice*	1998	0	10	15	52	3	352
Miley, O'Melia, and DuBois	*Generalist Social Work Practice*	1998	0	16	6	68	0	509
Total			16	423	159 (1%)	435 (3%)	35 (0.0002%)	14,681 (3%)

Combined index pages (ethnicity/culture/multicultural issues) 629 (3%)

TABLE 1-2 *Articles in Social Work Practice Journals, 1970–1997*

Journal	Year	General Multicultural Articles	African American Articles	Latino American Articles	Asian American Articles	Native American Articles	Total Multicultural Articles	Total Articles	
Social Casework	1970	3	6	0	1	0	1 0	56	
Social Service Review		1	3	0	0	0	4	26	} 133
Social Work		0	2	0	0	0	2	51	
Social Casework	1971	1	0	9	0	0	10	59	
Social Service Review		2	1	0	0	1	4	26	} 131
Social Work		0	0	0	0	0	0	46	
Social Casework	1972	3	2	1	1	0	7	62	
Social Service Review		2	1	0	0	0	3	25	} 163
Social Work		9	3	1	1	1	15	76	
Social Casework	1973	4	0	0	0	0	4	50	
Social Service Review		0	2	0	0	0	2	23	} 144
Social Work		1	3	2	2	3	11	71	
Social Casework	1974	0	1	9	0	0	10	61	
Social Service Review		0	1	0	0	0	1	25	} 154
Social Work		2	1	0	0	0	3	68	
Social Casework	1975	1	1	0	1	0	3	57	
Social Service Review		0	0	0	0	0	0	33	} 148
Social Work		0	1	1	0	1	3	58	
Social Casework	1976	0	0	1	13	1	15	68	
Social Service Review		0	0	0	0	0	0	36	} 157
Social Work		0	1	2	0	1	4	57	
Social Casework	1977	2	0	2	0	0	4	57	
Social Service Review		0	0	0	0	2	2	33	} 144
Social Work		3	1	0	0	1	5	54	
Social Casework	1978	2	0	0	1	1	4	59	
Social Service Review		0	1	0	0	0	1	33	} 147
Social Work		1	0	0	0	0	1	55	
Social Casework	1979	0	0	1	1	0	2	57	
Social Service Review		0	0	0	0	0	0	34	} 157
Social Work		1	2	1	0	0	4	60	
Social Casework	1980	1	0	0	1	12	14	66	
Social Service Review		1	0	0	0	0	1	34	} 157
Social Work		1	0	0	0	3	4	57	

TABLE 1-2 *(continued)*

Journal	Year	General Multicultural Articles	African American Articles	Latino American Articles	Asian American Articles	Native American Articles	Total Multicultural Articles	Total Articles	
Social Casework	1981	0	3	2	1	0	6	56	
Social Service Review		0	0	0	0	0	0	33	} 142
Social Work		1	0	0	1	0	2	53	
Social Casework	1982	2	2	0	1	1	6	63	
Social Service Review		1	0	0	0	0	1	36	} 157
Social Work		7	4	3	1	1	16	58	
Social Casework	1983	1	2	0	0	0	3	60	
Social Service Review		0	0	0	0	0	0	35	} 150
Social Work		1	0	0	0	0	1	55	
Social Casework	1984	0	0	0	0	1	1	58	
Social Service Review		0	0	0	0	0	0	32	} 152
Social Work		2	0	1	1	0	4	62	
Social Casework	1985	0	0	1	1	1	3	59	
Social Service Review		0	2	1	0	0	3	37	} 153
Social Work		0	1	0	0	0	1	57	
Social Casework	1986	1	0	1	0	2	4	62	
Social Service Review		0	0	0	1	0	1	33	} 146
Social Work		2	1	1	0	0	4	51	
Social Casework	1987	0	2	0	0	2	4	63	
Social Service Review		0	0	0	0	0	0	37	} 165
Social Work		0	1	0	3	0	4	65	
Social Casework	1988	0	1	2	1	0	4	68	
Social Service Review		1	2	0	0	0	3	34	} 154
Social Work		2	2	1	1	0	6	52	
Social Casework	1989	2	3	1	1	0	7	62	
Social Service Review		1	0	0	0	0	1	38	} 138
Social Work		0	3	0	0	0	3	38	
Families in Society (formerly Social Casework)	1990	1	1	0	1	0	3	57	
Social Service Review		0	0	1	0	0	1	31	} 148
Social Work		5	0	1	0	0	6	60	
Families in Society	1991	1	1	0	1	0	3	67	
Social Service Review		1	0	0	0	0	1	28	} 160
Social Work		0	0	0	0	0	0	65	

TABLE 1-2 *(continued)*

Journal	Year	General Multicultural Articles	African American Articles	Latino American Articles	Asian American Articles	Native American Articles	Total Multicultural Articles	Total Articles	
Families in Society	1992	4	3	1	1	1	10	43	
Social Service Review		2	1	0	0	0	3	30	} 133
Social Work		1	5	1	1	0	8	60	
Families in Society	1993	2	3	1	1	1	10	58	
Social Service Review		0	0	0	0	0	1	27	} 157
Social Work		1	3	0	1	0	5	72	
Families in Society	1994	2	1	0	2	0	5	39	
Social Service Review		0	0	0	0	0	0	28	} 132
Social Work		2	0	0	1	0	3	65	
Families in Society	1995	2	4	0	0	0	6	58	
Social Service Review		0	1	0	0	0	1	27	} 160
Social Work		2	3	0	2	1	8	75	
Families in Society	1996	1	2	1	1	1	6	54	
Social Service Review		0	0	0	0	1	1	26	} 136
Social Work		6	3	1	1	2	13	56	
Families in Society	1997	1	3	2	0	0	6	60	
Social Service Review		1	2	1	0	0	4	27	} 136
Social Work		1	2	3	2	0	8	49	
		112 (3%)	100 (2%)	57 (1%)	42 (1%)	27 (1%)	349 (8%)	4,148	

	Multicultural Articles	Total Articles
Families in Society (formerly *Social Casework*)	167 (10%)	1,635
Social Service Review	38 (4%)	867
Social Work	144 (8%)	1,646

- In two years (1980 and 1984) none of the journals published articles on African Americans.

- None of the journals published articles on Latinos in five years (1970, 1978, 1980, 1983, and 1987).

- In four years (1971, 1974, 1977, and 1983) none of the journals published articles on Asian Americans.

- In eleven years (1970, 1974, 1979, 1981, 1983, 1988, 1989, 1990, 1991, 1993, and 1994) none of the journals published articles on Native Americans.

The investigation revealed that multicultural concerns were addressed in 8 percent of the articles in the three leading social work journals, versus 3 percent of the total pages in practice texts. The overall conclusion is that cultural diversity has been largely neglected in practice journals and professional journals over twenty-five years.

Underemphasis in the Profession

Citing evidence from several sources, Dieppa (1984) has reached the following conclusions:

1. There has been little indication that social work curricula are providing the knowledge, skills, and intervention strategies required to work effectively with people of color.

2. The social work profession has become more conservative, reflecting American society.

3. Social work faculty and administrators do not know how to incorporate cultural diversity into social work curricula.

4. People of color have raised doubts about the validity of information provided on multicultural issues and the qualifications of faculty working in this area.

5. The social work profession has made limited efforts to develop its own body of knowledge about cultural diversity and has relied on sociological, psychological, and literary materials.

6. More research is needed on specific practice situations and differences between workers and others in race, class, sex, and sexual orientation and on the life experiences, culture, strengths, and history of specific ethnic groups.

7. Professional publications have paid only limited attention to important and timely contributions to knowledge about particular ethnic populations.

One might argue that the presence in practice texts of general material applicable to clients from any culture compensates for the lack of content pertaining explicitly to people of color. For example, there has been recent emphasis on environmental stress, the extended family, and natural support systems. These themes are relevant to people of color, although the texts do not indicate how they apply to particular cultural problems. However, the fact remains that there was a shortage of material relating explicitly to people of color in social work practice books and articles published during the 1970s, 1980s, and early 1990s. To point out that applicable content exists does not alleviate the responsibility of social work practice writers to address cultural diversity. Social work practice has assumed that practice principles are generic, even in their application to people of color. That position is no longer defensible.

Some signs of improvement are emerging. First, economic recession and massive unemployment in the early 1990s refocused national attention on the plight of the poor and of people of color, in particular. Second, many university social work programs now have multicultural practice faculty as a result of affirmative action and specific efforts to recruit culturally diverse social work students and doctoral fellows. Between 1974 and 1984, according to the 1984 Annual Report of CSWE's Commission on Minority Group Concerns, 178 students were supported through the CSWE Ethnic Minority Doctoral Fellowship Program. Other CSWE activities include computerizing a categorized bibliography on ethnic groups relevant to social work education and practice, publishing a multicultural faculty directory and regional listing of CSWE Minority Fellows, and addressing tenure issues that relate to people of color (*Commission, Committee, and Task Force Reports*, 1984). Third, social work education practice material has moved away from the generic approach of the 1970s toward more specialized topics in the 1980s and 1990s. Focal interest on multicultural practice remains high among social workers who recognize the increase in culturally diverse clients and wish to cultivate appropriate skills. Moreover, we may hope that multicultural faculty, students, and practitioners will themselves be producing high-quality practice texts in the near future.

SOCIAL WORK AND CULTURALLY DIVERSE CURRICULUM AND TRAINING

Under the auspices of the National Institute of Mental Health (NIMH), the University of Utah's Graduate School of Social Work was commissioned to study multicultural aspects of mental health clinical training programs in graduate schools of social work. Four position papers on the needs of American Indians/Alaskan Natives,

Asian/Pacific Americans, African Americans, and Latino Americans in such training programs were written and disseminated. Furthermore, a survey of graduate MSW programs addressed the development of multicultural mental health curriculum in the 1980s; the survey accurately assesses the progress made in multicultural mental health training in the 1980s and the planning needs of the 1990s.

The following recommendations on multicultural training in mental health practice are guidelines for social work educators and practitioners as they plan personnel, curriculum, and services.

Personnel

Culturally diverse mental health professionals are needed at the master's and doctoral levels. Although NIMH funding support for people of color is adequate at the doctoral level, its financial commitment to MSW students needs to be increased. In addition, if culturally diverse training is to be successful, multicultural social work faculty must be recruited and provided with support services to assist in promotion and tenure. As students, people of color need assistance and positive recognition to adjust to, and cope with, graduate programs in social work. It is also necessary to rejuvenate and reestablish coalitions of culturally diverse groups for mutual support and political action.

Curriculum

A multicultural curriculum component should be in place that emphasizes social systems theory as a conceptual framework, comparative cultural values and the development of ethnic and racial identity, the history of immigration and related policies, the impact of institutional racism, and components of appropriate service delivery systems. Field placements should expose students to cultural diversity, in terms of both the communities they serve and the professional staff by whom they are trained. Every social work student should have practicum placement assignments with clientele from different cultures.

The curriculum should emphasize the strengths of people of color, with specific courses related to appropriate social work intervention. The focus should be on public social services, particularly on prevention and intervention services. All students should be encouraged to develop an understanding of multicultural issues and to prepare themselves for competent and ethical professional practice with all prospective clientele.

Mental Health Issues and Intervention

Mental health training programs for people of color should emphasize individual and structural/institutional change within a broad spectrum of rules and skills oriented to diverse ethnic populations. People of color should be meaningfully involved in planning, implementing, and operating social work programs in their communities. The planning and delivery of services should incorporate indigenous strengths and resources based on traditional cultural values and practices. Of special concern is the development of culturally sensitive programs related to children and families. Within this emphasis, it is necessary to develop appropriate models to strengthen ethnic families and foster ethnic leadership.

A number of mental health–related issues are of concern for people of color. Long-term care of the aged in culturally sensitive facilities and primary prevention programs for the healthy elderly are of critical importance. Ethnic interventions must deal with schizophrenia and major mood disorders (particularly depression); substance use and abuse; sexual abuse of children; and family, domestic, and racist violence. These issues must be tied to appropriate and accessible services and to creative mental health prevention and intervention programs for people of color.

The NIMH should fund demonstration programs that provide research strategies to evaluate effective programs that address both these mental health–related problems and mental health clinical training programs for people of color (Egbert-Edwards, 1989).

These recommendations address the commitment of the CSWE's Curriculum Policy Statement, which calls for special-populations content areas. Social work educators should prepare students to understand and appreciate cultural and social diversity; patterns and consequences of oppression and discrimination; social, economic, and legal group bias; and theoretical and practice content about people of color. The CSWE and the National Association of Social Workers (NASW) should work closely to implement the intent of the Curriculum Policy Statement on Special Populations with the NIMH Report Recommendations on Ethnic Minorities (Commission on Accreditation, 1994; Egbert-Edwards, 1989).

CULTURALLY DIVERSE SOCIAL WORK PRACTICE THEORY DEVELOPMENT

Despite the small representation of social work ethnic and cultural content in major practice texts and journals, there has been a growing literature in social work and related area texts devoted to culturally diverse practice. The first substantive ethnic minority social work text was Barbara Solomon's (1976) *Black Empowerment: Social Work in Oppressed Communities.* This book sent the message that ethnic minority social work contained unique themes: powerlessness and empowerment in the midst of social oppression. Solomon immediately influenced the content of ethnic minority social work articles. For the first time social work educators began to analyze clinical and community cases from a powerlessness perspective and offered an empowerment intervention strategy as the solution.

Second, about the same time we were searching for an alternative term. Ethnic minorities emphasized ethnic groups who were outnumbered in size, power, and influence by the dominant society. June Gary Hopps (1982) began to speak about people of color as another way to describe African, Latino, Asian, and Native Americans. It was a term that reflected cohesiveness among the various racial groups who faced common oppression and exclusion based on skin color barriers. People of color described the interconnectedness of the American minority experience and sought to link Black, Brown, Yellow, and Red people together. I wrote (Lum, 1986) *Social Work Practice and People of Color,* which implemented Hopps's notion and identified culture common

(etic) themes and differentiated culture specific (emic) distinctions among the four major ethnic groups. In the 1988 presidential election, the Reverend Jesse Jackson seized on the people of color concept and called his supporters "The Rainbow Coalition" to connote separate and distinct colors yet unity in the whole.

The third step came with the publication of two important books: Devore and Schlesinger's (1981) *Ethnic-Sensitive Social Work Practice* and Green and associates' (1982) *Cultural Awareness in the Human Services.* For the first time in social work practice the four major ethnic groups of color were discussed in one text with generalist principles applied to them. Devore and Schlesinger embedded in the mind of social work education the principle of ethnic sensitivity. The scope of the book covered ethnicity, social class, and social work practice and adapted sociological and psychological insights to practice needs. The term *ethclass,* taken from Milton Gordon and applied to social work practice, was an important contribution. Ethnic sensitivity, according to Devore and Schlesinger, embodied the history of ethnic group oppression, the past and accompanying problems affecting the present, ethnic reality, nonconscious phenomena affecting functioning, microindividual and macrosystematic change, understanding of the ethnic community, knowledge of human behavior and self-awareness, data gathering, problem identification, contracting, and problem solving. These social work practice themes were set in an ethnic-sensitive context.

Likewise, Green and associates are remembered for their contribution in cultural awareness. Emphasizing the background of cultural groups, Green fashioned a cross-cultural framework model called help-seeking behavior based on cultural anthropology. Green taught social workers that it is important to find the client's definition and understanding of the experience as the problem, to understand the client's use of language to describe the problem, to use indigenous community resources in the decision making of problem intervention, and to determine the client's cultural criteria for problem resolution. The cultural content, significant others, and cultural behavioral practices were key concepts taught by

Green. The use of the term *cultural awareness* must take into account Green's cultural participation model.

The fourth step brought social work education into the nineties. Diversity and multiculturalism replaced the concept of ethnic minorities during this period. Part of the reason was the changing perspective of persons who wanted to move ethnic people of color away from an inferior and powerless status of minority to an inclusive view of increasing numbers, economic strength, and sociopolitical organization. *Human diversity* became a term that included all people and recognized the uniqueness of the individual at the same time.

Multiculturalism also became a recognized term denoting the coexistence of many groups with different cultural practices and traditions expressing themselves and interacting with each other. However, multiculturalism also became the object of criticism. It became politicized on many college campuses in terms of what was "politically correct." Yet many social work educators and practitioners embraced the term, teaching and practicing multicultural social work. An important journal appeared called *The Journal of Multicultural Social Work*.

As a result of the rise of cultural diversity, I revised the third edition (1996) of *Social Work Practice and People of Color* using the concept of cultural diversity as my focus. Recognizing the influence of the diversity movement and the emphasis on multiculturalism, cultural diversity was a combination concept that selected diversity as the primary focus and multiculturalism as the secondary idea. Cultural diversity placed the boundaries of diversity around the cultural components. It recognized and respected the importance of differences and variety in people and the crucial role of culture in the helping relationship. It encouraged practitioners to draw on the positive strengths of diverse cultural beliefs and practices. It affirmed that each population has color, language, and behavioral characteristics that must be distinguished as unique in a multiracial society.

The fifth step in the development of culturally diverse social work practice is cultural competency. In one sense cultural competency included the previous steps mentioned. To be culturally competent, one must understand the historical oppression of ethnic minorities, the similarities and differences among people of color, the practice principles of ethnic sensitivity and cultural awareness, and the practice emphasis on cultural diversity. Yet in another sense, cultural competency breaks new ground with the delineation of cultural competencies (specific practice guideline statements) and a new thrust on outcome measurement, teaching effectiveness, and student mastery. I have written (Lum, 1999) *Culturally Competent Practice* to delineate a framework model that addresses the cultural awareness, knowledge acquisition, skill development, and inductive learning aspects.

CONCLUSION

This chapter has presented the various foundational themes of culturally diverse social work practice with people of color. The parameters of this practice approach have been defined for students to gain basic concepts, and the development of the field from the early 1970s to the end of the 1990s has been described to demonstrate the progress made in culturally diverse practice.

Chapter 2 considers the historical events, ethnic groups, and special populations that comprise people of color. As you read about the history of Native, African, Latino, and Asian Americans in their historical and current situations, I hope that you will gain a perspective of how these groups were affected by the dominant society and how to work initially with new arrivals, women of color, gays and lesbians of color, children of color, the racially/ethnically mixed, and older persons of color.

REFERENCES

Barringer, F. (1990, August 28). Population tops 29 million as California widens gap. *New York Times*, p. A16.

Chin, J. L. (1993). Toward a psychology of difference: Psychotherapy for a culturally diverse population. In

J. L. Chin, V. De La Cancela, & Y. M Jenkins (Eds.), *Diversity in psychotherapy: The politics of race, ethnicity, and gender* (pp. 69–91). Westport, CT: Praeger.

Colburn, D. R., & Pozzeta, G. E. (1979). *America and the new ethnicity.* Port Washington, NY: Kennikat.

Commission on Accreditation, Council on Social Work Education. (1994). *Handbook of accreditation standards and procedures.* Arlington, VA: Council on Social Work Education.

Commission, Committee, and Task Force Reports. (1984). New York: Council on Social Work Education.

Compton, B. R., & Galaway, B. (Eds.). (1989). *Social work processes.* Belmont, CA: Wadsworth.

Cox, F. M., Erlich, J. L., Rothman, J., & Tropman, J. E. (Eds.). (1979). *Strategies of community organization.* Itasca, IL: Peacock.

Davis, A. F. (1967). *Spearheads for reform: The social settlements and the progressive movement, 1880–1914.* New York: Oxford University Press.

Davis, L. E., & Proctor, E. K. (1989). *Race, gender, and class: Guidelines for practice with individuals, families, and groups.* Upper Saddle River, NJ: Prentice-Hall.

De La Cancela, V., Jenkins, Y. M., & Chin, J. L. (1993). Diversity in psychotherapy: Examination of racial, ethnic, gender, and political issues. In J. L. Chin, V. De La Cancela, & Y. M. Jenkins (Eds.), *Diversity in psychotherapy: The politics of race, ethnicity, and gender* (pp. 5–15). Westport, CT: Praeger.

Devore, W., & Schlesinger, E. G. (1981). *Ethnic-sensitive social work practice.* St. Louis: Mosby.

Dieppa, I. (1984). Trends in social work education for minorities. In B. W. White (Ed.), *Color in a white society* (pp. 10–21). Silver Spring, MD: National Association of Social Workers.

Dixon, E., & Taylor, L. (1994, March 17). Workshop on cultural diversity in the workplace. The Center for Human Services Training and Development, University Extension, University of California, Davis.

Drachman, D. (1995). Immigration statuses and their influence on service provision, access, and use. *Social Work, 40*(2), 188–197.

Dumpson, J. R. (1970). Special committee on minority groups. *Social Work Education Reporter, 18,* 30.

Egbert-Edwards, M. (1989). *Ethnic minority social work mental health clinical training programs: Assessing the past-planning the future* (survey commissioned by the National Institute of Mental Health). Salt Lake City: Graduate School of Social Work, University of Utah.

Espin, O. M., & Gawelek, M. A. (1992). Women's diversity: Ethnicity, race, class, and gender in theories of feminist psychology. In L. S. Brown & M. Ballou (Eds.), *Personality and psychopathology: Feminist reappraisals* (pp. 88–107). New York: Guilford.

Fiske, E. B. (1991, February 22). New York City's population gain attributed to immigrant tide. *New York Times,* p. B16.

Green, J. W. (1982). *Cultural awareness in the human services.* Upper Saddle River, NJ: Prentice-Hall.

Ho, M. K. (1987). *Family therapy with ethnic minorities.* Newbury Park, CA: Sage.

Hoffman, K. S., & Sallee, A. L. (1994). *Social work practice: Bridges to change.* Boston: Allyn & Bacon.

Hopps, J. G. (1982). Oppression based on color. *Social Work, 27,* 3–5.

Ishisaka, A. H., & Takagi, C. Y. (1981). Toward professional pluralism: The Pacific Asian-American case. *Journal of Education for Social Work, 17,* 44–52.

Jenkins, Y. M. (1993). Diversity and social esteem. In J. L. Chin, V. De La Cancella, & Y. M. Jenkins (Eds.), *Diversity in psychotherapy: The politics of race, ethnicity, and gender* (pp. 45–63). Westport, CT: Praeger.

Kirst-Ashman, K. K., & Hull, G. H., Jr. (1993). *Understanding generalist practice.* Chicago: Nelson-Hall.

Longres, J. F. (1990). *Human behavior in the social environment.* Itasca, IL: Peacock.

Lum, D. (1986). *Social work practice and people of color: A process-stage approach.* Monterey CA: Brooks/Cole.

Lum, D. (1996). *Social work practice and people of color: A process-stage approach* (3rd. ed.). Pacific Grove, CA: Brooks/Cole.

Lum, D. (1999). *Culturally competent practice: A framework for growth and action.* Pacific Grove, CA: Brooks/Cole.

Magill, R. S. (1985). *Ethnicity and social welfare in American cities: A historical view.* In L. Maldonado & J. Moore (Eds.), *Urban ethnicity in the United States* (pp. 185–209). Newbury Park, CA: Sage.

McLeod, R. G., & Schreiner, T. (1991, February 26). State's astonishing population changes. *San Francisco Chronicle,* pp. A1, A7.

Munson, C. E. (Ed.). (1980). *Social work with families.* New York: Free Press.

Northen, H. (1982). *Clinical social work.* New York: Columbia University Press.

Pinderhughes, E. (1989). *Understanding race, ethnicity, and power. The key to efficacy in clinical practice.* New York: Free Press.

Pins, A. M. (1970). Entering the seventies: Changing priorities for social work education. *Social Work Education Reporter, 18,* 2.

Policy Analysis for California Education. (1989). *Conditions of children in California.* Berkeley, CA: Author.

Rounds, K. A., Weil, M., & Bishop, K. K. (1994). Practice with culturally diverse families of young children with disabilities. *Families in Society, 75*(1), 3–15.

Sasao, T. (1996). The cultural context of epidemiologic research. In A. H. Bayer, F. L. Brisbane, & A. Ramirez (Eds.), *Advanced methodological issues in culturally competent evaluation for substance abuse prevention* (pp. 183–212). Rockville, MD: U.S. Department of Health and Human Services, Substance Abuse and Mental Health Services Administration.

Schreiner, T. (1990, February 19). Growth, but not power, for state's minorities. *San Francisco Chronicle*, p. A11.

Silva, J. S. (1983). Cross-cultural and cross-ethnic assessment. In G. Gibson (Ed.), *Our kingdom stands on brittle glass* (pp. 59–66). Silver Spring, MD: National Association of Social Workers.

Solomon, B. B. (1976). *Black empowerment: Social work in oppressed communities*. New York: Columbia University Press.

Suinn, R. M. (1987, March). Minority issues cut across courses. *ADA Monitor*, p. 3.

U.S. Bureau of the Census. (1987). *Statistical abstract of the United States: 1987* (107th ed.). Washington, DC: U.S. Department of Commerce.

U.S. Bureau of the Census. (1993). *Statistical abstract of the United States: 1993* (113th ed.). No. 12. *Resident population—Selected characteristics 1790 to 1991, and projections 1995 to 2005;* No. 21. *Components of population change, by race and Hispanic origin: 1980 to 1991 and projections, 1995 and 2000*. Washington, DC: U.S. Government Printing Office.

U.S. Bureau of the Census. (1997). *Statistical abstract of the United States 1997* (117th ed.). No. 12 *Resident population—Selected characteristics, 1790 to 1996, and projections, 2000 to 2050*. Washington, DC: U.S. Government Printing Office.

Vobejda, B. (1987, June 2). Education leaders warn of crisis for U.S. youth. *Washington Post*, p. A-16.

CHAPTER 2

People of Color

People of color is an inclusive term that describes the similarities yet acknowledges the differences among and between the four major ethnically diverse groups in the United States: Native, African, Latino, and Asian Americans. We must have a sense of the unique historical journey of each of these ethnic groups. Yet as we examine their specific histories, we are struck with the similar themes of racism, prejudice, and discrimination inflicted on them by the dominant society. At the same time we witness the triumphant way each group has coped with their historical and contemporary problems as they draw on their cultural resources of family, community, faith, belief, and tradition.

Social workers must see that our profession reacted as part of the nineteenth and twentieth centuries. Social work and social welfare practiced segregation of social services as they excluded people of color from their helping base. Ethnic churches, family association, and limited government resources made up the difference between existence, survival, and provision. People of color supported themselves and called on their ethnic family, extended family, and community systems to cope with their economic, social, and political plight.

History is a great teacher of the past, present, and future. It reminds us of past problems, solutions, and mistakes and challenges us to learn from our past shortcomings. History often repeats itself, giving us a clue to how to resolve present challenges. Finally, history sets a chart and map for the future confrontations that we can anticipate and the next steps to take in our historical journey on the road of life.

ROOTS OF CULTURALLY DIVERSE SOCIAL WORK

Ancient Origins

Social welfare originated in Western civilization's view of the individual and society. During the Golden Age of Greece, Hippocrates strongly advocated the belief that problem behavior was a function of natural illness and prescribed medical treatment. Plato further believed that a person should not be punished if he or she committed a criminal act as a result of diminished understanding of right and wrong (Mehr, 1980). This humanistic view of people, morality, and helping merged into caring for the needs of society. Later, Western religion communicated a horizontal and vertical perspective of God and people; Judeo-Christian beliefs in the Old and New Testaments emphasize the importance of loving both God and one's neighbor, as well as providing for the needy. The early church was instrumental in instituting social welfare services through its network of parishes and monasteries. With the beginning of the Industrial Revolution came the breakdown of the medieval feudal system, the centralization of political power in national governments, and the transfer of church power to secular government. As church funds declined, responsibility for the needs of persons displaced from feudal estates shifted to local and national government units.

Modern Trends

The Elizabethan Poor Law of 1601 was major social legislation designed to protect the affluent from displaced and starving persons. It established three categories of poor people: the helpless, who were aged, decrepit, orphaned, lunatic, blind, lame, or diseased; the involuntarily unemployed, who were poor through situational misfortunes; and the vagrants, who were drifters, strangers, squatters, and beggars. The Poor Law created a parish welfare structure that consisted of almshouses, outdoor relief, workhouses, and the indenture system. It set the precedents of national coverage and administration of public welfare, funding through voluntary contributions and a public land tax, and a work ethic for the able-bodied. During the eighteenth and nineteenth centuries, social reformers such as Philippe Pinel of France, William Tuke of England, and Benjamin Rush and Dorothea Dix of the United States sought to reform these institutional structures with the humanitarian beliefs of Hippocrates and Plato.

Modern social work in the United States arose from two models: the Charity Organization Society and the settlement house movements. Begun in England in 1869, the Charity Organization Society came to the United States in 1877 and set up a relief system based on investigating claims, meeting individual needs, and providing minimal relief payment for the truly needy. Workers kept case records and visited recipients regularly. In 1887, settlement houses appeared in New York, Boston, and Chicago to help European immigrants newly arrived in America. These community centers offered practical education, recreation, and social cohesion for those in the inner-city ethnic ghettos. Hull House under Jane Addams exemplified community resources such as a free kindergarten, day nursery, playground, clubs, lectures, library, boardinghouse, and meeting rooms (Federico, 1980).

AMERICAN MULTICULTURAL SOCIAL HISTORY

While social welfare agencies served mainstream society and white immigrants, people of color struggled to exist in isolated geographic ghettos. They were targets of exploitation and oppression in the United States. Without the rights of citizenship, legal protection, and resource provision, each group suffered through its history of struggle to survive.

Native Americans

Before white settlers arrived in the early seventeenth century, approximately 1.5 million Native Americans lived in North America, and 30 to 40 million occupied the Western Hemisphere. A wide variety of tribal groups flourished, with distinct languages, customs, and habitats (Collier, 1956). It is estimated that 173 different Native American groups remain, each with its own culture and language (Spicer, 1980).

The history of the relationship between various Native American tribes and white settlers is a saga of exploitation and oppression. Tribal groups were systematically dispossessed from their traditional lands through treaty negotiation, massacre, and removal. The Indian Removal Act of 1830 is a case in point. Five tribes (the Cherokee, Choctaw, Chickasaw, Seminole, and Creek) were forcibly removed from their lands in southern states to the Oklahoma Territory. Over one hundred thousand Indians participated in a forced march called the Trail of Tears. Thousands suffered, and many died along the way. The California Gold Rush of 1849, continuous westward expansion of white settlements, and military occupation through a series of outpost forts were critical contributors to the fate of the Native Americans. Glamorized as "the age of the western frontier" in history, literature, and film, this era witnessed systematic genocide of Native Americans and the ultimate control of the federal government over them.

In 1871, Congress decreed that no Native American tribe would be recognized as an independent power and that all Native Americans were wards of the federal government. The U.S. government then forced Native Americans onto reservations and into farming. Land ownership, agriculture, and geographic confinement were alien to the history and culture of the Native American people. With the passage of the Dawes Act in 1887, each Native American adult male was given 160 acres and each male child 80 acres. However, much of the land was unsuitable for agriculture, and no funds were allocated for its development. Moreover, the land was not to be sold for twenty-five years and was to be divided equally among the male heirs of the landowner upon his death. This meant less land would be available for succeeding generations (Rose, 1990). Between 1887 and 1932, 90 million of 138 million acres held by Native Americans passed to white ownership through exploitation (Howard, 1970).

During the early part of this century, Native Americans were confined to isolated reservations in rural areas. The federal government did not acknowledge tribal authority. Rather, the government attempted to deal with Native Americans as individual farmers and their children as wards of distant boarding schools. These patterns of work and education were foreign to Native American traditions. Native American culture, language, and family life were destroyed in an effort to Americanize and Christianize the Native American people.

By 1924, all Native Americans were granted full citizenship, a token in exchange for years of exploitation and annihilation. The Indian Reorganization Act of 1934 was an attempt to move away from a policy of assimilation. It recognized the cultural distinctiveness of the tribes and preserved them from annihilation. It allowed Native Americans to sell their land to tribal members, to establish tribal councils to manage local affairs, and to incorporate into self-governing units. It also permitted the purchase of new land and the creation of loan funds for individuals and tribes; in addition, it extended the trust of Native American lands (Taylor, 1972). Tribal governments were helped to develop constitutions and to carry out the functions of local government for tribes. The states were urged to provide the same services for Native Americans as for other citizens (Garvin & Cox, 1979).

The Bureau of Indian Affairs and the U.S. Public Health Service have made some efforts to maintain the way of life of Native American people. Irrigation and programs to prevent land erosion, improve local education, and increase birthrates and health and welfare programs have stabilized the Native American population. The Self-Determination and Educational Assistance Act of 1975 gave tribal leaders the right to allocate federal funds to serve the special needs of their people (Rose, 1990). This aided the move toward decentralization and local autonomy. In 1985, the U.S. Supreme Court ruled in a landmark case, *Oneida Nation of Wisconsin v. The State of New York*. In 1970, the Oneida tribe had challenged the legality of a 1795 purchase by New York State because it was made without the authority of the federal government, which had the exclusive jurisdiction to deal with Native Americans under the Constitution and the Indian Trade and Intercourse Act of 1793. The Supreme Court ruled that a Native American tribe holds a common-law right to recover land that was wrongfully taken after the effective date of the Constitution. Several tribes are pressing land claims based on this ruling (Longres, 1990).

Adopting the principle of self-determination, the Indian Child Welfare Act of 1978 addressed the need to protect Native American children through placement within the tribe or extended family. Prior to this, children regarded as neglected or abused were placed in adoptive and foster homes among the white population. This law provided for the jurisdiction of tribes in child custody proceedings and gave preference in adoptions to the child's extended family, to members of the child's tribe, and then to other Native American families. It also authorized the establishment of child and family service contracts with tribes and indigenous people's organizations to prevent the breakup of Native American families. Management of the foster care of Native American children by Native American agencies is critical to ensure that the 1978 act is implemented in an indigenous service context.

However, MacEachron, Gustavsson, Cross, and Lewis (1996) consider the balance between individual rights versus cultural rights regarding the 1978 Indian Child Welfare Act:

> From a policy perspective, tribal control, in a broader sense, is the continual redefining and strengthening of Indian internal sovereignty within the contexts of Indian lands, languages, education, religion, and protection of its children. Indian culture may then surround a child in a unique communal meaning that strengthens a child's Indian identity while also protecting the child from being completely assimilated into dominant culture. This tribal focus on the rights of the collectivity places tribal child welfare decisions somewhat at odds with national policy in which an individually based definition of rights predominates in interpreting what is in a child's best interests. As debates regarding transracial adoptions demonstrate, a child's best interest may not coincide with a minority culture's right to survival or with the sovereign right of a child to be brought up and derive identity from his or her culture of origin. (p. 460)

Open transracial adoptions and Indian self-contained arrangements are part of the current child welfare adoptions arena.

Native Americans on reservations and in urban settings still await the restoration of land, freedom, and autonomy. Through long centuries of extermination and oppression, Native Americans have survived in spite of the treaties and laws of the United States. The story of the restoration of social justice between Native Americans and the U.S. government is still being played out in the courtroom.

The Clinton administration has promised more positive policies toward Native Americans. There is a need to strengthen existing Indian health care programs, self-government within the tribal communities, and economic renewal (light industry and gambling casinos on the reservation). Native Americans are in transition, finding areas of stability amid a legacy of inconsistent and contradictory government policies. With an economic base in the Indian gaming business, many tribes have an economic source of providing employment for its members. At the same time, the income from Indian gaming has been the source of providing better education for Indian children, social services for Indian families and the elderly, and housing and tribal facilities on Indian land and reservations. There has also been a restoration of cultural pride and celebration as Indian people have gathered for ethnic powwows, festivals, and ceremonies remembering historical events.

African Americans

African Americans first entered America in 1619 as indentured servants. Some gained freedom after a period of servitude from their masters, while others became free through conversion to Christianity. Most were unfreed men and women but were not considered slaves until the expansion of agriculture and the need for cheap labor in the second half of the seventeenth century. At that time, the South was part of an economic structure that depended on plantation labor. The invention of the cotton gin in 1793 and the demand for raw cotton to satisfy the needs of British textile mills created the plantation system, with its slave labor.

Seized from their native villages by white slave traders and fellow Africans, African slaves were taken to coastal ports in Africa to be transported by ship to the New World. These slaves were then sold at auction without regard to their families.

African Americans were considered to have the lowest social status and were segregated and labeled inferior to whites. Within the slave community, various levels of class stratification existed. Some African Americans worked in their masters' houses as servants, while the majority worked as field hands responsible for planting, harvesting, and clearing the fields for the next crop.

In the Civil War, the South fought to defend its way of life and the slave system, and the North sought to preserve the Union. The Emancipation Proclamation of 1863 was a political and moral strategy to rally and unify the North. All slaves in the South were declared free, and, by the summer of 1863, the Union Army recruited African Americans to fight in its ranks. Of the two hundred thousand African American troops who fought in the Civil War, over half fought for the North.

During the Reconstruction era that followed the Civil War, many efforts were made to secure equality for African Americans. However, in 1866 a civil rights bill was vetoed by President Andrew Johnson. In 1883, the Sumner Act of 1875, which secured equal rights in public transportation and accommodations, was declared unconstitutional by the U.S. Supreme Court. The Hayes-Tilden Compromise of 1876 returned local autonomy to the southern states. By the late 1800s, Jim Crow statutes divided southern society into two segregated classes, with separate ways of life and institutions. Several African American colleges were established during this period, including the Tuskegee Institute, founded in 1881. Southern states also ignored the Fourteenth Amendment, which granted citizenship to African Americans, and the Fifteenth Amendment, which guaranteed that the right to vote could not be denied on the basis of race. In 1896, in the *Plessy v. Ferguson* decision, the U.S. Supreme Court declared the principle of "separate but equal" to be the law of the land. The rise of the Ku Klux Klan intimidated African Americans in the South, and numerous lynchings of African Americans occurred without government intervention or enforcement of laws protecting the rights of all citizens.

Between 1910 and 1920, with the wane of European immigration after World War I, many African Americans moved to industrial urban areas of the North in search of factory work. They settled in old tenement buildings in the urban inner city. There they met subtle forms of housing, employment, and economic segregation and discrimination. However, during the post–Civil War era, African Americans began to organize as political, social, and educational forces. Frederick Douglass and George R. Downing were among the leaders who represented the best interests of recently emancipated African Americans. In 1888, the Colored Farmers' Alliance and Cooperative Union was formed to deal with political rights. By 1890, the Afro-American League was organized to advocate legal redress, with emphasis on legal and voting rights and school funds. In 1896, the

National Association of Colored Women was formed. At the turn of the century, Booker T. Washington represented an African American constituency that sought accommodation with whites to maintain white support. However, W. E. B. Du Bois spoke out against racism and started the Niagara Movement in 1905, which led to the formation of the National Association for the Advancement of Colored People (NAACP) in 1909. The National Urban League, formerly the Committee on Urban Conditions among Negroes in New York City, was also formed during this period. Social workers active in the formation of these two organizations included Jane Addams, Florence Kelly, Lillian Wald, and George Edmund Haynes.

African Americans in the 1920s and 1930s strove to improve their socioeconomic position but endured severe oppression. Nevertheless, the lynching of African Americans, the Chicago race riot of 1919, chronic unemployment, and poverty were offset by African American children's increased school attendance, industrial employment of African Americans in the North and West, and recognition of African American artists.

President Franklin D. Roosevelt's administration cultivated the support of African American leaders but, despite the liberalism of its New Deal programs, failed to deliver on crucial civil rights issues. At that time, America was in the midst of the Great Depression and concerned about the threat of war in Europe and Asia. The economic and totalitarian threats overshadowed African Americans' struggle for equality and justice. Local control of federal programs based on states' rights continued to exclude African Americans from necessary benefits and civil rights. Roosevelt did, however, issue Executive Order 8802, which sought to ensure fair employment practices.

During World War II, over a million African Americans entered the armed forces and were placed in segregated units. In 1946, President Harry S. Truman issued Executive Order 9981, which required integration of the military. However, the order was not implemented until 1952, during the Korean War under President Dwight D. Eisenhower. On the federal level, government civil service positions were opened to African Americans during World War II. In 1948, President Truman created the Civil Rights Section of the Justice Department. In 1954, the U.S. Supreme Court struck down restrictive housing policies and outlawed segregation of interstate bus travel. Martin Luther King, Jr., and the Southern Christian Leadership Conference became active proponents of civil rights. Together with the NAACP, the Congress of Racial Equality, and other religious and political groups, they mobilized a broad movement for African American civil rights.

In the 1960s, urban riots in major cities and the rise of the black power movement forced the political system to confront the effects of racism in major cities. Civil rights voting legislation resulted in the election of African American candidates on the local level and the shift of southern politicians to accommodating the needs of their African American constituents. However, the impetus of the civil rights movement and the influence of African American leaders on the political climate in Washington, D.C., waned during the 1970s and 1980s, primarily on account of economic recession, with its attendant inflation, unemployment, and homelessness. An attitude of benign neglect, the retrenching of social welfare programs for minorities, and a conservative political environment slowed the progress of African Americans (Garvin & Cox, 1979; Rose, 1990).

In the 1990s there has been an upsurge of African American people coming together in a national self-help movement and a spiritual revival of identity and culture. The Million Man March in Washington, D.C., held in 1996 was a national effort to commit the moral and spiritual resources of African American men to their families and communities across the country. A counterpart movement on a smaller scale was held for African American women in 1997 in Philadelphia. The spiritual faith of African American people has been demonstrated in their resolve to stand up against church burnings and racial hate crimes. A growing number of African Americans have turned to Islamic religion as a source of ethnic faith and unity. The Reverend Jesse Jackson has led the political and moral battle against the dismantling of affirmative action in higher education in California, uniting women who have been the

major beneficiaries of educational and employment admissions and students who were people of color. President Bill Clinton has also been aware of the problem of racism facing the United States, appointing a presidential commission on racial equality to study the problems and issues of race and racism and make recommendations for change. These are small but significant steps that reflect the dynamic nature of how African American leaders and community people have come together to respond to the unique set of problems facing them.

Women of Color

No organized multicultural feminist movement has united all women of color. However, the history of the modern feminist movement began in England and the United States in the nineteenth century. The term *feminist* arose during the 1880s and was used to indicate "support for women's equal legal and political rights with men" (Bryson, 1992, p. 1).

There has been, however, a split between white feminists and multicultural feminists due to the racism of the former who believed that the white world was the norm. Bryson (1992) observes:

> Much as feminists have attacked traditional political theory for excluding or marginalising women, feminism itself has been accused of universalising the assumptions and needs of white women in Europe and America and largely ignoring the very different perspectives of black and third world women—indeed its very use of such terms suggests that white first world women are seen as the norm to which other groups may be added, as well as concealing the vast differences amongst the women so labelled. (p. 5)

The present direction in the history of feminist thought is to move toward the inclusion of the multicultural experiences and history of women of color as a central starting point and to enlarge on a global view of women.

White Feminism and African American Women.
The history of African American women in the nineteenth century began with the abolition of

slavery movement championed by Elizabeth Cady Stanton (1815–1902). Stanton saw an analogy between the plight of the slave and the woman. Bryson (1992) states:

> The movement for the abolition of slavery was also related to the growth of feminist ideas in a number of ways. Most obviously, at a time when a married woman was effectively her husband's possession, there was a clear analogy between the situation of women and slaves. The movement was both a moral crusade and a liberal republican campaign, for the institution of slavery could be seen not only as an affront to God, but also as a violation of the spirit of the American constitution; in both cases the arguments against negro slavery could be used on behalf of women, while the frequently cited argument that slavery involved the sexual exploitation of women (both of the female slave by her owner, and of his wronged wife) introduced a gender-specific aspect to the debate. (p. 38)

Stanton along with Susan B. Anthony and William Lloyd Garrison were the leaders of the abolition movement before and after the Civil War.

The primary argument was against slavery and for the freedom of the slave. The argument for women was the abolition of women as slaves to husbands and the need for the suffrage of women. When it appeared that Congress and the nation were headed toward the Fifteenth Amendment to the Constitution (universal suffrage for all adult males, including African American men), the women's movement was not averse to harnessing racial prejudice against the African American male at the expense of white women suffrage. Stanton and Anthony moved to include southern white women, maintaining white supremacy and excluding black women from the movement.

The history of African American women is a series of historical events: slave women as field workers, separation of African American women from their children and husbands during slavery, sexual oppression of slave owners who viewed African American women as slave children breeders, the social and political oppression of white feminist suffragists who cut off African American women from participation in the women's movement of the nineteenth and twentieth centuries.

This history has led Davis (1989) to observe, "[W]omen of color are the most oppressed human beings in our society" (p. 29).

Kopacsi and Faulkner (1988) trace the interaction between African American and white women from the early 1800s in the struggle for the abolition of slavery, through the suffrage campaigns between the 1850s and the early 1900s, to the tensions between the civil rights and women's movements of the 1960s and 1970s. They identify ideological and racist attitudes on the part of white women, particularly toward African American women.

Kopacsi and Faulkner cite at least two reasons for the failure of white and African American women to work together for common feminist causes:

1. White women have not understood and recognized that race is the primary issue for African American women's feminism and that there can be no separation between the fight against racism and sexism.

2. White feminists have treated African American women as inferior or dependent partners in the social change enterprise.

They point out that white feminists had a social privilege agenda, whereas the agenda of African American women was to survive in spite of racism. However, both groups were targets of dehumanization, stereotyping, and discrimination. Kopacsi and Faulkner call for current mutual collaboration between them, suggesting two spheres of concern that could be the basis of cooperation for social change: work and family. Specific components of a cooperative agenda might include the elimination of racism in personal life, workplace, and politics; increase in the minimum wage and standards for health; job training and development for women; the reform of social programs—in particular, AFDC—to ensure a minimum level of health and decency and child care; recognition and acceptance of women's competence in the workplace; and increased appreciation of cultural diversity on the part of white feminists.

A few crucial junctures in the feminist history of African American women deserve separate discussion: (l) exclusion of African American women from the early women's rights campaign, (2) racism of the early twentieth-century women's suffrage movement, and (3) black women club movement.

Exclusion from Early Women's Rights. The 1848 Seneca Falls Convention in New York state was organized by two leading women's suffragists, Elizabeth Cady Stanton and Lucretia Mott. It marked the forming of the Seneca Falls Declaration, which included a list of grievances over the institution of marriage and women's inferior and dependent status within marriage. It was the articulated consciousness of women's rights and analyzed the female condition. It advocated the suffrage of women—the electoral power—as a way to fulfill the political equality of women. However, it ignored the plight of white working-class women and did not mention the dilemma of black women in the North and South. Only one black man was present among the Seneca Falls conferees, while not a single black woman was in attendance.

In 1851 Sojourner Truth, an escaped slave woman, addressed a women's convention in Akron, Ohio. In her famous speech, "Ain't I a Woman," she answered the male supremacist argument regarding female weakness and its incompatibility with suffrage. She declared:

> I have ploughed, and planted, and gathered into barns and no man could beat me! And ain't I a woman? I could work as much and eat as much as a man—when I could get it—and beat the lash as well! And ain't I a woman? I have borne thirteen children and seen them most all sold off to slavery, and when I cried out with my mother's grief, none but Jesus heard me! And ain't I a woman? Where did your Christ come from? From God and a woman! Man had nothing to do with him. (Stanton, Anthony, & Gage, 1881, pp. 115–117)

Sojourner Truth was a constant reminder that black women were in need of their rights as well as white women. At the same time, she was the lone African American feminist voice to speak, despite the constant efforts not to allow her to address meetings.

Racism in Women's Suffrage. By 1867 the women's suffrage movement made a major shift away from male black suffrage in favor of women's suffrage. At the 1867 Equal Rights Association, both Henry Ward Beecher and Elizabeth Cady Stanton argued for Anglo-Saxon white women enfranchisement rather than for the black male right to vote. This was a response to the impending enfranchisement of all adult males, especially blacks, in the Fifteenth Amendment to the Constitution, which passed in 1870. Stanton believed that this would render black men superior to white women. Her rationale was that women's rights proponents had fought for the abolition of slavery with the understanding that their reward would be women's suffrage. Now the Republicans were ready to extend the vote to black men.

Although Frederick Douglass, the leading advocate for black enfranchisement, supported the political equality of women, he was equally insistent that black people needed electoral power as a guarantee of the survival of the masses of his people. In the South, the Democratic party represented the former slave owner class and defended women's suffrage as a means to prevent black male enfranchisement. It was the issue of black male versus women's suffrage that dissolved the alliance between black liberation and white liberation.

By 1894 Susan B. Anthony broke with Frederick Douglass to recruit southern white women into the women's suffrage movement. She also refused to support Ida B. Wells, founder of the first black women's suffrage club, who wanted to form a branch of the suffrage association. Such an inclusion would cause the withdrawal of southern white women members from the organization. Anthony's capitulation to racism based on expediency was her public stance as president of the National American Woman Suffrage Association from 1894 to 1900. During this period, southern states were in the process of disfranchising black people from voting, legalizing racial segregation, and lynching black people as examples.

A profound sense of racial violence and white supremacy prevailed at the turn of the century. In 1898 Ida B. Wells called on President William McKinley to order federal intervention in the lynching of a South Carolina postmaster. By 1899

Wells compiled the findings of research on lynchings in the United States. McKinley chose to remain silent on this matter.

Black Women Club Movement. In 1895 the National Federation of Afro-American Women was established, while the National League of Colored Women was founded in 1896 as a response to the exclusion of black women from predominantly white women clubs. These two organizations eventually merged to form the National Association of Colored Women's Clubs, which became a powerful political force for black freedom and antilynching laws.

Mary Church Terrell, first president of the National Association of Colored Women's Clubs, became an advocate for black liberation, particularly black equality and women's suffrage, freedom for her people, and the rights of working people. Her rival, Ida B. Wells, a newspaper journalist, was a crusader against lynching of black people in the United States. Touring cities in the United States and Europe, she organized public sentiment and solidarity to protect black people from the reign of lynching mobs (Davis, 1983).

Mexican American, Asian American, and Native American Women at the Turn of the Twentieth Century. Mexican American women in the southwestern and western United States were predominantly middle-class people who in the first wave immigrated from Mexico across the border to the United States in search of a better life. After the Mexican Revolution at the turn of the century, the southwestern United States was in the midst of economic growth. Mexican families were able to establish small businesses in the United States. In successive waves Mexicans worked for the Southern Pacific and Santa Fe railroads and agricultural, mining, and midwestern industries. Historically, Mexico provided a source of cheap labor for agriculture and unskilled work. Mexican adults—male and female, husband and wife with children—were recruited as *braceros*, or contract laborers. They entered the United States with legal work permits, while illegal aliens without proper authorization slipped across the border in search of jobs.

Mexican American women were concerned about socioeconomic issues (such as steady employment), survival (for example, sufficient food and housing for the family), social class oppression (including the new underclass of California), and exploitation (for instance, low wages, long hours, and minimal living conditions). They were nurturers and caregivers of their husbands, children, and homes.

Almquist (1984) observes:

> Initially, many, but not all, Mexican-Americans worked as migrant laborers. Entire families worked in the fields, because the work was seasonal and the wages of all members were required to earn a living. Women and girls worked under the watchful eye of husbands and fathers, who made certain that the females did not violate traditional norms of behavior and were protected from unwelcome sexual advances. As industrialization occurred, Mexican-Americans were increasingly employed as factory operatives. Women especially were preferred for sewing jobs in garment factories. (pp. 432–433)

Thus, Mexican American women moved from the home to the fields and factories while attempting to maintain their families.

Asian American women—particularly Chinese and Japanese—were minimally represented in the early part of the twentieth century. The Chinese Exclusion Act of 1882 and the 1907 Gentlemen's Agreement between the United States and Japan effectively curtailed the flow of immigrants, particularly women, into this country during the first half of this century. The Immigration Act of 1924 was designed to close U.S. borders to immigrants from Asia, particularly China and Japan. Moreover, Asian American males already in this country were unable to marry white women because of antimiscegenation laws. As a consequence, for example, Chinese and Filipino males remained single or either married African American, American Indian, or Mexican American women. As a result of the lack of Asian women, there was no early Asian American feminist movement.

From a historical tradition viewpoint, Native American women and men shared common responsibilities and had complementary roles in the tribe. In some instances, Native American women participated in tribal councils, were respected as elders, and were able to share viewpoints and shape tribal decisions. They were part of the psychohistorical victimization by the white settlers and U.S. government and military who forcibly removed tribe after tribe from land in the westward movement.

Some Native American groups were matrilineal; that is, sons and daughters recognized their female ancestors, property was handed down from generation to generation through the female line, and women relied on female kin for support and assistance in work and time of crisis. The Hopi, Choctaw, and Iroquois tribes were matrilineal, whereas the Apache and Sioux were patriarchal and fierce, warring, and nomadic groups. Depending on these orientations, Native American women were regarded and treated accordingly.

Women of Color Feminism. There were vestiges of multicultural movements among various ethnic groups of women. Terrelonge (1984) points out that African American women have not developed a strong sense of black feminist consciousness for a number of reasons:

• Sexism has been viewed as a racially divisive issue that could trigger internal conflict between African American males and females.

• Racism is so identified in American culture, particularly among many white women, that African American females have been reluctant to participate with them.

• The emphasis in the African American social movement of the sixties was the liberation of the African American man rather than the African American woman.

• The idea of black matriarchy caused the suppression of feminist consciousness among black women and negated the fact of black female oppression.

• The church has supported the biblical notion of sexual inequality and has been oriented to patriarchal gender views.

Native Americans have been concerned about bicultural integration between the reservation and urban Indian women. Currently half of the Native Americans live in rural areas, on or near reservations, and the rest are in urban areas. Indian women on reservations traditionally in some cases tend to have large families, contribute to the household through gardens, raise sheep and cattle, and make clothes and household objects. There has been a slow growth of light industry on the reservation. Indian sponsored bingo and casino gambling have stimulated employment for the tribe in recent years. Women in the cities have lived bicultural lives. On the one hand, they enter the Anglo world of education, employment, and daily living while, on the other hand, maintain the native values of sharing material goods, being noncompetitive, and avoiding criticism and manipulation.

Chicana feminists participating in the 1910 Mexican Revolution were called *Jesucitas*, functioning as nurses and healers who followed the battle encampments and took up arms. Many pioneer feminists were involved in labor union movements in the southwestern United States, including Arizona mine workers. Jovita Idar, a woman whose family owned a Mexican American newspaper in Laredo, Texas, was instrumental in organizing El Premer Congreso Mexicanista de Laredo, which drew on professionals and others to develop labor unions. Many Mexican American feminists worked on the issue of unfair property taxation in the 1920s and 1930s. In Los Angeles and Texas Mexican American women organized garment workers in the Farah Garment disputes in El Paso and the International Ladies Garment Workers Union during the 1930s.

Gonzalez (1983) has documented the role of Chicanas as feminists who were in Mexican immigrant families between the 1920s and 1940s. Her history parallels the woman's movement from the time of suffrage to the struggles for just work conditions for women.

During the late sixties and early seventies, the Chicana feminist movement arose from a need to enhance political, educational, and economic opportunities. With strong roots in the working class and unions, this force was instrumental in encouraging labor activities, securing better health care, and supporting women candidates for public office. At the same time, unlike the white feminists, Chicanas held to the traditional feminine roles of being mother and wife in a positive light. They did not depict Chicano men as the enemy or lay blame on them for placing limitations on them as women (Almquist, 1984). In the 1990s women were still concerned about personal, familial, and societal issues: compensation for work at home and office, sexual harassment and abuse violence, reproductive rights, spousal sharing of responsibilities in child-rearing and household tasks, and related concerns. Moreover, women of color want to broaden the issue of gender oppression and include racism, social class, poverty, culture, and ethnicity to the discussion on women.

The 1996 Personal Responsibility and Work Opportunity Reconciliation Act has changed the face of welfare assistance for single women heads of households and their dependent children. No longer a part of the federal entitlement for single women and dependent children under the 1935 Social Security Act, the 1996 welfare reform legislation has moved single women and dependent children as a group to the responsibility of the states. The law has replaced the Aid to Families with Dependent Children (AFDC) entitlement program with a new block grant program called Temporary Assistance for Needy Families (TANF). A five-year lifetime limit has been placed on welfare assistance. TANF recipients must engaged in work after receiving aid for two years. The two-year limit forces a person off of public assistance and into a work situation. Recipients must work a minimum of twenty hours per work, with child care assistance and an attempt to place persons in private industry or public service work situations. There is an effort to establish paternity and to pursue child support on the part of "deadbeat dads" who have not supported their children.

Regarding these turns of events in welfare reform, the question becomes, Why have single women with dependent children been forced to carry the brunt of this legislation? Welfare reform is an appeal theme for American voters who demand changes in welfare assistance. However, does the American public realize that it is women, particular women of color, who are recipients of this legislation?

Davis (1989) has a sense of feminist history, particularly of compatible multicultural and socioeconomic dimensions. In Cultural Study 2-1 she raises several important questions and gives specific directions.

CULTURAL STUDY 2-1

Opening Up the Women's Movement

During this decade we have witnessed an exciting resurgence of the women's movement. If the first wave of the women's movement began in the 1840s, and the second wave in the 1960s, then we are approaching the crest of a third wave in the final days of the 1980s. When the feminist historians of the twenty-first century attempt to recapitulate the third wave, will they ignore the momentous contributions of Afro-American women, who have been leaders and activists in movements often confined to women of color, but whose accomplishments have invariably advanced the cause of white women as well? Will the exclusionary policies of the mainstream women's movement—from its inception to the present—which have often compelled Afro-American women to conduct their struggle for equality outside the ranks of that movement, continue to result in the systematic omission of our names from the roster of prominent leaders and activists of the women's movement? Will there continue to be two distinct continuums of the women's movement, one visible and another invisible, one publicly acknowledged and another ignored except by the conscious progeny of the working-class women—Black, Latina, Native American, Asian, and white—who forged that hidden continuum? If this question is answered in the affirmative, it will mean that women's quest for equality will continue to be gravely deficient. The revolutionary potential of the women's movement still will not have been realized. The racist-inspired flaws of the first and second waves of the women's movement will have become the inherited flaws of the third wave.

How can we guarantee that this historical pattern is broken? As advocates and activists of women's rights in our time, we must begin to merge that double legacy in order to create a single continuum, one that solidly represents the aspirations of all women in our society. We must begin to create a revolutionary, multiracial women's movement that seriously addresses the main issues affecting poor and working-class women. In order to tap the potential for such a movement, we must further develop those sectors of the movement that are addressing seriously issues affecting poor and working-class women, such as jobs, pay equity, paid maternity leave, federally subsidized child care, protection from sterilization abuse, and subsidized abortions. Women of all racial and class backgrounds will greatly benefit from such an approach.

From A. Y. Davis, *Women, Culture, and Politics*, pp. 6, 7. Copyright 1989 by Random House. Reprinted by permission.

Most feminist groups in the nineties have recognized the need for a multicultural emphasis that addresses racism, social class inequality, and homophobia along with sexism. Renzetti and Curran (1995) state, "If the movement is to remain strong and make up ground lost as a result of the conservative backlash of the 1980s, then the needs and experiences of diverse groups of women must not just be taken into account by the powers that be within feminism, they must reshape the focus and course of the movement itself" (p. 566). As mainstream feminists seek to incorporate more multicultural concerns, there must be an adequate body of women of color literature.

Latino Americans

The history of the relationship between Latino Americans and Anglo Americans began in 1848 with the Treaty of Guadalupe Hidalgo, which formally ended the Mexican-American War. Before this conflict, Mexico owned four provinces: Texas, New Mexico, Arizona, and California. Texas, New Mexico, and California were fairly extensively settled during this period. Both California and Texas, provinces with large Anglo populations, rebelled against Mexico and caused border disputes that drew the United States and Mexico into

war. The United States offered to purchase the southwest territories from Mexico. However, Mexico refused the offer, and the United States attacked and overran the territories, capturing Mexico City in 1848.

Article 8 of the Treaty of Guadalupe Hidalgo gave Mexicans the right to remain or to withdraw to Mexico in two years, the option of either Mexican or American citizenship, and guaranteed property rights. Eventually, however, Mexicans lost their land because the burden of proof of ownership fell on Mexican landholders. The U.S. government vigorously suppressed any form of armed resistance by Mexicans to American imperialism. Mexican Americans became second-class citizens, deprived of land and social status. Some became bandits. Others worked in agriculture and unskilled jobs.

Poverty and difficult economic conditions in Mexico forced many to immigrate across the border to the United States. After the Mexican Revolution at the turn of the twentieth century, the Mexican economy was poor, whereas the southwestern United States was in the midst of economic growth.

As a result of the 1910 Mexican Revolution, many thousands fled from central Mexico northward into the United States, and by 1920 more than one million crossed into this country. These migrants came from varied social class and economic backgrounds. They settled in Mexican American communities along the border. The first waves escaped with sufficient capital to go into business as middle class, whereas successive waves were without financial resources and worked in agriculture and industrial jobs. Between 1900 and World War I, many Mexican Americans worked for the railroads in the Southwest, particularly the Southern Pacific and the Santa Fe railroads. During the war there was a need for a labor pool because of Americans in the armed forces. Mexican laborers were recruited in agriculture and copper mining in the western and southwestern United States and iron foundries and coal mining in the Northeast and Appalachia. By then, Mexican Americans were employed in midwestern industrial cities (Meier & Rivera, 1972).

Zuniga (personal communication, September 10, 1998) points out that in the first two waves of immigration, educated Mexican Americans settled in the Southwest and provided the leadership for such organizations as the League of United Latin American Citizens, which was developed in the early 1920s to protect the civil rights of persons of Mexican heritage and continues to monitor activities today, and La Alianza, which provided life insurance and social group events.

The establishment of substantial Mexican American middle and blue-collar classes and a strong business sector in large cities in the West and Southwest resulted in the upward movement of Mexicans into all segments of American life. However, Mexico has provided a source of cheap labor for agriculture and unskilled work. Mexican citizens with green cards are contract laborers who enter the United States with legal work permits, while illegal aliens are those people who, without proper authorization, cross the border in search of jobs. At the end of the 1980s, the U.S. Immigration Service offered amnesty for illegal aliens who had lived in the United States for a certain period of time. The U.S. government made a major effort to offer citizenship to those who had lived as undocumented aliens.

Mexican Americans have been forced to fight for union representation and collective bargaining for farm workers. The living conditions, wages, and benefits of farm laborers have been major issues between the produce growers and union representatives. The Mexican American community has been the source of political power and cultural pride. The rise of the La Raza movement in the 1960s coincided with the black power and yellow power movements in other ethnic communities. In addition, Mexican Americans have held local, state, and national political offices.

Puerto Ricans have migrated from their island home to the eastern coast of the United States, facilitated by air transportation, ever since Puerto Rico became a territorial possession of the United States in 1917. New York City has been the gateway to the United States for Puerto Ricans, with job opportunities in the garment industry and commercial and tourist services. Unfortunately, many Puerto Rican migrants have lived in pover-

ty, inhabiting substandard apartments in congested inner-city neighborhoods. High rates of unemployment, drug use, and crime exist among Puerto Rican youth and male adults.

Refugees from the Castro regime during the 1960s and 1970s created a large Cuban American population in Florida, particularly in Miami. The first wave of Cubans were the professional classes and the intelligentsia, who formed a close-knit business and professional community in a section of Miami that came to be known as Little Havana. However, the second wave of Cuban immigrants were poor and uneducated. They depended on government social services to assist them with basic survival needs.

Many Central Americans in the United States have been displaced by war and unrest in Nicaragua and El Salvador. Some of these refugees have been forced to return to their own countries; others have remained, and their needs have strained the limited resources of local, state, and federal assistance.

Latino Americans have many socioeconomic needs, especially in the areas of language communication, job training, employment, housing, education, and health care. In California, Latino Americans constitute the largest ethnic group, followed by Asian Americans and African Americans. Throughout the United States, Latino Americans face widespread racism, prejudice, and discrimination based on stereotypes, along with limited employment opportunities. As they increase in number, Latinos need to become an effective political force to advocate their rights as American citizens. At the same time Latino Americans are facing a unique set of problems particularly related to legal and illegal immigrants and the rights to social service resources, the erosion of affirmative action programs and their impact on Latino admissions to university programs, and the need to organize Latinos who are able to vote and elect political leaders who are sensitive to their needs.

Asian Americans

Asian Americans comprise diverse and conflicting groups of ethnic nationals who historically fought each other on the Asian continent. Yet, during the mid-1800s and early 1900s, Asians of many nationalities came to the United States to pursue economic opportunities, to escape political oppression, and to migrate to the West. Many Chinese and Japanese entered as laborers who expected to return to their homeland and retire in comfort after making their fortune in the United States. During this period, the Chinese referred to America as "Gold Mountain," or the land of opportunity.

The Chinese were the first Asian immigrants. They came voluntarily in large numbers to Hawaii as sugar plantation laborers and stayed to establish a new generation of businessmen and farmers. In California, the Chinese were attracted by the Gold Rush of 1849 and competed with white miners in the Mother Lode country. Chinese workers constituted the major labor force in the construction of the Southern Pacific Railroad. They also worked in canneries and were a major part of the agricultural farm labor force. Their agricultural ventures included planting orchards of cherry, pear, lemon, and other fruit and harvesting rice fields. As the Chinese succeeded in these endeavors, growing anti-Chinese sentiment spread among white miners and farmers. Riots, hangings, and evictions of Chinese spread throughout the West Coast. The Chinese were restricted in their movements in the United States and were ultimately barred from entering the country through the Chinese Exclusion Act of 1882. They were also denied American citizenship and the right to intermarriage. The immigration of Chinese was labeled the "Yellow Peril" and likened to a spreading disease engulfing the United States. "Chinatowns" were established in major American cities as segregated communities that sought survival and group protection in the face of racial discrimination.

Large numbers of Japanese immigrants arrived in the United States from the turn of the twentieth century through the 1920s. These early immigrants were contract farm laborers who stayed to cultivate agricultural land in California. Japan and the United States signed the 1907 Gentlemen's Agreement, which established self-imposed quotas to limit immigration. By 1913, California had passed the Alien Land Bill, which prevented the Japanese from purchasing farmland. In other words, the Japanese were denied citizenship and ownership of land on account of racism and fear of competition.

The Immigration Act of 1924 closed U.S. borders to immigrants from Asia, particularly from China and Japan. Immigration policy favored those from European countries. In particular, there were high quotas for fair-skinned northern Europeans and low quotas for dark-skinned southern Europeans. Also discriminated against were individuals from Africa and Central and South America. Before this law was enacted, many Chinese and Japanese men married "picture brides" from their native countries. The Chinese who came without families were denied access to their families in China. Chinese males remained single or married into other races.

Intermarriage between whites and Asians was forbidden in many states. Chinese Americans were segregated in or near Chinatowns in large cities and worked as restaurant, grocery, and farm laborers. The Japanese Americans also established their communities, worked in agriculture, and raised their second generation in America, or *nisei*, who attended high school and college and entered occupations associated with the American middle class.

However, in the hysteria after the bombing of Pearl Harbor on December 7, 1941, Japanese Americans along the West Coast were compelled to give up their homes, businesses, and properties under Executive Order 9066 issued by President Roosevelt on February 12, 1942. They were forcibly removed to rural internment camps for the duration of the war, with the resulting loss of Japanese American property and income amounting to millions of dollars. Their family life was disrupted because many young Japanese Americans chose to join the military. Ironically, Japanese Americans fought with distinction in European combat divisions and served in intelligence units during the Pacific campaign.

Many were later allowed during World War II to move to cities in the Midwest, and many studied in university settings there. Most Japanese Americans were economically ruined and forced to restart with minimal resources after the war. In

1944, the U.S. Supreme Court ruled that the relocation of Japanese Americans was unconstitutional. After Japanese Americans spent years petitioning Congress for redress, in 1988 Congress passed a bill granting token remuneration for the property loss sustained as a result of internment. Every Japanese American still living who was in a relocation camp will eventually be paid $20,000.

Between 1942 and 1965, individuals from various Asian American ethnic groups entered the United States, in subservient economic positions. During World War II, China was an ally of the United States; therefore, provision was made to allow war refugees from China into the United States for relief purposes. Likewise, because the Philippines was an American possession that fell to Japan in the early stages of World War II, many Filipinos entered the U.S. Navy as mess stewards. Before this time, Filipino men worked in the United States as farm laborers, while Filipino women became domestic workers. During the early part of the twentieth century only a few Koreans entered the United States, as farm laborers. After the Korean War, Korean wives of U.S. servicemen also immigrated.

The 1965 Immigration Act was pivotal legislation that opened the United States to all countries. Political unrest and oppression in the Philippines and Korea caused many educated professionals and middle-class people from these countries to immigrate to the United States. Other groups of Asian immigrants became small-business owners, who worked as family units to ensure their livelihood.

During and after the Vietnam War, Southeast Asian refugees from Vietnam, Laos, and Cambodia fled the incoming communist regimes. The first wave of these refugees arrived after the fall of Saigon in 1975. Most were highly educated and affluent individuals who had been friends and coworkers of Americans. Later influxes of immigrants brought fishermen, farmers, and peasants, who, unlike the first wave, have experienced significant difficulty in adjusting to life in the United States. The total population of these groups (Vietnamese, Hmong, Mien, Laotians, Cambodians) in the United States numbers roughly nine hundred thousand.

Many Southeast Asian refugee families were sponsored by American churches through Church World Services and were accepted into American communities. Some Americans, however, expressed resentment of competition for public welfare benefits and the limited job opportunities that already constrained many low-income Americans. Nonetheless, the 1970s and 1980s were characterized by unprecedented population growth of Asian American groups—some who have lived in the United States for four generations and a new group of Southeast Asian refugees in the midst of acculturation.

In the 1990s Asian Americans are still aware of their weak influence on the political scene in the United States. With few Asian American politicians on the state and national levels, there have never been cabinet-level appointments at the presidential level. (An Asian American governor was elected in the state of Washington in 1997, which was a major breakthrough.) Asian Americans were the focus of investigation in the 1997 Senate and House Investigation on presidential campaign reform and abuse as a result of the 1996 presidential election. The selection of a Chinese American, Bill Lee, as the civil rights head of the Department of Justice in 1998 was heavily contested by the Republican Congress and sent a message about conservative politics and Asian Americans. Asian Americans need to organize themselves in an effective way on the par of the Japanese American Citizenship League, which has chapters in major cities where there is a Japanese American constituency and is a lobbying force at the national level in Washington, D.C. As the population of Asian Americans exceeds the ten million mark in a few years, Asian Americans will be heard as a formative political and financial force to shape and influence the American political scene.

PEOPLE OF COLOR GROUP EXPERIENCES

The preceding history of people of color describes the encounter with racism in the United States. Subjected to dominance, oppression, and exploitation by the majority white society, ethnic groups were denied access to land and civil rights and underpaid for their labor. Federal and state laws were enacted to force them into compliance with the wishes of the majority society. By and large, people of color endured these injustices; when they revolted, the police and military used force to subdue them. Often religion provided a source of strength for these oppressed groups. They also began to organize social, political, and legal organizations in response to rising exploitation and stress. Providing needed social services, these organizations arose from within the oppressed groups rather than from external social welfare institutions.

The early part of the twentieth century saw the rejuvenation of the Ku Klux Klan, race riots, large-scale immigration of ethnic laborers, the subsequent institution of quota restrictions on such immigration, and the erosion of tribal government. Despite constitutional protections, widespread racism and segregation dominated the national scene. Minimal gains were offset by widespread oppression.

The powerlessness of people of color persisted through the Depression and World War II. Fair employment and housing laws were enacted, but no significant improvement in human rights ensued. African Americans still lived in segregated neighborhoods, were limited in their employment, and sent their children to inferior schools. Native Americans were warehoused on rural reservations without an economic and employment future; their children were displaced to distant boarding schools, their able-bodied to the cities for work. Illegal Mexican aliens were used as cheap laborers and exploited for the interests of agriculture. To find factory jobs, Latinos moved to northern cities, especially Chicago, New York, and Boston. Japanese Americans on the West Coast were detained in relocation centers (in effect, American concentration camps) as a consequence of war hysteria and the wishes of white agricultural business interests.

The 1950s was a period of consolidation after the war years characterized by growth and prosperity. This conservative era gave way to the years of change in the 1960s. During the mid-1960s, the civil rights movement, urban riots, and the War on Poverty moved issues of racial equity briefly to center stage. With support from political leadership, people of color, especially African Americans, made important gains in voting rights, public accommodations, and social service programs. The Civil Rights Act of 1964 was landmark legislation. The 1965 McCarran Immigration Act eliminated restrictive quotas and allowed freedom of immigration for Asians and Central Americans.

In the 1970s, shaken by the Vietnam War and the Watergate scandal, the United States examined its moral values and reaffirmed the preeminence of constitutional government. The resignation of Richard M. Nixon as president was a watershed event; afterward, the nation felt cleansed and moved forward. The 1980s witnessed the waning of civil rights and lack of program commitment from a conservative political administration. However, propelled by political oppression and regional conflict in their native countries, immigrants and refugees continued to seek a better way of life in the United States.

The 1990s has been a decade of unprecedented growth of immigrants and refugees of color. Along the way have come women, children, and older people of color from other countries and from the populations who have been in the United States for many generations.

Portes and Rumbaut (1990), in their *Immigrant America: A Portrait*, are optimistic about the future:

> Immigrants and refugees will continue to come, giving rise to energetic communities, infusing new blood in local labor markets, filling positions at different levels of the economy, and adding to the diversity of sounds, sights, and tastes in our cities. The history of America has been, to a large extent, the history of its immigrants—their progress reflecting and simultaneously giving impulse to the nation's expansion. Although problems and struggles are inevitable along the way, in the long run, the diverse talents and energies of newcomers will reinforce the vitality of American society and the richness of its culture. (p. 246)

These observations emphasize the importance of exploring and understanding the impact of recent immigrant and refugee population growth. At the same time women, children, and older people of color are also groups who have dominated the special practice needs of cultural diverse social work practice.

In the following sections, the practice themes of these six groups (new arrivals, women, gays and lesbians, children, racially/ethnically mixed, and older people) are examined in detail.

Practice with New Arrivals

At this time, the United States is in the midst of an unprecedented increase in international immigration. Portes and Rumbaut (1990) observe, "Never before has the United States received immigrants from so many countries, from such different social and economic backgrounds, and for so many reasons" (p. 7). Yet at the same time, the immigrants moving to this country are a self-selective group. There is a greater proportion of professionals and technicians among immigrants than in the average American labor pool. Immigrants tend to be well represented at higher educational and occupational levels. Even unauthorized immigrants tend to be better educated and possess a higher level of occupational skills than their counterparts in their countries of origin. Few of these immigrants were unemployed in their own countries.

Why do immigrants come to the United States? The major reasons are their motivation and means to fulfill life aspirations and expectations in terms of lifestyle and consumption. An improved standard of living, which they are unable to find in their country of origin, tends to be immigrants' motivation for coming to the United States.

Four types of immigrants are representative of the groups migrating to this country: labor migrants, professional immigrants, entrepreneurial immigrants, and refugees/asylees. *Labor migrants*, in search of menial and low-paying jobs, represent the bulk of immigrants. Some cross the border on foot, with the help of smugglers, or overstay their U.S. tourist visa. Others enter legally, through the family reunification policies of the immigration law, as the spouse of a U.S. citizen. Still others come as contract laborers when

domestic workers are unavailable. The flow of foreign labor to the United States is constant because of the higher minimum wages, the economic savings realized by urban employers and rural growers, and the willingness of immigrants to perform jobs that American workers are unwilling to do.

Professional immigrants represent a "brain drain" of talented workers to the United States for higher salaries and better working conditions. These immigrants are probably among the best in their professions in their own countries; they must pass difficult entry tests or attract U.S. job offers. In some cases, university graduates from developing nations receive their education in the United States and recognize the poor job opportunities and lack of equipment in their own countries.

Entrepreneurial immigrants are self-employed businesspeople who establish themselves in their own ethnic enclave. They must have substantial business expertise, access to capital, and access to labor to succeed in their ventures. These immigrants generally hire employees from their own ethnic groups and cater to low-income groups in the inner city.

Refugee and asylum status, the fourth classification of immigrants, was formerly granted to those escaping from communist countries in Southeast Asia and Eastern Europe. However, the U.S. government's designation of *refugee* has broadened to include a combination of legal guidelines and political expediency based on changing world situations.

Among refugee groups entering the United States, the first wave of a group tends to be an elite consisting of notable professionals and intelligentsia who left their country because of ideological and political opposition. Successive waves of immigrants come from more modest backgrounds and have endured economic and political oppression from the same regime that caused the first wave to emigrate.

Based on 1987 statistics from the U.S. Immigration and Naturalization Service, 71 percent of 601,516 immigrants admitted for legal permanent residence went to six states: California (26.8 percent), New York (19.0 percent), Florida (9.1 percent), Texas (7.0 percent), New Jersey (5.1 percent), and Illinois (4.3 percent). New York City remains the premier destination of immigrants, particularly Puerto Ricans, Dominicans, Chinese, and East Indians. These groups are attracted to the industrial and garment employment opportunities in the area. Even with industrial decline, enough economic growth in services and construction remains to support the large urban population. Los Angeles attracts many Mexican and Asian immigrants, particularly Chinese, Vietnamese, and Koreans. These groups are prominent in the produce retailing, food, and garment industries. Washington, D.C., has been a center for entrepreneurial Asians and political refugee groups, such as the Vietnamese and Salvadorans. San Francisco is the choice of Chinese and Filipinos; it has the largest Chinatown in the United States, and refugees and immigrants seek employment in its food and commercial industries. Miami's predominant immigrant group is Cubans, three-fourths of whom settle in southern Florida. Latinos account for nearly half the metropolitan population of Dade County. However, New York City and Los Angeles remain the overall preferred initial destinations of new immigrants.

Will these immigrant groups remain clustered in major cities or, after a period of assimilation, disperse and scatter throughout the country? Evidence based on the repatterning of Indochinese refugees points to the maintenance of ethnic communities clustered in key settlement areas. The preservation of these ethnic community clusters helps ensure continued working capital, protected markets, and labor pools, as well as mutual support and the survival of cultural practices.

It is important to understand the education, employment, and income backgrounds of immigrants and refugees. Between 1975 to 1980, immigrants from India, Iran, Taiwan, and Nigeria were among the best educated, whereas those from Mexico, Latin America, Italy, and Portugal were from low-average educational levels. Initial waves of refugees from communist-dominated countries came from high socioeconomic and educational strata, but succeeding waves were composed of people with low incomes and low levels of education. The Southeast Asian refugee groups followed the same pattern. Among the various immigrant groups during 1980, Russians (predominantly

Jews) and Middle Eastern and Mediterranean nationalities (particularly Lebanese, Greeks, and Syrians) had the highest rate of self-employment. Far Eastern groups (Japanese, Chinese, and Koreans) had above-average self-employment rates; East Indians, Portuguese, and Canadians had average rates; and Cubans' self-employment rates were somewhat below the national average. At the bottom of the self-employment scale were new arrivals from Southeast Asia and Latin America. Self-employment is an important economic indicator of self-reliance; it has implications for wage-earning potential and upward mobility. Income levels tend to support these self-employment trends. Japanese, Greeks, and Cubans are among the most entrepreneurially oriented groups and earn close to the national median income, whereas Chinese and Koreans have above-average household incomes. In the middle-income bracket are the French, Greek, and Portuguese. At the bottom of household income, near poverty level, are Laotian, Cambodian, and Dominican immigrants.

An important immigrant trend is the movement toward citizenship acquisition. Asian immigrants, particularly Vietnamese, Filipinos, and Koreans, have high rates of naturalization. Asian groups tend to have high levels of education and to include large proportions of professionals; these immigrants recognize the political oppression in their country of origin and want full citizenship to exercise political and social rights as Americans. European and South American immigrants exhibit intermediate rates of naturalization, whereas immigrant groups from Canada, Cuba, Mexico, the Dominican Republic, and Jamaica exhibit low rates of naturalization. A number of factors explain these low rates: political reasons for leaving their native countries and residing in the United States, a desire to return to the country of origin, and geographic proximity and access to nearby countries.

Acculturative stress and related mental health needs are major problems among ethnic minorities. High stress is found particularly in women, the elderly, the non-English-speaking, the uneducated, and the unemployed. Contributing factors to good mental health include social support systems (sponsors, coethnic friends, and relatives);

high levels of education, professional training, and income; a pervasive sense of cultural heritage; and proficiency in English. People from intact families with relatively high levels of education, income, and knowledge of English are generally fluent bilingual speakers. By contrast, people with limited bilingual ability, particularly in English, tend to come from lower-class groups—for example, immigrant workers and peasant refugees (Portes & Rumbaut, 1990).

These profiles of new arrivals in the United States during the 1980s indicate the range of social service needs and programs that must be created to serve this influx. The variety of immigrants and their patterns of settlement and mobility, occupational and economic adaptation, mental health and acculturation, and language acquisition are major factors that infuse and alter existing social programs. As social service delivery systems address these needs, the social well-being of immigrants and refugees is improved, thus aiding their quest to become a part of American society.

With the passage of the 1996 Personal Responsibility and Work Opportunity Reconciliation Act (HR 3734), restrictions have been placed on aid to noncitizens such as legal immigrants and refugees who do not have American citizenship. Title IV of the federal welfare reform law restricts federal assistance programs for refugees/asylees in the country less than five years, who have worked forty qualifying quarters and who are veterans or active duty military including their spouses and children. There is the prohibition of aid to undocumented immigrants and limited emergency and in-kind services (for example, nutrition for mothers and children) at the local level. There is a loss of food stamps and Supplemental Security Income (SSI) for noncitizen immigrants, although some provisions are being made for elderly immigrants and refugees as far as medical benefits (Medicare) are concerned. As a result, many noncitizens have enrolled in citizenship classes, committed suicide in the face of despair, or relied on their American-born and citizenship children for economic support.

Padilla (1997) urges social workers to respond to the crucial needs of immigrants in light of this welfare reform and related immigration policy changes.

First, social workers can help clients obtain appropriate lawful immigration status, because this is a first step in becoming eligible for social welfare services. Second, by keeping abreast of changes in program eligibility requirements for immigrants, social workers can provide more accurate information and referral services. Third, social workers need to be aware that the unqualified use of public services by certain categories of immigrants can be a cause for deportation or future denial of lawful permanent resident status under the "public charge" rule. The *public charge rule* refers to the expectation that immigrants will obtain support from family members or other sponsors rather than from government sources during the initial years after arriving in the United States. Consequently, social workers may need to focus on finding alternative nongovernmental sources of support for specific immigrant clients in need. (p. 601)

Descendants of Immigrants of Color. Throughout U.S. history, people of color have been cast as immigrant laborers and refugees who either voluntarily or involuntarily came to the United States. By and large, the dominant majority society has not recognized the contributions of people of color as conscientious American citizens. Many were born in the United States as sons and daughters of immigrants or as family members of first-born American fathers and mothers.

A typical experience of my generation is described by Ronald Takaki, professor of ethnic studies at the University of California, Berkeley. Both Dr. Takaki and I were raised in Honolulu, Hawaii, during the 1950s and educated in the 1960s and rose to make contributions to American higher education during the 1970s and 1980s. Both of us finished Ph.D. programs—in American history and social welfare, respectively—without studying the cultural diversity of the United States.

In Cultural Study 2-2, Ronald Takaki describes familiar experiences of multicultural living—being mistaken on the U.S. mainland for a foreigner who speaks good English and studying in academic disciplines without multicultural course content.

Culturally Deficient Experience

In the community where I lived as a child, my neighbors were Japanese, Chinese, Hawaiian, and Portuguese. Nearby there were Pilipinos and Puerto Ricans. As I grew up, I did not ask why— why were we from so many "different shores," from Asia and Europe as well as Hawaii itself, living together in Palolo Valley on the island of Oahu? My teachers and my textbooks did not explain the reasons why we were there.

After graduation from high school, I attended a college on the mainland where I found myself invited to dinners for "foreign students." I politely tried to explain to my kind hosts that I was not a foreign student; still they insisted that I accept their invitations. My fellow students (and even my professors) would ask me where I had learned to speak English. "In this country," I would reply. And sometimes I would add, "I was born in America, and my family has been here for three generations." Like myself, they had been taught little or nothing about America's ethnic diversity, and they thought I looked like a foreigner.

The college curriculum itself contributed to their perception of me. Courses in American literature and history, by not including knowledge about racial minorities, had rendered them to be outsiders. "American," in effect, was "white." All of the readings assigned in my course on American literature, for example, were written by white authors. We did not read works by Richard Wright (Native Son), Carlos Bulosan (America Is in the Heart), and Toshio Mori (Yokohama, California). Here was a course on the literature of America, but it did not teach the literature of all Americans.

For graduate study, I entered a Ph.D. program in American history. And there I studied the history of America as if there had been no racial minorities in this country's past, certainly no Chicanos and no Asians. The war against Mexico was studied, and the Chinese were given a brief reference in discussions of the transcontinental railroad. Blacks were there, in the antebellum South, as slaves. And Indians were present, too, as obstacles to progress or as an ill-fated race. I was in an American history Ph.D. program, but I was not studying the history of all the peoples of America.

Major American universities now have ethnic studies programs that include courses on the history and current issues of people of color. Several universities have adopted an ethnic studies course requirement as part of their undergraduate degree program. However, most universities lack the faculty resources, course offerings, and funding commitments necessary to disseminate ethnic studies course content to all students. Additionally, as noted in Chapter 1, few scholars in higher education are publishing articles and books on ethnic groups and themes.

Progress toward cultural pluralism in the United States is also hindered by problems of communication among ethnic groups. Differences of culture, needs, and expectations between African Americans, Asian Americans, Latinos, and Native Americans present obstacles to sustained creative dialogue and consensus. These groups must resist the temptation to compete for limited existing resources and instead work together to ensure funding for all people of color. State and local funding based on a demographic profile that was drawn from 1990 U.S. Census figures is a tangible result of such mutual cooperation.

In considering the ideal of cross-cultural unity and the reality of cross-cultural understanding, William Mamoru Shinto (1977) found that people of color wanted to discuss white racism and oppression, but whites wanted to learn about other cultures for their own education. He concluded that people of color resented white denial of racism and that whites reacted angrily to these accusations and to the withholding of basic information. Shinto suggested that both sides need to take risks; people of color and whites need to share knowledge and experiences that will have educational benefits for both.

Can information exchange take place between the dominant white society and people of color? To some extent, university and school classrooms afford a forum for the reading, discussion, and publishing of material on cultural diversity for active teaching and learning, and for the promotion of shared experiences among students from different cultures. Churches constitute a major avenue of education and training in cross-cultural communication and diversity. Popular books and articles are needed to educate the public about the multicultural richness of the United States.

As long as diverse populations exist, the United States will face cross-cultural dilemmas. Yet this country has always grown and thrived on the talents and contributions of its people. Like many who have come before, the immigrants of the 1980s and 1990s are pursuing the American dream of liberty and prosperity. The tasks that lie ahead are to integrate these new Americans and to enlarge the perspective of all Americans, so that all can benefit from our greater diversity.

Practice with Women of Color

There is little literature on social work practice with women of color. One reason for this is that most studies on racial and ethnically diverse groups are not sex-specific; they focus on individuals, families, and communities. In addition, limited research has been done on gender differences and feminist issues in a multicultural context, because clinical researchers have not had the academic background or interest to pursue these areas. Today, however, multicultural feminist practitioners are beginning to reflect and write on the unique problems and issues facing diverse female clients.

Interest in exploring this emerging field is increasing for several reasons:

• The changing demographics of the population growth patterns in the United States that reflect significant increases in Latino and Asian populations and the steady state of African and Native American groups (U.S. Bureau of the Census, 1998)

• The growth of multicultural individual and family principles that lend themselves to application of gender issues related to women of color (Ho, 1987; Lum, 1996)

• The development of an alternative knowledge base (social constructionism) that relies on personal narrative experiences of individual women of color and lays the basis for establishing common experience themes (Gergen & McNamee, 1992; Holland, Gallant, & Colosetti, 1994; Radtke & Stam, 1994)

• The recognition of white feminist therapy that racial, ethnic, social class, and related issues need to be addressed along with gender oppression (Greene, 1994a; Kliman, 1994; Kopacsi & Faulkner, 1988)

• The growth of women of color text literature (Comas-Diaz & Greene, 1994) which has made contributions about women in various ethnic groups, intervention frameworks in a feminist context, and special populations of women of color.

Concerns of Women of Color. Gould (1987) points out that there has been a lack of communication between feminist and multicultural theorists regarding "how the elimination of racism will eradicate the effects of sexism on the lives of minority women" (p. 6). Women of color are in double jeopardy, as the objects of both sexist and racist practices, but feminist theorists have not addressed the relationship between sexism in nonwhite cultures and the white racism in which white women have participated. Moreover, feminist theories have not incorporated race, ethnicity, class, and sexual orientation in relation to gender.

Gould (1987) reports that some Third World feminists, uncomfortable with the white feminist movement and aware of the need for white women to educate themselves about racism, look to the development of a multicultural feminist consciousness movement that addresses racism, misogyny, and homophobia and, ultimately, to an international universal women's movement. Such a movement must dispel prejudice and ignorance among women of different cultures about each other, and recognize the value of the family and also the role of women of color as mother and housewife. Many women of color perceive that white middle-class women have glossed over race and class issues, have a power structure that makes pragmatic use of sex and color for personal gain, and have a lack of concern for the well-being of lower-class women. In short, the feminist movement is viewed as racist and classist by many women of color.

In a study of the strains and tensions between African American and white women, Lee See (1989) interviewed ninety-four African American and white women from social service agencies in Philadelphia and Atlanta and Atlanta colleges. On the whole, African American women tended to be critical of the white middle-class character of the women's liberation movement, dating and marriage between African American males and white females, the performance of white women in management positions, and dominant-culture attitudes to strong African American women in the workplace. Lee See concludes that, despite the unresolved antagonism, African American and white women share similar burdens and must strive for common goals.

Greene (1994a) restates the basic difference in perspective. Feminist therapy asserts that social inequity between men and women and the resulting power imbalance are responsible for many of the problems that women face in their lives. Gender-based social inequality and gender oppression have been the rallying cry to unite women in the feminist movement. However, women of color have been reluctant to participate because they regard white middle- and upper-class women as participating in the institutional power and racial oppression of white society. Historically, African American women were pieces of property for labor and slave breeding, whereas white women remained in the home and were elevated to a pedestal of sexual purity and virtue. Likewise, for many African American families, European physical features, especially light skin color, have been used as an indicator of social worth in the dominant society. Greene (1994a) explains:

> These presumptions of similarities and presupposed unity between white women and women of color, under the banner of gender oppression, may often serve to avoid confronting antagonisms between them by obscuring the power differentials in their experiences. Avoiding the examination of race may allow women who benefit from the prevailing power structure to avoid an examination of their own participation in oppression, most specifically, the ways in which white women who are gender-oppressed may engage in oppressive behavior themselves. (p. 337)

Greene's emphatic message is that gender must be balanced with equal emphasis on race, sexual orientation, culture, socioeconomic class, and other forms of oppression. The elevation of these concerns to the same level of legitimacy and attention as gender is the next step for the feminist movement.

Even McGoldrick (1994), a leader in ethnic, family, and feminist therapy, confesses a lack of academic training and personal awareness:

> I have myself only recently become aware of the constraints of class, culture, gender, and race on the structure of who I am. I have been coming to realize that most of us have never been safe, since home in our society has not been a safe place for women, children, or people of color, in light of the pervasiveness of abuse in the form of corporeal punishment of children, child sexual abuse, mistreatment/devaluing of women, and the appalling institutionalized racism of our society. I had no awareness of these issues until a very few years ago. They were, to borrow a phrase from Betty Friedan, issues with "no name"—invisible issues that I only now realize defined the entire construction of relationships in my family, my schooling, and the communities in which I have lived. None of these issues was ever mentioned in my childhood, my adolescence, my college or graduate experience, or in my study of family therapy.*

Regarding racism, McGoldrick confesses:

> I also did not realize that I benefited from the effects of slavery and racism, and do to this day. I

*From "Foreword," by M. McGoldrick. In M. P. Mirkin (Ed.), *Women in Context: Toward a Feminist Reconstruction of Psychotherapy*, xiii–xv. Copyright © 1994 by Guilford Press, New York. Reprinted by permission.

am coming slowly and painfully to realize what it means that we who are white carry around, in Peggy MacIntosh's terms, a kind of "invisible knapsack of privilege" containing special provisions, maps, passports and visas, blank checks, and emergency gear. We cannot see it, but those who do not have one can. I have been trying to think differently about these issues. I am beginning to see the racism in much of my work—when I spoke about couples or families and did not really mean black couples or families; when I spoke about women and did not really include nonwhite women. (p. xv)

A new day must dawn in feminist therapy and related areas of interest. Women of color active as academicians and practitioners, along with concerned and committed feminist therapists, must begin to integrate race, ethnicity, culture, and multicultural diversity in their analysis of gender issues. There are a number of areas for development: the feminist history of women of color, socioeconomic and political issues facing feminists of color, multicultural feminist knowledge theories, and growth development and therapy interventions. These themes are vital arenas for collaboration among those in feminist practice who want to develop a multicultural feminist therapy.

Social-Cultural Issues. Wilkinson (1989) has provided a concise summary of the social-cultural issues facing women of color:

• Their special mental health problems and socioeconomic needs

• The function of gender and race as culturally conditioned variables affecting the judgments of human services professionals

• The tendency of researchers to focus on women with severe emotional disorders, which results in the stereotyping of women of color

• The dynamics between a white male therapist and a nonwhite female client

• Practitioners' tendency to regard African American women as the most frequently focused-on group among women of color

• Psychoanalytic and psychotherapeutic myths about the racial causality of psychopathology

• Stereotypical attitudes, beliefs, and behaviors of the white male therapist

Given this context, multicultural feminism should liberate itself from the deficit pathology model and construct a positive, growth-centered framework that will be helpful to ethnic and gender development. Multicultural feminist research must develop a body of work on culture-general similarities common to ethnic women and culture-specific differences among women within their ethnic groups, on the positive cultural strengths of women, and on multicultural perspectives for development, as well as other related areas.

New Perspectives for Women of Color. Several multicultural feminist theorists and practitioners have articulated new perspectives for women of color. For African American women, Collins (1990) identifies knowledge themes essential to an epistemological foundation of ethnic feminist practice. Her epistemology is centered on struggle and survival. Collins sees a legacy of struggle that unites all African American women through the generations and across economic lines; that is, African American women have continued to struggle for survival and to create conditions in which their families can survive. This shared legacy shapes the consciousness and thought processes of the African American woman: On the one hand, she was never meant to survive; on the other hand, she needed to construct the necessary skills and strategies for survival. Moreover, the African American woman has emerged from the deconstruction of four controlling images:

1. The mammy, who was the cheerful provider of comforts in the homes or businesses of white people

2. The matriarch, who was forced to become head of household and work outside the home to become self-supporting and who was accused of neglecting her children and blamed for their academic failure and subsequent life problems

3. The welfare mother, who is a matriarch without the energy to work outside the home, who passes

on bad values to her children, and whose fertility must be controlled by regulations

4. The jezebel, the sexually uncontrollable woman, whose aggressive sexual appetites explain why she is the victim of sexual assault

African American women must replace such images with accurate positive self-definitions that reflect their creativity and activism. For instance, a study of the African American community reveals networks of women who share child care responsibilities and work and raise children cooperatively, with the hands-on help of male family members.

For Collins (1990), an African American feminist epistemology embraces interpretation of concrete experience on the basis of personal knowledge and subjective wisdom; dialogue as a method for validating knowledge claims; an ethic of caring that acknowledges the uniqueness of each individual and the importance of individual expression (the heart wisdom of each person) and asserts the appropriateness of emotion in cognitive pursuits; and an ethic of personal accountability, where knowledge makers are held accountable for their knowledge claims.

Strengths of Women of Color. The foregoing principles of multicultural epistemology provide guidelines on how feminist theorists and practitioners ought to approach practice with women of color. Without demythologizing pathological stereotypes and identifying cultural and behavioral strengths and sources of personal validation, multicultural feminist knowledge building cannot proceed with its work.

One example of research on the strengths of women of color that derive from their personal, family, and community traits is an exploratory study by Aguilar and Williams (1993) on factors contributing to the success of 164 Latino women and 160 African American women. Aguilar and Williams found that the women defined success in terms of personal and professional accomplishments, hard work, responsible positions, satisfaction with life and work, recognition from others, perseverance in spite of obstacles, acting as good role models, the realization that service has a payback, positive thinking, having choices, pride in

raising children, pride in having made it without help from others, and setting and attaining realistic goals. Significant support systems included their families—particularly their parents, who encouraged them to pursue higher education—and religion, especially faith in God. Cultural strengths were pride in culture, family, and ethnic group identity, responsibility at an early age, religious values, the ability to set goals, hard work, dedication, honesty, coping with racism, and belief in education and God. The women's personal strengths were persistence, determination, hard work, assertiveness, faith in God, the desire to succeed, an optimistic point of view, strong self-esteem and self-motivation, a desire to help and to be role models for other women in their ethnic group, a sense of responsibility and independence, resilience, a sense of service, a love for what they do, inner strengths (belief in themselves and a good feeling about life), family support, and being achievement or goal oriented.

Aguilar and Williams report that religious orientation and parental encouragement to pursue higher education had a more positive impact on African American women than on Latino women, who completed their education after marriage, sacrificed to send brothers to college, and, in some cases, received support from their husband.

Carter et al. (1994) have sought to integrate women's issues into social work curriculum. They cite the need for a paradigm shift that accounts for gender-integrated knowledge; their new paradigm consists of elements from ecological theory and social justice theory associated with self-determination and the historical and organizational factors shaping particular groups. The focus is on the specific experiences of women and the awareness of within-gender variations. Specific themes center on gender stratification, societal oppression and stereotypes, empowerment, and the role of power and conflict. However, further work is required to develop a gender-specific knowledge paradigm that systematically establishes a feminist social work epistemology and moves the field of social work education away from male-oriented theories. Transition toward this knowledge base will require specific historical-structural paradigms.

Kliman (1994) has offered a threefold paradigm to focus attention on gender, class, and race. She proposes a three-dimensional matrix of culture class gender, with one axis for race and ethnicity and another for class; each cell is divided by gender. In this way, the class and race components can be considered along with gender. Kliman is aware that ethnicity and race are often marginalized in family therapy training and writing; they are generally presented as afterthoughts and are not woven into the particulars of a given theory or practice. Likewise, the effects of class position and cultural experience for all social classes and multicultural families are obscured, overlooked, or pathologized. Kliman admits that discussions of race encompass whites as the dominant group and African Americans as the oppressed group, which renders other families of color invisible and ignored; certainly, no distinction is made among the various subgroups of Latino, Asian, and Native Americans and between Christian and non-Christian religions and philosophies.

Kliman acknowledges that gender roles and expectations and the dynamics of patriarchy for oppressed cultural groups are easily misperceived by the dominant white culture. For example, job discrimination against African American men has forced African American women to work more and to be financially less dependent on their men than white women. This adaptation to racism has been cast as the role and function of African American matriarchy. Furthermore, women of color are generally more oppressed on the basis of race than of gender; for them, unlike white women, gender oppression is secondary to institutional racism. Kliman argues that race must be the primary focus, although gender must be factored into the analysis. In the end, she asserts that the multiple lenses of gender × class × race/ethnicity in family life must shape our fundamental understanding and assumptions about gender differences.

People of color and white feminists are aware of the issues that have separated them. The efforts described here are clearly benchmarks for new knowledge theory and framework models in multicultural feminist studies.

Practice with Gays and Lesbians of Color

Social work and gay and lesbian issues have become visible with the Council of Social Work Education (CSWE) Commission on Gay and Lesbian Concerns, the Lesbian/Gay/Bisexual/Transgender Symposium (CSWE) at the Annual Program Meeting, and the *Journal of Gay and Lesbian Social Services*. Up to the early 1970s the *Diagnostic and Statistical Manual of Mental Disorders*, second edition (DSM-II), listed homosexuality as a mental disorder. Clinical diagnosis articulated a clinical pathology of gays and lesbians based on a punitive father and a distant mother. Even DSM-III contained a psychosexual disorder called "Ego-dystonic Homosexuality" that appeared in 1980.

Homosexuality has remained a moral pathology from a biblical and Christian basis. There is a gay and lesbian church movement: the Metropolitan Community Churches. However, among Protestant churches, with the exception of the United Church of Christ, no mainline denominations have ordained gay or lesbian clergy. Gay and lesbian weddings or celebration ceremonies in churches vary from acceptance to controversy in many churches. Church clergy, laity, and the American public require reeducation on the civil rights of this group.

The civil rights of gays and lesbians remain a major concern. There is no federal protection of sexual orientation in the 1964 and 1965 Civil Rights Acts, although state and local ordinances protect the rights of gays and lesbians. The "don't ask; don't tell" policy of the Clinton administration in 1993 gives limited protection to gays and lesbians in the U.S. military. Same-sex marriages, employment protection, health benefits to gay and lesbian partners, and artificial insemination and adoption among gay and lesbian couples are current issues. The civil rights battle for gays and lesbians is being fought in the courts of the United States. The First Amendment guarantees freedom of worship, speech, press, assembly and petition to the government for redress of grievances. The issue of freedom of speech and rights for redress of grievances are paramount in the arguments for gay and lesbian civil rights.

Gay and lesbian people of color are a growing issue of concern, since this population represents a non-visible minority. Greene (1994b) observes that lesbian women of color represent a triple jeopardy. They face racism by the dominant society in general and white lesbians in particular; sexism by their own ethnic culture that denies and rejects lesbian identity, particularly family and ethnic elements of their community; and isolation by the heterosexual and homosexual society. Being a gay and lesbian person of color may be a lonely experience, unless there is linkage and support from other gay and lesbian persons of color, particularly among their ethnic group.

Gay and lesbian persons of color recognize that the family is a source of economic and emotional support. Procreation and the continuity of the family line are important cultural values and motivators. There is particular fear about coming out in the ethnic culture, because cultural values from African, Latino, and Asian society dictate a strong bias against homosexuality and mean certain rejection and exclusion from family. Among Native Americans, however, from a historical perspective, gays and lesbians were seen and accepted as a part of the tribe. They were people who spiritually combined masculine and feminine styles in one person, or so-called "two spirited persons."

Appleby and Anastas (1998) have a helpful chapter, "Culture, Community, and Diversity," in their landmark text, *Not Just a Passing Phase: Social Work with Gay, Lesbian, and Bisexual People*. Under their principles for practice they recommend the following guidelines:

• Assessing community and cultural resources, connections, and involvements must be part of any social work assessment; relevant resources include friends and family members.

• Being lesbian, gay, or bisexual in any racial and ethnic minority social environment can be quite different than for those who identify with the dominant racial and ethnic group; relevant ethnic social systems must be taken into account such as values, religious and folk beliefs, and language and communication channels.

• Psychosocial well-being assesses the individual's ability to perform three fundamental developmental tasks: play, work, and love.

Gay and lesbian persons of color require affirmation from personal, professional, and interpersonal strength perspectives. Social workers who help this target group must keep in mind a number of guidelines. Greene (1994b) cautions:

> Mental health practitioners must make themselves aware of the distinct combinations of stressors and psychological demands impinging on lesbians of color, particularly the potential for isolation, anger, and frustration. Aside from being culturally literate, the practitioner must develop a sense of the unique experience of the client with respect to the importance of their ethnic identity, gender, and sexual orientation and their need to establish priorities in an often confusing and painful maze of loyalties and estrangements. (p. 422)

Aoki (1997) writes about Asian American gays and lesbians:

> Gay and lesbian Asian Americans are entering psychotherapy in increasing numbers. Some seek therapy from openly identified gay or lesbian therapists, whereas others seek out Asian American or other ethnic minority psychotherapists. For others, the issue of sexuality and sexual identity arises in the course of an ongoing psychotherapy relationship. In each case, the psychotherapist is faced with understanding the relevant cultural context and influences affecting the Asian American client and the client's level of progress toward a constructive adaptation to his or her sexuality and, ultimately, with responding in affirmative and culturally specific ways to facilitate this process. (p. 411)

In the process of walking a helpful line the social worker must remember to advocate and ensure social justice for all, to speak out against gender and sexual oppression as a profession and as an individual.

Practice with Children of Color

The publication of *Children of Color* (Gibbs, Huang, & Associates, 1989) focused attention on the unique problems and special needs of ethnically diverse children and adolescents. Gibbs and colleagues presented a conceptual framework consisting of developmental, ecological, and cross-cultural perspectives and highlighting the importance of ethnicity and mental health, individual psychosocial adjustment, family relationships, school adjustment and achievement, relationships with peers in the community, and adaptation to the community. (See Chapter 5 of this text for a treatment of their framework.)

A seminal text, *Transcultural Child Development*, edited by Johnson-Powell, Yamamoto, Wyatt, and Arroyo (1997) has reiterated the importance of child development and the influence of culture on children. Johnson-Powell (1997) observes:

> The United States is now in the midst of large population increases associated with major shifts toward a population composed of more elderly and more likely to be non-White or to belong to a Hispanic minority group. Thus, the experience of American children in the coming decades will increasingly be the experience of culturally diverse minority children in a society where children constitute a decreasing proportion of the dependent population and the elderly are increasing more rapidly than the birth rate. (pp. 28–29)

Furthermore, she reports:

> By 2030, only 50 percent of the children under age 18 will be White, 59 percent of adults 18–64, and 73 percent of the elderly. Thus, in the 21st century, children are more likely than the elderly to be minority group members, and the elderly will be more dependent on minority group working adults for their economic support. The implications for the health and human services as well as education and training provided to today's children and those in future decades are enormous if we are to achieve financial security for all our citizens. Cultural diversity will be the portrait of America's children, and these children must be helped to become part of the mainstream. (p. 29) Yamamoto, Silva, Ferrari, and Nukariya (1997) identify a number of cultural issues affecting children: multiple social and economic stressors affecting families, child rearing, and child

development; the development of moral values and value conflicts between independence and individualism versus interdependence and familism; bilingualism in relation to language versatility versus a stigmatized hindrance; migration and cultural conflict of adjustment to mainstream cultural systems; and racism and a lack of self-respect.

Social work with children of color brings a unique context to this area of practice. It is concerned about the protection and well-being of children in general and children of color in particular because of the social-cultural context. Child welfare policy has been concerned about child protective services, foster care, adoption, and permanency planning. The 1974 Child Abuse Prevention and Treatment Act established the National Center for Child Abuse and Neglect as an integral part of the U.S. Department of Health and Human Services. It also mandated state- and county-level child protective services and established a standard definition of child abuse and neglect, reporting and investigative methods for abuse and neglect, immunity for those reporting suspected injuries to children, and prevention and public education to reduce incidents of abuse and neglect. Recent high-profile and sensational cases involving the death of abused children in various parts of the country have heightened awareness and concern for separating abused children from abusive parents and live-in boyfriends who are addicted to drugs, particularly cocaine and metamphetamines.

The Adoption Assistance and Child Welfare Act of 1980 addressed the issues of reuniting children from abusive and neglected family and home situations with their biological parents, foster care and adoption in their kinship relative system, permanent adoption, and institutional placement with laying the groundwork for emancipation.

However, many ethnically diverse children have difficulty finding adoptive parents and homes. McRoy, Oglesby, and Grape (1997) report:

> The number of children in out-of-home care has increased from about 273,000 in the mid-1980s to almost 500,000 in 1992 (Children's Defense Fund,

1994). The proportion of all children of color in the out-of-home care system is three times their proportion in the nation's population (McKenzie, 1993). For example, in states such as New Jersey, Maryland, Louisiana, and Delaware, over 50 percent of the children in care are African American. Although accurate statistics on children in care needing adoptive placements are unavailable, experts estimate that between 30,000 and 50,000 U.S. children are legally free for adoption (North American Council on Adoptable Children, 1995). About 40 percent of these children are African American; in major urban areas like New York City and Detroit, about 80 percent of the children needing adoptive placement are African American (McKenzie, 1993; Jones, 1993). (p. 86)

The primary reasons for adoption are parental drug abuse, poverty, and increasing reporting of abuse and neglect. Child protection and permanency planning are the foundation of child welfare services and must be understood in working with children of color.

Gleeson, O'Donnell, and Bonecutter (1997) suggest that social workers work within the kinship foster care structure. In a 1993 Chicago study of kinship foster care consisting of ninety-one cases and forty-one caseworkers, they set forth a number of cultural competence and casework skills. They report:

> These findings also suggest that child welfare caseworkers must participate in an ongoing striving for cultural competence that includes efforts to become increasingly self-aware, to value diversity, and to gain knowledge of traditional strengths of the cultures of children with whom they work. Understanding the traditional roles of members of the kinship networks of African American children is one example of the need to strive for cultural competence (Bonecutter and Gleeson, 1996). Results of this study also suggest that caseworkers need to develop skills in facilitating collaboration in decision-making between members of the child's kinship system and the formal child welfare system (Bonecutter and Gleeson, l996). This requires skills in convening relevant members of the kinship net-

work, engaging the kinship network in a plan to ensure the child's safety and well-being, and helping the family develop a permanent plan for the child, and in some cases, facilitating the family's (re)definition of relationships in their family. To facilitate collaborative decision-making, caseworkers must also have adequate knowledge of all permanency options available to the family, such as private guardship, and must be committed to principles of self-determination and family empowerment. (pp. 822–823)

These recommendations involving cultural competence, cultural strengths, collaborative consultation and decision making, institutional and community resources, and family empowerment are common themes in social work practice.

Child development and child welfare policy and legislation are a part of working in a cultural family situation. From a psychosocial child development perspective, Huang (1997) describes a number of developmental assessment issues that are helpful in working with children of color, particularly Asian American adolescents: the *individual-person system*, taking into account the establishment of accurate age, physical appearance conformity to peer group, English and native language fluency, expression or suppression of affect, independent or interdependent interpersonal relations, the degree of anxiety and somatic, sleep, and school disruption complaints, sexuality and family dynamics; ethnocultural assessment pertaining to generational status and level of acculturation, immigration history, and ethnic identification; the *family system*, examining composition and nuclear and extended family, role relationships, patterns of communication, and socioeconomic status; the *school system*, analyzing the racial/ethnic composition, achievement philosophy of the school, patterns of communication with teachers, administrator, and parents, academic performance, and social behavior and integration; and the *peer system* pertaining to the composition of the group, age and gender, degree and types of involvement, and peer values with family and school.

Running through a child development perspective is the importance of self-esteem regarding children of color. Wu and Smith (1997) observe the differences among European, Native, and African American children:

> Empirical studies have also linked the development of self-esteem to the values of the particular cultural group to which individuals belong. For example, Rotenberg and Cranwell (1989) examined the specific attributes that were important to the self-esteem of Native American and European American children. They reported that Native American children, in describing themselves, referred frequently to traditional customs, beliefs, and moral worth, while European American children placed more emphasis on intellectual concerns and formal education. Studies summarized by Smith, Johnson, and Findlay (1994) and Harter (1990) suggested that while the self-esteem of European American children is strongly associated with the attitudes of peers, that of African American children is more influenced by the African American family and community. Further, African American children placed greater value on athletic prowess, musical talent, acting ability, and sexuality than their European American peers. Hence, those activities are salient to the self-esteem of that particular group. (pp. 1–2)

Asian American children tend to be influenced by parental expectation and educational achievement as far as their self-esteem is concerned. House (1997) reports:

> Hsu (1994) found that the self-esteem of Chinese-American university students was significantly correlated with specific parental behaviors and acculturation. Similarly, Tsai (1992) has identified a number of family values related to the achievement of Chinese-American students; those parental influences include an emphasis on hard work and effort, positive attitudes toward education, and respect toward teachers and elders. Finally, other research has shown that those cultural beliefs are similar to attitudes held by Asian parents regarding the value of students' efforts on academic tasks; for example, Chinese parents have been found to instill an attitude of self-improvement in their children that leads to high levels of dedication to their academic work (Chen and Uttal, 1988) and to higher parental expectations for children's achievement in mathematics (Stevenson et al., 1990). (pp. 105–106)

In sum, ethnic children of color tended to be influenced by parental and community structures.

Of all the children of color, African American children, particularly males, must cope with racial and situational barriers. In response to Jensen's (1960) study on African American IQ, Jenkins and Guidubaldi (1997) conducted a national study of 613 European American and 52 African American children from grades 1, 3, and 5. They found that divorce and gender were significant factors in racial differences in IQ scores. They report:

> In the absence of a positive male role model, a strong sense of identity may be particularly difficult to achieve given the highly publicized negative image of the African-American male in American society. This may lead to the gradual devaluing of academic and behavioral standards for conduct, in favor of other behaviors, to gain a sense of acceptance and personal worth from peer groups.
>
> As was found for girls in general, African-American females from divorced families are less adversely affected by divorce than African-American males. An alternative explanation for these academic effects may lie within the supportive structure of the educational system. African-American males may feel more distanced from the educational environment than the African-American female, thus, lacking an opportunity to strengthen their acquired knowledge and develop strong and more flexible problem solving skills. School strategies should be sought to supportively reach and stabilize the African-American male child experiencing family disruption. (p. 157)

Social workers who assist children of color must take into account an array of psychosocial factors that impact these clients. We must study and assess the unique characteristics of children of color that are emerging in the literature and the daily lives of their families.

Practice with the Racially/Ethnically Mixed

Racially/ethnically mixed persons of color literature is emerging in terms of recognizing the growing reality of interracial marriages and children (Crohn, 1995; Root, 1992, 1996; Rosenblatt, Karis, & Powell, 1995). Oriti, Bibb, and Mahboubi (1996) recommend a number of guiding principles for working with racially/ethnically mixed families:

• Examine your knowledge and beliefs about what race and ethnicity mean to you in terms of how they shape how you interact with others and with whom you interact publicly and privately in your family regarding race, ethnicity, class, and sexual orientation.

• Be open to people with different political positions regarding racial/ethnic issues in terms of monoracial/ethnic identity and intolerance for bi- or multiracial union.

• Help people see that racially/ethnically mixed people's conflict around identity is a reaction to the political hierarchy and oppression of our culture and the internalization of prejudiced thinking that frames identity conflicts.

• Help multiracial/ethnic families give voice to the traditions, rituals, political aspirations, and aesthetics that make up their legacy as well as the fear and anger that biracial/ethnic children may experience.

• Question the system—not the individual—to determine whether there is equal understanding by the family, school, workplace, and community as well as the management of the inequities of the social system.

• Be patient and persistent with yourself and your clients to deal with the effect of oppression based on race/ethnicity on our patterns of thought and behavior.

At the same time, social workers must recognize the traditional and historical separation of European, African, Asian, Latino, and Native Americans in which state laws were passed forbidding intermarriage between European and non-European Americans. Preservation of ethnic, racial, and cultural groupings is strongly associated with keeping ethnic group and family identity intact for succeeding generations of the family line. The majority of Americans still adhere to marriage within their broad (and in many cases, specific) ethnic groups, whereas a growing number of individuals have crossed racial/ethnic boundaries and intermarried across major racial groupings.

Practice with Older Persons of Color

Age has become a critical factor in understanding our life and the lives of others. Settersten (1997) observes:

> In sum, most investigators seem to assert that citizens of modern, industrialized nations are now (and have become increasingly) conscious of age as a core dimension of social life, and that this is true of both men and women alike. At some level, this is ironic, given that most modern societies, especially the United States, would like to think that they have made great strides in battling ageism and in making age irrelevant (Kertzer, 1989). At the heart of most research on the life course is also an implicit assumption that age is a natural part of the way we understand ourselves, others, and the world around us, and with which we present and experience the life course. (p. 261)

In most cultures of people of color, the elderly are not devalued because of their age but rather are respected and honored for their wisdom, maturity, and life experiences. Older persons of color are an integral part of their families and ethnic society.

According to the United Nations Conference on Human Settlements-Habitat (1993), on a worldwide basis, one million persons a month reach the age of sixty. By the year 2025, 1.2 billion will be age sixty and over. In the United States one of every eight Americans (33.2 million) was age sixty-five or older in 1994, and by the year 2050, the older population will reach eighty million, when one of every five Americans will reach age sixty-five (U.S. Census Bureau, 1995). In 1994, one of ten elderly was nonwhite; by 2050, this figure will reach two of ten (U.S. Census Bureau, 1995).

Older persons universally are confronted with at least four major areas of concern: (l) housing considerations, where there is home ownership or affordable housing in a family setting rather than living alone in isolation; (2) health care coverage, where there is adequate care for primary and extended care needs through Medicare, Medicaid, private insurance, and other means; (3) economic considerations, where adequate pension, life savings, Social Security, Supplemental Security Income, and other means are available to provide economic security; and (4) social considerations, where a social network of family, friends, neighbors, church, and community makes available meaningful relationships.

To meet these challenges, Butler (1996) focuses on several areas of new responsibilities for society and the older person in the new century:

The first overall response to population ageing must be dominated by a *new vision* of the responsibility of one person to another and a restoration of the somewhat frayed and misunderstood intergenerational compact of responsibilities of children to their parents and of parents to their children. This moves us away somewhat from the intense and important 20th-century preoccupation with the welfare state, and suggests the wisdom of building a broader base to sustain social protections. (p. 24)

We must also implement *productive ageing*—people live longer and therefore they must work longer. In order to have a full participation society and avoid both perceived and actual marginality, there should be job sharing, shorter work weeks, and more vacations. These measures can help create and assure more opportunities for people to work. People need to have a sense of purpose. (p. 28)

We need genuine reforms within the health enterprise. For example, we need a new kind of health practitioner school to replace conventional medical schools in order to create a new kind of *holistic health practitioner system*. Presently in the United States, medical training is geared to high technology, acute care medicine. We need doctors, nurses, social workers *and all other health workers* to see patients in nursing homes, in the community, and at home as well as to provide hospice service. (p. 29)

Butler's remarks reinforced the notion of ethnic caring for the older by family members, the value of meaningful work in the work place and ethnic community, and community health efforts that draw on psychosocial health care resources and personnel. Here social work and the older person of color are relevant partners.

McNeely and Colen (1983) edited a landmark text on social work and older persons of color called *Aging in Minority Groups*. They covered a number of interesting areas related to older persons of color such as social research and the minority aged involving life span and social integration; theoretical perspectives on aging and the minority aged including disengagement, activity, character development, and related historical perspectives involving discrimination and coping structures; selected historical events (for example, legislative acts affecting the life of an ethnic group); the demography of minority aging; aging in a cultural context; and selected social problems, including housing, crime, health and mental health, employment and income maintenance, local decision making and political involvement, and service delivery. Although these topics could be dealt with in depth, the focus on this section of older persons of color is on psychosocial/cultural dimensions.

In contrast to dominant societal values on individualism, youth and glamour, and nuclear family autonomy, ethnic families of color have been viewed as close-knit social units from which its members derived support, security, and a means for meeting their needs. Family may range from nuclear and extended blood and fictive relatives, church as a caring family unit, to the ethnic family association who are bound together by geographic vicinity in the country of origin or by the same surname. For example, older persons of color are cared for according to the family composition of the particular culture. Among African Americans, the elderly grandparents may care for their grandchildren and in turn be cared for by working sons and daughters who are the parents of the children. African American churches may be responsible for a selected group of their elderly in the community and may treat them as surrogate grandparents. Latino families may house grandparents in or near their homes and may look out for their welfare, stopping by daily to check on them, provide them food, and meet their needs. Asian families have been traditionally influenced by the concept of filial piety that venerates the older person. China has been described as a "gerontocracy" because of the position of the elderly in the family. Professors at Peking University, according to my friend and colleague, Dr. Anthony C. Yu of the University of Chicago on his trip to China, do not retire but are kept on and number the same size as the student body. The value of retaining wisdom and providing meaningful work for these venerated scholars and teachers is a Chinese societal value. Among Native Americans the elders of the tribe and village were exalted in the tribal council for their individual and collective wisdom and experiences.

Older persons of color are increasingly confronted with problems of poverty, isolation, language and communication difficulties, racial discrimination, poor housing, poor health, lack of transportation, and general dependency as the aging process increases and as their family and friends shrink because of time and distance. Their children may not live in the same neighborhood or city or may be unable to care for them owing to work responsibilities during the week. Brief care or weekend visits may be the only means of providing a lifeline. In many instances elderly persons of color may rely solely on friends, neighbors, ministers and church members, or social workers. Ethnic senior activity centers, adult day care centers with a health component, telephone reassurance programs with home visitation, and related community senior extender services are the answers. In major cities with extensive ethnic populations, ethnic agencies can mount their own programs for their elderly, offering programs, food, and staff who are ethnically oriented and responsive to particular cultural needs.

In the Asian American communities on the West Coast, several social service models meet the needs of the older person. In Los Angeles, Keiro is a convalescent care center primarily for Japanese Americans that has been duplicated for Asian Americans in nursing home facilities in Seattle and Sacramento. In San Francisco, Self-Help for the Elderly in Chinatown has an indigenous philosophy of service delivery to the elderly and provides information dissemination, employment, welfare, health, housing intake referral and follow-up, nutrition, and consumer advisement programs. It serves both Chinese and non-Chinese elderly and has bridged traditional family association services and public and private social services. On Lok Center, a geriatric day health program founded in 1973, serves several community groups (primarily Chinese, Filipino, and Italian) in San Francisco. It offers social, financial, legal, recreational, restorative, residential care, and referral. Its philosophy is that individuals should remain in the community as long as they wish and as long as it is medically feasible. The individual, not community service providers, should have the freedom of choice. People should be helped to help themselves.

Social work and ethnically diverse gerontology should come together as we begin a new century to lay out a strategic plan to meet the needs of a growing elderly population among people of color. Social work gerontological education should provide curriculum content, social and ethnically based research, and relevant and helpful publications to social work educators, students, and older persons of color clients. There should be an evaluation of existing services for older persons of color and social planning efforts to anticipate geriatric problems of the next ten years. Public transportation networks, ethnic health care workers, special bilingual and bicultural programs, extended care coverage as a natural outgrowth of Medicare and Medicaid, and related areas of progress must be addressed now. Social casework services must focus on restoring and maintaining family solidarity and fostering communication and understanding among the different generations. These are time-honored cultural and ethnic family values that are easily lost by acculturation and the stress of modern urban work and home demands. Increasingly home health care for the elderly of color must involve the family, the provider, and the surrounding community in efforts to keep the elderly independent in their own living environment.

CONCLUSION

This chapter has described how people of color have interacted with the dominant society from a historical perspective. Social welfare arose from religious and secular humanism and the social needs of the poor and disabled. However, it tended to exclude people of color, particularly African Americans, as a result of the racism and segregation that pervaded white society. People of color suffered alienation, oppression, and exploitation. The early history of social welfare reveals a failure to address the effects of racial prejudice. As public opinion and federal legislation moved toward civil rights, the social work profession developed a commitment to people of color. As a profession, it has served and advocated multicultural causes and clients during the past three decades. Particular attention has been given to how to practice with new arrivals, women of color, gays and lesbians of color, children of color, and older persons of color. Social workers must sensitize the American public to social justice and be effective practitioners with clients from all cultures.

In subsequent chapters, we will explore the values and knowledge base of people of color and formulate a culturally diverse practice process model. This particular framework details the stages of contact, problem identification, assessment, intervention, and termination. Multicultural practice principles and case studies appear throughout. Social workers will, I hope, be stimulated to apply these perspectives to their diverse clientele.

REFERENCES

Aguilar, M. A., & Williams, L. P. (1993). Factors contributing to the success and achievements of minority women. *Affilia, 8*(4), 410–424.

Almquist, E. M. (1984). *Women: A feminist perspective.* Palo Alto, CA: Mayfield.

American Psychiatric Association. (1968). *Diagnostic and statistical manual of mental disorders* (2nd ed.). Washington, DC: Author.

American Psychiatric Association. (1980). *Diagnostic and statistical manual of mental disorders* (3rd ed.). Washington, DC: Author.

Aoki, B. K. (1997). Gay and lesbian Asian Americans in psychotherapy. In E. Lee (Ed.), *Working with Asian Americans: A guide for clinicians* (pp. 411–419). New York: Guilford.

Appleby, G. A., & Anastas, J. W. (1998). *Not just a passing phase: Social work with gay, lesbian, and bisexual people.* New York: Columbia University Press.

Bonecutter, F. J., & Gleeson, J. P. (1996). *Achieving permanency for children in kinship foster care: A training manual.* Chicago: Jane Addams College of Social Work and the Jane Addams Center for Social Policy and Research, University of Illinois at Chicago.

Bryson, V. (1992). *Feminist political theory: An introduction.* New York: Paragon House.

Butler, R. N. (1996). Global ageing: Challenges and opportunities of the next century. *Ageing International, 23*(1), 12–32.

Carter, C., Coudrouglou, A., Figueira-McDonough, J., Lie, G. Y., MacEachron, A. E., Netting, F. E., Nichols-Casebolt, A., Nichols, A. W., & Risley-Curtiss, C. (1994). Integrating women's issues in the social work curriculum: A proposal. *Journal of Social Work Education, 30*(2), 200–216.

Chen, C., & Uttal, D. H. (1988). Cultural values, parents' beliefs, and children's achievement in the United States and China. *Human Development, 31,* 351–358.

Children's Defense Fund. (1996). *The state of America's children yearbook.* Washington, DC: Author.

Collier, J. (1956). The United States Indian. In J. B. Gittler (Ed.), *Understanding minority groups* (pp. 34–36). New York: Wiley.

Collins, P. H. (1990). *Black feminist thought.* Boston: Unwin Hyman.

Commission, Committee, and Task Force Reports. (1984). New York: Council on Social Work Education.

Comas-Diaz, L., & Greene, B. (Eds.). (1994). *Women of color: Integrating ethnic and gender identities in psychotherapy.* New York: Guilford.

Commission on Accreditation, Council on Social Work Education. (1987). *Handbook of accreditation standards and procedures.* Washington, DC: Council on Social Work Education.

Commission on Accreditation, Council on Social Work Education. (1992). *Handbook of accreditation standards and procedures.* Arlington, VA: Council on Social Work Education.

Crohn, J. (1995). *Mixed matches.* New York: Fawcett Columbine.

Davis, A. Y. (1983). *Women, race, and class.* New York: Random House.

Davis, A. Y. (1989). *Women, culture, and politics.* New York: Random House.

Federico, R. C. (1980). *The social welfare institution: An introduction.* Lexington, MA: Heath.

Garvin, C. D., & Cox, F. M. (1979). A history of community organizing since the Civil War, with special reference to oppressed communities. In F. M. Cox, J. L. Erlich, J. Rothman, & J. E. Tropman (Eds.), *Strategies of community organization* (pp. 45–75). Itasca, IL: Peacock.

Gergen, K. J., & McNamee, S. (1992). *Social constructionism in therapeutic process.* London: Sage.

Gibbs, J. T., Huang, L. N., & Associates (1989). *Children of color: Psychological interventions with minority youth.* San Francisco: Jossey-Bass.

Gleeson, J. P., O'Donnell, J., & Bonecutter, F. J. (1997). Understanding the complexity of practice in kinship foster care. *Child Welfare, 76*(6), 801–826.

Gonzalez, R. (1981). Chicanas in Mexican immigrant families: 1920–1940. In J. Jensen & L. Scharf (Eds.), *Decades of discontent: The woman's movement 1920–1940.* Westport, CT: Greenwood.

Gould, K. H. (1987). Feminist principles and minority concerns: Contributions, problems, and solutions. *Affilia, 2*(3), 6–19.

Greene, B. (1994a). Diversity and difference: Race and feminist psychotherapy. In M. P. Mirkin (Ed.), *Women in context: Toward a feminist reconstruction of psychotherapy* (pp. 333–351). New York: Guilford.

Greene, B. (1994b). Lesbian women of color: Triple jeopardy. In L. Comas-Diaz & B. Greene (Eds.), *Women of color: Integrating ethnic and gender identities in psychotherapy* (pp. 389–427). New York: Guilford.

Harter, S. (1990). Self and identity development. In S. S. Feldman & G. R. Elliot (Eds.), *At the threshold: The developing adolescent* (pp. 352–387). Cambridge, MA: Harvard University Press.

Ho, M. K. (1987). *Family therapy with ethnic minorities.* Newbury Park, CA: Sage.

Holland, T. P., Gallant, J. P., & Colosetti, S. (1994). Assessment of teaching a constructivist approach to social work practice. *Arete, 18*, 45–60.

House, J. D. (1997). The relationship between self-beliefs, academic background, and achievement of adolescent Asian-American students. *Child Study Journal, 27*(2), 95–110.

Howard, J. R. (Ed.). (1970). *Awakening minorities: American Indians, Mexican Americans, Puerto Ricans.* New Brunswick, NJ: Transaction.

Hsu, E. A. (1994). *Parental authority and its impact on the self-esteem of Chinese American college students.* Unpublished doctoral dissertation, California School of Professional Psychology–Berkeley/Alameda.

Huang, L. N. (1997). Asian American adolescents. In E. Lee (Ed.), *Working with Asian Americans: A guide for clinicians* (pp. 175–195). New York: Guilford.

Jenkins, J. E., & Guidubaldi, J. (1997). The nature-nurture controversy revisited: Divorce and gender as factors in children's racial group differences. *Child Study Journal, 27*(2), 145–160.

Jensen, A. R. (1960). How much can we boost IQ and scholarship achievement? *Harvard Educational Review, 35*(1), 1–123.

Johnson-Powell, G. (1997). A portrait of America's children: Social, cultural, and historical context. In G. Johnson-Powell, J. Yamamoto, G. E. Wyatt, & W. Arroyo (Eds.), *Transcultural child development: Psychological assessment and treatment* (pp. 3–33). New York: Wiley.

Johnson-Powell, G., Yamamoto, J., Wyatt, G. E., & Arroyo, W. (Eds.). (1997). *Transcultural child development: Psychological assessment and treatment.* New York: Wiley.

Jones, C. (1993, October 24). Role of race in adoptions: Old debate is being reborn. *New York Times,* p. 1.

Kertzer, D. I. (1989). Age structuring in comparative and historical perspective. In D. I. Kertzer & K. W. Schaie (Eds.), *Age structuring in comparative and historical perspective* (pp. 19–61). Hillsdale, NJ: Erlbaum.

Kliman, J. (1994). The interweaving of gender, class, and race in family therapy. In M. P. Mirkin (Ed.), *Women in context: Toward a feminist reconstruction of psychotherapy* (pp. 25–47). New York: Guilford.

Kopacsi, R., & Faulkner, A. O. (1988). The powers that might be: The unity of white and black feminist. *Affilia, 3*(3), 33–50.

Lee See, L. A. (1989). Tension between black women and white women: A study. *Affilia, 4*(2), 31–45.

Longres, J. F. (1990). *Human behavior in the social environment.* Itasca, IL: Peacock.

Lum, D. (1996). *Social work practice and people of color: A process-stage approach* (3rd ed.). Pacific Grove, CA: Brooks/Cole.

MacEachron, A. E., Gustavsson, N. S., Cross, S., & Lewis, A. (1996). The effectiveness of the Indian Child Welfare Act of 1978. *Social Service Review, 70*(3), 451–463.

McGoldrick, M. (1994). Foreword. In M. P. Mirkin (Ed.), *Women in context: Toward a feminist reconstruction of psychotherapy* (pp. xiii–xv). New York: Guilford.

McKenzie, J. (1993, Spring). Adoption of children with special needs. In I. Schulman (Ed.), *The future of children* (vol. 3, no. 1, pp. 62–76). Los Altos, CA: David and Lucile Packard Foundation.

McNeely, R. L., & Colen, J. L. (Eds.). (1983). *Aging in minority groups.* Beverly Hills, CA: Sage.

McRoy, R. G., Oglesby, Z., & Grape, H. (1997). Achieving same-race adoptive placements for African American children: Culturally sensitive practice approaches. *Child Welfare, 76*(1), 85–104.

Mehr, J. (1980). *Human services: Concepts and intervention strategies.* Boston: Allyn & Bacon.

Meier, M. S., & Rivera, F. (1972). *The Chicanos: A history of Mexican Americans.* New York: Hill & Wang.

North American Council on Adoptable Children. (1995, Summer). Multiethnic Placement Act policy guidelines issued. *Adoptalk,* pp. 2–3.

Oriti, B., Bibb, A., & Mahboubi, J. (1996). Family-centered practice with racially/ethnically mixed families. *Families in Society, 77*(9), 573–582.

Padilla, Y. C. (1997). Immigrant policy: Issues for social work practice. *Journal of Social Work, 42*(6), 595–606.

Portes, A., & Rumbaut, R. G. (1990). *Immigrant America: A portrait.* Berkeley: University of California Press.

Radtke, A. L., & Stam, A. J. (Eds.). (1994). *Power/gender: Social relations in theory and practice.* Thousand Oaks, CA: Sage.

Renzetti, C. M., & Curran, P. J. (1995). *Women, men, and society.* Boston: Allyn & Bacon.

Root, M. M. P. (1992). *Racially mixed people in America.* Newbury Park, CA: Sage.

Root, M. M. P. (Ed.). (1996). *The multicultural experience.* Thousand Oaks, CA: Sage.

Rose, P. I. (1990). *They and we: Racial and ethnic relations in the United States.* New York: McGraw-Hill.

Rosenblatt, P. C., Karis, T. A., & Powell, R. D. (1995). *Multiracial couples.* Thousand Oaks, CA: Sage.

Rotenberg, K. J., & Cranwell, F. R. (1989). Self-concept in American Indian and White children: A cross-cultural comparison. *Journal of Cross-Cultural Psychology, 20*(1), 39–53.

Settersten, R. A., Jr. (1997). The salience of age in the life course. *Human Development, 40,* 257–281.

Shinto, W. M. (1977). *Colorful minorities and the white majority: A subjective analysis* (UHME Monograph Series No. 1).

Smith, D. E., Johnson, M. E., & Findlay, A. J. (1994). Pregnancy status, self-esteem, and ethnicity: Some relationships in a sample of adolescents. *Family and Consumer Science Research Journal, 23*(2), 183–197.

Spicer, E. H. (1980). American Indians. In S. Thernstrom (Ed.), *Harvard encyclopedia of American ethnic groups* (p. 58). Cambridge, MA: Belknap.

Stanton, E. C., Anthony, S. B., & Gage, M. J. (1881). *History of woman suffrage: I. 1848–1861.* New York: Fowler & Wells.

Stevenson, H. W., Lee, S. Y., Chen, C., Lummis, M., Stigler, J., Fan, L., & Ge, F. (1990). Mathematics achievement of children in China and the United States. *Child Development, 61,* 1053–1066.

Takaki, R. (Ed.). (1987). *From different shores: Perspectives on race and ethnicity in America.* New York: Oxford University Press.

Taylor, T. W. (1972). *The states and their Indian citizens.* Washington, DC: U.S. Department of the Interior, Bureau of Indian Affairs.

Terrelonge, P. (1984). Feminist consciousness and black women. In J. Freemen (Ed.), *Women: A feminist perspective* (pp. 557–567). Palo Alto, CA: Mayfield.

Tsai, D. (1992). *Family impact on high achieving Chinese-American students: A qualitative analysis.* Unpublished doctoral dissertation, University of Connecticut, Storrs.

United Nations Conference on Human Settlements-Habitat. (1993). *Improving the quality of life of the elderly and disabled people in human settlements, Nairobi.* Nairobi: United Nations.

U.S. Bureau of the Census. (1995). Sixty-five plus in the United States. On-line: http://www.census.gov/socdemo/agebrief.html

U.S. Bureau of the Census. (1998). *Statistical abstract of the United States 1998: The National Data Book* (p. 31). Washington, DC: U.S. Department of Commerce, Economics, and Statistics Administration.

Wilkinson, D. Y. (1989). Minority women: Social-cultural issues. In M. McGoldrick, C. M. Anderson, & F. Walsh (Eds.), *Women in families: A framework for family therapy* (pp. 285–304). New York: Norton.

Wu, Y. J., & Smith, D. E. (1997). Self-esteem of Taiwanese children. *Child Study Journal, 27*(1), 1–19.

Yamamoto, J., Silva, J. A., Ferrari, M., & Nukariya, K. (1997). Culture and psychopathology. In G. Johnson-Powell, J. Yamamoto, G. E. Wyatt, & W. Arroyo (Eds.), *Transcultural child development: Psychological assessment and treatment* (pp. 34–57). New York: Wiley.

CHAPTER 3

Culturally Diverse Values

The perspectives on culturally diverse social work practice and various people of color groups presented in the previous chapters require an understanding of social work values and ethics and the unique values of ethnic people of color cultures. *Values* influence how the client and social work practitioner formulate and interpret social problems. *Ethics* determines how values are implemented in choices and the ensuing behavior. However, social work values and ethics must connect and mesh with the cultural value system of the client of color to be meaningful to both the client and the worker.

As a professional discipline, social work offers a value perspective and a code of ethics that advocate the social well-being of persons. But do social work's beliefs and ethical code speak to culturally diverse values and ethical perspectives? Professions have value preferences that give purpose, meaning, and direction to professional workers. Hepworth, Rooney, and Larsen (1997) point out that professional values do not exist apart from societal values. Professions champion selected societal values, and society gives professions legal, legislative, and program sanction and recognition. A profession tends to serve as society's conscience for particular values.

At its worst, social work has been identified with the dominant society and criticized as a social control agent against elements that endanger the institutional status quo. At its best, it embraces values and ethics that reflect the moral good of a society committed to service, provision, and advocacy for the poor and oppressed. Social workers must be aware of societal influences on the values and ethics of their work. A middle-class social worker and a ghetto resident may respond to different physical, economic, and cultural realities. This chapter examines culturally diverse values and knowledge bases, as well as traditional social work values.

VALUE CRITERIA

Social Work Values

According to Rokeach (1973), a *value* is a belief that a particular mode of conduct or end state is preferable to an opposite or converse one. *Professional values* refer to vested beliefs about people, preferred goals for people, means of achieving those goals, and conditions of life. They represent selected ideals as to how the world should be and how people should normally act (Hepworth et al., 1997). Compton and Galaway (1989) list three social work values: respect for the dignity and uniqueness of the individual, client self-determination, and legal authority and self-determination. Northen (1982) identifies the values of the individual's inherent worth and dignity and mutual responsibility or interdependence for survival and need fulfillment. The value ideology of social work is *humanistic*, in that it prioritizes the client's welfare and protection and the client's own participation in the helping process; *scientific*, in that it prefers objectivity, factual evidence, and rational practitioners' judgments and actions; and *democratic*, in that it governs relationships with people by principles of reciprocal rights and obligations and the welfare of the individual, group, and society.

Hepworth et al. (1997) stress the unique dignity, worth, and individuality of every person and mutual participation, acceptance, confidentiality, honesty, and responsible handling of conflict; the individual's right to make independent decisions and active participation in the helping process; assisting the client to obtain needed resources; humane social institutions responsive to human needs; and respect for and acceptance of the unique characteristics of diverse populations. The emphasis on self-determination and individuality highlights the tension between the rights of the individual and the demands of society.

Keith-Lucas (1971) contrasts the period of individual rights in the 1950s with the focus on social and psychological adaptation of the client in the 1960s. As social work moved into the 1970s, 1980s, and 1990s, it found that it had to adapt its values to culturally diverse clients and groups. The 1997 National Association of Social Workers Code of Ethics reflects several culturally competent and related values in its tenets. These statements are long overdue.

Social work values are rooted in Judeo-Christian principles that emphasize justice, equality, and concern for others. Addams (1907) speaks of love and justice as regulators of human relations. She refers to the practical difficulties confronting immigrant groups who settled in the ghettos and to the principles of love and justice as the forces motivating social work. Addams also alludes to Judeo-Christian beliefs in the integral worth of a person and in responsibility for one's neighbor. In Christianity, love possesses qualities of devotion, loyalty, and social responsibility. Justice relates to actions that strengthen relationships in society. Social work applies love through the expression of empathy, genuineness, warmth, and acceptance of

the individual. Justice is demonstrated through social equality, rights, and such responsibilities as access to economic opportunities and education. Justice is the fulfillment of reciprocal expectations of fairness (Kent & Tse, 1980). Regarding the theme of social justice and human rights, Clark (1988) states, "Social justice is the end that social work seeks, and social justice is the chance for peace. There is no other basis on which social stability can or ought to rest" (p. 3). Thus, Clark links social justice, social work, and social stability and seems to challenge the profession to work toward these universal goals.

Social work values reflect humanistic and democratic concepts of freedom, individuality, and social concern. These precepts are implemented in an ethical code that governs professional social work. The following section examines relevant components of the National Association of Social Workers (NASW) Code of Ethics to illustrate how social work values are translated into standards of conduct.

Social Work Code of Ethics

The 1997 NASW Code of Ethics sets personal and professional standards of behavior for its members. It specifies rules of conduct for social workers in relationship to clients, practice settings, professionals, and the broader society. Hepworth et al. (1997) point out that a code of ethics has the following formal functions:

1. Accountability of the profession to society, consumers, and practitioners
2. Regulations to safeguard the professional behavior of members
3. Competent and responsible membership practices
4. Protection of the public from unscrupulous and incompetent practitioners

Professional ethics involves translating values into a standard of practice that governs individual and group character, actions, and ends.

Principles of the NASW Code. The 1997 NASW Code of Ethics establishes six values and ethical principles that permeate the ethical standards and their resulting responsibilities:

- The value of service and the ethical principle of the social worker's primary goal of helping people in need and addressing social problems
- The value of social justice and the ethical principle of the social work challenge of social injustice
- The value of the dignity and worth of the person and the ethical principle of the social work respect of the inherent dignity and worth of the person
- The value of the importance of human relationships and the ethical principle of the social work recognition of the central importance of human relationships
- The value of integrity and the ethical principle of social work behavior in a trustworthy manner
- The value of competence and the ethical principle of social work practice in competence and the enhancement of professional expertise

Social workers have ethical responsibilities to clients in a number of areas: commitment to the well-being of clients; respect for client self-determination; provision of services based on informed consent; competence based on education, training, license and certification, and consultation and supervision; development of cultural competence and understanding of diversity; avoiding conflicts of interest; respecting client privacy and practicing confidentiality; providing reasonable access of their own records to clients; no sexual relationships, physical contact, and sexual harassment with clients, their relatives, or acquaintances; no derogatory language; fair, reasonable, and commensurate payment for services; safeguarding of the interests and rights of clients who lack decision-making capacity; and reasonable and appropriate termination of services.

Social workers have ethical responsibilities to colleagues in terms of respect and the avoidance of unwarranted negative criticism; confidentiality of information shared by colleagues; interdisciplinary collaboration on clients; nonexploitation of disputes involving colleagues; collegial consultation in the best interest of clients; referral for services; no sexual relationships with or sexual harassment of colleagues, supervisees, students, or trainees; consultation about the impairment and incompetence of colleagues; and appropriate action over unethical conduct of colleagues.

Social workers have ethical responsibilities in practice settings to provide and engage in supervision and consultation; relevant education and training as field instructors for students; fair and considerate performance evaluation of others; accurate, sufficient, and timely client records; accurate billing practices; clear and preparatory client transfer; administrative advocacy for adequate and available resources, allocation procedures, and ethical work environment; adequate continuing education and staff development; commitments to employers for improved agency policies and procedures, ethical dealings, nondiscrimination, fair personnel practices, diligent use of resources; and ethical settlement of labor-management disputes.

Social workers have ethical responsibilities as professionals to become and remain competent in professional practice and performance of professional functions; to practice nondiscrimination; to separate private conduct from professional responsibilities; to avoid dishonesty, fraud, and deception; to disallow impairment to interfere with professional judgment and performance; to avoid misrepresentation and uninvited solicitation of potential clients or testimonial endorsements; and to acknowledge credit for their own work and the work of others.

Social workers have ethical responsibilities to the social work profession to maintain and promote integrity and high standards and to monitor and evaluate policies and programs through research. Finally, there are ethical responsibilities to the broader society to promote the general welfare of society, to participate in the public shaping of policies and institutions, to provide professional services in public emergencies, and to engage in social and political action.

Implications for Culturally Diverse Practice. The NASW Code of Ethics has implications for culturally diverse clients. Under social workers' ethical responsibilities to clients, section 1.05, "Cultural Competence and Diversity," addresses the understanding of culture, a cultural knowledge base, and education on social diversity and oppression.

It asks social workers to understand culture and its function in human behavior and society and takes a strengths perspective on culture. It advocates a knowledge base of client cultures and the demonstration of competent service provision that is sensitive to client cultures and to people and cultural differences. It mandates education about social diversity and oppression regarding race, ethnicity, national origin, color, sex, sexual orientation, age, marital status, political belief, religion, and mental or physical disability.

CULTURAL VALUES

Social work has emphasized the dignity and uniqueness of the individual, self-determination of the client, and accessibility of resources. These values tend toward a high regard for persons and for individual rights and freedom. They form the basis for workers' relationship to clients in practice situations. In contrast, people of color espouse collective values, such as family interdependence and obligation, metaphysical harmony in nature or religion, and ethnic group identity.

Values are not either/or propositions. A person's belief system might include values that seem conflicting. For example, a person can affirm individual freedom of choice and yet believe in the collective-value obligation to his or her family. In some situations, one value may have higher priority than another. The hierarchy of values may be different for different ethnic groups, families, and individuals. Moreover, people of color may be bicultural, in the sense that they endorse values held by the majority society as well as those considered important by their own group. The issue for these persons may be under what circumstances the dominant or group values will prevail. For example, a young adult may assert his or her freedom to socialize with and date individuals of many races, with the object of experiencing many different kinds of people. However, the young person's collective family obligation in many cultures is to marry a person of the same race; the marriage might be arranged by both sets of parents or by a professional matchmaker. In honoring that obligation, the individual accepts the primacy of collective values—namely, to marry a person of the same race and to preserve the family name and ethnic identity.

Although social work values are oriented toward client rights, social work should address and incorporate the collective values of other cultures. A culturally diverse value base for social work implies the establishment of social policies, programs, and procedures that emphasize family unification, recognition of the leadership of elders and parents, and mutual responsibility among family members. Arising from family values is a respect for religious institutions and spiritual practices. African American and Latino communities have tended toward Protestant and Catholic Christianity within their cultural adaptations. Asian Americans participate in Christian and Buddhist churches and are aware of the moral ethic of family honor. Native Americans have rediscovered spiritual values in native rituals.

Longclaws (1994) offers insight into Native American approaches to healing in his account of practices of the Anishinabe (Ojibway-Saulteaux tribe). These holistic practices draw on the ecological and medicine wheel models, as Longclaws explains in Cultural Study 3-1.

CULTURAL STUDY 3-1

Anishinabe Healing Principles and Values

Anishinabe healing principles recognize the inherent rights of the individual but simultaneously believe in the interconnectedness of all so that the healing of the individual is necessary not only for the person but for family and clan. Holistic values, with ceremonial supports, contribute balance to the spiritual dimensions of life. The Anishinabe experts base their qualifications on life experience and giftedness. The key is to respect the family and clan in order to establish a relationship so that reciprocity can occur. Reciprocity is necessary for the person to become centered so that balance and harmony can be restored both to the person and to those affected, such as family and clan, thereby strengthening relationships within the environment.

Anishinabe revere age, believing that elders have gained the wisdom to understand the family's reality and can use the dynamics of that reality to guide people to healthier lives. Therefore, elders serve as mentors in guiding unhealthy families beyond their trapped reality. This guidance, provided within the medicine-wheel framework, suggests that behavior is determined by environment. In other words, to change behavior requires that the environment be changed. Yet crucial to this is the principle that a centered self (includes one who is in harmony with spirituality) will effectively balance the realities of the physical world or environment.

The centering of oneself is an empowering process; less emphasis is placed on expertise while acknowledging self as the principal resource. Utilization of extended family is encouraged to support this self-empowering process and contributes to the overall healing of the person within the context of the environment. The process may also include isolating parts of the person that do not permit self to provide leadership. Ceremonial activities support the person in reaching an agreement with all parts of the self. These healing practices are driven by spiritual principles in which secular values are not considered. Holistic principles are rooted in ancient wisdom, are humanistic in nature, and do not permit the isolation of person or problem from environment.

The interconnectedness of all cannot be overemphasized, but assistance is personalized in order to provide meaning and mutual healing. Person is not viewed as client but referred to as family. This is in direct contrast to labeling people as clients or patients, with the emphasis to remain problem or task oriented. Instead there exists a person-oriented focus throughout an indefinite treatment time span. Unlike short-term intervention, in which independence is viewed as progress, the Anishinabe healing principles emphasize restoring balance and harmony, which can only occur if there is interdependence.

After acceptance of a sacred offering, the elder's role is to identify the source of imbalance in the person requesting healing. Throughout the healing process and within the corresponding ceremonial supports the elder accepts responsibility as a mediator in the healing of the person's spirit. Additionally, throughout the entire process, there is acceptance and encouragement of the person's free will to influence self and environment. Centering of the person is encouraged by elders through the use of extended family and ceremonial supports. These important components are part of the process needed by people to achieve the balance and harmony necessary to function within the realities of their environments.

From "Social Work and the Medicine Wheel Framework" by L. Longclaws. In B. R. Compton and B. Galaway (Eds.), *Social Work Processes*, p. 32. Copyright ©1994 Brooks/Cole Publishing Company, a division of International Thomson Publishing Inc., Pacific Grove, CA 93950. Reprinted by permission.

Pedersen (1979) observes that Euro-American cultural values have dominated the social sciences and have been accepted as universal. In turn, these values have been imposed on non-Western cultures. Recently, however, an interest has arisen in examining non-Western value assumptions that offer alternatives to the dominant-culture value system. Likewise, Higginbotham (1979) points out that psychotherapy is determined by culture-specific values. For example, the emphasis of psychoanalysis on individual growth is in contradistinction to kinship- and group-centered cultures.

The following sections set forth multicultural values related to family, spirituality, and identity. It is important for social work to incorporate these elements into its value schema.

Multicultural Family Values

People of Color Family Patterns. Multicultural values revolve around collective structures. For example, the individual wishes of a particular family member are subordinate to the good of the family as a whole. The family unit is considered the most important transmitter of cultural values and traditions, and therefore the value of the family is emphasized over that of individual members (Mokuau, 1983).

Argyle (1982) states that the family is more important in developing countries than in developed ones. It encompasses a wider range of relatives with closer relationships and greater demands than in Western countries. The family is the primary source of relationships and is called on to pay for education, help obtain jobs, and assist when members are in trouble.

Among people of color, the family has three major characteristics, as follows.

1. *Maintenance of ethnic identification and solidarity.* Mindel and Habenstein (1981) point out that the family socializes its members into ethnic culture through family lifestyles and activities. Family gatherings and community celebrations of cultural holidays perpetuate ethnic awareness. Fritzpatrick (1981) further observes that, in Latin America, the individual is deeply conscious of family membership. Puerto Ricans, in particular, feel a deep sense of family obligation—to the extent of using advancements in public office or private business to benefit their families. Alvirez, Bean, and Williams (1981) have coined the term *familism* to emphasize the importance of this central point of reference and place of refuge. The individual turns to other family members for advice and help.

2. *Extended family and kinship network.* Multicultural extended family and kinship networks function on the principles of interdependence, group orientation, and reliance on others. For example, the Puerto Rican family often has the institution of compadres. People are designated as "companion parents." These compadres become godparents of the child, particularly as sponsors at baptism and confirmation. In other instances, they witness a marriage or consider themselves compadres because of common interest or intense friendship. They feel free to advise or correct and are expected to be responsive to the parents' needs. Among African Americans, there is an extensive reliance on kinship networks, which include blood relatives and close friends called "kinsmen." These networks arise from mutual need—need of such things as financial aid, child care, advice, and emotional support. Furthermore, elderly grandparents take young African American children into their households in infor-

mal adoption (Staples, 1981). The Hopi tribe practices bifurcate merging, which means that the mother's and father's sides are divided into separate lineages and that relatives of the same sex and generation are grouped together in helping clusters. The mother's sister is close to her and the child and behaves toward the child as the biological mother would (Price, 1981).

3. *Vertical hierarchy of authority.* Multicultural families generally operate within parental authority structures. Jenkins (1981) states that ethnic parents, particularly fathers, value obedience to parental authority. Children, however, may be at odds with this hierarchy, because of the influence of the dominant society. Alvirez, Bean, and Williams (1981) identify the principle of subordination of the younger to the elder in the traditional Mexican American family. The elderly receive respect from youth and children, who speak to them using the formal rather than the familiar form of address. Furthermore, the hierarchy of authority for Mexican Americans is male centered. Older male children have a degree of authority over younger children and sisters. In the absence of the father, the eldest son assumes authority or shares it with the mother. Variations on a strict vertical hierarchy of authority exist in families who have become acculturated to the dominant society.

Longres (1990) underscores the hierarchical nature of African, Asian, European, and Latin American family structures. The historical origins of family are exhibited in recent immigrant families. These families are more likely to manifest greater control over family life by the older generation, greater emphasis on male dominance, and greater respect for parental authority than do middle-class American families. Eventually, acculturation alters these structural characteristics.

Thus, among African Americans, Asian Americans, Latino Americans, and Native Americans, the family tends to function as a collective structure, stressing parental obedience and respect for elders. The family takes precedence over the individual, and a dominant family figure presides over a multigenerational, interdependent extended family and kinship system.

Zuniga (1992) shares her findings regarding Latino families in Cultural Study 3-2.

CULTURAL STUDY 3-2

The Family as a Support System

[E]ven when Latino families become acculturated to U.S. values, one of the last value stances they give up is their sense of familialism and family loyalty. In many non-Western cultures, the guiding framework is a collective orientation that supports family and community life (Roland, 1988). Latinos, as a whole, adhere to this collective sense, which often results in extended family configurations that often offer valuable support services (Vega, Hough, & Romero, 1983). Although many Latino families now live in nuclear households, support may emanate from each household to the other. Moreover, the godparent system or compadre system offers support through additions to the family through marriage and the consequent uses of godparents at baptism, confirmation, and at the *quinceaneras* (15 year-olds' coming-out celebrations) of daughters.

Thus, many families may have these resources to call upon for help in child care or babysitting. Interventionists can discuss this area with families, particularly when there is a need for the parent to obtain some form of respite from a child with a disability, for example, from demands for extensive attention and caregiving. Likewise, the parents may be asked to designate certain family members to be trained along with them in special medical regimens for the child.

As noted previously, examination of central tendencies in family life among the Latino subgroups denotes traits that are often attenuated by class, migration, and acculturation phenomena. The legacy received from the Spanish culture contributes to viewing the man as the provider and the woman as the main one who takes care of the children. In speaking about Cubans, Bernal (1982) noted that when the wife has to work outside the home, this affects the power balance of the family and may undercut the male's role. If the man is unable to obtain work, he loses face, self-esteem, and respect, and marital and intergenerational difficulties will likely develop.

From "Families with Latino Roots," by M. Zuniga. In E. W. Lynch and M. J. Hanson, *Developing Cross-Cultural Competencies: A Guide for Working with Young Children and Their Families*, p. 162. Paul Brookes Publications, 1992.

People of Color Value Variations. The preceding principles of family function vary among the principal ethnic groups in the United States. For Native Americans, grandparents retain official and symbolic leadership in family communities, as witnessed by the behavior of children who seek daily contact with grandparents and by grandparents who monitor parental behavior. In this milieu, grandparents have an official voice in child-rearing methods. Parents seldom overrule corrective measures from their elders. Younger people seek social acceptance from the elders of the community, whose norm-setting standards are seldom ignored. Unrelated leaders are incorporated into the family. These functional and flexible roles of "grandparents," "aunts," and "uncles" establish an important structure of relationships (Red Horse, Lewis, Feit, & Decker, 1978).

In African American families, there is a sense of corporate responsibility. Children of family systems belong to the extended family clan, not merely to the parents. The extended family is responsible for the care and rearing of children and for teaching them appropriate skills and values. As a consequence, uncles, aunts, cousins, and grandparents have considerable power in the family. It is not uncommon for these relatives to informally "adopt" children whose parents are unable to care for them or for children to be given to relatives temporarily or permanently. Kenyatta (1980) states:

> As in past times, the extended family exists largely as a response to and, let it be stressed, as a triumph over the impact of racism. Within the extended family, bartering of goods and services helps to buffer against the sharp edges of economic insecurity. The extended family both strengthens and is often strengthened by broader social institutions

within the black community, especially the black church. Extended families serve as grapevines for information of economic as well as affectionate significance and the extended family also serves as a reserve of affection, affirmation, encouragement, empathy, love, and sanity. It is "how we got over" and how we get over, one of various survival mechanisms to insure the continuity of black life. (p. 43)

The most valued ties for many African Americans are the mother-child and sibling relationships. In many families, the mother keeps the family together (Mendes, 1983).

Asian American families have specific roles and relationships. The family is patriarchal, with father as the leader of the family, mother as the nurturing caretaker, and sons of more value than daughters. The family relationship is based on filial piety and mutual obligation. The child is expected to obey parents and elders. In exchange, parents are responsible for the upbringing, education, and support of the child (Kitano, 1974). Parents and children demonstrate respect for their ancestors, and, in return, ancestral spirits provide protection for the family. These interdependent roles are intended to keep the family intact (Sue, 1973). Knowing one's place in the family arrangement is a primary aspect of group loyalty (Mokuau, 1983).

As Wong (1985) explains, "In Eastern cultures, the family rather than the individual is considered the unit of focus and identity. Southeast Asian refugees tend to view themselves as members of an extended family with strong emphasis on family obligations, mutual dependency, and collective responsibilities and decision-making" (p. 354).

Latino Americans value the extended family structure and interaction in their daily lives. Ruiz and Padilla (1977) observe that family therapies probably yield higher success rates among Latinos than among non-Latinos, regardless of whether the problem is intrapsychic or extrapsychic. An understanding of Latino family dynamics is crucial for social work practice. In the Latino family, fathers have prestige and authority; sons have more and earlier independence than daughters; sex roles are rigidly defined; and the aged receive respect and reverence.

Mexican American children have respectful attitudes toward their fathers. Even if children see their father unsuccessfully cope with life and begin to drink, they remain loyal to him as the family authority and head of the household. He is recognized as the provider for the family. *Dignidad* is a fundamental value for the Mexican American family; therefore, children are not likely to turn their father in for out-of-control behavior. The father demonstrates the *machismo* of the Latino male (Arnez, 1987).

Married Latino sons visit their parents frequently, a custom that does not connote the pathological dependency implied in other cultures. It is not unusual in Latino families for married children to move to a mobile home on the parents' land and share the same property. For Latinos, staying close to home has a different meaning. The motivations may be positive: the desire to maintain contact with several generations, to accept responsibility for older people, and to guide and protect younger brothers and sisters (Roll, Millen, & Martinez, 1980).

It is interesting to compare family strengths in different cultures. Fong and Peralta (1994) conducted research in Hawaii and New Mexico on family preservation, providing a valuable comparison of strengths in an Asian family and a Latino family. Their findings are summarized in Tables 3-1 and 3-2.

CULTURAL STUDY 3-3

Family Strengths

The findings of the individual and family strengths in the Asian family reiterates the literature's emphasis on the role of the elderly and the importance of their involvement in Asian families. The concern for children is a priority for Asian culture, especially where the role of the mother is to care for the children. The son plays an important role of carrying on the family name and having an impact on the community, positively or negatively. The finding of the Asian family's strengths of valuing respect, having extended family, living together, and offering support to each other are reiterated in the Asian family literature.

TABLE 3-1 *Strengths of the Asian American Family*

Grandmother	Mother	Son	Family
Helps with housing	Values respect	Is energetic	Attempts survival
Is involved	Has concern for child	Attends school	Lives together
Has life experiences	Admits limited skills	Acts out for family	Has three generations to help
Concerned for daughter	Is willing to attend school	Is a good climber	Values sharing and caring
Has influence on daughter	Is concerned about the son	Is independent	Wants to stay in the U.S.
Concerned about the grandchildren	Desires to discipline son	Seeks attention from the mother	Has extended family in the U.S.

The findings of the individual and family strengths in the Hispanic family also parallels the literature's emphasis on the role of the elderly and the extended family. The high value that is placed on respect for elders and authority was apparent in the findings. Both the mother's commitment for the children and the reliance on the grandmother and the family for support were noted. The three generations of family functioning together as a unit was observed.

From the study the findings emphasize the importance for social work practitioners to realize that cultural values are initial places to look for resources in developing treatment plans and interventions. In planning for services in family preservation situations with Asian and Hispanic families, the study directs the attention to the importance of being sure to include the elderly in treatment planning. They are respected and honored for their experiences in Asian and Hispanic cultures and should not be neglected but must be included in the treatment plan and the interventions suggested. Despite age, they are a resource. The families view them as a resource, unlike other ethnic family systems, who view them as a burden.

The strength of the extended family and the commitment to the importance of the intact family is a value despite the mom's two unsuccessful marriages. Asian and Hispanic women are committed to their children. Their roles as caretakers and disciplinarians allude to the high expectations they have for appropriate children's behavior. Despite family calamities, it is evident that loyalty and caretaking are qualities evidenced in the mother and the grandmother.

Both the Asian and the Hispanic data cite respect as a value in both cultures. Strong cultural values on respect for people in roles of authority are reiterated in the literature and in the perceptions of the social work practitioner and student respondents. This value of respect exemplifies traditional values to the Asian and Hispanic families and need to be heeded in treatment planning and intervention implementation.

From *Family Preservation Values and Services: Cultural Sensitivity Towards Asian and Hispanic Families*, R. Fong and F. Peralta, pp. 4–7. Unpublished paper presented at the Annual Program Meeting, Council on Social Work Education, Atlanta, GA, March 1994.

To sum up, multicultural family values stress a family's sense of mutual obligation to support, care for, and provide for each other. They emphasize family collectivity rather than individual independence. Social work professionals should explore the meaning of family responsibility with culturally diverse clients.

Multicultural Religious and Spiritual Values

Religion and spirituality represent external and internal values for people of color. Pedersen (1979) observes that non-Western cultures have an appreciation of religious and spiritual participation in the universe. Health and illness are

TABLE 3-2 *Strengths of the Latino Family*

Grandmother	Mother	Son	Family
Supports the daughter	Understands her limitations	Is creative and intelligent	Has extended family support
Wants better for daughter	Is able to access resources	Is energetic	Is an intact family
Expects good decision making from daughter	Is concerned for children	Is in SED[1] classes	Values respect for others
Has years of experience	Is involved and attends school conference	Responds to mother	Is willing to accept help
Provides child care	Is aware of son's inappropriate behavior	Is not bad	Has family support
Has strong values	Attempted to deal with problems on her own	Is humorous	Has children attending school
Is self-supporting	Is a committed mother	Is strong enough to test limits	Values education

[1]Seriously emotionally disturbed.

defined in terms of harmony or disharmony with the universe. The concept of the spiritual incorporates a metaphysical affinity with environmental forces in nature. Chestang (1976) portrays religion as sustaining an individual in adverse social stress and becoming a rallying point for social change. He states that religious institutions "serve the psychological purpose of strengthening the individual in the face of his impotence against the social structure and the sociopolitical function of providing an outlet for his talents and abilities as well as furnishing a focal point for community organization" (p. 72).

Religion was an integral part of the lives of African slaves who were brought to the United States and, as Staples (1976) asserts, has sustained African Americans through the hardships of slavery, prejudice, and racism. Religion has given credibility to cultural heritage, validated the worth of African Americans, and provided hope for the future.

The African American churches remain a strong force speaking out for civil rights and political justice. African American Protestant theologians have articulated a liberation theology, analyzing the sins of society in terms of oppression and proclaiming the good news of liberation and freedom in Christ. The value structure of the African American community is still strongly

influenced by biblical passages and stories, prayer, and the role of the African American clergy. Lefley (1986) notes:

> The role of the church in black survival is well established; it has served both as a social and spiritual resource, providing collective human support and a reference point for meaningfulness in life. Therapeutic aspects of the religious experience are so profound that it has been suggested that "the black church service is a functional community mental health resource for its participants." (p. 32)

For the Latino family, the church is a moral force that shapes the ethical behavior of family members and a spiritual influence for religious instruction and community change. For families involved in various church activities, the church also serves as a social vehicle for meeting with friends and interacting with the community.

In the Catholic church, the priest participates in the life of the Latino community through religious observances and holidays, confirmations, children's classes, and social services. Catholic Social Services maintains an extensive Latino program and identifies with local barrio churches. Protestant Latino churches provide emergency financial aid, home visitation, care for the ill, newcomer services, housing, employment, and rehabilitation programs for addicts and other outcasts.

In Cultural Study 3-4, Rothman, Gant, and Hnat (1985) recommend the inclusion of religion in the helping process for Mexican American families.

CULTURAL STUDY 3-4

The Importance of Religion

Religion and religious symbols appear to be an important source of identification and of internal support.

Discussion.—The pervasive influence of religion and religious symbols in Mexican American culture has been well documented, but is rarely considered in studies on effects upon treatment.

Application guidelines.—Early in the intervention, therapists should identify and consider the importance of religion and religious symbols to the client. Depending upon the degree of significance to the client, the following range of options could be exercised: (1) Refer the client to another therapist with similar values and beliefs if one cannot operate comfortably within the limits of the client's faith. (2) Include priests (or clergy) in the intervention. The range of solutions available for a given problem is delimited in part by the religious system. For example, suggesting divorce to an orthodox Roman Catholic would probably be counterproductive. The inclusion of religious factors would alleviate much emotional stress by placing the authority of the Church behind a decision, and would provide a means of tapping spiritual resources of resolve and hope.

From "Mexican-American Family Culture," by J. Rothman, L. M. Gant, and S. A. Hnat. In *Social Service Review, 59,* p. 208. Copyright 1985 University of Chicago School of Social Service Administration. Reprinted by permission.

For Asian Americans, formal religions include Buddhism, Protestantism, and Roman Catholicism. Asian Americans in the Catholic church are generally integrated with other ethnic groups in a geographic parish. Protestant and Buddhist churches serve a single Asian group, such as the Japanese, Chinese, Filipino, Korean, or Vietnamese. Asian Americans tend to practice such values as respect for ancestors, filial piety, and avoidance of shame. These moral principles assist many Asian Americans in family and social functioning by defining their obligation, duty, and loyalty to others. Good performance and achievement bring honor to the family. Shame and dishonor are powerful motivators to minimize unacceptable behavior. Mental illness and retardation, criminal behavior, job failure, and even poor school grades are kept in the family. To share negative information outside the home is to bring disgrace on the family name. This standard of morality may seem harsh and rigid to the outsider, but to many Asian Americans it maintains honor and harmony in the family.

Spirituality is at the heart of Native American cultural practices, as illustrated in Cultural Study 3-5. While Catholic and Protestant clergy have sought to Christianize Native Americans, indigenous religious rituals and beliefs in the healing power of nature have been maintained. Natural forces are associated with the life process itself and pervade everything that the believing Native American does. Community religious rites are a collective effort that promote nature and increase inward insight and experiential connection with nature. In the helping process, Native Americans can use the positive experiences that result from ceremonial events, power-revealing events (omens, dreams, visions), and contact with a tribal medicine man. In working with Native Americans, social workers must learn to explore and reinforce the therapeutic significance of religious and cultural events (Lewis, 1977).

CULTURAL STUDY 3-5

Plains Indians' Spiritual Retreat

Among the sacred ceremonies of the Plains Indians are the rites of purification, the annual tribal Sun Dance, and the individual spiritual retreat. The purification rites are centered in a dome lodge made of intertwined willows and covered over tightly with bison robes. In the circular form of the lodge and in the materials used in its construction, the tribesman sees a symbolic representation of the world in its totality. The lodge is the very body of the Great Spirit. Inside this lodge of the world, participants submit to intensely hot steam produced when water is sprinkled on rocks previously heated in a special sacred fire located to the east of the lodge. As the men pray and chant, the steam, conceived as the visible image of the Great Spirit, dissolves both physical and psychic coagulations, permitting a spiritual transmutation to take place. The elements contribute their respective powers to purification so that participants experience the dissolving of illusory separateness and the achievement of reintegration or harmonious unification within the totality of the universe. Going forth from the dark lodge, the men leave behind all physical impurities and spiritual errors and are reborn into the wisdom of the light of day. All aspects of the world have been witnesses to this cycle of corruption, death, wholeness, and rebirth. The cosmic powers have all contributed to the process.

The Sun Dance rites are performed annually by the entire tribe. This prayer dance is the regeneration or renewal of the individual, tribe, and entire universe. It takes place within a large circular pole lodge. At the center is a tall cottonwood tree representing the axis of the universe, the vertical link joining heaven and earth, and thus the path of contact with the solar power, the sun, symbol of the Supreme Principle or Great Spirit. Supported day and night by a huge drum beaten by many men and by heroic and nostalgic songs, the dancers hold eagle plumes and continually orient themselves toward the sacred central tree or toward one of the four directions of space. Blowing whistles made from the wing bone of the eagle, the men dance individually with simple and dignified steps towards the central tree, from which they receive supernatural power, and then dance backward to the periphery of the circle without shifting their gaze from the center. The power of the sacred center, realized within participants, remains with each individual and unifies the people.

The individual spiritual retreat or vision quest involves a total fast for a specified number of days at a lonely place, usually a mountain top. Alone and in constant prayer, the individual is in utter humility of body and mind and stands before the forms and forces of nature. He seeks the blessing of sacred power, which comes to him through a dream or vision of some aspect of nature, possibly an animal who offers guidance for the future direction of the man's life. These natural forces are an iconography that expresses the ultimate power or essence of the Great Spirit. In silence within the solitude of nature is heard the voice of the Great Spirit. Their quest for supernatural powers is essential to the spiritual life of the Plains Indians and influences their quality of life. The sacred tobacco pipe is central to all the rites and expresses sacrifice and purification, the integration of the individual within the macrocosm, and the realization of unity.

From "The Persistence of Essential Values among North American Plains Indians," by J. E. Brown, *Studies in Comparative Religion*, 3, pp. 216–255. Copyright 1969 Perennial Books, Ltd. Reprinted by permission.

Social workers and other human service professionals should ascertain the meaning of religion or a spiritual perspective for particular clients. Gary (1978) remarks that mental health professionals often minimize the functional usefulness of religion for African American clients:

Unfortunately, there is a tendency for professionals to ignore or downplay the role of the black church. One thing is apparent, many of these professionals, especially whites, do not understand this religious orientation in the black community. Some, because of their ethnic and religious backgrounds and for a variety of other reasons, have difficulties in advocating or emphasizing the positive role of religion (Protestantism) in mental health. (pp. 31–33)

Church-related social services have no difficulty in understanding the link between family and church in the African American and Latino communities.

In summary, many—though not all—people of color rely on religion to sustain and nurture them. For African Americans and Latinos, the church is a social and spiritual resource. For Asians, religion is a source of moral precepts. For Native Americans, the spiritual experience is expressed in rituals that symbolize renewal and change.

Multicultural Identity Values

Chestang (1976) defines individual identity as the conglomerate of consciousness, personality, attitudes, emotions, and perceptions that is termed the *self*. Identity is forged in the interaction between the individual's heredity and life experiences shaped by the physical and social environment. In developmental terms, many people of color become aware of the negative societal attitudes toward their racial group, and those attitudes have a devaluing or destructive effect on their identities. Within their own ethnic community, they find positive elements to reshape their identity.

In the past two decades, ethnic groups have rediscovered their cultural backgrounds. Ethnic history and cultural awareness are integral parts of university ethnic studies curricula. More recently, inspired by the television series *Roots*, many people have researched their genealogies and the history of their ancestors and relatives.

Greene (1992) emphasizes the vital importance of cultural awareness to children who must cope with discrimination and racism in the external environment. In Cultural Study 3-6, she explains the role of cultural values in coping strategies.

CULTURAL STUDY 3-6

Cultural Values and Coping with Racism

Despite the existence of pervasive racial discrimination and realistic barriers to their optimal development, African American children have succeeded against the odds for many generations. Their socioemotional environment represents a major factor contributing to their adaptive development. In this context, African American families constitute an important buffer between the child and the outside environment (Bowman & Howard, 1985; Boyd-Franklin, 1989; Comer,

1985; Greene, 1990; Hopson & Hopson, 1990; Norton 1983; Spurlock, 1986). An important aspect of this role of the family as a buffer, not unlike that of the therapist, is to help the child understand the outside world's messages and how to tell when those messages are true or not.

All parents face difficult challenges raising children in adverse circumstances, but African American parents face added stressors and special tasks. They must teach their children how to handle the special nuances of a bicultural existence without losing a core sense of themselves. This is particularly difficult because functioning in and between two often contradictory cultures can produce competing and conflicting developmental tasks and tensions (Baker, 1988; Chestang, 1973; Pinderhughes, 1989). African American parents must accomplish this task in the ubiquitous environment of real or potential racial discrimination, where there is always the potential for being devalued and/or physically and psychologically harmed, a condition beyond one's control. This context further changes and intensifies the meaning and impact of life's normal and catastrophic events, thus increasing the day-to-day level of stress. This pressure of racism and the effort by African American parents to minimize its damaging effects on their children is, in fact, a major stress not shared by their white counterparts. This stress is reflected in the amount of energy that must be consumed and in the distraction presented by the ongoing requirement of anticipating and coping with the dominant culture's barriers.

African Americans have used a variety of strategies to cope with racism throughout their history, yet they must be flexible in their strategies. The sensitivity of many African American persons to the potential for exploitation by white persons has been referred to as cultural paranoia (Grier & Cobbs, 1968). Faulkner (1983, p. 195) uses the term *armoring* to describe behavioral and cognitive skills used by African Americans as well as other persons of color to decrease their psychological vulnerability in encounters with racism. For the most part, such strategies have been pathologized by the mental health community of the dominant society, which often refers to such maneuvers as hypersensitivity or paranoia. This is the result of the mental health community's reluctance to view the behaviors of the African American individual in the context of a specific set of social conditions. Once viewed in that context, the adaptive value of such behaviors becomes obvious.

An important set of strategies for coping with racism consists of introducing and sharing derivatives of African cultural values and practices. According to Spencer (1987), an African American child's preparation by parents and other socializing agents to understand and take pride in their culture can be a major source of resilience and coping, a racial consciousness that provides a necessary foundation for the coping strategies needed. Sanchez (1989) notes that the first time African American children discover that they are "black" is usually through a negative experience; hence, many authors (Bowman & Howard, 1985; Boyd-Franklin, 1989; Harrison-Ross & Wyden, 1973; Hopson & Hopson, 1990; Peters, 1981; Sanchez, 1989; Spencer, 1987) strongly suggest that parents discuss the issue of race directly with their children before problems occur.

From "Racial Socialization as a Tool in Psychotherapy with African-American Children," by B. A. Greene. In L. A. Vargas and J. D. Koss-Chioino (Eds.), *Working with Culture: Psychotherapeutic Interventions with Ethnic Minority Children and Adolescents*, pp. 68–69. Copyright © 1992 Jossey-Bass, San Francisco. Reprinted with permission.

A number of variables are common to multicultural identity values. The most obvious distinguishing feature is skin color. All people of the earth have been classified according to color: white, brown, black, yellow, and red. Ethnic identity has been undermined by a color hierarchy. White symbolizes innocence, purity, and fairness. Black is associated with evil, darkness, and dirt. Yellow conjures up cowardice, impurity, and discoloration. Red is associated with rage. The derogatory tone of such idioms as "dirt black," "yellow belly," and "red skin" have caused them to become racist slurs, and they are still with us. Moreover, these terms depreciate ethnic identity value. In the 1960s the theme "Black is beautiful" was a way of reinforcing the physical aspects of ethnic identity as a positive attribute.

Names are another important factor in ethnic identity. Many people of color have forgotten or changed their native names for Anglo-European ones. African Americans adopted or were given the surnames of their plantation owners. Some African Americans have legally adopted African names, as Native Americans have reverted to their native names. Latinos are named after relatives and ancestors, and their full names can consist of four or five words. Asian Americans have combined an English first name with their ethnic middle and last names. An ethnic native name has a significant cultural meaning for the person. In some cultures, a person's invested worth and life mission are found in his or her given name. In other cultures, the name perpetuates the memory of important ancestors.

The language of an ethnic group is another important component of its identity. Many immigrants are unable to speak English and therefore converse in their native language at home. Within the ethnic community, language ability is a criterion of social acceptance. Inability to speak the community's language confers ignorance and shame. Language shapes unique patterns of thoughts, thus producing cognitive differences between English and, for instance, Spanish. Thus, English speakers and non-English speakers think and express themselves differently. Differences in language nuances influence behavior patterns.

A number of generic principles relate to ethnic identity. DeVos and Romanucci-Ross (1982) categorize two types of ethnic identity: past-oriented cultural identity and expressive-behavioral cultural identity. Past-oriented identity involves four characteristics:

1. *Competence.* Ethnic identity determines a person's confidence to take on goal-oriented activities, builds group competence based on collective confidence and supportive attitudes, and fosters freedom of expression to shape one's position or standing in the ethnic community.
2. *Responsibility.* Ethnic identity defines ethical obligations and the ethnic community's moral code, has an internalized moral dimension of both negative and positive heritage, and sometimes causes conflict about ethical standards.

3. *Control.* In a society, groups are placed in a superordinate or subordinate position with respect to one another on the basis of ethnicity. Those in the superordinate status legitimate their authority and dominance when they feel social insecurity or individual impotence. The subordinate group is subjected to pressures to demonstrate its submission, for reasons of survival or dependency. In other instances, the ethnic identity of the subordinates consists in a moral imperative to seek liberation, autonomy, and independence from the oppressor.

4. *Mutuality.* Ethnic traditions define modes of competition and cooperation expected by the group. In-group activities may demand concerted behavior and mutual trust to act together, emphasizing cooperation and minimizing competition. In other instances, competition is directed toward people outside the ethnic group.

Ethnic identity factors that influence the expression and understanding of behavior include the following five traits:

1. *Harmony.* Peace is maintained at the expense of conflict in ethnic group relationships. Harmony is used to maintain group continuance, whereas hostilities are projected onto outsiders in the process known as *scapegoating*.

2. *Affiliation.* An ethnic group maintains mutual contact and communication on the basis of shared past experiences. In some instances, ethnic peers maintain more intimate companionship than do family members of different generations. Loss of a sense of belonging—social isolation or the threat of separation—are social sanctions against violators of group norms.

3. *Nurturance.* Ethnic identity forms the basis for interdependence in terms of caring, help, and comfort. Ethnic membership fosters benevolent care of one generation for another. Because of their ethnic identity, professionally trained members of an ethnic group have an advantage in helping their own people.

4. *Appreciation.* Ethnic identity fosters pride in one's group, creating a sense of humanity, dignity, self-respect, and proper status. Situations in which others devalue highly positive cultural traits

or a group is forced to acknowledge the merits or superior technology of an alien group obviously pose a threat to ethnic identity.

5. *Pleasure and suffering.* Ethnic identity is related to a person's social satisfaction—in terms of personal identity and relationship to a group—and tolerance of suffering and death. Ethnic beliefs, cultural knowledge of history, and other systems form the basis for meaning in life.

These ethnic identity themes are useful to our understanding of common meanings that apply to a psychocultural theory of particular groups. To a certain extent, the nine variables listed apply to all cultures. However, in the case of people of color, these factors are crucial to self-survival and group sustenance. For this reason, it is important for social workers to locate and mobilize these centers of ethnic identity.

SOCIAL WORK AND MULTICULTURAL VALUES

The preceding sections have examined traditional social work values and ethics and multicultural values that center on family, spirituality, and identity. Social work values and ethics have been based on individualistic democratic ideals of self-determination, freedom of choice, and social responsibility. Multicultural values deal with collective entities, such as the family, church, and nature. The individual derives his or her point of reference from these ethnic structures. To bridge the gap between individuality and collectivity, social work must incorporate a cosmological orientation that accounts for the importance of family, spirituality, and nature. The individual draws meaning, relationship, and direction from these areas. These concepts should be reflected in broader social work definitions of values and ethical code. The following crucial multicultural values, among others, could be incorporated into the NASW Code of Ethics:

• Social work values family unification, parental leadership, respect for the elderly, and collective family decision making.

- Social work encourages the healthy application of religious and spiritual beliefs and practices, which join the individual and family to collective institutions and cosmic forces in the universe, resulting in harmony, unity, and wholeness.

- Social work seeks to use family kinship and community networks as supportive means of treatment for persons who are able to benefit from collective helping.

- Social work values the rediscovery of ethnic language and cultural identity, which strengthen a person's relationship to his or her heritage.

- Social work promotes the harmony or sense of congruity and agreement in feelings, actions, ideas, and interest within and between persons. Harmony is essential to the balance of the person in relationship to others, society, and the universe.

- Social work fosters cooperation that brings families and groups together in a common sense of purpose. This sense of purpose may include pooling resources for survival and coping with problem situations, meeting a common crisis, and working with the extended family and as part of the ethnic community.

These propositions serve as useful bridges to link traditional social work values with multicultural values that reflect a range of cultural beliefs, practices, and behaviors from ethnic traditions. Social workers must understand and respect these cultural values.

Value Implications for Practice

We have seen that the social worker must consciously understand social work and multicultural values and seek to apply them in practice situations. To get a better idea of what that means, we now consider some examples specific to Southeast Asian cultures, focusing on three values: harmony, confidentiality, and family obligations.

Harmony. Ishisaka, Nguyen, and Okimoto (1985) point out that conflict-avoiding behavior is characteristic of Indochinese culture. Consequently, Indochinese clients or interpreters will often deny or suppress information that they perceive as threatening to harmonious role relationships between the worker and client. Such information might include client complaints that are disrespectful of the worker's authority role or important aspects of the client's situation that could be a source of personal shame.

The worker should be sensitive to subtle cues that the client is withholding information or avoiding confrontation. For Indochinese clients, the value of maintaining positive harmony may take precedence over accurate disclosure.

Confidentiality. In multicultural practice, the ethical value of confidentiality may require careful explanation. Some cultures, for example, the Indochinese, have no sense of confidentiality. The Vietnamese believe that a single disclosure of information means widespread dissemination. In Vietnam, according to Ishisaka et al. (1985), "people believed that if one agency knew something, the whole government knew; or if one American knew, then every American in Vietnam knew" (p. 47).

Naturally, these beliefs deter clients from divulging information. Unless the worker recognizes a refugee client's misunderstanding of confidentiality and explains the concept to the client's satisfaction, important information might be withheld, with serious consequences for problem identification, assessment, and intervention.

Family Obligations. In many cultures, the individual self is construed as part of a larger collective whole, the family. The individual has an obligation to the family and to others in the extended family and ethnic community.

Many Indochinese refugees have suffered severe role and status loss in coming to this country. As a result, they may have difficulty in maintaining coping efforts. Family obligation can be used to motivate such clients.

In Cultural Study 3-7, the practitioner gains a relationship with the client through the use of family obligation; the process is facilitated by involving the client's friend.

Family Obligation

The client, a 31-year-old man, was a major in the army of Vietnam. The client came to the United States in the first group of Vietnamese refugees to arrive in this country. Because of circumstances surrounding his escape, the client came to the United States alone. The client's two brothers were also in the Vietnamese army but had been captured and were in a prison camp in North Vietnam. The client was enrolled in an English-as-a-second-language class but complained that he could not concentrate during class. He had applied for several jobs but failed in the interview process. The client began to complain about difficulties in living in the United States and began to withdraw increasingly from his friends and his usual activities. The client received a letter from his sister-in-law that his brothers had died in prison camp. He also learned that both his sisters-in-law had attempted suicide. One sister-in-law succeeded, but the other was rescued and decided to stay alive to take care of the children of both families. The client learned of the deaths in his family while depressed, and the information exacerbated his mood disorder. With growing hopelessness, the client decided to commit suicide by hanging. He was found and hospitalized, during which time he made two more suicide attempts. During hospitalization, the client was not receptive to treatment attempts. Attempts at providing treatment having failed, the case was referred to Asian Counseling and Referral Services, Inc., in Seattle. A Vietnamese-speaking counselor was assigned to the case. After obtaining information from the hospital and from the client's friend (networking), the counselor decided to make his first hospital visit with the client's friend. It was felt that introduction of the counselor by the client's friend (formal introduction) would help to gain the client's confidence and trust. Moreover, the friend could introduce the counselor along the lines suggested earlier. Over the course of discussion between the client and his friend, the counselor could observe how traditional values were

affecting the client's attempts to cope (transactional assessment). The counselor participated in parts of the discussion, providing illustrations of other newly arrived Vietnamese refugees and their attempts to adjust to life in the United States, often with the added strains of devastating news from home about relatives and friends (universalization and role induction). The counselor was also able to instruct the client about how others have been helped to cope with the grief of losing loved ones (normalization and attribution). The counselor acted in ways that would help the client to regain hope, to understand that help was possible and that in many instances the future could not be predicted from the client's present pain (motivating the client). As his work with the client continued, the counselor brought up the courage and sense of family which had caused his sister-in-law to choose life over death so that she could continue to care for her children and nephews and nieces. Using the sister-in-law as a model of how an individual can continue to honor her obligations during times of extreme hardship, the counselor was able to motivate the client to find meaning in his renewed attempts to help his surviving family in Vietnam. As the client's sense of meaning and purpose returned, the major symptoms of depression weakened. Over time, the client was helped to direct his energies toward finding work and establishing community ties. At this time, the client is employed and is supporting his family in Vietnam. He is an active member of the Vietnamese community. Throughout the counselor's efforts to assist the client, the client's friend continued to play an important role in treatment as the principal extratherapeutic source of emotional support to the client.

From "The Role of Culture in the Mental Health Treatment of Indochinese Refugees," Hideki A. Ishisaka, Quynh T. Nguyen, and Joseph T. Okimoto. In Tom Choken Owan (Ed.), *Southeast Asian Mental Health: Treatment, Prevention, Services, Training, and Research* (pp. 57–58). Washington, D.C.: U.S. Department of Health and Human Services, National Institute of Mental Health, 1985.

Using the client's sister-in-law as a role model, the worker points out that the sister-in-law honored her obligation to care for the family during periods of hardship. The counselor's emphasis on the value of cultural family obligation to the client marked the turning point in the client's treatment.

The preceding examples illustrate the importance of sensitivity to multicultural values in social work practice. This discussion on values emphasizes the need for social work students and practitioners to understand the value orientation of their clients. However, it is important to summarize these value themes and apply them to our life situation and experiences. The following cultural values clarification exercise is designed to put closure on the themes of this chapter and to involve the reader in personal and professional application.

CULTURAL VALUES CLARIFICATION EXERCISE

This values clarification exercise is designed to help you identify and clarify your own values and to prepare you to engage a multicultural person of color client with an understanding of his or her cultural values. Consider the following questions:

1. How would you explain the meaning of values?
2. Briefly describe your personal values, family values, and ethnic and cultural values.
3. Briefly describe your values about your neighborhood, community, and society.
4. Are your values reflective of your ethnic and cultural group? If yes, please explain how your ethnic and cultural group influences your values. If no, please explain how the dominant American society influences your values.
5. Are you able to understand the ethnic and cultural values of the following groups: African Americans, Latino Americans, Asian Americans, and Native Americans? If yes, please explain the essential ethnic and cultural values of the groups that you understand. If no, please explain why you are unfamiliar with the groups' ethnic and cultural values.

Rate yourself on the following value areas on a scale of 1 to 4: 1 = all of the time; 2 = most of the time; 3 = some of the time; 4 = none of the time. Circle the appropriate number.

Personal Values

1. I am an honest person in my dealings and communication with others.
   Circle one:
   1 = All of the time   2 = Most of the time
   3 = Some of the time   4 = None of the time

2. I am guided by a sense of right and wrong.
   Circle one:
   1 = All of the time   2 = Most of the time
   3 = Some of the time   4 = None of the time

3. I strive to be fair to others.
   Circle one:
   1 = All of the time   2 = Most of the time
   3 = Some of the time   4 = None of the time

4. I have a positive attitude when I relate to others.
   Circle one:
   1 = All of the time   2 = Most of the time
   3 = Some of the time   4 = None of the time

5. I strive to help people rather than harm and alienate them.
   Circle one:
   1 = All of the time   2 = Most of the time
   3 = Some of the time   4 = None of the time

Family Values

6. I listen to my parents and respect their wishes.
   Circle one:
   1 = All of the time   2 = Most of the time
   3 = Some of the time   4 = None of the time

7. I subordinate my individual wishes and make decisions based on the good of the family as a whole.
   Circle one:
   1 = All of the time   2 = Most of the time
   3 = Some of the time   4 = None of the time

8. I have regular contact with my grandparents and other elders in my extended family.
   Circle one:
   1 = All of the time   2 = Most of the time
   3 = Some of the time   4 = None of the time

9. I strive to maintain family harmony rather than compete with members of my family.

Circle one:
1 = All of the time   2 = Most of the time
3 = Some of the time   4 = None of the time

10. I have a good relationship with members of my family.

Circle one:
1 = All of the time   2 = Most of the time
3 = Some of the time   4 = None of the time

Ethnic and Cultural Values

11. I consider myself to be a spiritual person and practice a personal faith.

Circle one:
1 = All of the time   2 = Most of the time
3 = Some of the time   4 = None of the time

12. I practice ethnic and cultural beliefs and values such as observing ethnic holidays, speaking ethnic language, and attending ethnic community activities.

Circle one:
1 = All of the time   2 = Most of the time
3 = Some of the time   4 = None of the time

13. I am an active member of an ethnic organization in my community.

Circle one:
1 = All of the time   2 = Most of the time
3 = Some of the time   4 = None of the time

14. I am active in learning about my ethnic and cultural background and other ethnic and cultural groups in my community.

Circle one:
1 = All of the time   2 = Most of the time
3 = Some of the time   4 = None of the time

15. I am involved with members of my ethnic group as well as other ethnic groups on a social level.

Circle one:
1 = All of the time   2 = Most of the time
3 = Some of the time   4 = None of the time

Please count up your score on the fifteen value clarification items and rate your value level. Circle the appropriate level and write your raw score in one of the following levels:

Level 1: High cultural/ethnic values (score 15–29)

Level 2: Moderate cultural/ethnic values (score 30–44)

Level 3: Slight cultural/ethnic values (score 45–59)

Level 4: Minimal cultural/ethnic values (score 60 and over)

Discuss your answers in a value clarification classroom session.

CONCLUSION

We started with an examination of traditional social work values and ethics that are familiar to social work practitioners. However, along with these concepts, we discussed culturally diverse values that clearly point to an alternative direction. Traditional multicultural values tend to be collective and center on family, authority hierarchy, spirituality, and identity. Issues in culturally diverse values must be examined by social work students and practitioners who need to sort out their own personal, family, and ethnic and cultural values. These value components form the basis for an examination of culturally diverse social work knowledge theory that follows in the next chapter.

REFERENCES

Addams, J. (1907). *Newer ideals of peace.* New York: Chautauqua.

Alvirez, D., Bean, F. D., & Williams, D. (1981). The Mexican American family. In C. H. Mindel & R. W. Habenstein (Eds.), *Ethnic families in America: Patterns and variations* (pp. 269–292). New York: Elsevier.

Argyle, M. (1982). Inter-cultural communication. In S. Bochner (Ed.), *Cultures in contact: Studies in cross-cultural interaction* (pp. 61–79). Oxford: Pergamon.

Arnez, L. (1987). *Theory/case study integration.* Unpublished manuscript, California State University, Sacramento.

Baker, F. M. (1988). Afro-Americans. In L. Comas-Diaz & E. Griffith (Eds.), *Clinical guidelines in cross-cultural mental health* (pp. 151–181). New York. Wiley.

Bernal, G. (1982). Cuban families. In M. McGoldrick, J. Pearce, & J. Giordano (Eds.), *Ethnicity and family therapy* (pp. 187–207). New York: Guilford.

Bowman, P., & Howard, C. (1985). Race related socialization, motivation, and academic achievement: A study of black youths in three generation families. *Journal of the American Academy of Child Psychiatry, 24*, 134–141.

Boyd-Franklin, N. (1989). *Black families in therapy: A multisystems approach*. New York: Guilford.

Brown, J. E. (1969). The persistence of essential values among North American Plains Indians. *Studies in Comparative Religion, 3*, 216–225.

Chestang, L. (1973). *Character development in a hostile environment* (Occasional Paper No. 3). Chicago: Social Service Administration, University of Chicago.

Chestang, L. (1976). Environmental influences on social functioning: The black experience. In P. San Juan Cafferty & L. Chestang (Eds.), *The diverse society: Implications for social policy* (pp. 59–74). Washington, DC: National Association of Social Workers.

Clark, R. (1988). Social justice and issues of human rights in the international context. In D. S. Sanders & J. Fischer (Eds.), *Visions for the future: Social work and Pacific-Asian perspectives* (pp. 3–10). Honolulu: University of Hawaii, School of Social Work.

Comer, J. (1985). Black children and child psychiatry. *Journal of the American Academy of Child Psychiatry, 24*, 129–133.

Compton, B. R., & Galaway, B. (Eds.). (1989). *Social work processes* (4th ed.). Belmont, CA: Proofreader.

DeVos, G., & Romanucci-Ross, L. (1982). Ethnicity: Vessel of meaning and emblem of contrast. In G. DeVos & L. Romanucci-Ross (Eds.), *Ethnic identity: Cultural continuities and change* (pp. 363–390). Chicago: University of Chicago Press.

Faulkner, J. (1983). Women in interracial relationships. *Women and Therapy, 2*, 191–203.

Fong, R., & Peralta, F. (1994, March). *Family preservation values and services: Cultural sensitivity towards Asian and Hispanic families*. Paper presented at the Annual Program Meeting, Council on Social Work Education, Atlanta, GA.

Fritzpatrick, J. P. (1981). The Puerto Rican family. In C. H Mindel & R. W. Habenstein (Eds.), *Ethnic families in America: Patterns and variations* (pp. 189–214). New York: Elsevier.

Gary, L. E. (1978). *Support systems in black communities: Implications for mental health services for children and youth*. Washington, DC: Howard University Mental Health Research Center, Institute for Urban Affairs and Research.

Greene, B. (1990). Sturdy bridges: The role of African American mothers in the socialization of African American children. *Women and Therapy, 19*, 205–225.

Greene, B. (1992). Racial socialization as a tool in psychotherapy with African American children. In L. A. Vargas & J. D. Koss-Chioino (Eds.), *Working with culture: Psychotherapeutic interventions with ethnic minority children and adolescents* (pp. 63–81). San Francisco: Jossey-Bass.

Grier, W., & Cobbs, P. (1968). *Black rage*. New York: Basic Books.

Harrison-Ross, P., & Wyden, B. (1973). *The black child. A parent's guide*. New York. Wyden.

Hepworth, D. H., Rooney, R. H., & Larsen, J. A. (1997). *Direct social work practice: Theory and skills* (5th ed.). Pacific Grove, CA: Brooks/Cole.

Higginbotham, H. N. (1979). Culture and mental health services. In A. J. Marsella, R. G. Tharp, & T. J. Ciborowski (Eds.), *Perspectives on cross-cultural psychology* (pp. 301–332). New York: Academic Press.

Hopson, D. P., & Hopson, D. S. (1990). *Different and wonderful: Raising black children in a race conscious society*. Upper Saddle River, NJ: Prentice-Hall.

Ishisaka, H. A., Nguyen, Q. T., & Okimoto, J. T. (1985). The role of culture in the mental health treatment of Indochinese refugees. In T. C. Owan (Ed.), *Southeast Asian mental health: Treatment, prevention, services, training, and research* (pp. 41–64). Washington, DC: U.S. Department of Health and Human Services, National Institute of Mental Health.

Jenkins, S. (1981). *The ethnic dilemma in social services*. New York: Free Press.

Keith-Lucas, A. (1971). Ethics in social work. In R. Morris (Ed.), *Encyclopedia of social work* (pp. 324–328). New York: National Association of Social Workers.

Kent, R., & Tse, S. (1980). *The roots of social work in Christianity*. Unpublished master's thesis, California State University, Sacramento.

Kenyatta, M. I. (1980). The impact of racism on the family as a support system. *Catalyst, 2*, 37–44.

Kitano, H. H. L. (1974). *Race relations*. Upper Saddle River, NJ: Prentice-Hall.

Lefley, H. P. (1986). Why cross-cultural training? Applied issues in culture and mental health service delivery. In H. P. Lefley & P. B. Pedersen (Eds.), *Cross-cultural training for mental health professionals* (pp. 11–44). Springfield, IL: Thomas.

Lewis, R. (1977). *Cultural perspective on treatment modalities with Native Americans.* Paper presented at the National Association of Social Workers Symposium, San Diego, CA.

Longclaws, L. (1994). Social work and the medicine wheel framework. In B. R. Compton & B. Galaway (Eds.), *Social work processes* (pp. 24–33). Pacific Grove, CA: Brooks/Cole.

Longres, J. F. (1990). *Human behavior in the social environment.* Itasca, IL: Peacock.

Mendes, H. A. (1983). *Black American family.* Unpublished manuscript, University of Southern California School of Social Work.

Mindel, C. H., & Habenstein, R. W. (1981). Family lifestyles of America's ethnic minorities: An introduction. In C. H. Mindel & R. W. Habenstein (Eds.), *Ethnic families in America: Patterns and variations* (pp. 1–13). New York: Elsevier.

Mokuau, N. (1983). *Asian American individuals.* Unpublished manuscript, University of Hawaii School of Social Work.

Northen, H. (1982). *Clinical social work.* New York: Columbia University Press.

Norton, D. (1983). Black family life patterns: The development of self and cognitive development of black children. In G. J. Powell, J. Yamamoto, A. Romero, &A. Morales (Eds.), *The psychosocial development of minority group children* (pp. 181–193). New York: Brunner/Mazel.

Pedersen, P. (1979). Non-Western psychology: The search for alternatives. In A. J. Marsella, R. G. Tharp, & T. J. Ciborowski (Eds.), *Perspectives on cross-cultural psychology* (pp. 77–98). New York: Academic Press.

Peters, M. F. (1988). Parenting in black families with young children: A historical perspective. In H. McAdoo (Ed.), *Black families* (pp. 228–241). Newbury Park, CA: Sage.

Pinderhughes, E. (1989). *Understanding race, ethnicity, and power: The key to efficacy in clinical practice.* New York: Free Press.

Price, J. A. (1981). North American Indian families. In C. H. Mindel & R. W. Havenstein (Eds.), *Ethnic families in America: Patterns and variations* (pp. 245–268). New York: Elsevier.

Red Horse, J. G., Lewis, R., Feit, M., & Decker, J. (1978). Family behavior of urban American Indians. *Social Casework, 59,* 67–72.

Rokeach, M. (1973). *The nature of human values.* New York: Free Press.

Roland, A. (1988). *In search of self in India and Japan: Towards a cross-cultural psychology.* Princeton, NJ: Princeton University Press.

Roll, S., Millen, L., & Martinez, R. (1980). Common errors in psychotherapy with Chicanos: Extrapolations from research and clinical experience. *Psychotherapy: Theory, Research, and Practice, 17,* 156–168.

Rothman, J., Gant, L. M., & Hnat, S. A. (1985). Mexican-American family culture. *Social Service Review, 59,* 201–202.

Ruiz, R. A., & Padilla, A. M. (1977). Counseling Latinos. *Personnel and Guidance Journal, 55,* 401–408.

Sanchez, S. (1989). Sonia Sanchez. In B. Lanker (Ed.), *I dream a world: Portraits of black women who changed America* (pp. 868–869). New York. Stewart, Tabori, & Chang.

Spencer, M. B. (1987). Black children's ethnic identity formation: Risk and resilience of castelike minorities. In J. Phinney & M. J. Rotheram (Eds.), *Children's ethnic socialization: Pluralism and development* (pp. 103–104). Newbury Park, CA: Sage.

Spurlock, J. (1986). Development of self-concept in Afro-American children. *Hospital and Community Psychiatry, 37,* 66–70.

Staples, R. (1976). *Introduction to black sociology.* New York: McGraw-Hill.

Sue, D. W. (1973). Ethnic identity. In S. Sue & N. Wagner (Eds.), *Asian Americans: Psychological perspective* (pp. 140–149). Ben Lomond, CA: Science and Behavior Books.

Vega, W., Hough, R., & Romero, A. (1983). Family life patterns of Mexican Americans. In G. Powell, J. Yamamoto, A. Romero, & A. Morales (Eds.), *The psychosocial development of minority group children* (pp. 194–215). New York: Brunner/Mazel.

Wong, H. Z. (1985). Training for mental health service providers to Southeast Asian refugees: Models, strategies, and curricula. In T. C. Owan (Ed.), *Southeast Asian mental health: Treatment, prevention, services, training, and research* (pp. 345–390). Washington, DC: Department of Health and Human Services, National Institute of Mental Health.

Zuniga, M. (1992). Families with Latino roots. In E. W. Lynch & M. J. Hanson (Eds.), *Developing cross-cultural competencies: A guide for working with young children and their families* (pp. 161–175). Baltimore: Brookes.

CHAPTER 4

Social Work Knowledge Theory

Social work knowledge theory is essential for understanding the theoretical foundation of the content of our practice and its later application to skills with working with clients. In social work knowledge theory with people of color, our concern is to build a sufficient knowledge base for our study of Native, African, Latino, and Asian Americans in the field of social work practice and to impart it for use by social work students and practitioners.

Theories of social work knowledge include theories of human behavior and practice. This chapter focuses on practice, but there are also multicultural theories of behavior that draw on the concepts of ethnicity, culture, minority, and social class. *Culturally diverse knowledge* encompasses the complete range of information, awareness, and understanding regarding the multicultural experience. It includes the history, cognitive-affective-behavioral characteristics, and societal dilemmas of people of color. *Culturally diverse theory* refines knowledge into a series of general principles that attempt a systematic explanation of these phenomena. It includes the examination of the dynamics underlying prejudice, for example. These theoretical principles have been verified to some extent.

Likewise, social work knowledge tends toward Western social sciences. Western knowledge theory emphasizes the individual. With the assistance of a helping person and through reliance on verbal exchange and analysis, the client changes so as to become free of behavioral dysfunction. Culturally diverse knowledge theory, on the other hand, emphasizes the individual's membership and functioning within the collective (family, community, and ethnic) group; it involves ethnic helpers, customs, and cosmic forces in the process of personal change.

To implement applied values, the social worker needs a body of knowledge from which to develop an ethnic theory base. This section surveys these knowledge parameters and details representative theory.

SOCIAL WORK PRACTICE THEORY

Systems Theory

Systems theory is a framework used to analyze complex situations and the relationships that comprise them. General systems theory originated in the physical sciences and was adopted by the social sciences and later applied to social work (Compton & Galaway, 1979; Goldstein, 1973; Pincus & Minahan, 1973). In general systems theory, complex adaptive systems describe relationships between individuals and other subsystems such as family, relatives, neighborhood, school, job, church, and community. People's problems are viewed as products of transactions between systems. Theorists of social work practice have used systems theory as the knowledge theory base to explain the interaction of person and environment (Germain & Gitterman, 1980; Meyer, 1976).

Systems theory has provided social work practice with a new set of terminology. For example, a *boundary* is a semipermeable demarcation line that defines the components of a system. Boundaries define individual and relational components and filter information entering or leaving the system. The term *equifinality* refers to the accomplishment of similar outcomes by different developmental routes from different initial conditions. Individual systems are in the process of change and seek multiple goals. Equifinality is concerned with emergence, purpose, goal seeking, and self-regulation.

The main contribution of systems theory is its orientation of the client and the worker to a field of interrelated systems. The individual, family, group, organization, and community conduct transactions with each other, and these transactions result in dynamic changes. Subsystems include, among others, the client system, worker system, change system, target system, and action system. The worker and the client are able to analyze various change efforts, target and task systems, and appropriate change strategy methodologies. These interactive systems have a cyclical relationship to each other; that is, there is a circular sphere of interacting systems rather than a linear cause-and-effect explanation of the client's problem. Systems are connected through input, throughput, output, and feedback loops.

In multicultural practice, the worker and the client use systems theory to explain and examine the interaction of various systems. For many cultures, an interdependent relationship exists between the individual and the family. The individual is a subsystem of the collective family system. The family system consists of nuclear and extended components that provide a support system for socioeconomic needs and supportive care. The church and family association are examples of primary community systems that nurture the individual and family.

Systems theory identifies the problem need in the system where problem changes must be effected, assesses the other significant resources in the client system, and determines information exchange in the communication-feedback system. Systems theory focuses on the target system (the specific situation and peoples), which must be altered through an intervention plan. Organizing an action system consists of devising goal outcomes, behavioral objectives, and task assignments. System groupings facilitate relationship building, problem identification, assessment, intervention, and termination and provide a schematic framework to conceptualize interaction in the helping process.

Systems theory places less emphasis on psychopathology and more emphasis on the influence of interaction between the client and the various systems in the environment than other theories do. In systems theory, the problem is not considered intrapsychic but rather an interaction of numerous systems impacting each other. Likewise, the intervention strategy is based on modifying particular systems rather than focusing exclusively on changing the client system. Systems theory brings social work practice back to the person in the situation and emphasizes the range of systems that surrounds the client.

Psychosocial Theory

Psychosocial theory stresses the relationship between the environmental stressors that impact the person and the person's psychoindividual reaction. The objective of psychosocial theory is to mobilize the strengths of the individual and the available social resources. As a result, the social problem environment changes.

Psychosocial theory builds on the individual's biological-physical condition, psychological development, social environment, and cultural influences, which are a part of human growth and development. Moreover, the interaction of these components shapes the current reality for a person. For example, members of the African American underclass are victims of racial discrimination that affects psychological development and social environment. Low self-esteem, survival stress, and related factors of poverty result from these psychosocial influences. Asian Americans tend to exhibit psychophysiological symptoms of stress. Cultural factors demand the suppression of psychological stress, which is then manifested in physical complaints. Psychosocial theory explains the interrelationship between, in this example, the psychological and physical levels. It reiterates the principle that changes in one aspect of a person's functioning affect other dimensions of the psychosocial condition.

However, the major contribution of psychosocial theory is that it focuses attention on the role of the social environment. The external environment has a complex and powerful impact on people—particularly people of color. The worker must carefully learn about and thoroughly understand the client's socioenvironmental history. In turn, the worker and client must identify the changes that need to be made to a particular social environment.

This type of psychosocial study examines the positive strengths and negative limitations of the person and the social situation, the resources available in the person's environment and social service community, and knowledge about the social situation that might be useful for change strategy. In contrast to intrapsychic and interpersonal theories, psychosocial theory underscores the social orientation of social work.

KNOWLEDGE THEORY AND PEOPLE OF COLOR

Community Level

Because the experience of people of color is multifaceted, it is important to conceive of a range of knowledge theories applicable on several levels. On the community level, conflict theory speaks to the domination of the "haves," who have power and authority over the "have-nots." Murase (1983) explains that proponents of conflict theory view inequality as resulting from a struggle or competition for scarce resources, privileges, and rewards. In this struggle, the groups in power get what they want and prevent the less powerful from getting what they want.

People of color are kept in a subordinate position because it serves the interests of the dominant

groups to maintain such a stratified system. The concept of domestic colonialism, a specific application of conflict theory, states that whites use culture as an instrument for dominating other groups. White Americans in the eighteenth, nineteenth, and early twentieth centuries sought to impose Euro-American family patterns on people of color while attempting to destroy indigenous family systems. Implicit in the application of conflict theory to people of color is the knowledge of their history, which illustrates the conflict between the minority and majority society, particularly oppression and exploitation of the former by the latter. Conflict and power dominance are expressed in institutional racism and blaming the victim. In the process of being dominated, ethnic communities in this country have been relegated to a position of underdevelopment and dependency on a social structure similar to a colony in the classic sense. Conflict between the dominant society and colonized groups occurs when the latter attempt to break free of those controls (Murase, 1983).

In this analysis, social work has been cast as the social control arm of society. Ethnic clients seek out public welfare workers, who offer limited cash and material assistance in accordance with social regulations. Naturally, people of color are suspicious of social workers, who represent the distributors of human resources. In multicultural practice, social workers should personalize their contact with clients and learn to be advocates of social justice and equity in human services.

Family Level

On the family level, systems theory explains the role of the individual within the family social system. A social system is a configuration of identified subsystems with prescribed roles and functions. In many cultures, the family is the major integrative entity for individual participation and interaction. This entity prescribes individual role performance within the values and beliefs of the family. A natural support system involves a network of individuals and groups brought together by a common bond. The extended family, friends, neighbors, minister, and community comprise an extensive support network.

A relevant multicultural family theory is the concept of psychohistorical experience. For people of color, cultural intrusion and the attendant disruption of family systems are central to that experience. According to Red Horse (1983), the psychohistorical experience of Native Americans has been that whole generations have been separated from the family system. For example, Native American children have been removed from natural family systems for what the United States termed "protection from abusive environments" and "cultural enrichment." The government's rationale was to provide socioeconomic opportunities and education programs away from the nuclear family. Young adults were removed from kin systems to participate in employment training programs at urban industrial sites. The elderly were isolated on reservations or placed in long-term care facilities far from their homes. As a result of this experience, most Native American families strive to preserve culture and are suspicious of outside authorities and human service professionals.

In the African American community, cultural intrusion takes its toll on families through economic stress. Elements of the intrusive cycle include job loss, public assistance, alcoholism, spouse and child abuse, and desertion. Latinos, too, have experienced cultural intrusion. For example, when economic forces drive poor Mexicans across the border to work for subminimum wage in California's fields and sweatshops, the legacy of family disruption is felt through generations.

For Asian Americans, cultural intrusion took the form of a series of exclusion acts in the early twentieth century. Unable to marry women of their own ancestry because of these immigration quota restrictions, many Chinese American, Japanese American, and Filipino American men who came to the United States as laborers remained single and still live alone in urban and rural ghettos; these elderly men have lost contact with relatives in their native countries.

Individual Level

On the individual level, role theory is useful in understanding interactional behavior. George Herbert Mead (1934) developed the concepts of *role* and *generalized other.* In Mead's view, the self is composed of the attitudes of various individuals with whom the person interacts in his or her sphere. It reaches full development when a person's self consists of the attitudes of particular individuals and the internalized attitudes of the community, the generalized other. In many ethnic communities, individuals learn family and community role relationships. The eldest son or daughter is invested with the role of a surrogate parent to younger brothers and sisters. The father's role is that of authoritative decision maker, and the mother's role is that of mediator between the children's wants and the father's authority. Role diffusion occurs when individual prescribed roles are rejected and the generalized other of the ethnic community is set aside; role conflict arises between community role expectations and the wishes of the individual. The intent of role reintegration is to reach a balance between intended roles and personal choices.

ISSUES IN CULTURALLY DIVERSE KNOWLEDGE THEORY

In multicultural practice, the social worker encounters clients who present varying degrees of ethnic group membership, ranging from traditional ethnic to Americanized. Armed with an analytical framework that incorporates concepts of ethnicity, culture, minority, social class, racism, prejudice, and discrimination, the worker confronts an individual client, who may or may not have been affected by those phenomena. The client is a unique representative of an ethnic group with a collective personality. In collaboration with the client, the social worker must carefully evaluate the influence of each factor—for example, ethnicity—on the client's psychosocial identity as a person and as a member of a particular group. An awareness of the scope of culturally diverse knowledge theory is the first step toward the subsequent use of ethnic information relevant to the problem situation of a particular client.

It is crucial to delineate issues of culturally diverse knowledge theory that address the situation of people of color. A case can be made for developing a multicultural theory base that influences social work practice rather than drawing implications for people of color from existing social work knowledge theories.

This section deals with issues of culturally diverse knowledge theory related to ethnicity, culture, gender, minority, and social class. Each concept contains a body of knowledge crucial to understanding people of color. Social work theorists should integrate these themes into practice knowledge.

Ethnicity

The concept of ethnicity is fundamental to culturally diverse knowledge theory. Davis (1978) defines *ethnicity* as a sense of identity based on loyalty to a distinctive cultural pattern that is related to common ancestry, nation, religion, and/or race. Mindel and Habenstein (1981) explain that the ethnic group consists of those who share a unique social and cultural heritage passed on from generation to generation and based on race, religion, and national identity. DeVos (1982) further places ethnicity in a time frame: (1) present-oriented membership as a citizen of a particular state or a member of an occupational group; (2) future-oriented membership in a transcendent, universal, religious, or political sense; or (3) past-oriented self defined by ethnic identity based on ancestry and origin. Ethnic definitions, according to DeVos, refer to an independent past culture that shares common religious beliefs and practices, language, historical continuity, and/or ancestry of place or origin.

Ethnicity is a powerful unifying force that gives the individual a sense of belonging based on commonality. Gordon (1964) observes that an ethnic group possesses a feeling of peoplehood. Likewise, Green (1982) states that members of an ethnic group have a sense of sharing. Ethnic consciousness—that is, an awareness of distinctive ethnic culture—came to new prominence in the 1960s and 1970s with the growth of the African American civil rights movement, which was part of a wave of ethnic group mobilization. Stimulated by these developments, white ethnics became more conscious of their distinctive cultures (Mindel & Habenstein, 1981). Ethnicity has become an organizing force that provides a sense of community, a way of coping with an impersonal world, and a means of social mobilization in a multicultural context (Greeley, 1969).

Aspects of Ethnicity. Green (1982) differentiates two dimensions of ethnicity: categorical and transactional. *Categorical ethnicity* refers to the manifestation of distinctive characteristics, in terms of skin color, music, food, and socioeconomic status, for example. *Transactional ethnicity* is concerned with the ways people behave and communicate their cultural distinctiveness. It defines social boundaries in terms of ceremonies, technology, language, and religion. Furthermore, Green argues that idiosyncratic differences in ethnicity between the worker and client can become the basis for a healthy sense of individual identity and capability. He notes ethnic resources such as culturally based communication styles, healthy cultural values, and family and peer support. DeVos and Romanucci-Ross (1982) categorize four approaches to ethnicity:

1. Ethnic or social behavior that ranges from organization to disorganization within social structure and produces social change

2. Patterns of social or ethnic functioning and deviancy in ethnic interaction, including patterns of conformity behavior and social conflict accommodation

3. Focus on the self as the subjective experience of ethnic identity in terms of adaptation and maladaptation and changes in the life cycle or in social conditions

4. Personality patterns in ethnic behavior that emphasize adjustment and maladjustment as well as psychosexual and cognitive development

These views of ethnicity tend to emphasize the ethnic person, ethnic social influence, or an interaction between the two.

Harwood (1981) points out that differences exist among people within a given ethnic group, but its members nevertheless have common origins, a sense of identity, and shared standards of behavior, to which professional providers from other ethnic groups may be unable to respond appropriately. He identifies three aspects of ethnicity that form the basis for collectivities or groups:

1. Ethnic social ties of common origins
2. Ethnic shared standards of behavior or norms shaping the thoughts and behavior of individual members
3. Ethnic collective participation of members with one another in a larger social system

A distinction may be made between behavioral and ideological ethnicity. According to Harwood, *behavioral ethnicity* refers to distinctive values, beliefs, behavioral norms, and languages learned by members of an ethnic group during the socialization process. These distinctive cultural standards serve as the basis for interaction within the group and with members of other ethnic groups and for participation in mainstream social institutions. *Ideological ethnicity* is based on such customs as special food preferences, the celebration of certain holidays, or the use of dialect phrases or words from an ancestral language when speaking English.

McGoldrick (1982a) identifies seven factors that influence ethnicity:

1. The stresses of migration to a new situation and the potential abandonment of much ethnic heritage

2. The preservation of the languages spoken in the home

3. The identity of race and country of origin

4. The family place of residence in an ethnic neighborhood

5. The socioeconomic status, educational achievement, and upward mobility of family members and the relationship of these factors to ethnic dissociation (the process by which individuals sever ethnic identity and social class ties and reduce identification with their ethnic group as they move socioeconomically into the dominant society)

6. The emotional process (loyalty, ambivalence) in the family

7. The political and religious ties to the ethnic group

McAdoo (1993) asserts that the family is primary in ethnic identification. She interprets family ethnicity in terms of strength in diversity. Cultural Study 4-1 explains her viewpoint.

CULTURAL STUDY 4-1

Family Ethnicity

Ethnic identification has evolved so that it now transcends individual differences and has become *family ethnicity*, or the identification of entire families or clusters of individuals, who may or may not be aligned in racial grouping or land of origin, with certain ethnicities. Immigrants have come to the United States and have found commonalities that transcend individual countries. They have formed into clusters that are closely aligned with their continents of origin.

Family ethnicity is the sum total of our ancestry and cultural dimensions, as families collectively identify the core of their beings. Our ethnicity is fundamental to our identity. Families differentiate themselves from other groups and form linkages with families who assume similar identifications and provide reference groups for their members. Ethnicity involves unique family customs, proverbs, and stories that are passed on for generations. It includes the celebrations, the foods that are eaten, the religious ceremonies that are shared, and the stories of how the first family-members came to this land. A family's involvement in its ethnicity may be ongoing and intensive or may arise only occasionally. Almost all of us are from families with ties to ethnicities. Our ethnicity is one of the most basic elements of our being.

From "Introduction," by H. P. McAdoo. In H. P. McAdoo (Ed.), *Family Ethnicity: Strength in Diversity.* Copyright © 1993. Sage Publications. Reprinted by permission of Sage Publications.

Behavioral Characteristics of Groups. An effort has been made to differentiate the behavioral characteristics of various ethnic groups. McGoldrick (1982b) has made preliminary observations on seven ethnic groups. Although they tend toward stereotypic generalizations, they are useful as a starting point in discussing ethnic group behavior. The following is McGoldrick's tentative typology, derived from working with ethnic groups in a Bowen[1] family systems approach to therapy.

Irish. The Irish rely on personal responsibility, privacy, and humor. They often have difficulty with closeness and tend to be cut off emotionally. There is a need to respect their personal boundaries and privacy. They may respond minimally but significantly. The Irish often use humor to create distance. They also tend to silently cut off communication without discussing the issues, thus submerging emotional response. They need individual encouragement, particularly feedback about continued work on their own.

Italian. The Italian nuclear family is extremely enmeshed within family subsystems and has personal relationships with extended family. Separation is perceived by the family as betrayal. Small independent moves of family members can create great waves in the family. Disclosure of family secrets and breaking taboos can also be problematic. Separation of children, especially daughters, from the family feels threatening to fathers, who fear they will lose their position. Italians feel a need to maintain family unity and strength.

Jewish. Jews tend to have extremely close and supportive relationships, tend to understand themselves, and are family-oriented. They acknowledge the positive value of Jewish heritage, but many Jewish families have closed off their feelings about experiences in the Holocaust. Trips to Israel can put them in touch with cut-off aspects of family and culture. Family conflicts tend to center around money, family businesses, and attendance at family gatherings. Complaints about family members, meant to help, may instead escalate the problem. Jewish families are brought together around family gatherings (for example, a bar mitzvah or wedding).

WASP. WASPs (White Anglo-Saxon Protestants) are interested in family genealogy and background. They exhibit a need for personal space, distance, and boundaries. WASPs tend to cover over family triangles and issues for reasons of respectability. It is difficult to persuade WASP families to talk about feelings, particularly negative ones; everyone keeps up appearances. Whites from this background value personal responsibility and privacy, being an individual in the family, and independent thinking and planning ahead.

Puerto Rican. Puerto Ricans are attached to the informal kinship network of extended kin, godparents, and neighbors who assist with child-rearing. Puerto Ricans feel a need to be connected with their family. Enmeshment and a lack of differentiation from the family can create problems, particularly for daughters.

African American. Pride and a sense of connection to family and culture have special meaning for African Americans. It is important to ask African Americans about informal kinship systems and significant family connections. At times, African Americans may be reluctant to find out about their history. They may feel anxiety about relating to certain dysfunctional family members and shame about aspects of the family's past.

Greek. Greeks have a strong sense of ethnic pride and cultural heritage. There is often much competitiveness among family members. Rigid family roles lead to cultural conflict, particularly as the younger generation differentiates itself and becomes acculturated in the United States. Greeks prefer individual work because it would be difficult for them to expose themselves as a group.

Chinese. Chinese family structure is based on a formalized system with deep historical roots, unlike the family emotional system of Americans. An emphasis on the natural system and its allegiances would be appropriate in working with this formal multigenerational structure.

---

1. Murray Bowen's approach emphasizes interaction among family systems. See *Notes on Bowen Systems Therapy with Different Ethnic Groups*, by M. McGoldrick. An unpublished discussion paper, 1982. Reprinted by permission of the author.

As previously noted, ethnicity is the basic foundation for individual and group identity. It is the unifying force that brings a people together on the basis of race, ancestry, nation, and/or religion. Social work practice uses these aspects of ethnicity to help a person "belong to," "relate to," and "take pride in." In addition, some ethnic characteristics and qualities tend to differentiate groups: for example, behavioral reactions, family structure, sense of cohesion, and interactional intensity. Further investigation of ethnic dynamics and working with particular ethnic groups would be helpful to social workers and other human service professionals.

Ethnic Implications for Practice. Pinderhughes (1989) underscores the importance of ethnic identity: "How one feels about one's ethnic background very often is a reflection of how one feels about oneself" (p. 40). In other words, when a person internalizes negative feelings about personal ethnic worth, he or she often experiences insecurity, anxiety, and psychological conflict. The dominant society may communicate messages about being a "despised minority" and may attribute low status to, and express denigration of, a particular ethnic group. Such negative societal attitudes impact on the individual's sense of identity and personal meaning as part of that ethnic group.

The practice task in this instance may be to separate larger societal group prejudices about an ethnic group, which have been internalized by the client, from individual and ethnic group understanding of the group's ethnic identity, which has positive meaning for the client. This is no easy task, but the client must learn to differentiate between these two perspectives. Two natural responses to ethnic identity conflict are denial and avoidance. Denial eases the pain of conflict and negative identity, whereas avoidance creates distance from the ethnic group (Pinderhughes, 1989).

Cultural Study 4-2 describes how denial and avoidance of Jewish identity created a lifelong problem for one person.

CULTURAL STUDY 4-2

Ethnic Identity

A university instructor had lived with her family in a predominantly Anglo-Saxon, anti-Semitic community. Her family acknowledged its Swedish connection through her immigrant mother, celebrated Swedish holidays, was careful to "attend the right church, right schools, and make the right friends." When she was a teenager, her parents announced that her father was Jewish with the gift of the book, *One God, Three Ways*. She had reacted to this knowledge of ethnic connection with fear, horror, and nightmares. Her father's real cultural identity was kept a secret from other family and friends, or so she thought. Later she learned that his conflict over Jewish identity reached back to her paternal grandparents. Her grandmother had refused to attend her father's bar mitzvah, which was held at the insistence of the grandfather. After many years, she encountered a friend who told her that her Jewish identity had been suspected by many. With this revelation, she said, "Many unexplained incidents that had occurred during those years, such as slights, and not being included, suddenly clicked." Interaction with colleagues after this description revealed her ongoing struggle to master the sense of conflict she had internalized. When addressed by one as Jewish, she bristled and said it felt as though she were being forced to choose one identity instead of both. Later in acknowledging her ethnic identity first as neutral then as dual, she expressed the conflict she felt: "It's anti-Semitic to disown who you are but it's destructive to not be who you want to be," i.e., she did not feel Jewish. Her helpfulness to students and clients struggling to clarify ethnic identity confusion was, according to her own admission, severely compromised by this conflict.

Ethnic pride and strengths are vital assets for a person's self-esteem. Therefore, it is important to help a client through an ethnic identity conflict and to find positive worth as a part of an ethnic group. This means exploring negative feelings of self-hatred, isolation, and rejection due to societal racism, prejudice, and discrimination and contacting positive feelings associated with ethnic heritage and accomplishment and the structural strengths of an ethnic group. Exploration of negative feelings of ethnic identity is the precursor to building a positive sense of identity on the basis of the pain and anguish suffered.

Culture

Culture deals with our social heritage. Gordon (1978) defines *culture* as the way of life of a society, consisting of prescribed ways of behaving or norms of conduct, beliefs, values, and skills. Brislin (1981) views culture from a cross-cultural contact perspective in terms of interaction with unfamiliar people and focuses on people's characteristic behavior, ideas, and values. Hodge, Struckmann, and Trost (1975) refer to culture as the sum total of life patterns passed on from generation to generation within a group of people. Culture includes institutions, language, values, religious ideals, habits of thinking, artistic expressions, and patterns of social and interpersonal relationships. Green (1982) explains culture as elements of a people's history, tradition, values, and social organization that become meaningful to participants in an encounter. The essential idea of these explanations is that culture reflects the lifestyle practices of particular groups of people who are influenced by a learned pattern of values, beliefs, and behavioral modalities.

Cultural Pluralism. Pantoja and Perry (1976) define *cultural pluralism* as "a societal value and a societal goal [that] requires that the society permit the existence of multicultural communities that can live according to their own styles, customs, languages, and values without penalty to their members and without inflicting harm upon or competing for resources among themselves" (p. 81). Gordon (1978) observes that American society is a composite of groups who have preserved their own cultural identities. Within the cultural patterns of the national society is the cultural diversity of the ethnic subsociety. Gordon refers to this as "the subculture of the ethnic subsociety." Within cultural pluralism, ethnic groups maintain their own communal social structure and identity, values and behavior patterns. In group relations, a level of tolerance persists as long as there is no conflict with the broader values, patterns, and legal norms of the entire society.

Cultural pluralism initially envisioned a utopian society in which ethnic groups maintained their distinctiveness and coexisted in harmony and respect. Each group would participate in the common culture, thus resulting in a federation of ethnic groups. However, a realistic view of cultural pluralism recognizes the right of multicultural groups to coexist as recognized entities within a larger society that tolerates and encourages multiple cultures.

Cultural pluralism has superseded previous notions of assimilation and the "melting pot," or the Americanization of all ethnic races and cultures. According to Jiobu (1988), assimilation is the blending of the culture and structure of one ethnic group with the culture and structure of another group. Assimilation allows two possible outcomes: Anglo conformity or the melting pot. Anglo conformity describes the maintenance of the dominant group and modification of the ethnic group, which loses its distinctiveness and merges into the dominant group. In the melting pot model, by contrast, the dominant group and the ethnic group both lose their distinctiveness and blend homogeneously together, to form a unique product.

Within the context of cultural pluralism, where society remains heterogeneous, some people confront the problem of biculturalism and marginality. As Gordon (1978) explains, the marginal individual stands at the border, or margins, of two cultural worlds and is a member of neither. Such individuals may be from a racially mixed or interfaith marriage or may have personality traits and experience that place them between the dominant group and an ethnic group. They can choose among a number of alternatives: remain in the marginal position indefinitely, return to their ethnic group of origin, or participate in a subsociety of marginal people who have a commonality of lifestyle.

Galan (1992) writes about biculturalism among Mexican Americans. He introduces the concepts of bicultural conflict and bicultural tension and notes the role of acculturated children in bicultural socialization. Cultural Study 4-3 presents Galan's views.

CULTURAL STUDY 4-3

Bicultural Socialization

Bicultural conflict occurs when an individual's family values and behaviors are different from those of the society at large; there is a high degree of incongruence, or contrast, between family values and societal values. Although bicultural conflict need not necessarily be a problem, it can lead to bicultural tension. Typically, "new Americans" who have immigrated to the United States experience bicultural conflict immediately, whereas native-born Mexican-Americans usually experience conflict when they enter child-care or school situations outside the home.

Bicultural tension occurs when an individual's available coping skills are based on only one value system: either that of the family or that of society. The individual therefore is not able to use his or her coping skills in both family and societal situations. For example, if an individual learns coping responses from the family, such responses are used to adapt to family situations. Those same family-prescribed coping responses, however, may be socially problematic and not useful in adapting to situations outside of the family.

When adaptation is difficult, particularly adaptation to the majority culture, issues of adjustment may surface. The pressure to adapt to one's environment is, in part, integral to mastery of situations outside the family. Individuals who are not able to develop coping responses to adapt to societal situations experience stress that can sometimes be displaced on other family members.

Where one parent is culturally traditional (high adherence to family values and low adherence to societal values) and a child is more acculturated (integrated family and societal values) or assimilated (high adherence to societal values to the exclusion of family values and behaviors), the child may be cast in the role of helping a parent relate to society. Interactions with the representatives of social systems can strongly affect the individual's or family's self-esteem (Cohen, 1970). Acculturated or assimilated children who speak Spanish and English usually have the coping skills necessary to adapt to societal situations, whereas their monolingual parents may not. "Dual-frame-of-reference" children are placed in family roles that correspond to the needs they help their "single-frame-of-reference" parents meet. (Saenz, 1978). . . . As the children develop coping responses and skills in the majority culture, and as they discover a new power to manage societal situations, they may find themselves in conflict with one or both parents, whose coping repertoire is limited to family situations. Perceived threats to family unity may precipitate crises. . . . [C]hildren who have the coping skills to adapt to both family and societal situations may find themselves plunged into adult roles in order to help alleviate family stress.

From "Experiential Focusing with Mexican-American Males with Bicultural Identity Problems" by F. J. Galan. In K. Corcoran (Ed.), *Structuring Change: Effective Practice for Common Client Problems*, pp. 236–238. Copyright © 1992 Lyceum Books, Inc. Reprinted by permission.

The marginal individual confronts difficult choices. However, cultural resolution—whether it be with the dominant group, the ethnic group of origin, or another subculture—is vital for the individual's well-being and purposeful direction.

Behavioral Effects of Culture. Various functional characteristics of culture underscore its importance as a major behavioral influence. Price-Williams (1979) believes that culture is central to

FIGURE 4-1 *The Individual, Culture, and Group*

Individual ◄────── Culture ──────► Group
(bearer of culture)   (intersubjective factor)   (locus of culture)

an understanding of the dynamic ways people function and interact in their primary environment. Bilmes and Boggs (1979) view culture as the intersubjective phenomenon that connects the individual as the bearer of culture with the group as the locus of culture. A major implication of this view is that, without a cultural tie, the individual is unrelated to his or her primary group, from which identity and meaning derive. With the cultural linkage as the interface, the individual is able to relate to and communicate with his group locus. Figure 4-1 illustrates this foundation of culture.

Bilmes and Boggs (1979) state that culture—conduct, habit, and customs—governs behavior. Likewise, Draguns (1979) asserts that culture shapes behavior and personality and that behavior rooted in individual personalities produces degrees of cultural change. According to Bilmes and Boggs, culture constitutes a code that guides the interpretation of behavior. Thus, culture is a primary element of the cognitive system that makes actions intelligible to others (Bilmes & Boggs, 1979) and provides ways of communicating, thinking, and interacting with others and with one's environment (Ciborowski, 1979). Finally, culture is a system of knowledge; parts of the behavior code exist in the minds of some members of the cultural group (Bilmes & Boggs, 1979).

Certain elements of culture interact in clusters, as follows (Cuellar, 1984):

1. Collective cultural influences (ways of relating within the group, view and use of time, language, beliefs, group experience, group identity, and way of life)

2. Cultural choices (food, dress, accepted norms and values, lifestyle, religion, emphasis on education)

3. Cultural arts (music, dancing, architecture, and other forms of expression)

4. Cultural coping systems (child-rearing practices, family structure and network, ways of identifying problems, ways of problem solving, and use of available resources)

Theories of Culture. The impact of culture on human behavior and social functioning may be described within the framework of three different theories, each with particular emphases: the systems, cultural-duality, and cross-cultural relations theories. All the theories underscore the primary influence of culture on the client's makeup.

Culture-Centered Systems Theory. Bates and Harvey (1975) present a culture-centered systems theory, in which culture is conceptualized as society in a latent state. Culture is society stored in the memories of the society's members or latent behavior patterns, awaiting the conditions that will reactivate that portion of the social system. Personality combined with culture produces certain individual capabilities:

1. Organic capacities, disabilities, drives, or motivations
2. Perception mechanisms and equipment
3. Organic memory, recall, and associational mechanisms
4. Neurological motor control mechanisms
5. Learned-memory content, such as experiential and factual information and learned attitudes toward culture, self, and others

Situational and interactional factors within the social system account for the way latent behavior becomes active; that is, these factors serve as the mechanism whereby society as stored cultural patterns meets society as actual action.

Figure 4-2 illustrates the relationship among culture, personality, and society. In the view of Bates and Harvey (1975), culture consists of behavioral rules that are stored as a learned program for action. Culture interacts with personality to result in overt behavior. In turn, society is the behavior members perform in relation to one another.

FIGURE 4-2 *Culture-Centered Systems Theory*

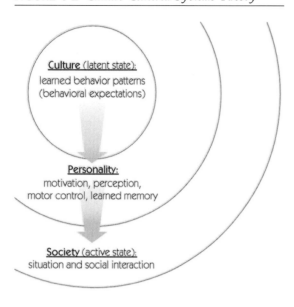

Culture (latent state):
learned behavior patterns
(behavioral expectations)

Personality:
motivation, perception,
motor control, learned memory

Society (active state):
situation and social interaction

Cultural-Duality Theory. Chestang (1976) has presented a social work knowledge theory that highlights the environment as an influence on social functioning. In the African American experience (which may be generalized to other ethnic groups), three socioenvironmental conditions affect the individual: social injustice, societal inconsistency, and personal impotence. *Social injustice* is the denial of legal rights and as such is a violation of social agreements. *Social inconsistency* is the institutionalized disparity or contradiction between word (affirmation of self-worth and esteem) and deed (societal rejection, demeaning of African American culture and ethnicity). *Personal impotence* is the individual's sense of powerlessness to influence the environment. The African American is tied to the larger society through his or her incorporation of its values, norms, and beliefs. This incorporation of the dominant culture means that the individual has been acculturated by the prevailing social system. The social conditions that confront African Americans cause a split in the acculturative process.

In consequence, the African American has established a cultural duality, distinguishing between sustentative and nutritive aspects of culture. *Sustentative aspects* consist of tools, weapons, shelter, material goods and services necessary for livelihood, physical comfort, and safety; they pertain to the instinct for survival. The sustentative aspects are associated with the dominant culture. *Nutritive aspects* relate to attitudes and beliefs, ideas and judgments, codes, institutions, arts and sciences, philosophy, and social organization for expressive thinking, feeling, and behavior; these aspects fulfill needs for psychological and social gratification, identity, intimacy, and emotional support.

Brown (n.d.) has applied cultural duality to Native Americans:

> Native Americans, as other ethnic minority populations, have experienced much incongruence between the two systems. The nurturing culture has validated the individual and family and generally produces feelings of positive self-worth and being valued. The sustaining system has given messages and structural rigidity which devalued Indian people and their ways. The difference between these two systems has led to institutional racism. To cope with the situation, it becomes necessary for [Native Americans] to develop two ways of relating and coping: one set of behaviors for the nurturing system and another set for use in the sustaining system. In the nurturing system, one can have status, respect and clearly-defined roles and contributions. In the sustaining system, the same person or family may be roleless and be judged as worthless, resistant, inadequate or problematic. Self-esteem is high in one system; it is challenged and eroded in the other. (p. 114)

Cultural duality affects character development. Adaptation to the sustaining and nurturing environments is associated with two types of character development. The depreciated character incorporates society's negative attributions and emerges from the sustaining environment. The transcendent character incorporates positive ethnic community images and is supported by the nurturing environment. Culture plays a strategic role in both types of character development. From Chestang's (1976) perspective, culture—that is, cultural duality—is a response to socioenvironmental

FIGURE 4-3 *Cultural-Duality Theory*

Social environmental conditions		Cultural duality		Character development
Social injustice Social inconsistency Personal impotence	Acculturative process	Sustentative aspects of culture (survival) Nutritive aspects of culture (support)	Adaptation	Depreciated character Transcendental character

conditions and results in character development adaptation (see Figure 4-3).

Cross-Cultural Relations Theory. Bochner (1982) presents a cross-cultural relations theory that begins with the premise that human beings are social creatures who interact as individuals, as groups, and as societies. Individuals belong to family, work, recreational, worship, artistic, and political groups, all of which tend to be hierarchically organized. Social groups reflect culturally homogeneous and heterogeneous societies. In the United States, culturally diverse groups are composed of many different ethnic subgroups. Societies and cultures can be compared internally and externally. Societies differ internally in cultural homogeneity and externally in terms of cultural dimensions between members of the same or different societies.

Given these groups and subgroups, major differences exist between interactions among members of the same society and interactions that cross group boundaries. Race, skin color, language, and religion are factors that determine these differences. In-group and out-group ("us" and "them") differentiation suggests that out-group members are seen in more stereotypic terms than are members of the in-group. Bochner asserts that discrimination against out-group members could be reduced by individuating them. He summarizes research that explains surges and declines in prejudicial attitudes, social perceptions, attributions, and behavioral indexes.

When contact occurs between groups within the same society or between two or more societies, the range of possible outcomes includes genocide, assimilation, segregation, and integration. *Genocide*

is the systematic and ruthless killing of members of a group by a dominant or technologically superior group. *Assimilation* takes place when a group or society gradually adopts or is forced to adopt the customs, beliefs, and lifestyles of a dominant culture. Through assimilation, members of ethnic groups become culturally and physically indistinguishable from the mainstream after a few generations. The working assumption of the dominant group seems to be that assimilated groups are inferior and self-rejecting and the majority culture is superior. *Segregation* occurs when the dominant group adopts a policy of separatism with respect to one or more areas—such as geography, culture, schools, or marriage—to keep out unwanted people, ideas, and influences. *Integration* takes place in a culturally pluralistic society when different groups maintain their cultural identity and yet merge into a single entity. Integration allows differences in worship, politics, recreation, occupation, and other areas to coexist within a broad framework of identity, values, and goals. Cases of successful social and/or ideological integration between differing cultures are known. For example, various ethnic groups have come together for a political purpose or over a community issue. On the individual level, the outcomes of cross-cultural contact can range from cultural rejection to acceptance; each of these has its effect on the person.

Bochner (1982) suggests that cross-cultural relations can be enhanced if each person regards others as different but interesting. Contact with an outsider is an opportunity to learn about the world in general and another culture in particular. Both parties must be sensitive to the impact they have on each other, and each must make an effort to learn about the other's culture.

FIGURE 4-4 *The Transcultural Perspective*

Cultural Implications for Practice. Culture is a key factor shaping multicultural practice. Pinderhughes (1989) asserts that culture defines the problem perspective, the expression of the problem, the treatment provider, and the treatment options. For example, it is well known that there is a high rate of treatment dropout after the first interview among ethnic clients. The primary reason for termination may be cultural insensitivity on the part of workers unaware of cultural behavior patterns and protocols. In other instances, the problem might be caused by the worker's focus on negative and dysfunctional aspects of culture as a response to the systemic situation rather than on positive aspects. If this is the case, the worker should consider reframing the problem to include positive cultural strengths within a strategy toward change. Likewise, the treatment approach must be consistent with a cultural framework that values directive task-centered approaches, environmental approaches to changing the problematic condition, the interdependent extended family, and practical advice giving. Ethnic clients respond readily to these practice emphases. Proceeding from this treatment framework, practice must be culturally relevant to ethnic clients (Pinderhughes, 1989).

The worker must strive to master those aspects of cultural pluralism that have implications for practice. Essential to this understanding are various notions of cultural interaction. Five perspectives are applicable for the practitioner: the transcultural perspective, the cross-cultural perspective, the paracultural perspective, the metacultural perspective, and the pancultural perspective. These dimensions of culture relate to the practice emphases the worker must consider when interacting with people of color.

The *transcultural perspective* (see Figure 4-4) involves the social worker who must make a transition from one culture to another. The prefix *trans-* means "across; over; on the other side of" and denotes a movement in one direction. The worker's task is to move from the dominant culture to the client's culture of origin. It requires the worker to learn to understand at least one other culture—its values, beliefs, customs, language, and related practices. The objective of the transcultural perspective is to enable the worker to relate to a designated client who is part of that particular culture.

Culturally diverse social work practice has tended to adopt a transcultural perspective, in that it has generated practice knowledge and skills about the four major groups: African Americans, Latino Americans, Asian Americans, and Native Americans.

The *cross-cultural perspective* (see Figure 4-5) concerns the mutual interaction and synthesis of two distinct cultures. The word *cross* means "to go from one side to the other; to pass across"; therefore, *cross-cultural* means moving between two cultures. To achieve cross-cultural integration, the worker moves back and forth between the client's culture of origin and the client's experiences with the dominant culture. In the process, the worker sees relationships between distinctive similarities and differences of the two cultures. A cross-fertilization of conceptual and behavioral patterns occurs in the process of mutuality. The cross-cultural perspective views each culture as a separate and equal entity, and the cross-cultural worker links essential cultural traits between the two cultures.

In some respects, cross-cultural psychiatry and psychology have focused on East-West clinical

FIGURE 4-5 *The Cross-Cultural Perspective*

FIGURE 4-6 *The Paracultural Perspective*

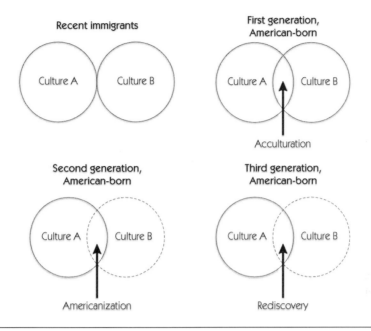

personality and therapeutic distinctions. Social work practice should examine the clinical findings of these two emerging subdisciplines and apply their knowledge bases to its own professional viewpoint.

The *paracultural perspective* examines the relationship between recent immigrants and multigenerational (see Figure 4-6) American-born descendants. The prefix *para-* means "alongside; by the side of," and the paracultural perspective offers a side-by-side comparison of at least four generations of ethnic family structure. To apply this perspective, the worker must be familiar with multigenerational family therapy that involves immigrant or refugee parents and their American-born children, grandchildren, and great-grandchildren. Each generation is involved in acculturation, Americanization, or rediscovery of the culture of origin.

Jung (1998) describes his multigenerational experiences with his parents and himself in Cultural Study 4.4.

CULTURAL STUDY 4-4

Multigenerational Cultural Integration

For me, life has been a process of integration. I learned to integrate and heal the emotional wounds of my childhood by finding peace with my parents. I learned to integrate the early conflicts in my marriage by relinquishing angry and resentful feelings and focusing instead on what was good and loving in our relationship. My exposure to various ethnic communities has allowed me to admire and accept the good every culture has to offer. My understanding of Catholicism, Confucianism, Taoism, and Buddhism has allowed me to integrate the beauty each has to offer into an eclectic philosophical view of life. Finally, my comprehension of various clinical models has permitted me to integrate them into a varied approach for working with families in therapy.

As with all immigrant families, my parents' task was to integrate and find peace in their adopted country. Even though they were confronted with the typical adversities faced by immigrants, including discrimination, financial hardship, and intergenerational conflicts, they were able to achieve their dreams and provide a home life that allowed their children and grandchildren to succeed in taking advantage of the opportunities this country has to offer. Their success was the result of their ability to adapt to their host culture while honoring their own cultural values of reciprocity, loyalty, respect, honor, self-efficacy, and altruism.

My parents, for the most part, adjusted to the American culture rather than becoming assimilated into it. They identified with being Chinese, and their primary cultural, social, recreational, and psychological needs were met within the Chinese community. They carried their culture of origin with them.

I, on the other hand, like others belonging to the first generation in America, have had to integrate aspects of both Chinese and American culture. I was able to accomplish this by accepting, knowing, and taking pride in my ethnic heritage. As a therapist, I recognized that to deny my Chinese heritage would be to deny my very existence. Once I accepted my ethnicity, I could select from it and from the broader culture the elements that were meaningful and enhancing and disregard those that were meaningless and detracting.

From *Chinese American Family Therapy: A New Model for Clinicians* by M. Jung, pp. 28–29.

The worker may be involved with a family in which the father and mother are recent immigrants or refugees and are familiar with their culture of origin but unfamiliar with the dominant culture. For them, the two cultures exist side by side without penetration. However, their American-born children are in the midst of acculturation, which involves a merger of both cultures. Misunderstanding and conflict may arise between parents and children over culture-related issues. In other cases, the worker may work with second-generation American-born parents and third-generation American-born children. A father and mother of the second generation may be Americanized to the point where the culture of origin has minimal influence and residual effects and the values and beliefs of the dominant culture predominate. At the same time, their third-generation American-born children may be in the midst of rediscovering their great-grandparents' culture of origin.

FIGURE 4-7 *The Metacultural Perspective*

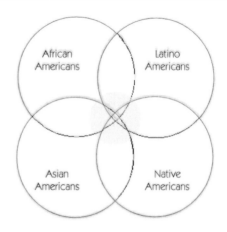

eration American-born children. A father and mother of the second generation may be Americanized to the point where the culture of origin has minimal influence and residual effects and the values and beliefs of the dominant culture predominate. At the same time, their third-generation American-born children may be in the midst of rediscovering their great-grandparents' culture of origin.

The *metacultural perspective* addresses the commonalities of people of color in terms of cultural values, beliefs, and behavior (see Figure 4-7). The prefix *meta-* has traditionally been understood to mean "beyond," in the sense of transcendence. However, *meta-* also means "between; among," and the metacultural perspective is concerned with comparisons between and among cultures. A worker who adopts a metacultural perspective is concerned with cultural linkages that bind the major ethnic groups. The metacultural framework acknowledges differences and affirms common cultural themes among people of color. Shared cultural themes include racial oppression, collective family, and religious strength.

This book emphasizes cultural themes common to all people of color. It offers a generalist culturally diverse practice model that addresses process stages. The decision to generalize information applicable to all people of color rather than to stress distinctions between particular

FIGURE 4-8 *The Pancultural Perspective*

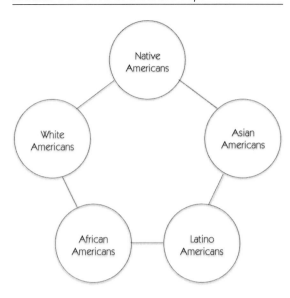

groups has attracted some criticism. However, there is a pressing need for a metacultural overview that draws together themes from different ethnic cultures. This effort will continue, as no doubt will the debate between those who support it and those who do not.

The *pancultural perspective* articulates universal cultural characteristics that are common to people throughout the world (see Figure 4-8). The prefix *pan-* means "universal; common to all," and the pancultural perspective reaffirms the notion of the common culture of humanity. In a real sense, multicultural social work must offer a pancultural perspective, which encompasses the various ethnic groups and also the dominant white culture with which they must coexist.

In previous generations, social work practitioners were concerned with developing a generalist practice framework that could be universally applied to all clients. Only within the last fifteen years have practitioners come to recognize clients' different cultural needs. A growing literature deals with cultural issues for people of color in general and for particular ethnic groups. The pancultural perspective seeks to build on this foundation by the continuing development of culturally diverse knowledge theory. Fundamental to the pancultural perspective is the conviction that the culture and ethnicity of *all* people are important factors in the helping process.

Takaki (1993) invokes a pancultural vision at the end of his history of multicultural America. Pointing out that this country fears its own diversity, he makes a passionate appeal for us to recognize our wholeness as members of humanity and one nation. He pleads his case in Cultural Study 4-5.

CULTURAL STUDY 4-5

America's Dilemma and Diversity

America's dilemma has been our resistance to ourselves—our denial of our immensely varied selves. But we have nothing to fear but our fear of our own diversity. "We can get along," Rodney King reassured us during an agonizing moment of racial hate and violence. To get along with each other, however, requires self-recognition as well as self-acceptance. Asked whether she had a specific proposal for improving the current racial climate in America, Toni Morrison answered: "Everybody remembers the first time they were taught that part of the human race was Other. That's a trauma. It's as though I told you that your left hand is not part of your body." In his vision of the "whole hoop of the world," Black Elk of the Sioux saw "in a sacred manner the shapes of all things in the spirit, and the shape of all shapes as they must live together like one being." And he saw that the "sacred hoop" of his people was "one of many hoops that made one circle, wide as daylight and as starlight, and in the center grew one mighty flowering tree to shelter all the children of one mother and one father." Today, what we need to do is to stop denying our wholeness as members of humanity as well as one nation.[2]

As Americans, we originally came from many different shores, and our diversity has been at the

2. Rodney King's statement to the press, *New York Times*, May 2, 1992, p. 6. Interview with T. Morrison, *Time*, May 22, P. 121. Black Elk. (1988). *Black Elk Speaks: Being the Life Story of a Holy Man of the Oglala Sioux*, as told to J. G. Neihart (Lincoln, NB), p. 43.

center of the making of America. While our stories contain the memories of different communities, together they inscribe a larger narrative. Filled with what Walt Whitman celebrated as the "varied carols" of America, our history generously gives all of us our "mystic chords of memory." Throughout our past of oppressions and struggles for equality, Americans of different races and ethnicities have been "singing with open mouths their strong melodious songs" in the textile mills of Lowell, the cotton fields of Mississippi, on the Indian reservations of South Dakota, the railroad tracks high in the Sierras of California, in the garment factories of the Lower East Side, the canefields of Hawaii, and a thousand other places across the country. Our denied history "bursts with telling." As we hear America singing, we find ourselves invited to bring our rich cultural diversity on deck, to accept ourselves. "Of every hue and caste am I," sang Whitman. "I resist any thing better than my own diversity."

From *A Different Mirror: A History of Multicultural America*, pp. 427, 428, by R. Takaki. Copyright © 1993 Little, Brown and Company, Boston. Reprinted by permission.

Gender

Most studies on racial and ethnically diverse groups are not gender-specific and focus on individuals, families, and communities of color. Culturally diverse studies were more concerned with developing general principles of how to work with people of color rather than distinctions about the unique concerns of ethnic women. There is limited research on ethnic gender differences and diverse feminist issues due to the domination of feminist therapy by white women writers. Gender oppression and therapeutic solutions to this issue dominated the scene at the expense of admitting the problem of ethnic/racial oppression and its resulting consequences in the lives of women of color.

There is a gradual dawning of awareness that racial, ethnic, and cultural factors are just as important as gender oppression concerning women. Moreover, women of color practitioners (Aguilar & Williams, 1993; Collins, 1990; Comas-Diaz &

Greene, 1994; Greene, 1994; Kliman, 1994) have begun to reflect and write on the unique problems and issues facing multiethnic and culturally diverse female clients. These contributions represent crucial components to delineating the particular helping approaches for this group.

The Need for a Multicultural Gender Perspective. Brown (1990) has analyzed the limitations of existing feminist therapy and the need to increase a multicultural theory-building perspective. On the one hand, she points out that feminist therapy and feminist therapy theory were developed by white women who excluded diversity issues that were the concerns of women of color, poor or working-class women, and non–North American women. Past feminist therapy theory was based on a sociological description of the external reality and social context (for example, gender and societal oppression) and a phenomenological recollection of the lived and inner reality of women's life experiences. Both approaches attempted to describe the interactive relationships of internal and external realities of predominantly white working- and middle-class women.

Brown, on the other hand, advocates the development of a multicultural gender therapy theory base with four goals:

• The creation of a multicultural, nonwhite and non-Western feminist database on the varieties of female experiences connected with research questions and data gathering that are guided by a feminist consciousness

• The deemphasis of gender oppression as the primary central issue for women of color, poor women, and women from non-Western cultures and the inclusion of multicultural female socialization experiences, which may vary according to ethnic and cultural gender social factors

• The search for how internal reality is shaped by diverse external experiences using phenomenology (observable, reported descriptive experiences) and introspection (personal sharing of an ethnic-cultural perspective in relationship to one's culture of origin and participation in the dominant society) as tools for theory development

- The place of cultural factors outside the control of particular group members that shape the internal experiences of individual women and women related to a particular ethnic group and become symbolic representations of how women accept culturally defined roles and yet transcend them to become liberated persons in their cultural society

Comas-Diaz and Greene (1994) summarize the tasks ahead for the inclusion of multicultural themes into a feminist approach of working with women of color. In Cultural Study 4-6, they set forth areas of concern.

CULTURAL STUDY 4-6

The Creation of Multicultural Feminist Themes

As therapists and scholars, we need to reconstruct our psychological knowledge of women by incorporating a more inclusive thinking into our approaches to psychotherapy. When scholarship relevant to women of color infuses our psychological paradigms, it challenges both our traditional definitions of womanhood and our conceptualization of mental health. This informed context necessitates a revision of the assumptions made about normalcy and deviance, adaptive and maladaptive (dysfunctional) behavior, and psychotherapeutic success or failure. Race, gender, class, and sexual orientation are examples of variables that may profoundly affect women's lives. The importance of these variables makes it essential to recognize the significance of racism, sexism, and heterosexism; oppression and domination; and power and powerlessness as critical and often ignored realities in the lives of women of color.

The dominant mainstream culture places expectations on women of color that are often a mass of contradictions and a series of paradoxes: They find themselves in circumstances that require them to be strong, resilient, instrumental, and self-affirming in order to survive, yet cultural norms frequently define "normal" women as weak, fragile, vulnerable, submissive, and oppressed. Many women of color have spent so little time focusing on their own needs rather than others' that in mental health treatment they are often unaware of what their needs even are. When they seek clinical services they bear the additional burden of determining whether the practitioner will be familiar with the worldviews of their cultures. In addition, traditional mental health treatment has been an institutional voice that tends to invest White middle-class values with the legitimacy of psychological normalcy. Hence, when White middle-class women seek mental health services they often correctly presume that the treatment and the clinician incorporate their worldviews in some way. This is not the case for women of color.

From Preface by L. Comas-Diaz and B. Greene. In L. Comas-Diaz and B. Greene (Eds.), *Women of Color: Integrating Ethnic and Gender Identities in Psychotherapy*, xv. Copyright 1994 by Guilford Press. Reprinted by permission.

Current Multicultural Feminist Issues. Pinderhughes surveys the multiple issues confronting multicultural women of color in Cultural Study 4-7:

CULTURAL STUDY 4-7

Women of Color Issues

Women of color, living as they do in a racist social system that is also patriarchal, are a "double minority." Along with men of their cultural groups, they are trapped in roles that maintain the equilibrium of the larger social system. These dynamics operate through a societal projection process, which encourages the dominant group in society to perceive and treat subordinate groups as inferior and incompetent, and thereby to benefit from the continued exploitation of these groups (Bowen, 1978).

Being victimized by the societal projection process and serving as systems balancers and anxiety reducers for the larger social society has had profound consequences for people of color in their individual, family, and group functioning. It has also had profound consequences for the beneficiaries of this process, creating high vulnerability to an intolerance for cultural differences, an unrealistic sense of entitlement, poor reality testing, and unsound judgment of self and others (Pinderhughes, 1989). These are issues that remain largely out of the dominant group's awareness, and unexamined by them.

Whether a woman of color is considered a member of an oppressed cultural group and it is her subordinate sex-role status that must be understood, or whether she is considered a member of an oppressed sex group and it is her subordinate cultural identity that must be understood, her circumstances are unique. In belonging to two groups whose positions are determined by oppression, her experience differs from that of her fellow victims, the man of color and the White woman, because her reality involves the dynamics of both racism and sexism. Not only must she cope with the confusion and contraction inherent in her position as a member of a minority cultural group that functions at the boundary of society, but she must also cope with expectations related to her role of nurturer and supporter of others. This role pushes her to fulfill the role of provider and protector from which men of color have been blocked. At the same time it is expected that she will nurture men in her life and cope with their reactive anger as well as nurture and support their children's attempt to thrive in a hostile environment.

Women are generally expected to relieve tension and reduce anxiety within their families, but this expectation for the woman of color must be realized with fewer resources and societal supports than are available to White women.

The woman of color is called upon to compensate for the costly consequences of her family's and cultural group's role as balancer in the larger social system. In so doing, she herself becomes a balancing mechanism within her family and cultural group. Such a role places her at a nodal point in the overall functioning of a society.

Viewed then via stereotypes that too often have determined societal treatment of her; confined by the dynamics of the societal projection process to low-paying, low-status work; with a weakened or absent extended family and few alternate forms of support to buffer her interface with a nonsupportive, frequently racist, external world; and blamed for consequent family conflict and breakdown, the woman of color finds her nodal role a formidable one.

Mental health intervention with women of color requires an understanding of this nodal societal role, the dynamics that maintain it as a significant contextual factor in the problems of women of color and those of their families, the solutions they might seek, and even the intervention process itself. Empowerment of these women so that they can cope effectively with the consequences of their societal entrapment becomes a fundamental goal in the work. Clinicians, if they are beneficiaries of this unjust social system, are, like their minority women clients, nevertheless trapped in it. They may find their ability to help compromised by the automatic benefits inherent to their beneficiary status, making them susceptible to the perpetuation of their clients' victim status.

From "Foreword" by E. Pinderhughes. In L. Comas-Diaz and B. Greene (Eds.), *Women of Color: Integrating Ethnic and Gender Identities in Psychotherapy*, xi, xii. Copyright 1994 by Guilford Press. Reprinted by permission.

Morris (1993) observes, "Women of color stand at the intersection of two worlds, subject to the interactions of racism and sexism in every arena of their lives. Indeed, many women of color also suffer from economic discrimination; others face social stigmatization because of sexual orientation" (Morris, 1993, p. 100). These interrelated issues lock the woman of color into a series of dilemmas: racism, sexism, economic discrimination, and social stigmatization due to gender and ethnicity.

Morris (1993) identifies five current issues facing multicultural women of color: societal oppression, interacting oppression, family bonds and oppression of men of color, stereotypes and myths, and power/power differentials.

Societal Oppression. The societal oppression of multicultural women of color is grounded in the beliefs and practices of a sexist and racist society.

Historically, minority women were exploited as cheap domestic and agricultural workers, while today's professional women of color often gain access as token appointments in an organization. Comas-Diaz and Greene (1994) identify the double bind of racism and sexism in the workplace. They point to tokenism, stereotyping, isolation, balancing of multiple responsibilities, conflicted self-esteem, depression, stress and anxiety, psychosomatization, and addictive behaviors as possible fall-out reactions of professional women of color.

Moreover, multicultural women are doubly oppressed inside and outside their culture around a patriarchal value system that diminishes the value of their cultural or racial status. These women must walk a fine line between fulfilling the role expectations of their cultural groups and remaining authentic persons who value their autonomy as equals with their husbands and other males. There is a constant demand of the multiple roles as breadwinner, family spokesperson, and nurturer to husband and children that takes its toll on the modern woman of color.

Morris (1993) suggests a number of ways that multicultural women ought to deal with societal oppression. There is a need for consciousness-raising—that is, an opportunity to tell one's own story in one's own voice to other women, men, and mixed gender groups. This leads to action that changes the order of things. Some examples of change action involve sharing of household responsibilities with one's spouse, involvement in women's support groups and ethnic feminist organizations, and an attitude of self-assertiveness within the context of a profound respect for one's cultural expectations as a woman. One must define one's own life choices while remaining true to one's self, spouse, family, and community. Moreover, a woman of color ought to become politically active, asserting personal power and modeling a positive sense of self for one's children, while advocating social change regarding gender issues.

Interacting Oppression. Regarding interacting oppression, Morris (1993) believes that we must understand the lives of those who are multiply oppressed in terms of the simultaneity of oppres-

sions affecting Third World women. Root (1992) has coined the term *insidious trauma* to describe the cumulative effect of racism, sexism, dislocation, and other types of oppression. Comas-Diaz and Greene (1994) discuss "the exclusion, marginality, and invisibility of women of color in the mental health literature," which has been a subtle form of oppression, ignoring the plight of multicultural women (p. 7).

The theme of interacting oppression reminds us that we must not be absorbed in a societal oppression that engulfs the woman of color. Rather, we must be aware of interacting oppression that affects many sisters of color in a horizontal and circular manner. We must share the multiple burdens that test our coping system, interacting and healing each other in the process. We must address this common concern about our experiences with multicultural men who are similarly laden with multiple expectations and demands.

Family Bonds and Oppression of Men of Color. Morris (1993) identifies two unique issues that affect women of color: family and racial bonds and the oppression of men of color. For people of color, the family unit is considered the most important transmitter of race, ethnicity, and culture. The family is emphasized over that of individual members to the extent that the individual wishes of a particular family member are subordinate to the good of the family as a whole.

In traditional ethnic families of color, the mother is the nurturing, caregiving person for her husband and children. Multicultural parents, particularly fathers, value obedience to parental authority from the children. In many families the mother is the liaison between father and children. Both parties communicate their wishes and feelings through the mother. She discusses the concerns of the children with the father who, in turn, communicates the decision making through the mother to the children.

Family function varies among the major multicultural people of color groups in the United States. For Native Americans men and women have historically shared work and family roles in many tribes. American Indian men hunted for the family and tribe, shared in the responsibility of raising and teaching children about cultural practices, and protected the family from danger. American Indian women tended the crops, made clothes, and were responsible for the daily tasks of the village community. In many instances, American Indian women participated in tribal council discussions and decision making.

During the 1990s, American Indian women were elected tribal leaders who coordinated the education, health care, social services, and business activities of the tribe. They have been articulate spokespersons for the political, economic, and social concerns of Indian people.

In African American families, there is a sense of corporate responsibility among adult males, females, and children. The extended family clan has been the source of pooling resources for child care and rearing and for teaching appropriate values and skills. African American women believe in strong kinship bonds, achievement motivation, religious and spiritual beliefs and practices, and work orientation to keep families together.

Traditional Asian American families tend to be patriarchal with father as the leader of the family, mother as the nurturing caretaker, and sons of more value than daughters. The family relationship is based on filial piety and mutual obligation. The child is expected to obey parents and elders. In turn, parents are responsible for the upbringing, education, and support of the child.

The mother is particularly involved in helping the children with their problems and communicating their needs, concerns, and desires to the father. The children generally feel emotionally closer to the mother than to the father. Asian American women have had to cope with an external subordinate role and maintain harmony in the family, extended family, and ethnic community. This is expressed by a strong work ethic and deference to the authority of the father or husband. However, Asian American wives may be assertive with their husbands in private and may have decision-making power behind the scenes. The Asian American woman practices a dual perspective: assuming a serving role in her Asian culture and expressing assertiveness in the dominant society.

Latino Americans value the extended family structure and interaction in their daily lives. In the Latin American family, fathers have prestige and authority. He is recognized as the provider of the family. *Dignidad* is a fundamental value for the Mexican American family, while the father demonstrates the machismo (strong courage and protection) of the Latino male on behalf of the family. Latinas have been taught that the family is the most important value in the culture. The traditional role of Latino American women in the family involves devotion to her children and respect and assistance to her husband. There is an increasing recognition that there is equity in decision making and conflict resolution between the Latino father and mother. At the same time Latinas nurture and care for the family and maintain family unity and connections (Vasquez, 1994).

Related to the multicultural family and gender issues is the oppression of minority men. Historically the white male dominant society sought to exclude men of color from the ownership of land, political power, and meaningful employment opportunities. Minority men were the source of cheap labor and marginal employment. The minority male underclass consists of young adult and middle-age men who have been unable to secure steady skilled employment because of educational, familial, and economic problems. Often they turn to crime, are arrested, and sent to prisons that have predominantly African and Latino American inmates. Recently African, Latino, and Asian street gangs have been involved in drive-by shootings and home invasion robberies. These peer groups have turned to violence as an expression of their alienation and frustration with societal oppression.

Women of color have been reluctant to denounce men of color for gender oppression. Rather, multicultural women are concerned about job training and employment for their men. A steady job has a positive effect on family stability as far as the presence of father, anticipated income, and family cohesion are concerned. White male domination of the economic system has been linked to the exclusion of opportunities for men of color and the marginal employment of women of color as domestic and sweat shop workers.

Daly, Jennings, Beckett, and Leashore (1995) bring a new understanding of African American men. Rather than discuss the problem pathology or oppression of this group, the authors offer a positive perspective of the health, well-being, and success of African American males with their families. Cultural Study 4-8 focuses on the provider role and family life satisfactions of married African American men.

CULTURAL STUDY 4-8

The Success of African American Males

The health and well-being of African American males are examples of the efficacy of indigenous coping skills. Racism and discrimination have historically blocked the door to opportunity for many African Americans. Yet many African American males have been successful (Gary & Leashore, 1982; Hacker, 1992). Much of their success can be attributed to individual and family resilience, the ability to "bounce back" after defeat or near defeat, and the mobilization of limited resources while simultaneously protecting the ego against a constant array of social and economic assaults. To varying degrees, success results from a strong value system that includes belief in self, industrious efforts, desire and motivation to achieve, religious beliefs, self-respect and respect for others, responsibility toward one's family and community, and cooperation.

Traditionally and conventionally, social and behavioral science research has largely ignored African American males who actively assumed the role of provider for their families. However, there is an emerging body of literature that focuses on African American males from within rather than from without the context of family life. Their relationships and socialization with their children and family and spousal satisfactions are also of interest (Allen, 1981; Braithwaite, 1981; Cazenave, 1979; Gary & Leashore, 1982; Madhubuti, 1990; McAdoo, 1981; Staples, 1977). Two analyses of data from the *National Survey of Black Americans* 1979–1980 (Jackson & Gurin, 1987) illustrate the research that is emerging. In the first analysis, Taylor, Leashore, and Tolliver (1988) examined the provider role as perceived by 771 African American males. Over half (54 percent) perceived themselves as providing very well for their families. Generally, younger men were the least likely to perceive themselves as good providers, whereas those 65 and older were the most likely to report that they performed very well in the provider role. A second analysis (Stewart, 1990) examined family life satisfaction among married African American males and found that home ownership, family closeness, and general life satisfaction were positively related to family life satisfaction.

The findings of these analyses suggest that African American men perceive greater success and satisfaction as they mature. The African American community collectively may provide a major structure that enables the development of self-esteem and general life satisfaction for African American males over time. This structure includes the tradition of giving honor and recognition to those in the African American community who have faithfully fulfilled their responsibilities to their families and communities. These men are not dependent on individual achievements such as the amount of earnings to feel good about themselves. Instead, they celebrate fulfilling their role as providers within parameters defined by their community. This perspective is in contrast to the dominant culture, which rewards individualism, competitiveness, and material achievements. Thus, the propensity toward collective in contrast to individualistic identity continues to provide a coping mechanism that enables these African American men to be successful and, indeed, to resist the onslaught of negative images that the dominant culture attributes to them.

From "Effective Coping Strategies of African Americans" by A. Daly, J. Jennings, J. O. Beckett, and B. R. Leashore, *Social Work, 40*, 242. Copyright 1995 National Association of Social Workers. Reprinted by permission.

Stereotypes and Myths. Women of color have been the objects of stereotypes and myths. *Stereo-*

types are prejudicial generalizations about the behavioral characteristics superimposed on all members of a race or sex; *myths* are fictitious stories with no basis in reality. Women of color stereotypes and myths tend to be negative, degrading or positive, overidealized caricatures that serve to maintain the subordination and inferiority of women of color in relations to white women and white America.

African American women have been the subjects of a number of controlling images: the mammy who was the faithful, obedient domestic servant; the matriarch who symbolized the bad mother/absentee working parent, overly aggressive and unfeminine; the breeder of children; the welfare mother dependent on the welfare state who is not aggressive, collects welfare, shuns work, and passes on her bad values to her children; and the jezebel, whore, or sexually aggressive woman (Collins, 1990).

Similar stereotypes are made of other women of color. Latino women are cast as the Madonna (Virgin Mary), or the virtuous, self-sacrificing mother; and the Spitfire, or the volatile and sensuous woman who expresses her anger and makes sexual advances toward men. Asian women have been categorized as the China Doll (the classic traditional woman with the porcelain complexion), the Dragon Lady (the mean and conniving beauty who is plotting against the male hero), and Suzie Wong (the Asian hooker with the high-slit Chinese dress). Native American women are depicted as Princess Pocahontas, the lovely Indian who saved the life of Captain John Smith, or the Indian squaw who is the quiet, hardworking wife of the Indian brave. According to Wynn DuBray (personal communication, 1995) the word *squaw* means vagina and was used in a derogatory sense to refer to an Indian wife. White bounty hunters often cut out the vaginas of Indian victims, turned the organ over, and claimed it for an Indian scalp. They were paid for the number of scalps brought to a white trading post.

Greene (1994a) points out that, via gender stereotypes, African American women have been blamed for family dysfunctioning. African American males are encouraged to believe that strong women are responsible for their oppression, not racist institutions. Racism and sexism combine to cast blame on the African American male and female victims rather than focus on societal systematic causes.

Bradshaw (1994) observes that Asian American gender stereotypes move between two extremes: either exotic, shy, submissive, demure, erotic, and eager to please or wily, manipulative, inscrutable, and untrustworthy. Three stereotypical images of Asian women emerge: the image of sexual objectification (importation of Asian women for sexual labor), the image of the asexual, unattractive, impersonal, and efficient worker or androgynous being; and the image of the domestic servant who is faithful and reverent toward her white family employer.

Greene (1994b) discusses the dynamics of ethnosexual mythology:

> This mythology may include the sexual myths the dominant culture has generated and holds about women of color. Such myths and stereotypes often represent a complex combination of racial and sexual stereotypes designed to objectify women of color, set them apart from the idealized Western counter-parts, and facilitates their sexual exploitation and control. (pp. 393–394)

However, there is a need to move beyond gender stereotyping to achieve discovering the unique person. I have introduced the concept of unique personhood, which recognizes the individuality of each person and seeks to discover the individuality of each person and personal and collective ethnic and gender worth (Lum, 1996). It is the opposite of stereotyping, which prejudges a woman of color by a negative generalization about her group.

Bochner (1982) indicates that deindividualized persons are likely to behave less responsibly and be treated less favorably than individuated persons. Likewise, individuating out-group members could reduce discriminating against them. Valuing the individual woman of color as a unique person means acquainting, knowing, and understanding the total person. The woman of color becomes a person and a human being.

Gender Implications for Practice. Gender knowledge issues should have implications for practice with women of color. The following theme of power explores how a multicultural woman must navigate in her interactions with men of color and white women as well as people in general.

Power and Power Differentials. Women of color experience the imbalance of social, economic, and political power compared with white women and men of color. The term *power differential* describes this state of comparative powerlessness between women of color and white women and men of color. Balswick and Balswick (1995) describe the dynamics of power differentials in marriage from a cross-cultural perspective. The themes of power disruption, deprivation, and egalitarian marriage are important in this discussion. Cultural Study 4-9 introduces these concepts.

CULTURAL STUDY 4-9

Cross-Cultural Power Differentials

Cross-culturally, there seems to be an inverse relationship between how powerful a spouse is and how active and even "disruptive" the spouse must be in order to influence his/her partner. A powerful spouse is influential without having to assert power directly, whereas a less powerful spouse will aggressively make demands to control a partner. The husband who rants and raves, screams and yells, or bullies and badgers is communicating a *lack* of culturally prescribed power. Although wives can also be abusive, they usually disrupt in manipulative rather than violent ways. A wife who appears weak and frail can control her partner by withholding favors, feigning sickness, or appearing to be helpless.

From a multicultural perspective, the relationship between power and marital violence is a husband's feelings of *relative deprivation*. This means there is a greater likelihood of marital violence in marriages in which husbands lack personal powers but live within a society that expects them to be powerful. We expect that marital violence will be least where husbands possess personal power and live in a society that values equality.

In egalitarian marriages, husbands are content with equal sharing of power and mutual decision making with their spouse. In patriarchal systems, the husband whose wife is equally powerful may resort to drastic means to gain more power in the relationship. A powerful husband in a patriarchal system can influence his wife without resorting to marital violence. Therefore an act of marital violence is a sign that the husband wants to control his wife but in reality has little personal clout or power over her.

From "Gender Relations and Marital Power" by J. O. Balswick and J. K. Balswick. In B. B. Ingosdby and S. Smith (Eds.), *Families in Multicultural Perspective*, p. 310. Copyright 1995 by Guilford Press. Reprinted by permission.

Apart from these differences, women of color struggle with power conflicts and choices. Morris (1993) explains:

> These women [of color] are seen as being caught in a series of double binds because of the interactions of racism and sexism in their daily lives. These binds include balancing multiple and conflicting roles, "choosing one's battles" in response to numerous racist and sexist encounters, and coping with conflicting loyalties regarding allegiances to groups representing women and one's ethnic group. Minority women require self-esteem and self-assertion to deal with these conflicts. (p. 104)

In this sense, power differentials result in feelings of powerlessness for women of color.

Powerlessness is the inability to control self and others, to alter problem situations, or reduce environmental distress (Leigh, 1984). In the case of women of color, powerlessness arises out of a racist and sexist process that distorts or denies valued identities and roles as well as valuable ethnic social resources to individuals and groups. As a result, these individuals or groups are unable to exercise interpersonal influence or command the social resources necessary for effective social functioning (Solomon, 1976).

Balswick and Balswick (1995) view *power* as the ability to influence another person in all human relationships, including marriage. According to them, there are three types of marital power:

- The *legitimization of power* (authority versus dominance) means that legitimate power is authority and illegitimate power is dominance; legitimate power in marriage is based on resources (for example, education, material wealth) valued by society, is unevenly distributed in society, and can be used as justification to dominate others; illegitimate power or dominance attempts to control others by ways that are not sanctioned by society such as abusive behavior.

- *Ascribed* versus *achieved power* describes power from the status or position of the person given by society (the ascribed power of the husband) and power earned by contributing resources to those who need and value them (achieved power by proving his worth as a husband).

- *Orchestrative power* and *implementative power* occur when one delegates power to others or when one carries out the task that has been delegated by the person in power (the husband as the decision maker, the wife as the implementer of items delegated by her husband).

Along these lines, Balswick and Balswick (1995) present four models of marital power: the traditional patriarchal model, the resource theory model, the democratic exchange model, and the empowerment model. There is a natural continuum starting with a sexist model and concluding with a feminist model.

The traditional patriarchal model espouses that power in marriage is ascribed to the husband, because he occupies the position of husband (and later father) in the marriage. There is a religious belief that moral authority justifies male authority, to the extent that in religious fundamentalism the husband/father is just below God in authority over the wife/mother and children. Patriarchal male authority is invested through religious teaching about the family hierarchy.

The resource theory model reflects the changes in marriage from a clear division of labor between husband and wife to marital tasks that are allocated to either partner. Marital power comes from the resources held by husband and wife. Marital power becomes a bargaining tool for negotiating between spouses. Marital control of resources is connected to gender-controlled resources at the family and societal levels and cultural ideology. However, resource theory is not widely used in social systems, because cultural change may be more of an influence than power distribution between spouses.

The democratic exchange model holds that husband and wife are given equal power. However, each partner can use differing resources to bargain or negotiate for power. A *resource* is a personal quality or possession that is valued by the other person in a particular culture, such as affection, nurturance, money, and economic and social status.

In contrast to the preceding options, the empowerment model involves the active and intentional process of each spouse, who develops and affirms power in the other. Balswick and Balswick (1995) explain the egalitarian nature of the empowerment model, which speaks not only to multicultural partners but husbands and wives of all cultures, in Cultural Study 4-10.

CULTURAL STUDY 4-10

Marital Empowerment

Most of the research on the use of marital power has focused on how each spouse tries to influence or control the behavior of the other. The underlying assumption is that when one spouse is more powerful, the other partner is less powerful. It follows, then, that the person with more resources has the more powerful position in the marital dyad.

The empowerment model, in contrast, purports that each spouse can use personal resources to move the other from a position of weakness to one of strength. Empowering is not merely one spouse yielding to the wishes of the other. It does not involve giving up one's power to empower others. Rather, *empowering is the active and intentional process of each spouse developing and affirming power in the other*. Each spouse is encouraged to reach full personal potential. Empowerment is an interactive process in which each desires that the other become all that he/she can be. Each believes in the other and uses personal resources to build the other up. This mutually empowering process leads to interdependence in the best sense of the word (Balswick & Balswick, 1987, 1990).

The empowerment model also allows us to focus on autonomy instead of control "over" something or someone. The greater the degree of empowerment in a marriage, the greater the sense of autonomy by each spouse. If marriages are structured so as to encourage each spouse to use his/her respective power for the other, spousal autonomy, as well as mutual respect and interdependence, will result.

The concept of empowerment makes no sense within a theoretical framework that perceives power as a commodity that comes in limited supply. The operationalization of power within social exchange theory, for example, is based on the view that there are a maximum number of power units available in any relationship. *Quid pro quo* (i.e., I get something when I give something) is considered an equal exchange where two people keep a 50/50 account record.

According to the empowerment model, power is available to both partners in *unlimited* amounts. Each has 100 units and does not work toward keeping an equal balance. Rather, each spouse desires that the other be 100% powerful because it benefits and strengthens the relationship. Empowered partners live in a relationship of mutual and reciprocal empowerment of each other. The increase of power is interactive, as the power of one spouse increases the potential for empowerment in the other; in the process, *each* spouse must expand and extend toward growth and greater potential. It is not a simple or nonconflictual process, but the end product is satisfying because both spouses have equally grappled with personal and relational issues that develop character and integrity. Personal power becomes the cutting edge of growth for an empowering marriage.

From "Gender Relations and Marital Power" by J. O Balswick and J. K. Balswick. In B. B. Ingodsby and S. Smith (Eds.), *Families in Multicultural Perspective*, pp. 310–311. Copyright 1995 by Guilford Press. Reprinted by permission.

Rather than controlling each other, each partner is encouraged to be an autonomous person in the relationship. According to Balswick and Balswick (1995), "When feminists criticize patriarchy as self-serving, they are implicitly suggesting that the basis of marital relationships should be one of mutual empowerment. From a feminist perspective, the goal in marriage must be equality. This will only be accomplished when nonoppressive structures are replaced by egalitarian ones" (p. 307). The task is to change the one-down position of the woman built on control. Marital empowerment allows husband and wife to have equal access to all resources and to thrive in the relationship.

Minority

Along with the concepts of ethnicity, culture, and gender, minority is central to a discussion of issues in culturally diverse knowledge theory. Davis (1978) defines a *minority* as a group that is discriminated against or subjected to differential and unequal treatment. It is characterized as subordinate, dominated, relatively powerless, and unequal in other ways. Traditionally, the term *minorities* has referred to racial, national, and religious groups, but it has recently been applied to women, the aged, people with physical disabilities, and the behaviorally deviant. Mindel and Habenstein (1981) view a minority as having unequal access to power and as being stigmatized for traits perceived by the majority as inferior. (According to these definitions, a minority group may not always be smaller in *number* than the dominant majority; a larger population may still be subordinate or disadvantaged, hence a minority.)

Longres (1982) analyzes the dynamics of minority versus majority. Majority and minority interest groups differ in power and influence as well as in position of dominance or subordination. Minority group members tend to have fewer rights and less power than the majority, to have a history of disadvantage, and to lack privilege. Under these conditions, minorities seek to eliminate the domination of the majority. The success of minority groups in overcoming subordination depends on their capacity to work on their own behalf and on the response of the majority.

Davis (1978) likewise points out the discrimination of the dominant community against minority groups. Discrimination is manifested through the control of businesses, occupations, choice property, government, and public facilities and through exclusive organizational membership. Dominant groups value their sense of superiority and perceive action toward the improvement of minority status as a threat to peace and order. It is therefore important to estimate the possibilities and probabilities of change.

Minority Relationships with the Dominant Culture.

Minority status is particularly significant at several points of group contact and interaction. At the time of immigration, racial and cultural groups enter another's territory as minorities. Racial and cultural minorities are formed when political boundaries are created during territorial expansion and when war is declared or peace treaties are signed. Shifts of political power occur when a former minority becomes politically dominant and the ascendant group loses its controlling power, as, for example, at the decolonization of a country and the transfer of power and government to a formerly subjected people. Social groups also emerge with distinctive beliefs and practices in lifestyle, religion, or politics. Homosexuals, Mormons, and American Communist Party members are diverse groups who created new subcultures with marked differences from the dominant social patterns. Finally, minorities differentiated biologically (on the basis of sex, age, or physical condition) are assigned socially discriminatory status and receive prime attention in the public media.

Minority groups interact with the dominant society through competition and conflict. Groups compete for scarce resources such as jobs, housing, and welfare. Conflict occurs when groups meet in direct rivalry that ranges from verbal exchanges to elimination of the other group from competition. However, "small groups may become powerful if they have sufficient economic resources, unity, organization, coordination with other groups, community prestige, access to the mass media and to political decision makers, and other advantages" (Davis, 1978, p. 30). Social workers should assess the particular conflicts or competitive situations confronting minority group clients in their contact with dominant societal groups.

Cultural Assimilation. Davis (1978) defines *assimilation* as a process whereby a group gradually merges with another and loses its separate identity and pride in distinctive cultural traits. The degree of assimilation is based on the modification of minority cultural traits (such as native language, naming system, traditional values, and model personality characteristics). Partial assimilation refers to selective participation in the dominant culture; for example, individuals might work in the dominant society but participate in ethnic community activities in their own minority group (Brislin, 1981). Full assimilation is achieved when immigrant minorities and their children leave behind their ethnicity and blend fully into the majority group (McLemore, 1983).

Related to the degree of assimilation are two basic dimensions: cultural and structural assimilation. *Cultural assimilation* refers to acculturation, or the replacement of minority group cultural traits with those of the dominant community. *Structural assimilation* deals with the integration of social interaction, or the replacement of minority group institutions and informal social patterns with participation in the dominant community. The dominant society is more apt to allow minority assimilation on a cultural than on a structural level. It resists the assimilation of minorities into social institutions (intermarriage), organizations (social club, church), and primary social groups (family) (Davis, 1978). Although assimilation of dominant values and practices does occur, minority groups increasingly are maintaining their own culture. Assimilation, in this sense, relates to our previous discussions of ethnic distinctions and cultural pluralism.

Minority Implications for Practice. The social worker must be aware of the adverse effects of the minority status to which people of color are relegated. A minority person may feel intimidated, threatened, and inferior. Davis and Proctor (1989) have compiled evidence that the dominant society perceives minorities as "different." These differences include color, attitudes, beliefs, and social status. The perception of dissimilarities may play a role in the relationship dynamics between the worker and the minority client. To what extent are workers drawn toward people similar to themselves in ethnicity, attitudes, and beliefs? To what extent do workers avoid clients different from themselves? Davis and Proctor argue that whether a worker responds favorably or unfavorably to a minority client will be markedly affected by consensual validation and attraction—that is, the positive effect of similarity and the confirmation of our sense of social reality; we view others as unattractive if their attitudes, beliefs, and social realities are different from ours.

It is crucial for the worker to become aware of this dynamic in multicultural practice. Its presence requires the worker to make a conscious effort to become familiar with minority culture—in particular, attitudes, beliefs, and behavior patterns. Further, the worker must learn, appreciate, and understand alternative minority perspectives. Bridging the gap between similarity and dissimilarity in an increasingly multicultural society must be a primary professional goal for the social worker. Without this commitment and effort to master minority knowledge and practice skills, the worker becomes a part of the dominant society, which tends to "ghettoize" the minority client physically and mentally.

Davis and Proctor (1989) offer a number of practical suggestions to prepare the worker for multicultural practice. They include (1) development of knowledge about minority populations, particularly general knowledge of race, culture, and ethnicity and specific minority groups' histories, norms, and cultural values; (2) self-examination—and modification, as necessary—of racial attitudes and values regarding prejudice and stereotypes; and (3) development of a wide repertoire of helping responses.

In four states (New Mexico, Alaska, Hawaii, and California), people of color form or will soon form the majority population. Many states have local, state, and national elected officials who are members of ethnic communities. However, ethnic minorities are still subjected to racism, prejudice, and discrimination in subtle forms in the public and private sectors. The social worker must be aware of minority attitudes and must strive to exercise equity in dealings with all clients.

Social Class

A final issue in culturally diverse knowledge theory is social class. Gordon (1978) defines *social class* in terms of social hierarchical arrangements of persons on the basis of differences in power, political power, or social status. Gordon has coined the term *ethclass* to integrate ethnic identity and social class. Ethclass characterizes the social participation or identity of persons confined to their own social class and ethnic group. An ethclass constitutes a subculture within a society. It comprises a set of social relationships among its members and between its members and major social institutions.

Willie has conducted recent research on social class and people of color, particularly African American families. Willie (1979) views social stratification in terms of a horizontal dimension of class behavior and a vertical dimension of caste groups. Occupation, education, and income constitute the important horizontal variables of social class. Race or ethnicity, sex, and age make up the principal vertical categories of social caste. Furthermore, Willie (1981) asserts that racial discrimination, rather than differences in education, is responsible for inequality in employment and income. His case studies of affluent, working-class, and poor African American families illustrate class differences within a single ethnic group.

Affluent African Americans are termed "conformists" and belong to middle-class families with both husband and wife employed outside the home. Willie points out that middle-class African Americans traditionally entered employment initially in such occupations as postal worker and teacher. These jobs accommodated African Americans excluded from other public service positions. Both spouses cooperate on work at home, encourage education, and are involved in community affairs. They are achievement and work oriented and upwardly mobile, and they own personal property.

Working-class African Americans are the "innovators" who struggle for survival and depend on the cooperative efforts of husband, wife, and children. Their income is just above the poverty line, and families often include five or more children. Parents are literate, but their education is limited. As a result, racial discrimination and insufficient education delimit the employment opportunities for working-class African Americans. Long working hours and two jobs, after-school and weekend jobs for children, stable work history, and long-term neighborhood residency characterize this group. People in this group own their own homes, raise their children with a strong sense of morality, and are self-reliant.

Poor African Americans are considered "rebels." Families subsist near or below the poverty level and are often part of broken homes. Extended households allow them to cope with low-income status. They frequently change jobs, houses, communities, spouses, and friends. Unemployment is a constant threat; women usually hold jobs in service occupations, and men are unskilled factory and maintenance workers. Marriage and child rearing occur during the middle teenage years, and some families have eight or more children. First marriages may dissolve, with other marital arrangements taking their place. Parents of this group are grade-school or high-school dropouts. Juvenile delinquency may occur as a result of unstable parental relationships. Fierce loyalty exists among mothers, children, and grandmothers. Brothers and sisters may loyally help maintain family functions when both parents work outside the home. Because of this situation, poor African American families rebel and reject society and experience failure and disappointment. When their hope is taken away, they use violent rebellion as a means of resistance.

Harwood (1981) observes a relationship between ethnicity and social class.

> Within the larger American social system, some ethnic groups are to a significant degree confined to lower-class positions because of barriers to both power and economic resources that are built into the status system by informal and, to some extent still, legal norms. Individual mobility in the class system is also limited for members of these groups. Although the reasons for these political and economic barriers may be explained differently by social scientists of various theoretical persuasions, few would deny that Blacks, Native Americans, and Hispanics in the United States disproportionately occupy the lowest strata of the class system and have historically been restrained within these strata by legal and economic means. (p. 5)

For people of color, social class is influenced by racial discrimination and socioeconomic constraints. Although they may occupy different social class levels, people of color are bound together by the reality of racism and their struggle to survive.

Social Class Implications for Practice. *Social class* refers to a group of people who have certain available economic opportunities, economic goods and resources, and occupations or positions in the economy (Longres, 1990). Implicit in a discussion of social class is the concept of social stratification, which ranks various groups according to economic, educational, and occupational hierarchies. The term *ethclass* recognizes the existence of ethnic and social stratifications in society. Access to life-sustaining and life-enhancing resources differs according to ethnic group. Many people of color suffer material deprivation or poverty. As a result of their lack of access to life-sustaining resources, they feel a sense of individual, family, and community powerlessness. This feeling is expressed in terms of systematic oppression and control of resources by a dominant group in power over oppressed sectors, who experience deprivation and despair. Powerlessness is internalized in the forms of low social status, low self-esteem, and devalued individuals. Self-destructive and self-defeating behaviors of individuals, families, and communities result in social pathology, social and mental disorders, and despair.

Adequate clinical treatment for persons of color must be accompanied by economic, political, and psychological strategies to redistribute resources and to address the problem of differentiation by social stratification. Treatment service programs must include access to employment opportunities, public resources, and material and social support (Prigoff, 1990).

The worker must recognize that social class is perceived as the mark of a person's societal worth. A person's social ranking significantly influences social interactions with other groups. For example, low class status can result in low self-esteem and respect for members of that person's racial group. Because of social status differences, the client may question the appropriateness of the advice the worker gives. Again, the worker must attempt to overcome this barrier and understand the social realities that accompany the client's class status. The worker must not only recognize the boundaries of social class but also advocate social justice and equity despite the limitations imposed by social stratification.

The following practice insights relate to social class status. First, practitioners from lower social class origins tend to be willing to work with clients from a wider range of socioeconomic backgrounds than do workers from higher social classes. Second, low-income clients generally have an external locus of control and view life events as the consequence of factors external to themselves. Social work with these clients will focus on psychosocial external stressors and their impact on people. Third, poor people are similar to other social classes in their aspirations for their children, work orientation, general personality characteristics, and basic life goals. They share middle-class goals and need improved opportunities in the job market.

CONCLUSION

Social work knowledge theory is essential to understanding the underlying themes that motivate people of color in their relationships to others and to society. From the social work knowledge base, systems theory from the social sciences and psychosocial theory from traditional social work practice have been two elements of theory understanding for our discipline and profession. Social work understands working with individuals, families, groups, and communities in terms of a systems analysis and a psychosocial (person and environment) perspective.

Moreover, the themes of ethnicity, culture, gender, minority status, and social class are basic concepts that the student and practitioner must understand. The following chapter builds on this foundation, constructing the framework for culturally diverse social work practice.

REFERENCES

Aguilar, M. H., & Williams, L. P. (1993). Factors contributing to the success and achievements of minority women. *Affilia, 8,* 410–424.

Allen, W. R. (1981). Moms, dads and boys: Race and sex differences in the socialization of male children. In L. E. Gary (Ed.), *Black men* (pp. 99–114). Beverly Hills, CA: Sage.

Balswick, J. O., & Balswick, J. K. (1987). A theological basis for family relationships. *Journal of Psychology and Christianity, 6,* 37–49.

Balswick, J. O., & Balswick, J. K. (1990). *The family.* Grand Rapids, MI: Baker.

Balswick, J. O., & Balswick, J. K. (1995). Gender relations and marital power. In B. B. Ingoldsby & S. Smith (Eds.), *Families in multicultural perspective* (pp. 297–315). New York: Guilford.

Bates, F. L., & Harvey, C. C. (1975). *The structure of social systems.* New York: Gardner.

Bilmes, J., & Boggs, S. T. (1979). Language and communication: The foundations of culture. In A. J. Marsella, R. G. Tharp, & T. J. Ciborowski (Eds.), *Perspectives on cross-cultural psychology* (pp. 47–76). New York: Academic Press.

Bochner, S. (1982). The social psychology of cross-cultural relations. In S. Bochner (Ed.), *Cultures in contact: Studies in cross-cultural interaction* (pp. 5–44) Oxford: Pergamon.

Bowen, M. (1978). *Family therapy in clinical practice.* New York: Aronson.

Bradshaw, C. K. (1994). Asian and Asian American women: Historical and political considerations in psychotherapy. In L. Comas-Diaz & B. Greene (Eds.), *Women of color: Integrating ethnic and gender identities in psychotherapy.* New York: Guilford.

Braithwaite, R. L. (1981). Interpersonal relations between black males and black females. In L. E. Gary (Ed.), *Black men* (pp. 83–97). Beverly Hills, CA: Sage.

Brislin, R. W. (1981). *Cross-cultural encounters: Face-to-face interaction*. New York: Pergamon.

Brown, E. F. (no date). Social work practice with Indian families. In E. F. Brown & T. F. Shaughnessy (Eds.), *Introductory text: Education for social work practice with American Indian families* (pp. 109–152). Tempe: Arizona State University School of Social Work, American Indian Projects for Community Development, Training and Research.

Brown, L. S. (1990). The meaning of a multicultural perspective for theory-building in feminist therapy. In L. S. Brown & M. P. P. Root (Eds.), *Diversity and complexity in feminist therapy* (pp. 1–21). New York: Haworth.

Cazenave, N. A. (1979). Middle-income black fathers: An analysis of the provider role. *Family Coordinator, 28*, 583–593.

Chestang, L. (1976). Environmental influences on social functioning: The black experience. In P. San Juan Cafferty & L. Chestang (Eds.), *The diverse society: Implications for social policy* (pp. 59–74). Washington, DC: National Association of Social Workers.

Ciborowski, T. J. (1979). Cross-cultural aspects of cognitive functioning: Culture and knowledge. In A. J. Marsella, R. G. Tharp, & T. J. Ciborowski (Eds.), *Perspectives on cross-cultural psychology* (pp. 101–116). New York: Academic Press.

Cohen, R. E. (1970). *Preventive mental health programs for ethnic minority populations: A case in point.* Paper presented at the Congresso Internacional de Americanistas, Lima, Peru.

Collins, P. H. (1990). *Black feminist thought: Knowledge, consciousness, and the politics of empowerment.* Boston: Unwin Hyman.

Comas-Diaz, L., & Greene, B. (Eds.). (1994). *Women of color: Integrating ethnic and gender identities in psychotherapy.* New York: Guilford.

Comas-Diaz, L., & Greene, B. (1994). Preface. In L. Comas Diaz & B. Greene (Eds.), *Women of color: Integrating ethnic and gender identities in psychotherapy* (pp. xv–xvii). New York: Guilford.

Cuellar, B. (1984, March). *Components of culture.* Paper presented at the meeting of the Council on Social Work Education, Detroit.

Daly, A., Jennings, J., Beckett, J. O., & Leashore, B. R. (1995). Effective coping strategies of African Americans, *Social Work, 40*, 240–248.

Davis, F. J. (1978). *Minority-dominant relation: A sociological analysis.* Arlington Heights, IL: AHM.

Davis, L. E., & Proctor, E. K. (1989). *Race, gender, and class: Guidelines for practice with individuals, families, and groups.* Upper Saddle River, NJ: Prentice-Hall.

DeVos, G. (1982). Ethnic pluralism: Conflict and accommodations. In G. DeVos & L. Romanucci-Ross (Eds.), *Ethnic identity: Cultural continuities and change* (pp. 5–41). Chicago: University of Chicago Press.

Draguns, J. G. (1979). Culture and personality. In A. J. Marsella, R. G. Tharp, & T. J. Ciborowski (Eds.), *Perspectives on cross-cultural psychology* (pp. 179–207). New York: Academic Press.

Compton, B. R., & Galaway, B. (Eds.). (1989). *Social work processes* (4th ed.). Belmont, CA: Wadsworth.

Galan, F. J. (1992). Experiential focusing with Mexican-American males with bicultural identity problems. In K. Corcoran (Ed.), *Structuring change: Effective practice for common client problems* (pp. 234–254). Chicago: Lyceum.

Gary, L. E., & Leashore, B. R. (1982). High risk status of black men. *Social Work, 27*, 54–58.

Germain, C. B., & Gitterman, A. (1980). *The life model of social work practice.* New York: Columbia University Press.

Goldstein, H. (1973). *Social work practice: A unitary approach.* Columbia: University of South Carolina Press.

Gordon, M. M. (1964). *Assimilation in American life.* New York: Oxford University Press.

Gordon, M. M. (1978). *Human nature, class, and ethnicity.* New York: Oxford University Press.

Greeley, A. M. (1969). *Why can't they be like us?* New York: Institute of Human Relations Press.

Green, J. W. (1982). *Cultural awareness in the human services.* Upper Saddle River, NJ: Prentice-Hall.

Greene, B. (1994a). Diversity and difference: Race and feminist psychotherapy. In M. P. Mirkin (Ed.), *Women in context: Toward a feminist reconstruction of psychotherapy* (pp. 333–351). New York: Guilford.

Greene, B. (1994b). Lesbian women of color: Triple jeopardy. In L. Comas-Diaz & B. Greene (Eds.), *Women of color: Integrating ethnic and gender identities in psychotherapy* (pp. 389–427). New York: Guilford.

Harwood, A. (Ed). (1981). *Ethnicity and medical care.* Cambridge, MA: Harvard University Press.

Hodge, J. L., Struckmann, D. K., & Trost, L. D. (1975). *Cultural bases of racism and group oppression.* Berkeley, CA: Two Riders.

Jackson, J., & Gurin, G. (1987). *National survey of black Americans, 1979–1980* (ICPSR 8512). Ann Arbor: University of Michigan.

Jiobu, R. M. (1988). *Ethnicity and assimilation.* Albany: State University of New York Press.

Jung, M. (1998). *Chinese American family therapy: A new model for clinicians.* San Francisco: Jossey-Bass.

Kliman, J. (1994). The interweaving of gender, class, and race in family therapy. In M. P. Mirkin (Ed.), *Women in context: Toward a feminist reconstruction of psychotherapy* (pp. 25–47). New York: Guilford.

Leigh, J. W. (1984, March). *Empowerment strategies for work with multiethnic populations.* Paper presented at the Council on Social Work Education, Annual Program Meeting, Detroit, MI.

Longres, J. F. (1982). Minority groups: An interest-group perspective. *Social Work, 27,* 7–14.

Longres, J. F. (1990). *Human behavior in the social environment.* Itasca, IL: Peacock.

Lum, D. (1996). *Social work practice and people of color: A process-stage approach* (3rd ed.). Pacific Grove, CA: Brooks/Cole.

Madhubuti, H. R. (1990). *Black men: Obsolete, single, dangerous.* Chicago: Third World.

McAdoo, H. P. (Ed.). (1981). *Black families.* Beverly Hills, CA: Sage.

McAdoo, H. P. (1993). Introduction. In H. P. McAdoo (Ed.), *Family ethnicity: Strength in diversity* (pp. ix–xv). Newbury Park, CA: Sage.

McGoldrick, M. (1982a). Ethnicity and family therapy: An overview. In M. McGoldrick, J. K. Pearce, & J. Giordano (Eds.), *Ethnicity and family therapy* (pp. 3–30). New York: Guilford.

McGoldrick, M. (1982b). *Notes on Bowen systems therapy with different ethnic groups.* Unpublished manuscript.

Mead, G. H. (1934). *Mind, self, and society.* Chicago: University of Chicago Press.

Meyer, C. H. (1976). *Social work practice: The changing landscape.* New York: Free Press.

Morris, J. K. (1993). Interacting oppressions: Teaching social work content on women of color. *Journal of Social Work Education, 29,* 99–110.

Murase, K. (1983). *Asian American communities.* Unpublished manuscript, San Francisco State University, Department of Social Work Education.

Pantoja, A., & Perry, W. (1976). Social work in a culturally pluralistic society: An alternative paradigm. In M. Sotomayor (Ed.), *Cross cultural perspectives in social work practice and education* (pp. 79–94). Houston, TX: University of Houston, Graduate School of Social Work.

Pincus, A., & Minahan, A. (1973). *Social work practice: Model and method.* Itasca, IL: Peacock.

Pinderhughes, E. (1989). *Understanding race, ethnicity, and power: The key to efficacy in clinical practice.* New York: Free Press.

Pinderhughes, E. (1994). Foreword. In L. Comas-Diaz & B. Greene (Eds.), *Women of color: Integrating ethnic and gender identities in psychotherapy* (pp. xi–xii). New York: Guilford.

Price-Williams, D. (1979). Modes of thought in cross-cultural psychology: An historical overview. In A. J. Marsella, R. G. Tharp, & T. J. Ciborowski (Eds.), *Perspectives on cross-cultural psychology* (pp. 3–16). New York: Academic Press.

Prigoff, A. (1990). *Beyond cultural sensitivity: Ethnic and gender stratification in America.* Unpublished paper, Division of Social Work, California State University, Sacramento.

Red Horse, J. G. (1983). *Native American families.* Unpublished manuscript, Arizona State University, School of Social Service Administration.

Root, M. P. P. (1992). Reconstructing the impact of trauma on personality. In L. S. Brown & M. Ballou (Eds.), *Personality and psychopathology: Feminist reappraisals* (pp. 229–265). New York: Guilford.

Saenz, J. (1978). The value of a humanistic model in serving families. In M. Monteil (Ed.), *Hispanic families.* Washington, DC: Coalition of Hispanic Mental Health and Human Services Organization.

Solomon, B. B. (1976). Social work in a multiethnic society. In M. Sotomayor (Ed.), *Cross-cultural perspectives in social work practice and education* (pp. 165–177). Houston, TX: University of Houston Graduate School of Social Work.

Staples, R. (1977). *Black masculinity.* San Francisco, CA: Black.

Stewart, R. (1990). *Familial satisfaction among African American married men.* Unpublished doctoral dissertation, Howard University, Washington, DC.

Takaki, R. (1993). *A different mirror: A history of multicultural America.* Boston: Little, Brown.

Taylor, R. J., Leashore, B. R., & Tolliver, S. (1988). An assessment of the provider role as perceived by black males. *Family Relations, 37,* 426–431.

Vasquez, M. J. T. (1994). Latinas. In L. Comas-Diaz & B. Greene (Eds.), *Women of color: Integrating ethnic and gender identities in psychotherapy* (pp. 114–138). New York: Guilford.

Willie, C. V. (1979). *Caste and class controversy.* Bayside, NY: General Hall.

Willie, C. V. (1981). *A new look at black families.* Bayside, NY: General Hall.

CHAPTER 5

A Framework for Social Work Practice with People of Color

A framework is a structure that systematically arranges parts of a whole, so that an observer can understand the relationships of components to each other. It is a mosaic or a puzzle that has been completed for the viewer to behold. This chapter presents a variety of culturally diverse social work practice frameworks that have been articulated in the last twenty years with the hope that readers will construct their own framework for working with multicultural people of color. There are no right or wrong frameworks. A framework is like your proverbial view of the elephant. You may view the elephant from the front, the side, the top, the bottom, or the rear and gain various composites of this creature. Likewise, you may construct a framework that makes sense to you about a particular area such as culturally diverse social work practice.

How far has culturally diverse social work practice progressed in the human services? Jenkins (1981) declares, "The social welfare field, although deeply involved in serving ethnic clients and training ethnic workers, has only recently and in peripheral ways acknowledged the need for ethnic content in therapeutic and service approaches" (p. 4). A number of reasons explain this lag. Green (1982) cites major theoretical and methodological deficiencies in such areas as training techniques, evaluation schedules, and systematic case studies; abstract directives; and the anec-

dotal nature of multicultural data. Cheetham (1982) characterizes the response of social work to multiracial communities as patchy, piecemeal, and lacking in strategy. It has relied on generic problem analysis and treatment to the exclusion of recognizing ethnic and racial differences. A starting point for remedying these shortcomings is to develop a practice typology or framework that serves as a guideline for ethnic groups and the corresponding settings and service patterns.

A framework for direct practice is designed to orient social work practitioners to working with people of color. As a result, the social worker has a perspective on direct practice (working directly with clients as opposed to working in administration) from which to operate as a helper. The framework sets an operational perimeter and identifies certain procedural principles for workers to follow in the helping effort. It provides the social worker with a degree of flexibility within guidelines and emphasizes specific multicultural subthemes unique to working with people of color.

In this chapter, we consider existing culturally diverse frameworks in relation to the current state of the field. In the following chapters, we present an overview of a model framework for the direct practice of culturally diverse social work. Particular practice process-stage issues are explained in detail. Subsequent chapters discuss the various stages and include detailed ethnic-practice principles, case illustrations, and procedural recommendations.

EXISTING FRAMEWORKS FOR CULTURALLY DIVERSE SOCIAL WORK

Frameworks for culturally diverse social work practice have emerged as a result of individual and group efforts. In this section, we examine a traditional ethnic-sensitive approach to social work practice, a cross-cultural awareness practice perspective, a family therapy orientation, a youth assessment and treatment viewpoint, a cross-cultural practice model, a transcultural assessment and therapy framework for children and youth, a women of color perspective, and a black experience social work practice model. These treatments form the background to the development of our ethnic-practice framework model.

Framework for Traditional Ethnic-Sensitive Practice

In 1981 Devore and Schlesinger wrote the first book on ethnic social work practice—a work long overdue in the field of direct practice. In the broadest sense, the book covers ethnicity, social class, and social work practice and adapts sociological and psychological insights to practice needs. It particularly emphasizes the contribution of class and ethnic factors to the process of assessment and intervention. The need to relate traditional social work practice to ethnic content rests on two basic propositions: (1) that ethnicity and social class shape life's problems and influence problem resolution and (2) that problem-solving social work must focus simultaneously on micro- and macroproblems. These themes draw heavily on the human behavior and practice approaches of social work.

Foundation. Devore and Schlesinger (1981) stress that ethnic reality must be understood on the basis of general knowledge of human behavior and specific knowledge of ethnic group and social class.

Ethnic reality is composed of ethclass, ethnicity, and social class. Human behavior is explained in terms of Erik Erikson's (1959) theory of the life cycle, focusing on specific stages with ethnic content. Together with ethnic reality, several layers of understanding form the foundation of social work practice. The first layer is a basic knowledge of human behavior that incorporates human development and the life cycle; social role; systems theory; an understanding of personality; and a knowledge of agency structure, goals, and functions. These subjects are generally covered in social work courses on behavior and reflect human, social, economic, and cultural influences on people and the environment. The second layer involves self-awareness in terms of the client's ethnicity and its influence on practice. The focus is on cultivating the client's ethnic "who am I?" awareness from the dual standpoint of the parents' ethnicity and the client's religious heritage. The third layer is the impact of ethnic reality on the client's daily life. Work, housing, marital and family relations, child rearing, health, food, and institutional assistance interact with ethnic background.

Ethnic-sensitive social work practice draws on an understanding of human behavior, clarifying its relationship with problem causation and practice application. Devore and Schlesinger offer no new approaches to social work practice. Rather, they attempt to evaluate the dimensions of ethnic reality in the psychosocial, problem-solving, social provision and structural, and systems approaches. Part of the problem in adapting traditional social work practice theory to multicultural practice is the peripheral treatment traditional theory gives to cultural content. Because of its limited focus on ethnic issues, traditional theory leaves most multicultural content to inference. Consequently, few principles for practice with people of color can be drawn from traditional schools of practice.

Working Principles. The following assumptions, principles, and skills related to working with people of color are unique to the framework for ethnic-sensitive social work practice.

• History has a bearing on the generation and solution of problems. The history of ethnic group oppression and the experience of migration into the United States influence individual members of the group. This ethnic history affects personality and lifestyle.

• The past and accompanying problems affect the present. Ethnic group history can influence the perception of present problems, and the ethnic reality—the environmental conditions in which people of color must live—shapes the scope of the problem.

• Ethnic reality is a source either of cohesion, identity, and strength or of strain, discordance, and strife. Multicultural family values, extended family structure, cultural and religious rituals and celebrations, ethnic schools, and language may be sources of support or conflict. These variables influence individual behavior patterns.

• Nonconscious phenomena—particularly cultural routines and dispositions toward life—affect functioning. These phenomena are part of the self and evoke an emotional response.

• Simultaneous attention to micro- and macro-issues requires the integration of individual and systematic change. Economic and social inequity—in the form of racism, poverty, and discrimination—underscore the structural source of the problem and the effect on the individual.

• Understanding the ethnic community means that the social worker should be familiar with population characteristics, the availability of resources, and neighborhood networks that can assist clients. Census material, community publications, and interviews with community leaders are means of uncovering and mastering community dynamics.

• Knowledge of human behavior and self-awareness focuses on ethnic family-life trends and group cognitive, affective, and behavioral responses. Particular class and ethnic dispositions concerning language, culture, and social problems have a bearing on how clients respond to workers. Workers must likewise recognize how their own ethnic background affects their behavior.

• Gathering data before the worker-client encounter enables the worker to review, synthesize, and order information about the client, problem, and referral. It is particularly important to obtain information on ethnic background, social class, and issues of racism or prejudice involved.

• Problem identification consists of setting the stage, using empathetic community responses, and specifying or particularizing the problem. The worker should draw on available information as much as possible before the encounter, alternate between open-ended and directive questions, reflect facts and expressed feelings, share feelings appropriate to the situation and offer opinions and ideas that will increase knowledge of the situation, be responsive to requests for concrete services, move slowly toward reaching for feelings, convey facts readily, be imaginative in finding ways to learn about the problem, understand who the appropriate actors are, start with the client's perception of the problem, and ascertain the link between individual functioning and the social situation.

• Contracting occurs when agreement is reached on how to proceed, what might be accomplished, and what the goals are.

• Problem solving consists of ongoing reassessment of the problem, subdivision of the problem into manageable parts, identification of obstacles, obtaining and sharing of information, review of progress or setback, and termination.

The framework of Devore and Schlesinger (1981) was a preliminary effort to introduce ethnic and cultural meaning into social work practice and to interpret the multicultural implications of existing modalities of social work practice. Relationship building, problem identification, contracting, and problem solving, traditional concepts of social work practice, were applied to ethnic situations. This approach demonstrated that traditional social work practice could be infused with ethnic meaning.

Framework for Cross-Cultural Awareness Practice

In 1982, Green published his book *Cultural Awareness in the Human Services* as a group effort of the University of Washington's social work faculty. Committed to a multiethnic perspective on the delivery of human services, the book places a major emphasis on cultural awareness, or the background of cultural groups. The cross-cultural framework draws on the anthropological theories of Barth (ethnic group), Kleinman (health-seeking behavior), and Spradley (ethnosemantics and ethnographic interviewing). It recognizes that ethnic clients are entitled to competent social services but that social work has been insensitive to cultural differences and has rarely considered its relation to ethnic communities. A cross-cultural model of social work is designed to apply to cross-cultural encounters, organize ethnographic client information, and be useful to a range of social service activities. *Ethnicity* is a key term in this approach. *Categorical ethnicity* refers to manifest cultural differences of individuals and groups, whereas *transactional ethnicity* denotes the ways in which people communicate to maintain their sense of cultural distinctiveness.

Help-Seeking Behavior. Green (1982) adopts a model for what he terms *help-seeking behavior.* His model recognizes the diverse perceptions of ethnic groups in a pluralistic society. Language is a key communicative modality to explain and evaluate experience. A problem is both a personal and a social event; it elicits individual reactions and requires confirmation from others before action takes place. The model has four major components:

1. The client's definition and understanding of an experience as a problem
2. The client's use of language to label and categorize a problem
3. The availability and use of indigenous community resources and the decision-making involved in problem intervention strategies
4. The client's cultural criteria for determining problem resolution

As a support to the model of help-seeking behavior, cross-cultural social work uses ethnographic information in planning, delivering, and evaluating ethnic group social services. It focuses on the social worker's cross-cultural learning and ethnic competence. The worker must learn about

another culture in terms of its cognitive beliefs, affective expression, and behavioral relationships. Ethnic competence involves awareness of cultural limitations, openness to cultural differences, the opportunity to learn about client experience, use of the cultural network of community resources, and the acknowledgment of cultural values of morality, honesty, and integrity within each ethnic group. This knowledge is fundamental to procedural steps. The worker learns about and enters an unfamiliar community by studying background information, visiting the community, and making a social map of ethnic groups, social organizations, community beliefs and ideology, distribution of resources, patterns of mobility, and access to and use of human services. Contact with key ethnic leaders, or gatekeepers, who are willing to share community knowledge provides the worker with information and a continuing relationship. Participant observation is a means of collecting data with some notion of what ought to be observed and why a particular topic is important.

Delivery of Social Services to People of Color. The cultural awareness framework further delineates social services to African Americans, Asian Americans, Native Americans, and Latino Americans. Aspects of help-seeking and help-providing activity are examined in terms of community, family, and urbanization. Each of the principal ethnic groups is presented in the following paragraphs, to familiarize the reader with a specific cultural context.

African Americans. Leigh and Green (1982) trace the historical relationship of social work to the African American community and criticize the profession for its neglect of relevant intervention strategies, family role, and indigenous community institutions. From a historical perspective, the African American family has long existed within a well-defined, close-knit system of relationships. Authority and responsibility have been clearly assigned, and complex rules of behavior have embedded them in village and regional linkages. Family life in the United States was impaired by slavery, but the African American community has survived as an active unit to meet the needs of its members. The church is still a central community institution.

Underlying themes in the African American community include strong bonds of household kinship, an orientation to work for the support of family, flexible family roles, occupational and educational achievement, commitment to religious values, and church participation. African American families participate in extended family networks, which pool resources and provide economic and emotional security. These interdependent relationships form a system of mutual aid in such areas as finances, housing, and child rearing.

Asian and Pacific Americans. Ishisaka and Takagi (1982) use the term *Asian and Pacific Americans* as a collective designation of numerous, disparate, and self-contained groups whose ancestry is in Asia and the Pacific Islands. They trace the history of immigration and resettlement patterns of Chinese, Japanese, and Filipino Americans. Although Asian communities have been remarkably self-sufficient as a result of mutual aid associations, social service statistics have documented needs in the areas of unemployment, the economy, health, and mental health.

Asian Americans have characteristically placed strong emphases on cultural values and family structure. The Chinese American family is, for the individual members, a reference group and source of personal identity and emotional security. It exerts control over interpersonal conduct, social relations, and the selection of occupation and spouse. Japanese Americans are traditionally influenced by strong values of filial piety, respect and obligation, harmony, and group cooperation. Changes in values and family relationships have tended toward increasing individualism. However, avoidance of shame, indirect communication, self-effacement, and modesty appear to be maintained in recent generations. Among Filipino Americans, there are strong family-centered values and extended kinship relationships. Respect is given to the head of the family and to the elderly. Marriage is an alliance between kin networks. The values of group cooperation, mutual obligation, and personal pride and integrity combine to create an interdependent society and conflict-free

relationships. Asian Americans represent diverse subgroups with profound language and cultural differences from mainstream American culture.

Practice with Asian Americans must take into account length of stay and country of origin (foreign-born versus American-born), socioeconomic status, fluency in English, and the history of intergroup conflict. The foreign-born generally require information referral and concrete services, while the American-born seek counseling and treatment. There is a movement toward multiservice, indigenous social service organizations in the Pacific-Asian communities.

Native Americans. Of the four major ethnic groups considered here, Native Americans have the greatest needs in the areas of income, education, health, and mental health. Rates of arrest, drinking, and unemployment are higher among Native Americans than among other ethnic groups. Of Native Americans, one-third live on reservations, one-third live in urban areas, and one-third move between reservations and cities. The children of urban Native Americans have few contacts with traditional life and require coping skills to survive city life. Miller (1982) examined the following nine cultural traits in relation to social services:

- Suspicion and distrust of white professionals and institutions
- Passive nature, avoiding or withdrawing from assertive or aggressive situations
- Shyness and sensitivity to strangers, resulting in low verbal behavior
- Short-term orientation
- Fatalistic view of life
- Respect for individuality, reflected in lax child rearing
- Casual time orientation
- Strong family obligations and extended family relations
- Noninterference with others

She concludes that these traits have not been defined operationally and often result in generalizations and stereotypes. Two traits were highly evident in her study: passivity in seeking services and shyness in interaction with the research investigator and professionals. These seem to be natural responses to outside institutions. On the whole, a wide variety of personality traits, cultural practices, and lifestyles exists.

The study also revealed that Native Americans had difficulty using services and were dissatisfied with the services they received. Part of the reason for this was the presence of institutional barriers, such as direct and indirect cost, unclear agency procedures, transportation, lack of child care, waiting time, impersonal service provider demeanor, distance, and limited opening hours. Satisfactory contacts were those that involved professionals who were sincere, had a sense of humor, spent time, and were nonjudgmental.

Summarizing the literature relating to delivery of transcultural services, Miller (1982) points out that mental health professionals do not have adequate knowledge of transcultural client interaction. Professional providers do not traditionally receive training in skills essential to transcultural service delivery, such as discussing the family's Native American background and culture, exploring relevant areas, asking questions that elicit information without causing discomfort, and using cultural information in assessment.

Latino Americans. Aragón de Valdez and Gallegos (1982) describe the historical oppression of Latinos by white Americans from 1848 (the time of the Treaty of Guadalupe Hidalgo) to the present and Latinos' resulting powerlessness. As a response to their situation, Latinos have relied on the church, service organizations, and political movements. However, the Catholic church, although providing religious solace, has adopted positions implying an inferior status of Latinos. Clearly the church should engage in social involvement and advocacy on behalf of the Latino community. Community-controlled service organizations and mutual aid societies provide ongoing and emergency assistance. Latino political organizations have made an educational contribution to community life. Activities of La Raza Unida, the League of United Latin American Citizens, El Congreso, and other groups have included local and national voting drives, lobbying, campaigning, and endorsing candidates.

The socioeconomic, educational, and cultural needs of Latinos congregate in the areas of English-language skills, poverty, cultural coping mechanisms, racism and discrimination, and substandard housing. The delivery of human services continues to be inaccessible, class-bound, culture-bound, caste-bound, and monolingual. Social services need to regear and rely on culturally specific treatment models. Three components are relevant to social work practice: (1) bilingual/bicultural staff and indigenous paraprofessionals; (2) procedural protocols emphasizing *personalismo* and a medical examination process; and (3) intervention based on active, goal-oriented problem solving; family support networks; and family interaction and interdependence.

The framework for cross-cultural awareness practice is based on cultural awareness and sensitivity to people of color in general and to the unique characteristics of the major ethnic groups. This approach is unique because it applies anthropological theory that emphasizes problem investigation and community learning strategies. It stands in contrast to traditional social work practice, which has drawn on psychotherapy and has been treatment oriented. Green (1982) and his associates have demonstrated the need to continue a dialogue on designing multicultural services, learning about ethnic clients and agencies, and using the ethnographic setting for problem solving.

Framework for Therapy with Culturally Diverse Families

Ho (1987) has conceptualized a multicultural family therapy framework based on existing family therapy theories and experience in family therapy with people of color.

Basic Structure. Ho constructs his culturally sensitive family therapy framework in terms of six basic factors:

1. *Ethnic minority reality.* Racism and poverty are the fundamental experiences of many people of color. Their communities are devastated by unemployment and often characterized by a pre-

dominance of single-parent, no-earner families. At the same time, people of color underutilize the services of monolingual, middle-class family therapists whose practice orientation is ethnocentric.

2. *Impact of the external system on minority culture.* The dominant society tends to emphasize human control of nature and the environment, future orientation, individual autonomy, competitiveness and upward mobility, and the nuclear family. Ethnic minorities, by contrast, value harmony with the environment, reminiscence about the past and pleasure in the present, collectivity, self-discipline and the endurance of suffering, and the extended family. The conflict between these two value systems causes problems at the individual and family levels.

3. *Biculturalism.* People of color must function in two cultural systems, each requiring a different set of behaviors. As a survival mechanism, they become bicultural: They learn two distinct ways of coping with tasks, expectations, and behavior.

4. *Ethnic differences in minority status.* Ethnic groups that differ in skin color, immigration status, and other circumstances are treated differently by the dominant society. The experiences of African Americans and Native Americans are case studies in oppressed minority status; other groups have received less severe treatment. These differences affect the social adjustment and well-being of families in white society.

5. *Ethnicity and language.* Ethnicity is experienced through language. Together, they provide a psychic bond among members of a particular ethnic group. Bilingual family services are essential in assisting individuals with limited English skills. Even when clients are relatively fluent, the forced use of English can impede the expression of personal and intimate feelings and even lead to an impression of flat affect. Self-expression will be more spontaneous and more complete in the client's native language. For this reason, it is important to provide qualified bilingual family therapists.

6. *Ethnicity and social class.* The interaction between ethnic group membership and socioeconomic status may be complex. Individuals who

have achieved some degree of mainstream success may still be unaccepted by white middle-class society and yet may have distanced themselves from their ethnic group. The combination of ethnic identification and social status is sometimes referred to as *ethclass*.

Values and Skills. The Ho framework assumes distinctive minority cultural values related to family structure; traditional family structure and extended family ties; immigration, migration, and political and cultural adjustments; and the use of family help-seeking patterns and behavior before resorting to the professional community mental health system and health care services. Culturally relevant techniques and skills in family therapy involve the family therapist in the role of a physician, medicine man, or folk healer; the use of personalism (personal interest in the minority family) and collaterality (the family educates the therapist); mutual goal setting related to situational stress, cultural transition, and transcultural dysfunction; and problem solving related to mobilization and restructuring of the extended family network, positive reframing/relabeling, and the intensive team approach.

Framework for Assessing and Treating Children of Color

Gibbs and Huang (1989) have broken new ground with their conceptual framework for children of color. The framework uses three primary conceptual perspectives: a developmental perspective, an ecological perspective, and a cross-cultural mental health perspective.

Conceptual Perspectives

Developmental Perspective. In examining the influence of race and ethnicity on psychosocial tasks, Gibbs and Huang (1989) take as their starting point Erikson's five psychosocial stages from birth to late adolescence. According to Erikson (1959), prejudice, discrimination, and barriers to full opportunity are such that ethnic group and low-income children may experience more difficulty in achieving positive outcomes than do white middle- and upper-class children. However, Mead (1934) contends that a child's self-esteem and self-concept derive from appraisals by family, close relatives, and friends rather than from the broader society. Indeed, Gibbs and Huang (1989) cite sources indicating that children of color match or exceed their white counterparts in terms of self-esteem. However, their primary concern is not to resolve this controversy but to formulate an adequate view of psychosocial growth and development.

Ecological Perspective. Growing children and adolescents participate in a series of interlocking systems (the microsystems of family and school; the macrosystem of governmental, social, and economic policies). Each system poses risks and opportunities for children of color, who may need to cope with the impact of poverty, discrimination, immigration, and social isolation at various developmental stages. For example, poverty has a negative impact on children's nutrition, health care, housing, education, and recreation. As another example, recent immigration and language problems contribute to stress on children of immigrants and refugees. The dominant society's attitudes toward the immigrants, high unemployment, lack of educational skills in an industrialized urban economy, and conservative political attitudes are stressors tending to destabilize the children's environment.

Moreover, children of color are caught in a conflict between two competing sets of values and norms at home and in school. The resulting emotional stress manifests itself in somatic symptoms, behavior disorders, school adjustment problems, delinquency, depression, or suicidal behavior. Gibbs and Huang (1989) remind us to focus on environmental stressors and their effects on children of color.

Cross-Cultural Perspective. It is critical to compare children's culture of origin and the dominant culture. The following guidelines may be used in cross-cultural evaluation:

1. All behavior has meaning and serves some adaptive function.

2. Behavior is governed by a set of rules and norms that promote stability and harmony.

3. Dysfunctional or deviant behavior disrupts group functioning and is regulated by institutionalized control invested in shamans, spiritualists, or mental health practitioners.

These guidelines and related principles form the basis for comparing psychological dynamics among ethnic groups. In a mental health context, the cross-cultural perspective examines attitudes and belief systems regarding mental health and mental illness; differential symptomatology, defensive patterns, and coping strategies; help-seeking behaviors; and use of services.

Practice Areas. These developmental, ecological, and cross-cultural perspectives may be applied to three primary areas of practice: ethnicity and mental health, assessment, and clinical treatment of minority children.

Ethnicity and Mental Health. Ethnicity shapes the child's belief system about mental health and mental illness. It influences how the child expresses symptoms, defenses, and coping patterns. From parents and other significant adults in the social environment, the child learns culturally reinforced and tolerated patterns of illness and dysfunctional behavior. Ethnicity also determines the kind of help-seeking patterns that parents select for their children—whether they seek help from a religious resource, herbalist or acupuncturist, or family elder. It also shapes whether a child or adolescent uses and responds to treatment with openness, trust, and self-disclosure.

Assessment. Important areas of child or adolescent assessment are individual psychosocial adjustment, family relationships, school adjustment and achievement, relationships with peers, and adaptation to the community. We now consider these areas in more detail.

Individual psychosocial adjustment may be assessed in terms of physical appearance, affect, self-concept and self-esteem, interpersonal competence, autonomy, achievement, management of aggression and impulse control, and coping and defense mechanisms.

The assessment of family relationships requires information on gender and birth order (age and sex-role hierarchy), parental authority, respect for elders, extended family, shared household responsibilities, individual decision making, martial roles, and community norms and expectations. Children of color may assume household and child care responsibilities at earlier ages than white children do. This role may differ from that of the "parentified child" who acts as an interpreter and mediator between immigrant parents and the dominant society. Gibbs and Huang (1989) state that the clinician must distinguish between children who function in supportive roles and those who act as substitute parents.

Assessment of school adjustment and achievement is based on psychological adjustment (for example, transition from home to school); behavioral adjustment (internalized or externalized anxiety); academic achievement (native language verbal skills, attitudes toward school, study habits, level of family support); relationships with peers (ability to form friendships, express empathy, engage in social competitive and extracurricular activities); and adaptation to the community (church activities, youth groups, and language schools).

Clinical Treatment. The clinician should relieve the child's anxieties and fears about treatment through an informal, friendly approach to establish initial rapport. The clinician should also respect cultural norms, especially those regarding gender and age roles. The clinician should explain the purpose of therapy and the expectation of symptom relief. He or she can also communicate the desire to establish a trusting relationship through warm acceptance and brief disclosure of personal information. As treatment progresses, the clinician should negotiate with the child and family a number of treatment boundaries, such as confidentiality, a businesslike relationship, and a flexible structure with clear guidelines.

Children of color are a population at risk because of their minority status, low socioeconomic status, and limited access to health and mental health services. Yet most of these children adapt successfully to their environment. Crucial factors for adaptation are extended families, kin and social network, strong religious beliefs, and traditional help or healing.

To sum up, Gibbs and Huang have provided a workable framework for human services practice with children of color. Their conceptual perspectives—developmental, ecological, and cross-cultural—blend assessment and treatment in a helpful and practical manner.

Framework for Cross-Cultural Social Work Practice

Chau's (1990) cross-cultural practice model for social work consists of four quadrants, defined by two axes (see Figure 5-1). One axis represents the ideological value continuum from ethnocentrism to pluralism; the other axis defines the targets or goals of intervention on a continuum from individual change to sociostructural change. The resulting quadrants specify four cross-cultural practice processes:

Quadrant 1: Ethnocentric, individual change corresponds to psychosocial adaptation (survival,

FIGURE 5-1 *Chau's Cross-Cultural Practice Model for Social Work*

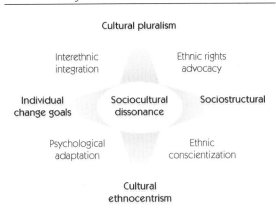

adjustment, and acculturation, for example, mainstreaming while attending to cultural factors)

Quadrant 2: Ethnocentric, sociostructural change corresponds to ethnic conscientization (critical ethnic consciousness-raising and empowerment through reinforcement of ethnic identity and group cohesion)

Quadrant 3: Pluralistic, individual change corresponds to interethnic integration (relationships and social integration among groups on the basis of cultural interdependence and mutual understanding)

Quadrant 4: Pluralistic, sociostructural change corresponds to ethnic rights advocacy (promoting and securing social equality and access to equal opportunities through advocacy and institutional change)

The Chau model permits a high degree of flexibility in addressing individual, group, community, and societal concerns confronting people of color. Chau points out that each of the four quadrants has a distinct set of practice goals and processes, corresponding to differences in the sociocultural dissonance between client and worker as they define the problem; in the focus of practice; in the role of the worker; and also in intervention strategies, methods, and skills.

Application of the Model. Chau applies this model to issues of cross-cultural coverage, teaching, and practice goals/outcomes.

Cross-Cultural Coverage. The model's four practice processes (adaptation, conscientization, integration, and advocacy) help broaden the worker's understanding of the reality confronted by ethnic clients, the sociocultural dissonance between worker and client, and appropriate intervention strategies. They also serve to differentiate ethnic client groups in terms of cultural congruence, available cultural resources, problem-solving patterns, perception of needs, and problem definition and solution. As a result, the practitioner becomes culturally attuned to the client's situation and sensitive to cultural considerations in problem solving.

Cross-Cultural Teaching. To explore values and attitudes, Chau initiates an ethnic self-profiling exercise. In this exercise, participants select words or concepts reflecting cultural or ethnic diversity and human differences and enter each word in a table according to whether they feel comfortable with that word, ambivalent about it, negative, or ignorant. Afterward, in small groups, participants identify and discuss common themes among their racial attitudes. Personal experiences, socialized attitudes, discriminatory behaviors, self-awareness, and empathy emerge in the form of expressive emotion or affective learning. This exercise tends to make participants more introspective about their cultural values and beliefs and their own cultural upbringing and also more sensitive to clients' cultural diversity and cross-cultural settings. Addressing the continuum from cultural ethnocentrism to pluralism, Chau points out that people are socialized to consider their own beliefs and ways of behaving as the best and their own values as universal.

Teachers can also promote cross-cultural awareness by the use of media depicting social justice, the assigned reading of cross-cultural material, care in preparing balanced lectures, the elucidation of appropriate social work practice skills (with a range of supporting case examples examining life dilemmas confronted by people of color), and role playing to develop practice skills in problem situations.

Cross-Cultural Goals/Outcomes. The goals of the cross-cultural practice course are an understanding of our pluralistic society and awareness of the need to work effectively with people of diverse ethnic and racial backgrounds and with social institutions impacting clients' lives. Specific outcomes include the worker's development of sensitivity and a pluralistic attitude toward cultural differences, an understanding of multicultural experience, and familiarity with an ethnic group or culture related to a practice area of concern.

Chau believes that interpersonal practice must be culturally responsible and be a balance between the needs of distinctive racial and ethnic groups and the concerns of the larger society. Culture-sensitive curriculum and practice must build on the acceptance of cultural differences and cultural integrity; social work students, faculty, and practitioners must affirm and embrace diversity in their thinking and behavior. Classroom and field faculty must collaborate with students in taking on this teaching and learning task.

Transcultural Framework for Assessment and Therapy with Children and Youth

Ho (1992) has offered a framework for working with children and adolescents that complements his contribution to multicultural family therapy. This framework is based on three components, as follows.

1. *Ethnicity and culture.* The influence of the distinctive life experiences of people of color on their mental health is analyzed in terms of the following categories: racism and discrimination, the impact of the external system (white America), bicultural competence, ethnicity and language, social class, skin color, belief systems, and help-seeking behavior.

2. *Psychosocial development.* The maturation and developmental processes of children of color are analyzed in terms of Erikson's stages of the life cycle, Norton's dual cultural perspective, and the ethnic socialization process.

3. *Social ecology.* The ecological perspective illuminates the interlocking transactional systems at the individual, family, cultural, and environmental levels.

Cultural Assessment. Within this framework, the assessment and treatment of a child or youth focus on issues of individual psychosocial adjustment, relationships with family, school adjustment and achievement, relationships with peers, and adaptation to the community.

Ho (1992) discusses the systematic assessment of Asian American, Native American, African American, and Latino American children and adolescents. His message is that the worker must understand the historical background (demographics, immigration, culture, and family), the particular mental health issues and problems (epi-demiology, diagnosis, and relocation), and the ecological aspects of assessment (personal system, family system, school system, and societal issues). The systematic approach is characterized by uniformity of purpose but variation in the particular issues confronting each group.

Cultural Therapy. Having laid a common basis for child and adolescent assessment, Ho concentrates on culture-specific methods, techniques, and skills in individual, family, and group therapy. For individual therapy, he outlines the rationale and criteria to indicate or contraindicate treatment and the goals of individual therapy. Ego-supportive, ego-modifying, cognitive-behavioral, play, and music therapies are examined, along with issues relating to the therapist's gender, age, credibility, communication style, use of empathy and authority, working relationship with the client's parents, and use of bilingualism and interpreters. The influence of ethnicity on mutual goal formation, problem solving, and termination is discussed. In discussing family therapy, Ho outlines a similar rationale and criteria, along with family therapy principles (adaptive functioning, problem-solving help, overt behavioral change, and family process modification). He covers the engagement, problem-solving, and evaluation and termination phases of family therapy. Finally, considering group therapy, Ho outlines the rationale and criteria regarding the appropriateness and goals of group therapy, as well as the pregroup, group interaction, and evaluation and termination phases.

Framework for the Integration of Ethnic and Gender Identitites in Women of Color

Comas-Diaz and Greene (1994) present a framework for the integration of ethnic and gender identities in women of color. Three working paradigms address the heterogeneity of women of color, their unique contextual experiences, and their intragroup diversity. First, the authors explore the heterogeneity of women of color by focusing on specific ethnoracial groups within a common format: a brief historical overview, sociocultural issues, family relations, gender roles, developmental issues, and appropriate therapeutic interventions. Second, they present a critical examination of existing treatment orientations: psychodynamic, cognitive-behavioral, family therapy, feminist, and integrative approaches. The emphasis is on gender and cultural sensitivity and theoretical applicability to women of color. Third, they consider the unique needs of special subpopulations: professional, lesbian, and battered women of color; mixed-race women; and refugee women from Southeast Asia. The framework is intended to provide a foundation for the clinical understanding and sensitive integration of racial, gender, and ethnocultural factors related to women of color.

Heterogeneous Women of Color. Women of color represent an ethnocultural mosaic; they are a part of the cultural pluralism in the United States. Race and color differentiate them from white women, while both women and men of color share the common life experiences of racial and ethnic discrimination. Yet gender and ethnic oppression facilitates a common bond—a connectedness—among women of color.

Women of color belong to specific ethnic groups: African American, Native American, Asian American, Latinas, West Indian, and Indian Subcontinent. Although these groups share common themes of historical background, culture and family, and therapeutic interventions and treatment, each group has unique distinguishing factors.

For example, African American women maintain specific African cultural characteristics (interdependence and collective responsibility, nonverbal communication, extended family network). Within the pernicious context of the dominant culture—in particular, racist and sexist stereotypes and economic subordination—African American women are vulnerable to internalized racism and must seek adaptive strategies to facilitate use of psychological resources.

By contrast, generations of Asian Americans and Asian newcomers to the United States have been shaped by the experience of immigration. Embedded in many Asian social systems are Confucianism, Buddhism, and other indigenous social philosophies, which have varying structural roles for women. Group dependency on the family and

community, harmonious relationships, and hierarchical structure are integral parts of Asian cultures. These are the bulwarks against the oppressive forces that Asian Americans face in the United States: socioeconomic, gender, and racial stereotyping; pressure to assimilate and acculturate; cultural conflict surrounding Asian feminism; and family structure stress over generational and interracial marriage issues. Asian American women are hesitant about seeking help and need to work through a range of pretherapy expectations. Depending on their level of cultural assimilation and the length of time since their arrival, they may respond to Western and/or indigenous approaches. Domestic violence, related sexual victimization, and lesbian lifestyle are some areas of concern.

Helping Approaches. A number of theoretical and applied interventions are relevant to women of color: psychodynamic, cognitive-behavioral, family therapy, feminist, and integrative approaches. Most suited to the needs of women of color is the integrative approach, which combines traditional helping models from various theoretical schools and takes thorough account of sociocultural, ethnoracial, and gender contexts.

The integrative approach views therapy in terms of decolonization and empowerment. Domination and oppression (both historically and psychologically) produce the colonized mentality (for example, the acceptance of a superiority/inferiority hierarchy). Decolonization means recovery of the self, the achievement of autonomous dignity, and action to change the self and/or the colonial condition. The therapeutic relationship calls on empathy, intuition, and the experience of being the other. The integrative approach confronts issues of gender, race, and internalized domination and is based on respect for the woman's culture and the recognition and use of her strengths.

The sense of self is important for women of color. Womanhood is defined within a collective context: family, group, community, and universe. The family role of women of color underscores that their identity derives from interpersonal relationships (the self-in-relation): mother-daughter, parent-child, work career–extended family assistance, grandmother-granddaughter. In these relationships, women care for significant others. Identity conflicts contribute to low self-esteem for women of color; self-esteem is related to the development of racial identity. Likewise, the development of the spiritual self is important for women of color. Spirituality provides a sense of oneness and harmony and is a source of personal strength in times of crisis and conflict. The end result of the integrative approach is the transformation and empowerment of women of color.

Special Populations of Women of Color. Professional, lesbian, battered, mixed-race, and refugee women of color constitute special populations with distinctive characteristics, problems, and treatment needs. Of the five groups addressed, the following three types are least mentioned in the literature on women.

The ethnocultural factors that come into play for professional women of color in the workplace include a long heritage of work outside the home, an adaptable gender role (being able to cope with work problems and stress in the white male–dominated business culture), the investment of education (the sacrifices involved in educating daughters for careers beyond domestic or service worker), internal and external fear of success, and strength to face adversity. On top of these issues are racism, sexism, and the double bind of tokenism and stereotyping in the workplace. Interpersonal relationships with white women coworkers, other women of color, and professional men of color pose challenging problems. Balancing family, community, and work implies coping mechanisms to link professional aspirations with community needs. As a result, professional women of color are vulnerable to such mental health problems as conflicted self-esteem, depression, stress and anxiety, psychosomatization, and addictive behaviors. Treatment is designed to reinforce and restore the client's sense of competence, self-reliance, and balanced functioning, as well as to manage the stress of discrimination and to teach coping skills for survival in the professional marketplace.

Lesbian women of color face triple jeopardy: heterocentric (appearance and behavior) stereotypes, androcentric (dominant male/submissive female) gender role stereotypes, and ethnocentric (tenacious ethnic homophobia) biases. Lesbians of color confront various cultural factors such as recent adjustment problems of immigration and acculturation to the United States, which involve separation from family members and homeland ties; and family and community attitudes to lesbianism. There is a continuum ranging from rejection to tolerance toward lesbian women of color in African American, Asian American, Latino American, and Native American families and communities.

Mixed-race women are seen against a legacy of American antimiscegenist thought; in some states, mixed-race marriage was still illegal barely twenty-five years ago. Such negative attitudes toward mixed-race persons cause identity problems. To define a self is essential to empowerment; however, rather than claim membership with more than one racial or ethnic group, the mixed-race person must cope with racial ambivalence in childhood and issues of physical appearance and social acceptance in adolescence. In some instances, multiracial heritage compounds adolescent girls' lower social status as female with a lower status based on color ambiguity.

To forge a distinctive identity that ensures stability and historical continuity, mixed-race people must confront issues of uniqueness, acceptance and belonging, physical appearance, sexuality, and self-esteem. On the whole, they tend to integrate their diverse experiences in a positive way, but difficulties result from an oppressive, dysfunctional environment based on notions of racial and cultural superiority.

The Comas-Diaz and Greene framework sets a new standard for the study of women of color. On the basis of a comprehensive survey of the major groups of ethnocultural women, it reinterprets intervention approaches to meet the particular treatment needs of women of color. It accommodates special populations spanning the full range of socioeconomic, lifestyle, spousal, racial, and newcomer statuses.

Framework for Black Experience–Based Social Work Practice

Martin and Martin (1995) have created a ten-step black experience–based social work model encompassing a historical perspective, a social analysis of problems, and a collective community-based problem-solving process. It is rooted in the black experience, but the practice intervention principles of the model transcend the particular group and are applicable in the etic (culture-common or universal) sense. Martin and Martin use the following definitions of terms: *Moaning* "bring(s) a deep-seated pain to the surface for collective affirmation of its reality"; *Mourning* is "a collective effort to overcome grief; a collective process of identification, empathy, and catharsis"; and *Morning* is a significant breakthrough, the arrival of a brighter new day, a new beginning, a transformation, or a change." The model uses the themes of moaning and mourning, the prerequisites to achieving morning, or a new dawning of hope.

Step 1 is (Moaning) Immersion in Black History and Culture. Immersion into black history and culture fosters historical empathy, strengthens ancestral connectedness, and enhances black identity or identification with black people.

Historical empathy provides the ability to moan over the sufferings of black people in the past and to connect their pain to contemporary suffering. A deeper sensitivity and a more sacred commitment to relieve one another's suffering result along with a resolve to continue fighting until the suffering stops.

Martin and Martin use bibliotherapy in which students read narratives, biographies, and autobiographies of black people throughout history. As a result, the student gains a sense of how previous generations suffered, struggled, and succeeded. The use of black history becomes a weapon for social cohesiveness and social change and strengthens ancestral empathy and connectedness as well as identity and consciousness.

Step 2 is (Moaning) Identification of the Problem. Immersion in blackness helps students make historical connections with current social problems. Martin and Martin observe that many individual contemporary problems are examples of collective unsolved problems of history. From a historical perspective one gains the sense of the depth of problems and how deeply entrenched they are in American society. A historical perspective tempers simple solutions and false hope. The

crucial problems of black people are loss and separation, troubled intimate relations, and racial oppression.

Step 3 is (Moaning) Creating Assessment Instruments. As a way to objectify problems, Martin and Martin have students create a loss/support chart that identifies major losses and separations on one side and significant other supports on the other side. This exercise helps social work practitioners spot core problems and asks students to write a narrative and make an oral presentation to explain their charts.

Step 4 is (Moaning) Clarifying the Objective. The objective is to help black people overcome personal, social, or mental disorders that thwart their maximum potential for upward social mobility. However, the objective is based on thorough knowledge of etiology, black people's reaction, and the impact on black individuals, families, and communities. Martin and Martin suggest the need for immediate and long-range life goals that analyze immediate pressing problems, societal barriers, internalized restraints, and a plan of action. Their goal is to help students to cultivate their cultural versatility. Martin and Martin teach:

> According to their "cultural versatility profile," black people are more culturally versatile when they are educated or skilled, intuitively in tune with the voices of their ancestors, racially conscious, historically knowledgeable, politically aware, communally oriented, and dedicated to the progress of black people in contemporary society and to the well-being of future generations. They are more versatile when they have confidence in themselves, faith in a higher power, and hope tinged with a firm grasp of reality. (p. 258)

Yet at the same time, there are five negative psychologies that keep black people from confronting core problems: cultural sickness, cultural paranoia, cultural claustrophobia, cultural amnesia, and cultural terminal illness. The most damaging is the psychology of cultural amnesia that cuts off black people from history and ancestral connections.

Step 5 is (Moaning) Clarifying the Goal. The ultimate goal is to create a healing-developing black community. Martin and Martin believe that the black community must heal its emotional, social, and historical wounds as a precondition for economic, political, social, cultural, and intellectual growth. Two examples of the negative psychologies are the psychology of cultural sickness and of terminal illness. The former is manifested through low self-esteem, whereas the latter is expressed by a grave feeling of mistrust of other black people and being hemmed in and thwarted by their environment. These negative psychologies must be worked through so that culturally versatile black people reach the goal of the healing-developing community.

Step 6 is (Mourning) Creating the Helping Atmosphere. The helping atmosphere consists of collective problem solving in which individual black people pinpoint the social origin of their personal pain as fellow sufferers who share a common history, problems, and racial identity. In an extended family group, students experience a warm, friendly, communal atmosphere; connect with other people's pain and with the suffering of their ancestors; and see one another as fellow sufferers and members of an extended family.

Step 7 is (Mourning) Wrestling with the Problem of Disclosure. Self-disclosure of personal problems comes through personal narratives about loss and separation, intimate relations, oppressions, and familial-ancestral-spiritual supports. Many students use stories from black literature and history, songs and poems that describe pain and problems, and particularly rap music and poetry to describe their life experiences.

In return, members of the class respond by probing or asking questions that carefully reach the deeper layers of inner feelings and experiences. The revelation of personal lives brings relief to all the students who share intimacy.

Step 8 is (Mourning) Mastering the Ability to Mourn. Lending group support is expressed through words and deeds of reassurance and encouragement and recognition of one another's strength and potential. Students experience positive worth and support in their suffering, recognizing that they have collectively suffered so much and have such strengths. Instilling and reinforcing hope are expressed through sharing a prayer of inspiration and encouragement, poems, songs, saying, and photos of people who serve as sources of hope and inspiration. Through these vehicles of instilling hope come the articulation of true self desires and aspirations and the inspiration toward excellence, uplift, and achievement.

Step 9 is (Mourning) Evaluating Growth. In this step growth is evaluated by identifying collective and common patterns of problems, exploring collective alternatives to problem solving, and making assessments of objective conditions and versatile strategies and skills. Students come together to look for common problem patterns and to explore collective alternatives and options. In the process they break the problem down into concrete, manageable, and solvable steps. They also discover that many fellow sufferers have the same problems and draw comfort from the support of their own extended families. Of considerable concern is the absence of fathers and the need to advocate suggestions to strengthen the role of black men and their family responsibilities and communal obligations.

There is also the need to explore collective alternatives such as taking responsibility for their own personal problems, which in turn involves examining the objective conditions to determine whether plans are realizable and manageable. It also means confronting problems and developing versatility strategies and skills, which entails listening to and trusting the intuitive self and carrying out tasks to reach goals.

Individual problems are reframed in the context of the group, and individuals are held accountable and responsible and seek help from others. Students are forced to become culturally versatile in light of their problems and the lack of external resources to meet them.

Step 10 is (Mourning) Engaging the Black Community. Engaging the black community means working in the social service institutions and creating the healing-developing community in its midst. It means going where the black client is and beginning social advocacy and political action. It involves creating black caregiving agencies and institutions to tackle the myriad of social problems.

Martin and Martin summarize the uniqueness of their approach when they explain:

Already, black experience–based social work is distinct from other social work methods in that it emphasizes developing skills as fostering historical empathy and ancestral connectedness, developing versatility skills and strategies, strengthening the ability to mourn, and mastering the art of collective problem solving, all based on black traditional ways. Black experience–based social work is also unique in that it uses concepts drawn from the black sacred and profane heritage and it uses the moaning, mourning, and morning themes of spirituals and the blues to guide the social change process. (pp. 276–277)

FRAMEWORK FOR CULTURALLY DIVERSE SOCIAL WORK PRACTICE

As we have seen, similarities and differences exist among the frameworks for ethnic-sensitive practice, cross-cultural awareness practice, therapy with families of color, youth assessment and treatment, cross-cultural social work practice, and integrative practice with women of color. Devore and Schlesinger's ethnic-sensitive approach delineates the scope of human behavior and practice when working with people of color. Green's cultural-awareness orientation further specifies appropriate practice steps and acknowledges the uniqueness of the principal ethnic groups. Ho's family therapy approach delineates relevant cultural and ethnic factors and has been extended and modified for youth assessment and therapy. Gibbs and Huang's youth assessment and treatment model underscores the need for multiple dimensions (developmental, ecological, and cross-cultural). Chau's cross-cultural practice model highlights the issues of adaptation, conscientization, integration, and advocacy. Comas-Diaz and Greene address treatment issues for women of color, identifying distinct subpopulations of women. Martin and Martin present a black experience–based social work practice model that emphasizes the history and culture of African Americans.

The framework for culturally diverse social work practice outlined in what follows recognizes that a basis for culturally diverse social work practice has been established and builds on this basis in three ways. First, the framework conceptualizes a systematic process-stage approach, following the classic formula of beginning, middle, and end. Second, it offers generalist practice principles universal to people of color and supports them with examples from each of the key ethnic groups. Third, it uses a representative sample of case material from the ethnic clinical literature and develops direct-practice continuity by following a single family case study through the various process stages.

Theoretical Foundation

The framework for culturally diverse social work practice is based on the notion that common themes pertain to working with people of color. At the same time, we recognize that each of the largest minority groups (African American, Asian American, Latino American, and Native American) has its own unique cultural history, socioeconomic problems, and treatment approaches. The concepts of cultural commonality and cultural specificity reflect these emphases. The question is, Can we articulate, from a social work perspective, a framework for culturally diverse practice that applies to people of color in general and yet recognizes particular subgroups? Vigorous debate stirs on this methodological issue, which is known as *etic versus emic goals.*

Etic Versus Emic Goals. The term *etic* comes from the linguistic study of sounds and refers to the categorization of all the sounds in a particular language. The term *emic* refers to all the *meaningful* sounds in a particular language. In the cross-cultural perspective, these two concepts are used to describe behavior. The etic goal documents principles valid in all cultures and establishes theoretical bases for comparing human behavior. The emic goal documents behavioral principles within a culture and focuses on what the people themselves value as important and familiar to them (Brislin, 1981). It is important to maintain both emphases in social work practice—that is, to focus on culture-common characteristics of people of color and on culture-specific traits of particular ethnic groups.

In Cultural Study 5-1, Sands and McClelland (1994) provide interesting background on the meaning and development of the terms *emic* and *etic*.

Etics—The Insider/Outsider Debate (Headland, Pike, & Harris, 1990).

From "Emic and Etic Perspectives in Ethnographic Research on the Interdisciplinary Team" by R. G. Sands and M. McClelland. In E. Sherman & W. J. Reid (Eds.), *Qualitative Research in Social Work*, p. 33. Copyright © 1994 Columbia University Press, New York. Reprinted by permission.

CULTURAL STUDY 5-1

The Emic/Etic Distinction

The terms *emic* and *etic* were coined by the linguist Kenneth Pike (1954), who extracted them from the terms *phonemic* and *phonetic*, respectively. Phonemics refers to sound units that are recognized as distinct and meaningful in a particular language (O'Connor, 1973). On the other hand, phonetics refers to the science of speech sounds that occur across languages, the range of which can be represented in a universal system of transcription, such as the International Phonetic Alphabet (Crystal, 1971). As Pike moved from an analysis of pronunciation units to an entire language, he realized that meaningful units existed not only within verbal data but also within nonverbal behavior (Pike, 1954, 1967). Recently, Pike (1990) explained that the linguistic terms were abbreviated to reflect this notion. Thus, the etic perspective refers to "generalized statements about data" (Pike, 1954, p. 8) that are constructed by the analyst on the basis of cross-cultural knowledge, whereas the emic perspective refers to patterns that appear in a particular culture. Pike (1954) described the etic approach as "external" or "alien," for the researcher is positioned outside the culture and compares one culture with others according to a preexisting system of knowledge; and the emic approach as "internal" or "domestic" because what is discovered about a particular culture is related to that culture as a whole (p. 10). Pike affirmed (1954) that no rigid dichotomy exists between the two perspectives, that both foster understanding, and that one approach can be transformed into the other. The differing interpretations of these concepts by Pike and Harris are juxtaposed in the recent volume, *Emics and*

Draguns (1981) poses emic and etic questions about the way to begin cross-cultural research or planning. The emic approach inquires, "Shall we start from within the unique and different culture which we have set out to study?" The etic approach asks, "Shall we proceed on the basis that all human beings are, in some important respects, alike?" (Draguns, 1981, pp. 3–4). Whether to focus on the distinctiveness of people or on their generally human universal experience is the choice of the therapist. Moreover, it is important to distinguish between what is different and what is maladaptive within the client's culture. The continual shift between discovering what is humanly universal and what is particular to the client's culture makes cross-cultural studies a challenging field.

Sundberg (1981) identifies universal/etic and culture-specific/emic aspects of counseling that are useful in social work practice. Important characteristics for the counselor to exhibit across cultures and clients are tolerance for anxiety in the client, positive flexibility in responding to the client, confidence in the imparting of helping information and a belief system, and an interest in the client as a person. Culture-specific counseling considers the unique background and personal resources of the individual, particularly his or her unique history, resources, strengths, and ability to use available cultural resources.

The social worker should use both etic and emic perspectives. The worker should discover the etic and emic characteristics of the client and cultural background during contact and relationship building. In a real sense, the worker communicates the message that the client is a human being with basic needs and aspirations (etic perspective) but is also a part of a particular cultural

TABLE 5-1 *Framework for Culturally Diverse Social Work Practice*

Practice Process Stages	Client-System Practice Issues	Worker-System Practice Issues	Worker-Client Tasks
Contact	Resistance, communication barriers Personal and family background Ethnic-community identity	Delivery of services Understanding of the community Relationship protocols Professional self-disclosure Style of communication	Nurturing Understanding
Problem identification	Problem information Problem area disclosure Problem understanding	Problem orientation Problem levels Problem themes Problem area detailing	Learning Focusing
Assessment	Socioenvironmental impacts Psychoindividual reactions	Assessment dynamics Assessment evaluation	Interacting Evaluating
Intervention	Joint goals and agreement Joint intervention strategies (planning, selection, and implementation) Micro-/meso-/macrolevel interventions		Creating Changing
Termination	Destination, recital, completion Follow-up strategies		Achieving Resolving

and ethnic group (emic perspective). Moving between these two points of reference is a creative experience for both worker and client.

The etic aspect of social work practice can draw on experience in related fields. Cross-cultural psychology and anthropology assume that cognitive processes are universal and have common denominators (Lonner, 1979). Our intention is to set forth a process model for social work direct practice with people of color that draws universal or common principles across cultures. Cross-cultural psychology asserts that its major function is to formulate laws that hold for human nature based on findings with a specified number of individuals who represent a logical class (Price-Williams, 1979). Similarly, a priority of cross-cultural social work is to identify a number of practice principles applicable to all people of color

before delineating specific principles for each major ethnic group.

THE FRAMEWORK

Table 5-1 shows the four categories within the framework for culturally diverse social work practice: practice process stages, worker-system practice issues, client-system practice issues, and worker-client tasks. Five process stages are used as major divisions of the framework. Practice process stages focus on the logical step-by-step sequence of client and worker movement in the helping process. Social work process has traditionally been characterized in terms of beginning, middle, and end. In this culturally diverse direct-practice framework, the beginning process stages are *contact* and *problem identification;* the middle stages include *assessment* and *intervention;* and the ending stage is *termination.*

The terms *client system* and *worker system* refer to those substructures (systems) of the framework that pertain to the individuals within the direct-practice relationship: the worker, on the one hand, and the client, on the other. Awareness of the client- and worker-system practice issues in Table 5-1 is essential to guiding both parties through the various stages. Whereas many of these practice issues (for example, problem area detailing, assessment evaluation, and joint goals and agreement) are common to most or all encounters between social worker and client, some (such as delivery of service, professional self-disclosure, problem orientation, and socioenvironmental impacts) must be highlighted and emphasized when the client is a person of color.

As a person in the midst of a growth experience, the client must deal with the client-system issues in collaboration with the worker. The worker-system issues are the crucial functions the worker must undertake to move the client through the process stages. Worker-client tasks entail the obligations of the social worker to nurture, understand, learn, and focus. Throughout the middle and ending stages, however, the client increasingly interacts, evaluates, creates, changes, and achieves, and, in the process, resolves.

In the following sections, the process stages are explained in terms of the framework here proposed.

The Process-Stage Approach

Contact

Practice Process Stage. The establishment of the relationship between the social worker and the client is basic to the contact phase. Relationship is the primary requisite for retaining the client. Fischer (1978) describes this stage as experiencing and exploration. The client and worker engage each other in the effort to develop a mutually trusting relationship. The worker responds to the client with empathy, warmth, and genuineness. Fischer suggests that "the more positive the emo-

tional responses in the client as evoked by the worker, i.e., the more he or she is liked, the greater will be the client's willingness to participate and be influenced" (p. 247). The social worker demonstrates listening and understanding, respect and concern for the client as a human being, and openness and spontaneity in the situation.

Client-System Practice Issues. There is a natural resistance on the part of clients who are entering the formal helping system. Suspicion and mistrust based on previous institutional contact, anxiety about the unknown, and shame about admitting the need for assistance are natural feelings of clients generally. For people of color, those feelings are exacerbated by racism and discrimination. The client often tests the worker to determine whether he or she has racist values and biases. Social workers should examine themselves for traces of racism and prejudice and evaluate their attitudes toward particular groups.

Personal and family background play a major role in the contact stage. Asking about ethnic family background may be an important signal to a client that his or her ethnicity is valuable information for the social work practitioner. The worker might ask, How do you identify yourself as a member of an ethnic group? What important ethnic customs and beliefs do you and your family observe and practice? Are you a participant in ethnic organizations? What are your favorite ethnic foods? Whom do you consider to be a local spokesperson or leader in your ethnic community? Are there any ethnic groups or individuals you would approach for assistance? These areas for preliminary conversation may or may not be relevant, depending on the client's reaction and the direction of the initial session.

It is important to determine the client's degree of acculturation. For decades, the United States has been termed "the melting pot" of all races. Unfortunately, this has resulted in the abandonment of native language and dress and adaptation to Americanized behavior patterns. Being Americanized meant discarding vestiges of past culture and custom and adopting the language idioms, mannerisms, dress, and mentality of the majority culture. *Acculturation* is the process of adapting to a new or different culture; in its usage, there has been the implication that a person who is becoming acculturated is from an inferior cultural background. The majority culture applies pressure toward social conformity; this affects children who are conditioned to the patterns of the new culture and parents who maintain ethnic cultural values. Fortunately, with the rise of ethnic awareness in the past two decades, many third- and fourth-generation minorities are rediscovering their past cultural heritage and learning the history and language of their forebears. These later generations have embraced cultural pride and identity, adopting an ethnic life pattern. Some new immigrants are moving toward partial assimilation of American lifestyle and behavior patterns, which conflict with traditional cultural values. Parents tend to preserve authoritarian family roles and traditional values and are thus at odds with their children, who are exposed to the independent and individualistic lifestyles of their school and neighborhood peers.

In confronting the adjustments demanded by acculturation, parents must deal with their experience of displacement and with economic and social uncertainty in their new homeland.

Another important variable is the client's sense of ethnic community identity. Does the client feel related to the ethnic community and participate in its activities? Are ethnic community resources available to the client? Helping a client or family adjust to life in this country, sort out cultural values and traditions, and stabilize family beliefs and practices is a starting point for contact in practice with people of color. For clients who have grown up in the United States and are aware of their own cultural identity issues, social work may focus on the rediscovery of past cultural values and tradition and the meaning of their ethnicity.

Worker-System Practice Issues. It is important for the social service agency to set up a responsive system of service delivery to meet multicultural client needs. Bilingual/bicultural workers, community education and prevention outreach programs, accessible facility location, and minimal fees can increase the use of services by people of color. To shape service delivery appropriately, social service agency administrators must understand the community. They should meet with ethnic community leaders and groups in their catchment area (mandated service area) to ascertain social needs, determine staff composition, and plan relevant programs. Social service staff should be oriented to various ethnic client communities and their socioeconomic needs, lifestyle, and other key elements. This groundwork must be performed before actual contact with clients.

When engaging an ethnic client, the social worker must observe certain relationship protocols, such as addressing the client by his or her surname, making formal introductions, acknowledging the elder or head of household as the authority, and conveying respect through other means. Rather than focusing immediately on the problem, the social worker should practice professional self-disclosure, whereby a point of interest common to the client and the worker becomes a means of forming a relationship. Further efforts to discover the ethnic family background of the client help the worker gain a sense of familiarity. The worker should also structure the initial session by explaining the functions and procedures of the agency, the purpose of the sessions, and the range of problems encountered among a broad spectrum of clients.

The social worker's communication style should convey friendliness, interest, and empathetic understanding; it is important to make the client feel at ease. By modeling a relaxed and open personal attitude, the worker evokes a similar response from the client. The worker should take cues communicated by the client, who eventually will allude to the reason for coming to the agency. At the point of disclosure, the focus moves from becoming acquainted with the client and his or her background to the presenting problem.

During the contact phase, the social worker gains a preliminary perspective on the client's psychosocial functioning. This perspective is based on the information that flows from the reciprocal interaction of the client and his or her environment. The basic demographic information on the intake form includes indicators of psychosocial state related to place of residence, occupation, health status, family, and other distinguishing variables. Where the intake form notes onset of a major illness, recent loss of a job, or change of address, for example, the social worker should determine the client's attitude toward such particulars. In this first stage, however, the emphasis is on obtaining a sense of adequate functioning or dysfunctioning as the person in the situation emerges. The worker surveys the biopsychosocial dimensions of the client (physical, cognitive-affective-behavioral, and environmental forces affecting the client) and notices the significant relationship and events, life experiences, and cultural/ethnic levels.

Worker-Client Tasks. Nurturing is crucial to the contact stage. The worker's actions and demeanor must indicate a willingness to engage in positive mutual involvement. Offering food and drink at the beginning of a session communicates the idea that physical refreshment and sustenance are important. Translating this symbolic act into emotional nurturing involves healthy doses of empathy, warmth, and genuineness, which develop into rapport, trust, and openness. A client may reciprocate by inviting the worker to his or her home for a social activity or by bringing fruit, candy, or a token of appreciation. If the worker is able to recognize and accept the meaning of this act, it can shape a mutually giving process.

Understanding is an important worker-client task. The worker should use open-ended reflection, recognizing the primacy of the client's feelings and thoughts. Understanding develops through careful listening and paraphrasing of the client's expressed thoughts and feelings to clarify or acknowledge the message communicated. Understanding is further expressed through the worker's support of the client in confronting issues of personal concern. These responses at the contact stage open up the client, releasing pent-up emotions and thought remnants that require later follow-up.

Problem Identification

Practice Process Stage. After the dynamics of contact are set in motion, a problem invariably emerges in the course of worker-client dialogue. Some clients continually face basic problems of survival such as unemployment, poor health, and substandard housing. These problems are often caused by inadequate funding for existing services. For example, state and federal budget cuts affecting Aid to Families with Dependent Children (AFDC) and Medicaid have sent shock waves through ethnic communities in which single mothers and the elderly struggle to survive with limited incomes and restricted access to medical care.

Client-System Practice Issues. During problem identification, the client will convey preliminary information to the worker about the problem. It may take time for the client to develop trust and overcome shame. Once the client can be assured that information about the problem will not be used against him or her, disclosure of the problem ensues. Sharing a problem with the professional gives the client the opportunity to understand it from another perspective. Defining a problem's chronological development aids understanding and allows the worker to gain insight into the individual client and his or her ethnic or collective family and community.

Worker-System Practice Issues. In the present framework, problems are regarded as unsatisfied wants. This problem orientation contrasts with the pathological viewpoint, which is detrimental to people of color. Rather than trying to uncover the dysfunctional aspect of a problem, the worker interprets the problem as symptomatic of a positive striving that has been hindered by an obstacle in the client's life. This perspective casts a new light on the identification of problems.

Various problem levels and themes are useful in categorizing the multifaceted problems of people of color. Recognition of micro- (individual, family, and small group), meso- (ethnic/local communities and organizations), and macro- (complex organizations, geographic populations) levels is part of problem identification. Oppression, powerlessness, exploitation, acculturation, and stereotyping are problem themes for people of color.

In problem identification, the psychosocial perspective focuses on the client's environment. Detailing the problem entails matching the appropriate problem levels and themes. Ethnic clients tend to confront multiple problems. For example, African Americans and Latinos in urban industrial jobs have been laid off because of economic recession. Depression, loss of self-esteem, and family conflict have led to behavioral problems such as alcoholism, child abuse, and attempted suicide. Detailing these problems implies matching macro- (state of the economy) and micro- (unemployed worker and his family) levels with the problem theme of powerlessness.

Worker-Client Tasks. Throughout problem identification, the tasks of the social worker and the client are learning and focusing. Learning consists of uncovering essential problem themes and then detailing them with facts. Focusing occurs when the worker and client decide to settle on a particular problem that both parties consider primary. As the worker probes and the client responds, both learn about dimensions of the problem. The worker describes the problem as a logical sequence of events on the basis of information supplied by the client. The client gains new insights into the problem. Which segment of the problem seems most manageable to the worker and client? What portion of the problem can most readily be detailed, studied, and analyzed? What is the sequence or pattern of problem events? Who are the actors involved? When does the problem occur? Where is the problem located? Problem identification moves from general learning about problem issues to focusing on a specific problem.

Assessment

Practice Process Stage. In social work practice, assessment generally involves an in-depth study of a psychosocial problem affecting the client. Its purpose is to analyze the interaction of client and situation and to plan recommendations for intervention. How does the problem affect the client? What resources are necessary to respond to the problem? With a person of color, it is useful to identify cultural strengths, significant others, and community support systems. Interactions of client and environment can change. It is important at each session for the client to brief the worker and for the worker to ask the client what has happened

since the last session, because the focus of the problem may have changed, new factors may have been introduced, and strategies for change may need revision.

Client-System Practice Issues. Psychosocial assessment concerns the impact of the social environment on the individual client. Socioenvironmental conditions affect and produce psychoindividual reactions. Numerous examples can be seen of the cause-and-effect relationship between the person and the environment. The influence of society is a strong force that shapes the reaction of people of color. For instance, societal caricatures forced African Americans toward behavior patterns that confirmed the stereotype in the minds of the dominant society. Leigh and Green (1982) observe:

> As stereotypes, these notions of restricted development persisted in popular ideas of racial differences. The belief that black people were conditioned by their genetic inheritance to develop only an inferior culture suggested that there was really very little justification for attempts to change, through social services, what seemed to have been established in nature. (p. 96)

Similarly, Wise and Miller (1981) point out that the media continue to perpetuate the image of the Native American either as a romantic, mystical figure of the past with a primitive and savage temperament or as a displaced, drunken individual. These stereotypes confuse the development of Native American self-esteem and identity.

Positive social environment affects psychoindividual reactions in terms of self-esteem and ethnic strength. To what extent does a particular client value and maintain his or her culture? For many people of color, cultural preservation and endorsement are fundamental values. For African Americans, extended family, church, art, music, and poetry are mobilizing forces. For Asian Americans, kinship and family ties, mutual obligation, and family welfare are elements of significant-other resources to be assessed. For Native Americans, respect for individuality, strong family relationships, and attendance at powwows are crucial to cultural development. For Latinos, family cohesion and helping networks, family interdependence, and respect for the elderly are factors in the assessment of cultural maintenance.

People of color should be aware of the range of effects that the social environment can have on them. The ethnic cultural environment and the discriminatory racist society are two forces that cause individual reactions. Social workers should assess the extent to which clients have cultural assets with which to fortify themselves.

Worker-System Practice Issues. The psychosocial perspective on assessment focuses on the interaction of client and environment. On the cognitive level, the ethnic mind-set of the person of color affects thought patterns learned from parents, experiences, and formal and informal learning in his or her ethnic group. The individual incorporates a past, present, and future life script of his or her ethnic history. For example, he or she experiences institutional racism through various early childhood stages. The location of the home, the racial composition of the neighborhood and school, and the degree of social segregation all play a part in the constructs incorporated into a person's ethnic experience. These learning situations form the basis of the individual's cognitive mind-set. In subsequent interactions with people, past experiences color a person's cognitive perception and response. Hepworth and Larsen (1990) observe:

> Perceptions, of course, do not exist separate and apart from the meanings that are ascribed to them; hence, we have considered perceptual and cognitive functioning as a single entity. It is the meanings or interpretations of events, rather than events themselves, that motivate human beings to behave as they do. (p. 182)

Assessment categories of cognition focus on intelligence, judgment, reality testing, coherence, flexibility, and self-concept. Assessment of the cognitive level ascertains to what extent these variables fall within an acceptable range of functioning. The worker must begin to assess the extent to which the client recognizes and analyzes the actions of a racist society and still functions with ethnic-oriented ideas and beliefs about living. The duality of an ethnic frame of reference and

intellectual comprehension and judgment is the basis of sound reality-tested decision making, logical and coherent thinking, and a self-concept influenced by ethnic values and history. A person of color can cope by means of cognitive thinking about who he or she is and about the reality of a racist society.

The client's affect involves the extent to which feeling states are expressed or masked to a range of persons: family, friends, acquaintances, people of color, and white persons. It is not unusual for people of color to change their affect responses according to their degree of familiarity with others present. For example, when members of the same ethnic group gather informally, a spirit of camaraderie is present. Bantering, jokes, and ethnic slang often characterize these moments; the affect is warm and open, and the person feels at ease. However, when a white person appears on the scene, the group may become quiet, with subdued affect. Discomfort with white people is responsible for this masking of affect. People of color do not want to make themselves vulnerable by disclosure of genuine affect. Only after considerable relating, testing, and trust building can people of color express positive affect in the presence of white people. Accordingly, white social workers must not use affective disclosure as a means of confrontation with ethnic clients. Loss of trust between worker and client may ruin the potential relationship with the client or with the local ethnic community.

Cultural limitations restrict the expression of feelings. To impose demands to "be totally open and let it all hang out" may be to ask for something beyond the client's cultural capacity. Recognizing and respecting those limits and striving to work with clients on the recognition and disclosure of feelings are realistic goals for the social worker. For some groups, affect is expressed through concrete action. For example, unable to express verbally their rage at years of economic exploitation by local merchants, police harassment and brutality, and inadequate human services, African Americans in the mid-1960s took to the streets in a series of urban riots. Those destructive protest actions expressed a collective feeling of frustration and exasperation over society's indifference to their plight. Surprisingly, after the civil unrest, federal and local funds, social programs, and national attention were directed to the predicament of inner-city African Americans.

Social workers must look beyond the traditional diagnosis of affective states. Affect is generally assessed according to the appropriateness of the client's functioning state vis-à-vis his or her clinical predicament. The psychiatric social worker looks for affective signs of depression and abnormality described as "flat or inappropriate affect." Although it is important to differentiate these affective categories, it is also necessary to consider the ethnic and cultural dynamics involving disclosure. How affect is expressed in nonverbal communication is a crucial consideration in assessing minority clients.

Akin to the cognitive and affective states are the actions of the person that result from conscious decision making. An individual acts for a specific reason. Behavioral therapy teaches that there are antecedent events that precipitate behavior and resulting effects. In a threatening situation, a person of color may respond passively and stoically. A client might choose to exhibit a cognitive and affective reaction based on environmental threats. Sometimes strategies for ethnic survival have given rise to racial stereotypes. For example, the seemingly happy-go-lucky, obedient African American slave behaved in such a manner to avoid the wrath and whip of the owner. The quiet, smiling Asian American exhibited survival behavior to avoid being attacked and lynched by angry white mobs at the turn of the century. The sleepy Mexican American, sombrero over his face, epitomized the maxim "hear no evil, speak no evil, see no evil" in the midst of vigilante rule. The stoic Native American with an expressionless face, wrapped in a blanket, concealed feelings of defeat and frustration over reservation restrictions. These behavioral responses are masks that cover ethnic despair at social, economic, and political oppression by a racist society.

A client may feel threatened in an unfamiliar setting or thoroughly at ease in a culturally familiar environment. The social worker can create an environment that puts clients at ease. Green (1982) terms this behavioral awareness *ethnic competence*.

The definition implies an awareness of prescribed and proscribed behavior within a specific culture, and it suggests that the ethnically competent worker has the ability to carry out professional activities consistent with that awareness. It does not propose that trained individuals are those who can mimic the behavioral routines and linguistic particularities of their minority clients. Nor does it rule that out. Its emphasis is on the trained worker's ability to adapt professional tasks and work styles to the cultural values and preferences of clients. (pp. 52–53).

The psychosocial perspective on the cognitive, affective, and behavioral dimensions of the ethnic client brings unique cultural knowledge to bear on clinical situations.

Worker-Client Tasks. In the assessment stage, the worker-client tasks consist of interaction and evaluation. In the interaction process, the worker and client sort through multiple cultural environmental factors and settle on those that have an effect on the problem. In this process, the worker is the inquirer and learner, and the client teaches and clarifies. The philosophy is patterned after Green's (1982) understanding of the ethnographic interview. Evaluation identifies individual and environmental factors useful in designing an appropriate intervention strategy. It appraises the changes necessary to alter the client's situation. When detailed information has been assembled about the problem, the client's cultural resources, and the community support system, the evaluation process culminates in the establishment of intervention goals, a contract, and procedural strategies to implement changes. Attention focuses on present conditions, selected past events that influence the current problem, and the client's capabilities and motivation to work on the problem.

Intervention

Practice Process Stage. Social work intervention is based on a strategy for change that modifies and resolves the problem situation. Intervention occurs when the client's biopsychosocial needs are met through material and supportive resources in the family community and through social or religious organizations. Turner (1978) identifies three contexts for psychosocial functioning: the medium of human relationships, the availability of material and service resources, and the client's significant environment. The purpose of intervention is to effect change in the client and in the environment for mutual improvement.

Client-System and Worker-System Practice Issues. The client and the worker participate jointly in the formulation of goals and the contract agreement and in the matching of intervention levels and strategies. Bloom and Fischer (1982) define *goals* as "statements of what the client/system (and practitioner and perhaps relevant others) would like to happen, do, or be when intervention is completed" (p. 64). Goals are terminal, or ultimate, outcomes that the client and worker would like to have achieved upon completion of the intervention phase. Objectives are intermediate subgoals or developmental procedures, a series of steps that begins with concrete action and ends with the accomplishment of outcome goals. The statements of goals and contract should be brief and prescriptive.

The selection of a particular intervention strategy depends on the nature of the problem, the client's background, and the worker's professional judgment. It should be based on certain objective criteria:

1. The intervention examines and resolves the problem.
2. The intervention focuses on immediate past and present time sequences related to the problem.
3. The intervention alters the psychosocial dimensions of the problem.
4. The intervention requires tasks to mobilize the client in focused positive action.
5. The intervention demonstrates in measurable terms that change has occurred in the problem area.

Levels of intervention are the same as the problem levels already named: micro-, meso-, and macro-. Direct social work practice tends to operate at the levels of micro- and mesointerventions. For example, the family and community provide natural helping resources that have an impact on the environment. Medicine (1981) advocates a psychosocial intervention based on extended family aid and collective survival. This kinship strategy results in the family's cooperation for the purposes of economic and social well-being. Medicine describes examples of reciprocity, such as maintaining joint use of an automobile, hauling water, cutting wood, running errands, exchanging child care services, and caring for the elderly.

These levels of intervention are matched with the following intervention strategies.

- *Liberation* is the client's experience of release or freedom from oppressive barriers and control when change occurs. For some, it accompanies personal growth and decision making: the client has decided no longer to submit to oppression. In other cases, liberation occurs under the influence of environmental change—for example, the introduction of a job-training program or the election of an ethnic mayor who makes policy, legislative, and program changes on behalf of people of color.

- *Empowerment* is "a process whereby persons who belong to a stigmatized social category throughout their lives can be assisted to develop and increase skills in the exercise of interpersonal influence and the performance of valued social rules" (Solomon, 1976, p. 6). Claiming the human right to resources and well-being in society, individuals experience power by rising up and changing their situational predicament. The first step to empowerment is to obtain information about resources and rights. Then, choosing an appropriate path of action, the client participates in a situation in which his or her exercise of power confers palpable benefits. Practical avenues of empowerment include voting, influencing policy, or initiating legislation on the local level.

- *Parity* relates to a sense of equality. For people of color, parity entails being of equal power, value, and rank with others in society and being treated accordingly. Its focal theme is fairness and the entitlement to certain rights. Parity is expressed in terms of resources that guarantee an adequate standard of living, such as entitlement programs (Social Security, Medicare), income maintenance, and medical care.

• *Maintenance of culture* asserts the importance of the ideas, customs, skills, arts, and language of a people. By tracing an ethnic group's history, worker and client can identify moments of crisis and challenge through which it survived and triumphed. Applying such lessons of history to the present inspires the client to overcome obstacles and provides a source of strength on which the client may draw. Maintenance of culture secures the client's identity as an ethnic individual.

• *Unique personhood* is an intervention strategy by which stereotypes are transcended. Functional casework asserts the view that each person is unique in the helping relationship and that there is something extraordinary in each individual. When people of color act to gain freedom from social stereotypes, they assert their unique personhood and discover their humanity.

Worker-Client Tasks. The worker-client tasks of the intervention stage revolve around creating and changing. In formulating new ways to deal with existing problems, the worker and client are creating. Like the God of the Old Testament, whose words and orderly actions produced creation, the worker and client originate a series of acts that they hope will result in the creation of a new system. By words, the worker and client communicate with each other and with their respective networks: family, extended support system, agency, and community resources. By action, the worker facilitates movement and direction to implement the creative formulations devised in collaboration with the client. The concept of creativity brings a new dimension to worker-client tasks. No longer does the worker go through the same motions and procedures again and again with the same type of client. Rather, each client poses a unique set of problems and interventive formulations that require creative imagination. The interweaving of worker, client, community, and service in infinite variations means that each case involves a new creation.

The task of changing provides movement from one situation to another. Rather than talking to the client about the general idea of change, the worker provides specific courses of action that alter the situation. Task-centered and behavioral-oriented changes are examples of approaches in clinical practice that emphasize change and measure its effects on the client: task-centered casework moves the client and situation from point to point in a series of goal-oriented changes; behavioral casework alters or modifies the behavior of the client and the antecedents and consequences of the environment. The ethnic community must change unjust and exploitative social policies, regulatory laws, and institutional practices. Thus, in multicultural practice, intervention must encompass both clinical and community dimensions.

Termination

Practice Process Stage. Termination denotes a closure of the present relationship between client and worker. The manner and circumstances of termination shape the future growth patterns of the client. Termination is the tentative ending of sessions that have focused on the identified problems. The problem, one hopes, has been resolved in an agreed-on number of sessions. Termination can also mean major adjustments of goals and interventive approaches, resulting in a new series of sessions. It is a time to redefine the problem and renegotiate new goals and intervention strategies. In some instances, termination results from counterproductive factors such as numerous absences of the client or lack of significant movement on the problem. These factors may be due to unresolved resistance on the part of the client, cultural and personal barriers, dissonance between the personalities of worker and client, or events beyond their control.

Client-System and Worker-System Practice Issues. Successful termination assumes arrival at destination points. Mature growth is one of those points. The client and worker are able to measure the amount of growth between the contact and termination stages. To differentiate the two stages as *before* and *after* is to recognize the changes that have occurred in the interval. *Recital* is an ingredient of termination: the client recites back the positive change that has occurred in the helping process. The client reflects on what has happened at certain points in his or her life. *Completion* is understood as the achievement of goals and resolution of issues, attended by a sense of accomplishment.

Follow-up strategies involve maintaining contact with the client after the conclusion of the practice sessions. Telephone calls and periodic follow-up meetings over the course of several months are helpful in evaluating the progress the client makes after completion of social services. Ethnic clients are known to have a high dropout rate for human services. Research is needed to determine which components of social treatment are responsible for premature closure.

Worker-Client Tasks. In terms of worker-client tasks, *achieving* carries the connotation of accomplishing and attaining a certain goal. For the worker, achieving consists of successfully helping the client through a problem situation. For the client, achieving means successfully sustaining the effort to change a psychosocial situation. *Resolving* places closure on decision making; it imparts a sense of finality.

CONCLUSION

This chapter has laid out a general framework for social work practice with people of color. Its major categories include practice process stages, worker-system practice issues, client-system practice issues, and worker-client tasks. Principles of social work practice have been integrated with insights into issues facing people of color. In the succeeding chapters, we will elaborate on the principles relevant to various process stages. The aim is to help social work practitioners implement this framework in their encounters with ethnic clients.

REFERENCES

Aragón de Valdez, T., & Gallegos, J. (1982). The Chicano familia in social work. In J. W. Green (Ed.), *Cultural awareness in the human services* (pp. 184–208).Upper Saddle River, NJ: Prentice-Hall.

Bloom, M., & Fischer, J. (1982). *Evaluating practice: Guidelines for the accountable professional.* Upper Saddle River, NJ: Prentice-Hall.

Brislin, R. W. (1981). *Cross-cultural encounters: Face-to-face interaction.* New York: Pergamon.

Chau, K. L. (1990). A model for teaching cross-cultural practice in social work. *Journal of Social Work Education, 26,* 124–133.

Cheetham, J. (1982). *Social work and ethnicity.* London: Allen & Unwin.

Comas-Diaz, L., & Greene, B. (1994). *Women of color: Integrating ethnic and gender identities in psychotherapy.* New York: Guilford.

Crystal, D. (1971). *Linguistics.* Middlesex: Pelican.

Devore, W., & Schlesinger, E. G. (1981). *Ethnic-sensitive social work practice.* St. Louis: Mosby.

Draguns, J. G. (1981). Counseling across cultures: Common themes and distinct approaches. In P. B. Pedersen, J. G. Draguns, W. J. Lonner, & J. E. Trimble (Eds.), *Counseling across cultures* (pp. 3–21). Honolulu: University of Hawaii Press.

Erikson, E. H. (1959). Identity and the life cycle. *Psychological Issues, 1,* 1.

Fischer, J. (1978). *Effective casework practice: An eclectic approach.* New York: McGraw-Hill.

Gibbs, J. T., & Huang, L. N. (1989). A conceptual framework for assessing and treating minority youth. In J. T. Gibbs & L. N. Huang (Eds.), *Children of color: Psychological interventions with minority youth* (pp. 1–29). San Francisco: Jossey-Bass.

Green, J. W. (1982). *Cultural awareness in the human services.* Upper Saddle River, NJ: Prentice-Hall.

Headland, T. N., Pike, K. L., & Harris, M. (Eds.). (1990). *Emics and etics: The insider/outsider debate.* Newbury Park, CA: Sage.

Hepworth, D. H., & Larsen, J. A. (1990). *Direct social work practice: Theory and skills* (3rd ed.). Belmont, CA: Wadsworth.

Ho, M. K. (1987). *Family therapy with ethnic minorities.* Newbury Park, CA: Sage.

Ho, M. K. (1992). *Minority children and adolescents in therapy.* Newbury Park, CA: Sage.

Ishisaka, A. H., & Takagi, C. Y. (1982). Social work with Asian- and Pacific-Americans. In J. W. Green (Ed.), *Cultural awareness in the human services* (pp. 122–156).Upper Saddle River, NJ: Prentice-Hall.

Jenkins, S. (1981). *The ethnic dilemma in social services.* New York: Free Press.

Leigh, J. W., & Green, J. W. (1982). The structure of the black community: The knowledge base for social services. In J. W. Green (Ed.), *Cultural awareness in the human services* (pp. 94–121). Upper Saddle River, NJ: Prentice-Hall.

Lonner, W. J. (1979). Issues in cross-cultural psychology. In A. J. Marsella, R. G. Tharp, & T. J. Ciborowski (Eds.), *Perspectives on cross-cultural psychology* (pp. 17–45). New York: Academic Press.

Martin, E. P., & Martin, J. M. (1995). *Social work and the black experience*. Washington, DC: National Association of Social Workers.

Mead, G. H. (1934). *Mind, self, and society*. Chicago: University of Chicago Press.

Medicine, B. (1981). American Indian family: Cultural change and adaptive strategies. *Journal of Ethnic Studies, 8*, 13–23.

Miller, N. B. (1982). Social work services to urban Indians. In J. W. Green (Ed.), *Cultural awareness in the human services*. Upper Saddle River, NJ: Prentice-Hall.

O'Connor, J. D. (1973). *Phonetics*. Middlesex: Pelican.

Pike, K. L. (1954). *Language in relation to a unified theory of the structure of human behavior. Part I: preliminary edition*. Santa Ana, CA: Summer.

Pike, K. L. (1967). *Language in relation to a unified theory of the structure of human behavior* (rev. 2nd ed.). The Hague: Mouton.

Pike, K. L. (1990). On the emics and etics of Pike and Harris. In T. N. Headland, K. L. Pike, & M. Harris (Eds.), *Emics and etics: The insider/outsider debate* (pp. 28–47). Newbury Park, CA: Sage.

Price-Williams, D. (1979). Modes of thought in cross-cultural psychology: An historical overview. In A. J. Marsella, R. G. Tharp, & T. J. Ciborowski (Eds.), *Perspectives on cross-cultural psychology* (pp. 3–16). New York: Academic Press.

Sands, R. G., & McClelland, M. (1994). Emic and etic perspectives in ethnographic research on the interdisciplinary team. In E. Sherman & W. J. Reid (Eds.), *Qualitative research in social work* (pp. 32–41). New York: Columbia University Press.

Solomon, B. B. (1976). *Black empowerment: Social work in oppressed communities*. New York: Columbia University Press.

Sundberg, N. D. (1981). Research and research hypotheses about effectiveness in intercultural counseling. In P. B. Pedersen, J. G. Draguns, W. J. Lonner, & J. E. Trimble (Eds.), *Counseling cross-cultures* (pp. 304–342). Honolulu: University of Hawaii Press.

Turner, F. J. (1978). *Psychosocial therapy*. New York: Free Press.

Wise, F., & Miller, N. (1981). The mental health of the American Indian child. In G. Powell, A. Morales, & J. Yamamoto (Eds.), *The psychosocial development of minority group children* (pp. 345–378). New York: Brunner/Mazel.

CHAPTER 6

Contact

Contact involves the establishment of a relationship between the social worker and the client. It is probably the most important phase of the helping process because retaining the multicultural client in the helping process is essential. Many people of color drop out after the first session because social workers have been taught to move directly into problem solving without laying the necessary groundwork of relationship building and engagement. The principles of contact described in this chapter are thus crucial to learn and practice with clients.

But even before the actual face-to-face encounter, the social service agency should carefully prepare its staff and procedural policy for working with people of color. To create a multicultural service delivery system, the administrative director and staff should have conducted an agency self-study, gathered relevant data on the ethnic population, and trained staff on approaches to culturally diverse practice.

This chapter identifies and explains the major subsystems that comprise client-worker contact (see Figure 6-1). The section on client-system practice issues contains subsections that discuss the client's resistance, barriers to communication, personal and family background, and ethnic community identity. We then move to worker-system practice issues: understanding the ethnic community, relationship protocols, professional self-

disclosure, and styles of communication. Finally, this chapter suggests practical ways to implement the client-worker practice principles in a planned strategy for people of color.

CLIENT-SYSTEM PRACTICE ISSUES

Resistance

A person of color often approaches a formal, professional social service organization with varying degrees of resistance. The person may feel anxiety and uncertainty over the unknown, shame and guilt over failure to solve his or her own problems, or anger when legal coercion is exerted to use the service. Moreover, going to a social service agency may represent the last resort after the client has asked family, friends, and the community's natural support systems for help.

Causes. From the psychoanalytic perspective, resistance has traditionally been understood as opposition to the bringing of unconscious, repressed material to consciousness. The therapist generally confronts the patient early in the interpretive process, because resistance builds from an unwillingness to accept insights into the problem. Recently, however, resistance has been recognized as a natural reaction to coming to the helping process. Clinicians are taught to ask, as a part of the initial session, "How do you feel about coming here?" to deal with natural resistance. This open-ended question is a tactful way of exploring any negative feelings that the client may have. It is also designed to clear the atmosphere and motivate the client. It seems natural to apply this technique to all clients.

However, in multicultural practice, understanding and coping with client resistance call for an alternative perspective. Clear distinctions are made between people of color and white people in social contexts. Bochner (1982) observes that, in situations of cross-cultural contact, people distinguish between hosts or owners, and visitors or newcomers; these labels refer to in-group and out-group designations. Members of ethnic groups are particularly distinguished by highly visible characteristics of race, skin color, and language. Green (1982) uses the term *cultural boundary* to designate the line that separates the professional social workers, organizational structure, and operational procedures from the ethnic client, community, and history. People of color are reluctant to approach human service agencies that are controlled and dominated by whites. Workers must overcome the resistance of ethnic clients by establishing trust.

Overcoming Resistance. The client has to work through his or her resistance. Leigh (1984) describes how a person of color sizes up a helper. At first, the client has minimal involvement and may be aloof, reserved, or superficially pleasant. He or she shows no overt interest in, or curiosity about, the worker. Then, the client checks out the helper by asking about his or her personal life, background, opinions, and values. These probes are intended not only to evaluate the worker but also to become acquainted and to establish a personal relationship. Fritzpatrick (1981) points out that the basic value of the Puerto Rican culture is personalism—the focus on the individual's inner qualities, which determine his or her goodness or worth as a person. What makes a person good and respected is an inner dignity *(dignidad)*. He

FIGURE 6-1 *Contact Stage: Client-System and Worker-System Practice Issues*

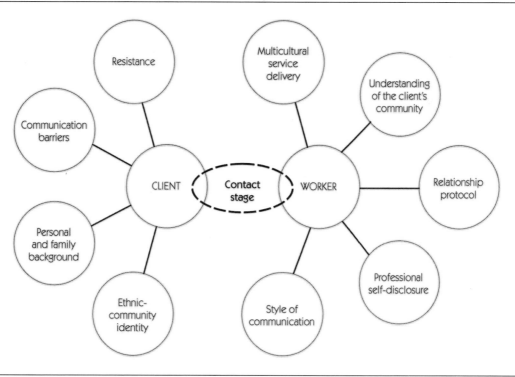

remarks that Puerto Ricans "are unusually responsive to manifestations of personal respect and to styles of personal leadership by men who appeal to the person rather than a program or a platform" (Fritzpatrick, 1981, p. 201). Perhaps the client instinctively searches for the inner qualities of the worker. Upon finding these traits, the client begins to lower his or her resistance and opens up to the worker. Otherwise, the client maintains resistance and drops out after an initial session, or seeks another helping resource.

Vélez (1980) further believes that *confianza en confianza* (trusting in mutual trust) is important to the extent that there is *deutero-learning*, a term that denotes mutualistic generosity, intimacy, and personal investment in others. Deutero-learning occurs with reciprocity of friendship, food, visits, labor, and other activities. Thus, the worker invests himself or herself in the client through the interpersonal helping process, and the client often reciprocates by bringing vegetables, fruit, candy, and other gifts of appreciation. *Confianza en confianza* further implies accepting the trustworthiness of self and others. That is, the multicultural client accepts the trustworthiness of the worker to an extent that eliminates the need for resistance. Not only does the client evaluate the worker's character, but reciprocal positive acts confirm the trust that has been established.

Lee (1981) observes that Indo-Chinese are reluctant to disclose problems to strangers; they generally share their problems and feelings with their families. Because of this cultural standard, Indo-Chinese have to establish a vicarious family relationship with the worker. This process can involve assigning the worker a family kinship position: The worker is given a highly respected title, such as uncle or aunt, elder brother or sister, and the client speaks of him- or herself as nephew or niece (a younger, lower rank in the family). By virtue of adoption as an honorary member of the family, the worker becomes someone with whom the client can share feelings and problems.

Thus, an ethnic client overcomes resistance by finding out about the worker, evaluating the worker's inner character, and perhaps bestowing family kinship. Social work practice should be aware of these alternative ways of dealing with clients' resistance. Rather than impeding the process, the social worker should participate in this reality testing and demonstrate genuine caring and empathy.

Communication Barriers

Social work practice generally teaches communication skills based on the assumption that worker and client communicate through primary verbalization and secondary nonverbal cues. Devore and Schlesinger (1981) suggest using empathy to identify feelings, attending skills that focus on verbal and nonverbal behavior, open-ended and directive questioning, and reaching for facts and feelings in a sensitive manner. However, a number of qualifications must be made for people of color. Otherwise, barriers to communication may form unbeknownst to the worker.

Special Concerns with People of Color. Valle (1980) suggests that, to facilitate communication, the worker and client should begin *plática*, or friendly conversation. Latinos are accustomed to mutual extended discussion, which is a recognized form of relationship building. *Plática* stresses mutuality and reciprocity, meaning an open and free exchange of information between the two parties. Helper-initiated friendly conversation about the weather, humorous incidents, or recent activities sets the stage for the development of a relationship. Brislin (1981) carries this goodwill approach a step further when he observes that the worker must gear the conversation to the level of the client's background:

> Much cross-cultural contact involves communicating with people who do not share the same types of information. People who personalize knowledge are able to judge the amount of information the other person possesses and to communicate their knowledge through appropriate examples based on the background that the other person brings to the learning situation. (p. 59)

It is important to find the personal fit between the communication levels of the worker and the client. As significant as the matching of communication levels is appropriate content. Talking

The Hernández Family, a Case Study

Mr. Hernández, age thirty-eight, is a Mexican American who works as a gardener. He and his family are making an inquiry at the Family Service Association agency regarding a problem that one of the children is having in school. Mr. Hernández speaks some English in his business, because much of his clientele is middle- and upper-class whites. From morning to evening, he drives his truck and maintains the yards and landscapes of many wealthy professionals who live in exclusive sections of the city. Mr. Hernández works hard and is friendly to his customers. During the holidays, many customers give him extra money and gifts for his family. When he returns home after a hard day of work, Mr. Hernández is tired. He has a few friends in the barrio who visit him in the evenings. He enjoys playing cards with them at home and drinking beer. Mr. Hernández is reluctant to talk about personal and family problems to outsiders. Rather, he confides in his wife on the rare occasions when he is deeply troubled over a situation.

TASK RECOMMENDATIONS

It is important to enter the world of a person of color. For thirty minutes you are to become Mr. Hernández. Role-play him getting up in the morning before dawn, eating his breakfast, and leaving for a full day of gardening. Imagine his feelings about his work, his gardening skills, his conversations with some of his customers during the day, and his evenings at home with family and friends.

Over the course of several months, Mr. Hernández tries to cope with a family problem that involves his eldest son, but he and his wife are unable to solve the problem. What would you do if you were Mr. Hernández?

- Would you approach a formal social service agency with your problem?
- How would you feel during the opening session?
- What kind of worker would you like to have help with your problem?
- How would you determine whether the worker is a person whom you can trust and in whom you are willing to confide?

---

prematurely about taboo topics can hinder the flow of communication. Brislin (1981) speaks of *conversational currency*, or the range of topics that are considered proper subjects for conversation. These topics differ from culture to culture. Workers must familiarize themselves with such topics as conversation shifts to serious issues. Allowing the client to lead the way into a restricted topic is a safe rule to follow. At times, an ethnic client may subtly introduce a problem and wait for the worker to open the dialogue around it. An impasse could form if the worker does not notice the opportunity. Leigh (1980) reminds us that a person of color often communicates latent content:

> Case workers will pick up on latent communication messages only if they have been trained to listen for such content and feelings. Racial references are probably passed by or when noted by the caseworker they will intervene and give another interpretation to the overt content. This action has the message in it that the subject is too dangerous, or immaterial to the process of help, or that the caseworker is too threatened by the mere perception of racial content in the relationship to manage his or her own feelings about the subject. (p. 1)

Offering a helpful suggestion to open communication about a client's ethnic group, McGill (1992) introduces the idea of the *cultural story* as a nonthreatening way to find out relevant background:

> The cultural story refers to an ethnic or cultural group's origin, migration, and identity. Within the family, it is used to tell where one's ancestors came from, what kind of people they were and current members are, what issues are important to the family, what good and bad

things have happened over time, and what lessons have been learned from their experiences. At the ethnic level, a cultural story tells the group's collective story of how to cope with life and how to respond to pain and trouble. It teaches people how to thrive in a multicultural society and what children should be taught so that they can sustain their ethnic and cultural story. (p. 340)

McGill (1992) suggests that, in a reflection period after the session with the client, the worker may wish to ponder the following questions:

- What is the family's central problem?
- How does gender relate to the problem?
- How do life cycle and intergenerational issues relate to the problem?
- How does ethnicity relate to the problem?
- How does class relate to the problem?
- How does migration relate to the problem?
- How might the relationship between the therapist and family (that is, similarities and differences in their cultural stories) affect the problem?
- How might the family "restory" the problem?

Breaking down the communication barriers and eliciting significant information is the thrust of the cultural story method.

Pedersen (1988) recommends a number of practical ways to increase cross-cultural communication, as outlined in Cultural Study 6-1.

CULTURAL STUDY 6-1

Decreasing Barriers

There are several obvious barriers to accurate communication across cultures. First, there is the obvious barrier of language differences. Language is much more than learning new sound symbols. Knowing a little of the foreign language only may allow visitors to make fluent fools of themselves if they are unaware of the implicit meanings behind the sound symbols.

Listed below are some ways that may help you decrease multicultural communication barriers.

Decreasing the Language Barrier

Learn the language.
Find someone who can speak the language.
Ask for clarification if you are not sure what was said.

Second, nonverbal communications such as gestures, posture, tone of voice, and timing often change what we say. There is some difficulty in recognizing unspoken codes that come so automatically that they may not even be deliberate in our own more familiar culture but communicate a definite feeling or attitude nonetheless.

Decreasing the Nonverbal Communication Barrier

Do not assume you understand any nonverbal communication unless you are familiar with the culture.
If the nonverbal communication is insulting in your culture, do not take it personally.
Develop an awareness of your own nonverbal communication that might be insulting in certain cultures.

The third barrier—preconceptions and stereotypes—consists of overgeneralized beliefs that provide structure in any ambiguous contact. We see or hear pretty much what we want to or expect to see or hear, screening out many contradictory impressions. When you first become slightly aware of another culture, these half-formed stereotypes are most likely to betray communications. The stereotype has a tendency to become realized through a "self-fulfilling prophecy" of the communicator.

Decreasing the Preconceptions and Stereotypes Barrier

Make every effort to increase awareness of your own preconceptions and stereotypes of cultures you encounter.
With this awareness, reinterpret the behavior of people from another culture from their cultural perspective.
Be willing to test, adapt, and change your perceptions to fit your new experiences.

A fourth barrier is the tendency to evaluate by an approving or disapproving judgment the content of communication received from others. "Everyone seems to speak with an accent except those people who talk like [me]." Premature evaluation frequently interferes with our accepting and understanding other persons from their point of view.

Decreasing the Evaluation Barrier

Maintain objectivity.

Recognize that you cannot change a person's culture overnight.

Do not judge someone from another culture by your own cultural values until you have come to know the people and their cultural values.

A fifth barrier is the typically high level of anxiety that goes along with the multicultural contact where the visitor is dealing with unfamiliar experiences.

Decreasing the Stress Barrier

Multicultural situations are often ambiguous and result in stress because you are not sure what others expect of you or what you can expect of them. As multicultural barriers are reduced, you can expect the level of stress to diminish.

A sixth barrier relates to the "organizational constraints" that may control what we do even when we know they are inequitable. Organizations shape our communications in ways that primarily protect their own interests.

Decreasing the Organizational Constraints Barrier

Identify the authority/responsibility/reporting relationships reflected in the formal organization chart.

Look for patterns of personal interaction that seem to deviate from the formal organization. These are your information communication channels.

Recognize that an organization does not exist apart from people; check and confirm the

limits of formal and informal personal influence.

Clarify your role, knowledge, and experience with the other person to the extent that you maintain the integrity and loyalties demanded by your position.

From *A Handbook for Developing Multicultural Awareness* by Paul Pedersen, pp. 23–25. Copyright 1988 American Association for Counseling and Development. Reprinted by permission.

Educational Outreach. To increase communication and to promote mental health, educational media programs have been designed for multicultural community outreach. When people of color are exposed to cultural presentations, they are responsive to the helping process. Boulette (1980) offers four ways to present mental health concepts to Latinos (Boulette also uses the term *Chicano/Mexicano*); the methods apply to people of color in general:

1. Spanish-language radio and television programming is a major vehicle of communication to the Chicano/Mexicano community. A series of fifty five-minute Spanish radio programs, entitled *Una Familia Sana* (a healthy family), focuses on child-rearing practices; child development, discipline, and conflict resolution; and constructive parenting and cultural practices. The material was transcribed to cassettes that were made available to organizations for parent education discussion groups.

2. A bilingual manual of preventive health care was written in Spanish and translated into English to retain a Chicano/Mexicano viewpoint. The manual was distributed to Spanish-speaking physicians, lawyers, public-health nurses, welfare case aides, Head Start workers, and others.

3. Educational coffee klatches and teas, called *meriendas educativas*, were organized to promote group mental health among low-income Spanish-speaking women. These gatherings were designed to share information about primary prevention, reduce the social distance and distrust between

The Hernández Family, a Case Study

Mr. Hernández is a quiet man who tends to demonstrate his feelings through hard, methodical work on his gardening route. Because his English is limited, he is accustomed to communicating in Spanish with his family and friends. He does, however, converse in English with his customers to maintain his business. In front of a helping professional, such as a social worker, Mr. Hernández is reserved and shy. He speaks only when he needs to answer the worker's questions and does not initiate conversation. Communication barriers exist.

TASK RECOMMENDATIONS

Continue playing the role of Mr. Hernández, who has come to a family social service agency with a problem about his son. Place yourself in his position as a reserved man who can speak some English but who feels more comfortable communicating in Spanish. If you were Mr. Hernández, what thoughts would run through your mind about communicating with the worker?

• What would be the best way to begin the conversation?

• When would be the appropriate time to talk about the problem I am having with my son?

• How can I maintain my role as a strong father when my son has a problem?

• Will I be blamed for my son's troubles?

• Are there other Mexican American families in similar situations?

These questions are pressing issues for Mr. Hernández. As a social worker, how would you communicate effectively with him and lower some of the communication barriers?

---

staff and clientele, impart information about available services, and encourage the resolution of child-rearing and marital problems.

4. Learning fairs—*fiestas educativas*—were all-day health workshops for high-risk Latino parents. The goals were to recruit distressed parents; offer support in building strong, healthy families; encourage the sharing of language, traditions, and values; and provide medical, psychological, and resource information.

Educational outreach in the community complements an awareness of the need to overcome communication barriers in a practice agency setting. In multicultural practice, both strategies can be helpful in communicating problem-solving information on individual and community levels.

Personal and Family Background

It is important to elicit and discuss information on personal and family background during the contact stage. Fritzpatrick (1981) points out that family solidarity is the major psychosocial support for its members. The family provides a helping resource, particularly for people of color. Marsel-

la (1979) observes that family structure and relationship patterns minimize depression in non-Western societies. Multicultural families have a support system composed of extended family and ethnic community agencies. Among Latinos and other people of color, there is a strong obligation to help each other as family members (Gonzalez & García, 1974). A worker gathers personal and family background about the client to build a psychosocial profile. Ethnic clients tend to be cautious about sharing information because the information may have been used against them in the past. It is critical for the worker to develop information-gathering approaches that recognize this reality and to work patiently with the client in the confidence that background information will come as trust develops.

Solomon (1983) asserts that the traditional mode of data gathering during the initial interview may not be advantageous when working with people of color. She indicates that clients are invariably required to answer questions that have little relevance to the problem-solving process. Examples of such questions are length of time in the community, place of employment, amount of family income, and religion. Some information,

The Hernández Family, a Case Study

Mr. Hernández has been under increasing pressure during the past few months to support his family and several in-laws who have moved to Los Angeles from Mexico. Because the unemployment rate is high, these recent immigrants are having a difficult time supporting themselves. Mr. Hernández feels responsible for their support and is working two jobs. As a result, he works from early morning to late night and is extremely tired when he arrives home. He is therefore unable to help his son Ricardo with his homework or play with him, and Mrs. Hernández, who works in a laundry part-time, cannot speak or read English. Moreover, Mr. Hernández has been under extreme stress and takes it out on the children. Ricardo has become disruptive in class, and his grades for the past six weeks have been poor.

TASK RECOMMENDATIONS

Obtaining personal and family information to increase knowledge of psychosocial interaction is important for the social worker. Some ethnic clients live in constant fear of revealing information that could be used against them—that might lead to deportation from the United States, for example. Disclosure of information should focus on relevant aspects of the problem.

- Review your agency's format for intake information. Discuss the possibility of revising it so that essential information is condensed to one page.
- Sort out general information received from the client and select material that is useful in the problem-solving process.
- Use the first two sessions to obtain the necessary information, which emerges during worker-client interaction.
- Find out about helping resources that the client has used in the ethnic community.

such as that pertaining to divorces, evictions, and last job held, reinforces the client's sense of personal deficiency. Solomon suggests that social workers ask questions that relate directly to the problem-solving work.

An alternative to the traditional data-gathering method is to take down basic information—such as name, address, phone number, and reason for coming to the agency—in an initial telephone interview. The worker then allows essential information—concerning family structure, socioeconomic living conditions, and natural support system—to emerge during the first few sessions and records relevant data after the client has left.

Ethnic Community Identity

It is important to determine whether the client relates to his or her ethnic community. Jenkins (1981) reports that people of color voiced positive feelings about going to their own community center staffed by bilingual/bicultural workers and having culturally oriented outreach programs. The choice of a worker depended on language fluency and cultural awareness. These findings support the need to establish ethnic social service agencies that have capable ethnic staff, are located in a geographic area accessible to the ethnic population, and stress preventive educational programs.

Helping Networks. Within an ethnic community are natural helping resources that the client uses in his or her search for help. Ethnic neighborhood networks operate on many levels:

Ethnic neighborhoods . . . were formed as places of refuge and protection in an alien world. The immigrants needed the support and assistance of others like themselves in order to establish a foothold in the new country. The ethnic neighborhood provided an economic base for the struggling newcomers. It also facilitated their efforts to organize and to participate collectively in the political system of America. In the neighborhood, they could exchange information concerning the location of jobs and the views of various candidates for politi-

The Hernández Family, a Case Study

Mr. Hernández is marginally involved with the local Mexican American community. Mrs. Hernández is more involved in community affairs than her husband is. She attends mass regularly at the neighborhood Catholic church. Apart from seeing his close friends and meeting his family responsibilities, Mr. Hernández scarcely has time for community activities. He arrives home tired after working two jobs. Sunday is the only day he is off work. On Sundays he usually goes fishing with his friends or with the children. He can be characterized as a person with a few close acquaintances who is trying to survive and meet his family's basic needs.

At the same time, Mr. Hernández is friendly and approachable in his community. He relates well to his neighbors and gives them advice about their landscape and gardening.

TASK RECOMMENDATIONS

If Mr. Hernández is open to help with family problems, ethnic community resources should be employed while guarding his confidentiality. He must have a guarantee that the whole Mexican American community does not find out about his family problems. Otherwise, Mr. Hernández would suffer a loss of face.

- What community resources are potentially available to Mr. Hernández to help him and his relatives with their job situations?
- How would a worker interpret these resources to Mr. Hernández?
- How could confidentiality be maintained if Mr. Hernández decided to use a particular community service resource?

---

cal office. Through neighborhood organizations, they could combine their forces to combat discrimination in employment or to negotiate with "city hall." In the neighborhood, they could engage in deeply satisfying human relationships with others who shared their language, religion, cuisine, and memories of the old country. The ethnic American neighborhood, in short, has been a device to enable immigrants to come to grips with the new while preserving many of the psychological satisfactions of the old. (McLemore, 1983, p. 382)

Various subsystems function within the networks to attend to particular needs. Newcomer services are vital to the constant influx of immigrants in many ethnic communities. Classes in English as a second language, job-finding services, clean and reasonably priced housing, and native-language media are essential for adjusting to the new environment. Fritzpatrick (1981) cites the role of the Puerto Rican Family Institute, founded by Puerto Rican social workers, who identified and matched well-established and newly arrived families with each other. The former served as *compadres* to the latter in the New York City area in the early 1960s.

The *tanda* or *cundina*, a rotating credit association, is an example of a related support system. A number of invited participants contribute an agreed-on amount of money over a specified period of time. The total amount rotates to each participant within a time limit. The *tanda* is designed to assist members with their financial needs; entrance is based on mutual *confianza* relations.

Vega (1980) describes an integrated natural health delivery system composed of three layers with distinct functions. Revolving around a natural healer support system, the primary level consists of a network of individuals and families who have reciprocal exchanges with natural healers. The second level is the natural healing/coping community system, whereby community residents are exposed to information about the healer. The third tier consists of formal health service providers, who are linked to the healer through treating the same individuals, having contact with each other and working arrangements for cross-referral and consultation.

Designated Helpers. Designated helpers, who assist with a variety of local needs, are basic to the helping networks of an ethnic community. In the Latino community, such people are called *servidores*. Mendoza (1980) has classified *servidores* according to their roles:

1. Historian *servidores*, who have resided in the community for forty-five years or more and have historical knowledge of the area and its actors
2. Young cohort *servidores*, who help their age peers in their thirties and forties and the elderly Latinos
3. Resident and mobile *servidores*, who either operate in one location or travel throughout the country assisting people
4. Program director *servidores*, who organize outreach group activities and are active on boards, in policy-making matters, and in advocacy
5. Casework counselor *servidores*, who work with individual clients as outreach workers and information and referral aides
6. Neighborhood caretaker *servidores*, who engage in supportive roles and make referrals to other *servidores* employed in agencies

Servidores have established a community reputation for helping; building trust; resolving problems; being willing to give and to provide for the needs of others; and providing planning, information, outreach, and services for the elderly. The extent to which a client maintains a relationship with a *servidore* is an indication of the client's use of natural community resources.

Within an ethnic community, several service resources are available to the client. Whether a particular person is identified with a neighborhood or an ethnic population is important to determine at the beginning of the contact stage. Involvement in a specific ethnic community presupposes the client's strong identification with the ethnic community, which can be drawn on for support systems.

WORKER-SYSTEM PRACTICE ISSUES
Multicultural Service Delivery

Effective design of a service delivery for ethnic clients is central to an understanding of culturally diverse social work practice. Watkins and Gonzales (1982) have summarized major barriers to ethnic clients' use of social services. In their review of the literature regarding Mexican Americans, Watkins and Gonzales identify the following factors:

1. Past compliance of social welfare agencies in identifying undocumented Mexicans for deportation
2. Perception of the public health worker as a representative of the government and therefore a potential threat
3. Group tension between whites and Mexican Americans, especially when the worker is white
4. Fear of discrimination in treatment and high sensitivity to criticism from white health personnel
5. Differences in culture and language
6. Previous demeaning contact with mental health agencies
7. Lack of mental health facilities in the Mexican American community
8. Differences in class-bound values of clients and agency staff
9. Biased diagnosis that imputes a high incidence of psychopathology to Mexican Americans
10. The absence of bilingual and bicultural staff

Other minority groups may voice similar concerns that make them hesitant to seek help from social service agencies. The crucial question is, How can social workers in multicultural practice lay foundations for contact with clients that will remove such barriers? Fortunately, research in multicultural social services has uncovered certain principles underlying clients' use of services.

Location and Pragmatic Services. Public and private agencies that offer health care, employment, housing, day care, and other tangible and practical services should be located in or near areas with a large ethnic population. Arroyo and López (1984) underscore the importance of the social service agency's geographic location:

> Locating services in the *barrio* can be advantageous to a family service agency because of the high concentration of Chicanos; it is beneficial to the community because the services are physically accessible to the people who are to be served. It also indicates that the agency is sensitive to the importance of the *barrio* to Chicanos and the Chicano culture. (p. 65)

People of color use services more often when facilities are located in their immediate neighborhood and are not advertised as mental health or counseling services (Catell, 1962; Yuen, n.d.). A home or storefront center, a unit of a multipurpose community complex, or a component of a community medical facility would be appropriate choices for an accessible location. Agencies stand a better chance for steady use if they offer concrete, pragmatic aid. Mental illness or emotional disturbance carries a social stigma in some cultures. After the agency has gained credibility and community trust, social and family casework can be applied to individual and group problems.

Murase, Egawa, and Tashima (1985) suggest:

> In order to reduce the stigma that is frequently associated with these services, entry is often somewhere other than a door specifically marked "Mental Health Services." Some programs, for example, have changed their names from one that obviously suggests a mental health facility to one suggesting a more neutral range of services (e.g., "children's services" or "family outreach services"). (p. 230)

Another alternative is to integrate mental health services with language, recreation, and social programs within various social service settings. Related services could be housed in the same building, or mental health workers could be stationed in various community sites.

To build trust, Murase et al. advise the worker to focus initially on satisfying, pragmatic assistance—for example, job assistance, translation services, and help in filling out a form. This lays a foundation for the future introduction of psychological and mental health programs.

Staffing. Bilingual/bicultural workers should be employed for non-English-speaking clients. Arroyo and López (1984) explain the strategic importance of a bilingual approach:

> The significance of the Spanish language cannot be overemphasized, for Spanish has been instrumental in maintaining personal, meaningful relationships that have provided emotional stability for many Chicanos. Even Chicanos who are bilingual often revert to Spanish because it is their first language—their mother tongue—and it has great emotional significance for them. Moreover, Chicanos frequently think in Spanish even when they speak English. It is important to remember this phenomenon, particularly when providing counseling services to Chicanos, because when people experience stress, they tend to regress and use their primary language to express fully their worries, anxieties, fears, and concerns. Furthermore, it must be kept in mind that language reflects an individual's philosophy of life, value system, and (most important) aspects of the personality that one may find difficult to understand or even may not notice without knowledge of the language. (p. 68)

Recent immigrants and elderly members of ethnic groups have difficulty understanding and communicating in English when they seek public services (Campbell & Chang, 1973; Lee, 1985; Chen, 1970; Sue & Wagner, 1973). Bilingual and bicultural workers should be fluent in the language dialects of clients and familiar with child-rearing and family practices, ethnic customs and beliefs, and other cultural nuances. In the absence of bilingual/bicultural staff, a community case aide with language and cultural skills can act as a co-caseworker with staff and client.

Lee (1985) reports, "Studies have demonstrated that service utilization is greatly enhanced when bilingual, bicultural personnel are employed. Ethnic, linguistic, and cultural similarities between client and therapist decrease the dropout rate and improve the effectiveness of care" (p. 309).

Crucial to staffing are a vigorous program for training staff in the language and culture of ethnic community populations and case consultation with a clinical resource in culturally diverse social work. In Cultural Study 6-2, Kahn et al. (1975) describe a staff training experience that included on-the-job and university sessions on Native Americans from the Papago tribe. Eugene Galvez, a Papago Indian and staff member of the Papago Psychological Service, narrates his experiences as an indigenous Papago mental health worker.

CULTURAL STUDY 6-2

Multicultural Staff Training

I learned the job mainly from on-the-job training, dealing with cases at the same time that I was learning and getting experience. We started with an introduction from the mental health staff that included the professional staff and the one already trained Papago mental health worker.

We then paired up with the trained people and learned as we went along. We had a lot of training sessions in the beginning, which included role-playing and explanations of things. The most important thing I think a mental health worker needs to learn is to develop a trusting relationship with people with whom he is working. Being honest with people about what you are trying to do and how you are trying to find ways to help them and maintaining confidentiality are important. Confidentiality is particularly sensitive on a reservation, where many people are related or know each other. The villages are very small and things can get around rapidly. Developing the interviewing skills is also quite important, as well as knowing what kind of information you need to have in order to understand the problem. Things like observing people's behavior and expression[s] during the interview and getting them to talk about their feelings and to trust you enough to tell the details of the problem are other important skills. We had to learn about neurosis and psychosis, and how these conditions can be changed or helped.

Our program tries to build ongoing training sessions using the professional staff to have regular weekly sessions about different topics in the field. We spend a lot of time learning about abnormal psychology and having in-depth case conferences. We also try to have a training session for the whole staff at the University of Arizona at least once every several months, where we can take up a topic sometimes through a film and discuss it.

We have developed our skills in helping people, both in Anglo ways and in Papago cultural ways and sometimes with a combination of both. While we see a good variety of types of cases, I tend to work a lot with couples with marital problems and often these involve problems of alcoholism. I've learned it's important when I work with a couple that I also involve a female mental health worker so that I'm not biased for the man.

It's also important in many of the Papago marital situations to get the husband to show the wife some affection. Papagos aren't people who show others their feelings very readily and this is often a problem in marital situations. Take, for example, the case of a middle-aged couple I worked with recently. The case involved alcoholism, as do many cases on the reservation. The husband had been intoxicated for some time, seemingly ignoring his spouse's feelings. This came to our attention as a result of his spouse being admitted to the hospital because of acute depression. I worked extensively with the wife providing supportive therapy while attempting to contact the husband.

We finally managed to get the couple together. I then enlisted the aid of a female mental health worker to provide marital counseling. There was a misinterpretation by the couple that the other member did not wish to continue the marriage. Our first task was to get the couple together to assure that each wanted to continue the marriage. Our second task was to get the couple to express their feeling for one another. After many sessions the couple began to realize that their situation was not as hopeless as it seemed. Since then they have been able to resolve some of their problems.

From "The Papago Psychology Service: A Community Mental Health Program on an American Indian Reservation," by M. W. Kahn, C. Williams, E. Gálvez, L. Lejero, R. Conrad, and G. Goldstein, 1975, *American Journal of Community Psychology, 3*, 88–90. Reprinted by permission of Plenum Publishing Corporation.

Sue (1978) suggests three strategies for linking clients to culturally relevant staff in the case of a mismatch or lack of fit between client community and provider services. The first strategy is to link the client to an existing culturally or linguistically appropriate service. The second strategy involves changing the person to fit the service; through agency education and information, the staff answer the client's questions, particularly those concerning the nature and procedures of treatment.

The intent is to work through the client's anxiety over the initial stages of the helping process. The third strategy focuses on changing the provider organization to meet the social and economic needs of a changing clientele. This is bound to stir up resistance from staff and board members who have become set in their ways of dealing with clients, or from those involved with particular programs needing revision. Organizational changes include establishing linguistic resources, improving the staff's cultural awareness, modifying existing therapy-treatment approaches to create better cultural fit, and offering more outreach and supportive services in ethnic communities.

Community Outreach Programs. Community outreach programs are effective for people who hesitate to come to a social service agency for help. Outreach programs offer preventive education in schools, family associations, ethnic churches, and other community groups. Arroyo and López (1984) suggest some alternative outreach approaches:

> [A]lthough home visits are viewed by some agencies as being unproductive and an inappropriate use of a worker's time, such visits can be a means of intervention with Chicanos when in-office sessions are not possible. Group sessions also may have to be scheduled outside the agency. They may be established in a school with the assistance of the principal, counselors, and teachers. These school contacts allow the development of parent education groups for parents of schoolchildren. (p. 67)

Agency follow-up interviews result as people of color make informal educational and social contact with social service staff in their community clubs. Bilingual brochures and community program announcements can answer questions that relate to issues of family interest. The Asian Pacific Counseling and Treatment Center in Los Angeles is an excellent example of an agency that offers preventive and outreach services, bilingual/bicultural staff, and an accessible location. Yamamoto and Yap (1984) report on the center in Cultural Study 6-3.

CULTURAL STUDY 6-3

Preventive Outreach Services, Bilingual/Bicultural Staff, and Accessible Location

The Asian Pacific Counseling and Treatment Center is a county- and state-funded facility near central Los Angeles. Initiated in the spring of 1977, the Center is deliberately located at a site which is accessible to but not identified with any of the ethnic communities such as Little Tokyo, Chinatown, Koreatown or Manilatown.

Since the opening of the clinic, a large number of patients have been seen from the different Asian Pacific Islander minority populations. A very high proportion of our patients are chronically psychotic and severely disordered. Approximately 50 percent of the patients seen at the Asian Clinic are psychotic, as contrasted with only 20 percent who are so diagnosed in the majority clinics.

For many Asians and Pacific Islanders, there is a persistent stigma attached to using mental health services which necessitates that efforts also be directed towards primary prevention. Therefore, in selecting staff to fill positions, a serious consideration must be their ability to relate to the community and to do outreach work.

Experience has shown that our clients are more likely to seek help from professionals who are Asian rather than non-Asian. Staff personnel are bilingual and bicultural: they all grew up in Asia or the Pacific Islands, and have been educated here in the United States.

Thus they are in an ideal position to better understand the problems of acculturation encountered by immigrants.

The generational differences among the staff are noteworthy. The overwhelming majority of the staff are first generation immigrants, all of whom received their graduate mental health training in this country. As a result, they are able to successfully bridge two cultures for our clients. One would, however, characterize the staff interaction as Asian. That is, while most identify themselves as Asian Americans, they still retain the major traits, values and attitudes of their cultural traditions (Yamamoto & Wagatsuma, 1980). The Indochinese staff have a somewhat different perspective on identity, having immigrated here more recently than the other immigrant staff, and also have been forced to flee their homeland as refugees.

Asian patients are mostly referred by outside agencies, with less than 20 percent being self-referred or referred by families, in contrast to majority patients who are mostly self-referred or referred by their families (Lam, Yamamoto, Lo, & Reece, 1980). Yet Asian and Pacific Islander patients are much more often still interdependent upon their families. When they come to the Asian Clinic, they often arrive with some family member. Therefore, the staff has initiated routine interviews of patients with their relatives, unless patients choose to be seen individually. That is to say, we much more often conceptualize the family as the unit to be evaluated and helped. We are aware, of course, that with some families where there is the question of high emotional involvement (Brown, Birely, & Wing, 1972; Vaughn & Leff, 1976), we may have to see the schizophrenic patients have some relief from relatives. For instance, we may try to arrange for patients to go to Asian Rehabilitation Services, a sheltered workshop where they learn important skills and have time away from relatives who are critical, intrusive, and overinvolved.

The responsible attitudes of our patients and their families is reflected in the fact that, of all the clinics in Los Angeles County, the Asian Clinic collects the highest percentage of fees. In addition, patients very often give gifts to therapists.

We have recommended that the staff accept such gifts and thank the patients and their families, despite the fact that county rules forbid the acceptance of gifts. Gift-giving is no more than a continuation of culturally syntonic behavior, that is, behavior normally responsive and adaptive to the social or interpersonal environment, and it would be insulting to reject them.

From "Group Therapy for Asian Americans and Pacific Islanders," by J. Yamamoto and J. Yap, 1984, *P/AAMHRC Research Review, 3*, 1. Reprinted by permission.

Asian Community Mental Health Services of Oakland, California, report that refugee staff spend 50 to 70 percent of their time providing indirect services such as mental health consultation, education, information and referral, community organization and client advocacy, and outreach and support services. Their reasons for providing these services include the lesser degree of cultural and social stigma associated with workshops or seminars, consultation, or social adjustment guidance; refugees' unfamiliarity with mental health concepts and resources and hesitance to use outpatient services; and the need to work with indigenous community leaders in prevention-oriented programs through mental health consultation (Lum, 1985).

Moreover, there is a need to train the indigenous helping resources whom a client approaches before seeking formal mental health services. For example, Chinese Americans seek help from family and relatives, English as a second language (ESL) teachers, translators, informal friendship networks, herbalists, martial arts masters, ministers and priests, and medical care providers. Consultation and educational activities with these community resources are crucial for meeting a community outreach need (Lee, 1982).

I have pointed out (Lum, 1985) that providers should develop community input into the policy-making and administrative practices of a service agency. The most effective levels of community participation include comprehensive orientation programs for new board members; accessibility of representatives to decision makers; broad-based support from diverse community groups;

and an effective team of administrators, board members, and community representatives committed to working together for more responsive services.

Agency Setting. The agency setting should be conducive to the comfort of culturally diverse clients. A bilingual receptionist should be stationed to greet clients and put them at ease with refreshments. Decorating the facility with ethnic art that reflects the clientele of the area conveys the nonverbal message to clients that the agency is sensitive to their community. Agency morale is quite important in terms of collegial support, teamwork, and good humor. Office staff should be friendly and informal. Staff should be on time for scheduled appointments and should not keep clients waiting for long periods. Most agencies employ a staff member on call to see walk-in clients so as to minimize the lag between the telephone contact and the first session.

Service Linkage. Social service agencies should establish linkage with community organizations; these organizations are a source of helpful suggestions for upgrading service provision. Arroyo and López (1984) suggest:

> One way of maintaining community awareness is to develop and maintain linkages with other agencies serving Chicanos. These connections ensure that the agencies will have knowledge of the evolving lifestyles and patterns of immigration-migration and of mobility through a mutual sharing of information. (pp. 66–67)

A directory of ethnic community information and referral is useful for linking clients with significant others such as ministers, community association leaders, and bilingual physicians and nurses. In many large cities, local and state funding has been obtained for ethnic group social service organizations composed of bilingual staff, with a governing board drawn from the various ethnic communities. Such organizations have targeted the needs of youth, immigrants, and the elderly and have created a network that links the program services of public and private institutions.

In San Francisco, the Indochinese Health Intervention Program has a referral and escort program. The worker sets up referrals by telephone, provides escort services for language assistance, facilitates client compliance with healthcare requirements, and implements follow-up services on prescription medication and appointments (Murase et al., 1985).

I have proposed (Lum, 1985) integrating program services into existing ethnic group support systems, particularly refugee clan structures and indigenous religious and medical support services. This integration is important because attitudes of community leaders to human service programs can be very influential. At the same time, the two overriding goals of such endeavors are treatment integrity and increased use by clients from the ethnic community.

Planning Multicultural Service Delivery. Creating a multicultural service delivery system requires the willingness of social service agencies to incorporate the principles already noted regarding location, staffing, community outreach, agency setting, and service linkage. Planning service programs to meet the unique needs of minority clients is a challenge for traditional agencies. Wong et al. (1983) identify ten principles for planning a culturally diverse mental health training center:

1. Community-based services with strong linkages, credibility, and a good reputation in the ethnic community and its networks

2. A critical mass of ethnic staff and clients for a diversity of programs

3. Internship training that augments and complements existing academic training programs by teaching special skills needed for working with ethnic populations and communities

4. Shared support and decision making among multidisciplinary staff

5. A mutual teaching and learning environment of peers and subordinates, with staff viewed as resources for the organization

6. A coordinated service delivery system in which staff selection and programs contribute to the total mission of the agency and recognize the importance of such things as the family and community networks

7. A longitudinal perspective on programs and staff, both of which have positive track records based on commitment, performance, and allocation of resources

8. Outreach services for home, churches, schools, and community centers

9. Problem consultation, mental health education, community organization, and program technical assistance

10. Fluent bilingual service providers

Understanding the Ethnic Community

Along with constructing a multicultural delivery system goes the need to establish staff understanding of the ethnic community. A social work staff should be well versed in the characteristics of local communities. It is important to learn about the history, problems, and demographics of an ethnic community. In Cultural Study 6-4, Laseter (1997, pp. 85–86) explains the importance of understanding the economic labor situation and its impact on culturally diverse populations, such as young black men.

CULTURAL STUDY 6-4

The Labor Market and Young Black Men

The demand-side findings confirm the influence of economic restructuring on respondents. Many respondents, but primarily the older respondents, had experienced labor market instability, believed that there had been a shift of employment from the inner city to the suburbs, and had experienced discrimination in hiring and on the job.

On the supply side, there were considerable differences in the aspirations and labor market hopes and expectations of two groups of youth in the younger cohort (sixteen to nineteen years old). The young aspirers, with effort, had been able to avoid early fatherhood, the widespread temptations of drug use, gang intimidation, and violence in the community. They faced the future believing that hard work and more education would result in success. The nonaspirers, in contrast, focused on the short term with modest aspirations. They did not like school, nor did they see the link between education and employment. They aspired to whatever was available. Opportunity defined their aspirations. Three of the four nonaspirers were teenage fathers.

The demand and supply framework proved useful in understanding the declining labor force participation of young black men. Yet alone, neither demand- nor supply-side explanations tell the entire story regarding why some young black men never enter the labor force, why several respondents had long spells of unemployment, and why a theme of disillusionment and hopelessness was evident. Almost all the factors are interrelated in complex ways.

For example, race, culture, and neighborhood context interact to produce unique social outcomes for black males. Many respondents believed that discrimination and racism, both subtle and overt, kept them from obtaining suburban employment. In the suburbs, they felt pressure to moderate their ghetto language and styles of dress. To be successful on a job where employers were primarily white, the worker had to control his temper and deal with other cultures and races. This subtle discrimination interacted with neighborhood factors (ghetto-specific styles, fast money, and street life) to keep many black youth unemployed. Wilson (1991) argues that young black men in inner-city neighborhoods are influenced not only by restricted opportunities but also by the behavior, attitudes, and norms and values of those around them.

When employers and society look at young black men in a stereotyped, negative way despite individual differences in motivation to work and a

The Agency

A Family Service Association agency is located in a large metropolitan area with a diverse minority population that is 25 percent African American, 20 percent Latino American, 12 percent Asian American, and 8 percent Native American. The one African American social worker and one Latino social worker at the agency are inundated with their own caseload and refer clients to other ethnic organizations. For several years the Family Service Association director and staff have discussed the need to increase multicultural services. A survey of social needs in the service population area revealed, as a major finding, a rapid increase in the number of Mexican, Vietnamese, and Indo-Chinese immigrants in the community.

Recently the county board of supervisors has designated block grant funds to develop multicultural mental health services. The director of the agency has decided to apply for a grant to fund positions for the agency's bilingual staff and to service more ethnic group clientele. A request for proposal (RFP) was recently sent to social service agencies in the county by the county mental health service agency.

As part of a multicultural mental health proposal for bilingual staff and expansion of service to culturally diverse clients, the Family Service Association staff reviewed its intake procedure for new clients. For several years the agency has employed two secretary-receptionists, one of whom could speak Spanish. The proposal asked for a Chinese-Vietnamese receptionist. Moreover, the association auxiliary was enlisted to secure local African American, Latino American, Asian American, and Native American artists. The auxil-iary persuaded these artists to lend some of their artwork for a month to the agency for display and sales. Their paintings and ceramics not only brightened up the agency but became conversation pieces for staff and clients as they greeted each other and walked to the interview rooms.

A psychiatrist has usually met with the staff weekly to consult with them on clinical cases. The psychiatrist has been paid through state mental health consultation funds. The county mental health proposal requested funds for a multicultural clinical consultant. The director of the Family Service Association asked an outstanding professor of culturally diverse social work practice from a nearby school of social work to write the proposal's section on multicultural consultation. Various bilingual social workers were scheduled to teach the staff cultural and linguistic

commitment to do something constructive with their lives, "the message is that it doesn't matter how hard they work, how honest and law-abiding they are, or how well they play by the rules; they can never escape discrimination and oppression because they are lifetime members of the group" (Netting, Kettner, & McMurty, 1993, p. 83).

From "The Labor Force Participation of Young Black Men: A Qualitative Examination" by R. L. Laseter, 1997, *Social Service Review*, 71(1), 72–88.

Suggestions for improving the worker's understanding of an ethnic community include the following:

- Study the demographic profile and social problems of the local community.

- Walk through the community as a participant-observer, noting the way people live and relate to one another in their physical surroundings.

- Patronize businesses and talk to store owners and customers about the news of the community.

- Show up at social and educational community events to understand how people enjoy themselves and learn in their ethnic groups.

- Become acquainted with the multicultural helping community to build working relationships with a wide variety of resource people.

The Agency (continued)

skills to use when working with ethnic group clients. Three positions for Latino, Chinese, and Vietnamese social workers with a master of social work (MSW) were written into the grant proposal.

TASK RECOMMENDATIONS

A number of strategic steps can be taken to implement multicultural service delivery:

1. Read and discuss the first three chapters of this book as a group. Find out the group participants' notions of culture, ethnic community values, and approaches to multicultural practice.

2. Conduct a study of the needs of culturally diverse clients, service programs, and staffing. Obtain local census tract data on ethnic community populations in your service area. Consult with community leaders on current social problems. Analyze present approaches to client contact and practice. Ascertain whether a comparable ratio exists between client populations and bilingual/bicultural staff.

3. Hire a case consultant in culturally diverse social work from a nearby school of social work. Initiate a consultation report on the multicultural mission of the agency; the service needs of the local community; and recommendations on culturally diverse programs, staffing, funding, and training. Have the case consultant interact with staff on ethnic group case issues and provide multicultural practice in-service training.

4. Chart a step-by-step program of culturally diverse service delivery: increase in qualified bilingual/bicultural staff, accessible facility location, community outreach programs, and so on.

5. Set up a steering committee of agency staff, ethnic community leaders, and culturally diverse social work practitioners and educators to oversee program development.

6. Establish support bases for multicultural service delivery with the agency administrator, governing board, and community organizations.

7. Obtain funding support for this project on a local, state, or federal level.

8. Implement a timetable for increasing clinical and community services to various ethnic populations.

Brownlee (1978) suggests some commonsense principles of community understanding: Look and listen before asking and acting, explore the community's attitude toward being studied, find out about special rules of protocol, and place human relations ahead of getting answers.

Solomon (1983) proposes the concept of the ethnosystem. The *ethnosystem* is a society comprised of groups that vary in modes of communication, control over material resources, and internal social structure. Involvement in the ethnosystem occurs in barbershops, churches, bars, and other community places. It is important for social workers to become acquainted with various parts of the ethnosystem (Solomon, 1983). Ghali (1977) argues:

Often when a poor Puerto Rican sees a professional worker he is wondering what that person thinks of the poor, of the dark-skinned, of those inarticulate in the English language. Does the professional worker understand how the ghetto has affected him? What it is like to be hungry, humiliated, powerless, and broke? Does he really want to help or just do a job? (p. 460)

Dryden (1982) reports on a community study that a social service department conducted with the Bengali community in England. Cultural Study 6-5 describes the practical steps that were taken. (*BWAG* is the Bengali Workers' Action Group, and a *patch* is an area.)

CULTURAL STUDY 6-5

Community Study and Learning Experience

As the community work with the BWAG developed, so work with individual Bengali families by the social workers in the area team increased. Both heightened the awareness of the needs of this community and the failure of the traditional services to meet them. The patch team responsible for the neighborhood where the majority of Bengali people were living undertook a patch needs and resources assessment exercise. When the area team had adopted the patch system some months before, the team had mapped out new referrals and existing cases. It became clear that there was a large area, the furthest from the office, which, though it came out high on indices of need such as overcrowding, lack of housing amenities, open space and facilities, and included some of the worst privately rented housing in the borough, produced very few referrals. The community work with the Bengali community centered on this area and the social worker who had taken on the original four referrals had become linked in to the network of Bengali families in the same district. The patch team struggled to make decisions about the special areas for investigation. The traditional needs of children, young people and the elderly population (which was known to be large), competed with the relatively recently identified needs of the Bengali community. Largely, I think, as a result of the alliance between the community worker (who had agreed to help the team with the exercise) and the caseworker involved with individual Bengali families, the assessment of the needs of the Bengali community was finally chosen as one of the four areas for special investigation.

Members of the team collected information in various ways including studying census material and analyzing referrals. Armed with some factual information they talked to workers in the local play centers, neighborhood advice agencies, schools, health clinics, and day care facilities about the needs they perceived in the Bengali community and the services they were providing.

A walkabout headcount was done in an effort to ascertain the size of the community. This produced a conservative estimate of about 550 people, about 7 percent of the patch's population. A byproduct of this exercise was the marvelous opportunity to talk to local Bengali people about what they were doing and thinking. All the information gathered was collated in a report which looked at the community with regard to housing, health, education, employment, recreation, immigration and nationality and social services.

Collecting this information alerted the patch team to the unmet need in this community. It also gave them a basis for planning their own work and supporting their arguments for the reallocation of resources and changes in departmental policy and practice. The team decided to run a weekly advice session in a neighborhood center in the district and a member of the BWAG is paid to attend the session as an interpreter. Team members decided also to use half a social work post to enable a worker to concentrate on developing services for the Bengali community. The needs assessment exercise was valuable both in process and product. Members of the team learned new skills in gathering and analyzing information. The results they achieved enabled them to re-distribute their own resources in an informed way and contribute to departmental knowledge and thinking. In 1978 the Social Services Committee set up a race relations working party to look at the Department's services to minority communities. With the evidence from the patch assessment the team made an impressive report to the working party and presented a good case for the employment of Bengali-speaking aides in the area office.

From "A Social Services Department an the Bengali Community: A New Response," by J. Dryden. In J. Cheetham (Ed.), *Social Work and Ethnicity*, pp. 157–158. Copyright © 1982 Allen and Unwin, Inc. Reprinted by permission.

Acuszaar (1990) has devised an interesting Cross-Cultural Personal Biography, which pinpoints the extent of contact with thirteen ethnic, lesbian/gay, and disabled groups. You are asked to state your cultural group and then to rate your interaction with these groups—positive, negative, mixed, or no interaction—in twelve chronological, work-related, relationship, community, socioeconomic, and religious categories. The biography rating usually discloses interaction patterns and opens up areas of discussion based on the extent of experience and contact. The Cross-Cultural Personal Biography, presented in Cultural Study 6-6, is an excellent staff training tool, permitting an evaluation of previous interchange and gaps in individual experience.

CULTURAL STUDY 6-6

Cross-Cultural Personal Biography

Your Cultural Group: _____

	Family/ Preschool	K–6	MS	HS	College	Military	Work	Significant Relationships	Neighborhood	Social	Religion	Business/ Real Estate
Asian American												
Asian National												
Black American												
Black National												
Disabled												
Hispanic American												
Hispanic National												
Jewish												
Lesbian/ gay												
Native American												
White American												
White National												
Other												

From L. Acuszaar, Executive Diversity Services, Inc. Seattle, Washington. Copyright © 1990. Reprinted by permission.

The Agency

The director of the Family Service Association would like to expose staff to the living conditions of the ethnic community. He has visited various leaders of the African American, Latino American, Asian American, and Native American communities and organizations and has talked with them about how his agency could effectively meet their needs.

TASK RECOMMENDATIONS

To establish multicultural community understanding, workers can take several steps:

1. Select a geographic area of the community and spend a day walking the streets. Observe people at work and at home. Eat lunch in a local ethnic restaurant; buy items in neighborhood stores. Talk with people on the street. Note the problem areas you see.

2. Visit an area of a local ethnic community with a staff worker or a community person who has rapport there. Meet community leaders and visit ethnic human service agencies in the area.

3. Spend a week as the houseguest of an ethnic family. Eat meals and spend evenings with them. During the day, shadow a local ethnic community worker, observing how he or she relates to people. Find out about local cultural customs, protocol, and the lifestyles of members of your host family.

4. Become a financial supporter of, and participant in, an ethnic community social service or political organization. Attend meetings and become involved in projects.

5. Establish a staff program between your agency and an ethnic counterpart, to cross-fertilize ideas. This can result in practical on-the-job training, mutual referrals, and alternative approaches to intervention.

A useful exercise in class is to divide up into small groups and explore on a life span development level the various ethnic contacts that individuals in class have made with the ethnic, lifestyle, cultural, and disabled persons. Life span includes chronological age periods, military and work contacts, and social/interpersonal relations. The cross-cultural personal biography is designed to open discussion on the spectrum of contacts that have been made in the life of an individual in terms of a narrow or broad span. It pinpoints areas of frequent, moderate, and slight contact with various groups and in a variety of life situations.

In the process of understanding the ethnic community, the worker becomes known to potential clients. Ho (1976) believes it is imperative that the worker express sincerity, concern, and caring and establish a reputation for integrity. It is also important for the worker to maintain positive working relationships and to win the support of community leaders. These accomplishments do not come instantly. Social distancing of the community from social service agencies reflects past neglect and institutional racism. Individual social workers must prove themselves over a period of time before they gain the ethnic community's acceptance and trust.

Relationship Protocols

Relationship protocols are observed in many ethnic communities. The greeter and the head of the household exchange formal expressions of respect before proceeding to the main conversation. Learning about relationship protocols is important during the initial contact with ethnic families. An indirect way to find out about family authority is to ask how family decisions are made. This question elicits information about family rules and customs, behavior patterns, and roles. Often family members nonverbally acknowledge a parent with a glance when a worker poses this question to the family. Usually the father is the acknowledged authority in the family. It is important that the social worker acknowledges this role and asks the father the major questions that arise during the initial session. This sends a message to the family that the worker recognizes the authority of the father and wants to show respect by eliciting his perspective on the problem situation.

In Cultural Study 6-7, Chao (1992) shares some practical ways of working with the father of an Asian family, which may also be relevant to fathers in other cultures.

CULTURAL STUDY 6-7

Working with the Father

When a family seeks help with an identified problem or "problem child," they are already dealing with issues of shame and guilt. Stepping into your office can be an act of losing face. A passage from *The Analects of Confucius* applies to every Asian family I have ever met. "What is meant by 'In order to rightly govern the state it is necessary first to regulate the family,' is this: It is not possible for one to teach others while he cannot teach his own family. Therefore, the ruler, without going beyond his family, completes the lessons for the state." Basically, every father is the king or "ruler" of his family. If there are problems that necessitate his going outside the family for help, the father of a family often suffers a terrible blow to his feelings of self-worth. How can he claim "kingship" in any other area of his life if there is unrest within his kingdom? The family has been referred to therapy by a social service agency or the courts, and the father experiences this as a direct assault on his authority and quite naturally resists the therapist's interventions.

For these reasons it is important to reach out to the father. I meet fathers the way one head of state meets another head of state; the ruler has been forced to seek help and must be treated with respect and dignity. These are delicate negotiations. Should this ruler trust you with the problems occurring in the kingdom or should he look elsewhere for help? How a therapist creates the trust that enables construction of a therapeutic container wherein everyone feels secure is up to each individual therapist, but there are some guidelines. I give clients information about my education, training, and clinical experience. (In some states, including the one in which I reside, there are mandatory disclosure laws regarding the therapist's education, mode of practice, fee schedule, the right to a second opinion, and the address of the grievance board.)

I tell the father something about the families of which I am a member, including my nuclear family, my family of origin, and my extended family. I tell him where I obtained my degree, what my training was, where I have worked. Without breaching confidentiality, I speak of other Asian families with whom I have worked. All clinicians are familiar with these concepts of "reframing" and "normalizing." While the family may look at me as the expert, I let the father know that he is the expert in terms of his culture and his country of origin. I explain that my "Americanness" will at times be so close to me that I will make mistakes with regard to his culture and not even realize it. I say he must point these mistakes out, even if it looks like I do not want to know about it or he fears it will be too impolite.

Basically I try to treat the father as a "head of state." Granted, his kingdom is in trouble—perhaps his subjects are rebelling—but he is still "king," and that position, with all of its responsibilities and stresses, must be acknowledged. I am an ambassador with whom he can consult for possible solutions. I am the guest in his kingdom.

From "The Inner Heart: Therapy with Southeast Asian Families," by C. M. Chao. In L. A. Vargas and J. D. Koss-Chioino (Eds.), *Working with Culture: Psychotherapeutic Interventions with Ethnic Minority Children and Adolescents*, pp. 175–176. Copyright © 1992 Jossey-Bass, San Francisco. Reprinted by permission.

Ghali (1977) points out that the Puerto Rican family is patriarchal. The man is the absolute chief and sets the norms for the entire family. Family members respect and even fear the father. He is the breadwinner and decision maker. His wife is responsible for child care and housekeeping. Other groups emphasize the importance of the family as a whole and define individual roles within this primary unit. For Asian Americans, the family unit serves as the link between the past and future. Each family member has a specific role and function (Wong, Lu, Shon, & Gaw, 1983). The development of affective ties and family relationships is central to resolving societal problems. The family provides stability, a sense of self-esteem, and satisfaction. Close family ties, family conformity, and role structures are important to the mental health of Asians (Sue & Morishima, 1982).

The social worker should not undercut or negate the importance of the family or of the father as family authority. Rather, the worker should suggest practical ways to support and strengthen the role of the father as a good authority and the importance of family functioning. The worker should not encourage individual freedom at the expense of the family.

The practitioner must also consider relationship protocols in determining which members of the family and extended family might be recruited to provide information and serve as supportive resources for the client. As Harwood (1981) notes, the appropriate choice will be different in different cultures:

> Among the Navajos, for example, matrilineally related women living in close proximity to the patient would be most appropriate; among Mexican Americans, the bilaterally extended family in general should be consulted and, for males, in particular, older male relatives; among Puerto Ricans, it might be sufficient to contact the wife/mother or, for elderly patients, their children. (p. 501)

In Cultural Study 6-8, Sue and Zane (1986) illustrate how an understanding of relationship protocols can be used in resolving family problems. In this case, the practitioner chose to address the conflict between a Chinese American daughter-in-law and mother-in-law by calling on an elder brother as intermediary, in keeping with a traditional family protocol.

Understanding Family Protocol

At the advice of a close friend, Mae C. decided to seek services at a mental health center. She was extremely distraught and tearful as she related her dilemma. An immigrant from Hong Kong several years ago, Mae met and married her husband (also a recent immigrant from Hong Kong). Their marriage was apparently going fairly well until six months ago when her husband succeeded in bringing over his parents from Hong Kong. While not enthusiastic about having her parents-in-law live with her, Mae realized that her husband wanted them and that both she and her husband were obligated to help their parents (her own parents were still in Hong Kong).

After the parents arrived, Mae found that she was expected to serve them. For example, the mother-in-law would expect Mae to cook and serve dinner, to wash all the clothes, and to do other chores. At the same time, she would constantly complain that Mae did not cook the dinner right, that the house was always messy, and that Mae should wash certain clothes separately. The parents-in-law also displaced Mae and her husband from the master bedroom. The guest room was located in the basement, and the parents refused to sleep in the basement because it reminded them of a tomb.

Mae would occasionally complain to her husband about his parents. The husband would excuse his parents' demands by indicating, "They are my parents and they are getting old." In general, he avoided any potential conflict; if he took sides, he supported his parents. Although Mae realized that she had an obligation to his parents, the situation was becoming intolerable to her.

Mae's ambivalence and conflict over entering psychotherapy were apparent. On the one hand, she had a strong feeling of hopelessness and was skeptical about the value of treatment. Mae also exhibited an initial reluctance to discuss her family problems. On the other hand, she could not think of any other way to address her situation.

The Hernández Family, a Case Study

Mr. and Mrs. Hernández have two other children besides Roberto: Isabella, age eight, and Eduardo, age six. A white staff member has been assigned the case because the Spanish-speaking worker has a full caseload. The assignment was made with the understanding that the Latino social worker would serve as a consultant and support base for issues in multicultural practice that arise during sessions. The present caseworker has worked with ethnically diverse clients in public welfare and in the present agency.

TASK RECOMMENDATIONS

It is important to observe family protocol during the early contact stage. The worker should acknowledge family authority and harmony. Here are some practical suggestions for implementing family protocol:

- Stand when the family enters the room. Greet the parents first. Speak initially to the father and take your cues for behavior and movement from him. Acknowledge his authority by asking for his insights concerning what has been taking place.

- Observe how family members interact and react to the father's behavior. Is there respect or hostility between several members of the family and the father? What is the relationship between father and mother and between father and children? How does the perspective of the father differ from that of other family members?

- When working with a single client, ask about the family to gain a sense of the family's influence on the individual. Determine whether to involve the family with the client during later sessions.

Then, too, her friend has suggested that she see me since I (Sue) had experience with Asian-American clients. In retrospect, I realize that my ascribed credibility with Mae was suspect. I was an American-born Chinese who might not understand her situation; furthermore, her impression of psychotherapy was not positive. Mae did not understand how "talking" about her problem could help. She, as well as her close friend, was unable to think of a solution and she would doubt how a therapist could help.

How can Mae's case be handled? During the case conference, we discussed the ways that Chinese handle interpersonal family conflicts. These conflicts are not unusual to see. Chinese often use third-party intermediaries to resolve conflicts. The intermediaries obviously have to be credible and influential with the conflicting parties.

At the next session with Mae, I asked her to list the persons who might act as intermediaries, so that we could discuss the suitability of having someone else intervene. Almost immediately, Mae mentioned her uncle (the older brother of the mother-in-law) whom she described as being quite understanding and sensitive. We discussed what she should say to the uncle. After calling her uncle, who lived about fifty miles from Mae, she reported that he felt that he should visit them. He apparently realized the gravity of the situation and wanted to help. He came for dinner, and Mae told me that she overheard a discussion between the uncle and Mae's mother-in-law. Essentially, he told her that Mae looked unhappy, that possibly she was working too hard, and that she needed a little more praise for the work that she was doing in taking care of everyone. The mother-in-law expressed surprise over Mae's unhappiness and agreed that Mae was doing a fine job. Without directly confronting each other, the uncle and his younger sister understood the subtle messages each conveyed. Older brother was saying something is wrong and younger sister acknowledged it. After this interaction, Mae reported that her mother-in-law's criticisms did noticeably diminish and that she had even begun to help Mae with the chores.

From "Therapists' Credibility and Giving: Implications for Practice and Training in Asian-American Communities," by S. Sue and N. Zane. In M. R. Miranda and H. H. L. Kitano (Eds.), *Mental health research and practice in minority communities: Development of culturally sensitive training programs*, 1986, pp. 168–170. National Institute of Mental Health: Rockville, MD.

Regarding contact and relationship building with parents and children of color, Gibbs and Huang (1989) recommend the following goals:

- Relieve anxiety and fear about treatment (negative attitudes), which may be based on their families' previous experience with the health and social welfare bureaucracy.
- Use an informal, friendly style to defuse anxiety and to establish initial rapport.
- Respect the traditional sex- and age-role relationships of a particular ethnic group.
- Offer a brief explanation of therapy, its similarity to familiar roles of cultural healers, and the relief it offers for the client's symptoms.
- Communicate warmth and acceptance to the client, who may have natural cultural paranoia and may be expecting distance and a superior attitude.
- Share some limited personal information for the purpose of self-disclosure.
- Build rapport and increase the client's self-disclosure level by accepting the pace at which culturally sensitive topics are discussed.
- Emphasize confidentiality in a businesslike relationship.
- Structure sessions with flexible, clear guidelines.

Professional Self-Disclosure

Research into multicultural practice indicates that clients are often apprehensive about professional help. Sue and Sue (1990) note a number of barriers: mistrust of the worker, who, as an agent of society, could use information against the client; cultural barriers against intimate revelations to a person of a different culture; and client anxiety and confusion in the face of an unstructured relationship. Solomon (1983) explains that African Americans in southern states distrust social welfare agencies because of differing benefit payment schedules for white and African American clients. In welfare offices, African Americans may express their feelings of frustration and powerlessness in the form of anger, hostility, passiveness, or dependency. Lewis and Ho (1975) observe that a Native American client may be reticent about disclosing sensitive or distressing topics until he or she is sure of the sincerity, interest, and trustworthiness of the worker. Sue and Morishima (1982) cite several studies that show the anxiety of Asian American university students about communication with helping professionals.

Professional self-disclosure addresses this anxiety and mistrust: The social worker takes the initiative in building a relationship by disclosing an area of interest that the worker and client share. Lee (1982) observes:

It is not uncommon for clients to ask the therapist many personal questions about his or her family background, marital status, number of children, and so on. The therapist will need to feel comfortable about answering personal questions in order to gain clients' trust and to establish rapport. Clients, in turn, find that they can reasonably depend on the competencies of the clinician because they have been able to "evaluate" the clinician's background. (p. 545)

Instead of hiding behind professional policies and practices, the worker meets the client as a human being and initiates the relationship. Instead of focusing on the client's problem, the worker seeks to humanize the relationship by disclosing a topic common to both their backgrounds. Professional self-disclosure lays the groundwork for the reciprocal response of client self-disclosure.

Sue and Sue (1990) state the case for counselor self-disclosure succinctly in Cultural Study 6-9. As the counselor takes the initiative to open up his or her thoughts and feelings, the ethnic client is in a more receptive mood than if the counselor took a nondirective or insight-oriented helping approach.

CULTURAL STUDY 6-9

Cross-Cultural Self-Disclosure

Giving advice or suggestions, interpreting, and telling the client how you, the counselor, feel are really acts of counselor self-disclosure. While the use of attending or more nondirective skills may also self-disclose, it tends to be minimal relative to using influencing skills. In cross-cultural counseling, the culturally different client is likely to approach the counselor with trepidation: "What makes you any different from all the Whites out there who have oppressed me?" "What makes you immune from inheriting the racial biases of your forebears?" "Before I open up to you (self-disclose), I want to know where you are coming from." "How open and honest are you about your own racism and will it interfere with our relationship?" "Can you really understand what it's like to be Asian, Black, Hispanic, American Indian, or the like?" In other words, a culturally different client may not open up (self-disclose) until you, the counselor, self-disclose first. Thus, to many minority clients, a counselor who expresses his/her thoughts and feelings may be better received in a counseling situation.

From *Counseling the Culturally Different: Theory and Practice*, by D. W. Sue & D. Sue, p. 71. Copyright © 1990 John Wiley and Sons. Reprinted by permission.

Unconditional positive regard for the client's ethnicity and culture will allow the client to share attitudes, feelings, and behavior openly with the worker. Respect for, and validation of, each other's uniqueness opens channels of communication between individuals. According to Shafer (1969), the important functions of the social worker include assessing the ethnic community structure and the functioning of the client in regard to cul-

ture, identifying strengths in the client's ethnicity, and anticipating and directing activities in a culturally sensitive approach to achieve desired results. This cannot be accomplished if the worker projects him- or herself as superior or more capable or chooses to participate in oppressive practices. Courage and affirmation from the worker are integral parts of the therapeutic process, especially for people of color (Pommells, 1987).

The following are some practical suggestions for professional self-disclosure:

- Introduce yourself.
- Share pertinent background about your work, family, and helping philosophy.
- Find a common point of interest with the client.

Self-disclosure signals the worker's openness and invites client response. Reciprocation on the part of the client may take longer than expected. A common question asked by Native Americans in formal helping situations is "How can I tell you about my personal life, which I share with my life-long friends, when I have met you only a half hour ago?" Mistrust and reservation are typical responses of ethnic clients until the social worker moves out of the category of stranger. Taking the first step of professional self-disclosure sets the stage for openness and relationship building.

Ivey and Authier (1978) suggest four components of self-disclosure for the worker:

1. The worker should use the "I" reference to express self-identity.
2. The worker should express feeling.
3. The worker should share a personal experience in order to develop a worker-client relationship and to help the client with his or her own situation.
4. The self-disclosure should be set in the past or present and should shed light on the problem at hand.

The following self-disclosure meets these guidelines: "A few years ago I went through an experience similar to yours. I was angry at my wife, but I felt I should tell her. We worked out the misunderstanding." The statement begins in

The Hernández Family, a Case Study

Mr. Platt is the social worker assigned to the Hernández family. He recognizes that ethnic clients have reservations about coming to an agency for assistance with family problems. Fortunately, Mr. Platt has traveled in Mexico and Central America and knows some Spanish phrases, but he cannot carry on an extended conversation in Spanish.

Mr. Platt begins by greeting the family and talking with Mr. Hernández. He shares his travel experiences in Mexico: the various cities, people, and food. He asks about the Hernández family and their upbringing in Mexico. Mr. Platt does not focus on the presenting problem; instead, he puts the family at ease with his Spanish, They laugh at his pronunciation of some Spanish words and phrases.

Mr. Platt talks about the agency's program and services. He explains the meaning of the helping process and gives them a brochure, written in English and Spanish, that explains the services and fee schedule. Mr. Platt notices that Mr. Hernández speaks some English and can make himself understood, although he hesitates over a few words and concepts. Mrs. Hernández speaks Spanish fluently but knows little English. The children speak English and assist in translation between the parents and the social worker. The parents speak to the children in Spanish throughout the session. Mr. Platt asks each family member how he or she feels about coming to Family Services and whether he or she is willing to continue the sessions.

TASK RECOMMENDATIONS

Practice professional self-disclosure with an ethnic client in an initial session. Do not wait for the client to begin with the problem. Initiate the conversation and allow the client to get to know you as a person.

- Introduce yourself and share some information about your background and your work at the agency. Personalize the relationship to the extent that the client finds out about an interesting facet of your life.

- Find a common ground for conversation with the client so the topic can serve as a bridge between you and the other person.

- Become a human being to your client by expressing humor or sharing a brief story about yourself. Put the client at ease by serving modest refreshments.

- Ask the client how he or she feels about coming to the first session. Support, and identify with, feelings of anxiety, discomfort, and uncertainty. Place yourself in the client's situation and verbalize those feelings back to him or her.

---

the past, moves to a personal experience that involved feelings, and identifies with a client problem. Note that this self-disclosure would not be appropriate as a means of building a bridge at the beginning of a relationship; rather, it reflects an intermediate stage, in which worker and client share similarities.

In a Council on Social Work Education (CSWE) videotape (*Diversity Issues in the Beginning Phase of Practice*), Clay and Shulman (1994) work with a group of social work graduate students to uncover a hierarchy of differences that separate the client and the worker: differences of ethnicity, culture, gender, age, social class, ability, religion, past painful experiences, behavior, thinking, communication, education, and social status. The presence of several differences, which will become obvious in the beginning stage of the helping relationship, introduces distance between the client and the worker; identifying common areas of background and experience by self-disclosure closes the gap between them.

Clay and Shulman (1994) make the following suggestions for practitioners:

- Tune in to the client through empathy (put yourself in the client's shoes).

- Establish rapport, trust, and caring.

- Switch the power and control from the worker to the client, by learning from the client as the expert in the situation.

- Humanize the relationship by sharing a similar experience and making a connection.

In Cultural Study 6-10, Hepworth and Larsen (1993) summarize research on self-disclosure. They caution about the self-disclosure of current problems. When practitioners disclose problems parallel to those of the client, this may undermine client confidence and divert attention to the practitioner. Hepworth, Rooney, and Larsen (1997) recommend self-disclosing statements that express the practitioner's personal reaction to the client in terms of support, identification, and empathy.

CULTURAL STUDY 6-10

Research on Self-Disclosure

Still another aspect of self-disclosure involves timing and level of intensity, ranging from superficial to highly personal statements. Giannandrea and Murphy (1973) found that moderate self-disclosing by practitioners, rather than high or low levels, resulted in a higher rate of returns by clients for second interviews. Simonson (1976) has reported similar findings. It is thus logical to assume that practitioners should avoid sharing personal feelings and experiences until rapport and trust have been achieved and clients have demonstrated readiness to engage on a more personal level. The danger in premature self-disclosure is that such responses can threaten clients and lead to emotional retreat at the very time when it is vital to reduce threat and defensiveness. The danger is especially great with clients from other cultures who are unaccustomed to relating on an intense personal basis. For example, in a study comparing the reactions of American and Mexican undergraduate students to self-disclosure, Cherbosque (1987) found that the Mexican students perceived counselors who did not engage in self-disclosure as more trustworthy and expert than those who did. This researcher concluded, therefore, that practitioners who work with Mexican-Americans need to maintain a degree of for-

mality that is unnecessary with Anglo clients. We believe that this caution is also applicable to American Indian clients. Formality, however, should not preclude honesty, for Gomez et al. (1985) have reported that manifesting honesty and respect and communicating genuine concern were positively correlated with satisfaction levels of Chicano clients treated as outpatients in a mental health system.

With respect to Asian-Americans, Tsui and Schultz (1985) indicate that self-disclosure by practitioners may facilitate the development of rapport:

> Personal disclosure and an *appropriate* [italics ours] level of emotional expressiveness are often the most effective ways to put Asian clients at ease. Considering the generally low level of emotional expressiveness in Asian families, the therapist is, in effect, role modeling for the client and showing the client how the appropriate expression of emotion facilitates the treatment process. (p. 568)

As clients manifest trust, practitioners can appropriately relate with increased openness and spontaneity, assuming, of course, that authentic responses are relevant to clients' needs and do not shift the focus from the client for more than brief periods. Even when trust is strong, practitioners should exercise moderate self-disclosure, for beyond a certain level authentic responses no longer facilitate the helping process (Truax & Carkhuff, 1964). Practitioners must exercise discretion in employing self-disclosure with severely mentally ill clients. Shimkunas (1972) and Doster, Surratt, and Webster (1975) report higher levels of symptomatic behavior (e.g., delusional ideation) by paranoid schizophrenic patients following personal self-disclosure by practitioners. Superficial self-disclosure, by contrast, did not produce increases in disturbed behavior.

With respect to social workers' actual use of self-disclosures, it is heartening to note that a recent study (Anderson & Mandell, 1989) indicated that self-disclosure gained increased acceptance by social workers between 1978 and 1989. Moreover, they were adhering to the guidelines advocated in this and other relevant references. As expected, however, psychodynamically oriented practitioners were less likely to use self-disclosure than were other practitioners.

In summary, professional self-disclosure has a number of levels. The first level is the self-disclosure of the professional worker about a common area of interest or concern to humanize the relationship and to reveal a sense of openness to the client. It usually occurs in the first session as a point of contact. Such professional self-disclosure is advocated in this text and is effective with ethnic clients who are looking for a worker to take the initiative and exercise genuine personhood. The second level of self-disclosure comes when the client is able to express genuine feelings that surround the problem and is looking for empathy and authentic response from the worker. A self-involvement statement indicating how the worker felt when the client expressed a significant thought or feeling is helpful to show support. The third level of self-disclosure occurs well into the problem identification stage, when the client is willing to share a pertinent problem and needs reassurance that other persons such as the worker have struggled with a similar problem situation. The worker should exercise discretion and determine whether his or her disclosure of a parallel difficulty will benefit this particular client.

Communication Style

The client encounters the social service agency's style of communication at the moment of contact. A friendly bilingual receptionist, an accessible location, and an attractive facility communicate a positive message to clients. A private interview room, comfortable furniture, light refreshments, and a casual approach create an open and relaxed atmosphere. This provides the setting for the positive communication style of the social worker.

Body language expresses acceptance. A posture in which the body leans slightly forward, attentive and relaxed, conveys willingness to listen with anticipation and understanding. The worker can exhibit sincerity and concern through facial expression, voice, and open-palm hand gestures.

Language is the major means of communication. Bilingual social workers convey familiarity and evoke responsiveness when they speak the client's language. The worker's ability to speak the client's language creates a common bond between them (Ghali, 1977; Bernal, Bernal, Martínez, Olmedo, & Santisteban, 1983). Bilingual people manifest different character traits, recall different sets of experiences, and feel a different sense of identity according to whether they are speaking English or their native language. Each language evokes a distinctive cognitive, affective, and behavioral pattern. Disturbed Latino patients manifest more psychopathology when they are interviewed in English than when they are interviewed in Spanish. Part of the reason is that the English-speaking frame of reference does not apply to the specific problems of Latino patients (Marcos, Alpert, Urcuyo, & Kesselman, 1973). The implications of this research for recruiting bilingual/bicultural social workers are obvious. The case for training social workers in ethnic group cognition, affect, and behavior is even more compelling.

Research with people of color has uncovered various culturally distinct communicative expressions. For instance, for a Japanese person, nodding the head does not necessarily signify agreement. Rather, it conveys attentiveness and assures the communicator that he or she has been heard. Unaware of its meaning, a social worker could totally misinterpret this gesture (Kuramoto, Morales, Muñoz, & Murase, 1983). Some streetwise African American youths relate antisocial exploits to force the worker to make value judgments. Raised eyebrows, furrowed forehead, and shifting in one's seat at sensational stories about drugs, sex, alcohol, and delinquency are nonverbal signs to these youths that the worker has made a value judgment. This tactic is employed to scare the worker off, test sincerity, and measure empathy for ghetto conditions (Franklin, 1983). The street language of African American youth employs slang words with a unique cadence, tone, and usage. Workers unfamiliar with these idioms should be honest about their ignorance and encourage the client to educate them (Franklin, 1983). Language incongruency between the worker and ethnic families creates a communication problem. Pseudodialogues or parallel monologues occur when both parties unsuccessfully attempt to communicate with each other. The worker terms this behavior "resistance," whereas family members refer to it as "social worker talk" (Minuchin, Montalvo, Guerney, Rosman, & Schumer, 1967).

Social workers should enhance their communication style with ethnic clients. In Cultural Study 6-11, Kahn et al. (1975) report some approaches to communication that they used when working with Native American clients from the Papago tribe.

CULTURAL STUDY 6-11

Ethnic Communication Styles

The Papago client brings several attitudes with him which influence the mode of therapy utilized. Many of these attitudes are due to the influence of the traditional culture and, more specifically, due to the influence of the medicine man or Mai Kai. Only he possesses the knowledge to heal and only a brief diagnostic interview is required before the healing ceremony begins. Clearly, this is much different from psychotherapy, wherein the client is an active participant and has a great deal of responsibility for his improvement.

Another attitude the Papago brings to therapy is that of secrecy regarding personal matters. Most Papagos loathe discussing personal information with anyone, and doing so with strangers is certainly most uncommon.

The paucity of verbal communication (as compared to the Anglo) is another variable which has considerable influence on therapeutic methodology. Impressionistically, it seems the Papagos really aren't very verbose among themselves and certainly not with Anglo professionals or, if you will,

authority figures. This brings us to another attitudinal factor of considerable importance when dealing with a Papago client.

Papagos treat age and social status with a great deal of respect. And respect within the Papago culture is often expressed by silence.

Avoiding eye contact can also be of considerable importance when dealing with Papagos in any social setting, and this includes psychotherapy. Establishing and maintaining eye contact are considered impolite among these desert people and may be interpreted as anger.

On the desert reservation, time is treated much differently than what urban dwellers are accustomed to. Papagos may be an hour late for a meeting and think nothing of it. This, we will discover, has a considerable influence on therapy.

These several factors then are of central importance when doing therapy with the Papagos. They include the importance of the mental health technicians, the influence of the medicine man, personal secrecy, a lack of verbosity, respect for age and social status, avoidance of eye contact, and an informal orientation to time. How these variables influence the approach to therapy is considered next.

As a group, the variables just mentioned dictate that therapy done with Papagos would involve, for the most part, at least one indigenous mental health technician and that the therapy would nearly always be of a crisis intervention nature. The need for the mental health technician is obvious. Perhaps the reliance on a crisis intervention approach has reasons which aren't so obvious. First, although a medicine man often needs only one treatment session to effect a cure, this one treatment session could last several hours. The therapist must remain flexible regarding his own time orientation. Rigid adherence to the fifty-minute session is simply of no value. As one graduate student extern recently pointed out when discussing marital therapy, the therapist should be willing to spend two to four hours with a couple and realize that this may be the only session there will be with them.

Not only does the variable of time orientation affect what will happen in one session, it also influences the execution of other sessions. That is, the client may be several hours late and the therapist must remain flexible and try to accommodate the client whenever possible.

The fact that the Papago client has had little to do when receiving other treatments (medicine man and physician) certainly affects what will happen in therapy. Quite often the Papago will present his problems (briefly) and ask "What is wrong with me?" and "What should I do?" A Rogerian reflection or question in return from the therapist may have little meaning. The therapist must be prepared to be directive—to make suggestions.

Confrontation in the therapeutic sense could be considered taboo with the Papago client. Socially, the Papago will religiously avoid confrontation. This is simply a matter of social courtesy. The therapist who confronts a Papago client in a manner that causes intense anxiety will lose the client.

Interviewing the Papago client has some unique features. The Anglo who attempts to establish direct eye contact with his client will make therapeutic rapport almost impossible. Similarly, an aggressive therapist with a loud voice will intimidate and perhaps anger the Papago client. The pace or tempo of the interview is also affected. That is, a longer period of time is needed to establish trust and rapport with the client. More time must be spent getting acquainted with the Papago client. Questions of a personal nature should be delayed. An opening question of "What brings you here?" could stimulate anxiety and defensiveness on the part of the client.

Because of language problems, interpretations and suggestions must be made crystal clear. A client may seem to understand but not understand at all. The pretended understanding and acquiescence are a result of trying to show respect and social timidity.

Group therapies have enjoyed considerable success in the Papago clinic. Every group has had at least one mental health technician and one university therapist. Different approaches have been used successfully, but with adaptation to the culture (Kahn, Lewis, & Gálvez, 1974).

In summary, some factors which we consider to be important in providing psychotherapy for the Papago are as follows:

1. Relying on the mental health technicians
2. Using a crisis intervention approach
3. Avoiding eye contact
4. Approaching therapeutic topics slowly and cautiously
5. Avoiding confrontations
6. Making interpretations very clear
7. Utilizing directive techniques
8. Remaining flexible in regard to time
9. Talking less than usual

From "The Papago Psychology Service: A Community Mental Health Program on an American Indian Reservation," M. W. Kahn, C. Williams, E. Gálvez, L. Lejero, R. Conrad, and G. Goldstein, 1975, *American Journal of Community Psychology*, 3, 91–93. Reprinted by permission of Plenum Publishing Corporation.

The social worker should be aware of these cultural dimensions of communication. Multicultural practice calls for highly developed communication skills. Lewis and Ho (1975) suggest frequent use of restatement, clarification, summarization, reflection, and empathy with Native American clients. These approaches apply to other groups as well. It is important to note that these responses enlarge on what the client has said rather than evaluating or probing for information. Reiteration is nonthreatening and allows the client to set the pace. When the worker asks a series of questions, the client may become exasperated and defensive.

When working with non-English-speaking clients, a joint practice approach between bilingual and monolingual workers is preferred. The goal is to increase the number of bilingual social workers so as to match the agency's caseload of non-English-speaking clients. Even monolingual workers should learn some important expressions in the client's language.

Listening Responses

Listening, the art of responding to thoughts, feelings, and behavior, is an important part of the contact stage, because it focuses on meaningful problem information from the client.

Listening is a sequential series of procedures. First, in the receiving phase, the worker asks an open-ended question and assumes a listening posture. Next is a processing phase, in which the brain interprets incoming messages and transmits outgoing responses. The third phase—the sending phase—depends on the message received. The worker's brain orchestrates a unique blend of cognitive, affective, and behavioral responses that is communicated to the client.

Listening times in to selected words and sentences, which generate thoughts and ideas. Listening for feelings involves observing facial expression, voice tone, and eye contact. The worker must also be attentive to behavioral responses—body language that supports or contradicts verbally expressed feelings. Generally, there is congruence among words, feelings, and behavior.

Listening involves five kinds of response skills: supportive, understanding, probing, interpreting, and evaluative (SUPIE). The following paragraphs examine these skills, paying particular attention to culturally diverse aspects.

Supportive Response Skills. Supportive responses reflect the speaker's essential thought patterns and feelings without using the same words. By restating the most meaningful part of the communicated message, the worker reassures the speaker that he or she has been heard and understood.

Supportive body language accompanies the verbal response. In American culture, the eye is the primary focus of contact; looking at someone conveys total concentration on that person. However, some cultures avoid direct eye contact: people look away or lower their eyes as a sign of respect and courtesy. In such cultures, prolonged staring or fixation on the eyes is a sign of rudeness.

In general, the listener communicates care and concern by leaning forward in a relaxed and earnest manner. In a listening posture, arms and legs are open and unfolded; the listener's open palms and appropriate facial affect support the speaker's current thoughts and feelings.

Thus, supportive responses restate the other person's thoughts and feelings. They communicate that the worker has heard the client and evoke an atmosphere of sustenance.

The following are examples of supportive responses for our case study of the Hernández family:

MR. HERNÁNDEZ: Ricardo has been getting poor grades in school. He is usually a good student. I can't understand what is going wrong.

SUPPORTIVE RESPONSE: It seems hard to figure out this situation. Ricardo has done well in school, but now there has been a change.

MR. HERNÁNDEZ: I get mad at him when he talks back to me. The least word from me makes Ricardo edgy.

SUPPORTIVE RESPONSE: There doesn't seem to be that sense of respect anymore. I imagine there was harmony in the family before this.

Understanding Response Skills. Understanding responses address the client's meaning and the significance of the problem. They do not simply support the other person's feelings and thoughts but explore the other's perceptions of the problem. Brammer (1979) uses the perception-check approach to verify the worker's understanding and, in the process, to clarify the client's perspective. The purposes of the perception check are to resolve miscommunication and misunderstanding and to further sharpen the accuracy of the understanding. To perform a perception check, the worker paraphrases what he or she understands has been communicated, asks the client to verify the accuracy of that perception, and permits the client to correct any inaccurate perceptions. The perception check then readjusts the communication so that accurate and perceptive understanding takes place.

Understanding response skills permit a comprehensive overview of the client and the environmental situation. A worker should use understanding responses until a sound relationship has been established, because they convey a caring and concerned attitude. A worker should also employ these responses when the client is involved in self-exploration. The client may require initial focusing on particular areas by the worker; once the client conveys significant thoughts and emotions, the worker should respond with support and understanding.

The following are examples of understanding responses, again for the Hernández case:

UNDERSTANDING RESPONSE: You mention communication problems with Ricardo. I can relate to this. I have two sons who are close to Ricardo's age. But it seems as though the family wants to make some changes.

UNDERSTANDING RESPONSE: It seems that Ricardo's school and home problems are getting you down and that you are at a low point. You thought that this wouldn't happen to your family. I sense that you are strongly determined to solve these problems.

Probing Response Skills. A probing response seeks further information about aspects of an issue that have been partially addressed. This type of response triggers further discussion in a certain area and conveys the message that the client ought to discuss a particular point further. An effective probing question guides the client into an area that requires further exploration. Probing opens up related topics of conversation. The client provides further information and explores important aspects of the problem. The goal is to articulate open-ended probing questions that move the dialogue toward a detailed exploration of a particular area.

The novice worker should refrain from excessive use of questions. It is easier to ask questions and to sit back and listen than to blend supportive and understanding responses with appropriate probing.

When probing, the worker must avoid directive questions and strive for open-ended responses. Directive questions restrict a client to an area defined by the questioner and result in a yes or no or a limited answer of a few words. Open-ended questions introduce relevant areas of interest, allow the client to shape answers, and convey meaningful information.

The following are examples of open-ended probing responses for the Hernández case:

PROBING RESPONSE: You mentioned that Ricardo talks back to you. Can you give me an example of what happens?

PROBING RESPONSE: You said the other day that you feel you would like to help Ricardo with his homework. I'm curious about how we could set this up.

PROBING RESPONSE: Well, I haven't seen you for a week. What's been happening to you lately?

Interpreting Response Skills. After the worker establishes support and understanding and uses selective probing, he or she has tentative information about people and problems. Interpretation offers an initial explanation and meaning for what has been happening. An interpreting response is based on various items of information that emerge from conversation with the client. The worker must constantly ask, What is going on? What has been happening to this client? How does this particular piece of information fit into the whole picture? The worker can then develop a hunch or a hypothesis that offers a reasonable explanation of events, places, and people.

An effective interpreting response is a preliminary explanation of what has happened, based on a careful understanding of the material elicited from the client, and draws on the client's participation in interpreting the situation. An *interpretation* is a tentative understanding of a situation based on the perspectives of the worker and the client. The client participates in self-interpretation of the situation. The worker reconstructs the order of events and provides a rational sense to the situation.

Interpreting responses should only be used sparingly, in the later stages of listening, after the worker and client have established a relationship. A premature interpretation based on limited information may harm the helping process. The worker should avoid making too many interpreting responses at one time; the client should assimilate one interpretation at once and think through its meaning. The worker should couch an interpreting response in tentative terms, ask for feedback from the client, and monitor the client's reaction. When the client agrees, he or she continues to respond positively and shares more information.

When the client senses inaccuracy, he or she may react with emotional withdrawal, defensiveness, or negative undercurrents. If the client

The Hernández Family, a Case Study

For Mr. Platt, the goal of the first session with the Hernández family was to become acquainted with them. He put the family at ease, acknowledged the authority of the father, and asked how the family felt about coming to the agency. The second family session is a home visit: Mr. Platt and the family meet around the kitchen table, Mr. Hernández shows Mr. Platt his Mexican artwork, while Mrs. Hernández serves a tray of Mexican pastries. Afterward Mr. Hernández tells the social worker about Ricardo's school problems: his poor grades, his absences without family knowledge, and his verbal abuse of his father. Mr. Platt listens and supports Mr. Hernández. He reflects feelings, restates thoughts, summarizes major points, and clarifies certain areas.

TASK RECOMMENDATIONS

The social worker creates a culturally sensitive relationship with the client through responses to communication. The following recommendations are designed to help you and your agency increase communication with ethnic clients.

1. Review your agency's procedures for intake of new clients. Do you employ a bilingual receptionist and bilingual staff for non–English-speaking clients? Is the waiting area for clients attractive and congenial? Do staff members convey a friendly, informal attitude to clients? Are refreshments available for staff and clients?

2. On the basis of the ethnic composition of your agency's clientele, establish a language program for staff to learn key phrases helpful in social work practice with non-English-speaking clients. (Spanish and Chinese phrases are especially important to learn in view of the influx of Latino and Indo-Chinese refugees. A fluent bilingual social worker can serve as a resource for teaching and writing important questions and answers in Spanish or Chinese.)

3. Try a clinical experiment. Divide your caseload into two groups: an experimental group, whose sessions are conducted in home visits, and a control group, whom you see in your agency. After six weeks, determine the extent of relative progress of the two groups in terms of communication, information disclosure, and problem resolution.

4. Using a case that involves an ethnic family, practice the following listening responses with a partner:

   • *Supportive*, or reflecting an important fact or feeling of the client in a different way

   • *Understanding*, or making clear the client's meaning and the problem situation

   • *Probing*, or asking for information about what the client has said at a crucial juncture in the session

   • *Interpreting*, or offering an initial explanation of what has happened

   • *Evaluating*, or conveying a preliminary indication of possible changes

Communicate feelings of warmth, acceptance, and concern as you engage in these response patterns. Have your partner give you feedback on your responses.

reacts negatively, the worker must review and modify the interpretation and ask for a response.

The following are examples of interpreting responses for the Hernández case:

MRS. HERNÁNDEZ: I don't feel that Ricardo should talk back to his father. I work hard to make this a happy family. Now everyone is miserable.

INTERPRETING RESPONSE: It sounds as though you have put much effort into the family and feel awful about what is happening. I sense that you want to work toward changing the situation.

RICARDO: It was my birthday last week, but things have not been going right for me. I have really messed up.

INTERPRETING RESPONSE: It must have been uncomfortable for you. It seems as though you have some unfinished business to work through with your father and at school. I would be happy to help you think through what you should do.

MRS. HERNÁNDEZ: I know I am a good mother. The children love me and I love them. But there is something missing in my life.

INTERPRETING RESPONSE: I'm glad you feel good about being a good mother. But there is a gap that has not been filled. I would like to hear more about what you think of this.

Evaluating Response Skills. An evaluating response makes a determination of the negative blocks that confront the client and of the positive potentials for change. The worker usually makes this kind of response toward the end of a session or after extensive problem exploration. Its intent is to summarize significant thoughts and feelings and to highlight the pros and cons of a situation.

The worker takes into account various strands of information before making an evaluation. The worker has seen a preliminary indication of possible changes in the person, the environment, and the problem situation. However, these areas are the basis for making decisions and choices as the helping process continues in later stages. An evaluation has a tentative quality. It is subject to the response of the client. It can be rejected, modified, or accepted to a certain extent. An evaluation is an opinion based on the results of all the preceding responses of listening; the worker serves as a provider of feedback.

An evaluating response contains several elements: expression of concern, willingness to change, recognition of barriers in life, and expression of positive outcomes. The following example incorporates these features:

EVALUATING RESPONSE: I am concerned about you and your family, particularly Ricardo. You want to help your son in school and can't figure out why he is irritable at home. However, you have some things going for you: You are here to get some answers, you want your son to do well,

and you are both good parents. All of you want to make some changes in the family.

CONCLUSION

Contact between the client and the worker is the most crucial phase of social work practice. Successful contact establishes a relationship and prevents client dropout. Preparatory work requires the agency's administrator and staff to rethink their service outreach to the local ethnic community. The future of culturally diverse social work practice is in the hands of public and private agencies that serve the poor and people of color. The philosophy of service delivery, bilingual/bicultural staff, appropriate language and culture training, an ethnic case consultant, and ethnic practice approaches are central ingredients for successful culturally diverse social work practice. Above all, the entire effort depends on the social worker's attitude toward the client. In spite of their training, behavioral science students, researchers, and practitioners are no more immune to racism than is the average person.

REFERENCES

Acuszaar, L. (1990). *Cross cultural personal biography.* Seattle, WA: Executive Diversity Services.

Anderson, S., & Mandell, D. (1989). The use of self-disclosure by professional social workers, *Social Casework, 70,* 259–267.

Arroyo, R., & López, S. A. (1984). Being responsive to the Chicano community: A model for service delivery. In B. W. White (Ed.), *Color in a white society* (pp. 63–73). Silver Spring, MD: National Association of Social Workers.

Bernal, G., Bernal, M. E., Martínez, A. C., Olmedo, E. L., & Santisteban, D. (1983). Hispanic mental health curriculum for psychology. In J. C. Chunn II, P. J. Dunston, & F. Ross-Sheriff (Eds.), *Mental health and people of color: Curriculum development and change* (pp. 65–94). Washington, DC: Howard University Press.

Bochner, S. (1982). *Cultures in contact: Studies in cross-cultural interaction.* Oxford: Pergamon.

Boulette, T. R. (1980). Mass media and other mental health promotional strategies for low-income Chicano/Mexicanos. In R. Valle & W. Vega (Eds.), *Hispanic natural support systems* (pp. 97–101). Sacramento: State of California Department of Mental Health.

Brammer, L. M. (1979). *The helping relationship: Process and skills.* Upper Saddle River, NJ: Prentice-Hall.

Brislin, R. W. (1981). *Cross-cultural encounters: Face-to-face interaction.* New York: Pergamon.

Brown, G. W., Birely, J. L. T., & Wing, J. K. (1972). Influence of family life on the course of schizophrenic disorders: A replication. *British Journal of Psychiatry, 121,* 241–258.

Brownlee, A. T. (1978). *Community, culture, and care.* St. Louis: Mosby.

Campbell, R., & Chang, T. (1973). Health care of the Chinese in America. *Nursing Outlook, 21,* 245–249.

Catell, S. H. (1962). *Health, welfare, and social organization in Chinatown, New York City.* Report prepared for Community Service Society of New York, Department of Public Affairs, Chinatown Public Health Nursing Demonstration.

Chao, C. M. (1992). The inner heart: Therapy with southeast Asian families. In L. A. Vargas & J. D. Koss-Choino (Eds.), *Working with culture: Psychotherapeutic interventions with ethnic minority children and adolescents* (pp. 157–181). San Francisco: Jossey-Bass.

Chen, P. N. (1970). The Chinese community in Los Angeles. *Social Casework, 51,* 591–598.

Cherbosque, J. (1987). Differential effects of counselor self-disclosure statements on perception of the counselor and willingness to disclosure: A cross-cultural study. *Psychotherapy, 24,* 434–437.

Clay, C., & Shulman, L. (1994). Program 1: Diversity issues in the beginning phase of practice [videotape]. In *Diversity videos, teaching about practice and diversity: Content and process in the classroom and the field.* Alexandria, VA: Council on Social Work Education.

Devore, W., & Schlesinger, E. G. (1981). *Ethnic-sensitive social work practice.* St. Louis: Mosby.

Doster, J., Surratt, F., & Webster, T. (1975, March). *Interpersonal variables affecting psychological communications of hospitalized psychiatric patients.* Paper presented at a meeting of the Southeastern Psychological Association, Atlanta.

Dryden, J. (1982). A social services department and the Bengali community: A new response. In J. Cheetham (Ed.), *Social work and ethnicity* (pp. 155–163). Winchester, MA: Allen & Unwin.

Franklin, A. J. (1983). Therapeutic interventions with urban black adolescents. In E. J. Jones & S. J. Korchin (Eds.), *Minority mental health* (pp. 267–295). New York: Praeger.

Fritzpatrick, J. P. (1981). The Puerto Rican family. In C. H. Mindel & R. W. Habenstein (Eds.), *Ethnic families in America: Patterns and variations* (pp. 189–214). New York: Elsevier.

Ghali, S. B. (1977). Culture sensitivity and the Puerto Rican client. *Social Casework, 58,* 459–468.

Giannandrea, V., & Murphy, K. (1973). Similarity of self-disclosure and return for a second interview. *Journal of Counseling Psychology, 20,* 545–548.

Gibbs, J. T., & Huang, L. N. (1989). *Children of color: Psychological interventions with minority youth.* San Francisco: Jossey-Bass.

Gomez, E., Zurcher, L. A., Farris, B. E., & Becker, R. E. (1985). A study of psychosocial casework with Chicanos. *Social Work, 30,* 477–482.

Gonzales, M., & García, D. (1974). *A study of extended family interactions among Chicanos in the East Los Angeles area.* Unpublished master's thesis, University of California, Los Angeles, School of Social Welfare.

Green, J. W. (1982). *Cultural awareness in the human services.* Upper Saddle River, NJ: Prentice-Hall.

Harwood, A. (Ed.). (1981). *Ethnicity and medical care.* Cambridge, MA: Harvard University Press.

Hepworth, D. H., Rooney, R. H., & Larsen, J. A. (1997). *Direct social work practice: Theory and skills.* Pacific Grove, CA: Brooks/Cole.

Ho, M. K. (1976). Social work with Asian Americans. *Social Casework, 57,* 195–201.

Ivey, A. E., & Authier, J. (1978). *Microcounseling.* Springfield, IL: Thomas.

Jenkins, S. (1981). *The ethnic dilemma in social services.* New York: Free Press.

Kahn, M. W., Lewis, J., & Gálvez, E. (1974). An evaluation of a group therapy procedure with reservation adolescent Indians. *Psychotherapy: Theory, Research, and Practice, 11,* 241–244.

Kahn, M. W., Williams, C., Gálvez, E., Lejero, L., Conrad, R., & Goldstein, G. (1975). The Papago psychology service: A community mental health program on an American Indian reservation. *American Journal of Community Psychology, 3,* 88–99.

Kuramoto, F. H., Morales, R. F., Muñoz, F. U., & Murase, K. (1983). Education for social work practice in Asian and Pacific American communities. In J. C. Chunn II, P. J. Dunston, & F. Ross-Sheriff (Eds.), *Mental health and people of color: Curriculum development and change* (pp. 127–155). Washington, DC: Howard University Press.

Lam, J., Yamamoto, J., Lo, S., & Reece, S. (1980, May). *Organizing mental health services for Asian Americans.* Paper presented at the Second Pacific Congress of Psychiatry, Manila, Philippines.

Laseter, R. L. (1997). The labor force participation of young black men: A qualitative examination. *Social Service Review, 71*(1), 72–88.

Lee, E. (1982). A social systems approach to assessment and treatment for Chinese American families. In M. McGoldrick, J. K. Pearce, & J. Giordano (Eds.), *Ethnicity and family therapy* (pp. 527–551). New York: Guilford.

Lee, E. (1985). Inpatient psychiatric services for Southeast Asian refugees. In T. C. Owan (Ed.), *Southeast Asian mental health: Treatment, prevention, services, training, and research* (pp. 307–328). Washington, DC: National Institute of Mental Health.

Lee, Q. T. (1981). Case illustrations of mental health problems encountered by Indochinese refugees. In *Bridging cultures. Southeast Asian refugees in America* (pp. 241–258). Los Angeles: Asian American Community Mental Health Training Center.

Lee, R. H. (1960). *The Chinese in America.* Hong Kong: University of Hong Kong Press.

Leigh, J. W. (1980). *Hearing racial references in the interview.* Unpublished manuscript, University of Washington, School of Social Work, Seattle.

Leigh, J. W. (1984). *Empowerment strategies for work with multi-ethnic populations.* Unpublished paper presented at the annual program meeting of the Council on Social Work Education, Detroit, MI.

Lewis, R. G., & Ho, M. K. (1975). Social work with Native Americans. *Social Work, 20,* 379–382.

Lum, R. G. (1985). A community-based mental health service to Southeast Asian refugees. In T. C. Owan (Ed.), *Southeast Asian mental health: Treatment, prevention, services, training, and research* (pp. 283–306). Washington, DC: Department of Health and Human Services, National Institute of Mental Health.

Marcos, L. R., Alpert, M., Urcuyo, L., & Kesselman, M. (1973). The effect of interview language on the evaluation of psychopathology in Spanish-American schizophrenic patients. *American Journal of Psychiatry, 130,* 549–553.

Marsella, A. J. (1979). Cross-cultural studies of mental disorders. In A. J. Marsella, R. G. Tharp, & T. J. Ciborowski (Eds.), *Perspectives on cross-cultural psychology* (pp. 233–262). New York: Academic Press.

McGill, D. W. (1992). The cultural story in multicultural family therapy. *Families in Society, 73,* 339–349.

McLemore, S. D. (1983). *Racial and ethnic relations in America.* Boston: Allyn & Bacon.

Mendoza, L. (1980). Hispanic helping networks: Techniques of cultural support. In R. Valle & W. Vega (Eds.), *Hispanic natural support systems* (pp. 55–63).

Sacramento: State of California Department of Mental Health.

Minuchin, S., Montalvo, B., Guerney, G., Rosman, B., & Schumer, F. (1967). *Families of the slums.* New York: Basic Books.

Murase, K., Egawa, J., & Tashima, N. (1985). Alternative mental health services models in Asian/Pacific communities. In T. C. Owan (Ed.), *Southeast Asian mental health: Treatment, prevention, services, training, and research* (pp. 229–260). Washington, DC: Department of Health and Human Services, National Institute of Mental Health.

Netting, F. E., Kettner, P. M., & McMurty, S. L. (1993). *Social work macropractice.* New York: Longman.

Pedersen, P. (1988). *A handbook for developing multicultural awareness.* Alexandria, VA: American Association for Counseling and Development.

Pommells, J. (1987, November). *Working with a Hispanic family's resistance.* Unpublished paper, California State University, Sacramento.

Shafer, C. (1969). Teaching social work practice in an integrated course: A general systems approach. In G. Hearn (Ed.), *The general systems approach: Contributions toward a holistic conception of social work* (pp. 26–36). New York: Council on Social Work Education.

Shimkunas, A. (1972). Demand for intimate self-disclosure and pathological verbalization in schizophrenia. *Journal of Abnormal Psychology, 80,* 197–205.

Simonson, N. (1976). The impact of therapist disclosure on patient disclosure. *Journal of Transpersonal Psychology, 23,* 3–6.

Solomon, B. B. (1983). Social work with Afro-Americans. In A. Morales & B. W. Sheafor (Eds.), *Social work: A profession of many faces* (pp. 415–436). Boston: Allyn & Bacon.

Sue, D. W., & Sue, D. (1990). *Counseling the culturally different: Theory and practice.* New York: Wiley.

Sue, S. (1978, September). *Mental health in a multi-ethnic society: The person-organization match.* Paper presented at the meeting of the American Psychological Association, Toronto, Ontario, Canada.

Sue, S., & Morishima, J. K. (1982). *The mental health of Asian Americans.* San Francisco: Jossey-Bass.

Sue, S., & Wagner, N. (1973). *Asian Americans: Psychological perspectives.* Ben Lomond, CA: Science and Behavior Books.

Sue, S., & Zane, N. (1986). Therapists' credibility and giving: Implications for practice and training in Asian-American communities. In M. R. Miranda & H. H. L. Kitano (Eds.), *Mental health research and practice in minority communities: Development of cultur-*

ally sensitive training programs (pp. 168, 170). Washington, DC: National Institute of Mental Health.

Truax, C., & Carkhuff, R. (1964). For better or for worse: The process of psychotherapeutic personality change. In *Recent advances in the study of behavior change* (pp. 118–163). Montreal: McGill University Press.

Tsui, P., & Schultz, G. L. (1985). Failure of rapport: Why psychotherapeutic engagement fails in the treatment of Asian clients. *American Journal of Orthopsychiatry, 55,* 561–569.

Valle, R. (1980). Social mapping techniques: A preliminary guide for locating and linking to natural networks. In R. Valle & W. Vega (Eds.), *Hispanic natural support systems* (pp. 113–121). Sacramento: State of California Department of Mental Health.

Vaughn, C., & Leff, J. (1976). The measure of expressed emotion in the families of psychiatric patients. *British Journal of Social and Clinical Psychology, 15,* 157–165.

Vega, W. (1980). The Hispanic natural healer, a case study: Implications for prevention. In R. Valle & W. Vega (Eds.), *Hispanic natural support systems* (pp. 65–74). Sacramento: State of California Department of Mental Health.

Vélez, C. G. (1980). Mexicano/Hispano, support systems and *confianza:* Theoretical issues of cultural adaptation. In R. Valle & W. Vega (Eds.), *Hispanic natural support systems* (pp. 45–54). Sacramento: State of California Department of Mental Health.

Watkins, T. R., & Gonzales, R. (1982). Outreach to Mexican Americans. *Social Work, 27,* 68–73.

Wilson, W. J. (1991, October). *Poverty, joblessness, and family structure in the inner city: A comparative perspective.* Paper presented at the conference on the Urban Family Life Project, Chicago.

Wong, H. Z., Kim, L. I. C., Lim, D. T., & Morishima, J. K. (1983). The training of psychologists in Asian and Pacific American communities: Problems, perspectives and practices. In J. C. Chunn II, P. J. Dunston, & F. Ross-Sheriff (Eds.), *Mental health and people of color: Curriculum development and change* (pp. 23–41). Washington, DC: Howard University Press.

Wong, N., Lu, F. G., Shon, S. P., & Gaw, A. C. (1983). Asian and Pacific American patient issues in psychiatric residency training programs. In J. C. Chunn II, P. J. Dunston, & F. Ross-Sheriff (Eds.), *Mental health and people of color: Curriculum development and change* (pp. 293–268). Washington, DC: Howard University Press.

Yamamoto, J., & Wagatsuma, H. (1980). The Japanese and Japanese Americans. *Journal of Operational Psychiatry, 11*(2), 120–135.

Yamamoto, J., & Yap, J. (1984). Group therapy for Asian American and Pacific Islanders. *P/AAMHRC Research Review, 3,*1.

Yuen, S. (n.d.). *Aging and mental health in San Francisco's Chinatown.* (Available from Self Help for the Elderly, 640 Pine St., San Francisco, CA 94108.)

CHAPTER 7

Problem Identification

Problem identification often conjures up in our mind something negative. Problems are typically seen as negative entities that must be eliminated and solved. In this chapter we view problems as indications of unfulfilled needs and unsatisfied wants. Problems are also opportunities that need to be reframed from a negative perspective to a discovery of the positive that is missing. In social work practice we must relearn the nature and dynamics of problems to reflect this perception. Otherwise, we will be caught in the traditional negative pathology that has been associated with problem identification.

The psychiatric and psychological literature has stereotyped people of color as problem-prone. This characterization may be traced to mental health researchers' practice of selecting ethnic group mental patients in state hospitals as their subjects; unsurprisingly, they have found gross and severe psychological traits in these subjects as compared with white subjects. In the literature, this pathology has been attributed to the ethnic family and to sibling rivalry, thereby exacerbating the already distorted picture of an extreme matriarchal or patriarchal system.

Typically, people of color in therapy have been subjected to classical psychoanalysis, in which the therapist is the primary authority and the client is regarded as a social misfit. Once again, the selection of seriously disturbed patients and the gener-

alization of findings to the entire ethnic groups has distorted problem identification. Even when psychoanalysis is not used, the therapeutic approach generally does not speak to the cultural milieu of ethnic clients in their community (Meadow, 1983). As a result, people of color have avoided white clinical research and traditional psychotherapy.

Fortunately, social work practice has moved away from a psychoanalytic approach. It has adopted a systems theory that recognizes natural support systems, ethnic family strengths, and normal problems of living. In our perspective on multicultural practice, problem identification begins with a nonpathological orientation. Hepworth and Larsen (1993) argue that problems involve unmet needs or wants. Translating complaints and problems into needs and wants enhances clients' motivation to work toward behavioral change that brings satisfaction and well-being. Current social work practice is deemphasizing diagnostic symptoms, disease, and dysfunction and instead seeks to identify strengths, resources, and healthy functioning.

The practice issues that emerge in problem identification are summarized in Figure 7-1: in the client system, issues of problem information (the client's problems, the cultural and environmental factors that contribute to them, and information on target age groups and their needs), disclosure of problem areas, and problem understanding; in the worker system, issues of problem

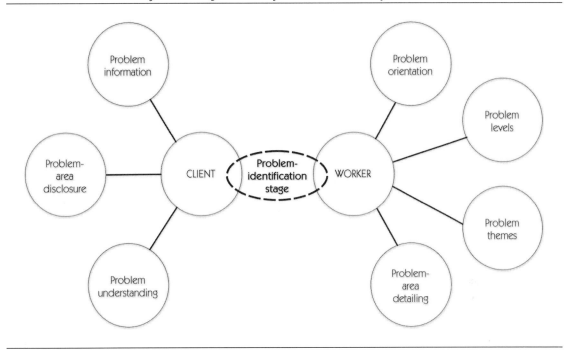

orientation, problem levels, problem themes, and problem area detailing. We consider these topics in detail in this chapter, which follows the format already established, presenting practice principles, case studies, and task recommendations.

CLIENT-SYSTEM PRACTICE ISSUES

Problem Information

Problem information tends to focus on the individual characteristics of the client and traditional approaches that have failed to uncover vital environmental factors. This classical view, often called *psychodynamic psychotherapy*, assumes an intrapsychic treatment approach to helping and builds a personal profile of the client. The intrapsychic model holds that the problems of clients stem from personal deficiency or disorganization rather than from institutional or societal dysfunction (Bryson & Bardo, 1975). However, it is important for social work practice to evaluate relevant problem information located in the patterns of the client's sociocultural environment.

Recent multicultural research has uncovered environmental issues that affect problem information. Jenkins (1981) reviewed multicultural literature over a ten-year period and summarized four common problem themes:

1. The lack of recognition that diverse cultural patterns exist and influence the change process. These variables include age, birthplace, education, recentness of migration, extent of acculturation, and social class. They form a unique configuration that affects the way a helping person works with an ethnic client.

2. The reality of language differences and the importance of bilingualism to effective service delivery. Although the dominant society does not value bilingual competency, bilingual and bicultural programs are essential services in mixed ethnic communities.

3. The existence of stereotypes that create barriers between the ethnic community and sources of help for their problems and needs. Stereotyping is a reality that all races confront.

4. The threat to group survival inherent in the adoption practices of child welfare agencies, which may place a child outside the group. Children are central to the survival of the ethnic group.

Vega (1980) identified a number of sociocultural issues that create service barriers. Racism and discrimination, in the form of cultural insensitivity, are manifested in style of service delivery, professional blindness to cultural norms, and other institutional policies. Faulty service delivery systems affect the problem-information interpretation. Culturally dissonant services fail to incorporate the client's ways of accepting and giving help. Methods of service delivery and treatment have not integrated cultural dimensions—for example, language and cultural values, community problems, and indigenous health practices. The inaccessibility of services is exhibited in the poor quality of such factors as bilingual communication, physical location of agencies, community relations, and client management. As a result, human services have low visibility for ethnic populations. Human services violate community integrity when they fail to understand and use existing cultural support networks. Instead, human services should reinforce, initiate, educate, organize, and engage community support networks, which are vital adjunct helping resources. Service delivery to people of color is problematic when it does not take cultural factors into account. The director and advisory board should review the social work agency's policies to ascertain whether they address unique ethnic behavior practices or create organizational barriers that complicate current social problems.

Research on problem information has identified target age groups and their needs. Sena-Rivera's (1980) report on Latino adolescents, young adults and parents, and elderly has implications for all people of color. Adolescents must struggle not only with confusion and ambivalence as a normal part of the life cycle but also with external threats to self-esteem. They are assaulted by an inferior and culturally demeaning educational system, crowded housing conditions, unemployment, cultural misunderstanding, and institutional racism. Some adolescents react to the stress through drug abuse, trouble with authority, dropping out of school, early pregnancies, and parent abuse. Young adults and parents in ethnic groups cope with poor socioeconomic conditions compounded by unemployment or employment with a limited future; discrimination that results in a lack of sense of self-worth, marginal self-identity, and alcohol and drug abuse; personal conflict, marital difficulties, and parental confusion about children and cultural values; and, for recently arrived immigrants, cultural shock. Elderly community members cope with anger and despair at the behavior of the young, lack of self-worth, loneliness, and fear of family separation. When gathering problem information, workers should take into account the potential high-risk areas for these age groups.

Problem information on people of color should be balanced between traditional personal data on the client and relevant socioenvironmental factors influencing the problem areas. Examples of the latter are the number of generations removed from immigrant status, birth (foreign-born versus American-born), language orientation, and family values. The acquisition of relevant problem information can be enhanced by the awareness of ethnic stereotyping; provision of an adequate number of bilingual/bicultural workers; communication with the ethnic community; and preventive education programs for needy age groups.

Problem Area Disclosure

Ethnic clients often feel shame and hesitation in the initial stages of the helping process. Certain cultural attitudes oppose the disclosure of problems outside the immediate family. Before disclosing the problem, the client may engage the worker in a rambling conversation to find out the worker's initial reaction. A client may ask a series of questions intended to test the situation. For example, the client might say, "I have a friend with a certain problem." After describing the situation,

The Hernández Family, a Case Study

The agency's recognition of the needs of Latino clients enhances the collection of problem information regarding the Hernández family. Mr. and Mrs. Hernández have migrated from Mexico and have adjusted to the local Mexican American community. Their social worker, Mr. Platt, is white but knows some Spanish phrases. A bilingual worker is available for consultation in the case, and stereotyping has been minimized by the agency's staff training in ethnic practice. Ample time has been allowed for discovering the unique character of each member of the Hernández family. Beyond learning about problem information from the family, the worker makes an effort to use ethnic-community resources—such as the school, the church, and employment-related contacts—to learn more about the family.

TASK RECOMMENDATIONS

To respond to the issues raised in this section on problem information, evaluate the information intake procedures and forms of a social service agency using to the following questions:

- What multicultural variables do these forms and procedures mention?
- How much attention is given to culturally diverse problem information such as generation and level of acculturation, language fluency, and factors of racism and discrimination?
- How would you revise the existing intake procedures and forms to raise the level of adequacy of information on ethnic clientele?

---

he or she may ask, "What would you suggest if this were the case?" Indirect questioning may occur under various pretenses until the client feels ready to risk disclosure and trust the worker with the problem. It is important to give the client enough time to acknowledge the problem. Devore and Schlesinger (1981) observe that ethnic-sensitive matters might not emerge early because of the worker's lack of knowledge, the client's reluctance to trust, a difference in the ethnic backgrounds of worker and client, or lack of awareness that ethnic factors have a bearing on the problem.

The same factors that can delay disclosure may also be primary reasons that ethnic clients drop out after the first session: too many barriers obstruct problem disclosure. Social workers learn the principles of direct interviewing skills, problem intervention, verbal communication, and the fifty-minute session. People of color must overcome cultural resistance and reticence about social service agencies. These people have ambivalent feelings about professionals who lack the client's cultural background and language skills.

In Cultural Study 7-1, Lewis and Ho (1975) illustrate how a worker might assist a client with problem disclosure.

CULTURAL STUDY 7-1

Problem Area Disclosure

The Redthunder family was brought to the school social worker's attention when teachers reported that both children had been tardy and absent frequently in the past weeks. Since the worker lived near Mr. Redthunder's neighborhood, she volunteered to transport the children back and forth to school. Through this regular but informal arrangement, the worker became acquainted with the entire family, especially with Mrs. Redthunder who expressed her gratitude to the worker by sharing her homegrown vegetables.

The worker sensed that there was much family discomfort and that a tumultuous relationship existed between Mr. and Mrs. Redthunder. Instead of probing into their personal and marital affairs, the worker let Mrs. Redthunder know that she was willing to listen should the woman need someone to talk to. After a few gifts of homegrown vegetables and Native American handicrafts, Mrs. Redthunder broke into tears one day and told the worker about her husband's problem of alcoholism and their deteriorating marital relationship.

Realizing Mr. Redthunder's position of respect in the family and his resistance to outside interference, the social worker advised Mrs. Redthunder to take her family to visit the minister, a man whom Mr. Redthunder admired. The Littleaxe family, who were mutual friends of the worker and the Redthunder family, agreed to take the initiative in visiting the Redthunders more often. Through such frequent but informal family visits, Mr. Redthunder finally obtained a job, with the recommendation of Mr. Littleaxe, as recordkeeper in a storeroom. Mr. Redthunder enjoyed his work so much that he drank less and spent more time with his family.

From "Social Work with Native Americans," by R. G. Lewis and M. K. Ho. In *Social Work* (September 1975), Vol. 20, No. 5, p. 381. Copyright 1975, National Association of Social Workers, Inc. Reprinted by permission.

Social workers should exercise patience, spend time in relationship building, learn culturally sensitive approaches, and allow the client to set the pace in problem disclosure. Lewis and Ho (1975) remind us:

> A Native American client will not immediately wish to discuss other members of his family or talk about topics that he finds sensitive or distressing. Before arriving at his immediate concern (the real reason he came to the worker in the first place), the client—particularly the Native American—will test the worker by bringing up peripheral matters. He does this in the hope of getting a better picture of how sincere, interested, and trustworthy the worker actually is. If the worker impatiently confronts the client with accusations, the client will be "turned off." (p. 380)

It is important for the social worker to recognize this hesitance as an integral part of problem identification and a hurdle for the ethnic client to overcome.

Research reveals potential client problem areas relevant to multicultural practice. According to studies of socioeconomic status and length of res-

idency in the United States, recent arrivals who do not speak English or lack marketable skills are often unemployed or underemployed. They need concrete services such as information, referral, and advocacy. American-born individuals or long-term residents exhibit a greater degree of acculturation and have a better knowledge of the service delivery system than do new immigrants and are more likely to seek counseling and related services (Kuramoto, Morales, Muñoz, & Murase, 1983). Immigrants, the poor, and the elderly are under particular stress: Immigrants are exposed to tremendous life changes that require a major adjustment and, as a result, the incidence of physical and psychological problems increases; the poor encounter adverse conditions because of their socioeconomic class; and the elderly face the problems of aging (Sue, Ito, & Bradshaw, 1982). Research on these at-risk groups reveals the kinds of problems each is most likely to encounter and helps the social worker anticipate the disclosures of a particular client.

History taking is encouraged as a way to gain familiarity with a client. The worker learns about crucial cultural factors, discovers important events in the client's life, and demonstrates empathy for the client and interest in the relationship between past and present situations. For example, history taking is important for Southeast Asian refugees. As a Southeast Asian client talks about his or her refugee experience, the worker receives important information about family life, loss of status and mobility, religious values, and related areas. Ishisaka, Nguyen, and Okimoto (1985) recommend exploring the following background areas:

1. Family life and experiences during childhood
2. Life experiences before the client became a refugee
3. Reasons for escaping, the escape process, losses, and expectations
4. Life in refugee camps, attitudes about camp life, and problems of sustenance
5. Sponsorship to the United States, expectations of life in the new land, experiences with culture conflict, survival problems, and coping strategies

The Hernández Family, a Case Study

At the next session, Mr. Platt shares some of the conversation he has had with Ricardo's teacher. He mentions that the teacher, Mrs. Villa, is concerned about Mr. Hernández's long hours. By relaying the teacher's expression of concern, Mr. Platt gives Mr. Hernández an opening to express his feelings about the past three months. Rather than confronting Mr. Hernández, Mr. Platt allows him to disclose the problem area. In turn, the social worker gives Mr. Hernández support as he tells about his two jobs, the long hours, and the economic burdens of the family. Mr. Hernández feels obliged to help his relatives. Since the two families of in-laws arrived from Mexico, the husbands have held part-time jobs washing dishes in Mexican restaurants and harvesting tomatoes.

Moreover, these three families feel they must send money to Mexico to support their elderly parents, who are retired and living on small pensions. Mr. Hernández feels a family obligation to support his in-laws until they can find steady employment. Mrs. Hernández states that her family in Mexico sent money to them when they came to the United States ten years ago. Now Mr. and Mrs. Hernández feel it is their turn to help members of her family. However, Mr. Hernández recognizes that he cannot spend more time with Ricardo and help him with his homework; the demands on his time are already too great.

TASK RECOMMENDATIONS

Disclosure of the problem area is based on mutual trust and accept-ance between the worker and client. The following are suggestions for working on problem area disclosure:

- Allow the client to lead you into problem area disclosure. Look for verbal and nonverbal cues. Let the client state the problem area in his or her own words, then restate and clarify what the client is saying.
- Discuss in a staff or student group some potential problem areas of ethnic immigrants, poor, and elderly.
- Determine practical ways to facilitate problem disclosure without demeaning clients who are sensitive to revealing personal problems to social workers and other helping professionals.

---

6. Family life adjustments, made over several years, that were necessitated by residency within the United States
7. Current concerns and expectations for the future
8. The client's present understanding of adjustment difficulties

Rather than short-circuiting problem area disclosure, proper relationship protocol may warrant understanding the entire background of the refugee client. The worker communicates interest in important past and present events that have affected the client. The sharing of these experiences has a therapeutic effect on the refugee client, who relives painful experiences that have shaped him or her. It also provides the worker with a broad overview of the problematic issues the client may face.

Problem Understanding

The client needs to develop a perspective on his or her problems. When the client understands the problem, he or she recognizes what has happened and owns the responsibility for coping with the problem. Green (1982) emphasizes the importance of finding out the client's definition and understanding of an experience as a problem. Cultures differ in their explanations of etiology, symptom recognition, treatment procedures, and desirable outcomes of problems. Members of the same culture share a cognitive map, an ability to understand and cope with a problem based on skills learned from personal, family, and community survival. Unifying themes bind members of a culturally distinct people to one another. Self-understanding is built on understanding one's own perception of how the world operates regarding a problem. According to Green, problem understanding occurs in a cultural, social, and economic context. Normality in the world of the ethnic client can look like pathology from the professional point of view.

The client's interpretation of the problem is as important as the client's understanding of it. Green (1982) stresses the meaning of reality and the reaction of the client, both of which influence the resulting course of action. Perceiving how culture influences behavioral responses gives the client an awareness of what happened and why he or she responded in a particular manner. In Cultural Study 7-2, the client indicates that there is widespread discrimination at school. However, she is in a transitional period of adjustment. The worker wisely concentrates on identifying concrete instances of discrimination, the goal being for the client to take action. As a result, the client is encouraged to establish a social network involving a cultural support group and ethnic activities.

CULTURAL STUDY 7-2

Problem Understanding

Ann is an attractive seventeen-year-old black high-school student who was referred for counseling because of her increasing depression and nervousness since she began attending a new school. She was an only child, living at home with her mother and father, who had recently moved into the new neighborhood as a consequence of the father's job transfer. The school she had attended before had been predominantly black. The new school was racially mixed, although a majority of the students were white. Ann told her counselor that there was a great amount of discrimination at the school, both within the black and white student groups as well as between them. Even though she knew that *some* black students seemed to be fairly well integrated into the social

network of the white students, she personally did not feel accepted by either group. She noticed that one small group of black students congregated daily at a certain table in the cafeteria, yet she was holding herself back from introducing herself to them. Ann expressed to the counselor who was also black her feelings of isolation and confusion as to what was happening to her in the school and what she wanted for herself.

The counselor reviewed the facts as perceived and presented to her by Ann. Two hypotheses or "choice points" stood out:

Ann was being discriminated against at school. (.60)

or

Ann was experiencing isolation, tension, and stress from the move, complicated by her own fears and expectations of others. (.40)

The counselor decided to develop an action hypothesis based on the first hypothesis, particularly since it was highly likely that by doing so, the issues present in the second hypothesis would emerge and could be taken care of at that time. The action hypothesis was described by the counselor in this manner: "If I focused in our counseling sessions on having her specify more concretely how and by whom she was experiencing discrimination, then Ann would become more aware of what she could *do* under the circumstances."

In subsequent sessions, the action hypothesis was implemented. Ann indicated that she felt she was being discriminated against by a large number of white students, evidenced by snide remarks about her hair or body odor as she walked in the halls, being pushed and shoved while in line for nutrition and lunch, and having students get up and change seats after she sat down next to them. In the process of having her define what was happening to her, she indicated that these things might not happen to her if she were not a "loner." At first, she was not very clear about her position with the other black students. When the counselor inquired whether she felt that other black students were also being discriminated against by white students, she replied that she did not know because she was not in contact with any of the black students. She spoke about being different from them, specifically in terms of her "conservative" clothes and the fact that she did not use the "hip" jargon that the other students did. The counselor asked her to exaggerate her "differentness" and try to convince her[self] (using a Gestalt technique) that she was so very different from the other black students that she could not hope to be their friend. As she tried this, Ann eventually concluded that she was not as different as she thought she was. She then spoke about the cafeteria activity and of her fear to approach the small clique of black students who gathered there daily. The counselor had her bring the cafeteria experience into the present and make it explicit by role-playing it in the office. Ann experimented with different ways to approach the group, for example by asking a question about a class assignment, or making a statement that she wanted to meet them. At this point, the counselor developed another set of choice points:

While discrimination was a realistic issue in Ann's life, she was generalizing it to include everybody and consequently was not approaching those black students who might be interested in meeting her, (.90), or

Ann's belief that everybody was discriminating against her was probably correct. (.10)

Again the counselor developed an action hypothesis: "If I suggest that Ann make contact with other black students where she could begin to establish a social network for herself through a collective identity, then I expect that Ann's feelings of isolation and being discriminated against would be significantly reduced and she would begin to feel an increased sense of her own significance and ability to handle the school situation."

The counselor followed the action prescribed and Ann agreed to try. She succeeded in making contacts with other black students and learned that many of them were also victims of racial discrimination. The students began discussing ways of actively dealing with this problem as a group. Ann also joined an ethnomusicology course on campus which taught African drumming and had both black and white students enrolled. Thus, Ann's success in establishing contacts with others, her efforts to "do something" about the issue of discrimination, resulted in reduced isolation and tension and

depression. The counselor discontinued sessions upon mutual agreement but with the understanding that counseling was available at anytime Ann thought she could use it to meet a need.

From *Black Empowerment: Social Work in Oppressed Communities*, by B. B. Solomon, pp. 306–308. Copyright © 1976 Columbia University Press. Reprinted by permission.

In Cultural Study 7-3, the social worker brings problem understanding to a Chinese American client. By acknowledging responsibility for his problem behavior, the client expresses cultural respect for his parents and his family obligation.

CULTURAL STUDY 7-3

Problem Responsibility

L. C., an American-born Chinese and a junior high school student, experienced a great many learning difficulties. He habitually skipped school and, as a result, was unaware of his homework assignments. Both of his parents were passive individuals who were confused by and ashamed of their son's behavior. Also they were having severe marital problems and were striving to present a facade, pretending their marriage was on solid ground and that it had nothing to do with their son's failing in school.

L. C. was aware of his parents' problems and defensiveness, and took advantage of their vulnerability by indulging himself whenever he pleased. A family treatment team consisting of one male and one female therapist was quite successful in helping the parents to gain some insights into their problems and to communicate more openly and fully; attempts to resolve their son's school problem, however, were met with continuous resistance, especially from L. C. himself, who accused the treatment team of conspiring with his parents against him. With the permission of the family, a child worker, actually the same age as L. C. and a personal friend of the male therapist, was introduced as an additional member of the treatment team. When L. C. repeatedly blamed his parents' marital problems for his own problems,

The Hernández Family, a Case Study

After disclosing his problem to Mr. Platt, Mr. Hernández realizes that economic conditions and family obligation have complicated his relationship with his eldest son. He is obliged to help his in-laws by virtue of the fact that they assisted him when he left Mexico for the United States. It is now his turn to assist them in their resettlement period. It seems a natural response for Mr. Hernández, but he is overwhelmed with his work schedule and family responsibilities. Mr. Hernández brings his cultural cognitive map—this feeling of obliga-tion and responsibility—with him. In turn, he receives from Mr. Platt understanding of what has hap-pened to him during the past sever-al months.

TASK RECOMMENDATIONS

Problem understanding is based on the assumption that a cultural cog-nitive map exists within each per-son. The client provides necessary information on when the problem began, how the problem has affect-ed him or her, and what can be done to alleviate the problem. To increase the client's problem under-standing, the worker might adopt the following suggestions:

- Trust the client, who has an innate cultural understanding of the problem.
- Facilitate a conversation in which the client is able to bring out the cultural meaning of the problem.
- Relate the chronology of prob-lem events to cultural dynamics that involve behavior.

---

the child worker pointed out that skipping school was a sign of "copping out" and that continuation of this activity would only bring him failure. "We all have problems, but we have ourselves to blame if we do not live up to our share of responsibili-ties," added the child worker. The child worker's intervention gradually lessened the guilt feelings of the parents, who later were able to better assume the limiting role in dealing with their son.

From "Social Work with Asian Americans," by M. K. Ho, *Social Casework* (March 1976), Vol. 57, p. 199. Copyright © 1976 Family Service Association of America. Reprinted by permission.

WORKER-SYSTEM PRACTICE ISSUES

Problem Orientation

Reid (1978) has described a problem as an unsat-isfied want or an unfulfilled need, recasting the dynamics of the problem in a positive perspective. A problem becomes a motivator and an impetus toward change. The focus moves from behavior pathology and blaming the victim toward positive attempts to focus and work toward satisfying wants and fulfilling needs. The client expresses his or her wants or needs and identifies barriers in his or her life situation. Then the refocusing is on moving away from problem pathology and reach-ing behind the problem to want satisfaction and need fulfillment.

Likewise, Hepworth and Larsen (1993) reframe the problem into unmet needs and wants. They encourage a focus not on problem pathology but on client assets—on strengths, resources, and potential in the client and his or her environment.

In Cultural Study 7-4, Ivey (1994) provides some helpful suggestions on how to focus a client on positive assets—in particular, refraining a prob-lem so that it uncovers strengths in the person. Ivey terms this approach the *positive asset search*.

The Positive Asset Search

Counseling, interviewing, and psychotherapy can be difficult experiences for some clients. They have come to discuss their problems and resolve

The Hernández Family, a Case Study

The Hernández family has been under increasing environmental stress since Mr. Hernández assumed the economic responsibility of assisting his in-laws. He has been forced to support his family and relatives. Socioeconomic factors and family disruption are reflected in Ricardo's school problems. Fortunately, Mr. Platt, the social worker, does not focus exclusively on Ricardo's behavior and relationship with his parents but is also aware of the family's environmental stress.

TASK RECOMMENDATIONS

Clinical psychotherapy tends toward individual-oriented personality theories. In multicultural practice, problem orientation starts with social community and environmental issues that affect individual reactions. The following are some practical suggestions for developing a psychosocial problem orientation:

- Discuss potentially oppressive factors that people of color confront in their environment.

- Identify human behavior and community theories that examine environmental aspects of the problem.
- Discuss the external problem orientation of a case involving an ethnic family.
- Establish procedures on how to uncover social causes of problems as you work with ethnic clients.

---

conflicts, so the session can rapidly become a depressing litany of failures and fears.

People grow from their strengths. The positive asset search is a useful method to ensure a more optimistic and directed interview. Rather than just ask about problems, the effective interviewer seeks constantly to find positive assets upon which the client can focus. Even in very complex issues, it is possible to find good things about the client and things that he or she does right. Emphasizing positive assets also gives a client a sense of personal power in the interview.

To conduct a positive asset search the interviewer simply uses the BLS [Basic Listening Sequence: summary of the issue, key facts of a situation, central emotions and feelings] to draw out the client's positive aspects and then reflects them back. This may be done systematically, as a separate part of the interview, or used constantly throughout the session. Specifically, the positive asset search appears in the interview in the following ways:

1. The interviewer may begin a session by asking what has happened recently that the client feels good about. Or the interviewer may comment on some positive strength in the client.

2. In the problem-definition phase of the interview, the interviewer may use the BLS to bring out positive client assets in detail. For example, a response to a client who has just lost a job and feels depressed and worried might be "You say you're worried and feel lost. At the same time, I know you held that job for four years. Could you tell me one thing you liked about the job or felt you did well?"

3. If a client constantly repeats negative self-statements, these may be paraphrased and then followed by carefully timed feedback from a more positive viewpoint. For example, "Yes, losing a job is traumatic and really hurts. At the same time, I see that you have several strengths—a good sense of humor, some valuable skills, and a history of perseverance in the face of difficulty. All of these will help you work through this."

4. One possible goal in counseling is to help clients find strengths in their weaknesses. An "overconcerned" parent may, for example, be redefined as a caring person. This redefinition may eventually lead to less involvement. The danger is that a caring person can at times become an interfering rescuer who denies others the chance to solve their own problems. Searching for

strengths helps a person let go. We grow from strength.

Highlighting specific concrete assets of a client in the context of real problems is a very helpful way of promoting positive change and is central to any intelligent approach to human problems.

Theoretically, the positive asset search may be described as a psycho-educational intervention that emphasizes human development rather than remediation of problems. . . . The concept appears under many different guises in the various forms of interviewing, counseling, and therapy. At times, the positive asset search can obviate the need for traditional problem solving in the session, as client strengths naturally overcome their weaknesses.

From *Intentional Interviewing and Counseling: Facilitating Client Development in a Multicultural Society*, by A. E. Ivey, pp. 144, 145. Copyright © 1994 Brooks/Cole Publishing Company, a division of International Thomson Publishing Inc., Pacific Grove, CA 93950. Reprinted by permission.

Hepworth and Larsen (1993) emphasize two basic components of the practitioner's problem orientation: positive reframing and a helpful expectation. To alter the negative cognitive sets that underlie client powerlessness, the worker reframes the problem so that the client sees that change is possible and conveys a genuine belief in the client's ability to improve the problem situation. If the problem is reframed as an opportunity for positive changes, the client is empowered to take constructive action. By affirming the client's ability to make changes, the worker imparts hope to the client that success is possible.

Sue (1981) points out that in multicultural practice, the client problem tends to not be internal or inherent in origin. Whereas traditional psychotherapy focuses on internal barriers within the person, the culturally sensitive social worker starts with the assumption that many client problems are rooted in a racist society; that is, environmental and societal conditions are responsible for clients' unsatisfied wants. Sue views sociotherapeutic aspects of problem identification and solution as a balance between services to individuals and social change. Extrapsychic sources of stress originate outside the person and are environmentally based. For African Americans, external environmental (extrapsychic) stress leads to the development of internalized negative (intrapsychic maladaptive) feelings about themselves: poor self-concept and feelings of hopelessness and rage (Smith, 1981). Middle-class counselors with individualistic and intrapsychic orientations tend to minimize the significance of the social and cultural forces that affect African American clients (Tucker & Gunnings, 1974).

Problem Levels

Social problems have been classified along a continuum of levels ranging from macro- (complex organizations, geographic populations) through meso- (ethnic/local communities and organizations) to micro- (individual, family, and small group). Social work practice has placed problems in various categories according to type. Reid (1978) catalogs the following problem areas:

Interpersonal conflict
Dissatisfaction in social relations
Problems with formal organizations
Difficulty in role performance
Decision problems
Reactive emotional distress
Inadequate resources
Psychological or behavioral problems not elsewhere classified

Northen (1982) has identified the following problem typology:

Lack of economic and social resources
Lack of knowledge and experience
Emotional reactions to stress
Illness and disability
Loss of relationship
Dissatisfactions in social relationships
Interpersonal conflict
Culture conflict
Conflict with formal organizations
Maladaptive group functioning

Problems in the aforementioned areas are caused by interaction of an individual with another person, group, or institution and by situations beyond the client's control. For people of color, problems are exacerbated by inadequate programs and service gaps, basic survival issues, and issues of acculturation and adjustment. Many individuals must cope with multiple problems beyond the limits of the average person's tolerance.

There are several ways to view problem levels in multicultural practice. Sue and Morishima (1982) indicate at least three areas of stress: culture conflict, minority group status, and social change. David (1976) illustrates these areas for Latinos. As people enter a new culture, they lose many reinforcing events that make life satisfying to them. Culture conflicts arise for many Spanish-speaking parents when, as heads of the family, they must rely on their children to translate and explain how things are done in the United States. Their sense of being a member of a minority group is heightened by the absence of familiar friends, family, and institutions. Problems of social change occur when a family from a rural area experiences the smog, crime, and crowded conditions of a city or the blatant prejudice of a predominantly white society.

Solomon (1983) notes that stress from external systems commonly contributes to the presenting problems of African American clients and comments, "If the theoretical frameworks that serve to guide social workers all relate primarily to intrapsychic functioning as the determinant of ability to cope with one's environment and not to institutional factors that might need to be changed instead or as well, the profession will have limited effectiveness in helping Afro-Americans" (p. 427). The starting point for the social worker is the stress of environmental problems and its effect on the client.

Traditionally, social work has focused on biopsychosocial reactions of the individual to the social environment. However, problems may involve a mixture of interactions at the macro-, meso-, and microlevels. In Cultural Study 7-5, Ghali (1977) shares an example of a Puerto Rican family facing such multilevel problems.

CULTURAL STUDY 7-5

Macro-, Meso-, and Microlevels of Interaction

Juan and Carmen R live in a tenement in the South Bronx. They have five children, three sons born in Puerto Rico and two daughters born in the United States. Juan was previously employed as a clerk in a New York City grocery store or *bodega*. He completed an eighth grade education in a small interior town in Puerto Rico but was unable to attend high school in the city because his parents, who had twelve children, could not afford the necessary shoes, uniforms, and transportation. Instead, Juan began working full time alongside his father in the *finca* (farm) of the wealthy L family. Juan asked God to forgive him for his envious thoughts toward his brother, Jose, who was the godson of Señor L and had his tuition paid by the wealthy farmer. Juan's own godparents were good to him and remembered all the occasions and feasts, but they were poor. When Juan was sixteen, his godfather, Pedro, got him a job on the pineapple farm of the coastal city of Arecibo. He enjoyed living with Pedro's family. At age twenty-four he fell in love with Pedro's granddaughter, Carmen, who was sixteen, in the tenth grade, and a virgin. Apart from family gatherings and Sundays in the plaza, however, he was unable to see her. Finally, he asked her father for her hand in marriage and the latter consented because he thought of Juan as a brother. The patron loaned his *finca* for the wedding and contributed a roasted pig for the occasion. Over fifty people from infancy to age ninety were there to celebrate the wedding.

Juan was very proud when his first-born was a son, but his pride as a man was hurt when Carmen had to return to work as a seamstress because of the increasing debts. Her family took care of the baby and fought over who would be the godparents. By the time a third child was born, a show of God's blessing, Juan was let go at the pineapple farm and he and his family moved to San Juan, where his brother, Jose, got him a job in a supermarket. This job did not last long and after a long period of unemployment and health problems with the youngest child, Juan moved to New York City with Carmen's brother, who obtained for him the job in the *bodega*.

Carmen was delighted with being reunited with her family, but when she became pregnant with their fourth child, the Rs moved into their own apartment. Carmen became depressed because for the first time she was not living with extended family; because of the stress of the change of culture; because of her inability to speak English; and because of the deterioration of the tenement which was impossible to keep sparkling clean. She suffered from headaches, stomach problems, and pains in her chest, but doctors told her these symptoms were due to nerves and her condition was chronic. When she felt better she would raise the volume of the *jíbaro* music on the Spanish station and talk to her saints. Finally, Juan sent for Carmen's aunt to come to live with them and her arrival helped Carmen. Carmen accepted Juan's arguments that in America job, schooling, and medical facilities were better than in Puerto Rico. (In some ways the job and medical facilities in Puerto Rico were nonexistent unless one had a car.) The years passed, and Carmen consoled herself that as soon as the children finished their education they would move back to Puerto Rico where Juan could set up a business. As the children grew they adopted the ways of the neighborhood children. They no longer asked for the parents' blessings as they came and left the house; they wanted to go to parties unchaperoned; they sometimes talked back; the girls wanted to wear makeup at age fifteen and dress in nonladylike clothes. The boys had friends who belonged to gangs and smoked pot, and the parents feared the same would happen to their sons. Juan and Carmen threatened to send them back to Puerto Rico or to a *colegio* (boarding school) if they did not sever these friendships. Another important and traumatic issue that the family was faced with for the first time involved the issue of color. The youngest daughter, Yvette, age twelve, entered junior high school and found herself placed on the black side of the two camps in school. This situation affected the entire family. Carmen reminded her daughter that she was a Puerto Rican and told her to speak Spanish loudly so the schoolchildren would not confuse her with the blacks. Inside, Carmen felt guilty that her daughter's dark skin led to problems.

During this very difficult period Juan injured his back while loading merchandise and became permanently disabled. Suddenly, the family had to receive public welfare assistance, and Juan's authority was gradually becoming undermined, particularly as he was no longer the breadwinner. He began to drink. Trips to Puerto Rico, while somewhat supportive, did not provide a solution to the problems the family was undergoing. Finally, Yvette came to the attention of school authorities because of her withdrawn behavior and she was referred to a mental health center.

From "Culture Sensitivity and the Puerto Rican Client," by S. B. Ghali. In *Social Casework* (October 1977), Vol. 58, pp. 464–465. Copyright © 1977 by Family Service Association of America. Reprinted by permission.

People of color often exhibit certain biopsychosocial problems through somatic complaints and emotional disturbances. Sue and Morishima (1982) cite research on Asian Americans that associates mental disturbances with organic or somatic factors. There are reasons for that relationship. Some Asian Americans see a unity between physical and psychological states, a perception that has consequences for the mind and body. Further, physical complaints carry less of a negative stigma than do emotional or mental disturbances. Checking out physical ailments with the client's physician and being aware of the psychophysiological relationship are crucial for the ethnic-sensitive social worker.

Morales and Salcido (1983) note that, for Latinos, psychological problems can often be interpreted as stress responses to external needs:

This is *not* to say that the poor are poor because of psychological problems; rather, their impoverished status may contribute to and exacerbate their stress. Indeed, it becomes a difficult task to help someone work through separation feelings regarding the loss of a loved one when they are starving, have no place to live, or are freezing to death. In this

The Hernández Family, a Case Study

The Hernández family's problems reflect the external stress encountered by clients who must cope with socioeconomic issues. Mr. Hernández has been placed under undue stress on account of the state of the job market: his relatives have been unable to find suitable employment on account of economic and transient factors. Sheer fatigue has placed Mr. Hernández in a position of inability to sustain an adequate relationship with his family, particularly his son. Mr. Platt notes the physical, psychological, and social aspects of the problem and its effect on Ricardo. The social worker identifies some concrete indicators of environmental stress on Mr. Hernández that are affecting his relations with his son.

TASK RECOMMENDATIONS

Problem levels are general indicators that help social workers identify problems. The focus is away from intrapsychic problems and toward external, environmental factors. The following exercises can be useful in helping the worker understand such principles:

- In a case study, identify macro- and mesoproblem stressors such as culture conflict (for example, entrance into a new culture, which sets up a conflict between ethnic traditions and white norms), minority group status (for example, the change in status from an ethnic majority in one culture to an ethnic minor-

ity in another), and social change (for example, the impact of the American metropolitan lifestyle on ethnic provincial ways).

- Continuing with the same case, find the biopsychosocial aspects of problems such as microsomatic complaints, the effects of external stress on the client's health, and socioeconomic factors that affect the client.
- Discuss problem categories with an experienced clinician who has worked with people of color. Determine whether other relevant problem categories have not been mentioned.

---

respect, certain basic human needs related to food, clothing, and shelter are universal, and a person's emotional response to stress also has universal qualities. (p. 397)

The state of the economy is a very important stressor for many people of color, especially for those with limited financial means. When the economy is good, jobs are more plentiful, and social policies tend to be liberal. During economic downturns, the job market is tight, and there is a trend toward conservative social policy, under which some individuals and groups gain at the expense of others and the most economically vulnerable are likely to be sacrificed (Myers, 1982).

Problem Themes

Ideological Belief: Racism. At the root of problem themes in multicultural practice is the problem of racism, which is manifested attitudinally in

prejudice and behaviorally in discrimination. This statement is not intended as an all-encompassing simplistic explanation of the problems confronted by ethnic clients. However, there is ample evidence that racist reactions of the dominant society contribute to and complicate the problems of people of color. Historically, in the United States, each ethnic group has suffered discrimination in its interaction with the dominant society. African Americans came to the United States predominantly as slaves, although some were free men and women. They have, as an ethnic group, suffered racial discrimination despite civil rights legislation. Latino Americans have faced economic exploitation as migrant farm workers and manual laborers. In the early part of this century, Asian Americans were excluded from immigration into the United States. Recent Indo-Chinese immigrants have encountered racism in various parts of the United States when they have competed with their white counterparts in Gulf Coast fishing.

Native Americans have been restricted to federal reservations and placed in a socioeconomically dependent role through the Bureau of Indian Affairs, Department of the Interior.

Racism has been defined as the domination of one social or ethnic group over another. It is used as an ideological system to justify the institutional discrimination of certain racial groups against others. Pinderhughes (1989) states:

> Racism raises to the level of social structure the tendency to use superiority as a solution to discomfort about difference. Belief in superiority of Whites and the inferiority of people-of-color based on racial difference is legitimized by societal arrangements that exclude the latter from resources and power and then blame them for their failures, which are due to lack of access. (p. 89)

Racism can take one of at least three forms: individual, institutional, and cultural. *Individual racism* refers to individual thoughts, feelings, and behaviors that are motivated by the attitude of generic superiority held by a person who considers others inferior. A racist person, according to Axelson (1985), has a psychological deficiency and needs to perceive that a person of another ethnic group is inferior compared with the racist's ethnic group. *Institutional racism* concerns educational, economic, social, and political organizations that intentionally or unintentionally perpetuate racial inequality. Institutionally racist practices relate to employment, housing, education, and inadequacies in program services. *Cultural racism* refers to the beliefs, feelings, and behaviors of members of a cultural group who assert the superiority of the group's accomplishments, achievements, and creativity, and attribute this claimed cultural superiority to genetic composition. In cultural racism, the in-group/out-group division is based on the supposed superiority of culture and racial background of one group over another (Axelson, 1985).

The concepts of symbolic racism and ethnocentrism reflect currently prevalent views in the United States. *Symbolic racism* rejects racial inferiority and segregation stances but focuses on the following themes:

- People of color push too much and demand too much in an attempt to obtain more than they merit.
- People of color want success but are unwilling to work hard or delay gratification to obtain it.
- People of color are linked to negative interpretations of welfare, urban riots, crime in the streets, affirmative action, and quota systems.

These themes border on racism to the extent that they perpetuate the belief in the dominant society's authority and belittle any "undeserving" challenge from other groups. Symbolic racism casts people of color as undeserving, lazy, and unable to check their impulses. They are lumped with negative elements in society that whites write off easily (McConahay & Hough, 1976).

In *ethnocentrism*, the individual's ethnic group forms his or her central point of reference, to the exclusion of other groups. Ethnocentrism has been criticized as representing a particularism that demands loyalty to a particular group. Critics of ethnocentrism have argued that college ethnic studies programs teach students about their racial and ethnic purity (Ravitch, 1990). This is a distortion of the goals of such programs, which aim to present the history, culture, social problems, and related areas of ethnic groups in a coherent context.

The systematic nature of the mistreatment people of color have experienced is a result of institutionalized inequalities in the social structure. Racism is one consequence of a self-perpetuating imbalance in economic, political, and social power. This imbalance consistently favors members of some ethnic and cultural groups at the expense of others. The consequences of this imbalance pervade all aspects of the social system and affect all facets of people's lives (Sherover-Marcuse, n.d.).

Racism operates as a "divide-and-conquer" strategy. It perpetuates a social system in which some people are consistently "haves" and others are consistently "have-nots." Although the haves receive certain material benefits from this situation, the long-range effects of racism shortchange everyone. Racism sets groups of people against each other and makes it difficult for us to perceive our common interests as human beings. Racism makes us forget that we all need, and are entitled to, good health care, stimulating education, and challenging work. Racism limits our horizons to what presently exists; it makes us suppose that current injustices are natural, or at best inevitable. "Someone" has to be unemployed; someone has to go hungry. Most important, racism distorts our perceptions of the possibilities for change. It makes us abandon our visions of solidarity, and it robs us of our dreams of community (Sherover-Marcuse, n.d.).

The following are common characteristics of racism (Davis, 1978; Hodge, 1975):

1. The belief that there are well-defined and distinctive races among human beings
2. The belief that racial mixing lowers biological quality
3. The belief in the mental and physical superiority of some races over others
4. The belief that racial groups have distinct racial culture to the extent that some races are naturally prone to criminality, sexual looseness, or dishonest business practices
5. The belief that certain races have temperamental dispositions, which is a form of stereotyping
6. The belief that the superior races should rule and dominate the inferior races

These beliefs can be overtly expressed or covertly felt by people of one race concerning other races. Racism generates prejudice and discrimination.

Attitude: Prejudice. Prejudice is an attitudinal response that expresses unfavorable feelings and behavioral intentions toward a group or its individual members (Davis, 1978). It primarily consists of negative affective reactions to others. Holding certain prejudices provides an organizational framework by which individuals can structure their world; it allows them to project blame onto the out-group and deny uncomfortable feelings about themselves (Brislin, 1981). Several theories of prejudice have been formulated. These theories view prejudice variously as the cultural transmission of beliefs about certain races that

result in degrees of social distance and as personality manifestations of frustration and aggression that lead to displacement of feelings onto the out-group (McLemore, 1983).

From a pragmatic standpoint, some conditions increase or decrease prejudice. Prejudice is heightened under the following circumstances (Amir, 1969, p. 338):

1. When the contact situation produces competition between groups
2. When the contact is unpleasant, involuntary, and tension laden
3. When the prestige or status of a group is lowered as a result of contact
4. When members of a group or the whole group is in a state of frustration
5. When the groups have moral or ethnic standards objectionable to each other
6. When the members of the minority group are of lower status or lower in any relevant characteristics than members of the majority group

Numerous incidents illustrate these principles: the competition between Vietnamese and Gulf Coast fishermen, which produced a volatile economic and social situation; racial slurs uttered in the heat of a political campaign; the covert exclusion of ethnic groups from the civil rights of voting, housing, and employment; and focus on the alcoholism and suicidal rates of Native Americans to the exclusion of favorable cultural characteristics such as survival skills, harmony with nature and the universe, and group sharing.

Likewise, prejudice is reduced when certain conditions are present (Amir, 1969, p. 339):

1. When there is equal-status contact between members of various ethnic groups
2. When there is contact between members of a majority group and higher-status members of a minority group
3. When an authority or social climate favorably promotes intergroup contact
4. When intergroup ethnic contact is pleasant or rewarding
5. When members of both groups interact functionally in important activities, developing

common goals or superordinate goals that rank higher in importance than the individual goals of each group

Examples of events that have lessened racial prejudice in the United States might include the achievement of voting rights and political power on the local metropolitan level for African Americans; the housing integration of middle-class professional whites with their nonwhite counterparts; the ethnic harmony and one-world spirit exhibited at the opening ceremony of the 1984 Los Angeles Olympics; and the 1984 election's appeal to an Americanism—pride of country, allegiance to God, and love of humanity—that transcends ethnic boundaries.

Behavior: Discrimination. Before the 1960s, cultural anthropology, encountered in the works of Margaret Mead and Clyde Kluckhohn, strongly influenced social work practice. During the 1960s the focus was on effects of discrimination that tended to impose deviant characteristics on people of color. Solomon (1983) observes that whites assumed African Americans were characterized by

> concern [only] for immediate gratification, lack of interest in personal achievement, and lack of commitment to marriage and family. Moreover these supposed characteristics were viewed as deterrents to the involvement of [African Americans] in problem-solving relationships with social work practitioners. (pp. 423–424)

The characteristics of ethnic groups were magnified and differentiated from those of white society (Solomon, 1983). These practices constitute a discriminatory interpretation of minorities. *Discrimination* refers to a behavioral response unfavorable to members of an ethnic or racial outgroup (Brislin, 1981; McLemore, 1983). Discrimination is preceded by prejudice, as a learned condition. A person discriminates against others because of a cognitive belief and affective attitude. Several theories of discrimination relate to (1) situational pressures (a person does not associate with people of color because of peer reaction); (2) group gains (competition for scarce resources and ethnocentrism result in ethnic domination and

subordination); and (3) institutional discrimination in employment, education, housing, and other life-sustaining areas. Discriminatory acts are likely to occur under the following conditions (Bonacich & Goodman, 1972):

1. Biologically, culturally, and socially distinct populations are present in a social system.
2. A segment of the population is threatened by another over competition for scarce resources.
3. A group is seen to be the common enemy of other groups, an enemy that unifies the other groups.
4. There are unequal degrees of power in populations.
5. Institutional discriminatory actions are legitimated in social structures and cultural beliefs.

Discriminatory behavior leads to denial of equal educational, economic, and political opportunities. It holds African Americans and other people of color back and contributes to inequality of employment and income. Discriminatory behavior represents a failure in relationships between minority and majority populations who do not recognize that they are interdependent on each other's welfare. In addition, it permits injustice to fester and erupt in race riots and other expressions of rebellion (Willie, 1981).

In Cultural Study 7-6 De Hoyos, De Hoyos, and Anderson (1986) share a poignant case in which discrimination occurred because of an ethnic individual's exceptional efficiency. This case shows how discrimination leads to sociocultural dislocation, which in turn results in social isolation.

CULTURAL STUDY 7-6

Employment Discrimination

Minority group members have only one basic institution based on their own values: the family. If they want to share in the social rewards available in their society (that is, money, status, recognition, and so on), they must take on that society's conditionally rewarding roles. Such roles, however, are rewarded for conforming to middle-class values, which are, to whatever degree, foreign to minority persons.

This problem is well illustrated by the experience of a young American Indian, just out of college in the early 1970s, who was hired by an industrial firm. The young man described the nature of his work in the competitive and busy world of business and industry as follows: "I go to my office every morning and find on my desk a number of papers that I must process. I typically finish by noon. So, some time in the afternoon, I take a book out and start reading." Needless to say, this intelligent young man is no longer in industry; he was eased out. Eventually, he returned to school and gained a higher degree. Now he holds a less competitive professional job on one of the Indian reservations.

Minority problems start when racial and/or ethnic discrimination closes the opportunity structure of society. When this occurs, social dislocation takes place. If this dislocation were temporary, it would not be so dysfunctional. However, when the opportunity structure remains closed for several generations, cultural dislocation takes place—the minority group members involved may be out of step with both their former culture and the majority group culture. When the opportunity structure finally allows them access, sociocultural dislocation takes place—they are blocked, unable to function in the mainstream of society.

From "Sociocultural Dislocation: Beyond the Dual Perspective" by G. De Hoyos, A. De Hoyos, and C. B. Anderson. In *Social Work, 31*, 64. Copyright © 1986 the National Association of Social Workers. Reprinted by permission.

We have briefly defined and described the essential characteristics of racism, prejudice, and discrimination. A thorough knowledge of the interaction between, and dynamics of, racism, prejudice, and discrimination is necessary to understand many of the psychosocial problems that people of color face in the United States. Racism can be viewed as an ideological belief that leads to prejudice. Prejudice is a negative social attitude toward a group of people, most often ethnic and other disadvantaged groups. In turn, prejudice leads to discrimination, which is manifested in unfavorable behavioral actions that relegate people of color to subordinate positions.

Expressions: Oppression, Powerlessness, Exploitation, Acculturation, and Stereotyping. Problems that can be traced to racism, prejudice, and discrimination find expression in five forms: oppression, powerlessness, exploitation, acculturation, and stereotyping (Figure 7-2).

Oppression. Turner, Singleton, and Musiek (1984) observe that oppression occurs when a segment of the population, systematically and over a prolonged period, prevents another segment from attaining access to scarce and valued resources. Oppression is a process and a structure: It is a process whereby specific acts are designed to place others in the lower ranks of society; it is also a structure that creates a bottom rank in a hierarchical system of ranks. In multicultural practice, clients' problems are usually not due entirely to personal deficiency; they are often personal reactions to oppressive social institutions. These extrapsychic problems are oppressive environ-

FIGURE 7-2 *Multicultural Problem Typology*

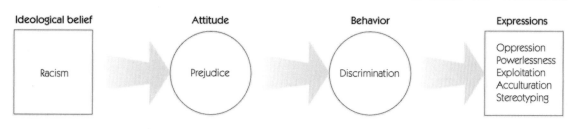

mental forces that trigger a reaction in the client (Leigh & Green, 1982). Group oppression is understood as the misuse of a group or class to perform the labor necessary to run society and the exclusion of the people who belong to that group or class from decision making that affects the course and direction of society (Leigh, 1984).

McMahon and Allen-Meares (1992) analyzed 117 articles on the four major ethnic groups published between 1980 and 1989 in four major social work journals (*Social Work, Social Casework, Social Service Review,* and *Child Welfare*) and drew four conclusions:

1. Much of the social work literature is naive, in that it decontextualizes clients, removing them from the racist context in which they live.

2. Remedies include awareness change in social workers, view of minority oppression as normal and natural, cultural awareness validation of the status quo.

3. The articles emphasize individual adaptation or resignation to oppression.

4. The articles endorse a status quo practice stance that adversely affects people of color.

The authors urge social workers to take nonracist transformative action to remove oppressive conditions; to shift social work practice to social activism and social change by working for racial equality and social justice; and to take an organized, advocative, proactive, and antiracist stance.

In Cultural Study 7-7, Song (1987) addresses gender oppression—specifically, the oppression of battered Korean women in immigrant families. This type of cultural oppression is rooted in certain husband-wife role expectations and behavior patterns.

CULTURAL STUDY 7-7

Gender Oppression

The battering of women, like other crimes of violence against women, has been justified in the context of Korean culture. A traditional Korean saying . . . that "the real taste of dried fish and women can only be derived from beating them once every three days" has been often quoted as a rationale for "beating" women, thus justifying the violent act as a means of improving her behavior. It perpetuates the notion that a man should beat a woman when she does something that makes him angry. In other words, the oppressed Korean woman's acknowledgment of her oppression would be a negation of her only source of pride, namely, to serve man as a "wise" mother and "good wife." A Korean woman who is repeatedly abused by her husband accepts this and considers it her personal shame and misfortune. She fails to see any relationship between these actions and the question of equality between the sexes.

Lee (1977) believes that Korean women developed an ability to absorb insults and injuries without protest and to assume responsibilities for others' faults; in contrast, Korean men were incapable of bearing responsibility for their own actions, always seeking to blame others.

From Y. I. Song, *Silent Victims: Battered Women in Korean Immigrant Families,* p. 16. Copyright © 1987 Oxford University Press. Reprinted by permission.

Powerlessness. Powerlessness is the inability to control self and others, to alter problem situations, or reduce environmental distress (Leigh, 1984). Solomon (1976b) explains that powerlessness arises out of a process that denies valued identities and roles, as well as valuable resources, to individuals or groups. As a result, these individuals or groups are unable to exercise interpersonal influence or to command the social resources necessary for effective social functioning. Solomon argues that powerlessness is also a problem for dominant-group members who must cope with interpersonal relationships, deficiencies in material resources, and life situations that assault their self-image. Pinderhughes (1989) defines powerlessness as individuals' inability to exert a positive influence on the forces that affect their life. Powerlessness in turn creates victimization.

In Cultural Study 7-8, Nguyen (1992) describes a form of cultural powerlessness. In cultures having strong family hierarchies, societal expectations regarding the parent-child relationship may generate unique feelings of powerlessness.

Cultural Powerlessness

Feelings of powerlessness and helplessness—not uncommonly found in children of any culture—seem to be inherent in the child's status itself, which subjects the child to a more or less strict submission to parental dominance. The Vietnamese and Chinese (and other Asians with a Confucian heritage) carry these feelings well into adulthood because of the early internalization of cultural ethics of a lifelong, unquestioned obedience to the absolute authority of the parents (Slote, 1972, 1986). Such feelings combined with narcissistic vulnerability may explain the similar attributes and attitudes that Asian and white children bring into therapy. Indeed, the transcultural literature reports that adult Asian American patients display high emotional inhibition and low verbal expressiveness; they demonstrate a propensity for somatizing or acting out their feelings rather than talking them out; more often than not, they are brought to the therapist against their will and are loaded with self-blame for having brought shame to their families. Because of a lifelong dependence on parents' approval, they feel awkward if not totally confused at being forced to discuss their most private feelings with a total stranger. This awkwardness can be easily transformed into a frightening sense of disloyalty, if the feelings happen to be negative feelings, such as anger, directed at family members or parents. In my view, these so-called "deficiencies," ascribed uniquely to adult Asian American patients, are in fact common occurrences in white as well as Asian American child-patients.

From "Living between Two Cultures: Treating First-Generation Asian Americans"' by N. A. Nguyen. In L. A. Vargas & J. D. Koss-Chiono (Eds.), *Working with Culture: Psychotherapeutic Interventions with Ethnic Minority Children and Adolescents*, pp. 209–210. Copyright © 1992 Jossey-Bass, San Francisco. Reprinted by permission.

Powerlessness stems in part from the relationship between the individual and oppressive social institutions. Solomon (1976a) has written about the African American experience in terms of powerlessness as a state of being and about the need for practical ways to experience empowerment. People of color often feel impotent. Underrepresented, outvoted, and manipulated, members of the different ethnic groups—social work professionals and clients alike—identify with similar experiences. Clients often feel at a loss about what to do. How does one cope with feelings of powerlessness, which are so overwhelming and devastating to a person of color? Solomon (1983) traces the vicious cycle of powerlessness as it affects African Americans. The cycle begins with racism, discrimination, and negative valuation. Because of white society's label of inferiority, African Americans are prevented from developing a positive self-concept or cognitive skills. In turn, African Americans are unable to develop interpersonal or technical skills, and their effectiveness to perform social roles is reduced. Finally, these shortcomings confirm and reinforce feelings of inferiority and negative value, and the vicious cycle begins again.

An example of oppression and powerlessness was the reaction to the influx of Vietnamese refugees into the United States at the end of the Vietnam War in the mid-1970s. Remarks by public officials and public fear of competition for jobs were almost identical to the oppression responses that Asian immigrants suffered at the turn of the twentieth century. Likewise, Southeast Asian newcomers in the 1970s were virtually powerless politically, economically, and socially when they entered the United States. They depended on the goodwill of churches and private sponsors. Cultural Study 7-9 illustrates the themes of oppression and powerlessness on the macrolevel (Tayabos & Pok, 1981).

Oppression and Powerlessness

The initial reaction of the American public to the admittance of the Southeast Asian refugees was essentially negative. Opinions were harsh and unfavorable. Indeed, a Gallup poll conducted in 1975 found that 54 percent of the American public were against admitting the refugees and only 36 percent were favorable. Former Representative Burt Talcott (R[republican], Calif.) said, "Damn it, we have too many Orientals already. If they all gravitate to California, the tax and welfare rolls will get overburdened and we already have our share of illegal aliens" (Liu, 1979, p. 63). Negative reactions were not only expressed in California. Senator George McGovern was quoted as saying "Ninety percent of the Vietnamese refugees would be better off going back to their own land" *(Time, May 19, 1975, p. 9)*.

In spite of all the negative reactions President Ford stood firm and reassured the public that "the people that we are welcoming today, the individuals who are in Guam or in Camp Pendleton or Eglin Air Force Base, are individuals who can contribute significantly to our society in the future" (Remark to the Advisory Committee on Refugees, May 13, 1975). President Ford was angry at widespread opposition because "we are a country built by immigrants . . . and we have always been a humanitarian nation" *(U.S. News and World Report,* May 19, 1975, p. 1). Various voluntary organizations (such as the Red Cross, International Rescue Committee), major American companies (for example, IBM), unions (for example, AFL-CIO), newspapers and magazines *(Time, Newsweek,* etc.) all endorsed Ford's stand on resettlement.

For many reasons the American public's reaction persisted even into the arrival of the second wave. The Southeast Asian refugees came at a time when the American public wanted to forget Vietnam, when interest was receding from social concern and social action efforts, and when the U.S. economy was at a low ebb (Liu, 1979).

The major argument against accepting the refugees centered around the American's fear of job displacement. It was argued that resettlement en masse in certain areas such as New York, Southern California, or Texas would unduly strain the employment markets. This meant resettlement could prove to be an economic threat.

From "The Arrival of the Southeast Asian Refugees in America: An Overview," by T. Tayabas and T. Pok. In R. F. Morales (Ed.), *Bridging Cultures: Southeast Asian Refugees in America,* pp. 7–8. Copyright © 1981 Special Service for Groups and the Asian American Community Mental Health Training Center. Reprinted by permission.

In the later 1990s Americans seemed almost helpless as a series of African American churches were torched by perpetrators of racial hate crimes in the United States. Many church burnings resulted in the arrest and conviction of local persons who harbored racial vendettas but many have been unsolved. Many elderly immigrants and refugees who held legal status in the United States but who were not citizens were helpless and suffered depression and suicide when certain benefits were threatened as a result of welfare reform. Many vulnerable people of color groups have experienced learned oppression and powerlessness in the face of external events and policies over which they have no control.

Exploitation. Exploitation occurs when a person of color is manipulated or used unfairly in an economic, political, or social situation for the benefit of the dominant society. Historically, people of color were exploited economically as cheap labor in agriculture and sweatshops. Most African Americans entered the United States as slave laborers in the rural South. Today poor Mexicans are migrant farm workers in agricultural fields of the western United States. Asians were imported to work on the transcontinental railroad and in agriculture at the turn of the twentieth century. Native Americans were the victims of political genocide, which forced them from their native lands across the United States and onto reservations. As a result, Native Americans have the highest rates of unemployment, illiteracy, alcoholism, and suicide of all ethnic groups in the country. Politically, both major parties have wooed African Americans and Latinos as a means of gaining their votes and appearing nonracist.

In Cultural Study 7-10, the exploitation takes the form of the appointment of a token person of color to a social service position. This incident took place in England but is similar to those that occur regularly in the United States. Exploitation occurs when an agency's intent to project a favorable image of affirmative action compels an individual to compromise his or her own integrity for the sake of the organization (Liverpool, 1982).

From "The Dilemmas and Contribution of Black Social Workers," by V. Liverpool. In J. Cheetham (Ed.), *Social Work and Ethnicity*, pp. 224–225. Copyright © 1982 Allen and Unwin, Inc. Reprinted by permission.

CULTURAL STUDY 7-10

Exploitation

The black social worker who is a victim of organisational prejudice may find that he is expected to conform to the organisation's stereotype of a "good black social worker." As one of the few black workers employed by the organisation, he may be expected to behave in an appreciative manner, serving as a symbol of the organisation's good record in race relations. When I was appointed to my first social work job, I wondered how easily I was accepted. A few months later, I was at a cocktail party for the department where I heard the clerk to the council discussing racial prejudice in the borough. When I responded unfavourably I was promptly reminded by her that if the borough was prejudiced they would not have employed me. She was in fact one of the interviewers at my job. The "good black social worker" is one who colludes with the organisation's view of its record in race relations.

The black social worker may also be made to feel he is different from other black people or that he is a "superior coloured." As a result he may feel obliged to collude with the organisation's stereotype of other blacks. Paradoxically, the "good black social worker," though viewed differently from other black people, may also fall victim to the way his organisation categorises them. Thus he may be expected not to be assertive or self-conscious. If he is he may be labelled as pushy, aggressive and over-sensitive. In other words he must be the "good black who knows his place." Similarly he may be judged according to the image created by the previous black worker or other blacks at present in the organisation, and their record of satisfying its expectations. If he does not react like some of his other black colleagues who fit the role of the "smiling nigger" he may be perceived as being anti-social, unfriendly and even anti-white. His individuality is lost.

Acculturation. *Acculturation* is an ethnic person's adoption of the dominant culture in which he or she is immersed. There are several degrees of acculturation; a person can maintain his or her own traditional cultural beliefs, values, and customs from the country of origin to a greater or a lesser extent. The term *Americanization* has been associated with the popular notion that people living in the United States gave up former cultural practices and adopted the American way of life.

Bogardus (1949) has identified three types of overlapping acculturation. *Accidental acculturation* occurs when individuals of various cultures in close proximity to each other exchange goods and services and incidentally adopt cultural patterns from each other in a hit-or-miss fashion. For example, people from two cultural groups that settle next to each other might shop in each other's stores, eat in each other's restaurants, and intermingle with each other at school. In the process, these people can influence each other to the degree that they acquire certain cultural practices that serve a functional purpose (for example, food dishes or cultural beliefs from the other group).

Forced acculturation imposes cultural patterns, behavior, or beliefs on ethnic populations and immigrants. The dominant cultural group tends to believe that their own beliefs, behavior patterns, and customs are superior to other cultural systems, which are less desirable. An example of forced acculturation is the strong pressure toward Americanization, which stresses the exclusive use of English, the relinquishment of foreign ideas and customs, and the adoption of certain forms of Christianity.

Democratic acculturation respects the history and strengths of differing cultures and demonstrates the equivalency of social and psychological patterns of all cultures. People from a particular culture are not forced to accept cultural patterns different from their own. Rather, they can choose either to adopt cultural patterns of other groups over time or to retain the patterns of their culture of origin. The prevailing approach to democratic acculturation is *cultural pluralism*, which recognizes the reality of a multicultural society and the individual's ability to construct a combination of cultural patterns.

Acculturation is not a continuum for those born in America, although for foreign-born there is a continuum of change and adjustment between the culture of origin and the dominant culture. Trimble (1996) explains the dynamics of acculturation:

> Not every individual from his or her culture will respond to the elements presented by the dominant culture. Individual variations in the adaptation, adjustment, and internalization of another culture's folkways and mores can be mediated by resistance, fear, anxiety, allegiance to one's own culture, and the level of perceived acceptance in one's own and the dominant culture. Moreover, an individual may make specific accommodations in certain settings and situations and in others cling to and maintain behaviors that are traditional and conventional in the individual's own culture. As a consequence, one's adjustments and accommodations, combined with the rejection of acceptable behavioral patterns, generates a good deal of variation in acculturative styles. (pp. 41–42)

In short, acculturation is very idiosyncratic according to the orientation of a particular individual.

Often a person moves between the culture of origin and the dominant culture, depending on the degree to which a person must interact with both. For example, a newcomer from the People's Republic of China who is unable to speak English and has no formal college education may be able to acculturate to an existence in San Francisco Chinatown without much acculturation stress. The person may be able to speak the language, get a job in a Chinese restaurant, and rent an apartment nearby in a residential part of Chinatown. A recent immigrant from Russia may have a difficult time settling in West Sacramento even though a Russian community of several hundred families is located there. However, because there are no Russian-owned businesses, the Russian person must learn English, interact with American employers, and find housing and a job in the gen-

eral community. The degree of acculturation from Russia to the United States with a large population to absorb that person places more demands for adjustment.

Trimble (1996) identifies a number of sociocultural and behavioral issues related to acculturation. Adaptation or adjustment to another cultural lifestyle brings about significant changes for some and little change for others. There is variation in acculturative stress or psychic difficulties in relation to changes in cultural surroundings, either by an individual's entry into a new culture or by the encroachment of a new culture or an already existing culture. Individual and family functioning also vary, although the younger the family member, the less difficulty one will experience. When acculturation produces confusion and duress, counseling is sought to focus on security and safety, integration of self and family, and future identity. Acculturating groups can adapt successfully to new environments in terms of intercultural effectiveness.

The person who acculturates may go through extreme changes depending on the extent to which his or her culture of origin is different from the dominant American culture. Persons acculturate in varying degrees to their own and other cultures.

Even when a second- or third-generation American-born person moves from one section of the country to another part, regional acculturation adjustment takes place. Acculturation to another culture does not require that a person be less acculturated to their own culture, although there is the process of enculturation that takes place to varying degrees. Enculturation involves the selective adaptation of one's culture based on functional pragmatism (what is functional and useful to keep and adopt or integrate into the dominant culture). There is a conscious choice to retain the essence of one's culture and to set aside aspects of culture that are not functional for the person. Enculturation is a development process of adopting to the prevailing cultural patterns of one's society.

Stereotyping. *Stereotyping* is the prejudicial attitude of a person or group that superimposes on all members of a race, sex, or religion a generalization about behavioral characteristics. For people of color, negative stereotyping has centered around skin color, low mentality, welfare freeloading, job competition, and pathological behavior. Stereotyping occurs in the context of racism as a means of explaining away ethnic populations as inferior or defective. It reflects the degree to which a dominant race views itself as superior to other ethnic groups in a pluralistic society.

Axelson (1985) describes stereotyping as a circular, self-reinforcing process in which a general mental picture is applied to an individual on the basis of a negative judgment of a group. Another formulation is that the dynamics of stereotyping ascribes to a single individual the characteristics associated with a particular group or extend to a group the characteristics attributed to a single individual. The stereotype generally represents a negative judgment of both the group and the individual and emphasizes negative differences (Axelson, 1985).

According to Draguns (1996), stereotyping is primarily a cognitive operation in which the perception of a person in an out-group is simplified and a set of exaggerated, unrealistic, or distorted characteristics are assigned to the person on the basis of minimal evidence. Stereotyping results in cognitive parsimony and reduced sensitivity and ability to perceive another person in a differentiated and individualized fashion.

Gonzales (1993) identifies five major characteristics of stereotyping:

1. Stereotyping is self-fulfilling in the way that it predicts the lives of some ethnic groups and allows limited lifestyle options. The social structure imposes these restrictions, locking particular ethnic populations into a monotonous, impoverished existence.

2. Stereotyping is based on selective perception. Once a mind-set about a particular group has been established, a search ensues for characteristics that will confirm the initial stereotype.

3. Stereotypes are often negative and support prejudicial attitudes about certain racial groups.

4. Stereotypes result in rejection and social isolation; the dominant group cuts off contact with the targeted individuals.

5. Stereotyping is based on an isolated characteristic of a group, which may or may not be true but is nevertheless generalized to all members of the group, without any supporting evidence.

Negative stereotypes of Native Americans persist in the media and in medical-health treatment, despite growing admiration for Native American culture and its value of harmony with nature. Cultural Study 7-11 addresses the stereotyping of Native Americans on the macrolevel and suggests the potential for alleviating hopelessness on the microlevel by the use of cultural rituals and support with individual clients (Hanson, 1978).

CULTURAL STUDY 7-11

Macrolevel Stereotyping

Tribal affiliation is the Native American's most basic identification. The tribal teachings and experiences determine to a great extent the personality, values, and life goals of the individual, including the meaning of death and customs surrounding the burial of the dead. Because of extreme forms of discrimination toward Indians in certain parts of the country, many Indians have denied their tribal affiliation in fear of losing their lives or suffering physical harm.

The attitude of American society towards Native Americans is a strangely ambivalent one. The popular holistic health movement with its emphasis on the harmony of body, mind, and spirit embraces to a great extent the worldview of Native Americans, with their emphasis on the natural harmony of all living things. Native American speakers have been invited to holistic health seminars to share their philosophy on many occasions. Native American art and jewelry have never been more popular. People everywhere seem to be wearing turquoise rings, bracelets, and necklaces handcrafted by Indian silversmiths. Indian symbols and designs are found on the wallpaper, bedspreads, and rugs of plush Fifth Avenue apartments. Indian-designed sweaters are seen from coast to coast. It would appear that the Indian culture is to be admired and embraced.

The Hernández Family, a Case Study

The problems facing the Hernández family are interwoven with their socioeconomic situation as people of color. The struggle to survive in a metropolitan area with immigrant relatives and family obligations affects the entire family. High unemployment compounds the existing stressful situation. Myers (1982) observes that current economic conditions influence the degree to which race and social class are a source of stress for people of color. Stress is magnified under conditions of poverty by recession and limited social supports. Race becomes the determining factor in the struggle. It is mediated by economics and social conditions and determines relative group status and power.

People of color, particularly new immigrants, have suffered under the present economic recession. At the same time, many white blue-collar and middle-class workers have lost their jobs and are now unemployed. The powerless ethnic family struggles to survive in an oppressive system that discriminates between the needy and the truly needy. In cases such as that of the Hernández family, Carrillo (1982) states, socioeconomic changes affect family structure. The Latino family in the United States has its roots in migration. One reason for geographic migration is the pursuit of educational achievements, job opportunities, and personal relationships. These new goals, which bring many immigrant families to the United States, require the family to restructure, reintegrate, and realign itself systematically to meet the needs of its members. The Hernández family is an example of those whose transition process following migration has been complicated by socioeconomic conditions.

TASK RECOMMENDATIONS

In this section on problem themes, we have discussed oppression, powerlessness, exploitation, acculturation, and stereotyping, from the perspective that external, oppressive social institutions adversely affect the ethnic client. The following exercises are helpful in exploring these issues:

- Identify current examples of oppression, powerlessness, exploitation, acculturation, and stereotyping that affect people of color on macro, meso, and micro levels. In the boxes of Table 7-1, write examples of these themes as they occur on all three levels. Brainstorm to bring as many incidents as possible to mind.

- Discuss present social, economic, and political conditions that are adverse to people of color.

- Outline positive strategies to cope with present forms of oppression, powerlessness, exploitation, acculturation, and stereotyping that affect ethnic clients.

On the other hand, social scientists, television, and the film industry portray a drunken Indian, suicidal and hopeless. Native Americans are either to be glorified and idealized as having mystical wisdom or ridiculed and stigmatized as being the shame of society. Mental health practitioners need to understand the self-image predicament Native Americans find themselves in when reacting to these extremely positive or negative stereotypes. The Indian client desires to be seen as a human being, with feelings of pride in his heritage and a desire for others to respect his beliefs and cultural traditions.

Negative stereotypes of Native Americans contribute to false impressions of behavioral adjustment (Shore, 1974). One commonly held assumption is that Indians as a group have many psychiatric problems and there is no hope for them (Beiser, 1974). After working with Native Americans of over a hundred tribes in the San Francisco Bay Area, I can recall a dramatic example of a young Hopi man experiencing auditory

The Hernández Family, a Case Study

For the Hernández family, problem details consist of three interrelated issues: (1) the recent arrival from Mexico of two immigrant families and the inability of the heads of those households to find steady employment; (2) the physical fatigue and emotional stress experienced by Mr. Hernández, who feels obliged to help these families and works at two jobs for extra income; and (3) the academic and social problems of Ricardo, the eldest child, which have prompted referral by the school to the Family Service Association. The social casework task is to decide which problems can be broken down into specific components that are amenable to solution. Making adequate resources for job finding available to the two immigrant families would eliminate the necessity of

Mr. Hernández's working at two jobs. He would then have time to spend with his son Ricardo. Which problem has a workable solution with reasonable closure? How can the social worker assist the family? How can Mr. Hernández facilitate employment for his in-laws? What natural ethnic community support systems are available?

TASK RECOMMENDATIONS

For purposes of problem detailing, it is important to obtain enough information about the problems and to identify a specific problem whose solution is feasible. Some aspects of problem detailing particularly relevant to multicultural practice include: facilitating problem information and understanding language analogies, selecting the

problems to be solved, and encouraging the client to make decisions. Try the following exercises:

- Discuss whether enough details of the Hernández family's problems have been given. What information is missing from the case study? Are there sufficient details to identify a workable solution to the problem?
- Select a focal problem area: unemployment problems of recent immigrant families, Mr. Hernández's job stress, Ricardo's school problems. What is your rationale for selecting one of these areas?
- How can the social worker assist the Hernández family and allow Mr. Hernández to carry the momentum?

---

hallucinations after a family death. The local psychiatric emergency ward erroneously interpreted the hallucination as a psychotic symptom rather than part of the symptom complex associated with unresolved grief. Our agency intervened and this man was returned to the reservation to participate in a series of rituals and tribal ceremonies appropriate for the burial of the dead. Shortly after the ceremony he was free from the hallucinations. This man could have been hospitalized in a state mental hospital as a psychotic patient if Native American mental health personnel had not intervened on his behalf. In most instances practices that are difficult to understand are usually interpreted as indicators of psychopathology by the dominant society. There are other examples of a

blending of healing and worship in the literature for the improvement of mental health as opposed to a diagnoses of pathology and long term treatment (Bergman, 1973).

From "Grief Counseling with Native Americans," by W. Hanson. In *White Cloud Journal, 1*, 20. Copyright © 1978 University of South Dakota. Reprinted by permission.

The emphasis on external forces is not to be construed as an excuse for avoiding individual responsibility and assertiveness. Rather, it is an opportunity to challenge and change the nature of oppressive social institutions (Solomon, 1983). The client cannot blame the system for his or her problems. To do so would be to surrender responsibility for mobilization and action. Focusing on the root causes of the problem provides an opportunity for the client, as a consumer, and the social worker, as a professional advocate, to correct discrimination.

Problem Area Detailing

Problem area detailing focuses on particular aspects of the client's problem. Bloom and Fischer (1982) discuss problem specification. The first step in specifying or detailing a particular problem is to conduct a survey of the problems or people posing the most difficulty to the client—whether an individual or a group. The next step is to select a specific problem about which the client is concerned. The problem selected then is defined in observable, clear, and quantifiable terms. However, covert problem details can surface under culturally understood conditions. Social workers should be aware of cultural dynamics that influence problem detailing.

During the 1970s and 1980s, large numbers of refugees and immigrants entered the United States. The majority of these people of color arrived from Cuba, Southeast Asia (Vietnam, Cambodia, and Laos), Korea, the Philippines, Thailand, India, and Pakistan. These patterns of immigration have produced reactions among several groups: the refugees themselves, who have experienced cultural readjustment; governmental and social service agencies, who have prepared for the transition; and the American public, who have expressed mixed feelings about the influx of immigrants. Brown (1982) has identified numerous problems that Indochinese refugees face: emotional responses to separation, such as guilt and a sense of obligation, as well as the problem of misapprehension; symptoms of vocational transition, such as frustration and violence; and intergenerational conflict, including acculturation of the young. Brown states:

> The loss of reference group, the destruction of vocational and social roles, and the drastic reorganization of family roles necessitated by survival considerations combine to create a threatening new world within which the refugees must begin the

painful process of defending and redefining the self. Immersed in a foreign culture and language, refugees are deprived of the feedback processes that normally help to guide role performance. (p. 159)

Timberlake and Cook (1984) suggest that Vietnamese refugees are likely to experience psychosocial dysfunction if they cannot make sense of the contradictions between the habits and beliefs of their old, familiar culture and those of the new culture of pluralistic America. Problems become manifest in confusion of thought, affect, and behavior, as well as in somatic and affective symptoms of depression.

Kitano (1969) reports that Japanese American clients cite parent-child difficulties, marital problems, intergenerational stresses, and problems of ethnic identity as central concerns. Yet Kitano asserts that mental health professionals are not meeting client needs in those areas. Some of the reasons for that lack of congruity between the client and the helping professional in multicultural practice are culturally motivated attempts to hide problem behavior, differing cultural styles of expressing problems, inappropriate service delivery, and lack of relevant connections to the therapeutic community. Human service helpers must be sensitive to the indirect expression of problem details. With some Asian Americans, the worker might have difficulty obtaining any details of a problem. For those clients, admitting a problem constitutes a lack of self-control, determination, and willpower and exposes a family defect (Ho, 1976). African Americans sometimes express problem details by analogy. Solomon (1983) explains:

> Thus, feelings of depression may be described as "I feel like I do not have a real friend in the world" rather than "I have feelings of intense loneliness." This tendency of a client to give examples of his or her experience of a problem rather than to isolate and analyze specific factors is often considered reflective of a lack of insight or ability to abstract when it maybe a style of communication instead. (p. 419)

Social workers should be ready to piece together and interpret details or cues interwoven in a conversation.

TABLE 7-1 *Problem Levels and Themes*

	Oppression	Powerlessness	Exploitation	Acculturation	Stereotyping
Macrolevel (complex organizations, geographical populations)					
Mesolevel (ethnic/local communities and organizations)					
Microlevel (individual, family, small group)					

Boyd (1982) suggests that many ethnic families present a variety of socioeconomic problems related to the welfare system, housing, child welfare, schools, courts, churches, police departments, and other institutions. From the multiplicity of problems, it is important to pick out one that can be solved within a reasonable time frame. Problem detailing involves determining who is involved, what the major issues are, and when and where the problem dynamics take place. Cultural dimensions of the problem are included among the problem details.

by analogy or other indirect means. Social workers should be attuned to the various styles in which problems are communicated and be willing to piece together details interwoven in the conversation. It is important to reiterate and confirm the problem details with the client. Social work educators and practitioners must examine how they conceptualize, teach, and implement problem formulation with students and clients. In multicultural practice, an alternative set of problem identification principles must be used.

CONCLUSION

In multicultural practice, relationship building is a prerequisite to problem formulation. Problem identification focuses on environmental and societal conditions that affect the client. Problem disclosure may be delayed as the client evaluates the social worker's character and style. Problem themes include racism, prejudice, and discrimination, which are expressed through oppression, powerlessness, exploitation, acculturation, and stereotyping. Problem detailing can be expressed

REFERENCES

Amir, Y. (1969). Contact hypothesis in ethnic relations. *Psychological Bulletin, 71,* 319–342.

Axelson, J. A. (1985). *Counseling and development in a multicultural society.* Pacific Grove, CA: Brooks/Cole.

Beiser, M. (1974). Indian mental health. *Psychiatric Annals, 4,* 6–8.

Bergman, R. L. (1973). Navajo medicine and psychoanalysis. *Human Behavior, 2,* 9–15.

Bloom, M., & Fischer, J. (1982). *Evaluating practice: Guidelines for the accountable professional.* Upper Saddle River, NJ: Prentice-Hall.

Bogardus, E. S. (1949). Cultural pluralism and acculturation. *Sociology and Social Research, 34*, 125–129.

Bonacich, E., & Goodman, R. F. (1972). *Deadlock in school desegregation: A case study of Inglewood, California.* New York: Praeger.

Boyd, N. (1982). Family therapy with black families. In E. E. Jones & S. J. Korchin (Eds.), *Minority mental health* (pp. 227–249). New York: Praeger.

Brislin, R. W. (1981). *Cross-cultural encounters: Face-to-face interaction.* New York: Pergamon.

Brown, G. (1982). Issues in the resettlement of Indochinese refugees. *Social Casework, 63*, 155–159.

Bryson, S., & Bardo, H. (1975). Race and the counseling process: An overview. *Journal of Non-White Concerns in Personnel and Guidance, 4*, 5–15.

Carrillo, C. (1982). Changing norms of Hispanic families: Implications for treatment. In E. E. Jones & S. J. Korchin (Eds.), *Minority mental health* (pp. 250–266). New York: Praeger.

David, K. H. (1976). The use of social learning theory in preventing intercultural adjustment problems. In P. Pedersen, W. J. Lonner, & J. G. Draguns (Eds.), *Counseling across cultures* (pp. 123–138). Honolulu: University of Hawaii Press.

Davis, F. J. (1978). *Minority-dominant relations. A sociological analysis.* Arlington Heights, IL: AHM.

De Hoyos, G., De Hoyos, A., & Anderson, C. B. (1986). Sociocultural dislocation: Beyond the dual perspective. *Social Work, 31*, 61–67.

Devore, W., & Schlesinger, E. G. (1981). *Ethnic-sensitive social work practice.* St. Louis: Mosby.

Draguns, J. G. (1996). Humanly universal and culturally distinctive: Charting the course of cultural counseling. In P. B. Pedersen, J. G. Draguns, W. J. Lonner, & J. E. Trimble (Eds.) *Counseling across cultures* (pp. 1–20). Thousand Oaks, CA: Sage.

Ghali, S. B. (1977). Culture sensitivity and the Puerto Rican client. *Social Casework, 58*, 459–468.

Gonzales, J. L., Jr. (1993). *Racial and ethnic groups in America.* Dubuque, IA: Kendall/Hunt.

Green, J. W. (1982). *Cultural awareness in the human services.* Upper Saddle River, NJ: Prentice-Hall.

Hanson, W. (1978). Grief counseling with Native Americans. *White Cloud Journal, 1*, 14–26.

Hepworth, D. H., & Larsen, J. A. (1993). *Direct social work practice: Theory and skills.* Pacific Grove, CA: Brooks/Cole.

Ho, M. K. (1976). Social work with Asian Americans. *Social Casework, 57*, 195–201.

Hodge, J. L. (1975). Domination and the will in Western thought and culture. In J. L. Hodge, D. K. Struckmann, & L. D. Trost (Eds.), *Cultural bases of racism and group oppression* (pp. 9–48). Berkeley, CA: Two Riders.

Ishisaka, H. A., Nguyen, Q. T., & Okimoto, J. T. (1985). The role of culture in the mental health treatment of Indochinese refugees. In T. C. Owan (Ed.), *Southeast Asian mental health: Treatment, prevention services, training, and research* (pp. 41–63). Washington, DC: National Institute of Mental Health.

Ivey, A. E. (1994). *Intentional interviewing and counseling. Facilitating client development in a multicultural society.* Pacific Grove, CA. Brooks/Cole.

Jenkins, S. (1981). *The ethnic dilemma in social services.* New York: Free Press.

Kitano, H. H. L. (1969). Japanese-American mental illness. In S. Plog & R. Edgarton (Eds.), *Changing perspectives in mental illness* (pp. 257–284). New York: Holt, Rinehart & Winston.

Kuramoto, F. H., Morales, R. F., Muñoz, F. U., & Murase, K. (1983). Education for social work practice in Asian and Pacific American communities. In J. C. Chunn II, P. J. Dunston, & F. Ross-Sheriff (Eds.), *Mental health and people of color: Curriculum development and change* (pp. 127–155). Washington, DC: Howard University Press.

Lee, I. (1977). Women's liberation in Korea. *Korea Journal, 17*, 4–11.

Leigh, J. W. (1984). *Empowerment strategies for work with multi-ethnic populations.* Paper presented at the Council on Social Work Education Annual Program Meeting, Detroit, MI.

Leigh, J. W., & Green, J. W. (1982). The structure of the black community: The knowledge base for social services. In J. W. Green (Ed.), *Cultural awareness in the human services* (pp. 94–121). Upper Saddle River, NJ: Prentice-Hall.

Lewis, R. G., & Ho, M. K. (1975). Social work with Native Americans. *Social Work, 20*(5), 379–382.

Liu, W. T. (1979). *Transition to nowhere: Vietnamese refugees in America.* Nashville, TN: Charter House.

Liverpool, V. (1982). The dilemmas and contribution of black social workers. In J. Cheetham (Ed.), *Social work and ethnicity* (pp. 224–231). London: Allen & Unwin.

McConahay, J. B., & Hough, J. C., Jr. (1976). Symbolic racism. *Journal of Social Issues, 32*, 23–45.

McLemore, S. D. (1983). *Racial and ethnic relations in America.* Boston: Allyn & Bacon.

McMahon, A., & Allen-Meares, P. (1992). Is social work racist? A content analysis of recent literature. *Social Work, 37*, 533–539.

Meadow, A. (1983). Psychopathology, psychotherapy and the Mexican-American patient. In E. E. Jones &

S. J. Korchin (Eds.), *Minority mental health* (pp. 331–361). New York: Praeger.

Morales, A., & Salcido, R. (1983). Social work with Mexican Americans. In A. Morales & B. W. Sheafor (Eds.), *Social work: A profession of many faces* (pp. 389–413). Boston: Allyn & Bacon.

Myers, H. F. (1982). Stress, ethnicity, and social class: A model for research with black populations. In E. E. Jones & S. J. Korchin (Eds.), *Minority mental health* (pp. 118–148). New York: Praeger.

Nguyen, N. A. (1992). Living between two cultures: Treating first-generation Asian Americans. In L. A. Vargas & J. D. Koss-Chiono (Eds.), *Working with culture: Psychotherapeutic interventions with ethnic minority children and adolescents* (pp. 204–222). San Francisco: Jossey-Bass.

Northen, H. (1982). *Clinical social work.* New York: Columbia University Press.

Pinderhughes, E. (1989). *Understanding race, ethnicity, and power: The key to efficacy in clinical practice.* New York: Free Press.

Ravitch, D. (1990, December 2). Academe's ethnocentric true believers. *Sacramento Bee,* Forum 1-2.

Reid, W. J. (1978). *The task-centered system.* New York: Columbia University Press.

Sena-Rivera, J. (1980). La Familia Hispana as a natural support system: Strategies for prevention in mental health. In R. Valle & W. Vega (Eds.), *Hispanic natural support systems: Mental health promotion perspectives* (pp. 75–81). Sacramento: State of California Department of Mental Health.

Sherover-Marcuse, R. (n.d.). *A working definition of racism.* Unpublished manuscript.

Shore, J. H. (1974). Psychiatric epidemiology among American Indians. *Psychiatric Annals, 4,* 56–64.

Slote, W. H. (1972). Psychodynamic structures in Vietnamese personality. In W. P. Lebra (Ed.), *Transcultural research in mental health.* Honolulu: University Press of Hawaii.

Slote, W. H. (1986). The intrapsychic locus of power and personal determination in a Confucian society: The case of Vietnam. In W. H. Slote (Ed.), *The psycho-cultural dynamics of the Confucian family: Past and present.* International cultural society of Korea (ICSK) forum series no. 8. Seoul: International Cultural Society of Korea.

Smith, E. J. (1981). Cultural and historical perspectives in counseling blacks. In D. W. Sue (Ed.), *Counseling the culturally different. Theory and practice* (pp. 141–185). New York: Wiley.

Solomon, B. B. (1976a). *Black empowerment. Social work in oppressed communities.* New York: Columbia University Press.

Solomon, B. B. (1976b). Social work in a multiethnic society. In M. Sotomayor (Ed.), *Cross-cultural perspectives in social work practice and education* (pp. 165–177). Houston, TX: University of Houston Graduate School of Social Work.

Solomon, B. B. (1983). Social work with Afro-Americans. In A. Morales & B. W. Sheafor (Eds.), *Social work: A profession of many faces* (pp. 415–436). Boston: Allyn & Bacon.

Song, Y. I. (1987). *Silent victims: Battered women in Korean immigrant families.* San Francisco: Oxford.

Sue, D. W. (1981). *Counseling the culturally different. Theory and practice.* New York: Wiley.

Sue, S., Ito, J., & Bradshaw, C. (1982). Ethnic minority research: Trends and directions. In E. E. Jones & S. J. Korchin (Eds.), *Minority mental health* (pp. 37–58). New York: Praeger.

Sue, S., & Morishima, J. K. (1982). *The mental health of Asian Americans.* San Francisco: Jossey-Bass.

Tayabas, T., & Pok, T. (1981). Arrival of the Southeast Asian refugees in America: An overview. In R. F. Morales (Ed.), *Bridging cultures: Southeast Asian refugees in America* (pp. 3–14). Los Angeles: Special Service for Groups.

Timberlake, E. M., & Cook, K. O. (1984). Social work and the Vietnamese refugee. *Social Work, 29,* 108–113.

Trimble, J. E. (1996). Acculturation, ethnic identification, and the evaluation process. In A. H. Bayer, F. L. Brisbane, & A. Ramirez (Eds.), *Advanced methodological issues in culturally competent evaluation for substance abuse prevention* (pp. 13–61). Rockville, MD: U.S. Department of Health and Human Services, Substance Abuse and Mental Health Services Administration.

Tucker, R. N., & Gunnings, T. S. (1974). Counseling black youth: A quest for legitimacy. *Journal of Non-White Concerns, 2,* 208–217.

Turner, J. H., Singleton, R., Jr., & Musiek, D. (1984). *Oppression: A socio-history of black-white relations in America.* Chicago: Nelson-Hall.

Vega, W. (1980). Mental health research and North American Hispanic populations: A review and critique of the literature and a proposed research strategy. In R. Valle & W. Vega (Eds.), *Hispanic natural support systems: Mental health promotion perspectives* (pp. 3–14). Sacramento: State of California Department of Mental Health.

Willie, C. V. (1981). *A new look at black families.* Bayside, NY: General Hall.

CHAPTER 8

Assessment

Assessment often means a detailed analysis of the psychopathology of a client in the psychiatric understanding of the term. However, this chapter takes the position that there is an asset value in the assessment process stage. Social work assessment is more and more drawn toward the strengths perspective of highlighting those assets or elements of worth and value in the person, his or her culture, and the surrounding environment. There is also a move in this chapter to extend assessment beyond the biopsychosocial aspects of traditional social work assessment. We identify culturally diverse assessment in terms of six entities: the biological-physical, the psychological, the social, the cultural, the gender, and the spiritual.

Assessment, in social work practice, is an in-depth investigation of the psychosocial dynamics that affect the client and the client's environment. It analyzes the forces between the client and the situational configuration, with particular focus on the environmental impact on the client and the resources available for responding to the problem. In multicultural practice, assessment identifies positive cultural strengths in the client's ethnic background. It moves away from a pathological investigation, which tends to evaluate internal and external liabilities. Reflecting on the history of the helping professions, Dieppa (1983) notes:

Knowledge from sociology, psychology, and social work has been used to explicate the ethos of ethnic and racial minorities within an ethnopathological framework. Sociocultural and psychological theoretical analyses have frequently placed causative factors and solutions within the context of the individual and familial psyche. Why has a profession that views life, behavior, and social problems within the context of an ecological or systems theory (which should include culture as a significant element) focused its goals, priorities, and resources on a "mental health solution" to the problems of oppressed populations? (p. 120)

Ethnic-oriented assessment should strive for a psychosocial balance between objective external factors in the community and subjective internal reactions. Ethnic beliefs, family solidarity, community support networks, and other cultural assets are intervening variables.

The social work profession has taken into account that certain environmental stressors are associated with institutionally caused powerlessness. Institutional policies that have a negative impact on people of color include the lack of national commitment to their civil rights and social well-being and deep federal budget cuts, which impede social service delivery. Further, social work should recognize the cultural assets implicit in ethnic community support systems and incorporate knowledge of collective cultural strengths into its assessment base.

As Sue and Sue (1990) note:

> In a society where individualism prevails, it is not surprising to find that White counselors tend to view their client's problems as residing within the individual rather than society. Thus, the role of the counselor will be person focused because the problem resides within the individual. Skills utilized will be individual centered (attending) aimed at changing the person. Many minorities accept the importance of individual contributions to the problem, but they also give great weight to system or societal factors that may adversely impact their lives. Minorities who have been the victims of discrimination and oppression perceive that the problem resides externally to the person (societal forces). Active systems intervention is called for, and the most appropriate way to attack the environment (stressors) would be an active approach. If the counselor shares their perception, he or she may take a more active role in the sessions, giving advice and suggestions, as well as teaching strategies (becoming a partner to the client).[*]

This chapter focuses on the psychosocial aspects of socioenvironmental impacts on clients' psychoindividual—internal cognitive, affective, and behavioral—reactions. My contention is that the client interacts with and reacts to the social environment within an ethnic context. Environmental forces interact with societal and ethnic factors; the client draws on familiar ethnic coping mechanisms when confronted with these forces. In turn, the social worker should be aware of the client's unique psychosocial action and reaction. Our task is to identify the assessment factors that influence the client and the worker, who must frame the psychosocial situation, note unique assessment dynamics, and formulate an assessment evaluation.

As Figure 8-1 illustrates, client-system practice issues are understood in terms of socioenvironmental impacts that result in psychoindividual

reactions. Worker-system practice issues relate to the analysis of assessment dynamics and the formulation of an assessment evaluation.

CLIENT-SYSTEM PRACTICE ISSUES

Socioenvironmental Impacts

In the previous chapter, we sought to identify a particular set of problems affecting the person of color. In assessment we investigate the scope of socioenvironmental impacts and their effect on the client. Romero (1983) asserts, for example:

> It is the belief of this author that the majority of mental health problems exhibited by Chicanos are not pathological. Rather, they result from a combination of socioeconomic stresses that are compounded by poverty, racism, oppression, lack of access to educational and legal systems and institutions as well as to health care, and the experience of acculturation and culture shock. (p. 91)

Harwood (1981) makes the point that, in many ethnic groups, illness is understood to involve both interpersonal and environmental factors:

> The cultural traditions of most ethnic groups tend to view illness episodes in both a psychosomatic and an ecological framework. That is, in many ethnic subcultures both psychological stresses, worry, and strained interpersonal relations, on the one hand, and unfavorable environmental and living conditions, on the other, figure importantly among the multiple etiological factors that are used to interpret and understand illness. (p. 23)

Moreover, ethnic groups believe that psychological states—such as stress, worry, and grief—and situational factors—such as poor housing, loss of work, and family disputes—cause or contribute to disease. Likewise, their perception of illness is based on the duration, location, and intensity of symptoms and the extent to which the symptoms interfere with valued social activities or the fulfillment of role responsibilities (Harwood, 1981). It follows naturally that social work should focus on removing specific symptoms and helping the client gradually resume normal social activities and roles.

---

[*]From *Counseling the Culturally Different: Theory and Practice*, by D. W. Sue and D. Sue, p. 72. Copyright © 1990 John Wiley and Sons. Reprinted by permission.

FIGURE 8-1 *Assessment Stage: Client-System and Worker-System Practice Issues*

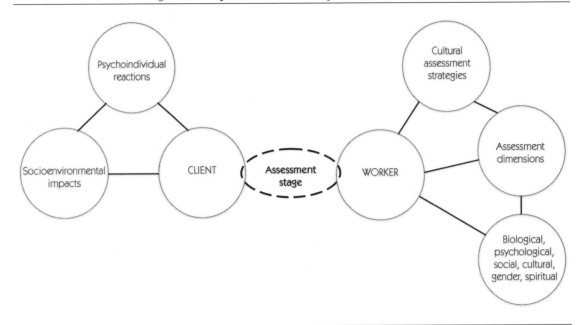

Kim (1981) presents an assessment that encompasses five major problem areas: newcomer survival, psychosomatic illness, psychological identity, mental illness, and problems of the elderly. Kim then groups several related problem clusters under each heading, as follows.[*]

1. *Newcomer syndrome (basic survival issues)*
   food, housing
   Job/welfare
   Culture shock/culture dislocation
   Language barrier
   Transportation
   Legal/immigration problems
   School for children

2. *Psychosomatic syndromes*
   Anxiety/depression
   Headache/back pain/shoulder pain

[*]Adapted from a lecture titled "Minority Assessment," Dr. Luke Kim, presented at California State University, Sacramento, Division of Social Work, Spring 1981. Used with permission.

Hypertension/gastrointestinal disturbance
Loneliness/isolation/alienation
Insomnia/weight loss/no energy

3. *Psychological/identity issues (second and third generations)*
   Ethnic identity confusion, conflict, ambivalence
   Self-hatred/negative identification/rebellion
   Cultural value conflict
   Family role conflict/husband-wife role conflict
   Women's liberation/emancipation/sexuality/ divorce
   Dating/mate selection/intermarriage
   Parent-child conflict
   Youth delinquency/gang/rebellion

4. *Major mental illness (acute, chronic psychosis, affective disorder)*
   Inadequate treatment in public, private facilities (few bilingual staff members)
   Stigma of mental illness
   Family rejection
   Lack of support system

5. Elderly problems
　Isolation/despair
　Confusion
　Disorientation

These five problem clusters form one dimension of Kim's (1981) model. The other two dimensions are temporal factors and acculturation.

The resulting model is geared toward mental health assessment with Asian American clients. However, it can be applied to other groups whose psychological, social, and cultural problems are affected by time factors (that is, length of stay and generational differences) and acculturation (that is, movement from native culture to Americanization).

Many socioeconomic impacts can be characterized in terms of these variables. For example, after living in the United States only briefly, a newcomer may struggle with survival problems such as culture shock, language barriers, and unemployment, which exacerbate acculturation problems in the critical initial period. For second-generation individuals, we might anticipate psychological/identity problems, such as ethnic identity confusion, value conflict, and issues raised by women's liberation. Temporal factors could involve first-generation parents and second-generation children. Acculturation tends to steer the children toward Western attitudes and behavior, while parents oppose total acculturation. Kim's model offers a helpful framework for assessment with certain groups of clients.

To conclude our consideration of socioenvironmental impacts, we discuss survival issues and environmental conflict.

Survival. Socioeconomic survival means maintaining basic necessities: food, shelter, clothing, and financial resources. These concrete survival needs may force the client to seek social services. Crucial client needs include adequate nutrition, housing, child care, health care, recreational activities, clean air, and police and fire protection. Myers (1982) identifies three environmental variables that influence survival stress:

1. The present social and economic conditions

2. The relevant racial and social class dynamics, which influence both exposure to stress and the contingencies governing options for coping with stress
3. The availability and accessibility of resources and support

These variables are particularly critical for immigrants. Although immigrants must have a sponsor who ensures employment and housing, newcomers are confronted with basic survival needs. American society and lifestyle are outside the experience of many immigrants, especially those who come from a non-English-speaking country and are accustomed to a rural environment. Newcomers undergo an initial period—commonly called *culture shock*—of stressful adjustment to unfamiliar culture. The immigrant must overcome the language barrier and learn alternative cognitive expressions. Finding reasonable housing, adequate employment, transportation, and school for the children are also hurdles of the transition period.

Language plays an important part in socioeconomic achievement. Monolingual minority clients without a command of English may be restricted to their own ethnic neighborhoods (such as Chinatowns or barrios). These people are able to express themselves in their native language, but their English is faulty and halting. Language restrictions curb mobility, produce social uncertainty, and limit employment opportunities. The result may be role and socioeconomic reversal for the immigrant, who cannot attain the social prestige and economic status he or she formerly enjoyed. The Vietnamese physician, the Filipino lawyer, and the Mexican schoolteacher must work toward state licensure and fulfill educational requirements in this country. Because of language difficulties, professional requirements, and field practicum, these professionals may need several years to obtain American credentials. Basic survival needs are a central reality for newcomers who have been economically displaced through loss of status, differences in professional credentials, and language problems.

To a large extent, socioeconomic survival depends on the state of the economy and public policy. Beginning in the 1980s, an economic recession, a tight federal budget, and a politically conservative administration have resulted in cutbacks in human services, political rhetoric about the truly needy, and subtle racial discrimination. The locus of problem assessment should be shifted from the individual to social recognition that people of color are placed in disadvantaged situations (Jackson, 1973). Jones and Seagull (1977) speak of survival:

> The therapist owes it to the client to deal with these more immediate real-life problems, either directly or through referral, before dealing with intrapsychic issues. In the statement, "I'll talk about my father if you want me to, but you have to know that there's no food to feed my kids tonight," lies a real dilemma. (p. 854)

Socioeconomic survival is a primary area of impact for assessment in multicultural practice.

Environmental Conflict. Issues of environmental conflict, another area of socioenvironmental impact, influence identity ambivalence and resolution. To what extent has a minority client resolved ethnic identity conflicts? Atkinson, Morten, and Sue (1979) offer a developmental model that traces the stages of conformity (preference for dominant cultural values), dissonance (cultural confusion and conflict), resistance and immersion (endorsement of ethnic community viewpoints and rejection of dominant society and culture), introspection (individual autonomy), and synergetic articulation and awareness (cultural self-fulfillment). Cultural conflict is expressed in ethnic religious values, family roles, loss of face, self-hatred, negative identity, and marginality. It is important to assess the points of conflict, the degree to which the client has acquired the internal skills and knowledge necessary to achieve a well-balanced minority identity, and family and kinship group resources.

Issues of environmental conflict tend to surface in second and third generations of immigrant families, who rediscover their ethnic roots and heritage in the midst of life crisis. They experience the tension of living in two cultures: American individuality, freedom of choice, and self-determinism, on the one hand, and collective decision making, family obligation, and self-restraint on the other. These two polarities produce a unique identity conflict between the personalities of parents and children, peers, and social-cultural values.

In Cultural Study 8-1, Ruiz and Padilla (1977) illustrate the dilemmas of ethnic identity conflict and their effects on a young Latino woman in her late adolescence who is struggling with an identity crisis. Geographic readjustment, the beginning of college, and the need for a support group have caused the client to question her past upbringing in light of a new situation confronting her.

CULTURAL STUDY 8-1

Ethnic Identity Conflict

This client identifies herself as "Spanish-American." Her ancestors have resided in Northern New Mexico under conditions of relative sociocultural isolation for generations. She is fluent in both Spanish and English, but her Spanish retains regional archaisms unfamiliar to other Latinos and her English is slightly accented. Her politics are conservative. She was educated in a Roman Catholic school system, is committed to the dicta of her faith, and was reared in the large extended family structure that is traditional in that region.

Maria's life adjustment was uneventful until she left home for the first time and enrolled in a California college. There she was shocked by her encounter with Chicanos and Chicanas who were personally assertive, less inhibited in personal decorum, and more liberal politically. She could not deal with the rejection and disdain she experienced when she identified herself as "Spanish," rather than Chicana. This is her opening statement when she sought counseling:

Moving away from home had a great psychological impact on me and my ideals. I had some difficulty adjusting myself to a completely new and independent form of life. Being Spanish-American, I was always closely bound to the family. When I tried to deviate from the norm, I was reprimanded and reminded of the obligation I had to the family. Living away from home taught me to appreciate them (family) and their conservative values more than I had before . . . but we sure are different from the people in California.

The brief history and presenting complaint identify Maria as a Latina whose sub-cultural identification is Hispano. Our comments on Latino ethno-history, as well as the client's own opening comments, confirm the contention of differences across Latino subculture groups. Maria voices awareness that she is "different from the people (Chicanos) in California," and we agree. Furthermore, we argue that Maria would become aware of other subculture group differences if her encounter had been with Puerto Ricans (or Cubans, or other Latinos), rather than California Chicanos.

With regard to degree of acculturation, Maria seems basically bicultural. Available history indicates she is a bilingual who is equally familiar with the values and traditions of both the majority culture and the Latino culture. Examining her personal value system stemming from identification with her Hispano subculture, she seems less assimilated into the Chicano subculture attending California colleges, than to the majority culture in some ways. This is an important point, expanded further in our discussion of sources of stress and recommendations for counseling.

Examining intra-psychic sources of stress first, Maria's major problem seems to be she is a college freshman away from home for the first time. Like other young people in a similar situation (regardless of ethnicity), Maria is almost certainly homesick and lonely. She probably misses friends, relatives, and familiar places. Her opening statement refers to problems in "adjusting." Her ability to tolerate and lessen distress is lowered because of her absence from familiar support systems (home, family, and church), while in a new, taxing, demanding, different, and frightening environment. At a less obvious level of analysis, there are hints that Maria is experiencing an identity crisis. She is clearly uncertain of subculture group identification as reflected by questions such as, "Am I Spanish as we call ourselves within the family, or Chicana as my new friends insist?" Maria has noted that fellow students are more assertive, striving, and goal-oriented; now she is beginning

to wonder if perhaps she would get more of what she wanted out of life if she were less passive. For example, feminism and the Chicano movement intrigue Maria, but the people involved seem "pushy" to her in many ways. And at a more personal and intimate level, Maria is beginning to question her traditional conservatism and her decorous sexual mores.

With regard to extra-psychic sources of stress, Maria denies any major hassles with the dominant culture. While she is subjected to the same general level of prejudice and discrimination that other Latinos are, it seems neither personal [n]or excessive at this time. Note, however, the anomalous situation with regard to her treatment by Chicanos and Chicanas. The Chicano student community rejects Maria because her self-designated "Spanishness" is misperceived as an attempt to deny her "Mexicanness."

How does the counselor respond to this complex of problems, and in what priority? We shall outline a culturally relevant treatment program but encourage the reader to anticipate our recommendations and to amplify upon them as he or she goes along. First, it seems to us the problem of priority is Maria's sense of personal isolation. We would recommend a supportive approach to minimize this intra-psychic source of stress. Although unstated, Maria is almost certainly experiencing dysphoric affect, probably depression ranging somewhere between mild to moderate degrees of severity. An initial approach that works well with problems of this sort is to minimize any tendencies toward apathy and social withdrawal by encouraging interpersonal interaction. Specifically, Maria, like any young person with depressive tendencies, should be encouraged to date, to go to parties, to mix with people her own age and so on. Simultaneously, Maria's major assets should be identified and reflected back to her, repeatedly if necessary, to enhance self-esteem. For example, if she is doing well academically she should be reminded of her intellectual assets: her bright mind, her good study habits, her perseverance, and so on. This supportive approach of confronting Maria with positive aspects of her life adjustment will tend to retard movement in the direction of increased depression.

A problem of second-order priority for Maria is her estrangement from the local Chicano student community. This is particularly lamentable for Maria because this group represents a "natural" but underutilized resource to combat what has been termed Maria's "first problem": her combined sense of low self-esteem, loneliness, mild depression, and isolation. Maria is a Chicana in more ways than she is not; and mutual realization of this aspect of her identity will facilitate Maria's admission into the Chicano group; in turn, it can provide her with much needed emotional support.

One reason Maria and the Chicano group have failed to achieve harmonious rapprochement may be a mutual misjudgment of how each perceives the other. It is conceivable that Maria is unaware that Chicanos perceive Mexican Americans who call themselves "Spanish" as denying their heritage; and some of the Chicanos may not know that Mexican Americans from Northern New Mexico refer to themselves in that manner with no connotation of deliberate efforts to "pass" from one ethnic group to another. Reconciliation may be achieved if both parties become more familiar with their own ethno-history. While this goal could be attained by the counselor bringing this issue to the attention of the ethnic studies department, if one exists, and having them plan a course or lecture on ethno-history, we propose an alternative course. We recommend Maria be informed of the possible source of the mutual misunderstanding discussed here, and that she be encouraged to confront those Chicanos who have been scornful. This approach has several advantages; Maria will be required to become more assertive; her approach behavior toward others will counteract her withdrawal tendencies; and everyone involved examines the problem from a fresh perspective.

The third problem for Maria is her blurred, changing, and developing sense of personal identity. She seems to be going through a psychological growth phase that involves questioning life values, but this process is evaluated by us as "normal" or "healthy" (Wrenn & Ruiz, 1970). She is not exactly certain "who she is" as yet, but continued self-exploration should be encouraged by her counselor because enhanced self-awareness will minimize subjective discomfort and expedite self actualization. The counselor maintains the responsibility, of course, for determining whether this third general recommendation is appropriate for Maria; and if so, of selecting the technique and methods thought to be maximally growth inducing for this client.

From "Counseling Latinos," by R. A. Ruiz and A. M. Padilla. In *Personnel and Guidance Journal*, 55, 405, 406. Copyright © 1977 American Association for Counseling and Development. Reprinted by permission.

Psychoindividual Reactions

Coping Skills. Individuals react to environmental impacts in various ways; Myers (1982) identifies a number of cultural and psychological effects. Individual temperament and disposition determine the degree of stress tolerance. Previous problem-solving success or failure influences present coping efforts to analyze situations and to determine the best course of action. Successful coping with problems engenders efficiency and competence, whereas failure to handle difficulties results in impotence and helplessness. The client should be encouraged to differentiate failure for which he or she is responsible from that which is due to external factors. People of color may experience failure and frustration because of institutional systemic barriers. When they can recognize externally controlled failure, they reduce the amount of subjective stress, self-blame, and sense of worthlessness. The perceptive client distinguishes personal responsibility from oppression by the system.

Negative discrimination has stimulated the development of a strong collective identity, an extended family network, creative coping strategies, personal and collective resilience, and even physiological and genetic resistance to disease. Hobbs (1962) observes that people build cognitive "houses" to protect themselves from the incomprehensibilities of existence and to provide some examples for daily experience. These built-in forms of cultural protection often form the basis for multicultural coping skills. In the assessment process, the worker should try to elicit information to answer the following questions: Does the client have coping skills that contribute to survival? How has the client withstood the pressures, stresses, and strains of meeting life's needs? What resources have been available or are potentially present for assistance?

Psychosomatic Reactions. Psychosomatic symptoms represent a reaction to environmental stress. Many cultures teach individual self-control as a method of dealing with life's problems. Negative feelings are held within. Sue (1981) reports that restraint of strong feelings and the shame and disgrace of having psychological problems cause many Asian Americans to express their difficulties through physical complaints, which represent an acceptable means of manifesting problems. Chinese tend to somaticize their depressive reactions (Marsella, Kinzie, & Gordon, 1973); Chinese and Japanese students in a psychiatric population exhibited more somatic complaints than their control counterparts did (Sue & Sue, 1971). Psychosomatic illness is socially acceptable because the individual consults a physician rather than a mental health professional. In Native American culture, a physical, mental, or social illness is understood as a disharmony with other forces. Physical, psychological, and cultural realities are interrelated. The assessment task is to find the forces of disharmony that pervade life (Lewis & Ho, 1975; Stuckey, 1975).

Many cultures have acceptable ways of expressing psychosomatic symptoms related to life disharmony, interpersonal stress, and other malfunctions. For example, among Latinos, the *ataques* reaction, a form of hysteria characterized by hyperkinetic seizures, is a response to acute tension and anxiety. It is a culturally expected expression of extreme displeasure over a negative act. Its purpose is to control other family members, such as a teenage son who gets out of hand or a husband who is going out to drink. Physical symptoms include vomiting spells, convulsions, and extreme fatigue, which lead to medical intervention and hospitalization (Ghali, 1977). Among Asian Americans, a mother expresses her extreme displeasure over a son's stealing or a daughter's promiscuous behavior by lying on the floor and going into a

hysterical fit of crying and irrational shouting. The fit is a maternal expression of suffering and anger over the misbehavior of a child. In turn, other family members impose sanctions against the guilty member for upsetting the mother. Rather than concluding that the client or family member has gone into an acute schizophrenic reaction, the social worker should recognize that this psychosomatic expression is a cultural behavior.

Green (1982) describes categories of disease among Latinos as an imbalance between physical and social well-being. *Empacho, mal ojo,* and *susto* are three disruptions of balance. *Empacho* (indigestion) is a physiological condition in which food lodged on the side of the stomach causes stomach pains. The food forms into a ball that can be broken up and eliminated by back rubbing and using purgatives. *Mal ojo* (evil eye) is the result of imbalance in social relationships; the sufferer exhibits headaches, sleeplessness, drowsiness, restlessness, fever, and vomiting. *Mal ojo* is precipitated by the covetous glances, admiring attention, or interest of another person; the eyes of another initiate the condition. It is treated by praying, by gently rubbing the body with a whole egg, or by having the perpetrator touch the head of the afflicted, thus drawing off the threatening power of the relationship. *Susto* (fright) is the loss of spiritual essence through an upsetting experience. Symptoms include depression, lack of interest in living, introversion, and eating disruption. The cure is to coax the lost spirit back into the individual's body. Treatment consists of prayers, body massages, spilling cold water over the patient, and sweeping the body with small branches while talking the spirit back into the body. The ethnic community recognizes this cultural means of dealing with stress.

WORKER-SYSTEM PRACTICE ISSUES

Assessment and Cultural Strengths

The term *assessment* denotes appraisal of the value or worth of a person and situation. Assessment comes from the root *asset*, which is an item of value or a resource owned. The asset aspect of the strengths perspective is explained by Saleebey (1996):

The strengths perspective demands a different way of looking at individuals, families, and communities. All must be seen in the light of their capacities, talents, competencies, possibilities, visions, values, and hopes, however dashed and distorted these may have become through circumstances, oppression, and trauma. The strengths approach requires an accounting of what people know and what they can do, however inchoate that may sometimes seem. It requires composing a roster of resources existing within and around the individual, family, or community. (p. 297)

However, Cowger (1994) points out: "Much of the social work literature on practice with families continues to use treatment, dysfunction, and therapy metaphors and ignores work on family strengths developed in other disciplines. The assessment literature, including available assessment instruments, is overwhelmingly concerned with individual inadequacies" (p. 262).

Cultural strengths are relevant for assessment. Saleebey (1996) states:

Extremely important sources of strength are cultural and personal stories, narratives, and lore. Cultural approaches to healing may provide a source for the revival and renewal of energies and possibilities. Cultural accounts of origins, development, migrations, and survival may provide inspiration and meaning. . . .

The building blocks of meaning making are, for the most part, found in the edifice of culture. Culture provides the means by which people receive, organize, rationalize, and understand their experiences in the world. Central elements of the patterns woven by culture are story and narrative. Individuals impart, receive, or affirm meanings largely through telling and retelling stories and recounting narratives, the plots often laid out by culture. (pp. 299, 301)

In multicultural practice, assessment means the estimation or determination of the significance, importance, or value of resources. Weaver (1982) declares:

Search for strength relates to the social worker's emphasis on positive aspects of individual and fami-

ly systems. It is crucial to begin with strengths of the family system: families move on strengths, not weaknesses. There are inherent strengths in the design of every family; the social worker must help the family use their own strengths in making choices and decisions that will enable them to achieve their desired goal. This skill, as it relates to the search for and use of strength within the family system, has the potential for being very empowering. (p. 103)

Cultural assets may include personal or religious belief systems, survival skills, natural healing practices, community networks, and other elements that contribute to functional coping. Lee (1982) identifies several cultural assets:

Strengths such as support from extended family members and siblings, the strong sense of obligation, the strong focus on educational achievement, the work ethic, the high tolerance for loneliness and separation, and the loyalties of friends or between employer and employee should be respected and used effectively in the therapeutic process. (p. 547)

Hepworth and Larsen (1993) note the Hawaiian tradition of generous hospitality, the Native American philosophy of harmony with natural forces, cultural folkways and values, and rituals—religious, seasonal, holiday, work, or entertainment—that preserve family ties.

Clinical psychotherapy has misused assessment as an evaluation of pathological defects, particularly with people of color. However, if we apply the root meaning of the word, assessment connotes the investigation of positive strengths, healthy functioning, and support systems that can be mobilized for goal planning and problem solving. Assessment is the link between problem identification and intervention strategy.

Positive Strengths. Moving social work away from the language of pathology and deficit, Saleebey (1992) embraces a strengths perspective. In this approach, the social worker's role in assessment is to identify cultural strengths in the client's past heritage, present family structure, and future potential; to build on these cultural strengths to

The Hernández Family, a Case Study

The Hernández family's case can be seen as an example of the interaction of socioenvironmental impacts and psychoindividual reactions. Social work family assessment reveals socioeconomic survival issues. The arrival of in-laws from Mexico as recent immigrants to an uncertain economy has shifted the burden to Mr. Hernández. He is approaching a point of inability to cope with the demands of extra work. His family obligation is to ensure adequate support for the other two families until his two brothers-in-law can find steady employment. However, Mr. Hernández complains of fatigue and the long hours he spends working on two jobs.

A major task for the social worker is to assess the community resources potentially available for job hunts, school tutoring, English classes, and newcomer services. At the same time, relevant assessment areas, such as role identity and stress tolerance, are affecting the family.

TASK RECOMMENDATIONS

To investigate socioenvironmental impacts and psychoindividual reactions, conduct a detailed assessment of the Hernández family. Answer the following questions that relate to this case:

- What are the family's practical needs pertaining to food and shelter, employment, finances, and other problems of living?
- Does the client feel a sense of powerlessness due to lack of adequate resources?
- What institutional barriers are obstructing socioeconomic survival and coping abilities?
- What is the client's level of stress tolerance?
- Does the client possess any problem-solving skills that could be applied to the present situation?
- Can the client differentiate between failures for which he or she is responsible and those caused by institutional barriers?
- Have any somatic symptoms accompanied the personal or family problems?
- Has the client seen a physician or ethnic healer in the past three to six months?
- What natural family and community support systems are available to the client?

---

foster client and situational changes; to facilitate the change process as a collaborator or consultant; and to latch onto the positive elements in the situational environment.

Saleebey (1992) explains this strengths perspective in Cultural Study 8-2.

CULTURAL STUDY 8-2

The Strengths Perspective: An Overview

RESPECTING CLIENT STRENGTHS

Social work practice is guided first *and* foremost by a profound awareness of, and respect for, clients' positive attributes and abilities, talents and resources, desires and aspirations. Furthermore, the practitioner must be genuinely interested in, and respectful of, clients' accounts and narratives, the interpretive slants they take on their own lives. These are the most important "theories" that guide practice (Goldstein, 1986). The discovery of who clients are does not unfold as the result of a litany of troubles, snares, embarrassments, lacks, and barriers. The client is best known as someone who knows something, who has learned lessons from experience, who has ideas, who has energies of all kinds, and who can do some things quite well. These may be immanent as the client begins the process of transformation or regeneration, and may be obscured or suppressed by the stresses and confusions of the moment.

Clients want to know if you actually care about them, that how they do makes a real difference to you, that you will listen to them, that you will respect them no matter what their history, that you believe that they can build something of value on the resources they have within and around them, and that you believe they can surmount the assault on their functioning (Cousins, 1989).

CLIENTS HAVE MANY STRENGTHS

Individuals and groups have vast, often untapped and frequently unappreciated reservoirs of physical, emotional, cognitive, interpersonal, social, and spiritual energies, resources, and competencies. These are invaluable in constructing the possibility of change, transformation, and hope. It is clear that individuals sometimes do not define some of their attributes or experiences as resources. It is likewise true that individuals sometimes are unaware of some of their own strengths, that some of their knowledge, talents, and experiences can be used in the service of recovery and development—their own and that of others (Saleebey and Larson, 1980; Weick et al., 1989).

THE SOCIAL WORKER IS A COLLABORATOR WITH THE CLIENT

The role of "expert" or "professional" may not provide the best vantage point from which to appreciate client strengths. A helper may be best defined as collaborator or consultant; an individual presumed because of some specialized education, training, and experience to know some things, but definitely not the only one in the situation to have relevant, important, even esoteric knowledge. Clients are usually the experts on their own situation . . . and we make a serious mistake when we subjugate their knowledge to official views. There is something liberating about genuinely connecting with clients and their hopes, fears, stories; much more liberating, perhaps, than trying to stuff them into the narrow confines of a diagnosis or assessment category. As we have said, to appreciate the strengths of the individual is to begin to understand the uniqueness of that individual.

AVOIDING THE VICTIM MINDSET

Emphasizing and orienting the work of helping around clients' strengths can help to avoid "blaming the victim" (Ryan, 1976). Victim blaming assumes may guises, but the "art of savage discovery" is its enduring face and is supported by an unwavering, destructive logic: discover a social problem; set about (as researcher or practitioner, agency or academy) to determine how those who suffer from the problem differ from those who do not; and then demonstrate how these differences actually cause or perpetuate the problem (Ryan, 1976). Ultimately, we find the problem within the individual and ignore two critical factors: how elements of the environment eventually pervade individual identity and energy, and how the individual has managed to survive, perhaps thrive in, an oppressive, even catastrophic environment. In the strengths orientation we want to understand as best we can the first factor, but our work with the client begins with an appreciation and investigation of the second.

ANY ENVIRONMENT IS FULL OF RESOURCES

No matter how a harsh environment tests the mettle of inhabitants, it can also be understood as a lush topography of resources and possibilities. This seems to run counter to conventional social work wisdom (and public policy). However, in every environment there are individuals and institutions who have something to give, something that others may desperately need: knowledge, succor, an actual resource, or simply time and place. Usually these individuals and institutions exist outside the usual panoply of social and public services. And for the most part, they are untapped and unsolicited (Saleebey and Larson, 1980). Such a view of the environment does not abrogate the responsibility for working, as citizens and social workers, toward social justice, but recognizes that while we await the Godot of political transformation, there are reservoirs of energy, ideas, and tools out there we can draw on. To regard the environment as persistently and totally inimical moves us to ignore these resources or mistakenly to regard them as disreputable.

From "Introduction: Power in the People," by D. Saleebey. In D. Saleebey (Ed.), *The Strengths Perspective in Social Work Practice*, pp. 5–8. Copyright © 1992 Longman Publishing Group. Reprinted by permission.

Following up on Saleebey's work, Cowger (1992) operationalizes client strengths into five factors: cognition, emotion, motivation, coping, and interpersonal. Cowger identifies several strengths particularly relevant to multicultural practice, such as a cultural view of the world; a cultural and ethnical understanding of right and wrong; a degree of self-control; coping with stressful situations; self-improvement through education and the seeking of understanding; and making sacrifices. Cultural Study 8-3 summarizes Cowger's approach to the assessment of client strengths

CULTURAL STUDY 8-3

Assessment of Client Strengths

A. Cognition
1. Sees the world as most other people see it in her culture.
2. Has an understanding of right and wrong, from her cultural, ethical perspective.
3. Understands how one's own behavior affects others and how others affect her. Is insightful.
4. Is open to different ways of thinking about things.
5. Reasoning is easy to follow.
6. Considers and weighs alternatives in problem solving.

B. Emotion
1. Is in touch with feelings and is able to express them if encouraged.
2. Expresses love and concern for intimate others.
3. Demonstrates a degree of self control.
4. Can handle stressful situations reasonably well.
5. Is positive about life. Has hope.
6. Has a range of emotions.
7. Emotions are congruent with situations.

C. Motivation
1. When having problems, doesn't hide from, avoid, or deny them.
2. Willing to seek help and share problem situation with others he can trust.
3. Willing to accept responsibility for her own part or role in problem situations.
4. Wants to improve current and future situations.
5. Does not want to be dependent on others.
6. Seeks to improve self through further knowledge, education, and skills.

D. Coping
1. Persistent in handling family crises.
2. Is well organized.
3. Follows through on decisions.
4. Is resourceful and creative with limited resources.
5. Stands up for self rather than submitting to injustice.
6. Attempts to pay debts despite financial difficulty.
7. Prepares for and handles new situations well.
8. Has dealt successfully with related problems in the past.

E. Interpersonal
1. Has friends.
2. Seeks to understand friends, family members, and others.
3. Makes sacrifices for friends, family members, and others.
4. Performs social roles appropriately (e.g., parental, spouse, son or daughter, community).
5. Is outgoing and friendly.
6. Is truthful.
7. Is cooperative and flexible in relating to family and friends.
8. Is self-confident in relationships with others.
9. Shows warm acceptance of others.
10. Can accept loving and caring feelings from others.
11. Has sense of propriety, good manners.

12. Is a good listener.
13. Expresses self spontaneously.
14. Is patient.
15. Has realistic expectations in relationships with others.
16. Has a sense of humor.
17. Has sense of satisfaction in role performance with others.
18. Has ability to maintain own personal boundaries in relationships with others.
19. Demonstrates comfort in sexual role/identity.
20. Demonstrates ability to forgive.
21. Is generous with time and money.
22. Is verbally fluent.
23. Is ambitious and industrious.
24. Is resourceful.

From "Assessment of Client Strengths" by C. D. Cowger. In D. Saleebey (Ed.), *The Strengths Perspective in Social Work Practice*, pp. 144–146. Copyright © 1992 Longman Publishing Group. Reprinted by permission.

Parenting Strengths. An example of the strengths perspective is parenting strengths. In a Greensboro, North Carolina, study of fifty-three African American parents who were associated with the National Black Child Development Institute, Hurd, Moore, and Rogers (1995) reported the following parenting strengths:

Trends

• Substantial parental involvement in the lives of their children
• Plentiful support for parenting from external caregivers
• Considerable male involvement in the lives of African American children

Themes

• Connection with family
• Emphasis on achievement and effort
• Recognition of the importance of respect for others
• Cultivation of spirituality
• Ability to foster self-reliance
• Recognition of the importance of education

• Acceptance of life's pain and instruction in coping skills
• Recognition of the importance of self-respect and racial pride

Uncovering and nurturing parental-child strengths interaction among people of color families is a vital area for strengths assessment.

Saleebey's (1992) message is for social work education and social work practice to move away from a "deficit, problem-focused, or pathology orientation" and toward a strengths "orientation that appreciates and fosters the power within and around clients" (p. 178). Later he gives social work a perspective when he writes:

> The strengths perspective honors two things: the power of the self to heal and the need for an alliance with the hope that life might really be otherwise. Helpers must hear the individual, family, or community stories, but people can write the story of their near and far futures only if they know everything they need to know about their condition and circumstances. The job is to help individuals and groups develop the language, summon the resources, devise the plot, and manage the subjectivity of life in their world. In a strengths approach, how social workers encounter their fellow human beings is critical. They must engage individuals as equals. They must be willing to meet them eye to eye and to engage in dialogue and a mutual sharing of knowledge, tools, concerns, aspirations, and respect. The process of coming to know is a mutual and collaborative one. The individuals and groups the profession assists, also must be able to "name" their circumstances, their struggles, their experiences, themselves. Many alienated people have been named by others—labeled and diagnosed in a kind of total discourse. The power to name oneself and one's situation and condition is the beginning of real empowerment. (p. 303)

There is an existential I-thou relationship quality of self, strengths, and empowerment in this perspective.

Dimensions of Assessment

In social work practice, assessment has traditionally been concerned with the relationship between biological, psychological, and social dimensions of the person. This has been termed *biopsychosocial assessment*, to reflect the dynamic interaction among the physical, mental, and social dimensions of the person and the environment. In the last two decades, there has been considerable interest in the cultural dimension of the individual. Psychosocial assessment of people of color is concerned with identifying significant cultural characteristics of the individual and the ethnic community. There is also a growing literature on multicultural gender dimensions of assessment. Moreover, there has been a growing recognition that a person is body, mind, and spirit. Spirituality and spiritual resources may be incorporated as assessment themes. In what follows, we identify biological, psychological, social, cultural, gender, and spiritual assessment variables appropriate to culturally diverse social work practice.

Biological Assessment. Biological assessment is concerned with the person's physical characteristics and life processes; the Greek word *bios* means life. Physical health assessment deals with the physical processes affecting the person. Asian, Latino, and Native American cultures take for granted the interaction and interpenetration of the body, mind, and spirit; balance and harmony are regarded as essential to maintain physical health. The ancient Chinese philosophies of Confucianism and Taoism reflect these beliefs. Confucianism was founded on respect for the social order and reverence for antiquity, whereas Taoism focused on the desire for harmony with nature, longevity, and immortality. These philosophical principles guided the actions of the individual and prescribed how life ought to be lived.

In this discussion of biological assessment, we address cultural concepts of health, the gathering and use of health information, and the meaning of somatic symptoms. The worker must become sensitized to multicultural perspectives on health.

Concepts of Health. Many cultures embrace a holistic view of health, which stresses harmony and balance, with self, family, friends, neighbors, acquaintances, community, and universe. DuBray (1993) notes Native Americans' orientation toward harmony with nature and balance among the various aspects of the universe. Similar attitudes are reflected in the Asian American Confucian and Buddhist concept of interpersonal harmony (Uba, 1994); the Latino understanding of *respeto*, *familismo*, and *personalismo* (Paniagua, 1994); and African American kinship bonds of helping and cooperation in flexible family role relationships (Ho, 1987).

A holistic model of health is based on the integration of the physical, psychological, and spiritual aspects of personality. Individuals are engaged in an ongoing inner exploration to find the essential purpose of life. According to Native Americans, this search for the light within is guided by the Great Spirit (DuBray, 1993).

Health and healing encompass physiological, psychological, social, and cultural components. Warm acceptance by a significant other, nurturing food as a symbol of love and respect, and cultural healing ceremonies contribute to the client's natural healing process (DuBray, 1993).

The worker must learn to assess these holistic components of healing and health, along with the physical signs of health traditionally recognized by Western medicine.

Gathering and Using Health Information. For some people of color, asking detailed questions about their history of physical and mental illness is a social taboo. For example, Chinese do not like to talk about sickness, mental illness, or death. They believe the mere thought of these tragedies may become a reality, as if one wished misfortune on another. Moreover, the whole Chinese community might learn about mental illness in a family, and the family could be ostracized as a result. Many Chinese fear that their children will marry into such families and have abnormal offspring. It is best to ask about general health and to have the client sign a medical waiver for consultation with the family physician. Workers should avoid asking explicit questions about sexual behavior, such as frequency of intercourse, menstrual cycle, masturbation, and homosexual relations. Ethnic clients hesitate to answer these private questions, particularly when they have no bearing on the problem. The social worker should be discreet in sensitive areas and allow the client to bring up those matters.

The assessment of health should emphasize the positive. Sena-Rivera (1980) asserts that the Latino family is a vital cultural and societal force that enhances the mental health of its members. The worker should focus on family wellness and strengths rather than on the identification of pathology. Social work assessment should reflect these assets.

Somatic Symptoms. Some cultures internalize stress and tend to manifest physical problems rather than psychological ones. Taught to suppress negative feelings and reactions rather than openly ventilate them, Asian Americans tend to express their mental health problems as psychosomatic complaints—for example, headaches, backaches, digestive troubles, and peptic ulcers. This is rooted in cultural values such as respect for parental and other authority, maintenance of harmony, and cultivation of a pleasant disposition. Moreover, physical aches and pains are culturally acceptable expressions, whereas mental health problems are taboo areas that cast a social stigma on the family and may result in social ostracism from the local Asian community (Uba, 1994).

If Asian American clients report physical ailments, the practitioner should refer them to a physician for a thorough physical examination but also proceed with a gradual and sensitive investigation of negative feelings that have been festering inside the person.

Psychological Assessment. Psychological assessment deals with the mental processes of the person. The ancient meaning of the term *psyche* referred to the soul; in a sense, psychological concerns deal with the relationship between the mind and the soul—between the mental and the spiritual. From a culturally diverse perspective, psychological assessment addresses the client's level of motivation for change, the relationship of self and others, the influence of the family environment, and language fluency.

Psychological assessment does not focus on processes internalized within the individual, but rather on the relation between the person's men-

tal state and his or her behavioral interaction with significant others in the cultural community and the society as a whole. The mind and spirit are nurtured by the quality of relationships with other people. Psychological assessment cannot be confined within a mental disorder diagnostic category. It is addressing a life process of mind and spirit, which are characterized by growth and interaction.

Level of Motivation. *Motivation* refers to the momentum toward change, whereas *resistance* suggests an unwillingness to cooperate or participate in the process of growth. People of color may be involuntary clients who have been ordered by the court system or the social service agency to undergo counseling. It is important that the worker acknowledge the unwillingness and anger of the client or the family who is forced to attend sessions. The worker's task is to offer assistance and deal with the barrier. Asking open-ended questions that lead to acknowledgement of both parties' uneasiness, triggering negative feelings from the client, and agreeing on a reasonable course of action are important to the relationship.

The meaning of prolonged silence may be culturally determined. It may simply allow the client time to think through and meditate on the worker's words. Or it may signal resistance, confusion, and uncertainty as to what the worker means or wants from the client. Silence is productive and helpful at crucial turning points when the client is able to select a course of action. It is important to verbalize what has been happening during long periods of silence. Many African Americans are not willing to disclose problems and feelings until significant rapport and trust have been established. In the meantime, they remain silent, become placid, and answer briefly. Likewise, Asian Americans may remain silent, briefly verbalize the problem, and wait for the social worker to take the initiative in the relationship. This use of silence is not an example of a defense mechanism. Rather, it is a culturally distinct way of relating and responding.

Relationship of Self and Others. It is important to assess self-image in relationship to others.

Huang and Ying (1989) report that children of color often have negative self-images that result from ethnic related insults (teasing or derogatory comments). They experience racism, prejudice, and discrimination early in childhood. Parents must prepare their children for these harsh realities.

As a result, the child might feel self-conscious or unsatisfied with racial behavioral characteristics that do not fit American standards or expectations (Nagata, 1989). A child derives a positive self-concept and high self-esteem from parents, relatives, and peers in the ethnic community. It is important to assess whether an individual grew up with this support. Gibbs (1989) reports that young African Americans possess self-concepts and self-esteem as positive as, or more positive than, those of comparable samples of young whites. Athletic ability, verbal skills, assertiveness, fashionable dressing, physical attractiveness, and social skills are major sources of esteem for African American males and females. However, young African Americans with behavioral or psychological problems tend to have negative self-concepts and low self-esteem. These feelings stem from their perceptions of physical appearance, atypical family structures, lack of competence in cultural values, or racial victimization. Parental and peer reinforcement and contributions from the environment are crucial to the development of self-image.

Peer groups of the same sex exert a strong bonding influence to conform to group norms. They also serve as a source for social identity and mutual protection. Peer bonding can lead to intense conflict and rivalry, reduced autonomy, and involvement in antisocial activities.

Adolescence is a period in which individual self-image and peer influence encounter and influence each other. Adolescent relationships are forerunners to later relationships of social intimacy with the opposite sex, relationships with school and work colleagues, and friendships.

Robinson (1989) explores racial and social identity in terms of self and others as they pertain to the client, problem, and clinician. Cultural Study 8-4 explains the racial issues that the worker and client must address and assess.

CULTURAL STUDY 8-4

Racial Issues

Four issues may present significant impediments to achievement of treatment goals: (1) racial congruence of the client, (2) influence of race on the presenting problem, (3) the clinician's racial awareness, and (4) the clinician's strategies. The clinician has specific therapeutic tasks related to each issue. The client's racial congruence is the client's acceptance of group identity. The clinician must clarify the client's relationships with individuals and subgroups of the client's race and the client's own identity as a member of the group. For the issue of influence of race on the presenting problem, the clinician must assess the extent to which race is a factor in the problems presented by the client. The clinician must assess this influence both in the client's own perception and in the clinician's independent contextual understanding of the circumstances. For the therapist's racial awareness, the clinician must address the racial attitudes and beliefs that he or she is bringing to the treatment process professionally and personally. Finally, the clinician must master strategies for addressing the other three issues during the engagement process and in the pursuit of treatment goals.

The questions that follow can aid the clinician in eliciting information regarding race as a factor in the treatment process with black clients. These factors are an addendum to the customary theoretical framework that underlies the process of clinical assessment and treatment. The style and training of the clinician will determine the manner in which the data are collected. For example, a question such as, "What do you think causes you difficulty?" may elicit a direct statement about racial factors or may lead to hesitation, which suggests that the client is reluctant to state an opinion at that particular stage of the interview. The client may respond with a socially acceptable response, which suggests a lack of understanding that the clinician is referring to the possibility that racial factors affect the problem. A relatively common error for the clinician during the early stage of treatment is premature clinical anticipation of the direction or content of the client's response and, further, presentation of a suggestion in that direction. To avoid discomforting exposure of a racially based concern, the client may accept direction implied by the therapist's suggestion all too willingly. Discussion of racial factors thereby may be delayed or eliminated in the treatment process. Any information elicited can be used to indicate the extent to which a particular racial factor relates to the problem and requires direct exploration. The clinician may inquire whether the client perceives a connection between the experiences of racism and the presenting problem or may postulate such a connection after hearing details of the situation. Although all black clients and all therapists (regardless of race) are influenced by the racism prevalent in American society, Helms (1984) noted that many black people enter sociopsychological treatment without major concerns either about racism as a factor in their problems or about the race of the clinician as a potential deterrent to the success of treatment.

Another series of questions will allow the clinician to assess the extent to which race is a factor in the presenting problem, from the client's perspective and from the clinician's understanding of the context in which the problem occurs. This area is the one most often addressed in the literature regarding race and psychotherapy, possibly because it is the topic most likely to be initiated by the client (Bowles, 1978; Gardner, 1970). At issue is whether the clinician's contextual view of problems includes an acceptance of the fact of racism as an integral part of current social interaction between black people and white people. The questions proposed can organize the clinician's attention regarding the level of importance that racism has in the problems presented by a particular client and can help the clinician in determining appropriate interventions:

- Does the client make any statements that suggest a belief that race contributes significantly to the presenting problem?
- Given the context of the problem, is there evidence or reason to believe that racism places a constraint on the client's power to resolve the difficulty?

These questions require particular attentiveness on the part of the clinician, because the answers are so easily obscured by concrete data, the emotionality surrounding the problem, or the crisis aspect of the situation. The contextual reality of the client influences his or her real and potential power to intervene on his or her own behalf. The attitude of individuals in the client's environment may be masked, ambivalent, ambiguous, or open. Clinicians should be familiar with the social context in which the intervention will occur.

Whether the goals of intervention include change in behavioral patterns, intrapsychic restructuring, environmental change, or change in interpersonal relationships, the presence of racist behaviors may contribute to difficulty in problem resolution. This realization allows the clinician to help the client acknowledge the complexity of the situation and clearly delineate the goals of treatment and the potential impact of planned interventions. Initiating a frontal attack on racist policies or behaviors usually is not appropriate or effective. It is extremely important for the clinician to have some ideas regarding the racial factors influencing a problem and the attendant implications for the alternatives that the clinician considers as interventions. The clinician accrues this knowledge base as a result of an awareness of the community in which he or she practices. The clinician's affirmation of the contextual reality of the client tends to increase the intensity of the treatment alliance and the client's availability to consider his or her own contribution to problem maintenance.

Adapted from J. B. Robinson, "Clinical Treatment of Black Families: Issues and Strategies," *Social Work*, 34, 325, 326. Copyright © 1989 National Association of Social Workers. Reprinted by permission.

Family Environment. The worker should assess the structure and roles of the client's family. Does the client come from a nuclear, single-parent, blended, or extended family? Or are elements of several family structural types embedded in the family? Are the parents foreign born or American born? Does the family have a clear sense of parental authority and interdependence, a sense of democratic autonomy, or a mixture of both? Does the eldest child function as a parental child in the sense of having household and child care responsibilities? Are the parents recent immigrants or refugees who are adjusting to a new environment? Is there cultural and social conflict resulting from a difference in the value system of parents from the country of origin and that of their Americanized children? Is the communication pattern between parents and children direct or indirect? Often the mother of the family acts as a go-between and mediator for the father and children. She is invested with child care responsibilities, whereas he provides for and protects the family. What are the parents' occupations and income levels? Where and how does the family live?

These structure and role questions provide information needed to determine the client's past and present life development. For example, family composition indicates the degree to which the client has been able to obtain adequate nurturing. Setting aside whether the client comes from an intact, nuclear, two-parent family, the major issue that concerns the worker is whether the person has received sufficient parenting to function as an individual. Whether parents are foreign born or first-, second-, or third-generation American born can indicate the degree of autonomy versus conformity that the parents expect from their children. Parents who were raised in their country of origin and have language problems and job skill limits necessarily depend on their children to help them deal with the American system. Children of refugees and immigrants are placed in the position of the family's advocate in American society. Their task is to assist parents in learning the language, obtaining necessary job credentials, and securing stable employment. In turn, parents' achievement of this transition will relieve the pressure on the children and promote family harmony and balance.

Whether the family consists of recent refugees or American-born individuals who have vestiges of ethnic culture, family assessment can uncover the degree of family conflict and role expectations. Most ethnic families retain residual cultural

and ethnic values. A primary theme for these families is the children's individual independence and the parents' collective interdependence. That is, the degree of independence that American-born youths exhibit can influence children of color. This independence may contrast starkly with the ethnic family norms. The collective interdependence of the family requires the worker to obtain a sense of the interrelated linkages among parents, children, grandparents, relatives, and the extended family. In this type of family structure, the individuals base their action on its positive or negative effect on the family as a whole. In this sense, the family becomes a check and balance to the action of individual members. Rather than taking independent action on a major decision, an individual learns to consult the rest of the family for wisdom and guidance. It may take longer to reach a major decision, because parents, grandparents, and other elders must process information. However, in the long run, the practice of mutual consultation proves an adequate testing ground for ideas about how the family should proceed in a situation. Many ethnic cultures have a family hierarchy that is used for mutual aid and final approval. The worker must find out whether a particular client comes from such a family system.

Lee has suggested ten areas of family assessment that serve as guidelines for pursuing areas applicable to a particular client (see Table 8-1).

Language Fluency. The client or the client's family may be unable to speak English; this can make survival in the United States extremely difficult. Often, the problem centers around non-English-speaking parents and bilingual American-born children who must speak on their parents' behalf. It is crucial for agencies to provide bilingual and bicultural workers so that clients can express themselves in familiar, personalized native language. Zuñiga (1987) points out that the Spanish-speaking client can benefit from catharsis and abreaction when speaking his or her native language. Likewise, the Spanish-speaking worker can interject *dichos*, or cultural parables, to illuminate and support the flow of the therapy. Familiar idiomatic phrases enhance the client's feeling of being fully understood and contributes to the helping process.

TABLE 8-1 *Suggested Guidelines for Family Assessment*

Area of Assessment	Assessment Content
1. Family migration and relocation history	1. Premigration Migration experience Impact of migration on individual and family life cycle
2. Degree of loss and traumatic experience	2. Losses Significant family members, relatives, and friends Material losses Loss of community support Trauma Physical trauma Psychological trauma
3. Cultural shock and adjustment problems	3. Language, housing, transportation, employment, child care, racism, etc.
4. Differences in rates of acculturation of family members	4. Years in the United States Age at time of migration Exposure to Western culture Professional affiliation Contacts with American peers English-speaking ability Work or school environment
5. Work and financial stress	5. Downward mobility Status inconsistency Long working hours Language difficulty Racism at workplace
6. The family's place of residence and community influences	6. Type of neighborhood Availability of support system Community stigma
7. Physical health and medication history	7. Degree of somatization Medical history of patients and family members Western and herbal medicines Consultation with physician and indigenous healers
8. Assessment of family problems	8. Integenerational conflicts In-law conflict Marital difficulty Sibling rivalries Hostile, dependent relationship with sponsor
9. Assessment of family strengths	9. Functional coping strategies Support from individual and family group Support from the ethnic community and service providers
10. Family's concept of mental illness, help-seeking behavior, and treatment expectation	10. Symptoms and problems as perceived by family Causes of the problems as perceived by family Relationship with posttraumatic events Family help-seeking behavior

Adapted from and by permission of Evelyn Lee, assistant clinical professor, Department of Psychiatry, University of California, San Francisco, California.

In Cultural Study 8-5, Rothman, Gant, and Hnat (1985) report that a relationship exists between Mexican American parents' facilitation of bilingual communication in the home and their children's academic achievement. The Mexican American child who is fluent in English is evaluated more favorably than are nonfluent children.

CULTURAL STUDY 8-5

Bilingual Fluency

English-speaking fluency is highly related to attitudes and performance in school. Both Anglo and Mexican-American teachers evaluate the English-fluent Mexican-American child more favorably than non-fluent children. Attitudes of Mexican Americans toward school may be determined by academic performance, which is directly related to English fluency of Mexican-American children. There is also a direct correlation between Mexican-American parental facilitation of bi-lingualism in the home and a child's academic achievement.

Discussion. The finding that English fluency of Mexican-American children is related to academic achievement is one that has been repeatedly replicated. Spence et al. found that children whose families were bilingual at home scored significantly higher in academic tests than monolingual Spanish- or English-speaking students. Stedman and McKenzie found that bilingual Mexican-American children in Head Start programs perform better academically than their Spanish-speaking peers. Anderson and Johnson report that the persistent use of Spanish as the only language spoken in the home is related to school failure. Stedman and Adams reported significant correlations between English fluency and objective reports of good classroom behavioral adjustment and teacher perception of competence. This finding appears to support an earlier study that noted a significant correlation between linguistic (i.e., English-speaking) ability, behavioral adjustment, and parents who were bilingual at home.

Application Guidelines for Practice. The practitioner might suggest that children need to develop bilingual fluency not only as a necessary end of education, but as a vital means of matriculation in the education process. This might require an effort to speak more English at home, or supplementation of the child's mastery of English in other ways, such as special classes. Practitioners could also organize teacher workshops concerning this issue, underscoring the critical role teachers play in the personal development of Mexican-American children, along with the positive and negative implications of the Pygmalion effect.

Essentially, practitioners would do well to discuss with the family Rosenthal's "Pygmalion effect" and the potential impact such teacher attitudes and behaviors can have (both pro and con) on their children. If teachers feel that the student is bright, the student will be treated accordingly, that is, with praise and encouragement, which in turn is internalized by the student. However, should the teacher think the student slow or inept—and here the above research suggests that such thoughts are intertwined with the teacher's evaluation of English-speaking fluency—the teacher may treat the student accordingly, thus inculcating in the student feelings of deprecation, self-doubt, and low self-esteem.

The practitioner could articulate the need for members of *la casa* to interpret and reconceptualize the development of English fluency as a vital strategy in pursuing the cultural emphasis on education and academic achievement. If recourse to academic support as a cultural fixture is not successful in developing the familial encouragement of education, the need for children to develop skills to survive within the Anglo culture could be emphasized, as well as pointing out the disadvantages of non-completion of primary and secondary education.

To enhance home use of English, the worker might suggest or form adult education classes to teach English to Mexican-American parents, stressing the importance of speaking English as well as Spanish in the home for the benefit of the child. Additionally, the worker might secure subscriptions to bilingual Spanish/English newspapers and magazines such as *Nuestro* for households unaware of or unable to afford such items.

For Mexican-American youth with little or no familial support (e.g., children of migrants) the worker might work with local churches, community youth centers, and the schools to establish peer support groups that would provide analogous familial functions and support, with special focus on the necessity of bilingual competence and the Mexican-American cultural emphasis on education.

Social Assessment. Social assessment focuses on the person's skills in group or community living. It explores how human persons live together as a group, how they deal with one another, and how they affect their common welfare. The cultural perspective underscores the meaningful social environment of the ethnic family and community.

Social assessment can be categorized into four major areas:

1. Immigration history—the family's transition from the culture of origin to American society
2. Acculturation—the adjustment, change, and maintenance of culture in the family
3. School adjustment, which is crucial in children's survival performance
4. Employment, which is critical for adults' self-esteem and respect in the ethnic community

For both adults and children, family stability helps determine how family members function in their larger social environment.

Immigration History Assessment. In working with refugees and immigrants, it is crucial to find out the client's previous history and learn facts about the client's country of origin. These are important elements in the assessment of the client's present problem situation. Crucial questions include the following: How old were you when you entered and settled in the United States? What do you remember about your country of origin? What did your parents do for a living in that country? What were some important events that occurred in transition from your country of origin to the United States? Who accompanied you on the journey? Who did you leave behind? Why did you come to America? The worker should select a number of relevant questions that will not overwhelm the client and will facilitate the sharing of worthwhile information about the client's previous experiences and present status.

Huang (1989) outlines three ecological stages of the migration experience that are important to this aspect of psychosocial assessment: premigration, migration, and postmigration.

Questions about the premigration period seek to understand the client's cultural beliefs and practices in his or her country of origin. Of particular importance are the structure and hierarchy of the family; filial piety and respect for elders, teachers, and authority; the goal achievement of children in the family (a behavioral expectation); behavioral reactions (for example, shame and loss of face, self-control, and the expression of emotions); and interpersonal relationships. The worker should discover the series of events that precipitated departure from the country of origin: social and political upheavals, family hardship, physical torture, or forced labor.

The migration period covers the process of flight and includes who migrated and who was left behind; the means of escape and the accompanying trauma; the refugee camp experience; and the resulting stress. Rather than have the client detail these experiences during the first few sessions, the worker should seek to gain a general sense of what happened. The worker and client should then revisit these events after the client has gained stability and growth in the helping process. Major posttraumatic stress results from the migration period. Adults and children may have witnessed or been victims of rape, beatings, and brutality by soldiers or pirates. Their rage, helplessness, and guilt from these experiences may still be festering. Moreover, the refugee camp experience may have been equally stressful in terms of basic survival, idleness, and boredom.

Questions concerning the postmigration period focus on entry into the United States in terms of family transition, acculturation, culture shock, and general readjustment. The family hierarchy is often in disarray as children acculturate much sooner than parents and as wives work for economic survival while husbands have difficulty finding employment on account of language barriers, minimal job skills, or differences in licensure standards. Role reversal occurs as parents depend on children to act as interpreters for them.

Acculturation Assessment. *Acculturation* is the adaptation of language, identity, behavior patterns, and preferences to those of the host/majority society. To some extent, acculturation involves modifying the existing culture of origin. Rejection and abandonment of the culture of origin is called *overacculturation.* A person who displays resistance and reluctance to adapt to the majority culture is termed *marginal.* A person who integrates positive qualities of both cultures has achieved *bicultural competence.* The client often does not recognize these particular stages in the acculturation process. The worker must identify the client's present acculturation status and work toward achieving bicultural integration.

In Cultural Study 8-6, Galan (1992) discusses the acculturation stress that occurs when parents are placed in dependent roles because of language and cultural limitations and children must assume adult bilingual and bicultural bridging responsibilities between their families and the dominant society.

CULTURAL STUDY 8-6

Acculturation Stress

In traditional family cultures or in low socioeconomic family situations, where interdependence and cooperation are operational values, children learn to adapt their roles to fit the needs of the family's limitations. Because children may have coping responses and skills that help them adapt in the majority culture, they may be called upon to be advocates, cultural translators, or problem solvers in a family. This has been observed repeatedly as later generations help traditional parents

adapt to the majority culture and thus increase their family's overall adjustment. Bilingual/bicultural children often are called upon to translate and mediate in situations involving their monolingual Spanish-speaking parents and monolingual English-speaking representatives of society. That children respond to these situations and exhibit their bicultural skills to help their parents is not in and of itself a problem. Bilingual/bicultural children who navigate between two languages and two cultures often develop incredible mediation abilities and sophisticated code-switching responses, as well as a high level of social sensitivity and an appreciation of the difficulties encountered by those who speak only Spanish. That they are referred to as "being like two people" is a tribute to an adaptive biculturality.

Thus, bicultural socialization is not inherently pathological. Nor does temporary adultification in itself necessarily create permanent role confusion. The negative circumstances in the environment that surround the acculturation process (in which a family finds itself changing from being solely monolingual/monocultural in the language and culture of origin to becoming bilingual/bicultural in succeeding generations) usually produces [*sic*] the stress attributed to role conflicts in the family. The acculturation stress of a family in transition in an environment of poverty, powerlessness, humiliation, lack of opportunity, and social injustice is sometimes too much for parents to manage. Spousification of children might not occur if negative circumstances in a family's environment were eliminated and appropriate supports were available for families undergoing the intergenerational transitions of acculturation. Many of the difficulties experienced by Mexican-American adolescents result from the inability of schools, media, neighborhood, and community to provide positive bicultural images and the skills with which to master their bicultural environment.

From "Experiential Focusing with Mexican-American Males with Bicultural Identity Problems" by F. J. Galan. In K. Corcoran (Ed.), *Structuring Change: Effective Practice for Common Client Problems,* p. 239. Copyright © 1992 Lyceum Books, Inc. Reprinted by permission.

School Assessment. School adjustment is an important determinant of academic and social functioning. The worker should gain a sense of the school environment. Is it a safe, pleasant place conducive to learning, or is it a violent-prone, conflicting, racist environment that detracts from learning and social growth? Ethnic students tend to be objects of white students' hostility or to act out negative behavior as a response to an unfriendly environment. Fights, drug use, property damage, and early sexual involvement are expressions of behavioral reaction to a social situation.

Schools often track children of color with academic and language problems in special education programs. However, the recent trend has been toward mainstreaming students in order to avoid labeling certain groups. Bilingual classes, work-study programs, and vocational and career internships are meaningful avenues to assisting students with special needs and interests.

The worker should contact the school counselor and selected teachers in order to determine how school environment, educational program, and peer relationships contribute to the client's problem needs.

Employment Assessment. It is important to assess the family's work history. To what extent do family members have stable employment? Given the state of the economy and a tight market for hiring, many adults are without jobs. For immigrants and refugees, language problems and educational requirements may limit employment opportunities. Many new arrivals are in English as a second language classes or job-training programs. Some are low-skill service workers or seasonal workers in agriculture. Others have given up, remain on welfare assistance, and are caring for children at home.

The single most important factor for family stability is the placement of an adult in a reliable, steady job. Many Southeast Asian refugees have pooled their resources to open restaurants, croissant and donut shops, and related business ventures; they are able to use their practical skills and create business opportunities. Many Native Americans are now employed in gambling casinos that have opened on reservations across the coun-

try. African Americans have taken out small business loans to start small enterprises in the inner city and have employed African American service and construction workers. Latino Americans are often agricultural and construction workers.

As culturally diverse families send their children to colleges and universities, many become middle-class government workers and upper-middle-class professionals, living in two-parent families with a stable home life and economic security. Many have returned to their ethnic community and reinvested their talents in service projects there.

Cultural Assessment. Culture consists of the ideas, customs, skills, and arts of a group of people that have been cultivated and passed on from generation to generation. Cultural beliefs and practices have enabled people of color to persevere in the face of racism, prejudice, and discrimination. Culturally diverse social work practice focuses on cultural assets from a strengths perspective and on the natural support system of people of color, which is an integral part of the cultural structure. Cultural assessment is the core contribution of ethnic-sensitive practice to the assessment stage.

Cultural Formulation in Diagnostic Assessment. The American Psychiatric Association has recognized the importance of cultural formulation in diagnostic assessment. In its *Diagnostic and Statistical Manual of Mental Disorders*, fourth edition (American Psychiatric Association, 1994), the section on cultural assessment discusses the influence of cultural considerations on comprehensive diagnosis and care. Four major components of cultural formulation cited there may be relevant to our understanding of the relationship between culture and assessment:

1. The cultural identity of the individual
2. Cultural explanations of the individual's illness
3. Cultural factors related to the psychosocial environment and levels of functioning
4. Cultural elements of the relationship between the individual and the clinician

Although social work does not subscribe to an illness model, it is interesting to note that psychiatry is concerned about the cultural formulation and psychosocial dimensions of individual functioning and social environment.

1. *Cultural identity.* Our ethnic or cultural reference group has an important bearing on how we view ourselves. For immigrants and other people of color, it is important to note the degree of involvement with both the culture of origin and the host culture—in particular, language abilities, use, and preference. The level of language adaptation is crucial in operating within two distinct cultures.
2. *Cultural explanations of illness.* Five areas are relevant here:
   a. *Cultural expressions of stress:* predominant cultural idioms of distress through which symptoms or the need for social support are communicated—for example, "nerves," possessing spirits, somatic complaints, and inexplicable misfortune
   b. *Cultural group norms and perceptions of symptom severity:* the meaning and perceived severity of the individual's symptoms in relation to norms of the cultural reference group
   c. *Local perspectives on cultural phenomena:* local illness categories used by the individual's family and community to identify culture-bound syndromes
   d. *Cultural explanations of dysfunction:* the perceived causes or explanatory models that the individual and the reference group use to explain the illness
   e. *Blending of professional and indigenous helping:* the current preferences for, and past experiences with, professional and popular sources of care

      In cultural assessment, cultural variables that previously were considered a part of the person's illness are instead viewed as integral to an understanding of how culture affects the individual as a whole person.
3. *Psychosocial environmental levels of functioning.* The cultural variables relevant here are culturally sensitive interpretations of social stressors; available social supports; levels of functioning and disability—particularly stresses in the local environment; and the role of religion

and kin networks in providing emotional, instrumental, and informational support. Social supports—particularly kin networks and religion—are cultural factors that contribute to the restoration of psychosocial functioning.

4. *Relationship between the worker and the client.* Culture has a critical influence on the dynamics between the helper and the client. Cultural elements of this relationship include differences in culture and social status between the client and the clinician and the problems that these differences may cause in diagnosis and treatment. Among such culturally determined problems are the following:
   a. Difficulties in communication in the individual's first language
   b. Difficulties in eliciting symptoms or understanding their cultural significance
   c. Difficulties in negotiating an appropriate relationship or level of intimacy
   d. Difficulties in determining whether a behavior is normative or pathological

Clearly, the clinician must take responsibility for rectifying the traditional treatment stance or adopting an alternative culturally sensitive approach; recognition of this responsibility will depend on exposure to cross-cultural training and text content.

These four aspects of cultural formulation have implications for social workers who are engaged in cultural assessment, as follows:

1. The worker must be aware of the client's cultural and ethnic background, group orientation, and acculturation.
2. Cultural explanations of the individual's problems include disharmony and imbalance manifested in psychophysiological or somatic symptoms, as well as shame and social withdrawal or isolation. Dreams, visions, and cosmic messages may be culturally accepted means of resolving problems.
3. Culturally significant resources are found in such social supports as self-help groups, extended family, and the church (perceived as a community of accepting people who are involved in practical helping programs).

4. The cultural gap between the worker and the client may be closed by means of an appropriate relationship protocol, professional self-disclosure, learning important helping phrases in another language, and the use of language interpreters.

Kutchins and Kirk (1997) in their critical analysis of the *Diagnostic and Statistical Manual of Mental Disorders (DSM-IV)* point out that there is a lack of connection between these preceding categories and their application to diagnosing clients, especially how to record a *DSM-IV* evaluation using cultural formulations. They observe:

> Whatever the virtues of the new culturally oriented features of DSM-IV, they do not solve the problem of racial bias. The manual does not even acknowledge the difference between race and culture. It does not take notice of the repeated finding that identical behavior by patients of different races who share the same culture will be interpreted differently. Poor Southern sharecroppers who are white are no less different from middle-class therapists than are African American sharecroppers, but there will be differences in the way these clients' symptoms are interpreted and their diagnoses are formulated. On the basis of repeated and convincing empirical evidence, we can predict that African Americans will be diagnosed as more severely disturbed than whites who manifest the identical symptoms. In short, there has been no significant correction of the biases incorporated into DSM diagnoses. (p. 237)

Use of the *DSM* should be balanced with the criticisms and limitations of these categories of classification.

The Culturagram. Congress's (1994) *culturagram* (Figure 8-2) comprises ten categories of cultural information for a specific family:

1. Reasons for immigration—why immigrants leave their country of origin

2. Length of time in the community—provides information on the degree of adherence to the original cultural beliefs and acculturation

3. Legal or undocumented status—legal immigration, student or work permits, secret arrival, remaining in this country after the expiration of visas

4. Age of family members at time of immigration—provides information on the degree of individual acculturation (for example, learning the new language) and family conflict caused by the rate of acculturation

5. Spoken language—native language, English, or bilingual ability

6. Contact with cultural institutions (ethnic churches, schools, social clubs) —provides information on cultural identity

7. Health beliefs—native attitudes of health, illness, and treatment, which differ from American medical practice

8. Holidays and special events—religious and life cycle transitional events (birth, marriage, death)

9. Crisis events or stressors—losing a job, death of a grandparent, rape, relocation to a different country or geographic area

10. Family, education, and work values—provides information on family patterns of support, education, and career selection

The completion of a culturagram reveals important differences among family members in terms of acculturation and family functioning. As a result, family stress and conflict areas are identified.

The following questions might be asked in completing the culturagram:

1. What brought you to the United States? Why did you decide to leave your country of origin?
2. How long have you lived in the United States—particularly in this community?
3. Do you have, or would you like to have, a green card?
4. How old were you when you came to the United States?
5. What languages do you speak at home and in the community?
6. What clubs or groups do you belong to?

7. When you are sick, what do you do? Where do you go? To whom do you turn for help?
8. What family occasions and holidays do you celebrate? How do you celebrate these events?
9. What particular events are stressful for your family?
10. Should everyone have a high school or college education?
11. Do you believe that the man should be the family breadwinner?

Congress (1994) believes that the culturagram helps us understand the complexities of family culture, individualize families beyond cultural generalizations, become sensitive to the daily experience of culturally diverse families, develop differential family member assessment, facilitate the family's understanding of its cultural background, and discover specific areas for intervention. In short, the culturagram is an assessment tool for multicultural practice with families—in particular, immigrant families.

Cultural Assets. Multicultural clinicians have been critical of the deviancy orientation of traditional assessment practice. Kuramoto, Morales, Muñoz, and Murase (1983) observe that the majority society defines cultural differences as deviant or abnormal by first imposing behavioral expectations and then penalizing those unable to meet such levels. Society superimposes a negative judgment on cultural resources, rather than viewing the unique strengths of cultural differences as assets. Foreign traits are immediately cast in a negative light.

Furthermore, many human service workers tend to impose American value assumptions on people of color. Bernal, Bernal, Martínez, Olmedo, and Santisteban (1983) differentiate the culture-specific values of Latinos from those of white Americans. A discrepancy exists between the American value of individualism, which fosters independence, and the Latino concept of the individual as a member of a close-knit family. Assessed in independence/dependence relations, the ethnic

FIGURE 8-2 *Culturagram*

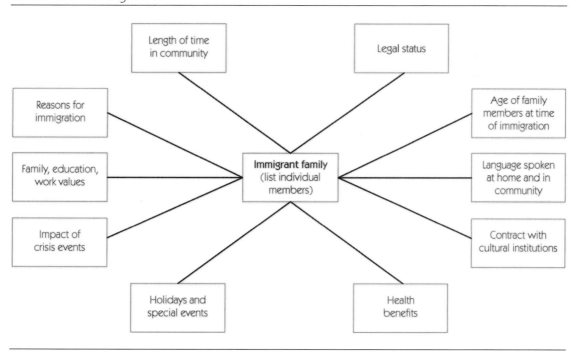

client may appear too dependent on the family. Actually the ethnic client is participating in a functional family hierarchy that maintains harmony and collective decision making. It is important to understand the cultural dynamics and tap into positive family assets rather than to superimpose the values of individuality and independence.

Both behavioral and social sciences have stereotyped African American intelligence and family structure. Bell, Bland, Houston, and Jones (1983) cite mistaken theoretical assumptions about the mental status of African Americans in American society. For example, the genetic fallacy holds that races differ in inherited mental qualities and that African Americans are inferior to whites in intellectual potential and achievement. Although social work rejects that theory, it has supported beliefs about African American inferiority in American scientific circles and has led to a focus on cultural liabilities. Sociological analysis of the African American family has propagated the idea of a pathological African American matriarchy. In this stereotype, African American women are unfeminine, promiscuous, and dependent on welfare; and African American men are inadequate fathers who have deserted their families, are unemployed, and are unable to provide for their children. The dissemination of this stereotype has contributed to African Americans' low self-esteem.

These examples provide evidence that behavioral and social sciences perpetuate a notion of deviance with respect to people of color. Human service workers may be prone to making certain assumptions in their assessments on the basis of these stereotypes. An alternative to focusing on stereotypes or pathological characteristics of ethnic groups is to emphasize the client's cultural assets and strengths, such as the abilities to cope with stress, to implement survival skills, and to use extended family and community support systems.

Cultural assets are found in the ethnic community. The term *ethnosystem* has been coined to describe the client's relationship to various ethnic systems. Solomon (1976) has defined the ethnosystem as a collective of interdependent ethnic groups who share unique historical and/or cultural ties and are bound together by a single political system. The task of assessment is to discover the assets of the ethnic individual, family, and community. The client may be related to an ethnosystem that has values, knowledge, and skills embedded in the person, family, and community. The client is the teacher best qualified to inform the social worker about his or her own ethnosystem. Writing of the informal and natural support networks within the ethnosystem of Asian and Pacific Americans, Kuramoto et al. (1983) ask:

> What is the potential for such networks to serve as mechanisms for identifying persons requiring services and for facilitating access to and utilization of services? Theory development is needed to comprehend the functions of informal support networks within each Asian and Pacific American community, to suggest ways in which they can be strengthened as resources and to provide the basis for promoting more effective communication between the informal and formal service networks. (pp. 143–144)

This statement has universal application for people of color. It is essential to incorporate assessment of clients' positive cultural strengths into the practice process.

Natural Support Systems. Psychoindividual reactions rely on indigenous community patterns. Multicultural literature has highlighted the importance of natural community support systems (friends, neighbors, church relationships) that provide support and opportunities for personal development (Rappaport, 1981). These natural settings "work to provide niches for people that enhance their ability to control their lives and allow them both affirmation and the opportunity to learn and experience growth and development" (Rappaport, 1981, p. 19). It is important to assess the significant components of the support system that already exist in the ethnic community for the client. Zuñiga (1983) reminds us:

> Recognition must be given to the fact that culturally based supports providing nurturing act as a buffer to hostile institutions such as unresponsive welfare departments, discriminatory housing authorities, or other negatively perceived institu-

tions that are supposed to foster social well-being. . . . Thus, attention must be given to the natural support systems that have been developed within one's cultural base. (p. 260)

Ethnic community social networks have been the focal point for assessing potential resources and for intervention strategies. These natural support systems help people of color to master their environment, retain or increase their self-esteem, participate in their communities (Kelly, 1977), and maintain individuals in relative health and comfort (Caplan, 1972).

There are a number of major network components. Central to this discussion are the kinship patterns among families. Boyd (1982) observes that African Americans have strong ties of kinship with extended families, which include blood relatives, friends, and acquaintances who are forged into a coherent network of mutual emotional and economic support. Members of the extended family interchange roles, jobs, and family functions such as child-rearing and household chores. Stack (1975) describes these patterns as "coresidence, kinship-based exchange networks linking multiple domestic units, elastic household boundaries, and lifelong bonds to three generation households" (p. 124). Among African American families, informal adoption and child raising form the basis for joint assistance. This network extends to the care of the elderly, who are often absorbed into the homes of family members and who care for children (Hill, 1972).

In the Latino family a bond of loyalty and unity exists in nuclear and extended families and in a social network of friends, neighbors, and community. The Latino family has obligations of loyalty. Children express *respeto* to their parents, to whom the children owe their existence. The debt of obligation can never be repaid. The father is the decision maker and disciplinarian concerned about the family's economic welfare and well-being. The mother oversees the upbringing of the children and provides emotional support. Extended family members supplement parental roles and form a network of reliance (Bernal et al., 1983).

Most Native American tribal groups function in extended family roles. Tribe, clan, family, and heritage are means of cultural system identity. The Native American extended family system encompasses traditional child-rearing practices, generational roles, and sex-role identity development (Trimble, Mackey, LaFromboise, & France, 1983). Likewise, Asian Americans have a social network consisting of nuclear and extended family and family associations in major cities. Relatives, friends, and neighbors are called "uncle" and "aunt," which are terms of endearment. This system functions for mutual support and assists with financial need, social activities, joint projects, and other ventures. Ethnic churches, food stores, and language/cultural schools are sources of communication and informational assistance.

Two case studies underscore the importance of family—particularly extended network—in working with ethnic clients. In Cultural Study 8-7, Red Horse, Lewis, Feit, and Decker (1981) present an example in which the public welfare system ignored the natural family helping network.

CULTURAL STUDY 8-7

Ethnic Identity Crisis

Nancy . . . was an eighteen-year-old mother identified as mentally retarded and epileptic by the department of welfare officials. Although retardation was subsequently disproved, the department assumed control and custody of Nancy's infant child.

Nancy's parents insisted that the family network was available for assistance, if necessary. The welfare staff, however, considered this offer untenable. The grandparents were deemed senile and unable to care for an infant. They were in their early fifties.

The staff ignored the fact that the grandparents had just finished caring for three other young and active grandchildren without dependence on institutional social intervention. Moreover, these children appeared to be well-adjusted. The officials simply insisted in this case that standard placement procedures be followed; a foster home was obtained for Nancy's child.

From "Family Behavior of Urban American Indians" by J. G. Red Horse, P. Lewis, M. Feit, and J. Decker, *Social Casework* (Feb. 1978), Vol. 59, pp. 67–72. Copyright © 1978 Family Service Association of America. Reprinted by permission.

Cultural Study 8-8, in contrast, highlights the use of the family network by the worker, who recognizes the natural helping system when preparing the client for reentry from a foster home. Attneave (1969) offers this case in support of tribal-network intervention. Mr. T. is the stepfather, Mrs. T. is Maria's mother. Mrs. T. married into a network clan organized around her husband's parents, his sisters' families, and their close friends. The network clan was concerned about Maria's problem and convened during the weekend.

CULTURAL STUDY 8-8

Family Network

Maria and the therapist arrived on a sunny afternoon . . . carefully prepared for Maria's reentry into the network. She had purchased a bag of candy and gum with the pennies she had "earned" in the foster home, and during the forty-mile drive she counted over and over one piece of candy and one piece of gum for each half sib and adult she knew, and a reassuring surplus for any others who might come. This time Maria was bringing the bag of sweets, and her anxiety was as high as if someone had explained that by doing so she could make amends for her past behavior and henceforth participate in the family ritual of sharing. Symbolically it was her bid for induction into the family.

This was indeed accomplished, but in even more dramatic and comprehensive fashion than the therapist had foreseen. As the car pulled up under a tree and the family came out to greet Maria, she suddenly gave a cry of recognition and thrust one of her offerings into the hands of a strange woman standing on the porch. The network, mulling over the therapist's remark ["It might help us understand if we knew more about your mother"], had stretched its links across two states and brought the absent grandmother to spend two weeks.

During the next twenty-four hours the bestowing of a tribal name at dawn and the eating of a very American birthday cake at the noon feast completed Maria's restoration to the family and network. During the ceremonial meeting of adults, the grandmother and her new husband sat as honored guests and had many things explained to them. Included were elements that had not been explicitly comprehended by Maria's mother, but which she now learned without embarrassment or loss of status. She was also able to fulfill an important ceremonial role, with her mother present, and thus symbolize the new integration of self and identity she had acquired without having to deny or bury her past. The husband also gained some sense of unsuspected dimensions of her as a person. Mr. T. was able to express his appreciation of his wife publicly as well as to secure the network's expressions of supportive interest and pleasure in her and in Maria.

The next afternoon sitting on the hillside the therapist observed Maria and her half siblings and cousins playing around a tire swing. Around an outdoor fire, Mrs. T. and some of the other women were showing the grandmother how to make "fry bread" and over further under the trees a group of men, including step-grandfather, were drumming softly, practicing songs, and shaving kindling.

Grandfather T., the eldest member of the network-clan, stopped beside the therapist and watched the same scene. After a few minutes he observed "Hum—a good idea to know that grandmother. . . . " Then with a piercing glance and the suspicion of a twinkle he gathered himself up to walk off. Turning, he raised an arm that embraced the group below in a majestic sweeping gesture— "*That* is much better than a lot of noisy talk."

From "Therapy in Tribal Settings and Urban Network Intervention," by C. L. Attneave. In *Family Process*, 8, 201, 202. Copyright © 1969 Family Process, Inc. Reprinted by permission.

These ethnic social networks practice understood codes that govern behavioral standards and values. Any action a family member takes is a reflection on the entire group. Social family and community systems are sources of aid and support and boundaries for ethical actions. Community leaders reinforce behavioral protocol in the ethnic community.

Several questions in assessment evaluation involve an understanding of the kinship and social network. Are supportive resources available for the client in the social network? Which particular significant others seem most helpful? Are persons, services, or institutions available that can be mobilized on behalf of the client? Focusing on these positive aspects of ethnic behavior and social networks is important for both social worker and client.

Gender Assessment. Related to biological, psychological, social, cultural, and spiritual assessment dimensions are a number of multicultural feminist resources that the woman of color may draw on as she moves toward multicultural self-fulfillment. For example, Schriver (1998) proposes alternative paradigms that recognize the interrelatedness and interconnectedness of all human beings. He is particularly concerned about the significance of relationship from multicultural and feminist perspectives.

On the one hand, many Afrocentric, Native American, and Asian worldviews share the sense of the interrelatedness of human beings with all elements of the environment: individual, family, ethnic group, ethnic community, nature, world, and universe. On the other hand, Miller (1986) observes that women stay with, build on, and develop connections with others. A woman's sense of self becomes organized around affiliations and relationships (Miller, 1986).

Four major resource areas are crucial to gender assessment: individual woman, family system relationships, group system relationships, and community system relationships. These are four major levels that identify natural linkages in multicultural settings. Under each level are four categories that cover associated themes: ethnic/gender identity, family interactions, social network, and cultural strengths.

A woman forms significant relationships as an individual who is part of a family, group, and community. These relationships develop over the course of the life span as a child, adolescent, young adult, mature adult, and older person. Crucial to each relationship system are the development of ethnic/gender identity (who am I as a person?), family interactions (what are the significant familial exchanges?), social networks (what are the informal and formal support resources?), and cultural strengths (what are the positive belief and practices systems of the ethnic community?). There are natural parallels between the relationship systems and the affiliated categories.

In the following sections, the multicultural resources levels are explained in terms of the categories.

Gender Assessment Levels

Individual Woman

Ethnic/Gender Identity. Whereas white feminists are generally concerned about gender issues, the multicultural woman has a dual identity perspective: her ethnicity and gender. Her ethnic personhood explains her individuality as much as her ethnic womanhood gives credence to her identity. Being an ethnic woman is her essence as an individual person. Ethnicity is related to a shared social and cultural heritage passed down from generation to generation based on race, religion, and native identity. Gender includes human physiological distinctions; the relationship among biological, rational, and emotional functioning; social roles; and societal expectations and biases. How a multicultural woman develops her ethnic/gender identity is an important area of concern.

Family Interaction. The multicultural woman interacts primarily with her immediate family, grandparents, and godparents in a socioeconomic environment. As a child she may be raised in a two-parent or one-parent family, by grandparents or an uncle/aunt. Multicultural child rearing has flexible patterns in some cultures such as African American or Native American. Godparents are supplemental parent figures to her, especially in Latino American families.

The family may experience a variety of socioeconomic conditions ranging from poverty to wealth, periodic unemployment to stable employment. Adverse stress may heighten the pressure on family interaction so that the family is forced to rely on survival skills. A sense of economic stability contributes to the security of the multicultural woman who thrives on positive experiences with family members.

These family interaction situations may be part of her childhood, adolescence, and adulthood. Hopefully the multicultural individual strives toward quality family interactions that are stable and supportive.

Social Networks. The multicultural woman establishes primary social networks linking her to other people in her ecological environment. Starting with peer relationships with brothers and sisters, cousins, neighborhood playmates, and school friends, she relies on the support and relationships from these social networks. Later she participates in social organizations that increase her sense of network building. These organizations range from neighbor and school sport teams, school clubs, and social groups in college and career settings. Meaningful relationships with individual persons emerge from these social network opportunities.

Cultural Strengths. Cultural strengths vary from person to person depending on the degree to which a woman learns cultural values and beliefs from her family and ethnic community. Cultural strengths may include personal or religious belief systems, survival skills, natural healing practices, community networks, and other elements that contribute to functional coping.

Lee (1982) identifies a variety of therapeutic cultural strengths:

> Strengths such as support from extended family members and siblings, the strong sense of obligation, the strong focus on educational achievements, the work ethic, the high tolerance for loneliness and separation, and the loyalties of friends or between employer and employee should be respected and used effectively in the therapeutic process. (p. 547)

Cultural strengths provide a number of character building assets for the individual woman: positive self-image (one's self-concept as a whole person),

positive self-esteem (one's self-worth and value), personal spirituality (cosmic meaning and purpose), and empowerment (the ability to take a proactive life stance).

Family System Relationships

Ethnic/Gender Identity. Multicultural family systems tend to revolve around collective authority structures. Rather than individual independence, there is an emphasis on interdependence within the family system. For example, the individual wishes of a particular family member are subordinate to the good of the family as a whole. In this traditional view of the multicultural family, there are variations of freedom and expressions of individuality which exist for the multicultural woman.

The multicultural family system is considered the most important transmitter of cultural values and traditions and is the primary source of identity and support in times of crisis. At the same time, ethnic parents, particularly fathers, value obedience to parental authority and respect from their children. In turn, children may be at odds with this hierarchy as second- and third-generation American-born.

The traditional functions of women in a multicultural family are caring, nurturing, and helping others in the immediate system. However, some adaptive strategies recognize flexible family social roles due to the demands of the social environment (Harrison, 1990). Sharing of responsibilities and equality of role functions are increasingly prevalent among multicultural families, particularly when both parents work outside the home. Multicultural husbands and fathers may be willing to assume some of the household chores when their spouses arrive home late from work.

At the same time, the ethnic and gender identity of the multicultural woman centers around bicultural competency and integration in the family system relationships. That is, the multicultural woman often functions differently in the dominant society of work and the culture of origin society of home. At the workplace, the multicultural woman may be expected to be a decisive, rational, and competitive employee. At home, the same multicultural woman may be quiet, show respect to her husband by deferring to his authority, and nurture and care for the children. There is no contradiction in this dual perspective of bicultural functioning. It is a matter of learning and practicing competency in cultural roles for both settings and integrating two sets of expectations and role functioning.

Family Interaction. In some traditional family systems, particularly Latino and Asian American, there is a modified patriarchal family structure. Family organization centers on the father as the acknowledged head of the family, mother as the nurturant caretaker and the indirect influential person, and sons of more value than daughters because they carry the family name for the next generation. The father is the provider and protector of the family. Children are expected to obey parents and elders. In exchange, parents are responsible for the upbringing, education, and support of the children (Kitano, 1974; Arnez, 1987).

Other family systems, especially African American and Native American, tend to interact as shared cooperative family structures. African American families, in spite of increasing one parent families among the adolescent and young adult years, share and exchange work roles among family and extended family members for survival and daily functioning purposes. Likewise Native American families share parenting responsibilities among several adults (father and mother, aunt and uncle, grandparents, and friends). There is the practice of sharing resources (money, food, possessions) with each other. From a historical perspective, American Indian women were highly regarded in some tribes which were matrilineal. Descent and kinship were derived through the mother's lineage rather than the father. Women were selected to participate in the tribal council and were respected because of their spiritual insights.

Multicultural women of color value their cultural family structure, recognizing the authority of the family and striving to interact as liberated persons within this cultural context.

Social Networks. Extended families and fictive relatives are major examples of social networks in family system relationships. They are a part of kinship networks that broaden the base of the family system. They function on the principles of interdependence, group orientation, and reliance on others.

Multicultural women of color are givers and receivers of these support systems. Among African Americans there is an extensive reliance on kinship networks which include blood relatives and close friends called "kinsmen." These networks offer mutual aid for financial assistance, child care, advice, and emotional support. African American women are primary organizers and participants of kinship systems (Staples, 1981).

Latino Americans have the institution of compadres who are companion parents. They become godparents of the child and are sponsors at baptism and confirmation, witnesses at a marriage. They show common interest and intense friendship, feel free to advise or correct their godchild, and are responsive to the needs of the parent. Latinas are particularly effective as teachers of culture to the younger generation.

In the Hopi tribe of the Pueblos of northeast Arizona, there is the practice of bifurcate merging. The mother's and father's sides of the family are divided into separate lineages. Relatives of the same sex and generation are grouped together in helping clusters. Women of all ages strive to help each other. The mother's sister is close to her and her child and behaves toward the child like her biological mother (Price, 1981).

Cultural Strengths. Drawing from cultural strengths of family system relationships, multicultural people of color manifest qualities of ethnic identity in family settings. DeVos and Romanucci-Ross (1982) identify two types of ethnic identity: past-oriented cultural identity and expressive-behavioral cultural identity.

Past-oriented identity involves four characteristics:

- *Competence*—the confidence to take on goal-oriented activities based on collective confidence and supportive attitudes that shape one's position or standing in the ethnic community
- *Responsibility*—ethical obligations and the heritage of the ethnic community's moral code that makes a person responsible

- *Control*—pressures toward submission for reasons of survival or dependence as well as the moral imperative to seek liberation, autonomy, and independence from the oppressor
- *Mutuality*—cooperation and mutual trust to act together, emphasizing cooperation and minimizing competition

Ethnic identity traits that influence the expression and understanding of behavior are as follows:

- *Harmony*—peace and harmony that maintain group continuance at the expense of conflict in ethnic group relations
- *Affiliation*—mutual contact and communication based on shared past experiences, companionship, and a strong sense of belonging
- *Nurture*—interdependence expressed in caring, help, and comfort of one generation for another
- *Appreciation*—pride in family and ethnic group that creates a sense of humanity, dignity, self-respect, and proper status
- *Pleasure and suffering*—meaning in life related to social satisfaction as a member of a family/ethnic group and tolerance of suffering, crisis, and death

These nine variables are observed in the lives of family and ethnic community members and are intuitively practiced in the lives of people of color. Multicultural women of color live these qualities and pass them on to their sons and daughters.

Group System Relationships

Ethnic/Gender Identity. The multicultural woman must determine her primary ethnic cultural gender reference group. Is she first-, second-, or third-generation? Was she born in her country of origin, which is crucial for Latina and Asian American women? Or is she American born with parents who came from their country of origin or who have been in the United States for many generations? Reference group orientation is critical for understanding ethnic/gender identity.

Coming from a culture of origin into a dominant culture is part of the acculturation process. One's culture of origin is identified with language, cultural values and traditions, cultural mind-set, and behavior protocols. Generally one's ethnic/gender identity is strongly related to family, friends, and acquaintances who are part of one's culture of origin.

However, for a multicultural woman who was raised in the United States as a second-, third-, or fourth-generation American, ethnic/gender identity is filled with ethnic culture of origin and dominant culture family and friends. There may be a predominant orientation toward American values, cultural practices, and behavioral traits. One may or may not have a motivation to rediscover beliefs, traditions, and language that are a part of the past cultural heritage. If there is an interest in one's culture of origin, the multicultural woman is engaging in a reacculturation process. Whereas a multicultural refugee or immigrant woman is involved in prospective acculturation, a multicultural American-born woman may be moving toward retrospective acculturation. Both require a culturally sensitive and competent practitioner who can assist with making cultural/ethnic/gender connections. Group reference identity becomes an important part of the group system relationship process.

Family Interactions. Family group system relationships involve levels of interactions with the nuclear family, extended family (blood relatives, fictive relatives) and kinship network (distant relatives, family association, tribal structure). The cast of characters in these family groupings influences the multicultural woman. Among the areas of family interactions and group system relationships are the following:

• Sources of support: nuclear, extended, and kinship persons who are available resources for support and assistance in times of crises

• Sources of wisdom and advice: persons among these levels who are listeners and advice givers and provide valuable suggestions during life transitions, such as entry into school, career decisions, and choice of marital partner

• Sources of social companionship: brothers, sisters, cousins, and close family friends who form a network for going out, travel, and group activities

Family group interactions and relationships may take place on a consistent or a periodic basis. In some communities, immediate, extended, and kinship groups may live within a general vicinity. These clan groups may see each other for Sunday dinners or special holidays. Other large family groups are scattered throughout the country and may arrange for family reunions where a large group of distant relatives are part of a genealogy tree. They may meet annually or biyearly in a central location for family group gatherings.

Among the multicultural women of these family groups are informal sharing of life experiences, values, and insights that strengthen each other as women of color and of a particular family clan.

Social Networks. Social networks are a part of a multicultural woman's world of group system relationships. Service groups, social groups, and professional groups are examples of various social networks for involved women.

Service groups are organized efforts to impact the needs of young and mature women who are part of the local ethnic community. Service groups include ethnic girls and women sorority groups who raise scholarship funds and assume the leadership for worthy projects in the ethnic community.

Social groups provide opportunities for ethnic women to meet and to learn relevant information, to support and participate in ethnic fine arts (music, art, and dance), and to initiate social change in the ethnic community. Social groups are found in ethnic churches for girls and women of all ages, in cultural dance performance, ethnic school social clubs, and related institutions and areas.

Professional groups are composed for career professional graduate women who combine an ethnic identity and a professional perspective. Examples of professional groups are African American Women's Lawyers Association, Latina American Nurses Association, Asian American Educators, and American Indian Social Workers. Among their activities are professional advocacy, student career recruitment, and group support and information exchange. These groups help multicultural women of color with social networking and linkage, which result in strong ties with other individual ethnic women.

Cultural Strengths. The ethnic gender group is a vehicle to identification and affinity with one's cultural group of origin, ethnic group members, and group action. According to ethnic tradition, the African American places personal goals as secondary to the primary value of the survival and well-being of the historical African American group who underwent the tribulation of slavery and discrimination. This value of group collectivity is a cultural strength recognized by African American women who have such a perspective of suffering and pain.

Similarly, among Latinos there has been a movement toward the reaffirmation of cultural roots, assertion of ethnic pride, and the active politicization of issues affecting Latino Americans. Latinas join their male counterparts and march with them in the struggle for racial and social justice.

Likewise, cases for the group cultural strengths of Asian Americans and Native Americans can be cited. For example, Chinese Americans have historically organized themselves according to the family name into family associations. In major cities such as San Francisco, Los Angeles, Seattle, New York, and Boston are family association buildings that provide benevolence funds, economic assistance, and cultural traditions to members of the same surname. Japanese Americans are organized according to surnames attached to a specific province or state in Japan. Many Japanese immigrants came to the United States from the same vicinity of Japan bearing the same last name. Over the years, Japanese from these areas helped each other as they worked toward establishing themselves in America. These group support and sharing efforts continue to the present time.

Community System Relationships

Ethnic/Gender Identity. Schriver (1998) explains community as a collective of people that "includes individuals, groups, organizations, families; shared interests; regular interaction to fulfill shared interests through informal and formally organized means; and some degree of mutual identification among members as belonging to the collective" (p. 475). In our sense, multicultural community system relationships involve ethnic community-oriented and wider service-oriented institutions, organizations, and people that encompass and relate to the multicultural woman and her family.

Among the multiple understandings of community with relevance for the woman of color are

• community as a geographic location or place where day-to-day activities are carried out in the midst of a predominant ethnic, multicultural, and/or mixed community (Schriver, 1998);

• community as functions of production-distribution-consumption of goods and services; socialization or transmission of knowledge, social values, and behavior patterns; social control to conform to community norms; social participation in activities with other members; and mutual support for community members in times of need (Warren, 1978);

• community as ways of relating in terms of identification or feelings of membership through sharing and connectedness (Schriver, 1998);

• community as celebration and tragedy where holiday festival occasions (social events, parties) as well as participation in suffering and death touch the community spirit (McKnight, 1987); and

• community as personal intimacy where residents experience a strong sense of relationship (friendship, marriage) and feelings (confidence, loyalty, and interpersonal trust) (Solomon, 1976).

Among the community system relationships is the importance of school and church, which shape the ethnic/gender identity of the woman of color. Both institutions provide teaching and learning experiences:

• Knowledge and skill development of language (reading spelling, and writing), mathematics and science, history, and related subject areas

• Knowledge, faith, belief, and morality of God, the world, others, and self

In the midst of the teaching-learning process, it is important to determine what a multicultural girl/woman learns about her ethnicity and gender. The ethnic and gender background of teachers often determines the content of the message which is transmitted about ethnicity and gender in school and church. A strong ethnic female teacher can impart a positive ethnic/gender identity to her students. Finding this person who shares this message along with knowledge areas is crucial in the identity process of a person. Encouraging multicultural parents to teach the ethnic cultural heritage and the gender implications for identity is an important factor to balance with school and church.

Family Interactions. In the community system relationships there is a community perception of the individual multicultural woman and her family, particularly in a close knit ethnic community. Family integrity—a sense of moral honesty—and family credibility—a sense of reliability—are important values to uphold and cultivate among friends, neighbors, and business associates. The multicultural family is recognized in the community and has a reputation to uphold in the eyes of people. Based on this family status, the multicultural woman of color is evaluated by other ethnic families.

In a metropolitan area, ethnic community members thrive and are scattered in various geographic pockets. However, these community members meet in churches on weekends, attend special ethnic events, and visit each other for special holidays and occasions. They become a close-knit community based on ethnic, language, and cultural ties. Individuals are very much aware of the latest development of certain persons, because they see each other weekly. The communication grapevine is very tight and current. The elderly may know the grandparents and parents of the family. Word of a family event or action spreads rapidly.

Social Networks. Social networks, particularly task-oriented project groups, are important to the development of community system relationships. Young In Song is a social work educator who illustrates community social network contributions on the local, regional, and national levels. She has been active on the local and national levels with community-based social task force networks. She was instrumental in the conception of a regional ethnic group senior citizen's center when she realized that her mother felt isolated from social activities of her own age group. Gathering together a representative planning group of influential members of the Korean American community, she spearheaded fund-raising efforts on behalf of Korean American senior citizens in her area. She spoke to many groups who donated money, time, and effort in the creation of this center. A building housing two hundred Korean elderly was secured, and three days of activities per week are offered also. She is the president of the East Bay Korean American Senior Citizen Center in Oakland, California.

A few years after this project, Young In Song was asked to be the national chairperson of Korean Americans for the Korean War Memorial celebration program in Washington, D.C. Based on her previous experience with the senior citizens' project and her national recognition as a Korean American leader, she coordinated a national steering committee with fund-raising and program planning groups in the major cities of the United States. Meeting on a regular basis and traveling from city to city and to Washington, D.C., and Seoul, Korea, she was instrumental in negotiating several Korean American features for the war memorial and in fund-raising a series of major donations from Korean individuals and business corporations in the United States and the Republic of Korea.

Song's efforts are a prime example of social networking among a series of project task groups related to an ethnic community on the regional, national, and international levels. These experiences illustrate the importance of social networking in the development of community system relationships with significant project groups which benefit a particular ethnic group.

Cultural Strengths. Community system relationships and cultural strengths are manifested in at least two areas: ethnic community involvement and spiritual/religious involvement. These spheres may or may not characterize a particular multicultural woman of color but are given to describe the range of possibilities.

Regarding ethnic community involvement there is a need for multicultural women to exercise leadership in their community. Native Americans have elected several women as presidents of their tribes. These women exercise a vast array of executive talent in the administration of educational, social service, economic, and related programs and funds. African American women have assumed the presidencies of the Children's Defense Fund and the National Association for the Advancement of Colored People (NAACP). They have been instrumental in the mobilization of organizational group consensus, social concerns over pressing issues, and national legislative program advocacy. These are examples of macroorganizations headed by multicultural women— African American women in these two instances. However, there are scores of local instances of women of color who are active in their children's schools, youth groups, and athletic programs. Belief in the ethnic community motivates a person to strengthen the quality of the cultural environment, which is essential to the lives of individuals, families, and groups.

Concerning spiritual/religious involvement, the church or spiritual celebration itself is a cultural strength from which a person, particularly a woman of color, draws as a purpose for living. A community of faith calls on members and friends to become involved in meaningful relationships through worship, prayer, faith-at-work, and related groups and experiences. Women are the backbone of the church because of their faith and relationships with others. Single mothers seek religion as a source of support and assistance for their children who are in need of moral teaching. The faith and prayers of a mother keep a family together in the midst of adversity and crisis. People reach out to help others in the church through the encouragement of the pastor-minister.

The ethnic community and church are instances of community relationships in which people meet and aid people. Together they form the basis of cultural strength through two bonds: ethnicity and religion. Martin Luther King, Jr., forged the civil rights movement through his appeals to African Americans (ethnicity) and to God, faith, and the church (religion). Through his leadership, a new era of freedom was born. But let us not forget that it was the faith, determination, and conviction of Rosa Parks, a lone woman on the bus in Montgomery, Alabama, who became the symbol of determination and defiance that segregation and discrimination were morally wrong. Her strength and conviction mobilized a community, a race of people, and a nation.

Spiritual Assessment. There has been a growing movement in social work education to recognize the importance of spirituality and religion. As stated earlier, the spirit cannot be separated from the body and the mind. The term *spiritus* means breath, soul, and life. Genesis 2:7 reminds us that "the LORD God . . . breathed into his nostrils the breath of life; and man became a living being." The spiritual is the essence of the breath of life for each living person.

Social work itself has religious origins. In the nineteenth century, social services were first provided by the church. Tracing that history, Marty (1980) argues for a "godly social service sense," in which social work recognizes the importance of religious dimensions.

A vigorous debate is under way regarding religious issues in social work education and their implications for social work practice and the religious client (Amato–von Hemert, 1994; Clark, 1994). It is important to clarify issues concerning the appropriate use of spiritual or religious issues in the helping process; professional limitations; collaboration with, or referral to, a pastoral clinical counselor; and the use of spiritual beliefs and practices in multicultural practice.

In my view, the assessment of spiritual dimensions provides information vital to the helping process for many clients. An understanding of spirituality and religion illuminates the nature of the problem situation and helps shape the intervention plan. Sheridan, Bullis, Adcock, Berlin, and Miller (1992) lay out four categories relevant to the assessment of spirituality and religion:

1. Self-examination
2. Client's religious or spiritual history (past and present attitudes and practices)
3. Assessment of possible religious or spiritual meaning assigned to a present or underlying issue
4. Knowledge of particular beliefs held by religious or spiritual groups that have an effect on a client

These areas provide helpful points of reference in the exploration of clients' spiritual orientation or religious background, in research and discussion with a religious resource (pastor, theologian, medicine man, shaman), or in collaborations with a clinically oriented pastor or pastoral counselor. We now consider each of these areas in turn.

Self-Examination. Asking a client about religious faith or spiritual existence may be a starting point for dialogue. At the social worker's prompting, the client engages in self-examination— reflection on personal beliefs, values, and attitudes concerning the religious or spiritual dimensions of human existence. To participate in a dialogue, the worker will need an understanding of spirituality and religion.

According to Canda (1989), *spirituality* is "the general human experience of developing a sense of meaning, purpose, and morality," whereas religion consists of the "formal institutional contexts of spiritual beliefs and practices" (p. 39). Nyquist (1994) explains spirituality as "the basic human drive for meaning, purpose, and moral relatedness among people, with the universe, and with the ground of our being" (p. 1). Likewise a person may be on a "human spiritual quest for a sense of meaning, purpose and morally fulfilling relationship" (Canda, 1990, p. 1).

Religion is a practical application of personal spirituality to self, others, community, and institution. Canda (1989) explains:

> Religion is an aspect of human culture and experience that significantly affects both individual and collective behavior. All human beings possess spiritual needs for a sense of meaning and purpose in life, including expressions both within and without formal religious institutions. Religious beliefs and practices often play a crucial role in the understanding of self and world, especially regarding the way they establish meaning and purpose in relationships between self, others, the environment, and the ultimate reality. (p. 36)

Many people of color do not have a relationship with a church. For them, spirituality is a personal philosophy of existence that provides meaning and purpose. Cultural and family remnants of beliefs and practices may indirectly influence a person's spiritual awareness. Native American spirituality, for example, is based on a deep reverence for nature and the Great Spirit and is expressed in cleansing and healing rituals. African Americans and Latinos, by contrast, are involved in institutional church settings. Netting, Thibault, and Ellor (1990) focus on African American churches, which perform social functions and social services for their communities, and on the role of the Catholic Church in providing social support for Latino families. Exploring spirituality and religious faith with an ethnic client may uncover key elements to understanding a particular life problem.

Client History. After initiating client self-examination, the practitioner may want to take a more detailed client history of religious or spiritual beliefs and practices: What beliefs and practices affect the client's past and present attitudes and behavior? Sheridan et al. (1992) suggest a number of areas that may be relevant: use of prayer and meditation; reading of scripture; faith and practices of the client's family of origin; change of faith as an adult, which may be an indicator of the motivation for change; and the nature and quality of religious or spiritual experience encountered during various stages of life.

Joseph's (1988) research on attitudes to religion over the life cycle reveals the following pattern:

1. Interest and curiosity in religion in the preschool stage
2. Family interaction with church groups during school years
3. Individualized view of God and church and service activities during preadolescence and adolescence
4. "Pulling away" from or "new closeness" to God and religious groups during young adulthood
5. Redefinition of the meaning of God or a cynical rejection of God and religion in the midlife stage
6. Importance of religion and God in the active elderly and frail elderly stages

In a research-interview study with eighteen social workers, Canda (1988) concluded that it is important to explore the spiritual meaning of life events for clients; to acknowledge the significance of a relationship with spiritual powers; and to use prayer, meditation, ritual, or scriptural study in practice whenever appropriate. If a social worker feels uncomfortable or lacks adequate training to explore a religious or spiritual practice, he or she should refer the client to an appropriate clergy or spiritual director.

Present Issues. Part of the assessment may involve determining whether a possible religious or spiritual meaning assigned to a present or underlying issue is therapeutic or debilitating. Has religion been used as a defense barrier or been distorted by the client? Or has spiritual faith been a source of strength to see a person through a crisis? Herein lies the difference between healthy and mature faith and sick and distorted religion.

At the turn of the twentieth century, psychology of religion undoubtedly helped expose the pathological extremes of American revivalism (jerks, trances, paralyzed will, mind made suggestible, shouting, and springing over benches). William James's book *The Varieties of Religious Experience*, first published in 1902, is a classic text in psychology of religion. James defined conversion (commitment of faith) as "the process, gradual or sudden, by which a self hitherto divided, and unconsciously wrong, inferior and unhappy, becomes unified and consciously right, superior and happy, in consequence of its firmer hold upon religious realities" (James, 1958, p. 157). His descriptions of healthy and unhealthy religion still have profound relevance for our discussion.

On the one hand, religion may be a means of escape from the responsibilities of life. Escapism may take the form of an overemphasis of "fear religion" or fanatical appeals to the emotions or a highly legalistic religion creating a gap between idealistic human conduct and realistic attainment. On the other hand, healthy faith comes from an understanding of the spiritual life as the balance between freedom and responsibility to God or as an ultimate source of reality that has a positive effect on the self, others, and the world.

Allport (1961) argues that mature religious sentiment has the following characteristics: (1) a reasoned faith, (2) a dynamic character, (3) a consistent social morality, (4) a comprehensive philosophy of life, (5) an integral pattern, and (6) an open relevance. Healthy religious clients should think through their faith in a reflective and critical manner. They should grapple with fundamental questions: What do I believe? Is my faith reasonable and practical to my life? By thinking through their faith, individuals strengthen their identity. This permits them to direct their motivation dynamically toward a goal that is not determined by self-interest; rather, mature religious individuals reach out to the needs of others. They exhibit a consistent social morality in relation to others in their world. To construct a comprehensive philosophy of life, these mature individuals ask, What is the purpose of life? What is the set of values that governs my life? How do I translate my observations and reflections on life into concrete behavioral actions? They look for an integral pattern or a common center that holds all the aspects of life together. A common center may be God, Christ, the Torah, the teachings of Buddha or Islam, Love, Peace, or Justice. However, this religious framework is not a source of complacency: Spiritual or religious individuals undertake a continuous journey or search to discover better and fuller answers to perplexing life questions; they are open to change in their lifestyle and faith, to address an emerging need or problem.

Amato–von Hemert (1994) encourages the social worker to initiate a discussion on religion and, where relevant, to examine its impacts on the client's situation. For the ethnic client, religion offers a number of resources: prayer for guidance and strength in the midst of crisis and adversity; faith in God as an individual life goal; the church as a corporate support resource and as a means for supplying needs for daily living; and the willingness to love, based on the religious and cultural heritage of family and ethnic group.

Knowledge of Client Beliefs. The social worker should acquire a knowledge of particular beliefs of religious or spiritual groups and their effect on a client. A particular social worker may be well versed in religion when a social work program has access to a department of religion in a college or university. A social work student may acquire such knowledge by taking required religion courses or by entering a joint master's of social work and master's of divinity program.

Netting et al. (1990) and Dudley and Helfgott (1990) give specific suggestions on the incorporation of religious content into social work course areas: the history of organized religion in social welfare history and policy; the influence of religious issues in social policy development; the role of churches in current community social movements; the relationship among religion, economics, politics, and other practice-related religious and spiritual issues to understanding the cultural, social, and individual aspects of client groups in a community.

Amato–von Hemert (1994) points out that several areas of religion are "relevant intellectual disciplines" and are sources for a primary social work knowledge base. Among them are philosophy, literature, ethics, pastoral counseling, comparative religions, psychology of religion, sociology of religion, the role of religion in global politics and economic policies, and the role of religion in public policy issues (for example, sexuality, poverty, health care, civil rights, the death penalty, animal rights, environmental policy, prison reform, and public versus private education). She further believes that religion is relevant to psychosocial assessment (for example, religious background) and intervention (for example, religious beliefs as a therapeutic resource).

Social workers must be able to determine when their own religious knowledge and skills are inadequate and collaboration with, or referral to, a clinically trained pastor or pastoral counselor is appropriate. A related question is "With what clients and at what point in the social work process should a worker ignore religious statements, engage them, or consult with and/or make a referral to a religious professional?" (Amato–von Hemert, 1994, p. 16). These issues of assessment, treatment, and referral must be based on the worker's evaluation of his or her own expertise and limitations.

Although Clark (1994) has reservations about the involvement of social workers in the religious dimensions of the client's situation, he makes a

The Hernández Family, a Case Study

Positive strengths are emerging from this family. Mr. Platt notices the husband's and wife's energy and determination to work overtime and provide for the needs of the other two families who have recently moved to the city. A sense of family obligation pervades the relationship. A clinical worker could easily have focused on the father's neglect of his family due to his working two jobs or on the poor academic performance of Ricardo. Instead, Mr. Platt assesses the strengths available from the support network in the ethnosystem of the local Latino community.

Although the Hernández family has been a part of the local Latino community for several years, family members are unfamiliar with community helping resources available. A major resource for the Hernández family is the newcomer services sponsored by Catholic Social Services. In addition, Mr. Platt has often worked with Latino social workers who provide job-finding,

tutoring, and housing services for families newly arrived in the city. This resource seems appropriate to the needs of the Hernández family. Rather than clinically assessing the relationship between the father and son, Mr. Platt evaluates how external ethnic services could be marshaled and implemented to realign the family and reduce family stress.

TASK RECOMMENDATIONS

Conduct a practice assessment on this case from two perspectives. First, focus on the problem aspect of the case—the aspect related to his or her client's malfunctioning. Investigate and uncover aspects of the intrapsychic problems that contribute to the problem configuration. Assess the client's ego coping mechanisms to determine the level of functioning. Identify the dynamics of the particular problem and their effects on the client, family, and community. Use the data to determine a clinical diagnosis from

the *Diagnostic and Statistical Manual of Psychiatric and Mental Disorders (DSM-IV)* (American Psychiatric Association, 1994).

Second, focus on the positive resources and strengths emerging from the client and his environment. What are the personal, family, and community strengths available to the family? What existing healthy functions can be increased for the client's benefit? What formal and informal community support networks are available? What cultural customs, beliefs, and traditions are useful in the change process? How can family support and ethnic pride become assessment resources? These basic questions lead toward positive assessment areas.

Which approach would you employ in client assessment? Is there merit in blending both perspectives? Are you inclined toward an assessment that uncovers client and community resources and strengths?

helpful suggestion: "When religion is implicated as a serious problem in the client's person-situation configuration, social workers need to turn to pastoral professionals who can work with them in an interdisciplinary collaboration for the client's benefit" (p. 12).

CONCLUSION

This chapter asserts that culturally diverse social work assessment should focus on positive resources of the client and ethnic community.

Cultural elements support the survival of people of color. Seidman and Rappaport (1974) have argued for the need to build on the existing cultural values and strengths in a multicultural community. They emphasize support for programs that provide cultural amplifiers or ways of expanding the community's resources into the agency's programs. This approach offers an alternative to the ideological environment of blaming the victim. This book's approach is to uncover helping principles embedded in culturally diverse communities and to apply those cultural elements to social work practice.

Multicultural assessment rests on the assumption that people of color are competent, adequate, and different. They are not inherently deficient or maladjusted. Social workers should identify resources in the ethnic community system that can benefit the client and should determine practical ways to obtain and use them. We have asserted that assessment means evaluation of clients' assets rather than of their dysfunctional defects. Such assets include coping abilities, natural support systems, problem-solving abilities, and tolerance of stress.

The assessment procedure adopts an ecosystem perspective that allows exploration of an ethnic social ecology. Rappaport (1977) states:

> The principle could be translated into an apparently simple imperative—"know the system before you try to change it." The problem from an action point of view is that it is not always clear when one does really "know" the system. It therefore could serve as a rationalization for inaction. There are some guidelines for assessment which suggest that key questions involve actual and potential roles of members, the resources and rules for their distribution, as well as the relationship of the setting to its surrounding environments. (p. 154)

The foregoing discussion of assessment covers basic information about family roles, community resources, ethnic rules, and setting. The practice-framework section of this chapter includes discussions of ethnic family history, behavioral protocols, physical and mental illness as a social taboo, the meaning of prolonged silence, and other nuances of working with clients in multicultural practice.

Social workers should select psychosocial assessment issues that are appropriate to each client. In the final analysis, we must study and understand the social ecology of the particular ethnic community as it pertains to the client, who is a part of the cultural community and the assessment process.

REFERENCES

Allport, G. W. (1961). *The individual and his religion*. New York: Macmillan.

Amato–von Hemert, K. (1994). Should social work education address religious issues? Yes! *Journal of Social Work Education, 30*(1), 7–11, 16, 17.

American Psychiatric Association. (1994). *Diagnostic and statistical manual of mental disorders* (4th ed.). Washington, DC: Author.

Arnez, L. (1987). *Theory/case study integration*. Unpublished manuscript, California State University, Sacramento.

Atkinson, D. R., Morten, G., & Sue, D. W. (1979). *Counseling American minorities: A cross-cultural perspective*. Dubuque, IA: Brown.

Attneave, C. L. (1969). Therapy in tribal settings and urban network intervention. *Family Process, 8*, 192–210.

Bell, C. C., Bland, I. J., Houston, E., & Jones, B. E. (1983). Enhancement of knowledge and skills for the psychiatric treatment of black populations. In J. C. Chunn II, P. J. Dunston, & F. Ross-Sheriff (Eds.), *Mental health and people of color: Curriculum development and change* (pp. 205–238). Washington, DC: Howard University Press.

Bernal, G., Bernal, M. E., Martínez, A. C., Olmedo, E. L., & Santisteban, D. (1983). Hispanic mental health curriculum for psychology. In J. C. Chunn II, P. J. Dunston, & F. Ross-Sheriff (Eds.), *Mental health and people of color: Curriculum development and change* (pp. 65–94). Washington, DC: Howard University Press.

Bowles, D. D. (1978). Treatment issues in working with black families. *Smith College Journal for Social Work, 4*, 8–14.

Boyd, N. (1982). Family therapy with black families. In E. E. Jones & S. J. Korchin (Eds.), *Minority mental health* (pp. 227–249). New York: Praeger.

Canda, E. R. (1988). Spirituality, religious diversity, and social work practice. *Social Casework, 69*(4), 238–247.

Canda, E. R. (1989). Religious content in social work education: A comparative approach. *Journal of Social Work Education, 25*(1), 36–45.

Canda, E. R. (1990). Editorial foreword: On the inaugural issue. *Spirituality and Social Work Communicator, 1*, 1.

Caplan, G. (1972). *Support systems*. Keynote address to the conference of the Department of Psychiatry, Rutgers Medical School, and the New Jersey Mental Health Association, Newark, NJ.

Clark, J. (1994). Should social work education address religious issues? No! *Journal of Social Work Education, 30*(1), 11–16.

Congress, E. P. (1994). The use of culturagrams to assess and empower culturally diverse families. *Families in Society, 75*, 531–540.

Cousins, N. (1989). *Head first: The biology of hope.* New York: Dutton.

Cowger, C. D. (1992). Assessment of client strengths. In D. Saleebey (Ed.), *The strengths perspective in social work practice.* New York: Longman.

DeVos, G., & Romanucci-Ross, L. (1982). Ethnicity: Vessel of meaning and emblem of contrast. In G. DeVos & L. Romanucci-Ross (Eds.), *Ethnic identity: Cultural continuities and change* (pp. 363–390). Chicago: University of Chicago.

Dieppa, I. (1983). A state of the art analysis. In G. Gibson (Ed.), *Our kingdom stands on brittle glass* (pp. 115–128). Silver Spring, MD: National Association of Social Workers.

DuBray, W. (1993). *Mental health interventions with people of color.* St. Paul, MN: West.

Dudley, J. R., & Helfgott, C. (1990). Exploring a place for spirituality in the social work curriculum. *Journal of Social Work Education, 26*(3), 287–294.

Galan, F. J. (1992). Experiential focusing with Mexican-American males with bicultural identity problems. In K. Corcoran (Ed.), *Structuring change: Effective practice for common client problems* (pp. 234–254). New York: Lyceum.

Gardner, L. (1970). Psychotherapy under varying conditions of race. In J. Dovidio & S. Gaertner (Eds.), *Prejudice, discrimination and racism* (pp. 61–89). Orlando, FL: Academic Press.

Ghali, S. B. (1977). Culture sensitivity and the Puerto Rican client. *Social Casework, 58,* 459–468.

Gibbs, J. T. (1989). Black American adolescents. In J. T. Gibbs & L. N. Huang (Eds.), *Children of color: Psychological interventions with minority youth* (pp. 179–223). San Francisco: Jossey-Bass.

Goldstein, H. (1986). Toward the integration of theory and practice: A humanistic approach. *Social Work, 31,* 352–357.

Green, J. W. (1982). *Cultural awareness in the human services.* Upper Saddle River, NJ: Prentice Hall.

Harrison, A., Wilson, M., Pine, C., Chan, S., & Buriel, R. (1990). Family ecologies of ethnic minority children. *Child Development, 61,* 347–362.

Harwood, A. (Ed.). (1981). *Ethnicity and medical care.* Cambridge, MA: Harvard University Press.

Helms, J. (1984). Toward a theoretical explanation of the effects of race on counseling: A black and white model. *The Counseling Psychologist, 12,* 153–165.

Hepworth, D. H., & Larsen, J. A. (1993). *Direct social work practice: Theory and skills.* Pacific Grove, CA: Brooks/Cole.

Hill, R. (1972). *The strengths of black families.* Washington, DC: National Urban League, Research Department.

Ho, M. K. (1987). *Family therapy with ethnic minorities.* Newbury Park, CA: Sage.

Hobbs, N. (1962). Sources of gain in psychotherapy. *American Psychologist, 17,* 741–747.

Huang, L. N. (1989). Southeast Asian refugee children and adolescents. In J. T. Gibbs & L. N. Huang (Eds.), *Children of color: Psychological interventions with minority youth* (pp. 278–321). San Francisco: Jossey-Bass.

Huang, L. N., & Ying, Y. W. (1989). Chinese American children and adolescents. In J. T. Gibbs & L. N. Huang (Eds.), *Children of color: Psychological interventions with minority youth* (pp. 30–66). San Francisco: Jossey-Bass.

Hurd, E. P., Moore, C., & Rogers, R. (1995). Quiet success: Parenting strengths among African Americans. *Families in Society, 76*(7), 434–443.

Jackson, J. J. (1973). Black women in a racist society. In C. Willie, B. Kramer, & B. Brown (Eds.), *Racism and mental health* (pp. 185–268). Pittsburgh: University of Pittsburgh Press.

James, W. (1958). *The varieties of religious experience.* New York: Mentor.

Jones, A., & Seagull, A. (1977). Dimensions of the relationship between the black client and the white therapist. *American Psychologist, 32,* 850–855.

Joseph, M. V. (1988). Religion and social work practice. *Social Casework, 69*(7), 443–452.

Kelly, J. G. (1977). *The ecology of social support systems: Footnotes to a theory.* Paper presented at the American Psychological Association convention, San Francisco.

Kim, L. I. C. (1981). *Minority assessment.* Lecture presented at California State University, Sacramento, Division of Social Work.

Kitano, H. H. L. (1974). *Race relations.* Upper Saddle River, NJ: Prentice-Hall.

Kuramoto, F. H., Morales, R. F., Muñoz, F. U., & Murase, K. (1983). Education for social work practice in Asian and Pacific American communities. In J. C. Chunn II, P. J. Dunston, & F. Ross-Sheriff (Eds.), *Mental health and people of color: Curriculum development and change* (pp. 127–155). Washington, DC: Howard University Press.

Kutchins, H., & Kirk, S. A. (1997). *Making us crazy. DSM: The psychiatric Bible and the creation of mental disorders.* New York: Free Press.

Lee, E. (1982). A social systems approach to assessment and treatment for Chinese American families. In M.

McGoldrick, J. K. Pearce, & J. Giordano (Eds.), *Ethnicity and family therapy* (pp. 527–551). New York: Guilford.

Lewis, R. G., & Ho, M. K. (1975). Social work with Native Americans. *Social Work, 20*(5), 379–382.

Marsella, A. J., Kinzie, J. D., & Gordon, P. (1973). Ethnocultural variations in the expression of depression. *Journal of Cross-Cultural Psychology, 4* 435–458.

Marty, M. E. (1980). Social service: Godly and godless. *Social Service Review, 54*(4), 457–481.

McKnight, J. L. (1987). Regenerating community. *Social Policy, 17,* 54–58.

Miller, J. B. (1986). *Toward a new psychology of women.* Boston: Beacon.

Myers, H. F. (1982). Stress, ethnicity, and social class: A model for research with black populations. In E. E. Jones & S. J. Korchin (Eds.), *Minority mental health* (pp. 118–148). New York: Praeger.

Nagata, D. K. (1989). Japanese American children and adolescents. In J. T. Gibbs & L. N. Huang (Eds.), *Children of color: Psychological interventions with minority youth* (pp. 67–113). San Francisco: Jossey-Bass.

Netting, E. F., Thibault, J. M., & Ellor, J. W. (1990). Integrating content on organized religion into macropractice courses. *Journal of Social Work Education, 26*(1), 15–24.

Nyquist, W. J. (1994). *Carefully reclaiming our past: Social work educators speak out on spirituality, religion, and social work education.* Unpublished master's thesis, California State University, Sacramento.

Paniagua, F. A. (1994). *Assessing and treating culturally diverse clients: A practical guide.* Newbury Park, CA: Sage.

Price, J. A. (1981). North American Indian families. In C. H. Mindel & R. W. Habenstein (Eds.), *Ethnic families in America: Patterns and variations* (pp. 245–268). New York: Elsevier.

Rappaport, J. (1977). *Community psychology: Values, research, and action.* New York: Holt, Rinehart & Winston.

Rappaport, J. (1981). In praise of paradox: A social policy of empowerment over protection. *American Journal of Community Psychology, 9,* 1–25.

Red Horse, J. G., Lewis, R., Feit, M., & Decker, J. (1981). Family behavior of urban American Indians. *Social Casework, 59,* 67–72.

Robinson, J. B. (1989). Clinical treatment of black families: Issues and strategies. *Social Work, 34,* 323–329.

Romero, J. T. (1983). The therapist as social change agent. In G. Gibson (Ed.), *Our kingdom stands on brittle glass* (pp. 86–95). Silver Spring, MD: National Association of Social Workers.

Rothman, J., Gant, L. M., & Hnat, S. A. (1985). Mexican-American family culture. *Social Service Review, 59,* 197–215.

Ruiz, R. A., & Padilla, A. M. (1977). Counseling Latinos. *Personnel and Guidance Journal, 55,* 401–408.

Ryan, W. (1976). *Blaming the victim.* New York: Vintage.

Saleebey, D. (1992). Introduction: Power in the people. In D. Saleebey (Ed.), *The strengths perspective in social work practice.* New York: Longman.

Saleebey, D. (1996). The strengths perspective in social work practice: Extensions and cautions. *Journal of Social Work, 41*(3), 296–305.

Saleebey, D., & Larson, S. (1980). *Resource development networks: Theory and practice.* Unpublished manuscript. Fort Worth, TX: Bridge Association.

Schriver, J. M. (1998). *Human behavior and the social environment: Shifting paradigms in essential knowledge for social work practice.* Boston: Allyn & Bacon.

Seidman, E., & Rappaport, J. (1974). The educational pyramid: A paradigm for research, training, and manpower utilization in community psychology. *American Journal of Community Psychology, 2,* 119–130.

Sena-Rivera, J. (1980). La Familia Hispana as a natural support system: Strategies for prevention in mental health. In R. Valle & W. Vega (Eds.), *Hispanic natural support systems: Mental health promotion perspectives* (pp. 75–81). Sacramento: State of California Department of Mental Health.

Sheridan, M. J., Bullis, R. K., Adcock, C. R., Berlin, S. D., & Miller, P. C. (1992). Practitioners' personal and professional attitudes and behaviors toward religion and spirituality: Issues for education and practice. *Journal of Social Work Education, 28*(2), 191–203.

Solomon, B. B. (1976). *Black empowerment: Social work in oppressed communities.* New York: Columbia University Press.

Stack, C. (1975). *All our kin: Strategies for survival in a black community.* New York: Harper & Row.

Staples, R. (1981). The black American family. In C. H. Mindel & R. W. Habenstein (Eds.), *Ethnic families in America: Patterns and variations* (pp. 217–244). New York: Elsevier.

Stuckey, W. (1975). Navajo medicine men. *Science Digest, 78,* 34–41.

Sue, D. W. (1987). *Counseling the culturally different: Theory and practice.* New York: Wiley.

Sue, D. W., & Sue, D. (1990). *Counseling the culturally different: Theory and practice.* New York: Wiley.

Sue, S., & Sue, D. W. (1971). Chinese American personality and mental health. *Amerasia Journal, 1,* 36–49.

Trimble, J. E., Mackey, D. H., LaFromboise, T. D., & France, G. A. (1983). American Indians, psychology, and curriculum development. In J. C. Chunn II, P. J. Dunston, & F. Ross-Sheriff (Eds.), *Mental health and people of color: Curriculum development and change* (pp. 43–64). Washington, DC: Howard University Press.

Uba, L. (1994). *Asian Americans: Personality patterns, identity, and mental health*. New York: Guilford.

Warren, R. L. (1978). *The community in America*. Chicago: Rand McNally.

Weaver, D. R. (1982). Empowering treatment skills for helping black families. *Social Casework, 63*, 100–105.

Weick, A., Rapp, C., Sullivan, W. P., & Kisthardt, W. (1989). A strengths perspective for social work practice. *Social Work, 37*, 350–354.

Wrenn, R. L., & Ruiz, R. A. (1970). *The normal personality: Issues to insight*. Pacific Grove, CA. Brooks/Cole.

Zuñiga, M. E. (1983). Social treatment with the minority elderly. In R. L. McNeely & J. L. Colen (Eds.), *Aging in minority groups* (pp. 260–269). Newbury Park, CA: Sage.

Zuñiga, M. E. (1987). Mexican-American clinical training: A pilot program. *Journal of Social Education, 23*, 11–20.

CHAPTER 9

Intervention

Intervention is the most exciting process stage because it represents the effort of the worker and the client to bring to bear a change in the person and his or her environment.

Intervention is derived from the verb *intervene*, which means "to come between" and connotes "an influencing force to modify or resolve." In the context of practice, intervention is a change strategy that alters the interaction between the client and the problem environment. As indicated in Chapter 5, intervention occurs when the client's biopsychosocial needs are met through individual, family, group, and community resources. In social work practice, intervention has traditionally been associated with several casework schools of thought (namely, psychodiagnostic, functional, problem-solving, crisis intervention, task-centered, and behavioral). The theories behind these approaches offer a range of alternatives for various case situations. However, mental health research has questioned the adequacy of traditional psychotherapeutic methods for people of color. Weems (1974) holds that, because of important cultural differences, the concepts, institutions, and practices of mental health are ill adapted to ethnic problems and needs. Moreover, Jones and Korchin (1982) assert that traditional interventional therapies lack sensitivity to the ethnic *Weltanschauung* and lifestyle and misunderstand cultural practices.

Clearly, culturally diverse social work must develop approaches to intervention that are compatible with clients' needs and their ethnosystems. Indigenous principles of intervention in ethnic cultures must be identified and integrated. Doubts regarding the effectiveness of existing mental health therapies (Jones & Korchin, 1982) necessitate the redefinition and reinterpretation of social casework emphases in a manner appropriate to multicultural practice.

This chapter presents interventional strategies and levels compatible with the multicultural experience. It draws from a range of practice theories. Figure 9-1 shows the interaction between the worker and client around joint goals and agreement, joint interventional strategies, and micro-meso-, and macrolevels of intervention. Although I am sympathetic to the criticism that traditional psychotherapy approaches may not be suitable for people of color, I am convinced that these approaches contain practice principles that are applicable in an ethnic setting. Culturally diverse social work practice is a new field that is developing knowledge theory and practical application. To this end, our task is to formulate interventions on the basis of previous stages and current culturally diverse practice trends.

FIGURE 9-1 *Intervention Stage: Client-System and Worker-System Practice Issues*

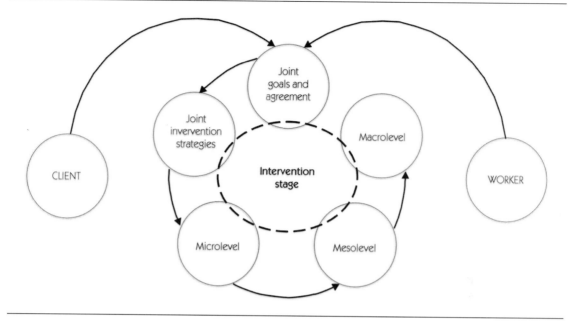

CLIENT-SYSTEM AND WORKER-SYSTEM PRACTICE ISSUES

Joint Goals and Agreement

How do we formulate appropriate goals, objectives, and a contract? Social work intervention begins with the establishment of goals for intervention from which a contract can be drawn between the worker and the client. *Goals* are terminal outcomes to be achieved at the end of the intervention stage. *Objectives* are intermediate subgoals, or a series of connecting steps that accomplish outcome goals. Goals and objectives should be tailored to the specific situation that confronts the client and the worker.

Solomon (1976, p. 26) identifies ethnic-related goals of intervention that enlist the mutual involvement of the client and the worker:

1. To help the client perceive him- or herself as a causal agent in achieving a solution to his or her problem or problems
2. To help the client perceive the social worker as having knowledge and skills that he or she can use

3. To help the client perceive the social worker as peer collaborator or partner in the problem-solving effort
4. To help the social worker perceive the oppressive social institutions (schools, welfare department, courts) as open to influence to reduce negative impact

These goals of intervention are general guidelines that affirm the client as a problem solver together with the social worker, who is also a source of knowledge and skill and an agent of institutional change. The goal statements imply both clinical and community intervention. Further, these broad goals are landmarks for articulating more specific goals that correspond to the assessment emphasis on socioenvironmental impacts. Intervention strategy is based on information derived from the previous stages of contact, problem identification, and assessment. For example, the worker and client can draw up specific statements of intervention goals relating to problem solving, peer collaboration, use of social work knowledge and skills, and institutional change, according to the particular problem-client-worker situation.

The Hernández Family, a Case Study

On the basis of what they have learned through contact, problem identification, and assessment, the Hernández family and Mr. Platt are ready to devise an intervention strategy for coping with the job situation confronting the three families as well as improving the eldest child's academic performance. From extensive discussion between the family and the social worker, a number of goals have emerged. Mr. Platt writes down the family's exact words in series of goal statements.

GOAL OUTCOMES

1. Job hunting: to assist the two families of new arrivals from Mexico in finding full-time employment
2. Father at home: to enable Mr. Hernández to work at his regular job and be home in the evenings with his family
3. Tutoring for the son: to provide Ricardo with tutoring assistance with his classroom assignments
4. English classes for mother: to teach Mrs. Hernández how to speak, read, and write English
5. Resettlement: to help the two families of in-laws with adjustment problems caused by their recent migration from Mexico into an urban setting in the United States

Mr. Platt will serve as a case manager who will coordinate various resources of the ethnic community in implementing these goal outcomes. Each family member will be responsible for following through on appointments that will be made for job hunting, tutoring assistance, classes in English as a second language (ESL), and newcomers' services. The family and Mr. Platt agree that, within the next two weeks, he will make contact with Catholic Social Services, located in the neighborhood Mexican American church. He will follow up on the effects of these services a few weeks afterward. A number of behavioral changes will be expected during the four-week process.

EXPECTED BEHAVIORAL CHANGES

1. Job hunting: the securing of full-time jobs for the two brothers-in-law
2. Father at home: adequate time in the evenings for Mr. Hernández to spend with his family, particularly in helping Ricardo and the other children with their homework
3. Tutoring for the son: improved academic performance of Ricardo—homework turned in on time and classroom work accomplished within the time frame established by the teacher
4. English classes for mother: free time two evenings a week for Mrs. Hernández to attend an ESL class in her neighborhood
5. Resettlement: periodic progress reports on social adjustments that the two newly arrived families make to urban life in the United States (driving a car, shopping in grocery and clothing stores, paying bills)

The Hernández family and Mr. Platt also decide that, before the intervention strategy is initiated, all three families will have a joint session with Mr. Platt to review these goal outcomes, responsibilities, time limits, and behavioral changes and to provide an opportunity for comments, suggestions, and revisions.

A brief session is subsequently held with all three families to review the intervention plan and to permit Mr. Platt to become acquainted with the two families who have lately migrated from Mexico. Rather than having the conference at the Family Service Association and causing a "misunderstanding" among the three families, the Hernándezes hold a dinner in their home. Mr. Platt is invited and brings wine for the occasion. After dinner, Mr. Hernández mentions to the men that Mr. Platt will be making some job contacts for them. Mr. Platt will also ask the newcomers' center to help the wives adjust to their new life. Catholic Social Services will be the organization that will help in these areas. The families seem agreeable to this plan, and the rest of the evening is spent in establishing rapport and finding out about each other.

Mr. Platt suggests several task objectives and the people involved agree to them.

The Hernández Family, a Case Study (continued)

TASK OBJECTIVES

1. Job hunting: The brothers-in-law will go to initial interviews with Catholic Social Services to find out about available jobs. They prefer to work for a Mexican American employer who owns a business in the city. If the brothers-in-law secure jobs, they will check back with Mr. Platt after two weeks to tell him how they feel about their work.

2. Father at home: During this period, Mr. Hernández will gradually taper off his second job and return home for dinner and spend the evening with the family. He will begin particularly to relate to Ricardo, assisting him with difficulties in homework assignments. During this two-week transition period, he will also let Mr. Platt know what is happening as far as his time and activities with the family are concerned.

3. Tutoring for the son: Mr. Platt will refer Ricardo for school tutoring service with the teenage unit of Catholic Social Services. Mexican American high school teenagers volunteer their time to assist elementary school children with school subjects. The volunteers receive credit from their high school and work closely with the classroom teacher and the tutoring coordinator, who assigns tutor-student pairs. The tutors focus on specific subject areas and skill problems and, in many cases,

tutor in both English and Spanish for bilingual children. Mr. Platt plans to monitor the tutoring experience with Ricardo in weekly family sessions and with the tutoring coordinator and assigned student helper.

4. English classes for mother: Mr. Platt will also check into ESL classes for Mrs. Hernández. He will investigate an evening class that meets in her neighborhood at the Catholic Social Services community center. Mrs. Hernández will attend classes after coming home from work and cooking dinner. Mr. Hernández will watch the children while she is at class. The class consists of twelve sessions, and students have an opportunity to join an intermediate class the following semester. Mrs. Hernández will begin her class after Mr. Hernández resumes his regular work hours. She will practice her English at home, and her husband and children will support and reinforce her conversations. She will report on her progress at weekly sessions with Mr. Platt.

5. Resettlement: Mr. Platt will ask the coordinator of the newcomers' center to get in touch with the two newly arrived families and to help them with shopping, paying bills, school, driving, and other adjustments. Although Mr. and Mrs. Hernández have taken the families around the community, the

families still need assistance in such areas of adjustment as registering for Social Security, buying a car, and reading newspaper advertisements.

CONTRACTING

No formal written contract is drawn up between Mr. Platt and the Hernández family with their relatives. Rather, a verbal agreement that delineates goal outcomes and task objectives is communicated at the session with the Hernández family and at the follow-up dinner meeting with the three families. Verbal consent is the substance of the contracting arranged between the parties involved.

The intervention strategy plan seems to examine and resolve the problems of the Hernández family, particularly the collective responsibility for the welfare of the two newcomer families, the work stress of the father, and the academic performance of the son. The plan focuses on the relevant past and present events that are affecting the family. It addresses the psychosocial dimensions of the problem by designating environmental resources in the ethnic community. The plan also initiates a series of behavioral tasks to implement the goal outcomes devised by the social worker and the families involved. Further, it fulfills the assumption that belonging to an ethnic community is important for family members' well-being, by tapping indigenous ethnic social services provided by

The Hernández Family, a Case Study (continued)

bilingual/bicultural workers who are familiar with the people and problems of the neighborhood. The services of the Catholic Social Services center, located in the church, symbolize the positive community assets that are available to Latino families under the stress of social adjustment. In a real sense, the intervention strategy uses the collective human services program of the ethnic community and reunites these three families with their local Latino community.

TASK RECOMMENDATIONS

Presented here is a clinical, community-oriented strategy for multicul-

tural intervention that relies on structure (goal outcomes, behavioral changes, and task objectives) as well as community (ethnic services, collective membership). To implement these guidelines, select a current or past case involving ethnic clients and apply an appropriate intervention approach:

1. Review each set of goal statements listed in the section on joint goals and agreement. Devise appropriate goal outcomes, behavioral changes, and task objectives for your case.
2. Explain how the intervention does the following:

a. Examines and resolves the problem behavior in a manner relevant to the minority client
b. Focuses on immediate past and present time sequences related to the problem
c. Addresses the psychosocial dimensions of the person and the environment
d. Initiates behavioral tasks to mobilize the client toward focused positive action
e. Demonstrates that intervention has occurred through a decrease in problem behavior during the social work practice process

---

For new immigrants, Fujiki, Hansen, Cheng, and Lee (1983) suggest the following intervention goals:

1. To clarify role expectations in therapy and in the client's personal life
2. To avoid situations in which parents act out their personal problems before their children (separate talks will work better in situations in which cultural attitudes inhibit intense feelings of anger)
3. To assist families in creating more successful problem-solving approaches
4. To assist children in their development in both cultures with minimal conflict
5. To assist families in learning how to establish an equilibrium as they live in two cultures
6. To provide community-supported programs in which ethnic clients participate
7. To recognize and provide help for clients with psychopathology regardless of symptom severity
8. To use ethnic and cultural communities, experts, and programs in assisting clients

Statements of outcome goals should be specific in detailing what is to be accomplished, clear as to what responsibilities each party will undertake, limited to a period of four to six weeks, and conditional in designating situations in which behavioral change will occur. Whenever possible, the client should define the outcome goals in his or her own words. The worker should write down the exact words in which the client states what he or she wants to change and accomplish. Consulting the client's significant others is useful in sharpening goal statements on the basis of cultural and personal preference. By this method, goal statements are established that are both acceptable and culturally relevant to the client. After goals have been stated, the worker and client must formulate specific tasks to implement the goals. These subgoals or intermediate steps are listed under each goal to specify a step-by-step strategy of change. After the goal outcomes and subgoals have been defined, the worker and client formulate a contract that designates areas of agreement and delineates responsibilities of the client, worker, and community resources. The contract should also specify the interventions to be employed, the time frame (expressed in number and frequency of sessions), mechanisms for monitoring progress, and practical activities for problem solving.

How do worker and client agree on an appropriate intervention strategy? There are at least five criteria for agreeing on a particular intervention:

1. *The intervention should examine and resolve the problem behavior in a manner relevant to the client.* The social worker and client should agree on an intervention that addresses and resolves the problem behavior and situation.

2. *The intervention should focus on immediate past, present, and future time sequences related to the problem.* It is important for the intervention to deal with the recent history of the problem (within the last three to six months) and to effect changes that influence and redirect the course of events in the near future. We are concerned with moderate, significant interventive changes that can occur in the present and alter the series of problems that have been mounting in the recent past.

3. *The intervention should address the psychosocial dimensions of the problem.* We have indicated that there are biological-physical, psychological-emotional, social-cultural, gender, and spiritual dimensions of the person and the environment that must be addressed and changed in the intervention stage. For people of color, changes in the external environment affect the client's cognitive, affective, and behavioral perspectives. Community helping services, surrogate helpers, and natural family systems have a tangible impact on psychosocial problem areas.

4. *The intervention should initiate behavioral tasks to mobilize the client toward positive action.* In social work intervention, change lies with the client, who implements a series of positive behavioral tasks to effect it. These interventional tasks are based on intervention goals, which are translated through practical activities the client performs.

5. *The intervention should demonstrate that change has occurred through a decrease in the prob-* *lem behavior following initial clinical contact and during the successive stages of problem identification, assessment, intervention, and termination.*

Joint Intervention Strategies

At least five interventional strategies are relevant in multicultural practice. These intervention themes must be seen as polarities paired with problem situations. Elsewhere (Lum, 1982) I have described a structure of problem situations and interventional strategies using the following themes:

> Oppression versus liberation
> Powerlessness versus empowerment
> Exploitation versus parity
> Acculturation versus maintenance of culture
> Stereotyping versus unique personhood

Chapter 7 deals with these problem themes in depth. This section applies each solution to its corresponding problem.

We assume the person of color can encounter a number of problem situations (oppression, powerlessness, exploitation, acculturation, and stereotyping) in his or her relationship with the dominant society. For each problematic state, there are corresponding interventional strategies (liberation, empowerment, parity, maintenance of culture, and unique personhood). These five pairs of problem situations and interventional strategies are Eriksonian polarities and are a means of explaining how a client can move from a problem situation to an interventional solution. Many multicultural cases contain multiple problem situations and intervention strategies. The introduction of the powerlessness/empowerment theme prompted culturally diverse social work practice to address related problems and strategies; identification of these five themes is an attempt to move practitioners beyond a single problem/intervention theme. At the same time, social workers should scrutinize the field to recognize emerging problem areas and devise interventional strategies that are not discussed in this section.

Liberation. Liberation involves the client's experience of release and freedom from oppressive restraints through psychosocial change. It is based on growth and decision making that occur when the client exercises choices in the face of oppressive conditions. One can also experience liberation through factual information about ethnic people of color. Cultural Study 9-1 reports facts that liberate oppressive thinking.

CULTURAL STUDY 9-1

Liberating Facts

As a guide for your own study, the U.S. Commission on Civil Rights has noted that increased immigration raises the following issues for both recent arrivals and Americans by birth:

Employment: The areas of occupation selected by or imposed upon various ethnic populations trace ethnic group mobility strategies and ethnic succession in the workplace, especially in manufacturing, hospitals, restaurants, and maintenance and custodial positions. Some ethnic populations appear to have greater numbers of highly educated persons in professional or semiprofessional positions.

Institutional and societal barriers: The job preferences and discrimination against the ethnic enclave and persons in small communities that are isolated from mainstream English-speaking society suggest the value of second-language competencies. Mutual accommodation is required to minimize the effect of inadequate language skills and training and difficulties in obtaining licenses, memberships, and certification.

Exploitation of workers: The most common form is the payment of wages below minimum standards. Alien workers have been stereotyped as a drain on public services. Such scapegoating is insupportable.

Taking jobs from Americans: Fact or fiction? The stunning fact is that immigrants are a source of increased productivity and a significant, if not utterly necessary, addition to the workforce as well as to the consumer power that drives the American economy.

Empowerment. Pinderhughes (1989) defines *empowerment* as "the use of strategies that enable clients to experience themselves as competent, valuable, and worthwhile both as individuals and as members of their cultural group. They no longer feel trapped in the subordinate cultural group status that prevents them from meeting their goals" (p. 111).

Simon (1990) emphasizes the self-determination and motivation inherent in client empowerment. That is, empowerment is initiated and sustained by the client, who must empower him- or herself. The social worker cannot empower the client; rather, the worker can only aid in the empowerment process by providing a climate, a relationship, resources, and procedural means to help the client enhance him- or herself. In other words, the worker participates in a collaborative alliance with the client to enhance empowerment (Simon, 1990).

Empowerment involves a change in the client's perception of him- or herself as a powerless victim. Rather, the client becomes a part of a group that has value and aims to change its powerless status by acquiring the necessary resources to cope with this reality (Pinderhughes, 1989).

According to Leigh (1982), empowerment consists of the development of skills that enable the person of color to implement interpersonal influence, improve role performance, and develop an effective support system. Helping interventions relevant to empowerment include educating the person regarding the effects of the oppressing system, mobilizing material and interpersonal resources, building support systems, informing people about their societal entitlements and rights, and strengthening a positive self-image (Leigh, 1984).

Cultural Study 9-2 details four dimensions of application situations and problem-solving activities when it is useful to employ an empowerment intervention.

<hr>

CULTURAL STUDY 9-2

Empowerment Intervention Dimensions

Empowerment practice centers on a continuum of factors regarding the personal, interpersonal, and political aspects of the problem at hand. Though focus on these factors may fluctuate, all remain critical to the empowerment process, which strives to achieve the most comprehensive analysis and approach for each problem-solving situation. [Four dimensions of intervention represent activities focused on client systems, from individual to sociopolitical.]

DIMENSION 1

Interventions consist mainly of initial work with individuals identified by themselves or by outreach or intake workers as needing assistance. The presenting problems may stem from lack of resources, interpersonal conflicts, emotional problems, specifically defined environmental problems, or any other concern of the client. With each client, the worker must first establish a working relationship and assess needs and resources. If indicated, securing entitlements is a first step in the helping process. One must do an initial assessment at this stage to determine the clients' needs and goals. At this point, clients' consciousness regarding the global aspects of their conditions and circumstances may be quite limited or hidden by an immediate need for critical resources. An assessment includes clients' views of the problem and their awareness of such problems in both themselves and their families. It also includes their perceived power to manage the problem or not.

DIMENSION 2

Interventions are designed to provide the knowledge and skills necessary to master identified problems, such as life transitions, developmental problems, or more specific conditions. The methods suggested for this second dimension include conferences, workshops, courses, small-group formats, newspapers, telephoning, and videos. Ongoing small groups allow the formation of support networks in which individuals can discover the strength of their common interests and have their perceptions and experiences validated by one another through discussion of the content of the training (Gitterman & Shulman, 1986; Lee, 1994). Educational programs and materials must take adult learning styles into account and must be determined in part by the interest and desires of the clients.

In dimension 2 interventions, the assessment of power dynamics involves larger systems. Because clients now understand these problems as common to many others, they define problems more broadly. The comprehension of a "common issue" often leads to self-help and collective action. Self-help approaches to empowerment actually require participation with other individuals in groups focused on alleviating a shared problem, such as alcoholism, illness, poverty, fear of crime, or housing issues. Further, knowledge made available through local, state, or national networks broadens the base of individual and collective knowledge.

A key factor in self-help is the action that group members decide to take. Reisman (1965) describes the essence of this action as the helper-therapy principle. Members of the self-help group seek not only to assist themselves in overcoming or coping with a problem but also to assist other members of the group in their struggle. Helpers appear to benefit greatly from this process. The development and use of interpersonal skills such as counseling, listening, and advocacy often proceed from such participation. At this level, consciousness regarding the public nature of the problem and the political nature of causality can be developed.

DIMENSION 3

Interventions center on change or mediation in the immediate environment. Learning about social service and health care resources and how to access them is one key activity. This dimension often proceeds from the consciousness process through which clients and workers continue to explore the impact of the environment on personal problems. For example, a single parent seeking employment may engage in training programs and support groups in dimension 2 and become engaged in job development and exploring gender discrimination and sanctions in dimension 3. The activities of dimension 3 also include an important focus on learning about professional helpers and how to communicate with them effectively.

DIMENSION 4

Interventions involve clients in the political aspects of their problems. This includes social action or other collective efforts to impact environmental forces that contribute to individual problems. The knowledge base in this dimension consists of the collective intelligence of participants and sources of formal knowledge such as national social action groups and academic institutions. For example, participation in the National Organization for Women (NOW) enables a woman to address health and other issues from an informed base of social action. Besides disseminating materials about current social policy of interest to all women, NOW offers training in skills necessary for social action.

From "A Model for Empowerment Practice" by R. J. Parsons, L. M. Gutiérrez, and E. O. Cox in *Empowerment in Social Work Practice: A Sourcebook*, L. M. Gutiérrez, R. J. Parsons, and E. O. Cox (Eds.), pp. 14–18. Copyright 1998 Brooks/Cole Publishing Company. Reprinted by permission.

Parity. Parity is the achievement of equality in power, value, and rank. It involves fairness and rightful access to services, compensations, and resources. Parity is the client's response to exploitation by manipulators in the dominant society. Cultural Study 9-3 illustrates the constant struggle for parity, illustrated in the affirmative action issue and the inequality that confronts us.

CULTURAL STUDY 9-3

The Rise and Fall of Affirmative Action

If you think that institutionalized racism, sexism and classism are no longer serious, structural problems in the United States, and that all that remains of these inequalities is individual prejudice, then you might argue that we no longer need policies of affirmative action. The evidence, however, suggests otherwise. In the critically important areas of public housing, health and education, we are returning to a highly segregated, separate and unequal, racialized society. The devastating economic polarization of the last twenty years, aggravated by a malign neglect of the public sector, has hit hardest at employment, and public resources in African American, Puerto Rican, Chicano, Latino, Afro-Cuban, Haitian, American Indian, South-East Asian and poor white communities, and disproportionately at immigrants, women and children.

When you look around at institutions of higher education, especially community and state colleges in California, you initially see considerable diversity. If you think that universities have done as much as is possible to diversify our students, faculty, curricula, and public discourse, then you might argue that affirmative action is no longer needed. What you see is accurate— California has the most diverse population, work force, and student body in the country. But look closer and you will find that this diversity generally stops as you climb the ladders of power. Walk on any campus these days and you will see a large number of employees of color, but over 80 percent of them work in clerical, support, or maintenance positions.

We reached the high point of affirmative action in higher education some fifteen years ago. To those who think that diversity is now the norm in academia, let me remind you that about 87 percent of all full-time faculty and some 90 percent of all full professors are Anglo. White males represent 59 percent of all full-time faculty and, in some departments, their over-representation is even greater—73 percent of Engineering, 71 percent of History, 82 percent of Philosophy, 70 percent of Economics. Close to 93 percent of all academics who have received Humanities doctorates since 1942 and are still active in their fields, are Anglos. Almost half of African American faculty still teach in historically black colleges. White females are still under-represented (28 percent) in full-time faculty and over-represented (40 percent) in part-time faculty; that of 57,000 tenured academics in the United States only 255 are Latinas; and that most curricula and textbooks have barely begun to diversify their contents.

Affirmative action, as we knew it in the 1960s and 1970s, has virtually disappeared. Unless reversed by the courts, Proposition 209 will eliminate what remains of its government-endorsed policies in California and encourage advocates of "reverse discrimination" to sue any institution or administration that retains a voluntary commitment to equity and diversity. It will not be enough to reverse Proposition 209. To continue the long journey to equality that we began some thirty years ago will require the renewal of a civil rights movement that, at its best, fought simultaneously and inclusively for class, race and gender-based policies of affirmative action. But we will also need to develop new models of social change that take into account the profound shift to the right in the political climate; the unprecedented demographic transformation taking place in states like California; a much more complicated alignment of constituencies, crisscrossed by issues of race, class, gender, sexuality, and disability; and a struggle for racial equality that, more than ever before, involves multiple and diverse struggles not only over economic access and upward mobility, but also over immigration policies, citizen rights, language, and cultural diversity.

From "The Rise and Fall of Affirmative Action" by A. M. Platt. In *Notre Dame Journal of Law, Ethics and Public Policy* (1997), Vol. 11, No. 1, pp. 67–78. Copyright 1997 Thomas J. White Center on Law and Government, Notre Dame Law School.

Maintenance of Culture. Maintenance of culture denotes the use of cultural beliefs, customs, celebrations, and rituals as means of overcoming social problems. Culture is a source of strength and renewal. When people of color rediscover their past heritage, they can use it to cope with present and future life problems, as we see in Cultural Study 9-4 (Lewis, 1977).

CULTURAL STUDY 9-4

Maintenance of Culture

Ben Dancewell is a thirty-four-year-old full-blooded Cheyenne-Arapahoe who was medically diagnosed as an alcoholic. He is married and has four children. He is an excellent dancer and has won several contests. The timing of the therapy was unique in that it was held after the ceremonial dances.

The ceremonial dances served Ben in many therapeutic ways such as (1) helping him to ventilate his feelings; (2) helping him possess a unique sense of identity and pride in his culture; (3) giving him a great sense of belonging through being with other Native Americans. (4) As he danced, one could see other Indians giving him support; therefore, he gained a unique support system. (5) This experience enhanced his altruistic feelings and made him uniquely ready for therapy.

In attendance was his entire primary family, as well as his parents. Each week, he began to ventilate, for example, about his pride at being an Indian but how he felt inferior when he was in the majority culture. After several sessions of ventilating and using the extended family as support, [his] drinking diminished and he was able to hold a job.

From "Cultural Perspective on Treatment Modalities with Native Americans," by R. Lewis. An unpublished paper presented at the National Association of Social Workers Professional Symposium, San Diego. Copyright © 1977 by Ronald Lewis. Reprinted by permission.

Unique Personhood. The theme of unique personhood recognizes the individuality of each person and seeks to discover personal and collective ethic worth. It is the opposite of stereotyping, which prejudges an individual by a negative generalization about the group to which he or she belongs. Bochner (1982) cites numerous studies that indicate that deindividuated persons are likely to behave less responsibly and be treated less favorably than individual persons. Similarly, individuating out-group members could reduce discrimination against them.

Cultural Study 9-5 reminds us about the uniqueness of the client in terms of self-respect, dignity, and worth.

CULTURAL STUDY 9-5

Unique Personhood

One needs to see the whole person in order to focus on both personal and environmental factors, on strengths instead of deficits, and on the person rather than on a diagnosis or presenting problem. Respect for the client's unique qualities, values, and experiences enables the practitioner to accept the client's definition of his or her problem. The client's personal and cultural background is important data for understanding the problem situation. At the same time, the practitioner engages with clients in expanding their view of problems to the environmental context.

The helping process provides opportunities for clients to experience capability, dignity and worth, and strength—to take risks, make their own decisions, gain knowledge and skills, learn critical thinking, participate in new roles, educate staff and other clients, participate in mutual aid and support groups, participate in collective action toward social change, and work with others on personal change and political change. This process also fosters clients' awareness of being an expert on their own problems, their understanding of rights and self-determination, and a change in how they see themselves—from passive beneficiary of services to active consumer of services.

From "Creating Opportunities for Empowerment-Oriented Programs" by L. M. Gutiérrez, R. J. Parsons, and E. O. Cox. In *Empowerment in Social Work Practice: A Sourcebook*, L. M. Gutiérrez, R. J. Parsons, and E. O. Cox (Eds.), p. 221. Copyright 1998 Brooks/Cole Publishing Company. Reprinted by permission.

Levels of Intervention

Social work practitioners have described practice in terms of intervention in the micro-, meso-, and macrosystems (Mullen, Dumpson, & associates, 1972). The microsystem involves the unit systems of the individual, family, and small group (Meyer, 1972). Examples of microlevel interventions include friendly neighborhood sharing (Blackwell & Hart, 1982) and support services linking clients to schools, churches, and other organizations (Weil, 1981). Leigh (1982) suggests that the worker and client begin with intermediate microlevel change that can be accomplished in the short term.

Intervention in the mesosystem entails study and analysis of the conditions and problems of the local community. Mesosystem-level intervention makes use of helping agencies and local organizations to effect social and political change and to assist with the socioeconomic needs of individuals, families, and ethnic groups (Turner, 1972). Mesointervention has included group-based services involving immigrant children, adolescents, and parents in transitional adjustment to the United States (Weil, 1981) and practical action in the community, such as improvement of street lighting, garbage collection, police protection, and neighborhood stores (Blackwell & Hart, 1982).

The macrosystem involves complex large-scale entities that affect large geographic populations. It has a bearing on poverty, racial and social class discrimination, substandard housing, drug abuse, mental illness, and other national problems. Macrosystem practice occurs in large organizations between population aggregates and social situations. Planning, policy, and administrative action are the modalities of intervention (Webb, 1972). Macrolevel change often requires changing power relations, which is a long-range aim (Leigh, 1984). Macrointervention for people of color includes social welfare programs and services for refugees that encourage individual productivity,

TABLE 9-1 *Intervention Levels and Strategies*

	Liberation	Empowerment	Parity	Maintenance of Culture	Unique Personhood
Microlevel (individual, family, small group)					
Mesolevel (ethnic/local communities and organizations)					
Macrolevel (complex organizations, geographic populations)					

responsibility, and sense of self-worth (Weil, 1981); better-quality education; and improvement in economic conditions (Blackwell & Hart, 1982).

The following sections describe intervention at the micro-, meso-, and macrolevels in depth. The social work practitioner and client should collaborate on the selection of appropriate intervention strategies and levels according to the nature of the problem. There is wide latitude for orchestrating an interventional approach based on the given criteria for selection, strategies, and levels. Both the worker and the client might ask, Are we dealing with a psychosocial problem that involves empowerment and cultural maintenance and affects the individual and family on a microlevel? Or are we struggling to formulate an intervention that calls for liberation and parity strategies at the local community and complex organization levels? Table 9-1 contains blank spaces for writing case problem situations in the appropriate categories to identify relevant intervention levels and strategies.

Microlevel Intervention. Microlevel intervention has traditionally focused on psychosocial change that affects the individual, family, and small group. Social casework, family casework, and group work have been formulated around offering interventional approaches to these target groups. Historically, clinical social work practice has been oriented to at least five theories: psychodiagnosis, which has combined Freudian psychoanalysis and systems theory; functionalism, which has been influenced by Rankian psychology and has reemerged in existential psychology; crisis intervention, which is oriented to ego psychology and the Eriksonian life-crisis stages; problem solving, which has its base in cognitive theory and was popularized by Perlman (the task-centered casework by Reid and Epstein is an effort to combine problem solving with an empirical behavioral approach); and behavioral therapy, which has its base in learning theory and has been adapted to social work by Thomas, Fischer, and others. Social work practitioners have been oriented to one or more of these theories of clinical practice by their academic and professional education. I take the position that a number of theories of social work intervention are applicable to multicultural clients, depending on the situation. An underpinning of intervention with ethnic clients is to apply social casework emphases selected for the particular problem.

Generalist Clinical Principles. Multicultural practice draws on three basic clinical principles:

changing the person and the environment; adapting to the language of the client; and practicing culturally appropriate listening. Aspects of these approaches have been detailed in previous sections; they are brought together here to reaffirm their importance.

Change the Person and the Environment. Microlevel clinical intervention reaffirms the central importance of the relationship between the person and the environment. As previously indicated, social work knowledge theory emphasizes the person-and-environment theme in systems theory and psychosocial theory. Ivey (1981) declares, "the person influences the environment and the environment influences the person" (p. 280).

In multicultural practice, it is important to investigate the cultural and ethnic characteristics of the person and environment on the community and individual levels. That is, the worker must study both the essential characteristics of a particular ethnic group and the unique, individual client as a member of that group. The object is to reduce the cultural difference between the worker and the client, so as to increase the likelihood for successful transaction.

Throughout the clinical process, the worker relates constantly to the particular cultural and ethnic dimensions of the client and the social environment. Each process stage must address this point of reference. The familiar phrase "which therapy for which individual at what time under what condition" might be reworded to say "which culturally relevant intervention strategy for this particular ethnic client, who is involved in this present problem, which is affected by a particular social/cultural environment." Ivey (1981) stresses that Western clinical treatment tends to obscure systemic, cultural, and environmental influences and concentrates on the self, individual behavior, and personal psychodynamics. Social work is the only discipline that emphasizes the social causes of distress and proposes helping strategies for the individual, family, small group, community, and organization. Social work practice restores the social and cultural meanings of clinical helping. It calls for a social awareness of the person in a social system context. Environ-mental interventions may be more effective and important for human growth and change in ethnic clients than traditional psychotherapy, which deals with internal problems in the person.

Adapt to the Language of the Client. *Language* is the expression or communication of thoughts and feelings through verbal sounds, nonverbal gestures, and written symbols. It involves the selection of particular word combinations that result in forms of expression and an identifiable style. The idiom "speaking the same language" means having the same beliefs and attitudes as another person. In a therapeutic helping sense, the worker must enter the client's linguistic culture to achieve mutual understanding and identification.

Language is a descriptor of culture and forms a base for culturally relevant treatment. Psycholinguistics and sociolinguistics are two specialized disciplines that study the meaning of communication and the effect of language on thought and conceptual abstractions. Culture influences the words, constructions, and sequences of thoughts expressed by an ethnic group. The social work profession must concentrate on the language communication of cultures. What is the particular expression of language used by members of the culture in relating to each other? How are problems formulated and explained in a particular culture? How are solutions constructed and implemented from a cultural perspective? Studying a particular group's language, customs, and behavior provides clues that may be used in answering these questions. If words, concepts, and interpretations are essential parts of language, social workers must understand personal, situational, and cultural contexts and respond appropriately to meet these linguistic expressions of problem situations.

Ivey (1981) asserts that counseling and psychotherapy are concerned with freeing people to generate new modes of responding and acting. Clients often learn clinical words and phrases and nonverbal communication, which cause them to act in a positive therapeutic manner. Different theories generate varying sentences and constructs, which clients learn from counselors. Each clinical approach emphasizes a particular interpretation of problem reality and solution. From a multicultural perspective, different counseling approaches lead to different ways of dealing with a problem.

Different cultures or groups of people, according to Ivey (1981), generate different sentences and constructions that must be recognized as culturally unique. Words and sentences from key constructions form the core of most counseling and psychotherapy theories. Each therapeutic theory represents a separate reality for explaining human behavior and problem perspective. The client tends to learn new words and constructions from the therapist. However, it is crucial for the client to generate his or her own sentences and constructions, which are a meaningful part of the client's cultural orientation. Each culture has its own pattern for movement and change; this pattern is reflected in its language. More attention to language expression and analysis is needed in counseling and therapy. Part of the problem might be that a worker and a client have different language-communication patterns and are working at cross-purposes.

Working from this orientation, experienced clinicians tend to draw from a wider range of client responses, use more interpretations and initiation, employ more exploration and less reflection, and ask more open-ended questions early in the interview and more directive questions to elicit details later. These helpers move toward an inductive approach to draw a broad range of information from the client's environmental situation and cultural perspective.

Given that language is central to the helping process, what are the language tasks for the worker? They may be grouped under three themes: relating, naming, and adapting.

Relating involves understanding how people relate to each other in a particular culture. For example, Latino culture involves the language of *personalismo* (friendly small talk), which builds on informality and humanness. Asian culture emphasizes silence and respect as a means of communication. The worker must learn about a culture's particular verbal and nonverbal means of communication.

Naming refers to focusing on important problem areas related to the client's cultural context. For African Americans, racism and discrimination

are associated with socioeconomic problem areas. Asian Americans are confronted with the lack of family obligation or loyalty related to cultural and social conflict between the generations. These and similar culturally relevant areas must be named or discussed in the problem-identification stage. Otherwise the worker may gloss over critical areas underlying struggle and conflict.

Adapting refers to cultural adaptation in which the worker forfeits the right to fit the client into his or her particular therapeutic casework framework. Rather, the worker chooses to cross over and to adopt clinical theory and skills to fit the client's cultural orientation. This culturally inductive helping approach is well suited to multicultural practice.

Practice Culturally Appropriate Listening. Although empathy, warmth, and genuineness have been associated with effective therapy, it is important to meet the individual client's specific need levels. The worker must decide whether these qualities are culturally appropriate at a given time. Various cultures express empathic qualities differently. Rather than using empathic listening responses in all cases, the worker should understand the cultural appropriateness or inappropriateness of empathy for a particular ethnic client.

Ivey (1981) makes a case for the importance of using attending in the listening process instead of empathy. Ivey sees the interview as a series of conversation blocks interspersed with periodic pauses between the end of an old topic and the negotiation for a new topic. The therapist keeps to a single topic and listens carefully. The listening style is more active and directive in response to the client's statements; the worker learns to listen and respond within the cultural and linguistic contexts of the client. This is antithetical to imposing the worker's language and theory orientation on the client. Ivey warns workers not to commit psychological and linguistic imperialism.

Intervention Strategies. The social worker has a repertoire of intervention strategies that are useful in multicultural practice. In this chapter, the following microlevel intervention approaches are discussed: problem-solving/task-centered intervention, crisis intervention, empowerment, existential intervention, woman-centered perspective, family therapy, group work, and treating refugees. Particular interventions seem to be appropriate for different ethnic groups. The worker should evaluate the particular client, problem situation, and psychosocial assessment factors and should select an intervention strategy approach that addresses the relevant problem needs.

Problem-Solving/Task-Centered Intervention. In general, the problem-solving/task-centered intervention strategy offers a cognitive-behavioral approach. Problem solving appeals to the cognitive need to reorder a series of events, persons, and problems that have overwhelmed the client, whereas the task-centered approach provides structure and specific instructions to achieve goals.

Task assignments are particularly helpful for the client who needs direction. Higginbotham and Tanaka-Matsumi (1981) note that people of color "desire a 'guidance-nurturant' oriented intervention. They want a helper to take an active, directive role and give them explicit directions on how to solve problems and bring immediate relief from disabling distress" (p. 261). Uba (1994) observes that Asian Americans expect the helping person to give advice, recommend courses of action, and tell them how to resolve their problems. In some ways, the clinical practitioners is expected to behave like a physician: to conduct an examination, make a diagnosis, and write out a prescription. The problem-solving/task-centered intervention addresses these expectations. Its emphasis is on a clear, detailed intervention plan and straightforward solutions to concrete and immediate problems.

Problem-Solving Intervention. The word *problem,* from the Greek word *problema,* which refers to "a thing thrown forward," suggests a projection of an obstacle. A problem is a barrier or an obstacle thrown in the path of a person. The word *solving,* or *solution,* is derived from the Latin word *solutus,* which means "to loosen." In chemistry, a *solute* is a substance dissolved in another substance. Thus, the joining of these two root words, *problema* and

solutus, to form *problem solving* evokes the metaphor of a solution that has the power to loosen an impediment blocking a person.

Problem solving is a rational step-by-step procedure that requires mental comprehension and behavioral action. It calls on a person's coping capacities and social competence to deal with daily problems. Problem solving is not only an individual endeavor but also a cooperative effort. Mutual and cooperative problem solving is used as the worker assists the client with decision making related to change. A network of people is organized into a support system for the client. It is important for all parties to commit to working collaboratively and cooperatively in problem solving.

Problem solving is a natural part of the client's survival skills. The immediate family and extended family act as a support system for collaborative and cooperative problem solving. The pooling of resources for housing, child care, and basic necessities is a problem-solving response to daily survival needs.

Moreover, as a practical and pragmatic approach that requires directive action in the current situation, problem solving appeals to clients who seek direction and structure. Hepworth and Larsen (1990) offer five guidelines on problem solving:

1. Specify problems accurately, so that the client's concerns can be determined. The worker must seek concrete details of the client's problems and pinpoint difficulties.
2. The focus should be on present problems rather than on past difficulties. Details of recent mishaps help to pinpoint problem behavior, but the client should not dwell on past problems.
3. Focus on only one problem at a time. A rapid shift in focus from problem to problem sidetracks progress toward problem solving.
4. Listen attentively to those who are sharing problems and offer your perceptions of what the client is saying. Summarize major points and provide feedback. Make sure there has been accurate understanding. The worker and client should periodically check and verify the successful transmittal and receiving of mes-

sages. Both parties should agree on the intended meaning of a message.

5. Problems should be presented and expressed without blaming or attacking the other person. Expressing problems in an accusatory manner can cause defensiveness or countercriticism and undermine the helping process.

It is more effective to express positive intent and to share personal feelings than to focus on what the client is doing wrong. As preparation for presenting a problem, the helping person should convey a positive, caring message before he or she states a concern. Moreover, it is helpful to assist the client with framing the problem in terms of positive intent rather than of negative pathology and victim-blaming. A problem should be stated as an unsatisfied want or an unfulfilled need.

Problem-Solving Steps. The counseling process consists of three basic stages: defining the problem; generating alternatives; and making a commitment to action (Ivey, 1981). The problem-solving approach asks, What is the problem? What is the range of possible solution alternatives? What is the most viable solution? How can the solution be implemented? What are the results of the solution? The problem focus of ethnic clients tends toward external social issues rather than internal individual ones.

The problem-solving process incorporates a decision-making framework, in the form of six specific steps the person can take to confront and deal with the problem: problem identification, problem analysis, solution alternatives, solution prioritization, solution implementation, and problem-solving evaluation. In the helping process, the worker and the client go through each step and discuss aspects of how to cope with the problem. The procedure becomes an intuitive part of the person's rational thinking and behavioral action responses. Problem solving formalizes the commonsense way in which a person handles a problem in daily living.

Problem Identification. It is important that the client acknowledge and define the problem he or she is facing. There is much cultural resistance to confronting a problem, and a person may procras-

tinate until the problem becomes so severe it can no longer be ignored. Admitting the existence of a problem and taking action to alleviate it are the first steps the client must take. In problem identification, the task is to examine the set of interrelated problems—the *problem cluster*—facing the client and to identify a manageable problem that can be solved in a reasonable time frame.

Assuming the worker has established trust and rapport and has overcome resistance and communication barriers, the worker can use the following questions to initiate problem identification:

- It seems that, as we have been talking about your problem, we need to focus on a particular problem and work on it. What is the most pressing problem facing you now?
- Tell me more about this problem. Do you think it can be solved? Would you like for us to work on it and see if some changes can be made in the next several weeks?

Problem Analysis. Analyzing a problem entails uncovering its history and assessing the needs of the persons involved. In Chapters 7 and 8, we discussed problem identification and assessment in detail. However, a rule of thumb for the worker is to find out what has happened to the client during the last four to six weeks. Often an event related to the problem can precipitate a crisis reaction in the patient during that time. The task is to pinpoint and detail problematic feelings and behavior that occurred in the last few months. The worker should take a brief history of problem information; this is a crucial part of problem analysis.

Assessing the client's needs as they relate to the problem requires the worker to consider the environmental impact on the client and the resources available for responding to the problem. Socioenvironmental stressors have an important impact on the individual's reactions. It is important to differentiate what can and what cannot be changed. The client must accept what cannot be changed, and the client and the worker must act on what can be changed. Together the worker and client make an effort to find ways of solving problems.

The following are examples of problem-analysis responses:

- Let's get some background on the problem. Can you tell me when it started and what has been happening recently?
- Can you give me a recent example of the problem? What were your feelings and thoughts in this situation?
- Is there anything in your surroundings that could be contributing to the problem?

Solution Alternatives. Based on an agreed-on problem to be solved, the next step in problem solving is to brainstorm a range of alternatives. The worker should ask the client to think about possible solutions to the problem. The worker and client then spend time developing several answers and write them on a piece of paper or on a chalkboard. If the client hesitates, the worker can suggest possible solutions to generate discussion.

The solution alternatives set forth in brainstorming should be open and spontaneous, and they should be received in a positive, accepting manner. No answer is unworthy of consideration.

- Let's brainstorm some possible solutions to your problems. Just think about the problem for a moment and feel free to say whatever comes to mind.
- Let me list these ideas on the board. I'll write them down. You keep saying them.

Solution Prioritization. The purpose of solution prioritization is to review each viable solution and find the answers most likely to solve the problem. It is also necessary to eliminate unrealistic or unlikely possibilities from the list. Which alternatives are unlikely to solve the problem? Which ones might solve the problem? Which ones are most likely to solve the problem? The client should weigh the pros and cons of the strongest solutions and make a tentative choice. If a particular solution does not work, the client can try other solutions that have the potential to solve the problem.

The following are examples of possible solution-prioritization responses:

- There are a number of good suggestions here for solutions to this problem. Let's go through the list and find out which ones you want to choose.
- Which solution would you like to work on?

Solution Implementation. After the client has selected a solution, the next step is to implement it in a problem situation. At first, it may be advantageous to conduct a "dry run." Ways to introduce the solution include role-playing a situation, conducting reality testing, or giving specific instructions. It is important for the worker to provide as much structure and guidance as possible for the solution to succeed.

After the client tries out the solution, it is helpful to obtain initial feedback on implementation. When and where did the client introduce the solution? What happened to the problem after the client tried the solution? How did the client feel during the implementation period?

Possible solution implementation responses include the following:

- I am pleased that you want to try out this solution. Let's imagine that you are in a situation and want to test it out. What would you say? How would you feel?
- It will take some time, but let's work on this together. I know progress will be made.

Problem-Solving Evaluation. Effective problem solving evaluates the outcomes that result from changing the problem. Monitoring the behavioral changes of the persons involved is a good way to determine whether change has occurred. Daily logs and records quantify the frequency of the problem behavior and its decline after the client introduces the solution. A decrease in the problem behavior means that the solution has worked.

To monitor behavioral change, the client should divide a piece of paper into four columns labeled "Date," "Problem Behavior," "Frequency," and "Solution" and should keep this record for at least two weeks. Then the worker and client can note the changes as the solution is steadily applied during this period.

Problem-solving evaluation should be ensured through frequent meetings between the client and the worker. Sessions should focus on what has happened during the week, the client's efforts toward solution implementation, and modifications necessary to maintain positive behavioral change. Supportive reinforcement is necessary to encourage and foster momentum.

If the original solution has not produced positive results over the course of several weeks, it is necessary to return to the solution priority list, select another possible solution, and repeat the process.

Possible problem-solving evaluation responses include the following:

- Well, how have things been going for you? What has been happening since we last talked about how you were going to deal with the problem?
- Tell me what happened when you tried out what we practiced the last time. How did you feel in the situation? What response did you pick up from the other person?

Problem solving is an opportunity to foster self-help for people who are able to figure out problems for themselves. It helps a person learn to identify and analyze a problem, generate a number of solutions, and test a possible solution. Problem solving enhances a person's social functioning by providing a way to cope with daily problems. These skills can be transferred to other areas of daily living. Problem-solving skills enable a person to gain confidence in his or her abilities, so that problems will not have an immobilizing effect. Gaining problem-solving skills helps a person function autonomously and independently.

Task-Centered Intervention. Task-centered social work integrates a short-term treatment/time-limited structure with the notion of the client's task as a focus or measurable progress. Task-centered social work theory has emphasized an empirical research knowledge base; client-defined problems and goals; problem focus and problem resolution intervention; contextual effects of problems on individual, family, and environmental systems; brief, planned services; collaborative work between the client and practitioner; well-defined, structured treatment activi-

ties; and problem solving that culminates in external action (tasks) (Reid, 1986).

The function of task-centered practice is to help the client develop solutions to psychosocial problems that the client defines and solves. The worker's role is to help the client with changes that arise from the client's motivation and will. Task-centered theory has formulated a problem classification, a problem context of obstacles and resources, and a time-limited service perspective. Problems are defined as unsatisfied wants or unfulfilled needs that serve as motivators for the client. Underlying these assumptions is the belief that a person has autonomous problem-solving capacities that initiate and execute action to obtain a desired goal.

The central and distinctive strategy of task-centered practice is the reliance on tasks as a means of problem resolution. The emphasis is on constructing, implementing, and reviewing tasks. A *task* is defined as a constructive action taken in response to a problem. The client takes responsible action on his or her own behalf, with the worker's assistance. The treatment relationship between the worker and the client is problem focused, task centered, and highly structured. Davis and Proctor (1989) state that it is important for people of color to incorporate environmental or social system changes. Focus on external action is a natural corollary to task-centered social work. In varying degrees, task-centered treatment incorporates action-oriented, cognitive-behavioral, structural, and problem-solving emphases.

Contracting is a vital part of task-centered social work because the contract is a statement of the client's goals, problems, and solutions to be effected. The contract also states the estimated limits of treatment, the formulation of tasks, and the planned implementation of tasks. Task planning defines specific action to alleviate problems. There are two types of tasks: general tasks and operational tasks. *General tasks* give the client a direction for action without a specific program for behavior, whereas *operational tasks* require the client to undertake a specific action. The worker and the client should first generate a range of possible alternative task-related actions that the client can use to solve a problem. These alternatives are then examined, and the client chooses the best alternative for the situation. It is important for the client to "own" and agree on the task or set of tasks.

After the tasks have been selected, a number of intermediate procedural steps, or *subtasks*, are plotted to accomplish the tasks. These subtasks are weekly assignments that the client executes between sessions. The client should experience initial success when he or she performs subtasks related to the problem. Task mastery and a sense of accomplishment are necessary ingredients for changing the problem situation. Identifying possible obstacles and conducting behavioral task rehearsal during the session before the client actually executes a task assignment lessen the difficulties the client encounters in the actual situation. At the beginning of each session, the worker reviews problems and tasks with the client to ascertain progress (task achievement and problem change). Important factors in the problem situation context include mobilizing the individual client's strength and family support and agency program resources.

To sum up, task-centered treatment is effective with people of color because it is based on the client's taking incremental and realistic external action on the problem situation in a measurable and effective manner. Task-centered treatment takes the problem out of the victim-blaming state and initiates step-by-step task assignments by the client. Through problem-solving tasks, the client is empowered to make definite behavioral changes (Reid, 1986).

Crisis Intervention. A crisis intervention strategy is a generalist approach applicable to a client who has experienced a significant loss and is temporarily overwhelmed. Crisis intervention provides an understanding of the dynamics of loss, the need for brief treatment to stabilize the client, and the use of problem-solving and task assignments. In this sense, the crisis intervention, problem-solving, and task-centered approaches work together in a complementary manner.

Crisis intervention has universal application to people of color who are undergoing a major loss or crisis in life. Its theoretical framework is ego psychology, which arose as a revision to psycho-analytic theory. In ego psychology, the ego is regarded as the major integrating force of the personality, bringing the internal person into relationship with the external world. The ego assumes the major functions of perception, adaptation, and equilibrium between psychophysical needs and outside demands. The major contribution of ego psychology is the notion of the ego as an autonomous self that functions independently of instinctual drives. Ego psychology categorizes ego development according to successive life stages. The ego adapts or misadapts at crucial life cycle development stage periods. During the life development stages, the ego relates early and past experiences to present and future anticipatory states. Mastery or failure at earlier stages affects the present course of the life crisis. Each state is accompanied by normal stress, which could result in crisis overload. Ego mastery involves mobilizing adaptive coping mechanisms to deal with stress.

Crisis intervention is applicable to many client problems, ranging from survival stress crisis with problems of living to posttraumatic stress syndrome resulting from loss suffered as refugees. Many people of color enter the formal helping system after they have exhausted family and ethnic community resources. The client's crisis state has often reached a chronic stage by the time of the initial interview.

Lydia Rapoport (1967), an early pioneer in crisis theory, points out that there are at least three types of crisis: (1) a biopsychosocial crisis of maturation, in which a person undergoes physical, mental, and environmental changes in various developmental stages; (2) a crisis related to role transition and social adaptation, such as marriage, promotion, or retirement; and (3) accidental crisis, in which the person experiences a significant loss (loss of job, divorce, death). One or more of these crisis predicaments are enough to immobilize a person temporarily. Refugees have already suffered significant loss of family members and are in the midst of acculturation transition. Language barriers and lack of credentials mean that many are unable to find employment positions comparable to those in their country of origin. These refugees are forced to accept menial work and suffer a consequent role reversal. A series of losses precipitates a crisis reaction. Likewise, gay and lesbian clients can experience tremendous crises due to resolving fears about the coming-out process, coping with discrimination and homophobia, and ensuring that there is lawful protection of civil and human rights.

Crisis theory has described the crisis reaction of a person. A *crisis reaction* is an upsetting disturbance of a normal psychic balance, called a *homeostatic state*. This disturbance results in a disequilibrium or a temporary disruption. The restoration of an organized state of equilibrium results in learning how to cope with this as a particular crisis stress experience. However, a person may be so overwhelmed that there is minimum functioning and loss of organization. A crisis reaction has four stages: (1) the initial rise in tension resulting from the impact of the crisis event, which calls for additional problem-solving responses within the person; (2) lack of success by normal problem solving and the continuation of the crisis, associated with a further rise in tension and a growing sense of ineffectual efforts; (3) more tension, which acts as a powerful internal force to mobilize internal and external resources; in an attempt to relieve this tension, the person uses reserve strength and emergency problem-solving abilities; and (4) further rise in tension to a breaking point and more disorganization of the individual, with drastic results unless the problem can be resolved (Caplan, 1964).

The crisis pattern consists of four basic stages: the crisis event, disorganization, recovery, and reorganization. Before the crisis, the person has a sense of balance or equilibrium in life and is able to cope with problems. The crisis creates an impact that causes a downward-spiraling state of disorganization. A person "hits bottom" and reaches the point of requesting help. A worker administers psychological first aid, which the crisis-ridden person readily receives. During the recovery stage, the worker applies crisis intervention techniques to help the client reach a point of reorganization. Crisis intervention reconstitutes the client's life, which may mean the client functions at the same level as before the crisis, at a higher level on account of learning and insight from the crisis situation, or at a lower level on account of inability to function adequately again.

The fundamental characteristics of crisis intervention may be summarized as follows:

- Crisis intervention is time limited; an acute crisis lasts four to six weeks. The practitioner must work intensively with the client during this period. However, the crisis usually resolves itself during this time.
- Crisis intervention focuses on problems of living rather than on psychopathology (the study of mental disorders).
- Crisis intervention involves one person helping another with a tangible problem that occurs in everyday life. It assumes that some problems temporarily overwhelm an individual, but concrete assistance and community professional help can resolve them.
- Crisis intervention concentrates on the here and now. It deals with what is currently happening, so that the immediate future can be a new beginning.
- Crisis intervention promotes a high level of activity based on the belief that immediate action and mobilization of resources can change the problem. Action-oriented change comes from the client and from work, family and community support systems, and helping agencies.

As indicated, the person of color is responsive to a present, time-limited, action-oriented approach to problems that temporarily overwhelm normal functioning. Understanding the crisis reaction state and crisis intervention procedures is helpful when addressing stress-prone situations in multicultural practice.

Empowerment Intervention. Since the publication of *Black Empowerment: Social Work in Oppressed Communities* (Solomon, 1976), the theme of empowerment has been widely used in social work, ethnic studies, women studies, theology and religion, and related disciplines. In particular, African American social workers and clients readily identify with the state of powerlessness and the need to devise practical strategies of empowerment. A history of racism, economic deprivation, and struggle for survival necessitates an empowerment approach.

The literature on empowerment intervention reflects a maturing discussion of its essential characteristics. Insights from recent work are summarized in this section.

Gutiérrez (1990) has broadened the concept of empowerment so that it applies to the micro-, meso-, and macrolevels—that is, the individual, interpersonal, and institutional levels. In Cultural Study 9-6, she outlines her view of empowerment.

CULTURAL STUDY 9-6

The Process of Empowerment

This definition of empowerment includes combining a sense of personal control with the ability to affect the behavior of others, a focus on enhancing existing strengths in individuals or communities, a goal of establishing equity in the distribution of resources, an ecological (rather than individual) form of analysis for understanding individual and community phenomena, and a belief that power is not a scarce commodity but rather one that can be generated in the process of empowerment (Biegel & Naperste, 1982; Kieffer, 1984; Rappaport, 1981).

Empowerment theory is based on a conflict model that assumes that a society consists of separate groups possessing different levels of power and control over resources (Fay, 1987; Gould, 1987a, 1987b). Social problems stem not from individual deficits, but rather from the failure of the society to meet the needs of all its members. The potential for positive change exists in every person, and many of the negative symptoms of the powerless emerge from their strategies to cope with a hostile world (Pinderhughes, 1983). Although individual clients can be helped to develop less destructive strategies, changes in the social order must occur if these problems ultimately are to be prevented (Rappaport, 1981; Solomon, 1982).

The process of empowerment occurs on the individual, interpersonal, and institutional levels, where the person develops a sense of personal power, an ability to affect others, and an ability to work with others to change social institutions. The literature describes four associated psychological changes that seem crucial for moving individuals from apathy and despair to action:

1. Increasing self-efficacy. Bandura (1982, p. 122) defined *self-efficacy* as a belief in one's ability "to produce and to regulate events in one's life." Although this term was not used in some of the empowerment literature, all authors described a similar phenomenon, using such concepts as strengthening ego functioning, developing a sense of personal power or strength, developing a sense of mastery, developing client initiative, or increasing the client's ability to act (Fagan, 1979; Garvin, 1985; Hirayama & Hirayama, 1985; Mathis & Richan, 1986; Pernell, 1985; Pinderhughes, 1983; Shapiro, 1984; Solomon, 1976).

2. Developing group consciousness. Developing group consciousness involves the development of an awareness of how political structures affect individual and group experiences. The development of group consciousness in a powerless person results in a critical perspective on society that redefines individual, group, or community problems as emerging from a lack of power. The development of group consciousness creates within the individual, or among members of a group or community, a sense of shared fate. This consciousness allows them to focus their energies on the causes of their problems, rather than on changing their internal subjective states (Burghardt, 1982; Friere, 1973; Gould, 1987a, 1987b; Keefe, 1980; Longres & McLeod, 1980; Mathis & Richan, 1986; Solomon, 1976; Van DenBergh & Cooper, 1986).

3. Reducing self-blame. Reduction of self-blame is tied closely to the process of consciousness raising. By attributing their problems to existing power arrangements in society, clients are freed from feeling responsible for their negative situation. Because self-blame has been associated with feelings of depression and immobilization, this shift in focus allows clients to feel less defective or deficient and more capable of changing their situation (Garvin, 1985; Hirayama & Hirayama,

1985; Janoff-Bulman, 1979; Keefe, 1980; Longres & McLeod, 1980; Pernell, 1985; Solomon, 1976).

4. Assuming personal responsibility for change. The assumption of personal responsibility for change counteracts some of the potentially negative results of reducing self-blame. Clients who do not feel responsible for their problems may not invest their efforts in developing solutions unless they assume some personal responsibility for future change. This process is similar to Friere's notion of becoming a subject, or an active participant, in society rather than remaining a powerless object (Bock, 1980; Friere, 1973). By taking personal responsibility for the resolution of problems, clients are more apt to make an active effort to improve their lives.

Although these changes have been described in a specific order, the empowerment process does not occur in a series of stages. Instead, the changes often occur simultaneously and enhance one another. For example, as individuals develop self-efficacy, they may be more likely to assume personal responsibility for change. Researchers who have studied the process also suggest that one does not necessarily "achieve empowerment" but rather that it is a continual process of growth and change that can occur throughout the life cycle (Friere, 1973; Kieffer, 1984). Rather than a specific state, it is a way of interacting with the world.

Gitterman (1994) defines empowerment practice as "the process and outcome of helping clients and staff to increase their personal, interpersonal, and political power so that they can exert greater control and influence in their personal and professional lives" (pp. x, xi).

Simon (1994) identifies five necessary elements of American social work practice in the empowerment tradition:

1. Collaborative partnerships with clients, client groups, and constituents, where there is an alliance between the social worker and the client, both of whom endorse their equality of dignity and human worth, while acknowledging the imbalance of power and authority in their agency-based relationship

2. Practice emphasis on expanding client strengths and resources

3. Dual focus on, and interconnection between, individuals and their social and physical environments

4. The operating assumption that clients are active subjects and members of a community and are claimants of resources, power, and relationships

5. Selective focus on historically disempowered and socially stigmatized persons, groups, and communities

Simon reviews these themes in the various historical periods of social welfare history and social work practice.

Simon (1994) also sets forth a number of social work guidelines for empowerment practice that are useful in working with programs and clients:

1. Shape programs in response to the expressed preferences and demonstrated needs of clients and community members by listening to clients and neighborhood members.

2. Make certain that programs and services are maximally convenient for, and accessible to, clients and their communities.

3. Ask as much dedication to problem solving from the client as from yourself.

4. Call and build on the strengths of clients and communities, particularly recognizing and tapping particular self-help talents and capacities.

5. Devise and redevise interventions in response to the unique configuration of requests, issues, and needs that a client or client group presents, without becoming wedded to a particular interventive method.

6. Make leadership development a constant priority of practice and policy through personal, group, and community involvement.

7. Be patient in the face of the time and continuity of effort required in empowerment-based practice.

8. Evaluate your own powerlessness (limitations) and power (authority) as a social worker.

9. Use local community knowledge of clients' problems, perspectives, and interpretations to contribute to the general good.

Parsons et al. (1998) identify a number of elements that contribute to process change in empowerment practice:

1. Attitudes, values, and beliefs regarding self-efficacy or a sense of self, which promotes action on one's behalf, a belief in self-worth, and a sense of control that affects the empowerment process
2. Validation through collective experience in which the self and others recognize shared experience, which motivates one to seek change beyond the individual level toward other systems such as the family or community
3. Knowledge and skills for critical thinking and action, which causes individuals to think about the internal and external aspects of a problem, identify macrolevel structures and their impacts, access information and take action, assess the outcome, and place problems in a sociopolitical context that reduces self-blame and recognizes that the roots of problems are in society
4. Reflective action, which results in the development of action strategies in which individuals learn to assume responsibility for their action, act with others to attain common goals and social change, and reflect on and learn from those actions

Cowger (1994) distinguishes between personal and social empowerment. *Personal empowerment* recognizes the uniqueness and self-determination of the client to take charge and control of his or her life, to learn new ways to think about the problem situation, and to adopt new behaviors that give more satisfying and rewarding outcomes. *Social empowerment* involves the acquisition of resources and opportunity for the client to play an important role in the shaping of his or her environment. Cowger states:

Clients, not social workers, own the power that brings significant change in clinical practice. A clinical social worker is merely a resource person with professional training on the use of resources who is committed to people empowerment and willing to share his or her knowledge in a manner that helps people realize their own power, take control of their own lives, and solve their own problems. (p. 264)

Empowerment is coming to be understood as a process (Cornell University Empowerment Group, 1989; Rappaport, Reischl, & Zimmerman, 1992)—specifically, as "an intentional, ongoing process centered in the local community, involving mutual respect, critical reflection, caring, and group participation, through which people lacking an equal share of valued resources gain greater access to and control over those resources" (Cornell University Empowerment Group, 1989, p. 2). Empowerment is both a process leading to resource acquisition and an outcome resulting from a resource gain.

Gibson (1993) summarizes the major components of empowerment theory and practice as follows:

1. A stress on the client's mastery of the environment, self-determination, and a recognition of the social forces that negatively affect his or her life
2. The client's movement toward an internal locus of control (over the outcome of his or her life) and an external locus of responsibility (perception of the external barriers of discrimination, prejudice, and exploitation as responsible for the problems in his or her life)
3. The client's capacity to improve his or her life as determined by the client's ability to control the environment, connect with needed resources, negotiate problematic situations, and change existing social situations that limit human functioning
4. A focus on the client's strengths rather than pathology, client responsibility rather than reliance on an authority figure, and the social worker as an advocate rather than as an expert
5. The examination of external or macrosociopolitical and economic forces on personal identity and problems as central to the client's difficulties
6. The collective group and people's ability to pool resources and power to effect social change and the transfer of power between groups in society

7. Group affiliation to discuss common experiences, receive social support, identify links between personal and political issues and problems, and promote racial pride and bonding among people of color

Family Empowerment. In Cultural Study 9-7, Solomon (1985) outlines four types of empowerment strategies that lend themselves to working with families: enabling families to use resources, linking families to connective networks, catalyzing families through obtaining resources, and priming the system. Each function involves family members, family strength, and the social worker.

CULTURAL STUDY 9-7

Family Empowerment

ENABLING

This strategy assumes that a family may have considerable resources that are not always recognized as useful in obtaining from a system what the family needs. Enabling refers to actions on the part of the social worker to provide information or contacts which will enable the family to utilize its own resources more effectively.

A family attempting to obtain special support services for a child who was failing in school was frustrated until the counselor made the parents aware of the legal remedies available to them in this situation. Given this new knowledge, the parents were able to confront the school authorities and obtain the services.

A single parent who could read only at a fifth grade level often experienced crisis situations due to the difficulty she encountered in reading utility bills, rental agreements, etc. The parent was helped to see that her teenage daughter could be a useful resource in interpreting written materials until the time that she could master basic reading and writing skills herself. The teenager viewed this request for consultation as an acknowledgement of her own growing maturity.

LINKING

This strategy assumes that families can augment their own strengths by linking with others who can provide new perceptions and/or opportunities. Families may link with others to provide a collective power which can be more successful in confronting a system than that available to any individual family.

Linking, then, refers to actions taken by the social worker to connect families to other families, groups, or networks. In the case of the single, illiterate parent above, she was also helped to join a support group of single parents, many of whom were enrolled in adult education classes. It was their influence which helped her to decide to increase her reading skills.

CATALYZING

This strategy assumes that families have resources, but additional resources may be needed before their own can be fully utilized. For example, if a parent has job skills, he or she will need an actual job before those skills can be used. Catalyzing refers to those actions taken by the social worker to obtain resources which are prerequisite to the family fully utilizing their existing resources.

One family had a relative who lived in another city but was willing to move in with the family and provide child care which the family could not otherwise afford. However, the family's apartment was too small to accommodate another adult and they had been unsuccessful in finding appropriate yet affordable housing. By finding a room for the relative in the same neighborhood, the social worker was able to provide a resource that made it possible for the family to use their own extended family more effectively to meet their needs.

PRIMING

This strategy assumes that many of the systems with which families have negative encounters can respond more positively, but only under conditions which would not be perceived as a "cost" to the system, e.g., any suggestion that the system was not adhering to its own policies and procedures or that the system was "caving in" to some external pressure.

A family was experiencing a great deal of conflict. Their junior high school–age son had become angry and even assaultive with his siblings and parents when he was feeling particularly stressed. The social worker pointed out to the parents that although he had not exhibited the behavior at school, he might do so at any time and the school would very likely suspend him. The mother was able, therefore, to discuss her son's reactions to the stress situation at home with the school counselor and homeroom teacher, indicating that in the case of any unacceptable behavior she could be called to school to handle it. Thus, the social worker assisted the parent in priming the system so that it would respond differently and more positively than it would have otherwise.

From "How Do We Really Empower Families? New Strategies for Social Work Practitioners," by B. B. Solomon. In *Family Resource Coalition Report 4*(3), pp. 2–3. Copyright © 1985. Reprinted by permission.

Existential Intervention. Existentialism is a philosophy of the late nineteenth and early twentieth centuries, with two branches: Kierkegaard represents the religious view, whereas Heidegger and Sartre represent the atheistic perspective. On the whole, existentialism was based on the philosophical premises that existence takes precedence over essence, that a person is totally free and responsible for individual acts, and that this responsibility and choice are the source of the dread and anguish that encompasses the person.

Existentialism as a philosophical perspective influenced Christian theologians, notably Tillich and Bultmann, who adapted the language of existentialism in the fields of systematic theology and biblical interpretation, respectively. Krill (1978) identifies four recurring themes in most of the philosophical literature on existentialism: the stress on individual freedom and the related fundamental value of uniqueness of the person; the recognition of suffering as a necessary part of the ongoing process of life for human growth and the realization of meaning; the emphasis on the individual's involvement in the immediate moment as the most genuine way of discovering identity and what life is about; and the sense of commitment that seeks to maintain a life of both discipline and spontaneity, of contemplation and action, of egolessness and an emerging care for others.

In social work, the forerunner of existential intervention was the functional school of casework, which was taught at the University of Pennsylvania as an alternative to the psychodiagnostic school of casework associated with Columbia University during the 1930s and 1940s.

In culturally diverse social work practice, existential intervention is of particular interest as an approach appropriate for use with Native Americans. DuBray (1993) points out that, for Native Americans, the intrinsic worth of the individual, the search for meaning in life, and a relationship where the worker and client are partners on a journey are very important. The worker must maintain an unobtrusive stance and respect the client's self-determination. A climate is created for the client to evaluate past choices and to have the freedom to make choices in the present. For DuBray, the existential approach helps the client experience liberation through individual decision making.

Functional Casework. Functional casework, the forerunner of humanistic and existential theory, holds a high view of societal relationships; it places implicit faith in the innate striving of each person to be human and healthy. The functional approach is based on a psychology of growth, an emphasis on the creative potential of the person, and the role of social and cultural factors in development. The client is at the center of the relationship; the worker facilitates the client's growth. This is in contrast to a psychology of illness, which focuses on the diagnosis and treatment of pathology and assigns a central role to the worker, who evaluates sickness and prescribes treatment.

The purpose of social work practice, according to functional casework, is to release human power in the individual for personal fulfillment and social good and to release social power for the creation of a society where self-realization is possible for all people. Traces of the human potential, empowerment, and social justice perspectives can be seen in this approach.

Human growth is purpose and process. It is purpose, in the sense that there is self-motivation toward life, health, and fulfillment; individuals are capable of modifying themselves and the environment. Human growth is process, because individuals move through a series of experiences, drawing on innate capacities and the immediate environment. As a result, they achieve task mastery and remain in control of their own growth.

As an organizing and controlling force, the self is will. The task is to free a person to claim and use his or her will in a positive manner and thus to choose and act on his or her own choice. The agency function is to provide structure and direction to the growth process. The purpose, role, and function of the agency and the social worker are explained to the client. The worker assists the client to release his or her potential in the discovery of specific actions.

The structure of the helping process makes creative use of time phases: In the beginning, emphasis is on the agency's services, conditions of availability, client expectations, and problem identification; during the middle phase, the client moves toward responsibility for part of the situation, a new sense of accomplishment and power to realize potential, and increasingly independent functioning; at the end, there is the new and developed self, a capacity for relationship, and autonomy.

Linkages between Functional Casework and Existential Intervention. Both functional casework and existential intervention operate from a psychology of growth that emphasizes the creative potential of the person, the stages of being and becoming, and self-actualization. The client is at the center of the relationship rather than the worker. The client-centered approach believes that the client is able to facilitate purposeful growth; the worker assists in this process. The purpose of the helping effort is to release human power in individuals for personal fulfillment and social good. Values involve the respect for the dignity and worth of the individual and the opportunity for each person to realize personal potentiality and social fulfillment. Human growth is a purposeful process: The person is self-directed toward life, health, and fulfillment.

Existential Approach. The existential approach has an optimistic and positive view of personhood. A person is in the process of self-actualization—of fulfilling his or her potential as a human being. There is an innate drive toward growth and need satisfaction. The worker facilitates this process and conveys awareness, feeling, and sensitivity to the person.

The focus is on the here and now. The client cannot change the past but can only act in the present. By responding and reacting to the concrete present, the client takes control of the future. The worker helps the client concentrate on the present experience, asking, What can you see, feel, and hear? The present interaction between the worker and the client represents a microcosm of the client's present relationships with other people.

The worker strives to be an authentic person who is empathetic, expresses unconditional positive regard, and communicates genuineness or congruence. Empathy involves placing yourself in the position of the client. Unconditional positive regard means nonjudgmental acceptance of the person as he or she is. Genuineness or congruence is to be real or to express your thoughts and feelings to the person.

Problems are incongruencies between the self (what I want and am heading toward) and experiences (what is happening to me). The worker creates a permissive nonthreatening environment to explore specific incongruencies. The worker uses clarification and reflection of feelings, restatement, and summarizing as means to foster client insight. However, the client's impulse to self-actualization knows the best course of action and decision making. The task is to allow the self-actualizing process to take over and to work with the person on decisions that have implications for future direction.

To sum up, the existential approach assumes the client's capacity and desire to make changes in him- or herself, the client's freedom of choice to accept or reject suggestions from the worker, and the uniqueness of the client's personal perspective (Pommells, 1987). The workers is a facilitator of the client's self-actualization. The existential approach can be useful in multicultural practice in that these basic assumptions of the theory cross all cultures.

Existential and Empowerment Combined Intervention. The Inter-Tribal Council of Arizona, Inc., combines a microlevel existential approach to intervention with the interventional strategy of empowerment. It makes the following suggestions for working with Native American communities (Inter-Tribal Council of Arizona, Inc., n.d.):

1. A nondirectional approach, which eliminates imposition and emphasizes cooperation and participation instead of competition between people
2. The maximum use of all local resources, specifically the extended family system, which is representative of tribal culture and lifestyle
3. The involvement of all community people in decision-making, thus reinforcing the old traditions of respect for all in community collaboration for community problem-solving

This existential intervention stresses the attitude of "I-Thou" terminology proposed by philosopher Martin Buber or a spiritual relationship with people. (An I-Thou relationship involves an existential, meaningful encounter between two persons that is significant for both.) There is also the element of collective community empowerment, which brings together the extended family, the tribe, and the total community.

Woman-Centered Perspective. The Woman-Centered Perspective framework was formulated by Young In Song, a Korean American social work educator. It focuses on five psychosocial stages (Before the Dawning, Awakening, Immersion, Emergence, and Woman-Centered Action) that reflect the personal journey of awareness and growth for the individual multicultural woman as well as affords a treatment approach for multicultural women who are confronted with the issues

of sexual harassment, spousal abuse, family violence, and related areas encountered in our current situation.

Woman-Centered Perspective Intervention. We are living through an important transitional period in which the traditional notions of womanhood in popular culture are rapidly becoming obsolete. Women can no longer rely on these prescribed models of role expectations, because the more that young women develop a clear sense of personal identity, the more stark the disjunction between traditional ideal and modern reality becomes for them (Song & Kim, 1992; Song, 1994). There are new visions of what a woman is and can be, while there are social and personal complexities and ambiguities that movements toward social change generate.

A woman-centered perspective believes that gender exerts a profound influence on all spheres of human experience and that gender and its relevancies in the lives of women and men should be reframed. Gender is a total experience for women as wives, mothers, caregivers, or simply as girls that should move beyond their sexual behavior and affirm their individuality as persons. The primary aim of a woman-centered perspective is to make women visible first and foremost as individual human beings. Women must become valued in and for themselves.

Making women visible requires a greater understanding of the conflicts women experience and of the demands placed on them as part of the problems of society encountered in the daily living by women and men.

A woman-centered perspective is oriented around social equality rather than the domination and control of some classes of people by others. Rather than viewing individual men as the cause, a woman-centered approach focuses on the social institution of patriarchy in all its forms as the problem. A patriarchal society is a male-dominated social system characterized by hierarchical, dominant-subservient relationships between men and women.

It may be asserted that patriarchy is the oldest form of the family, but Benston (1979) holds that patriarchy arose only after the demise of an original human family structure that was matrilocal and matriarchal (Banks, 1981). Patriarchal structures evolved as a consequence of the development of private property and capitalist economies that reflected the competition and acquisitiveness of societies. In these social orders, the dynamics of control and acquisition are cultural forces that affect not only the economic system but also the relationships between the sexes.

In the following section, five psychosocial stages of the Woman-Centered Perspective are presented to examine the growth process of women as they strive toward full realization.

Psychosocial Stages of the Women-Centered Perspective

Before the Dawning Stage. Occupational segregation and sociocultural disadvantages have historically relegated women and ethnic minorities in the United States to social positions that prevent access to acquiring economic and social status and legitimacy. As a result there is an inherent frustration over the denial of equal status that produces feelings of inferiority and powerlessness. This results in ways of seeking methods of numbing or supplanting self-perceptions as powerless and worthlessness.

During this stage, women accept their traditional social roles as women imposed by the male-dominated culture. There may be selective perceptions of cultural awareness and/or denial of their predicament that wards off cognitively dissonant information and experiences about their place in society. Physical and sexual abuse and related painful experiences are denied and carefully hidden. Women come to the conclusion that no matter what they attempt to accomplish or how they go about attaining their goals, they are bound to lose. This perception sets up a psychology of defeat that strengthens male domination and control and results in feelings of isolation, anomie, and despair on the part of women. Conformity to patriarchal capitalism promulgates social control and the imposition of power over others. Conforming to existing beliefs and norms overshadows the personal experience or philosophy of a woman as a person.

Awakening Stage. During the Awakening Stage, women experience events which cause them to question their state of existence. They become increasingly aware that things are not right with the world yet they have difficulty identifying the source of the discord. They experience a growing sense of anger and bitterness and a conviction that men are the enemy. Although anger is necessary and important, it may lead to inappropriate and ineffective actions. Still, there is a sense of restlessness and a searching for alternative ways to relate to others and a profound dissatisfaction for the present situation.

Immersion Stage. In the Immersion Stage there is a submergence of personal values, priorities, and beliefs, a searching for an emerging new value system as an alternative. There is a conviction that change must come and that the present assumptions and stereotypes about gender differentiation taught in education (gender roles, sexual behavior, career advice, ideas of parenthood) must be reconsidered. We must strive to avoid handing down misleading stereotypes about the capabilities, appropriate education, and moral obligations between men and women.

Part of the Immersion Stage involves accepting a fragile internal balance between the external world of the status quo and the growing self of the woman. Anxiety and fear are immersed and the self of the woman begins to transcend the past and moves toward changing the present.

Emergence Stage. The quiet revolution of the Emergence Stage calls women to make a response in their lives in terms of personal alternatives and their responsibility to make choices, although they may not yet see how their choices may affect changes in society. Women view patriarchal relations rather than individual men as the prime target for change and acknowledge the importance of the class dimension of women's oppression.

Woman-Centered Action Stage. During this final psychosocial stage, women recognize their own personal needs and priorities and commit themselves to work for social change in ways appropriate for women as individuals. A person defines her own direction, reality, or indicators for success rather than conform to conventional criteria or norms. The values and beliefs a person holds, the goals she sets, and the way she pursues her life can be considered political statements. The personal as political, however, is based on the philosophy of the values of individual worth, an inherent connection to others, concern with collective well-being, and the perspective that living is an ongoing process. It is a liberation philosophy promoting the nurture of the self as well as concern with collective well-being. It is concerned with ending domination, resisting oppression, and providing equality of opportunity for all women.

The values of the Woman-Centered Action Stage include working collaboratively, collectively, and co-operatively; valuing personal experiences; encouraging growth and development; caring for others; building supportive relationships; and believing in the interconnectedness of people and events.

Integral to the Woman-Centered Action Stage are four resource levels that are related to the individual woman, family system relationships, group system relationships, and community system relationships. Under each system level are four related themes of ethnic/gender identity, family interactions, social network, and cultural strengths.

Individual woman: The multicultural woman in the Woman-Centered Action stage draws on her ethnicity and gender as an individual. She is a part of her nuclear and extended family as she interacts with the significant other family members that are a part of her childhood, adolescence, and adulthood. These persons emerge as a part of her social network along with peer relations, which forms a part of her support system. Cultural strengths (values and beliefs) are learned from family and ethnic community and are the basis for character-building assets.

Family system relationships: The multicultural woman must navigate between collective authority structures, family interdependence, and her own autonomy as a person. Flexible family social roles, the sharing of responsibilities, and equality of role functions are increasingly important to her as a member of the family. The model of a shared cooperative family structure is central to family system relationships. Extended families and fictive relatives are examples of social networks in which multicultural women of color are givers and receivers of these support systems. They draw on such cultural family strengths as responsibility, mutuality, harmony, and affiliation.

Group system relationships: Reference group orientation is critical for understanding ethnic/gender identity: generation, acculturation, reacculturation, and related group issues. Related to family interactions and group relationships are persons who are sources of support, wisdom and advice, and social companions. Family groups are opportunities to share life experiences, values, and insights with each other. Among the social networks for a multicultural woman are service, social, and professional groups that link individual women and result in bonding. Group cultural strengths include identifying and affiliating with one's cultural group of origin, ethnic group members, and collective group action.

Community system relationships: The multicultural woman of color finds part of her ethnic/gender identity in her multicultural community, which may be a geographic location or place, ways of relating, celebration, and tragedy. There may be a community perception of the individual woman and her family, particularly in a close-knit ethnic community. Community task-oriented project groups are vehicles in which the multicultural woman makes her contribution to the progress and well-being of the larger ethnic community. Among the cultural community strengths expressed are ethnic community involvement and spiritual/religious involvement.

As a liberated person the multicultural woman of color is able to draw on these resource levels and interface her ethnic/gender identity and family interaction with group and community system interaction. However, her experience of liberation has implications for her male counterpart.

The Liberation of Women and Men. The Woman-Centered Perspective is committed to the liberation of women and men from class oppression, work alienation, and a corrupt male-dominated culture. Too often cultural stereotypes prevent men from expressing feelings in public as well as affection and sharing in marriage. Basic needs of companionship, warmth, and intimacy are not met. Relationships between men often deteriorate into competitiveness and assertiveness where one's pride is on the line and no one dares to admit being wrong or making a mistake. Patriarchal values of dominance and power seeking grip the relationships of men with women.

There is a present need to listen to one another, to realize the need to transcend the present patriarchal system, and to forgive each other. Nonsexist resocialization involves enacting liberating changes in family, education, religion, economy, and politics while preserving the best of traditional social values. A woman-centered perspective must therefore initiate research and direction for change in each sphere to generate new information for a different set of issues to be considered in society. To this end, it is hoped that gender barriers will be removed and that women and men as respected and genuine persons will be realized in significant ways.

Family Therapy. Family therapy has wide application for families of all cultural groups. However, I am concerned about people of color and particular intervention connections. This section applies family therapy to a specific ethnic group: Latino Americans. Family therapy is an appropriate intervention approach for Latinos. The family system is central to Latino culture. The nuclear family is embedded in an extended family consisting of a vertical hierarchy and a horizontal kinship system.

The hierarchical structure involves intergenerational roles for grandparents, parents, brothers, and sisters. Family functions are organized around age and gender. The grandparents are respected and have influence over the family system. The father and oldest son are the authority of the nuclear family and are responsible for its function. Male domination (*machismo*) is expressed as courage, protection, and manliness. In the best sense, *machismo* is good authority and leadership in the family. The father disciplines and controls the family. The mother provides nurture and support for the children. *Marianismo* reflects the self-sacrifice of the mother (as the Virgin Mary was the model mother), who is devoted to her home and children. The parents delegate authority to the older children. The boys chaperone and protect the girls, who perform household chores. There is *respeto* and mutual caring and help between parents and children.

The horizontal kinship system is a natural support system consisting of uncles, aunts, cousins, and *compadres* (godparents). Along with the nuclear intergenerational family, the extended family offers interdependence, support, affiliation, and cooperation. Child care, protection, and discipline of the children; financial assistance; group problem solving; and companionship are outcomes of *familismo*.

Paniagua (1994) advocates the use of family therapy as the primary approach for Latino clients, because it reinforces *familismo* and extended family. Ho (1987) suggests that Latino communication tends to be formal, indirect, and guarded in public. The worker should communicate in a respectful, nonconfrontational, and indirect manner. The use of humor, allusions, and diminutives softens the directness of the worker and blends into a Latino cultural transactional style of communication.

Family Practice Principles. Effective culturally diverse family practice focuses on the family system as the critical element for the helping process. At the beginning, it is important to interview the whole family together and, specifically, to recognize the father as the authority and spokesman of the family. Turning to the father for his perspective on the family sends a message of respect and acknowledgment. It also provides valuable information on the viewpoints of the head of household and the underlying family dynamics. Asking the father and mother and then children for their brief views on "what is happening in the family" provides an opportunity for each family member to have input into the process.

After the initial go-around, the worker should interview the father and mother, while the rest of the family is given a recess. The worker can pursue further information on the spousal system—

the husband-wife relationship—and the parental system—father/mother role functioning. It is important to remain on the side of the father and to show *respeto*. Responding with supportive and understanding statements ("Mr. Hernández, if I understand you, you are saying that . . . ") and identification statements ("Mr. Hernández, if I were you, I would feel like . . . ") conveys the message of friendship and helpfulness.

Next, the parents take a break, and the worker briefly interviews the children, to broaden the picture and to fill in the details of the family system. This provides an opportunity for the children to voice feelings without the presence of parents and for the worker to find out how the sibling system is functioning as part of the family structure.

Finally, the whole family is brought together, and there is a general discussion of the cultural understanding and behavioral history of the family. The worker should summarize the problem issues confronting the family; this makes clearer the extent of the work that is facing family members. Eliciting each family member's willingness and commitment to work on specific problems is important to determine the rate of change that can be expected from this particular family.

The worker should practice *personalismo*—that is, be friendly and flexible, and yet establish structure and boundaries for the family. The use of humor and storytelling to make a point establishes a relaxed emotional atmosphere in which the family can work on problems. Cultural storytelling is a useful device to relate the problem and the family's positive intent. What has been the story of this family? How can this family rewrite or rescript their story? What can be a happy ending to this family's story? Reframing the negative aspects of the problem into the family's unsatisfied wants or unfulfilled needs provides the incentive for a good family story. Perhaps the family wants respect, harmony, and cooperation. Uncovering these positive intents behind the negative problem statements reframes the problem and casts a new story line for the family. Incorporating the positive elements into the story is the beginning of a new chapter for the family.

Before the family leaves the first session, a practical intervention plan for positive action should have been established. Weekly family assignments create avenues for immediate change. What can the family do together this week to experience satisfaction? What does the family enjoy as a group? What can be done to reduce the problem symptomology of the family? How can the family begin to solve the most pressing problem confronting a particular family member? Asking these questions and eliciting commonsense answers from family members is the first step toward practical intervention. Several suggestions should be agreed on, implemented during the week, and brought back to the next session for discussion.

It is crucial to work on the alleviation of practical needs: the employment stability of parents, the medical care of the family, and the education of the children. Families who are in the midst of acculturation and social adaptation face situational stress and cultural transitions. Home visits offer a window of understanding on the actual living environment of the family. The use of the family and ethnic community networks is important to locate a family or community resource who can provide wisdom and counsel on a particular problem situation. In the Latino community, Catholic Social Services provide an array of services and bilingual/bicultural social workers in many major cities.

Group Work. Group work with people of color is an emerging area of the literature. Davis, Galinsky, and Schopler (1995) present a RAP (Recognize, Anticipate, Problem-Solve) group framework that has three leadership tasks.

> The RAP framework assumes that effective outcomes in any multiracial group require that leaders carry out three essential tasks. First, they must recognize (R) the critical importance of the racial dynamics of the group and their ability to act. Second, they must anticipate (A) the sources of racial tension and help members deal with these tensions. Third, they must be prepared to problem solve (P) if issues become problems. (p. 160)

In terms of *recognizing* critical racial, ethnic, and cultural differences in a group, leaders must be

- responsive to racial, ethnic, and cultural differences between leaders and members and among members;
- know and respect the respective group history, norms, and cultures of populations;
- examine their own racial, ethnic, and cultural attitudes and values;
- obtain supervision and consultation from practitioners and other leaders of ethnic group members when there are racial differences;
- become familiar with agency, professional, and community resources that are responsive to the needs of group members and refer when racial issues preclude effective helping in the group;
- be aware of institutional discrimination and the impact on different community population groups;
- be aware of racial tensions due to events, beliefs, and issues in society at large or in the neighborhood of group members; and
- be aware of concerns that individual members have about racial, ethnic, and cultural differences.

In terms of *anticipating* how group members and the group as a whole are affected by racial issues and problems, leaders should

- develop a repertoire of helping responses and select a culturally appropriate leadership style to a specific racial configuration;
- discuss potential problems and ensure equal status in the group when coleaders are of different races;
- avoid having one member of any race in the group and acknowledge the difficulty of having that person serve as a representative of that racial or ethnic group;
- strive for psychological and numerical balance of ethnicity in group composition;
- help the group formulate a purpose that is responsive to members' concerns and needs and take action and empower members to change environmental barriers to the achievement of individual goals;
- acknowledge early in the sessions the racial and ethnic differences in the group and potential difficulties and awkwardness about discussing race;

- encourage and develop tolerance and mutual respect; and
- discuss racially inappropriate statements and remarks that may be considered insulting.

Finally, *problem solving* may involve confrontation and resolution within and outside the group. Leaders should

- use culturally acceptable and appropriate interventions and goals;
- convey respect and genuineness through behavior and gear attending skills and nonverbal behavior to the culture of members;
- discuss and resolve racial, ethnic, and cultural issues and focus on the positive contributions of diversity;
- stop group action and confront and problem-solve when there is a problem between members of different races, allowing for a cooling-off period;
- provide problem-solving rules and a framework for discussion to avoid escalation of the situation;
- use structured problem-solving processes and exercises that facilitate interactions;
- foster skills to confront and deal with racial and ethnic problems; and
- be prepared to intervene and advocate in racial, ethnic, and cultural issues, conflict resolutions, and environmental systems to bring about justice.

These leadership functions and culturally diverse group work principles are examples of how group work increasingly needs to address people of color concerns.

Treating Refugees and Immigrants. In the past fifteen years, the number of refugees and immigrants from Southeast Asia, Central America, and Eastern Europe to the United States has increased significantly. Because the majority of these refugees and immigrants are people of color, it is important to develop an intervention strategy that meets their special needs.

A need exists to establish a specific treatment program geared to refugees, complete with an interdisciplinary mental health staff, bilingual and bicultural counselors and interpreters, and cultural training for professionals. Kinzie (1985) emphasizes the need to recognize cultural and value differences between clients and staff and to modify existing techniques to meet refugees' expectations.

The development of a strong worker-client relationship is crucial at the beginning of the helping process. Regarding social work with immigrant families Hulewat (1996) suggests:

> The beginning focus for the worker is to welcome the family and get to know them. Most families come with many questions but cannot fully comprehend the answers. At this point, it is imperative that the worker presents him- or herself as calm, confident, knowledgeable, and caring. Presenting too much information can overwhelm the family. It is more useful to give clients as much information as possible in writing to be reviewed at later appointments and to spend the first appointment discussing practical realities. Although several things need to be accomplished in the first interview, the primary task is to establish a relationship. In getting to know the client, the focus of the conversation initially will be on how and why the decision to emigrate was made and what losses resulted in making that decision. The discussion also needs to involve the clients' expectations of their new life in America. (p. 132)

The worker should concentrate on the client's presenting problem, which is often a somatic one.

At the same time there may also be loss and dependence in terms of adjustment. Hulewat (1996) crafts three kinds of groups requiring adjustment:

> The first and largest group, identified as the "help me get started" group, were those who were truly eager to gain control of their lives and move ahead to become independent. The second largest group, identified as the "take care of me" group, were those who were regressed to a dependent state in a way that created a control struggle. The focus of their energy was to get their worker to take care of them. They presented as entitled and grandiose. After a period of struggle, with sound case manage-

ment, this group would reconstitute their defenses and successfully resettle. The smallest group, identified as the "you must do it my way" group, were those would could not give up the control battle and who remained rigidly committed to having the community meet all of their needs. The need to control the worker and manipulate the system to get all their needs met took precedence over getting on with their lives. They were often borderline individuals who could not tolerate loss and who needed to continually assert the fantasy of their omnipotence. (p. 133)

The worker should use a slow, cautious, and ethnic-sensitive approach with the client and build trust and credibility.

Next, the worker should take a complete psychosocial history of the refugee's past life, escape, and transition periods. Major stages include life in the homeland (education, socioeconomic status, health, family, problems of war), the escape or exit from the country of origin (who left, who stayed, experiences during the escape), life in the refugee camp (length of stay, problems), adjustment in the United States (attitudes, problems, expectations, losses, progress), and current problems and future concerns.

Potocky (1996) has summarized a number of problems faced by refugee children upon their entry into the United States in resettlement: language barriers, intergenerational stress resulting in role reversal (quick adaptation of cultural change by children and the lag of language and cultural norms by parents), lack of respect for elders, lack of child discipline as a result of threatening the report of child abuse to child welfare authorities, parents with posttraumatic stress disorder as an effect of witnessing trauma during escape and refugee camp experiences, double-bind acculturation and cultural identity over traditional native cultural expectations and Americanization, and increasing involvement in criminal peer activities.

Open-ended, long-term supportive intervention is required, on account of the chronic nature of many refugee problems. Adjustment crises in a new culture precipitate a series of events. A regular worker and regular session time are stabilizing facets in a changing situation. Reality-based problem solving is a helpful approach to dealing with major symptoms, current stresses, children, and financial problems. The worker should communicate positive social behavior that the client can model in his or her life. Much family support and education are needed to maintain the interdependent functioning capacity of family members.

Posttraumatic stress is a major problem. The chief symptoms include the following: (1) recurrent or intrusive recollections of past traumas; (2) recurrent dreams and nightmares; (3) sad feelings, as if the traumatic events are recurring; (4) social numbness and withdrawal; (5) restricted affect; (6) hyperalertness, or hyperactive startle reaction; (7) sleep disorders; (8) guilt; (9) memory impairment; (10) avoidance of activities that might trigger recollection of events; and (11) reactivation of symptoms caused by exposure to events similar to the original trauma.

In Cultural Study 9-8, Song (1987) points out that posttraumatic stress often manifests itself in spousal violence as a result of a crisis reaction centering around loss.

CULTURAL STUDY 9-8

Immigrant Spousal Violence

Conjugal violence is sometimes the result of stress from cultural shock. Due to the complete lack of research in this area, empirical data has not been developed. However, the closest approach applicable concerning cultural loss could be . . . the crisis reaction. There have been some systematic attempts to describe the human experience of crisis from the loss caused by transition. Fink (1967) and Parkes (1972) have described some of the stages that people pass through in coping with bereavement. Mead (1955) examined the effects of change on traditional stable cultures.

Kim (1978) explained that the immigration process signifies disruption of a familiar lifestyle. It involves disintegration of the person's intrafamilial relationships, loss of social identity, and major shifts in the value system and behavioral patterns. It is an upheaval and disequilibrium of

catastrophic proportions which can be considered as a crisis. For immigrant Korean couples, the process is fraught with danger, and it challenges all their resources in order to cope with this crisis. It frequently places the marital relationship in a most vulnerable state which may lead to violence in the family.

Stress due to the culture shock may be an experience of a sudden trauma arising from disorientation, displacement, disappointment, alienation, loneliness, sometimes total inadequate feelings, cognitive dissonance, and loss of self-control during the cultural transition crisis.

From Y. I. Song, *Silent Victims: Battered Women in Korean Immigrant Families*, p. 54. Copyright © 1987 Oxford Press. Reprinted by permission of the author.

Kinzie (1985) found that supportive life adjustment intervention was effective for refugees undergoing posttraumatic stress: a regular, structured, and supportive approach that neither pushes for details of the past nor avoids discussing them when necessary; consistent financial stability and flexibility in school and work; reduced pressure and stress whenever possible; and the use of antidepressant medication, which decreased symptoms of depression and posttraumatic stress disorder.

In Cultural Study 9-9, Matsuoka (1990) shares a case of a Vietnamese adolescent who uses a variety of intervention approaches to help work through grief, guilt, and neglect.

CULTURAL STUDY 9-9

Intervention with a Refugee

The case of Phuc, a fifteen-year-old who arrived in America during a critical point in his development, illustrates a problem arising from differences between traditional Vietnamese culture and American customs. As a student in Vietnam, this young man excelled in mathematics and was encouraged by his parents to pursue a career in engineering. Although an only child, Phuc was part of a close-knit extended family and was often called upon to care for his grandparents and younger cousins. Upon the death of his father, and seeing little future for themselves in Vietnam, Phuc and his mother set out as "boat people" to seek a better life elsewhere. They eventually resettled in America.

After a year, Phuc's mother met and married another Vietnamese refugee, and they moved to a home in a middle-class community without a concentrated population of Vietnamese. Because of the lack of a Vietnamese community, reinforcement for appropriate Vietnamese behavior was unavailable beyond Phuc's family. The loss of reinforcement and role patterns that would ordinarily have given him a strong identity left him confused and depressed. In school, Phuc was having great difficulty understanding the lessons because he could not speak fluent English. Phuc felt inferior because he was doing poorly, and soon he began skipping classes and spending time in the city with other Vietnamese youth who were involved in gang activity. Because he lived so far away, Phuc was regarded as a marginal gang member although he experimented with drugs and participated in some gang-related activity.

The school officials became concerned about his truancy and reported it to his parents. When his stepfather and mother discovered that their son had not been attending school, they became very angry, because back home he was an outstanding scholar. The stepfather felt that Phuc was lazy and disrespectful, so he physically punished him for his truancy at school. As a result, Phuc ran away from home. The police eventually picked him up, and because he refused to return home, he was placed in foster care.

TREATMENT

Phuc remained in foster care until a bilingual and bicultural social worker was assigned to the case. The social worker became aware of the severity of the family problems and prescribed individual treatment for Phuc and family therapy for the entire family.

The therapist found that the severe consequences of events in Phuc's childhood were exacerbating current developmental issues associated with the ambiguity of adolescence. The untimely death of his natural father in a Vietnamese "reeducation" camp had been extremely traumatic and apparently had triggered a whole series of family disruptions. Phuc had been unable to appropriately terminate any of his family relationships before his clandestine escape from Vietnam. He had left behind cousins, aunts, uncles, and grandparents whom he could never hope to see again. This sense of loss at such a critical period of his development was extremely traumatic.

Much of Phuc's individual therapy was based on reminiscing about the past and analyzing his current feelings associated with those experiences. Phuc's feelings of guilt and depression over lost loved ones needed to be treated before he was able to move ahead to other concerns. He experienced a type of guilt that could be best described as "survivor guilt." He wondered why his life was spared when his relatives in Vietnam were forced to live under such oppressive conditions. The treatment focus was on reliving, analyzing, and working through the events contributing to his feelings of guilt and depression. The therapeutic objective was to help him accept the oppressive conditions of his relatives and to reconceptualize the traumatic events and thus reduce the feelings of self-blame. Next, he was encouraged to move away from the stressful events and the associated thoughts. Reminiscing about his natural father, with the support of his mother, Phuc was able to grieve his death for the first time. The grieving brought a degree of self-awareness and a connection with his past. It also brought him closer to his mother, who was able to support her son and reconcile her own unresolved feelings from the past.

Phuc generally felt neglected by his parents, who were working long hours. This may in part explain his decline in school performance and his acting-out behaviors. Family therapy was aimed at reestablishing a family culture that he would feel part of. The parents were encouraged to take more interest in Phuc's social and academic activities and to take time for family activities, especially those that linked them to the Vietnamese community. Family members were also taught to reward each other for desirable behaviors, which were defined by mutual agreement. Contractual agreements were made to prevent physical punishment from recurring. The social worker also advocated and received a bilingual educator to assist Phuc in his schoolwork.

This case illustrates the type of problems encountered by Vietnamese faced with the arduous task of finding reliable alignments between old and new cultures. The social worker in this case used psychodynamic techniques to enable Phuc to resolve past conflicts, existential techniques to help him examine his past in relation to his current life and develop self-awareness, and cognitive-behavioral techniques to encourage an atmosphere of family support.

From "Differential Acculturation among Vietnamese Refugees," by J. K. Matsuoka. In *Social Work, 35,* 344–345. Copyright © 1990 National Association of Social Workers. Reprinted by permission.

Preventive Programs for Refugees and Immigrants. Apart from directive treatment, there have been major preventive efforts to provide indigenous helping systems and education on acculturation among refugee populations. These services have been provided by public and private service organizations through funding from the Refugee Assistance Act. At the beginning of any program effort, it is important for program organizers to contact and consult with refugee community leaders for their input and reactions. At the outset, refugee community leaders should be contacted and consulted regarding mental health prevention efforts. Community power brokers range from clan leaders, religious leaders, and professionals, to former political or military leaders. It is necessary to build support and understanding for preventive intervention activities. High-risk refugees face problems of underemployment, breakdowns in the family network, and changing family roles. They need new programs to prevent stress and possible mental illness.

Community organizations, such as mutual assistance associations, can serve as vehicles for managing social skills training programs that have an educational thrust and a preventive effect. Community leaders can consult and contract with

program services whose trained mental health professionals either are people of color or are culturally sensitive and trained to address refugee issues (Bliatout et al., 1985).

Mental health education, competence training, support systems, and social system modifications are some primary prevention programs. The Owan and Miranda primary prevention community model is a prime example of a program that combines personal, social support, and institutional units to help refugees improve their mental health and coping skills. Figure 9-2 illustrates the interrelationship of these components.

The personal unit consists of family, extended family, and friends, who serve as a natural support system for the refugee. Efforts are made to include the family in psychoeducational classes, counseling, and community resource use.

Sherraden and Bariera (1997) conducted a 1992–1994 Chicago study of forty-one Mexican women immigrants and underscored the importance of the family as caregiver. Their results are presented in Cultural Study 9-10.

CULTURAL STUDY 9-10

The Role of Family as Caregiver

The results of this study indicate that families play a crucial mediating role in providing support and opportunity to second-generation immigrant women in impoverished and sometimes hazardous urban communities. Family is the key resource—and often the only dependable resource—for the women as they grow up. This resource is especially important during pregnancy, when proximity and interdependence enable families to provide assistance and guidance. Specifically, we find that high family support translate into care, guidance, and assistance during pregnancy, all of which have a positive relationship to babies' birth weight. However, the ability of families to provide guidance and support during pregnancy depends on relationships established in childhood and adolescence. When a positive relationship had not been developed in childhood and adolescence, the families had little influence over the women's behavior and were not in a good position to provide support during pregnancy.

Our findings also indicate that socioeconomic status influences the family's ability to provide support and protection to young mothers. Parents who were struggling economically but "making it" provided access to at least minimal resources and opportunities for their children. Moreover, we find that families with some resources were more likely to be supportive over the long term. Perhaps equally important, families that were improving their socioeconomic position had greater credibility as role models, enabling them to influence their children as they reached adulthood. Specifically, young women from less marginal families listened more closely to their family's advice regarding pregnancy care. In this way, socioeconomic conditions may solidify family ties.

Families that provided higher levels of support and protection also maintained stronger ties to Mexico, including visits back and forth between Mexico and the United States. Relatives in Mexico can provide an important resource for parents seeking a safer environment for their children during a particularly vulnerable stage in adolescence. Just as wealthy native families often send young people who are getting too deeply involved with the "wrong crowd" to summer camps or boarding schools, immigrant families sometimes send daughters to stay with relatives in Mexico, where they are less likely to get into trouble. Family members also come from Mexico for caregiving during illnesses, childbirths, and when adults are working. Some families enhance ties with Mexican relatives by sending money, purchasing real estate, and building homes in Mexico. Also, greater contact with Mexican relatives increases the likelihood that a child of immigrants will approach pregnancy more like the immigrant generation itself. Although the mechanisms are not entirely clear, culturally transmitted knowledge in immigrant families may have positive effects on birth outcomes.

From "Family Support and Birth Outcomes among Second-Generation Mexican Immigrants" by M. S. Sherraden and R. E. Bariera, *Social Service Review*, 71(4), 626—627. Copyright 1997.

The social support unit consists of mutual assistance associations. Southeast Asian refugees tend to cluster in social and fraternal groups; educational and cultural groups; religious and spiritual organizations; professional societies; political groups; student groups; groups formed to meet the needs of senior citizens, veterans, women, and refugees without families; and emergency refugee resettlement groups. These community-based self-help groups strengthen ethnic pride, facilitate coping, and lessen the impact of stress and the risk of mental illness.

The institutional unit consists of schools, churches, and public and private agencies that provide leadership training to develop client self-determination and coping skills. The institutional unit strengthens refugees' internal network for mutual problem solving and provides resources to develop educational programs for primary prevention (Owan, 1985).

Within the ethnic community, some community resources and program services have primary prevention effects. *Primary prevention* is understood to mean activities and services, directed at a target population, that will have a positive mental health outcome and will reduce the incidence of mental disorders. There are a number of refugee community resources that form a collective, protective network for Southeast Asians.

In Cultural Study 9-11, Tran and Wright (1986) identify several variables that are necessary when helping Vietnamese refugees in resettlement.

CULTURAL STUDY 9-11

Refugee Resettlement

According to the findings of this study, a happy Vietnamese refugee seems to be a person who has stronger social supports, who is not afraid to interact with Americans, who has a relatively high family income, and who is married. To be happy in America, a Vietnamese person also needs good English communication ability, a high level of formal education, and a relatively long time of living in this country, and that person also needs to be in the younger age cohort. English language com-

FIGURE 9-2 *The Owan and Miranda Primary Prevention Community Model*

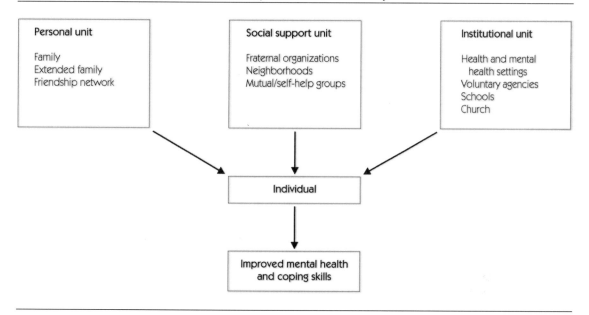

Personal unit	Social support unit	Institutional unit
Family Extended family Friendship network	Fraternal organizations Neighborhoods Mutual/self-help groups	Health and mental health settings Voluntary agencies Schools Church

Individual

Improved mental health
and coping skills

NOTE: Developed with Manual Miranda, Ph.D., School of Social Welfare, University of California at Los Angeles. From "Southeast Asian Mental Health: Transition from Treatment Services to Prevention—A New Direction," by Tom Choken Owan, 1985. In *Southeast Asian Mental Health: Treatment, Prevention, Services, Training, and Research* (p. 151), Tom Choken Owan (Ed.), Washington, D.C.: National Institute of Mental Health.

munication ability, as found in this study, had an indirect effect on well-being. This suggests that a Vietnamese refugee who has better English language communication ability tends to feel less anxious in interacting with American people and, as a result, tends to feel a greater sense of psychological well-being. Vietnamese refugees who have lived in the United States a relatively long time tend to speak English well and have stronger social supports, which tend to increase their sense of well-being. Length of time living in the United States and education had a direct effect on increasing family earnings or income, which presumably helps to increase the individual's sense of well-being. Finally, older Vietnamese refugees tend to have more problems in social interaction with American people than do younger Vietnamese. Thus, age is an important factor that indirectly influences a person's sense of psychological well-being.

Social supports from and within the ethnic community are crucial factors for producing high levels of well-being among new refugees and immigrants in their new host society. Social supports become even more crucial for nonwhite immigrants in American society, in which there has been a long history of systematic discrimination and prejudices against them. As Stonequist (1961) suggests, it is very hard for a nonwhite immigrant to assimilate into American society because of the constant rejection by members of the dominant group. For the Vietnamese in America, social supports provide them comfort and, to some degree, a sense of belonging in a strange social and cultural environment.

The findings reported in this study have some important implications for policymakers and professionals who are interested in working with the Vietnamese refugees. A good refugee resettlement policy must take into account the important role and function of social support systems. Future policies and programs must make systematic efforts to preserve and maintain these support systems. Refugees who are not familiar with the

American environment and culture must be trained in ways that will ease their attempts to adjust to American society. English language training must be made available to all refugees before their arrival in this country as well as after they have been resettled in new communities. Refugees must also be adequately trained and prepared with job skills that can be useful in the current and future job markets. A high level of well-being among Vietnamese refugees is one good indicator of successful and effective refugee policies, programs, and services.

In conclusion, the results of this study clearly indicate that social supports are crucial factors in determining Vietnamese refugees' sense of psychological well-being. Future research efforts should focus attention on trying to empirically identify and examine factors that facilitate or inhibit the refugees' and immigrants' efforts to assimilate into mainstream American society.

From "Social Support and Subjective Well-Being among Vietnamese Refugees," by T. V. Tran and R. Wright, Jr. In *Social Service Review, 60,* 456–457. Copyright © 1986 University of Chicago School of Social Service Administration. Reprinted by permission.

Many refugee groups live next to each other in apartment buildings or houses. This living style is called *cluster housing* and facilitates mutual assistance among persons who speak the same language and share similar culture. Cluster housing provides an extensive support system and self-help network when families and extended families live close to each other. Community centers and churches are facilities where refugees can come, make friends, and reestablish networks within a helping context. Existing churches have opened their facilities to refugee groups for worship and community services during the week at no charge or for a nominal fee. Mutual assistance associations provide social networks and support systems. Indigenous workers are available to assist refugees with filling out forms, job information, translation, and related basic survival and community service needs.

Social skill enhancement programs for various refugee age groups are important to maintain group contact. Programs for the elderly provide an orientation on American society, how to ride the bus, how to shop in American stores, how to use the hospital, and how to apply for Medicare and Social Security. These skill-building activities can be integrated with social and recreational programs. Programs for adult males, females, and parents help define their new roles in American society. Issues for men include Western versus Indo-Chinese male-female roles, raising children in the United States, urban lifestyles versus Indo-Chinese lifestyles, and American work ethic and setting. For women, topics include American versus Indo-Chinese women's roles, the role of a working mother/career woman, child rearing, family planning, and equal rights.

For parents, learning about new methods of disciplining children, acceptable child behavior in America, and changing parent roles is helpful on account of the breakdown of traditional child-rearing and disciplinary systems. Skill workshops for children and adolescents are crucial in helping them adapt to American life and in minimizing antisocial gang behavior. Parents and children should identify acceptable organizations and group activities for participation such as Boy Scouts, Girl Scouts, cultural school clubs, ethnic youth summer camp, and other social group experiences.

Cultural art activities provide opportunities for various age groups to participate. These activities include, for instance, Lao weaving, Hmong and Mien embroidery, Indo-Chinese cultural songs and dances, and the playing of traditional instruments (Bliatout et al., 1985).

Refugees respond to regular, supportive crisis intervention and group cultural activities. Community program activities are useful vehicles for promoting primary prevention.

Sherraden and Bariera (1997) discuss social work's responsibility to immigrants:

Social workers are in a position to influence the design and implementation of social policies related to immigrants, but unfortunately the profession has not assumed a leadership role in the current era. At the turn of the twentieth century, Addams and other settlement house workers were intimately involved in improving the lives of immigrants and their children. Today, at the dawn of the twenty-first century, immigration continues to be a central feature of the American experience, and the struggles of immigrants for a foothold in American communities and the economy will shape and define the nation we become. If left unchecked, the decline observed among some second-generation immigrants will have results that are quite different from those previous waves of immigration. In both humanitarian and practical terms, this is unacceptable. Social workers can and should again assume a leadership role in improving the life chances of the children of immigrants. The profession could begin by taking a page from *Twenty Years at Hull House* on involvement with immigrant families in the community. (p. 629)

Unlike the European immigrants of Addams' day, the immigrants of the twenty-first century are from Asia, Central and South America, and Eastern Europe. People of color immigrants abound and raise a serious challenge for social work educators, practitioners, and students.

Mesolevel Intervention. Mesolevel intervention is increasingly used as a means of working with clients in the context of extended family and community network resources. Culturally diverse family and community intervention have been developed. Jones and Korchin (1982) introduce *commitment therapy* as a multicultural alternative to existing helping models. Commitment therapy is based on the assumption that a person of color's well-being depends on membership in a community (Reiff, 1968; Sarason, 1972). A positive community is necessary; it offers meaning and hope to its members through their participation, and individuals can merge themselves with it. Cultures likewise serve this function as systems of religious, philosophical, or ideological integration.

Recently, ethnic communities have shown renewed interest in historical roots and ethnic culture, identification and affinity with the group of origin and other group members, and community solidarity and group action. At the same time, ethnic group psychology has developed. For example, according to African psychology, the African American retains a sense of being a communal person who subordinates personal goals to the survival and well-being of the historically African group. Similarly, among Latinos there has been a movement toward return to cultural roots, assertion of ethnicity, and the active politicization and pride of cultural differences. Commitment therapy emphasizes returning the individual to an ethnic community, membership in which results in an effective pattern of symbolic integration (Jones & Korchin, 1982).

The Community. Mesointervention focuses on the importance of the collective community as a primary modality. The goal of mesointervention is to rejoin the client with his or her own ethnic community, which provides the basis for identity, support, and cultural resources. Osborne, Carter, Pinkleton, and Richards (1983) stress that an understanding of the ethnic community and cultural supports is essential to treatment interventions. In working with the African American community, the practitioner requires a knowledge of personal groups, family, and community supports, as well as cultural elements such as philosophy of life, music, patterns of behavior, religion, morals, habits, rules, knowledge, art, language, beliefs, customs, and ways of living. The client experiences linkage with these collaborative networks as part of the treatment.

Delgado (1997) suggests that Latino small businesses can provide access to services for disempowered groups in their role as urban sanctuaries, as providers of cultural items and services, and as providers of information related to the homeland. Beauty parlors in Latino communities and other small businesses can distribute public education information, make referrals, perform listening and crisis intervention support, and interpret correspondence for non-English-speaking persons. Social service organizations should approach and collaborate with these resources, helping train and educate resource persons. Early in the community mental health movement in the 1960s there were training efforts of beauty parlor hairdressers and bartenders because these persons were natural supportive resources for women who share problems while getting their hair done and for men who talked about their troubles in the neighborhood bar. Delgado sees the value of these efforts with Latina hairdressers.

In the African American community one witnesses the importance of the community resources. In Cultural Study 9-12, for the example of the African American community, Tucker (1979) emphasizes use of the full range of family and community social supports for mesolevel intervention.

CULTURAL STUDY 9-12

Family and Community Social Supports

In this model of practice, intervention begins at the level of community social structure. The support has to be deliberately designed to support the family structures as they exist; observing functions as a measure of adequacy rather than design. Those aspects of family function that provide biological needs, emotional needs, and support for acceptable values and goals [are important], rather than the process by which they are achieved.

For example, the father role may be played by a grandfather, who enjoys, accepts, and is enhanced by the role. The child loves, accepts guidance, and turns to him for protection and help. The record should reflect this, rather than a long social monologue on illegitimacy, loose morals, absentee father, and weak parental involvement. The state of the family functioning must be reflected and supported.

The role of the black church and its influences must be recognized, accepted, and worked with to broaden its social structural involvement. Its institutional posture has historically evaded overt colonial interference to the degree that it has survived as a perpetuated institution over time. Since the interference with it is more pronounced and reacted to, it stands as a monument in the black community. Community mental health efforts must be tied to the spiritual and moral needs of the black community.

For example, the space available in black churches should be made use of when and on whatever conditions possible. [Churches] should be generously reimbursed for lending their community relations, moral sanction, and facilities to mental health services. The role of the minister in the leadership of the local congregation should entail a concentrated financially supported training program for black ministers in mental health leadership and a total congregational participation in a carefully designed, well-delivered membership training in community mental health and counseling knowledge. This is critical to insure the survival of mental health practice when the mental health funds are no longer available.

A deliberate program with local schools, businesses, and absentee vested interest to identify and plan their responsibility in local community mental health is necessary.

For example, the local movie theater owner who builds his business on the showing of "X"-rated movies in local neighborhoods might consider a matinee for the children as well as local residents on a continuous basis for human relations, community development, and black-oriented films on weekend afternoons. This is by no means a limit to local community support structures accessible to the community mental health practitioner.

From "Minority Issues in Community Mental Health," by S. Tucker. In B. R. Compton and B. Calaway (Eds.), *Social Work Processes*, pp. 122, 123. Copyright © 1979 The Dorsey Press. Reprinted by permission of Brooks/Cole Publishing Company, a division of International Thomson Publishing Inc., Pacific Grove, CA 93950.

Mokuau (1985) discusses the Hawaiian healing method of the *bo'oponopono* process, which is likened to an interactive interdependent family problem-solving approach. In the initial phase, the general problem is identified, and procedures for problem solving are specified. Participants deal with only one problem or issue related to the general problem at a time. Everyone is allowed to speak, so dimensions of the problem are revealed that caused misunderstanding and disruptive family behavior. Confrontation and negative feelings are minimized. Resolution is effected through confession of wrongdoing and seeking of forgiveness from family members. Wrongdoers make restitution if necessary. The leader summarizes the process and reaffirms the family's strength and mutual commitment. The family prays and offers food to the gods, then shares food together.

Sue and Morishima (1982) discuss the use of indigenous community workers and natural community caretakers such as ministers, relatives, prominent community members, and family physicians. They also differentiate between various natural resources in terms of individual skills and strategies, interpersonal support systems such as family and friends, and institutional systems such as churches, herbalists, family doctors, and folk healers. For Chinese Americans, family associations were historically responsible for community governance, financial support, and political ideology. Later, Chinese Christian churches functioned as learning and social service institutions that offered teaching of English and the Bible, provision for the poor, assistance with immigration, socialization, and counseling. More recently, Asian American professional workers and young activists have organized the poor and powerless into grassroots organizations that combine social service and politicization.

The Extended Family. Agbayani-Siewert (1994) emphasizes the responsive nature of the extended family.

> The bilateral extended family provides mutual support, protection, and interdependence to all its members, and the kin group takes precedence over unrelated persons, the community, and the law. When a member is threatened, the family will rally around the individual to provide protection and support. Through the conception of reciprocal obligation, the extended family will provide financial aid and career favors. (p. 431)

Morales and Salcido (1983) explain social network interventions in terms of formal and informal systems involved in Mexican American family life. The goal of social network intervention is to deal with the individual and family structure by rendering the network visible and viable and by restoring

its function. The social network includes extended kin, *compadres* (coparents), friends, *curanderos* (folk healers), and other concerned individuals. These subsystems provide emotional strength, support, and practical assistance to the family. The Latino extended family system is tightly knit and includes the nuclear family, relatives, and close friends in *compadrazgo* (coparenthood). Characteristics of this system include emotional displays of affection, hierarchical roles, and distinctive child-rearing practices. Family members seek advice and support from each other before going for professional help. The *compadre* and *comadre* are the godfather and godmother of a child who is baptized. They have important family roles and perform parental duties if anything happens to the natural parents (Carrillo, 1982). The Puerto Rican family in particular maintains good relationships with extended family, friends, and people with connections to receive help with job or educational opportunities. In some extended networks, children are raised by families other than their own, who offer opportunities for education, employment, and marriage. The extended family and friends of the family go out together for recreational and social purposes. In some small communities, storekeepers, teachers, and neighbors are all concerned about, and watch out for, each other's children.

Thus, in multicultural practice, the family and community are potent forces for intervention and support. Ghali (1977) states:

> It should be borne in mind that the family has within it the resources and strengths to restore the homeostasis. The therapist and other sensitive professional workers simply help the family to release the energy needed to meet their proper tasks so that the individuals can be free to grow. The family capacity to love, to share, and to be generous and hospitable is the foundation to build on. (p. 468)

In Cultural Study 9-13, Willis, Debrecv, and Sipes (1992), writing specifically about Native Americans, emphasize the importance of working with the extended family in the client's home rather than treating the individual in the office. This provides a valuable opportunity to observe interfamily dynamics.

The Extended Family Context

The culturally sensitive therapist will recognize that the American Indian has had little contact with mental health personnel. Members of a tribe may distrust non–American Indian personnel because of discrimination and oppression they have experienced in the past, and they will generally be distrustful of the therapist, at least in the beginning. Therapy may be nontraditional in that it may not be one-on-one therapy in the therapist's office but may be scheduled in the home of the client. This may include not only the immediate family but also the extended family, especially the grandparents. It is important to remember that the American Indian family is not just a single nuclear family but is rich and varied and may extend across several households and include grandparents, aunts, uncles, or nonkin who have become members of the family. The therapist working with children who have been sexually abused will often see the child while the child is in foster care. The child may also be distrustful, but, generally, therapy and therapy issues with American Indian children will not be different from those with non–American Indian children. When one begins working with the family for reunification, however, cultural differences may arise, because many American Indian families resist cultural assimilation. Because of the multitude of tribes (400 plus), therapists in a given locale may need to familiarize themselves with the customs and healing ceremonies of the tribes in their area.

From "Treating American Indian Victims of Abuse and Neglect," by D. J. Willis, A. Debrecv, and D. S. B. Sipes. In L. A. Vargas and J. D. Koss-Chioino (Eds.), *Working with Culture: Psychotherapeutic Interventions with Ethnic Minority Children and Adolescents*, pp. 284–285. Copyright © 1992 Jossey-Bass, San Francisco. Reprinted by permission.

The Church. The church is another influential institution for people of color. As Pinderhughes (1989) explains:

Some people use religion to help them cope with powerlessness, uncertainty, and depreciation. In addition to spiritual fulfillment and emotional support, institutionalized religion and the church meet social needs. Thus, practitioners' failure to consider the use of religion and church-based support systems as effective treatment resources can be particularly unfortunate. (p. 164)

The church has provided an extensive network of caregivers for persons in need. The English word *care* has the meaning of *concern, close attention, liking or regard, protection, responsibility, take charge of, look after,* and *interest.* These synonyms are action words that denote extending oneself in a helpful way to another. The biblical understanding of caring emphasizes the reassurance of God's concern and a concern or caring for others.

The Old Testament words for care involve concrete concern for others. The Psalmist exclaims, "What is man that thou art mindful of him, and the son of man that thou dost care for him?" (Psalm 8:4). Or as Jeremiah 23:2 says, "Therefore thus says the LORD, the God of Israel, concerning the shepherds who care for my people." The New Testament follows the practical and concrete caring of the Old Testament. I Peter 5:7 urges, "Cast all your cares on him, for he cares about you." This verse points to God's caring concern. However, in some instances, care is understood as self-reliance. Matthew 13:22 declares, "but the cares of the world and the delight in riches choke the word, and it proves unfruitful." In other instances care is directed toward responsibility for others. I Corinthians 12:25 says "that there may be no discord in the body, but that the members may have the same care for one another."

The caring ministry of the church affirms the concern for others and their needs and is the basis for pastoral and lay caregiving. Caregivers express their caring in a number of ways and are a rich source of volunteers in church and social service agencies for persons who are in need:

- Trust: developing trust and openness with another person
- Telephone contact: maintaining regular communication with a person in need

- Activity: using positive activities such as sharing a meal, shopping, going to public events to develop a relationship
- Sharing: meeting to talk about practical problems in a supportive environment
- Fellowship group: introducing a person to a church fellowship group with persons who have common interests and age similarity
- Individual and group Bible study: studying relevant passages of scripture on a regular basis with a Bible study guide and a layperson who understands the Bible
- Prayer: meeting a prayer support partner who listens to prayer requests and upholds the person in prayer for daily strength

Community service caregivers and volunteers have participated in such diverse activities as these:

- Helping another individual in personal support service such as home delivered meals, friendly visiting
- Advocating the rights and entitlements of people with institutional systems
- Participating as citizens on government boards and committees, channeling communication and information, and monitoring and evaluating public programs
- Serving on boards of directors and similar bodies in the voluntary private sector
- Participating in self-help activities such as neighborhood improvement
- Fund-raising for a community organization in a campaign

A church caregiving model involves a number of functions, each of which will be described in the following subsections.

Practical Help. The practical assistance of the caregiver involves friend helping friend and neighbor helping neighbor with daily needs. According to Luke 10:29–37, Jesus answered the question "Who is my neighbor?" by telling the story of the good Samaritan who stopped to assist a man who was robbed and beaten by thieves. The true neighbor, according to Jesus in this parable, was the person "who showed mercy on him." Practical help consists of home visitation, activity companionship, listening and advice giving, and supportive and friendly telephone conversation. Concrete help involves transporting a person to the doctor's office, cooking for the homebound or bereaved, and checking on an elderly person who lives alone. Practical need means helping a person fill out an application for Medicare, secure Social Security services, and find needed government programs. Neighborly assistance includes helping a family move into a new home, paint a house, and put in a fence.

Hooyman and Lustbader (1986) write about family and elderly caregiving and report that the elderly have practical needs as the primary problem. Families tend to respond to their elderly through socioeconomic support and practical activities. These include financial cash assistance to supplement living needs; emotional contact through visiting, companionship, advice giving, and telephone checkups; advocacy to secure social and health services from program agencies; concrete daily services such as cooking, cleaning, shopping, bathing, dressing, feeding, and transportation; and homebound tasks such as caring for the elderly who are unable to shop for themselves at the grocery store.

Befriending. Befriending people through helping provides an opportunity to get to know each other. Caregiving offers a growing relationship between the caregiver and the care recipient. There is a mutual giving that transpires in a relationship. As Luke 6:38 states, "Give, and it will be given to you; good measure, pressed down, shaken together, running over, will be put into your lap. For the measure you give will be the measure you get back."

Hooyman and Lustbader (1986) report that caregiving to the elderly develops a better relationship between parent and children. Caring for elderly parents offers an opportunity to become closer to each other. For example, helping an elderly parent dress in the mornings provides the experience of touching, a nonverbal message of tender intimacy. Or providing daily cooking for an elderly parent helps to discover strength that emerges in this kind of commitment. These experiences create freedom from interruption for intimate conversation and understanding of each other.

Natural Help Networking. Forming natural support systems is a major task for the caregiver. No single individual can meet the multiple needs of a person. It is important to involve others in the helping process to spread the responsibilities. Natural helpers consist of nurses and receptionists at doctors' offices, bank tellers, bus drivers, apartment managers, grocery store clerks, postal carriers, cab drivers, hairdressers and barbers, pharmacists, restaurant staff, neighbors, and home health aides. These natural helpers observe the needs and limitations of older persons and are adept with meeting their particular needs. In their own way, these natural helpers make sure that the elderly are protected, serviced, and cared for.

When natural helpers do not exist, volunteers from churches and social service groups provide concrete help and emotional reassurance. This information is important when the caregiver observes the presence or absence of a natural support system. Together with the pastor, the social worker, and the caregiver, efforts can be made to activate family, neighbors, and friends to aid in the assistance of a person.

Lay Caregiving Training Programs. Church lay caregiving training started in the early seventies and was influenced by the paraprofessional and volunteer movements of the War on Poverty in the sixties. Lay caregivers in the church have been called lay shepherds, lay counselors, and similar titles. Crucial to the success of a lay caregiver program is the commitment of the pastor who is the leader, trainer, and specialist of lay caregivers. In some instances the minister has shared these responsibilities with church-related social workers. Both have participated in training, guidance, and consultation with lay caregivers who must be well trained and supervised in these programs.

Several congregations have used laypersons to build a bridge between the church and a community need. Among the areas are visiting elderly in a nursing home, serving as halfway house spon-

sors for young adults with mental health problems, and working with families of prisoners. Lifeline Centers in many countries, particularly Australia, have used trained volunteers in church-sponsored crisis telephone answering help. The Stephen Series training program has been adopted by many churches and trains laity in helping others. The crucial success of this program depends on continuing support, pastoral supervision, and follow-up training. Lay training is used to enhance pastoral care activities in evangelism, hospital visitation, bereavement care, homebound visitation, stewardship canvassing, church school, and group ministries.

There are a number of ingredients for successful church lay caregiving programs. First, the *organization of the program* should involve the pastor and the church pastoral care committee. The board of deacons is a natural body to discuss the possibilities of establishing this program. It is important to involve this group in preliminary interaction to solicit ideas and to build a support base. Part of the understanding and agreement between the pastor and deacons is the time and resource commitment of the pastoral staff to this program.

Once the lay caregiving program has the support and endorsement of the church board and the church, the pastor and the planning committee must address a number of issues: What are the program purposes? What are the service areas of the program? How should recruitment be conducted? What are some areas of training and assignment? Who should conduct supervision? In the planning phase, these questions must be discussed and answered to formulate a detailed plan.

A rule of thumb is that each congregation defines the unique purposes of lay caregiving according to the particular church and community needs, individual caring gifts, and pastoral skills. For example, the needs of a suburban community church could focus on newcomers, family life needs, and child care, whereas the problems of an urban downtown congregation could center around the elderly, the sick, and the homeless. Shaping lay caregivers to fill missing gaps in either church situation results in differing and legitimate purposes. The program purpose depends on the unique situation.

There should be a series of messages on lay caregiving, a brochure on the program, and qualifications and responsibilities of the lay caregivers.

The *recruitment and selection process* entails an announcement about the program to the entire congregation to afford the opportunity for everyone. A flyer should describe the goals and responsibilities of the program with an application form. The application elicits information about the particular reasons for joining the program, family background, time constraints, previous helping experiences with people, educational background, occupation, and a preference for certain caring situations. It serves as a screening device and information database and becomes the basis for selecting trainees.

The selection process should involve a committee who are aware of the following selection criteria:

- Warmth and friendliness
- Willingness to listen and to help with a problem
- Ability to maintain confidentiality
- Emotional health
- Concern about others
- Commitment to training and supervision
- Commitment to the program for a period of six months to one year
- Awareness of personal limitations
- Ability to work cooperatively with others
- Sufficient time devoted to spouse and family

A particular church may not wish to follow these criteria and opt for simpler guidelines. Nevertheless, objective standards should be derived to guide the selection of trainees.

What about those who are not accepted into the program? The recruitment should be conducted in such a manner that elitism is avoided among those accepted and hurt feelings are minimized among those not accepted. The latter group should be sent a letter thanking them for their interest, stating that there is a limited number, and asking for their continued support for the lay caregivers. There is an opportunity for the next training group for those who were not selected in this round.

Group size should be established during the recruitment stage. How many lay caregivers can be adequately trained and supervised? A suggestion is that an initial training group be limited to twenty persons. This number allows for attrition and is feasible for class size, assignments, tracking, and supervision.

Trained formats vary depending on the schedule and needs of the group. A concentrated model sets aside a number of weekends (Friday evening to Sunday afternoon) for an intensive workshop experience. The advantage is that busy persons can concentrate on developing several skills and experiences away from their demanding schedules of family and work. The alternative training model is a weekly training session that spreads out the learning and affords time for the training group to absorb the material.

Content curriculum should cover crisis material, particularly the significance of loss and recovery; communication and listening skills, particularly the sharing and reflection of feelings; problem-solving steps on how to work through a problem situation; application of the problem-solving model to family, hospitalization, and personal crisis situations.

The curriculum model for caregivers revolves around befriending, listening, and problem solving. Let's consider each in more detail.

Befriending involves initiating and maintaining a satisfying emotional relationship with another. It is the beginning of the helping relationship. Bridging is a necessary ingredient in befriending. The minister initially builds a bridge with the person in a crisis problem situation. It means that the person and the helper have access to each other. Bonding is another aspect of befriending. Bonding occurs when the caregiver is referred to the person by the minister and initiates relationship building. The sharing of self, providing nurture, and spending time with the person in crisis are examples of how bonding is achieved. It is a process that occurs over a period of time when a helping relationship is formed between two persons.

Befriending reminds the person in need that there are church resources that are a part of a social support system. Hepworth, Rooney, and Larsen (1997) state:

Parishes and congregations are natural ecological structures and as such may offer many resources needed by clients such as a reference group, spiritual stimulation, social activities, recreational programs, home visits, short-term homemaking when clients are ill, and concrete services for elderly and home-bound persons. (p. 448)

A person in crisis tends to move toward isolation and noninvolvement. Befriending reaches out to reintegrate a person into the mainstream of life and activities.

Befriending a person in crisis involves entering the life situation of an individual, family, or group as a friend. It mobilizes individual and significant-other resources. It reduces the impact of the stressful situation through the presence of a friendly caregiver.

Listening is a helping process skill. It presumes that trust and relationship building are in process. Now the person is ready to disclose thoughts and feelings. Listening opens the door to the problem issues. It is a learned art. One must be trained to listen in a certain manner. Learned listening cuts through the conversation between the person in need and the caregiver. It identifies the most meaningful and significant message of the person. It asks, "What is this person really saying and feeling?" In brief, it trains the listener to decipher the meaning behind the message.

One understands another's problems by selecting the significant thoughts and feelings, summarizing communication patterns, and asking questions about unanswered or unexplored areas. The listener takes mental notes on the cognitive, affective, and behavioral messages; that is, the important ideas, feelings, and actions emerging from communication between two persons. Listening involves processing these messages. The listening task is to distinguish between the words that are heard, feelings perceived, and behavior observed and the real message being communicated. One provides feedback by summarizing what is being communicated or asking a question to clarify a point.

Problem solving involves devising an immediate solution to a particular problem after relationship building or befriending and problem listening. Problem solving is used to confront the daily tasks of living. A person is constantly problem-solving throughout the day. With each situation, the problem is defined in specific terms, alternatives are reviewed to determine the range of possibilities, and a solution is selected to deal with the problem. Problem solving involves a decision to change the person or social environment or both. It is a part of our thought and action process. It is an automatic response that a person performs in daily activities. When a person experiences a crisis overload, normal problem-solving procedures are temporarily interrupted until they are restored by focusing on a particular problem, alternatives, and a solution.

Generally a person in crisis has many interrelated problems to be solved. The person along with the caregiver must select a specific problem that can be solved within a reasonable period of time. In this sense, the problem solving must be with a manageable problem that is feasibly solvable with the person.

Brainstorming the needs of church and community caring and arriving at a decision to form pastoral and lay care teams for these areas is essential to develop structure to the program.

Initial calls on the newcomer, the homebound, or the aged provide lay caregiver trainees experience in applying principles from the training program. An assignment assumes that the pastor has made an initial visit with the person in need. From this contact has come the agreement between the pastor and person about follow-up visits with a lay caregiver from the church. The pastor explains that there will be further pastoral contacts but that lay involvement is part of the church's ministry.

The pastor should give to the lay caregiver sufficient background information on the person and particular instructions on caring issues before the visit. This briefing helps the visitor anticipate what might happen and to prepare for the visits.

Later, lay caregivers are brought together with a person in a life crisis by the pastor who has worked with the individual and who feels that a follow-up relationship would further the progress of the person. Mutual permission of both parties is essential to this process.

Periodic and regular supervision of lay caregivers and their cases is important to guide and instruct the group in the art of caring and helping. The pastor or the church-related social worker/trainer gives specific instructions on particular caring problems before and after the visit, offers back-up support and communication, and sets up a supervision time to discuss feelings and problems encountered in the relationship.

Regular supervision between the pastor or the church-related social worker and lay caregiver as individuals, in pairs, or as a whole group is crucial to a successful program. At the beginning regular weekly supervision may be necessary to build confidence and to focus on the interaction between the caregiver and the person in need. The caregiver should bring a written recording on a sample conversation between both parties for learning purposes. This will give the pastor-supervisor a good indication of what is happening during the visit. To avoid the obvious distraction the caregiver should write down the conversation after the visit.

During the supervision the pastor or the social worker should be helpful and tactful in feedback teaching and learning. It is helpful to be supportive and positive in supervision while remaining didactic about areas for improvement.

No doubt each visit elicits feelings and questions that serve as an opportunity for individual and group learning. Role-playing a situation to examine what was occurring in the process may be helpful. The caregiver involved may wish to assume the role of the person in need to sense that person's feelings. Group feedback and alternative suggestions for responding to the situation are likely to occur in the supervision process. Together a satisfactory solution to a situation is the end result.

Supervisory sessions are opportunities to discuss specific topics that are applicable to caregivers in a number of predicaments. The pastor or the social worker provides background information on such topics as understanding grief, depression, loneliness, and related crisis issues.

After the caregiver group gains considerable experience, the supervision could move to bimonthly conferences. Between these sessions are frequent telephone contacts between the pastor and caregivers to discuss interpersonal problems that occur in various helping encounters with people. In particular emergencies immediate supervision and consultation between the pastor, the social worker, and the caregiver are understood procedures.

The caregiver requires periodic support, continuous training, and a sense of direction from the pastor or the social worker. The minister recognizes that key laity are engaged in significant helping relationships in the church and community. A shared ministry is the outgrowth of this program.

The caregiver should be exposed to the wide knowledge of social services. Various social service and social work speakers should be invited to discuss important topics confronting the community in general and helping persons such as caregivers in particular. This information will enliven and enrich the quality of training and supervision. It will also serve as a bridge for enrolling in mental health and family life courses in community colleges and university extension programs, crisis intervention telephone volunteer programs, and related workshops and conferences.

The caregiving model is applicable for ethnic people of color churches. The ethnic church represents a natural support system that is part of the ethnic community and is infused into the fabric of family and community life.

Solomon (1983) emphasizes the role of the church in African American community life in the areas of civil rights and job discrimination. In addition to human rights, the church advocates prayer, African American unity, and the collection and distribution of funds on behalf of needy people. The church provides social leadership, mutual assistance, and spiritual strength. Solomon (1983) explains:

> God is never an abstraction not linked to the here-and-now. He is personalized and included in daily life situations. It is not uncommon to hear Afro-Americans relate a conversation they have had with God or with His son, Jesus Christ. Prayer is a frequent response to everyday crisis, even by those who do not profess to any deep religious convictions. (p. 422)

For African Americans, the church is intricately involved in personal, family, and social needs. It has a bonding effect on the African American community.

Latinos are also spiritual people. Ghali (1977) observes that Puerto Ricans turn to spiritualism and mysticism. Traditionally Catholic, they may not be regular churchgoers; some may attend services only on Christmas, Palm Sunday, and Easter and for weddings and funerals. Puerto Ricans love processions, rituals, and pageantry and make promises to God and the saints in return for favors. For other Latinos, the church represents a place of worship, ethnic socialization, strengthening of family moral values, and provision of community services.

Patterns of Helping. Extended family and community support systems play a vital role in mesointervention with people of color. However, research on informal support systems reveals that different components of the family and community systems are best for different roles. Siegel (1984) reports that, when helping the elderly, the roles are as follows: nuclear and kinship family for long-term crisis, friends for socialization, and neighbors for short-term assistance. Kin are best for functions that involve long-term commitment and require time, energy, or money—especially the long-term care of ill and helpless elders. Friends are important for companionship and leisure activities. Neighbors are useful in situations that require speed of reaction, as in emergencies; continuous observation and knowledge of the neighborhood; and the granting of a favor, such as picking up an item at the store.

Cantor (1970) found the following patterns among elderly African Americans, Latinos, and whites in New York City:

1. African Americans were most likely to have a wide-ranging support network made up of kin and nonkin.
2. Latinos' functional support systems were equally likely to be composed of family (spouse, children, and relatives) or nonfamily.
3. Latinos were most likely to have a living spouse and a greater number of functional children who saw them frequently.
4. Latinos were given more help by their children than were members of other groups.

Mesolevel intervention involves reuniting or joining together two entities—the client and his or her community, which offers a rich heritage and tradition of customs, beliefs, and person-oriented resources. The objective of mesolevel intervention is to tap the community's strengths to change the client's problem set. Cultural Study 9-14 reports the dramatic healing effect of a family network on a Native American client.

CULTURAL STUDY 9-14

Family Network Intervention

The . . . example . . . involves a network-clan with a single extended family at its core. At the time the therapist entered the picture, it was composed of a grandmother, several adult son's and daughters' families, and their close or significant friends. This network was deteriorating rapidly. There had been two murders, a suicide, a crippling assault, and the death from a heart attack of the grandfather who had healed the group.

The man upon whom the network then depended for survival was acutely and suicidally depressed. He was ambivalent about assuming the leadership role. He was not only concerned about his ability to cope with the task, but he was overwhelmed with a feeling of guilt and loss of face about a dishonorable Army discharge, after fifteen years of honorable military service. This element assumed real importance because of the cultural importance of honor in battle as an Indian tradition, which might not have parallel importance in another culture. In addition to suicidal ruminations, his symptoms included an inflammation of shrapnel induced arthritis sufficient to render him unemployable, at a time when many of his kin were also facing financial crisis.

Clinical judgment indicated that this man required inpatient hospitalization. Rather than arrange a quick admission to the United States Public Health Service Indian Hospital, the network-clan and the patient were invited to participate in finding a solution. This seemed imperative since it had appeared to the therapist even before this man presented himself as a patient, that the network-clan itself was sick.

The first stage was a rapid gathering of the network-clan at the grandmother's home. This permitted introducing two elements that had been lost: First, an element of hope in getting treatment for the potential leader and second, some success experiences in reaching short-term reachable goals. These quick success experiences actually consisted of raising $20.00 via a bingo game and finding temporary employment for one son. It was also possible for the clan to offer support and help for the therapist in treating the depressed patient, which could be received gratefully.

The network-clan, reeling from a series of disasters, had been unable to exchange positive experiences in this fashion between its members for some time and consequently had been resonating and amplifying pathology. Once this pathology was dampened, it was possible to discover that admission to a VA Hospital would symbolically expunge the dishonorable discharge. This was arranged through the therapist's liaison with the professional agencies and was ceremonially validated in a formal meeting.

As a result of the opportunities for interaction with individual network members during these activities, the therapist was able to share the grief with the grandmother and other individuals in such a way that they found a release in tears and could get about the work of mourning, which eliminated another source of pathology within the network.

Supportive contacts between the network-clan and the depressed man began within hours of his brief hospitalization. Although the VA psychiatry department found him "unsuitable" for psychotherapy, his somatic and suicidal symptoms disappeared and his arthritis was brought under medical control. The network worked through the patient's practical problems by helping him find a job, transportation, and so on, as well as providing the therapeutic relationships needed. He was able to show his own resilience three months later when he handled the details of a terminal illness and funeral of another of the network members. That event would probably have triggered another wave of suicidal-murder catastrophes had not pathology been halted within the group.

Within twelve months the destructive processes had been reversed and the reciprocal healing strengths of network and ex-patient network-clan leader were such that he and one or two others were visibly assuming interlocking leadership roles as tribal representatives at pow-wows and in the elected tribal business organization.

Evidence that real changes in network pathology had occurred is deduced from the fate of one family unit which for a variety of reasons (mainly job opportunities) moved several hundred miles away at the height of [the] pathological period. This family was not present during the period of therapeutic intervention and was out of touch with the network in an unusual fashion. Before contact was reestablished, the state newspapers headlined that this family had another "unexplained" murder and suicide incident which left only one surviving child. In an institution for delinquents at the time of the parents' deaths, the child continues to be both "incorrigible" and "isolated."

This continued antisocial experience of that one surviving delinquent is in contrast to the other children of the network-clan who survived similar family destruction during the pathological period. They have now faded into public anonymity. Local authorities ignore them since they are in school, not delinquent, and not in need of "public assistance" as they have been scattered among network-clan families. While clinicians might predict some psychic scar tissue, they probably could not write a better therapeutic prescription than the network's cooperative distribution of nurturing responsibilities. It is probable that a professional clinic or agency could not deliver these services as efficiently as the restored network-clan.

Southeast Asian refugees in particular have formed nuclear community organizations for mutual support and for the preservation of cultural heritage. These mutual associations have created among refugees a sense of self-confidence and a firm belief in the future. In Southeast Asia, mutual assistance and solidarity are a way of life. Villagers help one another and share responsibility for the security and development of the community. Community life centers are used for public meetings, ceremonies, and cultural performances. In the United States, mutual assistance and community activities are important for refugees who have experienced postwar trauma. Religious ceremonies, holiday celebrations, and social and cultural events reestablish a sense of belonging and identity.

These community organizations, called mutual assistance associations (MAAs), prevent and treat refugees' mental health problems. Community members share experiences and help each other with such adjustment problems as cross-cultural conflicts. They discuss and try to resolve issues of common interest.

Particular MAA services include maintenance of culture and spiritual integrity through social activities on traditional holidays among religious and secular groups; resettlement service provisions, which offer social services based on community needs; gender-specific, age-specific, and special-interest groups that organize program activities; economic development for local refugee business associations; and advocacy and political action that ranges from local elections to concerns in their native countries (Khoa & Bui, 1985).

In social work intervention, the social worker serves as an intermediary between a client and a helping resource of the client's community to ensure the appropriate referral and delivery of services. Social work intervention involves helping the client select a suitable ethnic service organization or helping person, arranging a referral, and establishing a working relationship for follow-up community intervention. At the core of intervention is a strategy for change that involves a joint decision by the worker and client to follow a course of action. This strategy engages the worker and the client in problem solving within the context of the client's community. Action is taken in consultation and concert with the spirit and values of the ethnic community. Problem-solving action takes place within the community's realm of influence. Problem solutions are not independent of the ethnic community; they have a point of reference from which they are formulated, agreed on, and implemented. At this interventional level, the ethnic community influences the outcome of action. For example, the client who is coping with a specific problem may need the support of, or feeling of belonging to, the caring and nurturing part of the community. In this sense, the feeling of oneness with the ethnic community, or finding one's place in it, involves identifying with a particular group of people who share a history and tradition, beliefs and values, customs and practices, and family and collective cohesion. Resolving a specific problem is an overt act of coping with stress or conflict and a symbolic way of finding one's ethnic lifeline.

Example of a Mesolevel Intervention. The mesolevel of intervention focuses on the use of the extended family and community network resources in working with clients. Among the interventional strategies relevant to the mesolevel is maintenance of culture. A prime example is the creation of an approach of collective cultural intervention when working with a local ethnic community. Red Horse (1982) suggests an ethnic collective interventional approach for Native Americans that involves an age-integrated developmental day care service. The service would be organized as a model of a cultural network that would bring at-risk families together for collective therapeutic support and incorporate individuals from allied community programs to serve as cultural and social role models. The network replicates a cultural community designed to meet the social and emotional needs of children, youth, adults, and elders and reaffirms Native American extended kin systems. Daily social contact would occur between at-risk families and professional staff, who could keep abreast of emerging family crises. Staff of allied programs could meet the developmental needs of children through natural informal relationships. The result would be a true ethos of family development. Red Horse outlines a multigenerational therapeutic community that draws on cultural and ethnic perspectives.

Macrolevel Intervention. Macrolevel intervention poses the challenge of formulating new approaches to change in the realm of perennial large-scale social issues that affect ethnic populations in a changing political and economic situation. Macrointervention emphasizes both individual betterment and social change in the direction of social equality, social justice, new institutional structures, and distribution of wealth and resources (Washington, 1982).

Social policy, planning, and administration have been macrointerventional tools for affecting social change in major problem areas. *Social policy* is the body of stated goals, directions, and guidelines that govern the implementation of programs, activities, and efforts related to public and private human services organizations. Presidential and congressional leadership, public and private interest groups, and the political and economic situation influence and affect social policy. In turn, social policy is translated into a rational formulation of program goals and objectives, design, implementation, and evaluative components that involves social planning. *Social planning* sets forth a systemic formulation that embodies goal priorities, program policies, and regulations. Accompanying funding incentives usually induce the participation of the public and private sectors and their compliance with the terms of the legislative program. *Social administration* oversees the funding of programs, the monitoring of program intent, and the implementation of program activities on behalf of the public legislation. Application proposals are written on the local level and submitted for review, approval, and funding on the state, regional, and national levels. Local city, county, and state departments act as liaisons between federal officials and local participants and assist in implementing national social programs.

Changing Social, Economic, and Political Situations.

Since the beginning of the Reagan administration in 1981, major changes in social policy have affected macrolevel intervention. Together with ethnic groups, social workers with policy, planning, and administrative skills are devising alternative policies, program designs, and strategies based on this changing context.

With the rise of a conservative political philosophy, social attitudes toward poverty and minorities have changed. Hopps (1982) observes that the new conservative philosophy has dismantled policies and programs that have worked for people of color and other vulnerable groups. This political conservatism has altered the funding of federal programs, which have been the most consistent source of social assistance for people of color. It has shifted the federal government's role from the public promotion of social welfare to the provision of incentives for the private sector to increase productivity and economic growth, create jobs for the able-bodied, and lessen public reliance on government. At the same time, social assistance programs have been cut, producing a devastating effect on the resources of ethnic communities because of their disproportionate reliance on these programs (Walters, 1982).

The prime factors behind these moves have been inflation, declining public social resources, shifts in national priorities, and majority power tactics. Rivera and Erlich (1981) point out that, on account of inflation, social work has sought to respond to rapidly expanding needs with ever-declining resources. National defense, energy supplies, and inflation have replaced social justice issues as top priorities and have shifted program resources away from ethnic communities. Competition for resources has taken place among people of color, who are in conflict over the meager remaining funds available to them. Latino Americans claim that the size of their population will soon surpass that of the African American population, and they will become the largest minority group in the United States. Latin American and Asian immigrants have gained access to public services and now compete for employment with African Americans, who have been denied or have made minimal gains for generations (Walters, 1982).

As a result, majority power tactics toward people of color have been overtly expressed through control of benefit distribution. Walters (1982) states:

To maintain this control, they use a variety of tactics in dealing with subordinated groups, such as suffocating minority demands by avoiding decisions, manipulating the bias of the demands by reinterpreting issues, developing manipulative actions that anticipate the reaction of the subordinate groups, co-opting subordinate groups' demands and denying their legitimacy, and denying minority groups entrance into the bargaining arena. (p. 27)

Institutional racism, which interferes with the social responsibility of delivering resources to people in need, is expressed through declining affirmative action, barriers in housing, and school segregation (Walters, 1982). These trends in public policy influence the social environment by limiting opportunities and resources available to people of color and reducing their self-worth and behavioral security (Longres, 1982).

Strategies for Macrolevel Intervention. As people of color have reinterpreted the changing social, economic, and political situation confronting them, macrolevel interventions for the 1980s and 1990s have assumed directions that address the conservatism and racism of this period.

Community Network Intervention. As a natural response to program cutbacks, reduced services, and restrictive eligibility-requirement tests, indigenous social networks have turned inward, toward their own survival resources. Rivera and Erlich (1981) describe neo-*Gemeinschaft* communities in which primary cultural, social, political, and economic interrelationships have been developed by new immigrants or ethnic groups occupying a geographic area. A support structure has been developed along horizontal lines in the face of an antagonistic environment and dwindling resources. For example, members of the Cuban immigrant community in the Miami, Florida, area employ bartering as a form of service sharing: Lacking money, many have turned to craft skills that they learned in their country of origin as a medium of exchange for necessary goods and services. Churches have been a primary source of help to newcomers through fundraising, housing, English classes, training in basic survival skills, and emergency food and clothing.

Intervention through community networks requires funding for the community's grassroots service organizations and churches. Delgado and Humm-Delgado (1982) suggest that community mental health funding should be directed to local churches to assist with multicultural youth programs. A national policy of family assistance payment would alleviate the burden of families who care for elderly and disabled at home. Moreover, the Department of Health and Human Services and its counterparts at the state level should establish strong bureaus to coordinate multicultural health care, housing, and services to children, youth, and the elderly. Local county revenue sharing and state block grants should give high priority to funding human services sponsored by indigenous bilingual/bicultural organizations.

Welfare reform and community change are relevant themes in organizing a community network. Gutiérrez, Alvarez, Neman, and Lewis (1996) observe:

> Welfare time limits and strong work requirements will leave large numbers of families in extremely precarious economic circumstances unless many of the barriers to employment for men and women currently in the low-skill labor force and moving on and off welfare are reduced. This problem cannot be approached piecemeal or within an individual focus; it requires a comprehensive approach to rebuilding the opportunities and supports for work in low-income communities. . . .
>
> Social workers must take the lead in changing the focus of welfare-related research from individual capacity to community capacity. This refocusing can be accomplished by including measures of the local community employment capabilities in all studies related to welfare reform. Welfare demonstration projects should be targeted not only at changing individual behavior but also at enhancing communities' abilities to provide access to and support for work. The research must convincingly demonstrate that individual success is, in part, contingent on community assets. (pp. 516, 517)

A community and economic strategy is required to respond to welfare reform policy on a practical grassroots level.

Community Organizing in a Diverse Society. Community organizing must be redefined for people of color. Rivera and Erlich (1998a) offer a paradigm that addresses three factors of diversity:

- The distinctive, ethnic, and cultural characteristics of people of color
- Their implications for such role variables as kinship patterns, social systems, power and leadership networks, religion, language, and particular community, economic, and political configurations
- The process of empowerment and the development of critical consciousness

Rivera and Erlich also identify three levels of community contact:

- The primary level—the racial, cultural, and linguistic identity of the community
- The secondary level—contact and influence expressed in language, liaison functions with the outside community and institutions, and technical expertise service resources
- The tertiary level—the outsider who works for the common interests and concerns of the community as an advocate and broker of services for communities of color

These variables form the basis for organizing issues of diversity and community contact.

Gutiérrez et al. (1996) remind us about the importance of cultural knowledge for organizing.

> Gaining knowledge of other cultures is essential for multicultural organizing. Knowledge includes awareness of the history, traditions, and values of other groups. Because ethnicity is formed from historical and social influences, learning about these external and internal factors helps one understand problems and strengths. Respect for another's culture means that one not only acknowledges the importance of the other's culture, but also shows interest in gaining knowledge about the differ-

ences. Through ethnic competence, community organizers can cultivate a respect for diversity among different groups, which will facilitate cooperation and break down barriers, and can maximize a group's potential through coordinated efforts with other groups. (p. 503)

In short, knowledge, ethnicity, culture, and diversity are critical elements for the multicultural social work organizer.

Rivera and Erlich (1998a) identify twelve qualities of an organizer who works in a diverse community setting:

1. Cultural and racial identification with a community
2. Familiarity with customs and traditions, social networks, and values
3. Knowledge of language style and subgroup slang
4. Leadership styles and development approaches that work with existing community leaders
5. A framework for political and economic analysis that accounts for the dynamics of oppression and highlights access and leverage points for political systems
6. Knowledge of past organizing strategies (strengths and limitations)
7. Skills in the development of critical consciousness and empowerment
8. Skills in assessing community psychology (the psychological makeup of the community)
9. Knowledge of organizational behavior and decision making
10. Skills in evaluative and participatory research that provide supportive information for communities of color
11. Skills in program planning, development, and administration management that position people of color for administrative positions
12. Awareness of self, personal strengths, and limitations

As organizers of color master these skills, they will be equipped to assume leadership for culturally diverse community needs.

Rivera and Erlich (1998b) identify the following agenda for community organizers in the future:

- *Coalition building:* Disenfranchised communities must be mobilized to identify common concerns and issues and present a united front to external political forces.
- *Politics and legislative reform:* The emphasis must be to resuscitate civil rights, to address economic bifurcation and rising poverty, and to meet the needs of refugees.
- *Racism:* As always, racism from outside the community must be addressed. In addition, the series of incidents between African American residents and Korean American business owners in South Central Los Angeles after the Rodney King verdict underscores the need for communities of color to come together and discuss mutual concerns.
- *Nurturing the growth of true cultural pluralism:* More effort is required in social work education recruitment, research, curricula, and organizer job prospects.

Political Impact Intervention. Electoral participation is a powerful strategy for influencing politicians and highlighting macroproblem issues that affect people of color. The Democratic party's 1984 presidential primaries witnessed the campaign of the articulate Reverend Jesse Jackson, who sought to form a Rainbow Coalition of disenfranchised groups. As a result, voter registration increased among people of color, especially African Americans. One political impact strategy is the encouragement of people of color to run as candidates for local, state, and national offices to maintain political visibility and gain leverage for social change. Hopps (1982) believes that, as a primary agenda, ethnic communities must return to political activism and organization at the grassroots level and speak out for necessary policies and programs. Coalitions must be formed with other groups who are affected by conservative policy cutbacks and human and civil rights retrenchment. People of color must register and vote for candidates who are willing to champion their cause. In short, the effectiveness of political impact intervention depends on the development of local political infrastructures of culturally diverse people around issues and candidates who are able to effect relevant social change.

Legal Advocacy Intervention. Legal advocacy is a long-term means of achieving social change through far-reaching landmark decisions in the courts. Morales (1981) asserts that we need advocates who plead the cause of clients before organizations and who represent the interests of an aggrieved class. Morales is particularly concerned about the need to continue class action suits on behalf of people of color. He cites the work of John Serrano, a social worker who initiated the now-famous case of *Serrano v. Priest*. In this class action suit before the California State Supreme Court, it was argued that the quality of a child's education should not be dependent on the wealth of a school district. The court ruled that the financing scheme of public education in California, which relied heavily on local property taxes, violated the equal protection clause of the Fourteenth Amendment to the U.S. Constitution. Wealthier school districts were favored to the detriment of poor districts. As a result, a financial plan must now assure equal funding for each child throughout the public school system of the state. Morales's point is that this argument could be extended to equal protection under the law in areas such as welfare, health, and mental health services. In light of government cutbacks, legal class action advocacy of a range of governmental services could be initiated on behalf of people of color. The distribution and quality of human services could be standardized under the equal protection clause in a class action suit.

Example of a Macrolevel Intervention. Macrolevel intervention addresses national and regional social problems and involves large-scale change with respect to entire communities and social classes. We have considered a number of macrolevel strategies, which correspond to particular intervention themes: Community network intervention and community organizing rely on the support structure of the community and emphasize empowerment and cultural maintenance. Political impact intervention calls forth the strategies of liberation and empowerment through the use of bloc voting and visible ethnic community candidates who achieve local, state, and national political offices. Legal advocacy

The Hernández Family, a Case Study

Having established a plan for an interventional strategy, Mr. Platt begins to implement various aspects with service resources and family members. Indispensable to the success of the plan is Father Carlos, a Catholic priest who directs the local satellite center for Catholic Social Services. He commands the respect of the community both as a Latino clergyman and as a competent, warm administrator of ethnic social service programs. Father Carlos is aware of the community's social needs and has been able to obtain program and funding resources and establish an indigenous program staffed with bilingual/bicultural service workers. It was natural for Mr. Platt to turn to this person and his organization, with their positive reputation and track record in the community, to provide assistance for the Hernández family. Over the years, Father Carlos has brought together job hunting, tutoring, child care, and newcomers' services under one roof and identified the church as a practical instrument for helping with the problems of the Latino community. His staff has also cultivated excellent relationships with the county welfare departments, general hospital, and housing authority and is able to refer clients to ethnic-sensitive, sympathetic workers in those agencies.

At the next session, members of the Hernández family report that initial contact has been made with the various unit workers. The two brothers-in-law were interviewed by a Spanish-speaking worker who had a number of job openings available with a local contractor. Although the brothers-in-law are not skilled trade workers, they have a promise of steady employment with apprentice-class status. They have been working on a local construction site for the past several days and seem to be adjusting to the work procedure. As a result, Mr. Hernández has taken a leave of absence from his second job as a night machine operator in a food-processing plant and begun to spend evenings with his family. Ricardo has been assigned a high school senior to tutor him in math, spelling, and social studies. Mrs. Hernández is involved in an ESL class through the adult education program of the local school district. A Mexican American woman who works as a volunteer at the newcomers' center has already spoken with the wives of the two immigrant families and has been helpful with practical problems of adjustment. All three women came from the same part of Mexico. Parts of the intervention plan are in motion and appear to be running smoothly.

TASK RECOMMENDATIONS

Principles of micro- and mesolevel intervention advocate the use of indigenous helping activities, programs, and persons in the ethnic community that are available to clients and ethnically aware human service workers. The following suggestions are designed to enhance your awareness and use of these resources:

- Identify and use appropriate ethnic community resources, such as a family system network, a community leader, minister, or service organization, to meet your particular needs and further your intervention plan.
- Serve as an intermediary advocate broker coordinator between the client and the ethnic helping resource. Support the relationship between the client and the community entity.
- If your city or county has a lack of ethnic community service organizations, conduct a preliminary study to identify ethnic social needs, key ethnic community leaders, funding sources, and specific services that can be initiated with seed money.

---

intervention pursues class action judicial decisions in a parity-based strategy.

A case example is the design of a macrolevel intervention to address the issue of unemployment. High unemployment among African Americans is a continuing social and economic problem. The majority society's perception is that African Americans have an aversion to work and exhibit personal and cultural defects. The multicultural view of unemployment is that systemic racial discrimination has excluded African Americans from the job force. In addition, educational inequality, technological/industrial innovation, and industry's pursuit of cheap labor abroad have severely restricted employment opportunities for people of color in the United States (Moss, 1982). It is estimated that, in 1973, African Americans lost $19 billion in national income on account of job discrimination and $5.9 billion in property on account of illicit activities (Thurow, 1975).

Moss (1982) recommends the following policy objectives for youth employment:

1. Ensure the accessibility of the labor market to all young people, regardless of race, sex, and national origin.
2. Provide means of identifying gaps in employment among youth and design programs to meet the needs of the hard-core unemployed.
3. Develop a monitoring and working procedure with employers who resist changes in discriminatory employment practices.

One means of implementing these objectives is subsidized on-the-job experience through direct federal grants to private employers. The subsidy would consist of a graduated wage increase over a five-year period, to a maximum of $5,000. Employers would receive bonuses for hiring the hard-core unemployed (Thurow, 1975). Improvement of the bleak outlook on unemployment for people of color in general and youth in particular depends on economic growth, federal funding, and presidential and congressional leadership. The current dominance of conservative policies in Washington, D.C., offers little hope for improvement in the near future.

Certainly a major interventional initiative in social policy is to devise a clear, effective program for employment training and placement of people of color. Such a program might adopt the following goals:

1. To *liberate* the person, by allowing him or her to select a career field from an open range of choices
2. To *empower* the person by providing relevant training experience and marketable skills

3. To target those who are most in need of economic stability and security (to address issues of *parity*)
4. To foster *cultural maintenance* by creating industrial work zones in the community
5. To recognize the *unique personhood* of the individual by providing jobs in which individual creativity can be demonstrated

The task of the social worker in multicultural practice is to design appropriate ethnic intervention strategies (liberation, empowerment, parity, culture maintenance, and unique personhood) on micro-, meso-, and macrolevels. Depending on the scope of the problem theme and level, the worker and the client can devise multiple interventional levels and strategies.

CONCLUSION

Intervention, which addresses social change for the client, is at the core of social work practice. This chapter has discussed in detail the elements of goals and agreement, interventional strategies, and interventional levels from a unique multicultural perspective. The social worker must create an appropriate intervention for each client's situation by drawing on a variety of strategy themes (liberation, empowerment, parity, maintenance of culture, and unique personhood) and considering micro-, meso-, and macrolevels of intervention. Of particular concern are the relevance of microlevel casework theories that speak to the individual family and small group; mesolevel extended family and community resources; and macrolevel interventional responses to socioeconomic and political dimensions of society. A wide range of interventions is presented, enabling the social worker to select pertinent combinations that fit the client's problem needs and assessment requirements.

REFERENCES

Agbayani-Siewert, P. (1994). Filipino American culture and family: Guidelines for practitioners. *Families in Society, 75,* 429–438.

Attneave, C. L. (1969). Therapy in tribal settings and urban network intervention. *Family Process, 8,* 192–210.

Bandura, A. (1982). Self-efficacy mechanism in human agency. *American Psychologist, 37,* 122–147.

Banks, O. (1981). *Faces of feminism.* New York: Oxford University Press.

Benston, M. (1969). The political economy of women's liberation. *Monthly Review, 21,* 13–27.

Biegel, D., & Naperste, A. (1982). The neighborhood and family service project: An empowerment model linking clergy, agency, professionals and community residents. In A. Jeger & R. Slotnick (Eds.), *Community mental health and behavioral ecology* (pp. 303–318). New York: Plenum.

Blackwell, J. E., & Hart, P. S. (1982). *Cities, suburbs, and blacks: A study of concerns, distrust and alienation.* Bayside, NY: General Hall.

Bliatout, B. T., Ben, R., Do, V. T., Keopraseuth, K. O., Bliatout, H. Y., & Lee, D. T. T. (1985). Mental health and prevention activities targeted to Southeast Asian refugees. In T. C. Owan (Ed.), *Southeast Asian mental health: Treatment, prevention, services, training, and research* (pp. 183–207). Washington, DC: National Institute of Mental Health.

Bochner, S. (1982). The social psychology of cross-cultural relations. In S. Bochner (Ed.), *Cultures in contact: Studies in cross-cultural interaction* (pp. 5–44). Oxford: Pergamon.

Bock, S. (1980). Conscientization: Paolo Friere and class-based practice. *Catalyst, 2,* 5–25.

Burghardt, S. (1982). *The other side of organizing.* Cambridge, MA: Schenkman.

Cantor, M. H. (1970). *The configuration and intensity of the informal support system in a New York City elderly population.* Unpublished manuscript, New York City Department for the Aging.

Caplan, G. (1964). *Principles of preventive psychiatry.* New York: Basic Books.

Carrillo, C. (1982). Changing norms of Hispanic families: Implications for treatment. In E. E. Jones & S. J. Korchin (Eds.), *Minority mental health* (pp. 250–266). New York: Praeger.

Cornell University Empowerment Group. (1989, October). *Networking Bulletin, 1,* 2.

Cowger, C. D. (1994). Assessing client strengths: Clinical assessment for client empowerment. *Social Work, 39,* 262–268.

Davis, L. E., Galinsky, M. J., & Schopler, J. H. (1995). RAP: A framework for leadership of multiracial groups. *Social Work, 40*(2), 155–165.

Davis, L. E., & Proctor, E. K. (1989). *Race, gender, and class: Guidelines for practice with individuals, families, and groups.* Upper Saddle River, NJ: Prentice-Hall.

Delgado, M. (1997). Role of Latina-owned beauty parlors in a Latino community. *Social Work, 42* (5), 445–453.

Delgado, M., & Humm-Delgado, D. (1982). Natural support systems: Source of strength in Hispanic communities. *Social Work, 27,* 83–89.

DuBray, W. (1993). *Mental health interventions with people of color.* St. Paul: West.

Fagan, H. (1979). *Empowerment. Skills for parish social action.* New York: Paulist.

Fay, B. (1987). *Critical social science.* Ithaca, NY: Cornell University Press.

Fink, S. L. (1967). Crisis and motivation: A theoretical model. *Archives of Physical Medicine and Rehabilitation, 48,* 592–597.

Friere, P. (1973). *Education for critical consciousness.* New York: Seabury.

Fujiki, S., Hansen, J. C., Cheng, A., & Lee, Y. M. (1983). Psychiatric mental health nursing of Asian and Pacific Americans. In J. C. Chunn II, P. J. Dunston, & F. Ross-Sheriff (Eds.), *Mental health and people of color: Curriculum development and change* (pp. 377–403). Washington, DC: Howard University Press.

Garvin, C. (1985). Work with disadvantaged and oppressed groups. In M. Sundel, P. Glasser, R. Sarri, & R. Vinter (Eds.), *Individual change through small groups* (pp. 461–472). New York: Free Press.

Ghali, S. B. (1977). Culture sensitivity and the Puerto Rican client. *Social Casework, 58,* 459–468.

Gibson, C. M. (1993). Empowerment theory and practice: With adolescents of color in the child welfare system. *Families in Society, 74,* 387–396.

Gitterman, A. (1994). Editor's note. In B. L. Simon, *The empowerment tradition in American social work: A history* (pp. ix–xi). New York: Columbia University Press.

Gitterman, A., & Shulman, L. (Eds.). (1986). *Mutual aid groups and the life cycle.* Itasca, IL: Peacock.

Gould, K. (1987a). Feminist principles and minority concerns: Contributions, problems, and solutions. *Affilia: Journal of Women and Social Work, 3,* 6–9.

Gould, K. (1987b). Life model vs. conflict model: A feminist perspective. *Social Work, 32,* 346–351.

Gutiérrez, L. M. (1990). Working with women of color: An empowerment perspective. *Social Work, 35,* 149–153.

Gutiérrez, L., Alvarez, A. R., Neman, H., & Lewis, E. H. (1996). Multicultural community organizing: A strategy for change. *Journal of Social Work, 41*(5), 501–508.

Gutiérrez, L. M., Parsons, R. J., & Cox, E. O. (1998). Creating opportunities for empowerment-oriented programs. In L. M. Gutiérrez, R. J. Parsons, & E. O. Cox (Eds.), *Empowerment in social work practice: A sourcebook* (pp. 220–233). Pacific Grove, CA: Brooks/Cole.

Hepworth, D. H., & Larsen, J. A. (1990). *Direct social work practice: Theory and skills* (3rd ed.). Belmont, CA: Wadsworth.

Hepworth, D. H., Rooney, R. H., & Larsen, J. A. (1997). *Direct social work practice: Theory and skills* (5th ed.). Pacific Grove, CA: Brooks/Cole.

Higginbotham, H. N., & Tanaka-Matsumi, J. (1981). In P. B. Pedersen, J. G. Draguns, W. J. Lonner, & J. E. Trimble (Eds.), *Counseling across cultures* (pp. 247–274). Honolulu: University of Hawaii Press.

Hirayama, H., & Hirayama, K. (1985). Empowerment through group participation: Process and goal. In M. Parenes (Ed.), *Innovations in social group work: Feedback from practice to theory* (pp. 119–131). New York: Haworth.

Ho, M. K. (1987). *Family therapy with ethnic minorities.* Newbury Park, CA: Sage.

Hooyman, N. R., & Lustbader, W. (1986). *Taking care: Supporting older people and their families.* New York: Free Press.

Hopps, J. G. (1982). Oppression based on color. *Social Work, 27,* 3–5.

Hulewat, P. (1996). Resettlement: A cultural and psychological crisis. *Journal of Social Work, 41*(2), 129–135.

Inter-Tribal Council of Arizona, Inc. (n.d.). Community resources for American Indians. In E. F. Brown & T. F. Shaughnessy (Eds.), *Introductory text: Education for social work practice with American Indian families* (pp. 201–230). Tempe: Arizona State University School of Social Work, American Indian Projects for Community Development, Training, and Research.

Ivey, A. E. (1981). Counseling and psychotherapy: Toward a new perspective. In A. J. Marsella & P. B. Pedersen (Eds.), *Cross-cultural counseling and psychotherapy* (pp. 279–311). New York: Pergamon.

Janoff-Bulman, R. (1979). Characterological versus behavioral self-blame: Inquiries into depression and rape. *Journal of Personality and Social Psychology, 37,* 1798–1810.

Jones, E. E., & Korchin, S. J. (1982). Introduction. In E. E. Jones & S. J. Korchin (Eds.), *Minority mental health* (pp. 3–36). New York: Praeger.

Keefe, T. (1980). Empathy skill and critical consciousness. *Social Casework, 61,* 387–393.

Khoa, L. X., & Bui, D. D. (1985). Southeast Asian mutual assistance associations: An approach for community development. In T. C. Owan (Ed.), *Southeast Asian mental health: Treatment, prevention, services, training, and research* (pp. 209–224). Washington, DC: National Institute of Mental Health.

Kieffer, C. (1984). Citizen empowerment: A developmental perspective. In J. Rapport, C. Swift, & R. Hess (Eds.), *Studies in empowerment: Toward understanding and action* (pp. 9–36). New York: Haworth.

Kim, J. K. (1978). Some value questions for ethnic orientation: An ethical perspective on Korean immigration motives. In M. Shin & D. B. Lee (Eds.), *Korean immigrants in Hawaii: A symposium on their background history, acculturation and public policy issues* (pp. 18–26). Honolulu: Korean Immigrant Welfare Association of Hawaii and Operation Manong, College of Education, University of Hawaii.

Kinzie, J. F. (1985). Overview of clinical issues in the treatment of Southeast Asian refugees. In T. C. Owan (Ed.), *Southeast Asian mental health: Treatment, prevention, services, training, and research* (pp. 113–135). Washington, DC: National Institute of Mental Health.

Krill, D. F. (1978). *Existential social work.* New York: Free Press.

Kromkowski, J. A. (1994). Immigration: The American experience in a new era of mobility. In J. A. Kromkowski (Ed.), *Race and ethnic relations 96/97* (pp. 38–39). Guilford, CT: Dushkin/Brown & Benchmark.

Lee, J. (1994). *The empowerment approach to social work practice.* New York: Columbia University Press.

Leigh, J. W. (1982). *Empowerment as a process.* Unpublished manuscript, University of Washington School of Social Work, Seattle.

Leigh, J. W. (1984). *Empowerment strategies for work with multi-ethnic populations.* Paper presented at the Council on Social Work Education Annual Program Meeting, Detroit, MI.

Lewis, R. (1977). *Cultural perspective on treatment modalities with Native Americans.* Paper presented at the National Association of Social Workers Professional Symposium, San Diego, CA.

Longres, J. F. (1982). Minority groups: An interest-group perspective. *Social Work, 27,* 7–14.

Longres, J., & McLeod, E. (1980). Consciousness raising and social work practice. *Social Casework, 61,* 267–277.

Lum, D. (1982). Toward a framework for social work practice with minorities. *Social Work, 27,* 244–249.

Mathis, T., & Richan, D. (1986). *Empowerment: Practice in search of a theory*. Paper presented at the annual program meeting of the Council on Social Work Education, Miami, FL.

Matsuoka, J. K. (1990). Differential acculturation among Vietnamese refugees. *Social Work, 35,* 341–345.

Mead, M. (1955). *Sex and temperament in three primitive societies*. New York: Morrow.

Meyer, C. H. (1972). Practice on microsystem level. In E. J. Mullen, J. R. Dumpson, & associates (Eds.), *Evaluation of social intervention* (pp. 158–190). San Francisco: Jossey-Bass.

Mokuau, N. (1985). Counseling Pacific Islander-Americans. In P. Pedersen (Ed.), *Handbook of cross-cultural counseling and therapy*. Westport, CT: Greenwood.

Morales, A. (1981). Social work with Third-World People. *Social Work, 25,* 45–51.

Morales, A., & Salcido, R. (1983). Social work with Mexican Americans. In A. Morales & B. W. Sheafor, *Social work: A professional of many faces* (pp. 389–413). Boston: Allyn & Bacon.

Moss, J. A. (1982). Unemployment among black youths: A policy dilemma. *Social Work, 27,* 47–52.

Mullen, E. J., Dumpson, J. R., & associates (Eds.). (1972). *Evaluation of social intervention*. San Francisco: Jossey-Bass.

Osborne, O., Carter, C., Pinkleton, N., & Richards, H. (1983). Development of African American curriculum content in psychiatric and mental health nursing. In J. C. Clunn II, P. J. Dunston, & F. Ross-Sheriff (Eds.), *Mental health and people of color. Curriculum development and change* (pp. 335–375). Washington, DC: Howard University Press.

Owan, T. C. (1985). Southeast Asian mental health: Transition from treatment services to prevention—A new direction. In T. C. Owan (Ed.), *Southeast Asian mental health: Treatment, prevention, services, training, and research*. Washington, DC: National Institute of Mental Health.

Paniagua, F. A. (1994). *Assessing and treating culturally diverse clients*. Newbury Park, CA: Sage.

Parkes, C. M. (1972). *Bereavement: Studies of grief in adult life*. New York: International Universities Press.

Parsons, R. J., Gutiérrez, L. M., & E. O. Cox. (1998). A model for empowerment practice. In L. M. Gutiérrez, R. J. Parsons, & E. O. Cox (Eds.), *Empowerment in social work practice: A sourcebook* (pp. 3–23). Pacific Grove, CA: Brooks/Cole.

Pernell, R. (1985). Empowerment and social group work. In M. Parenes (Ed.), *Innovations in social group work: Feedback from practice to theory* (pp. 107–117). New York: Haworth.

Pinderhughes, E. (1983). Empowerment for our clients and for ourselves. *Social Casework, 64,* 331–338.

Pinderhughes, E. (1989). *Understanding race, ethnicity, and power: The key to efficacy in clinical practice*. New York: Free Press.

Platt, A. M. (1997). The rise and fall of affirmative action. *Notre Dame Journal of Law, Ethics and Public Policy, 11*(1), 67–78.

Pommells, J. (1987). *Working with a Hispanic family's resistance*. Unpublished manuscript, California State University, Sacramento, Master of Social Work graduate program, Sacramento, CA.

Potocky, M. (1996). Refugee children: How are they faring economically as adults? *Journal of Social Work, 41*(4), 364–373.

Rapoport, L. (1967). Crisis-oriented short-term casework. *Social Service Review, 41*(1), 31–43.

Rappaport, J. (1981). In praise of paradox: A social policy of employment over prevention. *American Journal of Community Psychology, 9,* 9–25.

Rappaport, J., Reischl, T. M., & Zimmerman, M. A. (1992). Mutual help mechanisms in the empowerment of former mental patients. In D. Saleebey (Ed.), *The strengths perspective in social work practice*. New York: Longman.

Red Horse, J. (1982). Clinical strategies for American Indian families in crisis. *Urban and Social Change Review, 15,* 17–19.

Reid, W. J. (1986). Task-centered social work. In F. J. Turner (Ed.), *Social work treatment. Interlocking theoretical approaches* (pp. 267–295). New York. Free Press.

Reiff, R. R. (1968). Social intervention and the problem of psychological analysis. *American Psychologist, 23,* 524–530.

Reisman, F. (1965). The helper-therapy principle. *Social Work, 10*(2), 27–32.

Rivera, F. G., & Erlich, J. L. (1981). Neo-*Gemeinschaft* minority communities: Implications for community organization in the United States. *Community Development Journal, 16,* 189–200.

Rivera, F. G., & Erlich, J. L. (1998a). A time of fear, a time of hope. In F. G. Rivera & J. L. Erlich (Eds.), *Community organizing in a diverse society* (pp. 1–24. Boston: Allyn & Bacon.

Rivera, F. G., & Erlich, J. L. (1998b). Epilogue: The twenty-first century. In F. G. Rivera & J. L. Erlich (Eds.), *Community organizing in a diverse society* (pp. 243–257. Boston: Allyn & Bacon.

Sarason, S. B. (1972). *The creation of settings and the future societies*. San Francisco: Jossey-Bass.

Shapiro, J. (1984). Commitment to disenfranchised clients. In A. Rosenblatt & D. Waldfugel (Eds.), *Handbook of clinical social work* (pp. 888–903). San Francisco: Jossey-Bass.

Sherraden, M. S., & Bariera, R. E. (1997). Family support and birth outcomes among second generation Mexican immigrants. *Social Service Review, 71*(4), 607–633.

Siegel, D. I. (1984). *Primary group supports in age homogeneous versus age heterogeneous areas for the elderly.* Paper presented at the Council on Social Work Education Annual Program Meeting, Detroit, MI.

Simon, B. L. (1990). Rethinking empowerment. *Journal of Progressive Human Services, 1,* 27–37.

Simon, B. L. (1994). *The empowerment tradition in American social work: A history.* New York. Columbia University Press.

Solomon, B. (1976). *Black empowerment. Social work in oppressed communities.* New York: Columbia University Press.

Solomon, B. (1982). Empowering women: A matter of values. In A. Weick & S. Vandiver (Eds.), *Women, power, and change* (pp. 206–214). Silver Spring, MD: National Association of Social Workers.

Solomon, B. B. (1983). Social work with Afro-Americans. In A. Morales & W. W. Sheafor, *Social work: A profession of many faces* (pp. 415–436). Boston: Allyn & Bacon.

Solomon, B. B. (1985). How do we really empower families? New strategies for social work practitioners. *Family Resource Coalition Report, 4,* 2–3.

Song, Y. I. (1987). *Silent victims: Battered women in Korean immigrant families.* San Francisco: Oxford Press.

Song, Y. I. (1994). *Silent scream: Battered women in Korean immigrant families.* New York: Garland.

Song, Y. I., & Kim, E. (1992). (Eds.) *American mosaic: Selected readings on America's multicultural heritage.* Upper Saddle River, NJ: Prentice Hall.

Stonequist, E. V. (1961). *The marginal man.* New York: Russell & Russell.

Sue, S., & Morishima, J. K. (1982). *The mental health of Asian Americans.* San Francisco: Jossey-Bass.

Thurow, L. C. (1975). Poverty and discrimination: A brief overview. In T. F. Pettigrew (Ed.), *Racial discrimination in the United States* (pp. 240–247). New York: Harper & Row.

Tran, T. V., & Wright, R., Jr. (1986). Social support and subjective well-being among Vietnamese refugees. *Social Service Review, 60,* 449–459.

Tucker, S. (1979). Minority issues in community mental health. In B. R. Compton & B. Galaway (Eds.), *Social work processes* (pp. 119–124). Belmont, CA: Wadsworth.

Turner, J. B. (1972). Forgotten: Mezzosystem intervention. In E. J. Mullen, J. R. Dumpson, & associates (Eds.), *Evaluation of social intervention* (pp. 129–145). San Francisco: Jossey-Bass.

Uba, L. (1994). *Asian Americans: Personality patterns, identity, and mental health.* New York: Guilford.

Van DenBergh, N., & Cooper, L. (Eds.). (1986). *Feminist visions for social work.* Silver Spring, MD: National Association of Social Workers.

Walters, R. W. (1982). Race, resources, conflict. *Social Work, 27,* 24–30.

Washington, R. O. (1982). Social development: A focus for practice and education. *Social Work, 27,* 104–109.

Webb, G. E. (1972). Rethinking macrosystem intervention. In E. J. Mullen, J. R. Dumpson, & associates (Eds.), *Evaluation of social intervention* (pp. 111–128). San Francisco: Jossey-Bass.

Weems, L. (1974). Awareness: The key to black mental health. *Journal of Black Psychology, 1,* 30–37.

Weil, M. (1981). Southeast Asians and service delivery issues in service provision and institutional racism. In *Bridging cultures: Southeast Asian refugees in America* (pp. 136–163). Los Angeles: Special Service for Groups.

Willis, D. J., Debrecv, A., & Sipes, D. S. B. (1992). Treating American Indian victims of abuse and neglect. In L. A. Vargas & J. D. Koss-Chiono (Eds.), *Working with culture: Psychotherapeutic interventions with ethnic minority children and adolescents* (pp. 276–299). San Francisco: Jossey-Bass.

CHAPTER 10

Termination

In social work practice, *termination* refers to the ending stage of the social work process. Over the course of the process, the client and worker have built up a relationship that now must end. Ending a relationship is an emotional event. One person's investment of emotions and feelings in another can entail grief. Both client and worker must work through the dynamics of the separation process (Strean, 1978), though perhaps to different degrees. The client may go through the following reactions: denying termination, returning to earlier behavioral patterns or reintroducing problem situations, displaying explosive behavior at the worker's termination decision, or breaking up the relationship before the worker leaves the client (Compton & Galaway, 1979). Termination dynamics include separation and loss, clinging to therapy and the practitioner, recurrence of old problems, introducing new problems, and finding substitutes for the practitioner (Hepworth & Larsen, 1990).

Part of the client's reaction to termination is due to his or her dependency on the worker. A major aim of social work practice is to guide the client away from the worker, who must extricate himself or herself during the course of the process stages. Gambrill (1983) observes:

> Endings are often handled poorly because of the social worker's hangups about endings. It is thus important to explore your own beliefs and feelings about endings to make sure that these will not interfere with learning and using the skills necessary to bring about planned rather than unplanned endings. One of the requirements of planned endings is recognition of the limits of your own responsibilities for other people's lives. Some social workers have difficulty ending because they assume more responsibility than they should for the well-being and decisions of others. (p. 357)

The termination phase should not be structured so that the emphasis is on separation and overdependency. Rather, positive change dimensions can be built into termination (Gambrill, 1983).

From the standpoint of culturally diverse social work, hardly any adequate treatments of termination exist. In fact, Strean (1978) believes that superficial attention is paid to termination because it conjures up rejection, abandonment, and loss for the social worker and the client. Moreover, unsuccessful intervention is often the reason a case is closed, and many social workers may wish to overlook the reasons for premature termination (Strean, 1978).

Premature termination also occurs when people of color drop out of the helping relationship after the initial interview (Sue, 1981; Sue & Morishima, 1982). Strean (1978) points out that unsuccessful intervention is often the reason a case is closed. Beck (1962) reports in a family-agency study that one-third of clients do not return for a second interview and that 50 percent of all applicants have one interview or less. Strean (1978) believes that in cases of premature termination, the client has experienced some antagonism toward the worker and agency. He also suggests that many social workers wish to overlook the reasons why the client does not continue in the helping process.

Premature termination among people of color is a crucial area of concern for study. Hepworth and Larsen (1990) propose that premature termination is the result of unresolved resistance. The worker should provide the client with an opportunity to express negative feelings and to work toward resolving them. However, direct confrontation of unresolved resistance can drive away the person of color. It is important to personalize the relationship and become acquainted with the client. Putting the client at ease, structuring the purpose of the helping process, and allowing the client to set the pace for problem disclosure are effective ways of dealing with resistance. Another reason for premature termination is the client's claim that the problems have cleared up. Sudden and miraculous improvement can be symptomatic of problem denial or wishful thinking. For people of color, abrupt termination may be due to factors such as mistrust of the worker, pressure from the worker to disclose the problem, difficulties with transportation, problems with child care, and inability to pay. A client may be too embarrassed or polite to reveal the reason for termination. Gambrill (1983) offers some additional helpful suggestions about premature termination.

A social worker has professional and personal limits and will not be able to help all clients. However, when a client terminates prematurely, the agency needs to review its procedure, approach to casework, and techniques of practice to determine whether they address the needs of the ethnic client. The newness of the field of multicultural practice is reason enough for the lack of literature on termination. Few frameworks for culturally diverse practice adequately address the process stages of social work.

In view of the paucity of material, this chapter draws on several practice analogies that allude to,

and are applicable to, ethnic dimensions of termination. Elaborating on the core principles of termination presented in Chapter 5, we will speak of termination as destination, recital, and completion. In the course of the discussion, multicultural perspectives will be introduced at crucial points. Figure 10-1 illustrates the joint participation of client and worker in the termination process.

CLIENT-SYSTEM AND WORKER-SYSTEM PRACTICE ISSUES

We have spoken of termination as an end point that signifies closure of the present relationship and noted that the manner and circumstances of termination have a bearing on future growth patterns of the client. However, Locke, Garrison, and Winship (1998) write in terms of evaluating outcomes and making transitions. *Outcome evaluation* measures movement occurring during the change process, enhances client system competency by understanding how change movement is managed, and helps social workers become more effective in the helping process. Likewise, Parsons (1998) speaks about *outcome evaluation*, which addresses the intended goals of a program; *process evaluation*, which assesses the activities, methods, or means employed to achieve the desired outcome; and *impact evaluation*, which assesses the impact of an intervention on an identified problem. Locke et al. (1998) explain that "making transitions" rather than using of the term *termination* connotes the reality that the work has not been finished. Rather, the concept of transition helps us see the ongoing nature of the helping process.

> Transition, then, can be a time of affirmation of competence realized and identification of roads remaining to be traveled. Even when the results may not be realized in a way that was originally envisioned, this reflection process provides client systems with the opportunity to learn from the experience. (pp. 247–248)

Transition may mean the strengthening of our support system, behavioral changes for well-being, support to maintain efforts that have

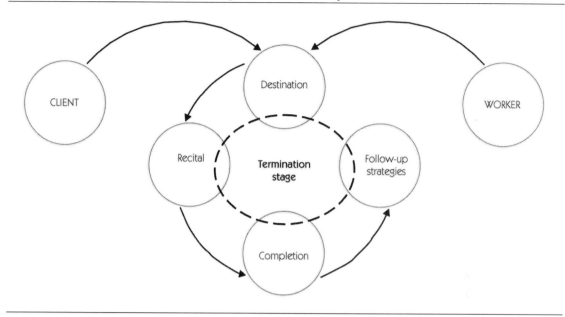

been realized, community alliance with others to achieve goals, and the next step to meet our concerns.

Not only is the concept of termination changed by outcome evaluation and transition thinking, but the purpose of the termination process is highlighted by a number of directions. The termination process can mean one of three things: resolution of the identified problems, major readjustments in intervention goals resulting in another series of sessions, or conclusion of the relationship because of barriers between the client and the worker. The functioning of the person's social system during this concluding phase is of paramount importance in termination. To what extent have intervention goals been achieved and measured against the problem? Is there partial resolution or adequate closure on a problem situation at the time of termination? These are some of the crucial issues relating to the dynamics of termination.

In Cultural Study 10-1, Hess and Hess (1994) point out a number of termination themes: separation and joining, reviewing and evaluation, and accomplishment and completion.

CULTURAL STUDY 10-1

Termination Themes

During termination clients must accomplish two general tasks: first, they must confront and begin to accept the impending separation from their helper, and second, they must come to terms with the outcome of the helping process. Client awareness of both loss and outcome is stimulated by the encroaching time limit of termination. At no other phase in the process is time such a powerful influence. The press of time requires client and practitioner to confront both the limits of their relationship and the importance of client self-responsibility and autonomy.

Because clients and practitioners often form close attachments, termination typically requires working through the grief resulting from a break in these ties. Movement through the grief process involves a giving up, or decathexis, of the lost object. This process is supported by the clear evaluation or review of accomplishments. The termination phase thus demands an intricate management of both loss and evaluation of gain. The presence of one theme stimulates the other, ultimately allowing termination to occur. If the goals of working together have been accomplished, clients can be helped to acknowledge the appropriateness of ending. Conversely, if the goals have not been accomplished, the client can be helped to determine whether the goals were realistic and how problem solving can continue after the end point with the practitioner. When the helping process is disrupted, the termination work should clarify the nature of the necessary referral or transfer. As the work is reviewed, clients often experience a blend of pride in accomplished change, hope for the future, and sorrow about the loss of a valued resource. As the themes of loss and evaluation resonate against one another, the client moves toward either a resumption of living exclusive of the helping process or continuation of the process with another helping person.

From "Termination in Context," by H. Hess and P. M. Hess. In B. R. Compton and B. Galaway (Eds.), *Social Work Processes*, p. 529. Copyright © 1994 Brooks/Cole Publishing Company, a division of Thomson Publishing Inc., Pacific Grove, CA. Reprinted by permission.

Termination means end, conclusion, or finish. It comes from the Latin root terminus, which refers to an outcome, result, or goal. *Terminus* is the name of the ancient Roman deity who presided over boundaries and landmarks. Termination thus implies the concept of *destination*—a predetermined end point, boundary, or landmark. Another aspect of termination is *recital*—the retelling of major events that brought the worker and client to the destination. In recital, worker and client review and play back the whole practice-process experience. Finally, termination connotes *completion*, in the sense of accomplishment of a goal or achievement of a result. We now consider these three aspects of termination.

Termination as Destination

We have stated that the well-being of people of color depends on membership in an ethnic community that has natural and social service support systems. This corporate entity provides identity, support, and cultural resources. It is important to rediscover supportive elements in the client's own ethnic family; community; and belief system of customs, rituals, and practices. We believe this type of reunification with ethnic roots is a significant dimension in termination. Ethnic identity, or a new sense of what it means to be African American, Asian American, Latino American, or Native American, is a powerful motivator for coping with the kind of living and problem situations that the client confronts. Moreover, gaining a sense of ethnic selfhood creates a source of personal integration. It involves establishing linkage with significant family and ethnic-community members who can play a meaningful part in the client's life. This direction runs counter to a misguided attempt on the part of the worker to alienate the client from his or her ethnicity and recognizes instead the importance of ethnic bonding, which has a positive, sustaining influence on the client. The worker-client relationship in termination should not focus on separation and loss. It should be the passage to ethnic wholeness through the joining of the client with ethnic resources.

Termination has a destination: reunifying with the ethnic community network rather than continuing the single worker-client entity. Devore and Schlesinger (1981) highlight the importance of alternative sources of support in the termination phase. They particularly suggest kinship and neighborhood networks, the church, or a heightened sense of ethnic identity. They view these ethnic community resources as effective safeguards against the client's interpretation of termination as rejection or abandonment. Carrillo (1982) observes that the focus of Latino culture is harmony through cooperation with the ethnic community. This focus emphasizes the development, maintenance, and enrichment of interpersonal relations through social gestures, friendliness, sentimentality, and an appreciation for lightheartedness and humor in conversation. This community bonding is linked to a deep respect for affiliation, affection, and the need to belong to a network of family and friends. It implies lifelong commitments, the cultivation of relationships, and presence in crisis.

Social casework trends on termination emphasize the importance of ongoing linkages to significant others, new activities, natural communities, and environmental resources. Gambrill (1983) discusses arranging for the maintenance of positive outcomes among a variety of community linkages. The involvement of significant others is important in light of their continuing role in influencing change. New behavior of significant others has a positive effect on the client for making and maintaining change. Socializing agents who impart positive feedback, such as teachers and parents, sustain progress and stability of change. Gambrill (1983) suggests introducing clients to local centers where social and behavior skills are amply supported in interactional situations. These centers are naturally reinforcing communities where people are taught to seek sources of feedback in order to maintain behavior. Praise for good work is an example of positively reinforcing feedback. Natural environments can be shaped to benefit clients along these lines. Identifying enriching programs, settings, and other community resources and encouraging clients to participate are ways of using environmental supports. Gradually the client is integrated into the group life of the ethnic community.

Miley, O'Melia, and DuBois (1998) offer some valuable suggestions in terms of evaluating destination points. They speak about knowing when to resolve closure and integrate gains. With respect to ending with individuals and families, they note the need to focus on goal achievement, the readiness to function independently, and the limited productivity of future sessions that lead to improved closure; referral elsewhere for service; and withdrawal of the client from service. At times preparing for resolution may provide convenient exit points for discussion and checking with the client; in other cases client progress may stop short of intended goals. It is important to discuss readiness in light of the work being done and to continually evaluate the nature of our work together as client and worker.

Termination as Recital

Termination as recital is an opportunity to review the worker-client relationship and to recount the major changes that have occurred from beginning to end. Recital involves review and playback. Like a piano student, the client has practiced both the parts and the whole of the composition with the worker's assistance and instruction. Through diligent effort, he or she has mastered those procedural steps needed for functioning in life situations. Now comes the opportunity for retrospective recital. The client reflects on the work and plays it back to the worker. The worker listens, comments, and focuses on various aspects of the life situation. The worker and client play their respective parts so both can hear, listen, and learn. Termination necessitates reciting back the growth process. It also previews the next steps of helping and future learning, much as a piano teacher previews the next lessons with the student, demonstrating crucial passages of a new selection, giving instructions on how to play, and teaching new techniques. The preview helps the student practice effectively, with a knowledge of what is expected. Likewise, termination is an opportunity to anticipate problems and to design ways of coping through role playing. Recital helps the client anticipate problems that may arise in the coming weeks and months.

The analogy of the piano recital is seen in the life enhancement model of psychosocial counseling. Szapocznik, Santisteban, Kurtines, Hervis, and Spencer (1982) have applied life enhancement counseling to their work with Cuban elderly. Life enhancement counseling builds on the elderly's strengths, reduces environmental sources of conflict and stress, and facilitates acceptance of past life experiences. The life review approach focuses on completion of unfinished business and identifies capabilities available to clients. Once strengths have been identified, the potential for mobilizing them in current conditions is assessed. The elderly client's past strengths are activated by strategies of directive counseling and ecological intervention, which emphasize the psychosocial development of present strengths in the client's life. Review of a client's past experiences is a source of meaning, life acceptance, and ego integration. Meaningful transactions are fulfilled in the here and now; fulfillment comes from acceptance of the past and from current interactions between the client and the environment.

The life review aspect of the life enhancement model enhances the recital dimension of termination. In life review, the worker encourages the client to reminisce and probes uncovered areas, to elicit further memories. This approach has a cathartic value because it allows expression of feelings and organization of thoughts, which bring closure to those experiences. The primary aim of life review is to identify events, incidents, and relationships that are filled with meaning for the client and to translate the corresponding themes to the present. Directive reinterpretation provides the client with an alternative perspective on past experiences that helps move the client toward a therapeutic goal. Throughout the life review, the worker listens for experiences that reflect the client's values and definition of meaning and reactivates them in the present. For example, a lifetime of work or dedication to raising a family provides a relevant and meaningful theme. Opportunities may also arise to develop areas that were secondary in the client's earlier life, such as interest in gardening, cooking, painting, fishing, or cultivating friends. These areas become a source of pride, hope, and meaning. Miley et al. (1998) discuss the importance of reviewing progress: "Reviewing progress solidifies changes and reinforces a client's sense of achievement. To do so, social workers reminisce with clients about the work from its inception to its current state, accentuating what clients did to make the positive changes that have occurred" (p. 433). It is vital to give clients credit for making situational change progress and developing competency. The worker similarly should share feelings about completing his or her work and ending the partnership in the recital or review process. Feelings of sadness and grief as well as positive opportunities for new possibilities are areas that should be covered, along with consolidating successes and anticipating how to cope with future and upcoming issues.

Miley et al. (1998) remind us:

> An effective closing process does not end the client's development. Instead, it is a beginning for the client to stabilize the progress achieved, to integrate the skills learned, and to function independently. The success of this transition rests not only on the closing activities, but it also requires a process that encourages client self-direction throughout the entire social work relationship. A collaborative social worker and client partnership that recognizes client strengths, creates productive alliances, and increases opportunities empowers clients with the resources to continue to function competently after the professional relationship is done. (p. 449)

Unresolved feelings or decisions can emerge. Recital provides an opportunity to learn about crucial junctures, client strengths, community resources, and effective coping. Recital of the past moves toward planning for the present and the future to maintain the patterns of change.

Termination as Completion

Termination as completion points to the theme of outcome. It addresses the pragmatic issue of goal accomplishment based on the agreement in intervention planning. Goal outcome depends on problem identification and on resolution at the time of termination. A primary issue of termination is whether the intervention approach based on assessment has had an impact on the identified problem. A number of questions are crucial to practice-process evaluation during termination:

- Have significant changes been made with respect to the identified problem?
- Can these changes be measured by conditions prevailing before and after the intervention plan was implemented?
- What intervention tactics contributed to the changes: resources, organizations, significant others?
- Over what time span did the process of change occur?
- Did change occur as the result of actions of the client, the worker, the client and worker, or a third-party resource?

These issues stress the need to document specific, objective data that contributed to change and that can be verified by an impartial third party.

Several criteria can be used to evaluate results in these areas of concern. Firestein (1978) offers the following criteria for termination:

1. Disappearance of symptoms: the problem that brought the client to the worker is eliminated, mitigated, or made tolerable.
2. Change in the client's personality: the client's ability to deal with crisis and conflict improves.
3. Social-situational change: improvement in psychosocial functioning, capacity for planning, and relationships with significant others.
4. Intuition: increased perception, particularly in observations and feelings.
5. Change in the client's relationship with the worker: the client is able to deal with the worker as one mature adult with another.

Muñoz (1982) identifies five factors relevant to the effectiveness of termination in multicultural practice:

1. Dropout rate, which can be evaluated by identifying the factors that increase the probability of continued treatment
2. Improvement rate by approach, which examines which therapies work most effectively with which problems for which clients
3. Time effectiveness, which shows which modality used fewer sessions than another, with similar results than the other
4. Maintenance rates, which demonstrate continued improvement after termination versus the "revolving door" effect
5. Consumer satisfaction with the way multicultural clients were treated

Research data on these areas have yet to be reported on a large scale regarding termination with people of color.

At the same time, there may be obstacles to the completion of intended goals. Rothman and Sager (1998) speak about obstacles to a valid intervention plan: lack of client motivation, loosely formulated goals, client resistance, unsteady client progress, uncooperative agencies, and time limitations and work pressures. These areas should be carefully assessed in evaluating the extent to which goals have or have not been completed.

Follow-Up Strategies

Termination is a crucial stage of practice process because it shapes the client's future growth patterns. In some instances, the worker-client relationship is dissolved because of such counterproductive factors as the client's numerous absences, the client's resistance, the worker's bias, and personality dissonance. The worker and client may renegotiate and schedule another series of sessions. It may be appropriate to define another problem area and to establish a contract for a different set of goals. However, when the client terminates the present helping relationship, follow-up strategies are needed to establish a transitional period of change and stability. Fischer (1978) views termination as the provision of procedures to enhance the transfer of positive change from the artificial situation to real life. Without this transfer and follow-up, gains witnessed in the office are limited to the client's learning to verbalize problems differently or to please the worker with reports of success.

Miley et al. (1998) raise some interesting questions in formulating follow-up strategies:

> Will there be additional contacts? Should clients schedule a check-up visit for three months to monitor if they are still on track? Will someone from the agency contact clients to check their continuing progress as part of the agency's outcome evaluation procedure? How will clients access their records if they choose to do so? What if clients really feel the need to contact the worker again—how do they do it? Is it acceptable for clients to get back in touch? Can they call with good news or are contacts limited to those requests for additional assistance? What are clients supposed to do if they coincidentally run into workers in other contexts, at the mall, the grocery store, or the movies? (p. 437)

These are interesting areas for client-worker conversations. Many of the questions are commonsensical but may need explanations so that a degree of comfort and rapport be maintained. Accomplishing the tasks of transfer and follow-up means that the behavioral change the client learned in the helping relationship must be adapted to his or her life situation.

The Hernández Family, a Case Study

After four weeks, it is apparent that the intervention strategy plan is taking hold with the Hernández family and the two immigrant families from Mexico. The two brothers-in-law are working steadily with the Mexican American contractor, who has received several bids from a number of housing projects in the barrio. Mr. Hernández is home nearly every night, spending time with the three children and particularly helping Ricardo with his homework. Mrs. Hernández is enjoying her ESL class, and several of her friends are classmates. The family is helping her practice English words and sentences. Ricardo is adjusting to school; the latest report from his teacher says that he is doing his work at school and is more relaxed and happier than he was a month ago. The two other families seem to be adjusting to urban American life.

Mr. Platt, the social worker, is satisfied with the progress the families have made. They have become linked to resources within their ethnic community. These community supports, located at Catholic Social Services in their neighborhood, have drawn them closer to the church and the Latino community. The families have gained a sense of satisfaction and pride in knowing that assistance is available in the Latino community. Together, the church, school, and social services have forged a strategy to help these families in need.

At the next session, Mr. Platt encourages review of the major progress and changes that have taken place. Most significant is the relief of stress on Mr. Hernández and Ricardo. Before, the father was overburdened with the strain of two jobs, and his son was a disciplinary problem in school due to his father's absence in the evenings. Now measurable progress has been made in job hunting, stability of home life, school tutoring, and English classes, which have brought a change to the family. Recounting the progress made during the sessions helps the family recall former negative affect and experience present feelings of happiness and contentment.

With respect to goal achievement, the two families from Mexico have been assisted in obtaining full-time construction work leading to apprenticeship. Mr. Hernández is therefore able to work at just his regular job and to spend his evenings with his family. Ricardo's classroom tutoring with a high school aide and his father's help in the evenings are having a marked effect on his grades (a B average) and his peer relations (no fights in the last three weeks). His teacher has noticed his happiness, contentment, and willingness to settle down and begin his work. Mrs. Hernández is learning to speak, read, and write English through her classes. She is well on her way, learning how to ask and answer questions in English about daily living situations. Through the assistance of the Latino volunteer and their friends, the two families from Mexico are able to find their way around the city well enough to shop, pay bills, and drive.

TASK RECOMMENDATIONS

The principles of termination have been expressed in terms of destination, recital, and completion. Select a case from multicultural practice that was completed successfully and review how termination as destination, recital, and completion might be applied to the case. The following questions demonstrate uses of the three principles:

- Was an effort made to connect the client with a positive element in the community for identity, support, and cultural resources? If so, elaborate on such use of kinship and neighborhood networks, the church, or community activities.
- Was there an opportunity to review and play back the major changes that had occurred in the client's life during the social work helping process? Were certain areas explored further or events interpreted and integrated into the client's life?
- Were criteria for goal outcomes established at the beginning of intervention and used as measures at termination? To what extent did the client complete the stated goals? What were the strategic changes and time frame for accomplishing the goals, and what significant others participated in the process of change?

The Hernández Family, a Case Study

At their termination session, Mr. Platt and the Hernández family agree to begin the process of tapering off. Mr. Hernández will call Mr. Platt weekly to brief him on the progress of the family. They will meet in a month to assess the extent of growth, to find out what has happened in the interim, and to evaluate the usefulness of the ethnic community's social service system. Mr. Hernández reflects on his period of crisis as a major transitional adjustment triggered by the arrival of relatives during a time of particular economic strain. He feels the family has been strengthened as a result and can now handle a similar situation, should one arise, because they know about the social services available in the local Latino community.

Mr. Platt states that, if the family is still functioning adequately at home and school after one month, a final termination will take place. However, the family should feel free to contact him at the Family Service Association in case of future need.

TASK RECOMMENDATIONS

We have mentioned strategies for follow-up beyond termination, for successful and unsuccessful cases. The case study of the Hernández family illustrates how an ethnic family moves through the process stages of clinical social work and responds to a number of ethnic-oriented practice principles. However, some cases are terminated prematurely when clients drop out after an initial interview.

Select a case of premature termination with an ethnic client and conduct a retrospective analysis of causal factors behind the dropout.

- Did the agency have an ethnically sensitive system of service delivery that was responsive to ethnic clients: tangible and practical services located near ethnic populations; bilingual/bicultural workers, extensive community outreach information and prevention programs, an agency setting congenial to people of color, and a culturally appropriate practice model? If some of these components were missing, how can they be introduced into your agency? Which ones would make a difference in retaining ethnic clients?

- During the initial session with the client, was an effort made to convey a sense of understanding of the community, to practice relationship protocol, to share professional self-disclosure, and to communicate empathetic, open-ended responses?

- Was adequate time set aside to become acquainted with the client's background and to permit the client to know the social worker as a person and as a professional?

The social worker facilitates continuity of change through several procedures. Sessions between the worker and client should gradually taper off. The worker and client may agree to meet every other week or once a month and evaluate the client's progress between extended sessions. What has happened to the client in the interval? Has the client been able to cope successfully when problem stress occurred? What lessons learned from the worker-client relationship has the client applied in life situations during the interval? How has the client used the support network of the ethnic community during this time? The gradual fading of contact offers an opportunity for reality testing.

During a one- to two-month trial period, telephone contact between the worker and client is helpful for monitoring progress. From a short distance, the worker is available to offer support and to assess whether the client has maintained changes. Telephone follow-up imposes minimal demands on the worker's and client's time and effort and is an efficient means of checking on carryover effects. Hepworth and Larsen (1990) recommend that a follow-up session take place two to six months after termination. They identify these advantages to follow-up: encouragement of clients to continue progress after termination, brief assistance for residual difficulties during a follow-up session, assessment of the durability of change, and continuance of the worker's interest in the client.

After formal termination, the worker should maintain an open-door policy. The worker should communicate the fact that the client is free to call for a return appointment. This offer does not mean that the client has failed in the process. Rather, it is a natural invitation based on friendship and concern. Gilbert, Miller, and Specht (1980) point out that former problems can recur, and new problems arise. Because some problems will not be solved in this helping relationship, the client should be assured that the worker is available to assist the client if the need arises. Should the client return, it is important to reassign the same worker to the client, if possible, to provide continuity of care. This saves much time otherwise spent in relationship building and obtaining relevant background information.

It may be necessary to terminate the present worker-client relationship if the client's changing needs necessitate referral to another resource. Every social worker has an individual personality and an orientation to practice that he or she imparts to the client. It may be helpful to refer certain clients to other community resources when the worker's capacity for helping them has been exhausted. Adequate referral is a three-way process involving the client, the worker, and the referral resource. The worker must prepare the client for the referral and discuss the need for, and importance of, the referral. The worker should discuss with the client any hesitations he or she might feel and any doubts and questions the client might have about the new agency. It is crucial that client and worker examine a range of referral resources. Usually the worker maintains a working relationship with colleagues in other community agencies. Developing an informal network of referrals facilitates the referral process when there are waiting lists at those agencies. It is important for the client and the worker to participate in the referral process. The client should make an appointment at the new agency after clearance has occurred between the two workers. This groundwork involves discussing the client's needs and advocating the new agency's acceptance of the client. The worker should make sure the client accepts the referral, contacts the agency, and becomes involved with its services.

This book has sought to distinguish characteristics of people of color that are pertinent to social work practice. Reviewing these principles of culturally diverse practice is useful in ensuring successful termination.

CONCLUSION

This chapter on termination has emphasized new dimensions in the ending stage of the practice process. Termination is explained as destination, recital, and completion. Destination underscores the importance of reunification with the ethnic community during the process of termination. Gaining a sense of ethnic selfhood is a powerful motivator for coping and integration. Striving to make this connection provides ethnic wholeness even after the dissolution of the worker-client relationship. Recital recalls the major changes that have taken place during the beginning, middle, and end of the practice process. It is a replay that has an analogy in the life enhancement model of counseling. The life review approach recounts major events and experiences that move toward achieving ego integrity. Directive reinterpretation and identification of meaningful themes are involved in the review process. Completion emphasizes the need to formulate and achieve goals. Criteria can be used to measure successful completion.

Several follow-up strategies aid the transition from practice process to the client's life situation. Among them are the gradual tapering-off of sessions, periodic telephone contact between sessions, and the prevention of premature termination. These efforts result, we hope, in successful termination that meets the client's needs and enhances the social worker's ethnic effectiveness.

REFERENCES

Beck, D. (1962). *Patterns in use of family agency service.* New York: Free Press.

Carrillo, C. (1982). Changing norms of Hispanic families: Implications for treatment. In E. E. Jones & S. J. Korchin (Eds.), *Minority mental health* (pp. 250–266). New York: Praeger.

Compton, B. R., & Galaway, B. (1979). *Social work processes*. Pacific Grove, CA: Brooks/Cole.

Devore, W., & Schlesinger, E. G. (1981). *Ethnic-sensitive social work practice*. St. Louis: Mosby.

Firestein, S. K. (1978). *Termination in psychoanalysis*. New York: International Universities Press.

Fischer, J. (1978). *Effective casework practice: An eclectic approach*. New York: McGraw-Hill.

Gambrill, E. (1983). *Casework. A competency-based approach*. Upper Saddle River, NJ: Prentice-Hall.

Gilbert, N., Miller, H., & Specht, H. (1980). *An introduction to social work practice*. Upper Saddle River, NJ: Prentice-Hall.

Hepworth, D. H., & Larsen, J. A. (1990). *Direct social work practice: Theory and skills*. Belmont, CA: Wadsworth.

Hess, H., & Hess, P. M. (1994). Termination in context. In B. R. Compton & B. Galaway (Eds.), *Social work processes* (pp. 529–539). Pacific Grove, CA: Brooks/Cole.

Locke, B., Garrison, R., & Winship, J. (1998). *Generalist social work practice: Context, story, and partnerships*. Pacific Grove, CA: Brooks/Cole.

Miley, K. K., O'Melia, M., & DuBois, B. (1998). *Generalist social work practice: An empowering approach*. Boston: Allyn & Bacon.

Muñoz, R. F. (1982). The Spanish-speaking consumer and the community mental health center. In E. E. Jones & S. J. Korchin (Eds.), *Minority mental health* (pp. 362–398). New York: Praeger.

Parsons, R. J. (1998). Evaluation of empowerment practice. In L. M. Gutiérrez, R. J. Parsons, & E. O. Cox (Eds.), *Empowerment in social work practice: A sourcebook* (pp. 204–219). Pacific Grove, CA: Brooks/Cole.

Rothman, J., & Sager, J. S. (1998). *Case management: Integrating individual and community practice*. Boston: Allyn & Bacon.

Strean, H. S. (1978). *Clinical social work: Theory and practice*. New York: Free Press.

Sue, D. W. (1981). *Counseling the culturally different: Theory and practice*. New York: Wiley.

Sue, S., & Morishima, J. K. (1982). *The mental health of Asian Americans: Contemporary issues in identifying and treating mental problems*. San Francisco: Jossey-Bass.

Szapocznik, J., Santisteban, D., Kurtines, W. M., Hervis, O. E., & Spencer, F. (1982). Life enhancement counseling: A psychosocial model of services for Cuban elders. In E. E. Jones & S. J. Korchin (Eds.), *Minority mental health* (pp. 296–330). New York: Praeger.

CHAPTER 11

Epilogue

Culturally diverse social work practice is a fertile ground for defining the unique knowledge and skills required to work with people of color. This epilogue is a closing commentary on a developing field of social work practice that emphasizes the need for specialists in multicultural practice. Competency-based practice is the current trademark of social work practitioners. Northen (1982) views competency in terms of values, purposes, and knowledge, which translate into effective performance. The social worker uses judgment in the practice process, executing techniques of planning, assessment, and intervention and facilitating the accomplishment of tasks in each process stage. The practitioner keeps abreast of current practice theory and research to base actions on researched principles. Northen's competency base integrates social principles in practice and application and reflects sound performance based on knowledge, judgment, and currency in the field.

Gambrill (1983) speaks of competency-based practice from an empirical perspective. Among its major characteristics are the pursuit of outcomes related to clients and significant others, cognitive and behavioral skills, empirical procedures of assessment and intervention, indicators for tracking progress, and personal assets and environmental resources. For Northen, competency reflects the performance of the social worker, who integrates and applies values, knowledge, purposes,

techniques, and research to the process of social work practice. For Gambrill, it is based on empirical information that governs the selection of procedures and behavioral outcomes for the client.

However, in the mid- and late 1990s, culturally competent practice has emerged primarily with multicultural counseling psychology and has influenced culturally diverse social work. Cultural competency views the client as the focus of developing his or her own sense of cultural orientations to the resources that are part of his or her indigenous culture. LaFromboise, Coleman, and Gerton (1993) viewed the culturally competent person as possessing a strong personal identity, knowledge of the beliefs and values of his or her culture, sensitivity to the affective processes of that culture, ability to speak the language of the cultural group, social relations within the cultural group, and familiarity with the institutional structures of that culture. About the same time, Sue, Arredondo, and McDavis (1992) began to articulate a culturally competent training model for multicultural counseling psychology that includes cultural awareness, a cross-cultural client worldview, and cultural intervention strategies and skills along with the counselor's beliefs and attitudes, knowledge and understanding, and intervention strategy skills. In social work practice Manoleas (1994) presented a preliminary social work culturally competent model in terms of knowledge, skill, and value cultural components, while Miley, O'Melia, and DuBois (1998) spoke about cultural competence dimensions involving the practitioner, agency, and community. I have written (Lum, 1999) about culturally competent practice in terms of a social work framework with generalist and advanced levels. The major areas of cultural competency for social work are cultural awareness, knowledge acquisition, skill development, and inductive learning. There are two definitions involving cultural competency and cultural competencies as well as a self-assessment instrument and questionnaire tools for student learning. Hopefully the field of culturally competent social work practice will grow in the coming years. Certainly there is interest in cultural competency among social work students, educators, and practitioners.

Competency-based culturally diverse social work practice integrates a multicultural service delivery structure, collective values, knowledge theory, and ethnic practice framework. In this book, principles of multicultural social work have been related to practice-process stages. This epilogue reiterates the essential characteristics of competency-based culturally diverse social work practice and points out new horizons and challenges for the practitioner-specialist. Toward this end, I hope to open a dialogue on distinctions between working with people of color and working with the majority society. I believe that social work practice has emphasized a generic systems framework and has not delineated factors of culture, ethnicity, and minority status and so have sought to present an alternative framework for multicultural practice.

COMPETENCY-BASED CULTURALLY DIVERSE SOCIAL WORK PRACTICE

A need exists to develop multicultural practice competency for the social work profession and for work with clients. Valle's (1986) discussion of cross-cultural competence offers clues to the development of similar social work efforts. *Cross-cultural competence* is defined as a working knowledge of symbolic/linguistic communication patterns; knowledge and skill of naturalistic/ interactional processes; and underlying attitude, value, and belief systems of ethnic target groups.

Language and symbols are important cultural expressions. They include written and spoken language, ethnic group heroes, folk art, ceremonies, and celebrations. Language contains different modes of address that differentiate strangers and intimates through speech patterns. Written and spoken language also conveys an understanding of ways of coping, accepting help, and group mutual assistance styles. Subtle nuances of feeling and protocol are communicated through language. The worker must understand these nuances to help the client.

Interactional patterns are located in three primary group networks: the family, the peer group, and the community. The family has been the focus of natural social networks. However, the peer and community groups are important dyadic and triadic relationships that also make up the individual's primary group relations. These resources establish contact with, and entry to, the client's ethnic culture.

Group norms, values, and beliefs include such values as Asian American obligation or Latino personal independence (*orgullo*, cultural and personal pride). These beliefs or value dynamics help the worker understand the client's worldview and the behavior rooted in this orientation.

In considering group norms, the worker must also assess the client's level of acculturation. Traditional individuals remain locked in their traditional cultural systems and maintain cultural normative expectations. Bicultural individuals relate both to their culture of origin and to the mainstream society and can function in both domains. Assimilated individuals have passed into the mainstream culture in all or most domains.

As mentioned earlier, I have discussed (Lum, 1999) four components of cultural competency: cultural awareness, knowledge acquisition, skill development, and inductive learning. Cultural awareness determines whether the social worker is aware of his or her life experiences as a person related to a culture, particularly family heritages and cultural beliefs and practices. Next the worker explores his or her contact with other cultural and ethnic individuals, families, and groups to ascertain whether there is an appropriate range of contact and perceptions of cultural groups. Knowledge acquisition covers the range of understanding of basic ethnic and cultural terminology and concepts related to demographic knowledge, critical thinking, group history of oppression, cultural values, and practice theories that impact people of color. Skill development involves the cultivation of technique and strategy process, case analysis conceptualization, and personal growth personalization skills related to the effectiveness of the social worker with multicultural clients. Contact, problem identification, assessment, intervention, and termination skills are stressed along with multicultural service delivery. Inductive learning is concerned about how the social worker continues to evaluate his or her own multicultural practice and carry out the learning process of exploring new information about culturally competent practice in his or her professional career. Qualitative research inquiry and analysis are tools to equip the worker for inductive learning.

These competencies must be linked to the actual behaviors of people of color in their social environment. These themes are played out in specific cultures and are crucial for competent cross-cultural practitioner understanding. Various practice principles are effective for an ethnically oriented social worker practitioner. The following themes are essential characteristics of competency-based culturally diverse social work practice.

Multicultural Service Delivery

Competency-based culturally diverse social work structures service delivery on the basis of trends in client usage. Sources of tangible and practical services are situated near areas with large ethnic populations. Bilingual/bicultural social workers are employed for non-English-speaking clients. Extensive outreach and educational programs are available for target community groups. The agency setting is conducive to the comfort of people of color. It features a bilingual receptionist, refreshments, and ethnic decor. The agency uses a cultural model of practice and participates in a clearinghouse for multicultural service organizations.

Multicultural Collective Values

Multicultural values involve collective structures such as the family, kinship clan, and church. A particular family member's individual wishes may be considered subordinate to the good of the family as a whole. The family is the vehicle for cultural values and traditions, child care, and decision making. The church plays the role of support in crisis, moral force, and provider of social services. A person's color and language reinforce his or her identity as a member of an ethnic community group.

Culturally Diverse Knowledge Theory

An appropriate theoretical knowledge base is essential for practicing with people of color. On the community level, conflict theory speaks to the domination of the "haves," who possess power and authority over the "have-nots." Racism, prejudice, and discrimination result. On the family level, systems theory offers an understanding of the individual in relation to a natural support system of family, friends, neighbors, and community. The network of caregivers is available, to a certain degree, whenever the occasion arises. On the individual level, role theory focuses on individual role relationships within an ethnic family and community. Each member of the family has an assigned role. Community spokespersons are in charge of speaking to public officials on behalf of an ethnic family or community.

Culturally Diverse Practice Framework

A framework for culturally diverse practice focuses on process stages, client-system and worker-system practice issues, and task recommendations. The *contact* phase involves establishing a relationship between the social worker and the client. The worker gains a preliminary sense of the psychosocial functioning of the person in the situation. Understanding the ethnic community involves becoming acquainted with the geographic area, leaders, and residents that comprise the ethnosystem. Relationship protocol acknowledges the authority of the father and the collective family.

The worker must also practice professional self-disclosure, which personalizes the relationship and fosters rapport and trust. It is the task of both worker and client, in collaboration, to ensure that the client is nurtured and understood.

In the *problem identification* stage, the practitioner views a problem—reframes it—as an unmet need or an unfulfilled want, rather than as a pathological symptom. People of color constantly cope with gaps in program services, crisis events, and survival needs. They are often hesitant about disclosing problems to helping professionals; a client may seek out the worker's initial reactions by asking a series of questions about a hypothetical situation. After the problem has been disclosed, it must be subdivided into observable, clear, and specific components. For people of color, racism, prejudice, and discrimination emerge as problem dynamics in the forms of oppression, powerlessness, exploitation, acculturation, and stereotyping. Worker-client tasks of problem identification involve learning and focusing.

The purpose of *assessment* is to understand and analyze the dynamic interaction between the client and the situation. The worker must assess the impact of the problem on the client and the resources available for helping. Rather than focusing on the pathological effects of the problem, the assessment stage emphasizes identifying strengths and support systems for coping with the problem.

Assessment categories include biological, psychological, social, cultural, gender, and spiritual dimensions from a perspective of cultural diversity. Biological assessment is concerned about a cultural perspective of health, health status, and somatic symptoms. Psychological assessment deals with the level of motivation, relationship of self and others, family and person, and language fluency. Social assessment relates to immigration history, school, and employment and work. Cultural assessment covers cultural formulation of diagnosis, the culturagram, cultural assets, and natural support systems. Gender assessment addresses levels related to the individual woman and her relationship to family, group, and community systems. Spiritual assessment pertains to spirituality, religious practices, self-examination of personal religious beliefs and attitudes, client history related to spiritual beliefs and practices, healthy religion, and knowledge of beliefs. The worker-client tasks include interacting with psychosocial functioning and evaluating resource supports.

Intervention is a change strategy that alters the client's interaction with the problem environment. Microlevel interventions apply relevant principles of problem-solving/task-oriented, crisis intervention, empowerment, existential, woman-centered, family therapy, group work, and working with refugees and immigrants approaches to a client's particular situation. Mesolevel intervention is based on the assumption that the client's well-being depends on membership in a positive and meaningful ethnic community. The family and church are essential components of natural community support systems. Macrolevel interventions draw on social policy, planning, and administration as practice skills for working with complex social issues and target populations. Strategies using the community network, political organizing, and legal advocacy are examples of intervention modalities. The worker-client tasks of the intervention stage are to create formulations to address present problems and to change the client's existing situation so as to produce different consequences.

Termination is an end point at which closure of the worker-client relationship takes place. It may occur for numerous reasons: resolution of problems, redefinition of goals, or counterproductive factors. There are three aspects of termination: destination, recital, and completion. Destination focuses on restoring supportive linkages to family, significant others, and community. Recital reviews the major changes that have occurred during the previous stages of the worker-client relationship. Completion focuses on the accomplishment of specific goals relating to the identified problems. Follow-up strategies associated with termination are gradual tapering-off of sessions, periodic telephone contacts, and an open-door policy; the prevention of premature termination is a particular concern. Termination marks the mature growth, dynamic change, and intuitive learning that have taken place in the interaction between the client and the worker. The worker-client tasks reinforce the achievement of a desired aim and the resolution of a problem situation.

NEW HORIZONS AND CHALLENGES FOR CULTURALLY DIVERSE SOCIAL WORK PRACTICE

As the twenty-first century begins, culturally diverse social work practice must address clinical and community issues facing people of color. A prototype example of such an effort is seen in the field of family therapy. McGoldrick (1998b) has edited an anthology of articles entitled *Re-Visioning Family Therapy: Race, Culture, and Gender in Clinical Practice*. She brings together a group of social work educators and practitioners, clinical psychologists, and marriage and family therapist to re-vision family therapy in the areas of race, culture, and gender, with seven goals:

- To re-vision family therapy in the direction of culture, social class, spirituality and transcendence, and hope and culture
- To challenge racism in ideology and training as it pertains to the field of family therapy, pro-racist ideology, and oppression and powerlessness
- To explore the meaning of white privilege and particularly white male privilege
- To reach for cultural legacies in terms of family genealogy, multicultural identity, returning to a place called "home" to experience belonging and liberation, racial unity, and personal family history
- To focus on family therapy with ethnic couples and siblings intercultural couples, families of lesbian women and gay men, and bicultural women
- To assess the impact of migration on refugee families, social network disruption, and multiple contexts on immigrant families
- To offer new approaches on intracultural issues, culture, and postmodern thinking, and cultural context

Allow me to focus on various parts of this effort to re-vision and reposition family therapy toward perspectives which encompass culture, class, race, gender, and sexual orientation. This is precisely the kind of dialogue that culturally diverse social work practice must engage in to respond to new challenges and reach new horizons in the next millennium.

Dynamic Notions of Culture

Culturally diverse social work practice must reexamine the nature and meaning of culture, moving from a static, fixed notion to a fluid, flexible meaning. Laird (1998) offers five characteristics of culture that reflect motion and change in meaning and definition. First, culture is performative and improvisational in that it is performed in various social contextual discourses through our cultural stories and narratives. Often we make culture up as we go along, re-creating the old and creating the new. Second, culture is fluid and emergent depending on our contextual location—what we are doing, where we are, and who we interact with as we express our multiple cultural selves. Third, culture is intersectional in the sense that it is like the turning of a kaleidoscope in which various colors and shapes fall into patterned arrangements (our age, gender, sexual orientation, ethnicity, social class, regionalism, job, education). Fourth, culture is definitional and constitutive, because it is a narrative cluster of meanings drawn from past, present, and future. Fifth, culture is political in that it is always contextual, emergent, improvisational, transformational, and political.

Multicultural Social Work Education

Culturally diverse social work practice educators ought to convene a conference to discuss and identify effective teaching content, process, and involvement (cpi) strategies for instructors and students. Green (1998) offers eleven guidelines for multicultural transformation of training programs:

- Multicultural competencies as goal statements of skills
- Outside program evaluation/consultation for preplanned, periodic assessment and resolution of organizational impasses

- Multicultural faculty leadership that is shared by all for multicultural teaching and transformation
- Numerical faculty and student body balance in which the program has a substantial proportion of people of color representative proportionately to the general population for effective training purposes (a minimum of 20 percent is recommended)
- Faculty multicultural training that includes lectures, workshops, peer case consultation, reading seminars, and group discussions on the inclusion of multicultural content
- Co-teaching of intercultural awareness by leaders of different cultural groups that reflect the student cultural composition; dispersion of multicultural content in all courses so that it is infused throughout the curriculum rather than compartmentalized into one or two electives or required courses
- Inclusion of multicultural content in clinical supervision that addresses cultural similarities/differences between worker and client
- Cultural norms and presenting problem, and intergroup relations and presenting problem
- Specialization of multicultural content in the educational training process for faculty and students
- Evaluation of instructors on their multicultural competencies and content for all instructors
- Evaluation of students on their multicultural competencies through mastery of content in exams, papers, and evaluation

White Privilege

Attention and writing have increasingly focused on the issue of white privilege or the favored vantage point of European Americans who are part of the dominant society. White privilege is a label on those who see themselves as the norm or who have established the norms and use them to measure and evaluate all others. McIntosh (1998) identifies twenty-six conditions related to skin color privilege, which is race bound. She discusses "this invisible knapsack of white privilege" that is an "unearned entitlement," provides an "unearned advantage," and reflects "conferred dominance" (pp. 150–151). Dolan–Del Vecchio (1998) documents the domination and bias of white male family authors and therapists and moves toward liberation that seeks to dismantle the hierarchy of power in white male heterosexual privilege.

Ethnic Life Narratives

With the rise of social constructionism and the strengths perspective, which both emphasize life narratives, culturally diverse social work ought to integrate ethnic life narratives into case studies and ethnic practice content. Regarding the discovery of cultural legacies, Pinderhughes (1998) traces two branches of her mother's family back to the eighteenth century. Her research shows how racism affected the lives of African American families which in turn helped her to restory her family in context. Colon (1998) shares his life chronology and his search for his multicultural identity in terms of four stages: mystery and confusion—birth to seventeen years; making his way "home" in the world—ages seventeen to thirty-three; identity search—ages thirty-three to thirty-seven; and integration—ages thirty-seven to sixty. It is a moving account of his growing up with foster parents in New York City and rediscovering his father and mother who lived in Puerto Rico.

McGoldrick (1998a) experiences her belonging and liberation as she recounts her sense of growing up and discovering her Irish heritage; three unsung "sheroes" (her mother, Helen McGoldrick; grand aunt, Mamie; and her African American caretaker, Margaret Bush); and her professional and personal struggles with gender, race, and class.

Scope of Different Populations

Culturally diverse social work practice ought to broaden its perimeters to address different populations. Mahmoud (1998) covers the dynamics of racist double binds where "a more powerful person tyrannizes and victimizes a less powerful person, communicating in a mystifying way that binds the victim and leaves him or her no room for safety" (p. 255). There are several applications made to African Americans and ways of escaping from a double bind and techniques to deal with double-binding relationships. Boyd-Franklin and

Franklin (1998) write about African American couples in therapy and coping with race and gender in terms of the experiences of African American men and women, socialization differences by gender, victimizing and contradictory messages, complexity of gender roles, extended family involvement, and therapy content themes such as rage over racism and the shortage of black men.

Focusing on the needed area of intercultural couples, Crohn (1998) documents growing intermarriage rates among Jews, Italians, Japanese Americans, Native Americans, and blacks and whites. However, there are issues of social status, cultural and religious differences, and related problems. Areas of concern include taking a cultural history; recognizing the issue of class background; and discussing positive and negative aspects of gender roles, family cohesion, cultural identity, emotional expression, religion, and parenting of mixed-race children.

Johnson and Keren (1998) identify four areas when working with families of lesbian women and gay men: (1) personal identity development, (2) gender roles, (3) sexuality in terms of the frequency of sexual activity, and (4) family construction. There are variations and exceptions, because no monolithic lesbian/gay community exists. Owing to diverse communities, there is a need to address family and relational norms assumed by lesbians and gays.

Migration

The migration experience of refugees and immigrants has been a theme of culturally diverse social work practice since the major influx of these groups in the last three and a half decades. Mock (1998) discusses individual and family assessment in terms of exploring the migration history and the relationship between refugeeism and family conflict. Major refugee family issues include language to negotiate old and new worlds; the changing cultural identities of family members and family subsystems; the strengths and resilience of refugee families; and the need for "ultimate listening" (Ting), which involves focused cultural empathy, compassion, heart, and sincerity. Murkin (1998) advocates expanding the context of family and life stories (a relational-narrative approach), looks at

the terror and multiple losses of the premigration and migration experience, and focuses on the racism and stereotyping and the class differences of the postmigration experience. Culture of origin, acculturation, and biculturality are important to determine regarding cultural differences within couples and parent-child struggles.

New Approaches

Culturally diverse social work practice is open to new approaches that expand intervention models. Almeida, Woods, Messineo, and Font (1998) offer a cultural context model that emphasizes a socioeducational orientation, using film clips, news magazine articles, and songs to address gender, race, class, and cultural issues. There are separate cultural circles for men and women designed to address relationship issues such as family-of-origin and couple relationships, parenting, work, and friendships. Family therapy is included, in separate sessions. Men's groups emphasize personal accountability to others, whereas women's groups focus on empowerment and the range of felt and expressed emotions. There are couple, individual, parent-child, sibling, whole-family, and family-of-origin sessions in the cultural circle, with/without the therapist. Children have their own cultural circles and talk about their perceptions of race, gender, culture, and sexual orientation. There is graduation from treatment to community connection and community outreach and coordination where coalitions are formed with sponsors who mentor families.

These themes are open windows that allow fresh ideas to enter our minds, areas of study, teaching, research, and writing. As culturally diverse social work practice educators, practitioners, and students, we need to think and talk about where this field of study is heading and the new ideas shaping it. These new horizons and challenges beckon onward to new heights.

CONCLUSION

Since 1986, the United States has observed the third Monday of January as a national holiday remembering Martin Luther King, Jr., the first person of color to be so honored. The designation of this holiday marks a milestone in the recognition of people of color and their contribution to our life. In a small measure, this book also represents a milestone. It is the first treatment of multicultural social work that uses a practice process-stage approach. It emphasizes the importance of service delivery relevant to people of color, collective multicultural values, a framework for culturally diverse practice, and major process-stage principles.

I hope that this book brings a culturally conscious dimension to the practice and teaching of social work. The integration of traditional and culturally diverse social work practice is essential to an understanding of the nature of the profession, its values and knowledge base, its framework for practice, and its process stages. With the increasing population of people of color in the United States and, correspondingly, among social work clientele, it is particularly important that practitioners acquire adequate multicultural knowledge and helping skills. I trust that they will find these insights and practice principles useful in enhancing their knowledge and skills. Above all, I hope scholars, educators, clinicians, and practitioners will use this text as a point of departure for further creative work in the field of social work practice with people of color.

REFERENCES

Almeida, R., Woods, R., Messineo, T., & Font, R. (1998). The cultural context model: An overview. In M. McGoldrick (Ed.), *Re-visioning family therapy: Race, culture, and gender in clinical practice* (pp. 414–431). New York: Guilford.

Boyd-Franklin, N., & Franklin, A. J. (1998). African American couples in therapy. In M. McGoldrick (Ed.), *Re-visioning family therapy: Race, culture, and gender in clinical practice* (pp. 268–281). New York: Guilford.

Colon, F. (1998). The discovery of my multicultural identity. In M. McGoldrick (Ed.), *Re-visioning family therapy: Race, culture, and gender in clinical practice* (pp. 200–214). New York: Guilford.

Crohn, J. (1998). Intercultural couples. In M. McGoldrick (Ed.), *Re-visioning family therapy: Race, culture, and gender in clinical practice* (pp. 205–308). New York: Guilford.

Dolan–Del Vecchio, K. (1998). Dismantling white male privilege within family therapy. In M. McGoldrick (Ed.), *Re-visioning family therapy: Race, culture, and gender in clinical practice* (pp. 159–175). New York: Guilford.

Gambrill, E. (1983). *Casework: A competency-based approach.* Upper Saddle River, NJ: Prentice-Hall.

Green, R. J. (1998). Training programs: Guidelines for multicultural transformation. In M. McGoldrick (Ed.), *Re-visioning family therapy: Race, culture, and gender in clinical practice* (pp. 111–117). New York: Guilford.

Johnson, T. W., & Keren, M. S. (1998). The families of lesbian women and gay men. In M. McGoldrick (Ed.), *Re-visioning family therapy: Race, culture, and gender in clinical practice* (pp. 320–329). New York: Guilford.

LaFromboise, T., Coleman, H. L. K., & Gerton, J. (1993). Psychological impact of biculturalism: Evidence and theory. *Psychological Bulletin, 114*(3), 395–412.

Laird, J. (1998). Theorizing culture: Narrative ideas and practice principles. In M. McGoldrick (Ed.), *Re-visioning family therapy: Race, culture, and gender in clinical practice* (pp. 20–30). New York: Guilford.

Lum, D. (1999). *Culturally competent practice: A framework for growth and action.* Pacific Grove, Ca: Brooks/Cole.

Mahmoud, V. M. (1998). The double binds of racism. In M. McGoldrick (Ed.), *Re-visioning family therapy: Race, culture, and gender in clinical practice* (pp. 255–267). New York: Guilford.

Manoleas, P. (1994). An outcome approach to assessing the cultural competence of MSW students. *Journal of Multicultural Social Work, 3*(1), 43–57.

McGoldrick, M. (1998a). Belonging and liberation: Finding a place called "home." In M. McGoldrick (Ed.), *Re-visioning family therapy: Race, culture, and gender in clinical practice* (pp. 215–228). New York: Guilford.

McGoldrick, M. (Ed.). (1998b). *Re-visioning family therapy: Race, culture, and gender in clinical practice.* New York: Guilford.

McIntosh, P. (1998). White privilege: Unpacking the invisible knapsack. In M. McGoldrick (Ed.), *Re-visioning family therapy: Race, culture, and gender in clinical practice* (pp. 147–152). New York: Guilford.

Miley, K. K., O'Melia, M., & DuBois, B. L. (1998). *Generalist social work practice: An empowering approach.* Boston: Allyn & Bacon.

Mock, M. R. (1998). Clinical reflections on refugee families: Transforming crises into opportunities. In M. McGoldrick (Ed.), *Re-visioning family therapy: Race, culture, and gender in clinical practice* (pp. 347–359). New York: Guilford.

Murkin, M. P. (1998). The impact of multiple contexts on recent immigrant families. In M. McGoldrick (Ed.), *Re-visioning family therapy: Race, culture, and gender in clinical practice* (pp. 370–383). New York: Guilford.

Northen, H. (1982). *Clinical social work*. New York: Columbia University Press.

Pinderhughes, E. (1998). Black genealogy revisited: Restorying an African American family. In M. McGoldrick (Ed.), *Re-visioning family therapy: Race, culture, and gender in clinical practice* (pp. 179–199). New York: Guilford.

Sue, D. W., Arredondo, P., & McDavis, R. J. (1995). Multicultural counseling competencies and standards: A call to the profession. *Journal of Counseling and Development, 70,* 477–486.

Valle, R. (1986). Cross-cultural competence in minority communities: A curriculum implementation strategy. In M. R. Miranda & H. H. L. Kitano (Eds.), *Mental health research and practice in minority communities. Development of culturally sensitive training programs* (pp. 29–49). Washington, DC: National Institute of Mental Health.

Index